THE CANADIAN YEARBOOK OF INTERNATIONAL LAW

1991

ANNUAIRE CANADIEN DE DROIT INTERNATIONAL

The Canadian Yearbook of International Law

VOLUME XXIX 1991 TOME XXIX

Annuaire canadien de Droit international

Published under the auspices of
THE CANADIAN BRANCH, INTERNATIONAL LAW ASSOCIATION
AND
THE CANADIAN COUNCIL ON INTERNATIONAL LAW
with the financial support of the Social Sciences
and Humanities Research Council of Canada

Publié sous les auspices de
LA SECTION CANADIENNE DE L'ASSOCIATION DE DROIT INTERNATIONAL
ET
LE CONSEIL CANADIEN DE DROIT INTERNATIONAL
avec l'appui financier du Conseil de recherches
en Sciences humaines du Canada

UBC Press
VANCOUVER, B.C.

ISBN 0-7748-0416-5
ISSN 0069-0058

Canadian Shared Cataloguing in Publication Data

Main entry under title:

The Canadian yearbook of international law

Vols. for 1963–   published under the
auspices of the Canadian Branch, International
Law Association and the Canadian Council on
International Law
Editor: 1963–   C. B. Bourne.
ISSN 0069-0058

1. International Law — Yearbooks
I. International Law Association. Canadian
Branch and the Canadian Council on
International Law. II. Bourne, Charles B.
JX21.C3   341′.05

UBC Press
University of British Columbia
6344 Memorial Rd.
Vancouver, BC V6T 1Z2
(604) 822-3259

The Board of Editors, the Canadian Branch of the International Law Association, the Canadian Council on International Law, and the University of British Columbia are not in any way responsible for the views expressed by contributors, whether the contributions are signed or unsigned.

Les opinions émises dans le présent *Annuaire* par nos collaborateurs, qu'il s'agisse d'articles signés, ou non signés, ne sauraient en aucune façon engager la responsabilité du Comité de rédaction, de la Section canadienne de l'Association de droit international, de la section canadienne du Conseil canadien de droit international ou de l'Université de Colombie Britannique.

Communications to *The Yearbook* should be addressed to:
Prière d'adresser les communications destinées à l'*Annuaire* à:

THE EDITOR, THE CANADIAN YEARBOOK OF INTERNATIONAL LAW
THE FACULTY OF LAW, 1822 EAST MALL
THE UNIVERSITY OF BRITISH COLUMBIA, VANCOUVER, BC V6T IZI

INTERNATIONAL LAW ASSOCIATION (CANADIAN BRANCH)
ASSOCIATION DE DROIT INTERNATIONAL (BRANCHE CANADIENNE)

Officers / officiers 1990-92

Life Honorary Presidents / Présidents honoraires à vie	Nicolas M. Matte Émile Colas Jean-Louis Magdelénat
Honorary Vice-Presidents Vice-présidents honoraires	Charles B. Bourne Maxwell Cohen
President / Président	Cameron DesBois
Vice-Presidents / Vice-présidents	Harry Bloomfield Armand De Mestral Brian Dickson Leslie Green Jennie Hatfield Lyon Valerie Hughes Mark Jewett Martin Low Jacques-Yvan Morin Gerald Morris
Honorary Secretary-Treasurer / Secrétaire-Trésorier honoraire	Jean-Marc Fortier
Executive Committee / Comité exétutif	Cameron DesBois Harry Bloomfield Martin Low Jean-Marc Fortier Émile Colas Valerie Hughes Nicolas M. Matte
Councillors / Conseillers	Charles B. Bourne Armand De Mestral Allan Gotlieb John Humphrey Edward McWhinney Daniel Turp Anne-Marie Trahan Ivan Vlasic
International Officers / Membres du bureau international	Charles B. Bourne Émile Colas Jean-Louis Magdelénat Nicolas M. Matte

Editor-in-Chief of the Canadian Yearbook of International Law
Éditeur-en-chef de l'Annuaire canadien de Droit international
Charles B. Bourne

Contents / Sommaire

BOOK REVIEWS / RECENSIONS DE LIVRES

THE CANADIAN YEARBOOK OF INTERNATIONAL LAW

1991

ANNUAIRE CANADIEN DE DROIT INTERNATIONAL

Leadership in Law:
John P. Humphrey and the Development of
the International Law of Human Rights

R. ST. J. MACDONALD*

JOHN PETERS HUMPHREY, first Director of the Division of Human Rights at the United Nations, author of the Secretariat draft of the Universal Declaration of Human Rights, is one of the most distinguished international civil servants of our time. As student and successor of Percy Ellwood Corbett at McGill University in Montreal, he also occupies a key position in the line of international lawyers who have struggled to develop that subject in Canada. As a Canadian patriot prominent for half a century in public debate, he has contributed creatively to the development of Canadian perspectives on human rights and international order. The article that follows reviews Humphrey's career as scholar, teacher, official, and human rights activist in Canada and in the world at large.[1]

---

* Professor of International Law, University of Toronto; Judge at the European Court of Human Rights, Strasbourg; Honorary Professor in the Law Department, Peking University, Beijing. The writer wishes to recognize with pleasure as well as gratitude the admirable assistance of Annemieke Holthuis, B.A., LL.B. (Dalhousie), LL.M. (McGill) of the Department of Justice, Ottawa, and Teresa Scassa, B.A. (Concordia), LL.B./B.C.L. (McGill), LL.M. (Michigan), of Dalhousie Law School, Halifax, in the preparation of this paper.

---

[1] Much of the information referred to herein is based on John P. Humphrey, *Human Rights and the United Nations: A Great Adventure* (Dobbs Ferry: Transnational Publishers, 1984, hereafter *A Great Adventure*); Humphrey's unpublished autobiographical manuscript (hereafter Original Manuscript); Kieran Simpson (ed.), *Canadian Who's Who* 486 (Toronto: University of Toronto Press, vol. 26, 1991); A. J. Hobbins, "René Cassin and the Daughter of Time: The First Draft of the Universal Declaration of Human Rights," (1989) 2 Fontanus: From the Collections of McGill University 7; A. J. Hobbins, "Human Rights Inside the United Nations: The Humphrey Diaries, 1948- 1959," (1991) 4 Fontanus 143; Humphrey's scholarly writings, many but not all of which are listed in Christian L. Wiktor, *Canadian Bibliography of Inter-*

THE EARLY DAYS

John Humphrey was born on April 30, 1905, in Hampton, New Brunswick. He never knew his father, a well-to-do businessman, who died only thirteen months after his birth. On the death of his father, Humphrey's maternal grandfather, "Squire" Thomas Peters, presided over the household, which included Humphrey's mother, his brother, Douglas, and his sister, Ruth. The "Squire" was a farmer, a businessman and, for twelve years, a deputy commissioner of agriculture in the provincial government. He was also authoritarian. Humphrey's relationship with his mother was close, but in 1916, when he was eleven, his mother died of cancer at the age of forty-two.

In addition to the loss of his parents, Humphrey's childhood was greatly influenced by an event that occurred when he was six. One day, when he and his friends were playing with matches, his sleeve caught fire. His arm, which had been badly burned, required numerous operations and skin grafts; eventually it required amputation. Having lost a year of school owing to the operations, transition to normal life was difficult.

Humphrey spent four years at the Hampton Consolidated School, where he was a poor student and always in trouble. The loss of his arm left him open to ridicule from the other children. It was decided to send Humphrey to Rothesay Collegiate School, a Church of England boarding school between Hampton and Saint John. With visions of English boarding school life in his head, Humphrey looked forward to this new adventure. Unfortunately, the four years at Rothesay were not as rosy as anticipated. Rather fat at this age, and possessing a temper,[2] Humphrey became the subject of bullies' teasing and the British boarding school practice of "fagging." Not unlike other boarding schools of its time, discipline at Rothesay was strict; punishment consisted of the strap and the cane and contact with members of the other sex was limited. In his own words,

national Law 714 (Toronto: University of Toronto Press, 1984); materials from McGill University libraries and archives; a series of taped interviews, and innumerable discussions with Humphrey that date back to our first meeting in the Third Committee of the General Assembly in 1965.

[2] Even later, reflecting on his years at the UN, Humphrey would say "It is true that I have a reputation for sometimes losing my cool, but I think I can say that, although I was often provoked, I always did keep my cool whenever I was acting in my official capacity" Speech, "Reminiscences of a One-Time International Official," Conference on Human Rights and the Protection of Refugees under International Law, Nov. 29, 1987, at 4.

Humphrey hated "nearly every minute" of those four years. He began to study secretly for the provincial matriculation examinations with a view to entering Mount Allison University in Sackville, which he succeeded in doing in 1920 at the age of fifteen. Nevertheless, the two years Humphrey spent at Mount Allison were wasted academically. He had no good reason for being there, save a compelling desire to leave Rothesay and its discipline, and, at fifteen, he was more interested in college pranks than in studying.

A visit to Montreal, where his sister was teaching at Baron Byng High School, piqued Humphrey's interest in the city and in McGill University. However, since his activities were still being underwritten by the executor of his father's estate, J. M. Scovil, the latter had to approve any major changes in his career moves. Scovil believed that Humphrey should pursue a career as a bank clerk, a belief that was reinforced by the fact that his academic career had not been impressive. However, by professing an interest in commerce as a course of study, Humphrey managed to get Scovil's consent to enrol in the commerce program at McGill in 1922.

Montreal Years: From Student to Professor

In Montreal, Humphrey shared an apartment on Hutchinson Street with his sister, Ruth. The lectures at McGill's school of commerce, on accounting, mathematics, economics, languages, and commercial law, left him uninspired, although a course by the inimitable Stephen Leacock, who later became an adviser, was a notable exception. He joined the commerce fraternity and made close friends. Following his graduation in 1925, Humphrey briefly worked in the Asiatic Freight Department of the Canadian Pacific Railway. The job had been secured with the help of a recommendation from Stephen Leacock to Sir Edward Beatty, President of the CPR and Chancellor of McGill. At eighty dollars a month, Humphrey was a "kind of super office boy lost somewhere in the higher labyrinths of Windsor Station."[3] Soon afterwards he decided that law was the appropriate stepping stone into politics, in which he had developed an interest.

Since the Faculty of Law at McGill required a B.A. degree for admission and Humphrey had a B.Comm., he decided, more or less by default, to attend Osgoode Hall Law School in Toronto. At only twenty, he moved to Toronto and began to look for a lawyer

---

[3] Original Manuscript, 45.

with whom he could article. He did this by systematically touring the law offices of Adelaide Street. In less than a week he had a position, a room at Knox College, and was registered at the law school, but he felt little affinity for the City of Toronto, where he had no friends. At the end of his first week in the city, he had packed his things and taken the night train back to Montreal. His small patrimony was still held in trust and no income would be received from it until the following April, when he would reach the age of majority. In these circumstances, he quickly accepted a job on the floor of the stock exchange in the firm of Mathewson, McLennan, and Molson, a job which had been offered to him before leaving for Toronto through the intervention of a second cousin. He lasted there about two months before a combination of boredom, lack of desire to become a stockbroker, and his unintentional insult of a senior partner, compelled him to leave.

Despite his Toronto experience, Humphrey was still interested in studying law. He wanted to study at the Université de Montréal to perfect his French; for the practice of law in Quebec, however, the strict B.A. requirement for entry into law school remained an obstacle.[4] Stephen Leacock suggested that Humphrey enter his classes in Arts after Christmas so that in the following year he could combine his first year of law with his last year of Arts. To follow such a program meant a return to McGill. Backed by a bank loan of $1,000, Humphrey returned to university after Christmas in 1926, this time to work in earnest: "The period of uncertainty was over; I knew where I wanted to go; and I soon fell in love with political science."[5]

In the summer of 1926 Humphrey worked selling ginger ale, and with the money earned from this endeavour he yielded to the temptation to see Britain, particularly Oxford, where his sister was graduating. While in England, he noticed not only class differences, which, in his opinion, "hardly existed in Canada," but, more particularly, that he had become a Canadian nationalist. "I prized the British connection but I was too wrapped up in Canada not to be conscious of the fact that England was, if not a foreign country,

---

[4] In his article on the history of the national law program at McGill, Professor R. A. Macdonald notes that, as late as 1949, "The Bar refused to recognize the McGill B.Comm. degree as a matriculation requirement, [and] maintained the additional requirement that students complete 'a regular course in philosophy'. . .'': R. A. Macdonald, "The National Law Programme at McGill: Origins, Establishment, Prospects," (1990) 13 Dalhousie L. J. 211, at 268.

[5] Original Manuscript, 51; Interview, May 5, 1989, at 6.

at least something quite different from what I want Canada to become."[6]

LAW SCHOOL AT MCGILL

Humphrey returned to Canada in the fall of 1926 to begin his legal studies at McGill and to complete the requirements for his B.A. in economics and political science. At first he disliked the study of law: it seemed the mere memorization of rules. Since he was concurrently completing an arts degree, his interest was drawn more towards his classes in political science. He was involved in the establishment of a model parliament and the short-lived Confederation Club, both of which aimed at introducing students to matters of interest in public affairs.[7]

In his second year, Humphrey developed a more serious attitude towards law. This was partly owing to the influence of Percy Corbett and H. A. Smith, both full-time teachers at McGill. Smith, a constitutional and public lawyer, later became professor of international law at the University of London, where he acquired an international reputation. Percy Corbett, a fellow of All Soul's College, Oxford, had been an assistant legal adviser to the ILO in Geneva. At McGill, where he taught Roman law and international law, he soon established himself as perhaps the most outstanding public international law scholar Canada has ever produced. Humphrey did not like Corbett much during his undergraduate days — "I thought he was stubborn...and he had a reputation of being a bit of an intellectual snob" — but that assessment would change "radically" during the years ahead.[8]

After completing his second year of law school, Humphrey decided to spend the summer in France. He had long had a liking for the French language, and had tried to make friends among the French-language community. At the time, however, Montreal was a city of "two solitudes." Even in "mixed" company, conversa-

---

[6] Original Manuscript, 52, 56.

[7] Editorial, "Make Good Canadians," *Montreal Gazette,* Spring 1925. This editorial refers to the book by John Lane entitled *The New Elizabethans;* "Confederation Club Formed at Central YMCA," *Montreal Gazette,* Spring 1925, Humphrey's clippings. Letter: John P. Humphrey (JPH) to his sister Ruth, Feb. 23, 1925, at 2, Mar. 10, 1925, at 1, Mar. 25, 1925, at 2.

[8] "Thank You Percy Corbett," undated three-page tribute by JPH to Corbett, typescript (hereafter *Thank You Percy Corbett*); Interview, May 5, 1989, at 17-18. On Corbett, see *infra* note 30.

tion was invariably in English, even where the French of the anglophones was as proficient as the English of the francophones. It seemed necessary to go abroad to learn French.[9] He enrolled in a summer French program at Grenoble, a favourite with McGill students, where he quickly became fluent and learned to love French literature and culture. He made friends, travelled in France, and returned to Canada via London. During the summer he decided that he would try for the Macdonald Travelling Fellowship offered by McGill, and return to France for a year after his B.C.L.

Humphrey's final year at McGill was uneventful, although he did acquire more experience to fuel his interest in politics:

Apart from law, my chief interest was politics. One night I went together with some friends to a Conservative Party meeting in the Mount Royal Hotel. They were drumming up enthusiasm for the forthcoming federal election, but my friends and I had been attracted as much as anything else by the free beer. We listened to the speeches which were on the light side. Jokingly I said to my friends that I was going to make a speech. They urged me on and, finally, I sent a note up to the Chairman: "There is a student here from McGill who would like to say something." He gave me to the floor. I had, of course, nothing prepared nor had I even had the time to marshall my thoughts. But I made a fiery speech in which I accused the politicians of neglecting young men. "You are dying of hardening of the arteries," I said, "yet you don't give us a chance." Much of this was nonsense, thought up on the spur of the moment, but it made an impression. That Saturday, the *Montreal Gazette* carried an editorial entitled, "The New Elizabethans" which referred to my speech; Dr. Tory, the national organizer for the Conservative Party, invited me to call at his office. He asked me to become the President of the Young Men's Conservative Party in Quebec. . . . I then talked to Professor J. C. Hemeon, who taught Economics at McGill, who advised me not to accept. "If you do," he said, "you will be a marked man for the rest of your life." I thought this was pretty good advice. . . . I am glad now that I had the good sense to follow it.[10]

Despite his early oratorical success, Humphrey did not consider himself a good speaker; but he joined the McGill Literary and Debating Society, becoming its President, and was also involved in Mock Parliaments at McGill.[11]

---

[9] Original Manuscript, 59. For a description of life in Montreal and at McGill at the time, see Eugene Forsey, *A Life on the Fringe* 19-35, 49-72 (Toronto: Oxford University Press, 1990).

[10] Original Manuscript, 65-66.

[11] "Liberal Leader Discusses Plans," Spring 1925; "Government was Sustained on Pulp Embargo Bill in Mock Parliament Session," Spring 1925: Humphrey clippings.

STUDYING AND TRAVELLING IN FRANCE

Humphrey obtained his B.C.L. with first class honours in 1929. He was also awarded the Montreal Bar Association Prize in Commercial Law and the Thomas Alexander Rowat Prize for study of old French law. On the basis of marked improvement in his class standing, he also received the Macdonald Travelling Fellowship for the academic year 1929-30.[12] Before leaving for France on May 26, 1929, he passed the Bar Examinations for the Province of Quebec and secured an articling position with the Montreal firm Wainwright, Elder, and MacDougal, where he had been employed during the summer of 1927 after first-year law. The firm agreed to hold the position open until he returned from France.

Humphrey originally booked his passage to France on a Canadian Pacific liner. Yet on the advice of Aubrey Elder, the senior partner of the firm where he would article, he switched to the Cunard line; Cunard was a client of the firm. Humphrey later said, "The change in plans was the most important I would ever make."[13] On the second night at sea, he met Jeanne Godreau, "the prettiest girl in the room," at a ship's dance. As she was a French-Canadian Catholic, and he a Protestant, the two would not likely have met under ordinary circumstances in Canada. After spending a great deal of time together on the voyage, Humphrey proposed marriage the night before the ship reached the French coast. Jeanne disembarked in Cherbourg without giving John an answer. Humphrey continued on to England, where he received a cablegram with a simple message, "oui."

He rushed to France, where the couple decided to marry as soon as French law would allow, but there were two obstacles. First, French law required a two-week residence in the same arrondissement; second, they were unable to find a church that would marry them, because of their mixed religious denominations. Instead, they decided to be married in a civil ceremony before the British Consul General, there being no Canadian Consul in Paris at the time. Although they were refused a dispensation to wed at one cathedral, Humphrey's sister Ruth photographed the couple as they descended the front steps, with the result that Jeanne Humphrey was able to send home wedding photographs from a Catholic Church.[14] They

[12] Original Manuscript, 64; Letter: JPH to R. St. J. Macdonald (RStJM), Nov. 13, 1975.
[13] Original Manuscript, 70; Interview, May 5, 1989, at 8.
[14] Interview, May 5, 1989, at 9, 10.

spent their honeymoon travelling in France with very little money. However, their long-term prospects were more promising: $5,000 "invested in the stock market on margin, under my brother's supervision," and a job waiting in Montreal. Then came the crash of 1929.

Humphrey learned of the crash while sitting in a barber's chair in Monte Carlo. He rushed back to the hotel in near panic. From then on, under pressure to save money, the couple travelled quickly to Montpelier, where Humphrey was to attend university. They had planned to winter in Montpelier, but after a month they felt they were missing something and moved on to Paris. There they found a room in the Hôtel d'Athènes, rue Guy Lussac, near the Sorbonne and the law faculty.

Humphrey began attending lectures at the law faculty in what is now known as Paris I, given by such giants in civil law as Henri Capitant and Demogues, but the lecture halls, crowded and noisy, were not satisfactory for his main purpose in France, which was to perfect his French. So in addition to attending classes in international law at the Haute École des Études de Droit International, he followed popular evening lectures on a range of subjects from vegetarianism and theatre to theosophy. A cousin, Jack Humphrey, an artist of growing importance in Canada, was in Paris that year, the year of the Paris World's Fair; he passed on the newlyweds many of the artist's survival techniques, such as free church suppers.[15]

BACK IN MONTREAL

In the summer of 1930, the Humphreys returned to a Montreal that was in the grip of the Great Depression.[16] They stayed with

[15] On the artist Jack Humphrey, see L. S. Loomer, *Three Painters: Boardman Robinson, Jack Humphrey, Miller Brittain* (Windsor, NS: L.S. Loomer, 1973).

[16] Writing to his sister Ruth in 1932, from 2080 Lincoln Avenue, Humphrey observed that:
> We're all sweating from the first to the last, under the fear of losing our jobs. We're afraid that we won't have the opportunity to sweat! Great system! Of course, I am one of the fortunate ones. I live in comparative security; but there are those who don't. When I think about these things — it's not theorization. Unfortunately there are too many concrete examples all around us — I want to go out and tear someone to pieces. Here I am, my mouth shut up and my feet tied, because I'm caught up in the same whirlpool as the rest. Walking downtown at noon today I made a prayer. God, I said, make me independent of this and then, my God, watch my dust! Letter: May 2, 1932, at 7-8.

The world depression of the 1930s struck Canada more severely than any other country except the United States. By 1936, two-thirds of Canadians entering the

Humphrey's brother and his wife on Roslyn Avenue, before settling
into an apartment of their own. They were to live on a starting
lawyer's salary of $125 per month. Wainwright, Elder, and
MacDougal, where Humphrey was employed, was engaged mainly in corporate, insurance, and real estate work, none of which
Humphrey liked very much. Though he was attracted to litigation,
the firm did almost none. Despite these shortcomings, he remained
with the firm for six years.

At the end of six years Humphrey was finding his work in the
practice of law to be "dry and intellectually unrewarding." He began the search for something more satisfying without any definite
career plans in mind. He was interested in international law and
had taken a course on the subject given by Percy Corbett; he had
also attended lectures in diplomatic history in Paris, especially lectures given by Professor Renouvin. This interest led him to investigate the possibility of obtaining a master's degree in the subject.
He was an idealist,[17] and there was an attractiveness about the study
of international law that stimulated sentiments of working for international peace and the abolition of war. "I may have had the
missionary spirit...being a youngster at the time of the First World
War did affect me. I was interested in applying the law to some
international purpose and with that in mind, I went to see Percy
Corbett."[18]

Showing remarkable generosity, Corbett, in the spring of 1935,
agreed not only to supervise Humphrey's thesis but also to devote
"the better part of an evening every week" to the gratuitous job
of tutoring him.[19] Within a matter of weeks, Corbett, who was suffering from eye trouble, asked Humphrey whether he would be interested in assuming responsibility for teaching Roman law.
Although hesitant about the opportunity at first, he later "jumped

---

work force couldn't find jobs; more than a million people were on relief. See Pierre
Berton, *The Great Depression 1929-1939* (Toronto: McClelland & Stewart, 1990); Cameron Smith, *Unfinished Journey: The Lewis Family* 246, 290 (Toronto: Summerhill Press,
1989); Thérèse F. Casgrain, *A Woman in a Man's World* 115-16, 173-74 (Toronto:
McClelland & Stewart, 1972).

17 "I'm starting to see that there are some pretty fine things that a fellow can achieve
if he goes at it in the right spirit. . . . It's the good that a chap can do for humanity
and his country that counts; not the good that he does for himself,": JPH to his
sister Ruth, Apr. 22, 1925, at 4. See too P. E. Corbett to Principal A. E. Morgan,
Jan. 30, 1936, referring to Humphrey's willingness "to sacrifice his very distinguished prospects at the Bar" if an opening occurred on the full-time faculty.

18 Interview, May 5, 1989, at 17.

19 *Thank You Percy Corbett, supra* note 8; at 2.

at it.'' Though it would mean a cut in his earnings, he understood that by beginning with Roman law he might, in the future, have the chance to teach international law.

Humphrey felt that he needed at least a year to prepare himself to lecture in Roman law. With Corbett's help, he obtained a $2,000 fellowship from the Carnegie Endowment for International Peace, to spend another year in France (1936-37).[20] At the time of his return to France in 1936, he described himself as ''a social democrat in my political thinking, strongly anti-fascist, deeply sympathetic with the Loyalist government in Spain, and shocked by the Italian aggression in Ethiopia.''[21] After a brief, unpleasant trip through Nazi Germany, the Humphreys settled down in Paris in the Square de Port-Royal, rue de la Santé.

Humphrey registered in the graduate course at the law faculty. Though unable to recognize its use in a Canadian context at the time, he followed lectures in administrative law by Rolland. In fact, he devoted most of his energy to learning French administrative law, which he found to be ''one of the monuments of legal science, as original a system of law as I have ever studied.''[22] Rolland's lectures later proved especially valuable when Humphrey taught one of the first administrative law courses in Canada. Other outstanding professors at the faculty included Basdevant, who later became a judge on the World Court, de la Pradelle, Le Fur, Grandclaude, and Barthelèmy.[23] At the end of the 1937 academic year Humphrey passed all of the examinations for the degree of docteur en droit in both Roman and public law. In the latter, he was the only foreigner and one of the few who received the mark ''très bien,'' but he did not complete his doctoral thesis. He returned in 1937 to devote his energies to grasping and teaching the tenets of Roman law as a sessional lecturer at the Faculty of Law at McGill University.

PROFESSOR AT MCGILL

Humphrey was appointed a lecturer in Roman law in 1936. At the same time, he was granted a leave of absence to continue his studies in Roman law and public law at the University of Paris,

---

[20] Original Manuscript, 82; *Thank You Percy Corbett, supra;* JPH to RStJM, Nov. 13, 1975.

[21] Original Manuscript, 84.

[22] JPH to Dean C. S. Le Mesurier, May 13, 1937, at 4.

[23] JPH to Dean C. S. Le Mesurier, Dec. 6, 1936, and May 13, 1937, at 2, describing his program of studies at Paris.

where he held a Carnegie Fellowship. In 1938 he was appointed Secretary to the Faculty of Law and also Sessional Lecturer in engineering law.[24] In the same year he was promoted to the rank of Associate Professor of Law for a five-year term, beginning September 1, 1939. His appointment as Associate Professor was renewed for a further term of five years from September 1, 1944 and on June 12, 1946, he was appointed Gale Professor of Roman Law, a title he retained only until his departure from McGill three months later.[25]

In September, 1937, the year in which he started to lecture, McGill's Faculty of Law had four career professors: Percy Corbett, Stuart Le Mesurier, F. R. Scott, and John Humphrey.[26] Humphrey admired both Corbett and Scott, and became close friends with Corbett, though he had not much liked him during his undergraduate days; it was as a colleague that he learned more about Corbett's "true character," which, "far from being coldly intellectual was essentially warm and generous."[27] In his estimation, Corbett was not only "the greatest scholar we have ever had," but he was also "one of the first international lawyers to welcome the development of an international law of human rights."[28]

Corbett had joined the Law Faculty in 1924 to teach Roman law, international law, and legal history. He had been Dean of the Faculty from 1928 to 1936 and remained Professor of Roman and International Law until 1938, when he assumed the duties of Acting Principal for a year. Frank Scott would later say that "[m]any of us at McGill hoped that he would be named Principal after Sir Arthur Currie died, but the Board of Governors thought otherwise and we sadly saw him leave Canada for the United States" to work

24 *McGill University Calendar, 1935-36,* at 48. The Board of Governors' Minute Books of Mar. 3, 1936 state that, though appointed a lecturer in law for two years from Sep. 1, 1936, Humphrey was granted a leave of absence during the session 1936-1937 in order to pursue advanced studies in Europe. See also, *McGill University Calendar 1937-38,* at 22; *McGill University Annual Report, 1945-46,* at 78; C. S. Le Mesurier to JPH, Apr. 2, 1937.

25 *McGill University Annual Report, 1945-46,* at 52; *McGill University Calendar, 1937-38,* at 22; *McGill University Annual Report, 1945-46,* at 78; Board of Governors' Minutes Books, June 7, 1944, at 1422, and June 12, 1946, at 1696.

26 Interview, May 5, 1989, at 28. On the history of the Faculty, see the splendid papers by Roderick A. Macdonald, *supra* note 4 and J. E. C. Brierley, "Quebec Legal Education since 1945: Cultural Paradoxes and Traditional Ambiguities," (1986) 10 Dalhousie L. J. 5.

27 *Thank You Percy Corbett, supra* note 8, at 3.

28 *Ibid.,* 4.

with the United States government in 1939.[29] Corbett returned to
McGill to teach legal theory in the Department of Political Science
before returning again to the United States in 1943, destined for
Yale and, later, Princeton and LeHigh universities.[30] On his departure, Humphrey took over his courses.

Roman law occupied an important place in the McGill curriculum. A mandatory course, it was taught for three hours a week in
first year. In 1937 it was also taught in second year, for one hour
per week throughout the year. Humphrey continued to teach the
subject until 1946, although the second year course, which was not
given in 1941-42, was dropped in 1944.[31] His lectures in Roman Law
were based on his own translation of Girard's *Manuel de droit roman*
and he comments that he was generally "never more than two or
three jumps ahead of the students." As an undergraduate, he had
had the usual disdain for the subject, unable to see its relevance
in a modern setting. To his surprise, he now found that he actually
liked it. "If the chief function of a law faculty is to train the minds
of students, no subject could be more important."[32]

In 1938 Humphrey became a Sessional Lecturer in the Faculty
of Engineering as well, teaching an engineering law course one hour
per week throughout the year.[33] That same year he introduced a
second-year administrative law course, given one hour per week.
Having taken a course in "droit administratif" under Rolland in
Paris, he decided to turn the municipal law course he had been
asked to teach into an administrative law course, one of the first
in Canada. In 1940 this course was increased to two hours per week

---

[29] Frank R. Scott (FRS) to RStJM, Nov. 14, 1979. Humphrey adds, significantly:
"I don't think he was getting any recognition in Ottawa," Interview, Saturday,
May 6, 1989, at 7.

[30] On P. E. Corbett (1892-1983) see B. M. Greene, ed., *Who's Who in Canada* 446 (Toron-
to: International Press Ltd., 1934-35); *The Canadian Encyclopedia* 516 (Edmonton: Hurtig
Publishers, 2d ed., vol. 1, 1988); Kathleen Fisher, a note in *Quid Novi*, McGill Law
Faculty, vol. 4, no. 9, Nov. 2, 1983, at 1; and Stanley Brice Frost, *McGill University
for the Advancement of Learning, vol. 2, 1895-1971* (Montreal and Kingston: McGill-Queen's
University Press, 1980). Unfortunately, Frost's account does not do Corbett justice.
McGill University Faculty of Law Newsletter, Oct. 1984.

[31] *McGill University Calendar, 1935-36,* at 48; *1936-37,* at 49; *1937-38,* at 50, 393-94; *1938-39,*
at 51, 408; *1940-41,* at 32, 609-10; *1941-42,* at 32, 610-11; *1942-43,* at 32, 610-11; *1943-44,*
at 32, 610-11; *1945-46,* at 36, 610-11; *1945-46,* at 35, 590-91; *1946-47,* at 35, 770-71.

[32] Interview, May 5, 1989, at 25; Interview, May 6, 1989, at 10; Interview, Dec. 27, 1991.

[33] Humphrey had ambitions for this, generally regarded, routine course which he
wanted to make into a course on jurisprudence: JPH to Dean C. S. Le Mesurier
Dec. 6, 1936, at 2-3; Apr. 20, 1937; see also *supra* note 31.

and in 1943, although not offered that year, administrative law was made a third-year course. Frank Scott took over this course on Humphrey's departure for New York in 1946. Humphrey's interest in administrative law and in the law of international organizations was important to the curricular development of McGill at the time:

The first signs of real development in curriculum, teaching methods or professoriate since the late 1920s occurred in 1943, when Scott and Humphrey finally succeeded in convincing Le Mesurier that the war effort was changing the nature of legal regulation and that Faculty would have to take concrete steps to reassert its scholarly and non-vocational orientation if it wished to avoid total domination by traditionalist elements within the Bar.[34]

Humphrey's interests and ideas at the time helped to push the teaching of law at McGill beyond exegetical and *cours magistral* teaching. In 1943 he began teaching two new first-year courses, "Introduction to Public Law," and, "International Law and Organization." These courses were an innovation not just at McGill, but in Canadian legal education: "In establishing these two courses, Humphrey became Canada's first 'institutionalist'."[35] He continued to teach until 1946, when Maxwell Cohen took over the international organizations course, and the introductory course was dropped.[36] Humphrey was an institutionalist whose ideas were strongly influenced by his study of French administrative law. His grasp of the value and potential of administrative law at the time was advanced well beyond that of his colleagues and contemporaries.

It was, however, on international law that he focused his teaching, both before and after his service at the United Nations, and it was on the theory of international law that he, more than any Canadian other than Corbett, concentrated his interest. Following in Corbett's footsteps, he delved deeply into the works of Kelsen, Anzilotti, Duguit, De Visscher, and Lauterpacht, and in due course published several fine articles on high theory.

EARLY SCHOLARSHIP

Humphrey's writings between 1936 and 1945 touch on not only Canada's position vis-à-vis the emerging Inter-American system

[34] R. A. Macdonald, *supra* note 4, at 271.

[35] *Ibid.*, 273.

[36] *Supra* note 31. See too, R. St. J. Macdonald, "Maxwell Cohen at Eighty: International Lawyer, Educator, and Judge," (1989) 27 *Canadian Yearbook of International Law* 3.

but also on broader notions of government, the separation of functions within government, the theoretical foundations of international law, and new developments in the framework and structure of the international legal community. It is appropriate to review these writings briefly in order to appreciate the range and depth of Humphrey's academic interests.

Some of Humphrey's early writings show a very strong interest in events in Latin America. He consistently emphasized the interests and responsibilities of Canada regarding its neighbours to the south. In December 1940, he published an article criticizing the prevailing Canadian isolationist view of Latin America; that article looked at developments in Mexican political structures and advocated stronger Canadian participation in Mexican attempts at agrarian reform.[37]

In 1942 Humphrey published *The Inter-American System: A Canadian View,* under the auspices of the Canadian Institute for International Affairs. This study was one of the first Canadian examinations of the Inter-American system.[38] At that time, and until very recently, the attitude of English-speaking Canadians towards Latin America had been one of indifference. Having only recently begun to perceive their own national identity, Canadians, said Humphrey, were leery of membership in the Inter-American system because membership would inevitably bring them into a closer relationship with the United States. Humphrey was among those in the 1940s who argued that Canada shared certain cultural similarities with Latin America, particularly as regards its French-speaking regions. Further, membership in the Inter-American system would enhance Canada's international status as an independent nation. There would be formal benefits from such membership; some of the responsibilities it had already assumed indirectly through Canada's signature of the Ogdensburg Agreement.[39]

[37] John P. Humphrey, "Canada and the Mexican Revolution," *The Canadian Forum,* Dec. 1940, at 269.

[38] *The Inter-American System: A Canadian View* (Toronto: Macmillan, 1942); this book won the David Prize in Quebec. Interview, May 5, 1989, at 30-31. For reviews, see H. McD. Clokie, (1942) 8 Can. J. Econ. and Pol. Sc. 615; R. G. Trotter, 49 Queen's Quarterly 252; H. G. Skilling, (1942) 36 Am. Pol. Sci. R. 964; Ricardo J. Alfaro, (1942) 36 Am. J. Int'l L. 735. On Canadian-Latin American relations, see too Escott Reid, *Radical Mandarin: The Memoirs of Escott Reid* 153-58 (Toronto: University of Toronto Press, 1989).

[39] *The Inter-American System* 1-6, 17-19; "Relationship of This Country to Pan-American Movement Described," *Sherbrooke Daily Record,* Mar. 10, 1945.

In Humphrey's opinion, the arguments in favour of member-ship (benefits of membership in a regional organization, economic and cultural advantages, defence considerations, and "an obvious international duty") outweighed any disadvantages, such as pos-sible difficulties in reconciling Canadian positions with Common-wealth policies.[40] Indeed, he thought that Canada's membership in the Organization of American States might be seen as "a logi-cal and necessary corollary to membership in the new universal security organization proposed at Dumbarton Oaks."[41] It was in this spirit that, after spending several months in Mexico in the Summer of 1942, he helped to found the Canadian Inter-American Association "to educate Canadians about Latin America."[42]

During the turbulent war years, Humphrey also turned his at-tention to problems of Canadian unity. He wrote about the cul-tural divide between French and English in Canada and was an early (and prophetic) advocate of Canadian bilingualism.[43] He iden-tified many of the problems and conflicts between French and English Canada that would later give momentum to Quebec's Quiet Revolution and flare into the linguistic nationalism and constitu-tional crisis which have dominated the political agenda of Canada in the 1970s and 1980s and which remain critical in the 1990s.[44]

[40] *The Inter-American System* 161-73. After twenty years at the United Nations, Hum-phrey changed his opinion:: membership was "a poor idea." If Canada joined the OAS, "we would be spending most of our time taking chestnuts out of the fire for our American neighbors": Interview, May 6, 1989, at 9; JPH to RStJM, Oct. 30, 1989. Although this view was shared by such distinguished experts as Alfred Pick, the first Canadian Ambassador-Observer to the OAS from 1972 to 1975, the government of Canada, urged by the United States, committed itself to joining the OAS, which it did in 1990. Alfred Pick, Letter to the Editor, *The Globe and Mail*, Nov. 3, 1989, at 6, wrote: "I was the first Ambassador-Observer of Canada to the OAS from 1972 to 1975. Since leaving the post...I have been strongly opposed to Canadian membership. The last time this issue came to the fore was in November 1982, when the House of Commons Committee on External Affairs was thinking of recommending membership. I wrote a piece that got some attention and I was also interviewed by CTV. In the essence, I said that membership 'would, to put it mildly, complicate Canada's already complex relations with the United States.' I feel even more strongly today that the government of Canada, especially the cur-rent government, has neither the will nor the capacity to pursue a responsible in-dependent policy in the OAS. We are bound to disappoint the Latin and Caribbean

[41] "Relationship of this Country to Pan American Movement Described," *supra* note 39.

[42] Interview, May 5, 1989, 31.

[43] John P. Humphrey, "Whither Canada?", *The Canadian Forum*, May 1940, at 44.

[44] John P. Humphrey, "A Recipe for Canadian Unity," *The Canadian Forum*, March 1943, at 345.

In 1945 Humphrey received his Ph.D. in political science. His thesis, later published in article form in the *University of Toronto Law Journal,* examined the theory of the separation of powers of government, though he preferred the label ''separation of functions.'' He began from the premise that governmental power resides in the state as a whole. Each branch of government in the exercise of different functions exercises one part of the larger whole of state power, whether that be legislative, judicial, or executive power. His central thesis was that the theory of the separation of functions ''will be found to be historically inaccurate, scientifically wrong, and undesirable as a principle of good government.''[45]

After outlining the British constitutional system, Humphrey discussed the overlap between different functions. He considered the extent to which the judiciary in Britain exercises legislative functions, and the extent to which the administrative and legislative branches exercise judicial functions. He concluded that ''[a]t no time has the theory of the separation of functions particularly as it has been stated by some of Montesquieu's followers, ever corresponded to the theory or practice of British government.''[46] He also found this to be the case in Canada. Even the United States, which recognized the separation of functions as a basic constitutional principle, had not strictly applied the doctrine in practice. Elaborating, Humphrey stated that, ''under modern conditions, when government is concerned with manifold problems unheard of in the eighteenth century, strict application of the doctrine would serve not so much as an instrument for the preservation of liberty as an obstacle to the achievement of the other purposes of government.''[47] Thus he suggested that the principle of the separation of functions has, in the United States, seriously affected the ability of government to conduct its international relations; the principle had been ignored or manipulated as administrative agencies exercised more and more legislative powers and the judiciary became a source of legislative authority by nature of its effective supremacy over the other branches of government.[48]

[45] ''The Theory of the Separation of Functions,'' (1946) 6 U. of T. L.J. 331.

[46] *Ibid.*, 342-43.

[47] *Ibid.*, 355-56.

[48] The ''rigid separation'' between the administration and the legislature was, in Humphrey's opinion, one of the reasons behind the failure of the U.S. to join the League of Nations, and therefore of the failure of the League itself, as President Wilson lacked the necessary support of Congress to achieve the League's success: *ibid.*, 356.

The theory of the separation of functions is better understood, Humphrey contended, as "an instrument of political action" than "as an objective statement of scientific principles of government." Arising out of "a passionate belief in liberty and a conviction that the legal order existed not only in the interest of the state but also in the interests of the people," this theory had often been relied on to weaken the control of a particular branch of government in favour of another and in the name of liberty. However, it may also be used "as a means of consolidating reaction and even of suppressing liberty." He put it thus:

In the twentieth century. . . men and women are as concerned with economic security and freedom from want as they are with political liberty. And when it appeared that the rigid categories that Montesquieu's followers had established were incompatible with the kind of governmental action that a new concept of democracy demanded, most people were ready to abandon a theory that had become an obstacle to political and social progress. There were others whose interests were opposed to change. Nothing could have been more natural than that these should have resurrected the shibboleth of separation in defence of a liberty that they interpreted as a perpetuation of their privileges. But the doctrine is dangerous even from the point-of-view of reactionary interests opposed to change; for a principle the rigidity of which can prevent social development and necessary change can eventually lead to the violent overthrow of the whole political order.[49]

In Humphrey's opinion, the solution to this stand-off lies in the reation and adoption of "adequate checks" against the arbitrary use of powers that have been concentrated in the various administrative agencies or other branches of government.

Having considered a basic principle of constitutional law in his doctoral work, Humphrey moved on to international law. In his well-known article, "On the Foundations of International Law," he examined the traditional international legal system founded on natural law and the consent of states after "the disintegration of the authority of the Pope and the Emperor."[50] In this article, he reviewed the thought of the classical writers, the Grotians, the positivists, and the naturalists. He concluded that the essential difference between them was the degree to which natural law or consent was given priority within their theoretical framework. He examined the nature of "consent" and concluded that consent to a system

---

[49] *Supra* note 45, at 360.

[50] "On the Foundations of International Law," (1945) 39 Am. J. Int'l L. 231.

of law in and of itself did not explain its character as ''law.'' After considering the customary rule *pacta sunt servanda,* he suggested that the search for an ''even more general'' fundamental norm must begin in order to explain the legal nature of international law. He then examined one such fundamental norm postulated by certain international jurists who sought to ground the validity of international law in ''the collective will of the subjects governed by it.'' This fundamental norm suggests that the will of the international community shall be obeyed. Humphrey argued that since the general will need not and perhaps cannot be shown, it was ''not possible to demonstrate the ultimate validity of any legal order by juridical reasoning.''[51]

The fundamental norm traceable to ''collective will'' presupposes the existence of an international community and the ''legal will'' of such a community. In the remainder of the article, Humphrey considered these two elements. While he found support for the existence of an international community, he arrived at the conclusion that the will of such a community cannot be a ''collective or common will'' separate from the will of each individual member of such a community. It is on this latter basis that the fundamental norm fails. In its place, Humphrey proposed ''the precept that international custom shall be obeyed,'' which, while not explaining the legal nature of custom, ''does, through the customary rule *pacta sunt servanda* explain the validity of treaties.'' That this norm fails to specify criteria for the development of custom or assumes the existence of law, is not a fatal flaw to Humphrey, who wrote:

the terms used in the suggested norm must carry within them their own definitions. By 'custom,' we mean a body of customary rules that emanate directly from the undifferentiated mass of the subjects governed by them and which are habitually obeyed because they are generally regarded to be binding. Whether or not a particular norm satisfies this definition is, we think, a question of fact the determination of which involves recourse to the judicial process.[52]

Nor does this norm deny the existence of other potential fundamental norms. Humphrey, a life-long advocate of the development of world order, perceptively identified as long ago as 1945, the potentiality of an even more fundamental norm, namely, ''that

[51] *Ibid.*, 239.
[52] *Ibid.*, 242.

the *constitution* of the world society shall be obeyed."[53]

In the same year that he examined the underlying theory of international law, Humphrey focused his attention on international legal order. Half a century later, he still regards his 1945 article, "The Parent of Anarchy," as his most important essay.[54] Relying on an article by Alexander Hamilton in *The Federalist* (no. XVI), he drew an analogy between federalism and the international legal order. Essential to the development of his timely and insightful exploration was the fact that in the classical inter-state system no legal relationship existed between the legal order and the individual men and women who were the objects of the law. Only states possessed international legal personalities and thus the rights and duties flowing therefrom. Similarly, few international organizations existed and, when later they did appear, they were typically inter-state organizations with powers subject to the limits of the doctrine of state sovereignty.

One of the first of these organizations, the League of Nations was, in Humphrey's opinion, "little more than an alliance of states." The United Nations Charter, an "agreement between states in their collective capacities," had not realized any further change in the relation between international law and the individual. In fact, for the five permanent members of the Security Council, the new international organization was "little more than a defensive alliance" in which the smaller states had formally accepted a legally inferior position. Because the five permanent members enjoyed a right of veto over almost all decisions save those on procedural matters, "the Security Council can hardly be considered a governmental organ possessing political or even legal superiority over the five states, which, because of their predominating international power and position are most in need of government."[55]

With no enforcement mechanisms, and no international police force, the United Nations would have to rely on the military might and co-operation of its member states, with the result that "if the members respect their undertaking to maintain the alliance," which many will be hesitant to do, against a state not complying with a Security Council decision, "the result will be equivalent to war,"

[53] *Ibid.*, 243, emphasis added. See too J. P. Humphrey, "Definition and Nature of Laws," (1945) 8 Modern L. R. 194.

[54] "The Parent of Anarchy," (1946) 1 Int'l J. 11.

[55] *Ibid.*, 15.

the very thing the United Nations was designed to remedy.[56]

Humphrey argued that the only real guarantor of peace is an international force under the control of the Security Council. The establishment of this force would have to overcome difficulties of recruitment, funding, raw materials, and issues of authority, and control. These difficulties, however, could not be overcome "as long as the world continues to be organized in the existing state system," for a government limited to collectivities and dependent on them "can govern only and so long as all of them or at least a preponderant number of them. . . remain in fundamental agreement." In the end, Humphrey argued that, to govern effectively, an international government must possess an effective monopoly over all the instruments of coercion, which, under modern conditions at least, is possible only when the authority of the government extends to individuals. Citing Hamilton's work on federalism in support of the federal principle of government, under which the powers of government are distributed between the different branches of government and within each branch of government, and imaginatively anticipating future developments, Humphrey insisted that there must be "a direct relationship" between the government and the citizens, who are "the only proper objects of government."[57]

Despite obvious obstacles, such as differences in language, religion, culture, political traditions, economic systems, and the "deeply imbedded and powerful vested interest which controls the various national governments," principles of federalism can be applied to the international community. Humphrey called for "the peoples of the world. . . [to]. . . somehow join in establishing a government that will be commensurate with the demonstrated needs of government; and, when their mandatories come together for that purpose, they must. . . finally reject that collective principle which has been a source of anarchy for centuries and the principal reason for the ineffectiveness of international law and international organizations."[58] For this purpose, Humphrey did not feel that the disappearance of existing states or "excessive centralization" was required. States would retain their sovereignty, subject to limited powers granted to the international government, through "radical amendments" to the United Nations Charter under the procedures of articles 108 and 109 of the Charter. This would enable in-

[56] *Ibid.*
[57] *Ibid.*, 19.
[58] *Ibid.*, 21.

dividual states to maintain their particular national traditions while existing co-extensively with "still larger loyalties," the possession of which by the international government would be as necessary in the performance of its high functions as its coercive powers, however strong.

The last forty-five years, twenty of which span Humphrey's tenure at the United Nations, have seen a dramatic change in the relationship between the individual and the international legal order. However, even today, the form of world government envisaged by him in 1946 remains distant and he seems resigned to that fact. In his article, "The United Nations in the Year 2000 A.D.," he refers to his 1945 article, stating that: "There is no lack of utopian plans based on principles which are familiar to political scientists, including formulae used in the constitutions of federal states; but they all come to grief at the point of implementation."[59] In 1945 Humphrey was one of a handful of Canadian professionals with the foresight to argue that the international legal system was "obsolete" primarily because of its "fundamental weakness," namely, the failure to incorporate a legal relationship between the legal order and the individual men and women who comprised it. In the years that followed, he continued to call for an increase in the status and rights of individuals, both within the framework of the state and the larger world community.[60] Yet in 1945 he could not have guessed that he would soon be involved personally "in a revolutionary attempt to dispel the parent of anarchy from its entrenched position in the international legal order."[61]

OTHER INVOLVEMENTS AT MCGILL AND WITHIN THE MONTREAL COMMUNITY

While Humphrey denies any direct political involvement during this early period at McGill,[62] the fact is that he began to pub-

---

[59] "The Main Functions of the United Nations in the Year 2000 A.D.," (1971) 17 McGill L.J. 219, 225.

[60] Speech, St. Mary's University Convocation Address, May 12, 1984, at 9; "Two Parents of Anarchy," June 4, 1985, at 5-7; "The Dean Who Never Was," (1989) 34 McGill L.J. 191, 198.

[61] "Two Parents of Anarchy," *supra* 5-7.

[62] In 1932, he had considered running as the Canadian Labour Party's candidate in the federal by-election in Maisonneuve; however, he realized that "I would be without a job the day my candidature was announced. There isn't much glory in being a defeated Labour candidate when you're without a job." JPH to Ruth, May 28, 1932, at 1, 4. Later Humphrey is reported to have been named by the

lish articles and speak out on political and legal issues, national as well as international.[63] He had come a long way from his first publication, a letter to the *Saint John Telegraph* written while a student at Rothesay Collegiate, in which he urged the union of the three maritime provinces. One of the first of his forthright articles, in which he attacked the Duplessis regime's Padlock Law, was published in *The Canadian Magazine* in 1939.[64]

Several institutions and organizations feature significantly at this stage of Humphrey's development, particularly the League for Social Reconstruction, the Canadian Institute of International Affairs, and the League of Nations Society (later the United Nations Associations). As former Canadian diplomat Escott Reid notes in his memoirs, thinking about foreign affairs and Canadian foreign policy in the thirties "did not take place in closed compartments of the CIIA, or the League of Nations Society, or the League for Social Reconstruction" because members of one organization were also active in another.[65] These associations all influenced Humphrey's thinking at the time.[66]

Board of Governors as one of its three representatives to the reorganized Montreal City Council: "McGill Names Three to City Council," *Montreal Daily Star,* Nov. 8, 1940, at 3.

[63] "Canadian-American Friendship" (1938-1939) 8 U. of T. Quarterly 242; "The Twenty-Second Chair: Is It for Canada?," (1941) 3 Inter-American Quarterly 5; "Homes Are Not Castles," *Canadian Magazine,* Mar. 1939, at 9; "Whither Canada?," *Canadian Forum,* May 1940; "Canada and the Mexican Revolution," *The Canadian Forum,* Dec. 1940, at 269; "Pan America in the World Order," *The Canadian Forum,* 1941, vol. XXI, at 199; "Argentina's Diplomatic Victory," *The Canadian Forum,* 1942, vol. XXI, at 362; "A Recipe for Canadian Unity," *The Canadian Forum,* 1942, vol. XXII, at 345; "Dumbarton Oaks at San Francisco," *The Canadian Forum,* 1945, vol. XXV, at 6.

[64] "Homes Are Not Castles," *The Canadian Magazine,* vol. 91, no. 3, Mar. 1939, at 12; Original Manuscript, 103; Interview, May 5, 1989, at 32.

[65] Escott Reid, *supra* note 38, at 74.

[66] On the general background, see especially Michiel Horn, *The League for Social Reconstruction* (Toronto: University of Toronto Press, 1980); Michiel Horn, "Lost Causes: The League for Social Reconstruction and the Cooperative Commonwealth Federation in Quebec in the 1930s and 1940s," Journal of Canadian Studies, vol. 19, no. 2, 1984, at 132-56. See also two important reviews of Sandra Djwa, *The Politics of the Imagination: A Life of F. R. Scott* (Toronto: McClelland & Stewart, 1987): Kenneth McNaught, (1989) 12 McGill L.J. 422; also, J. King Gordon, (1989) 12 Dalhousie L.J. 567; and see also J. King Gordon, "Scholarly Study Cannot Contain Old Radical Underhill," rev. of R. Douglas Francis, *Frank Underhill: Intellectual Provocateur* (Toronto: University of Toronto Press, 1986) in *The Citizen* (Ottawa), Sept. 27, 1986, at C5.

For him, the League for Social Reconstruction, of which he was a charter member of the Montreal branch, was both "[a]n important influence on my intellectual and political development and a source of new friends." Meetings were often combined with social gatherings. At the same time, he states that: "I regret, in retrospect, that I took no part in the serious and lasting work of the LSR which included the publication of some good books. Nor did I join or work actively for the CCF. I was, and remained, very much on the periphery."[67] This fact he attributes to his "over-riding preoccupation" with international affairs and, significantly, to the conclusion he had reached that the majority of participants in the socialist movement "seemed to have the least interest in international affairs."[68]

The Canadian Institute of International Affairs (CIIA), which Humphrey had joined while in law practice, was a significant institution for internationally minded Canadians of the time. It was formative of his education in international affairs.[69] It was in the first volume of the Institute's *International Journal* that one of his early articles, "The Parent of Anarchy" — "the best and most original article I ever wrote" — was published.

The membership of the CIIA was diverse. One group, which favoured close links between Canada, Britain, and a "closely knit empire," included prominent public figures, such as Sir Robert Borden, Newton Rowell, Vincent Massey, and Sir Arthur Currie. Another group, comprising younger members, generally academics, did not hold the same views. A third group included members of the Canadian League, formed in 1924 "to foster the national spirit as opposed to sectionalism, and to stimulate popular interest in public affairs."[70] At the beginning of Humphrey's involvement with the CIIA, its primary activity was the presentation of public lectures. He was Vice-Chairman of the Montreal Branch from 1943-44 and Chairman of the New York Branch from 1961-66. Later, he was active with the United Nations Association, which replaced the League of Nations Society, the object of which was "to foster the spirit of internationalism."[71] In October 1945, he was elected Presi-

[67] Original Manuscript, 105, 107; Interview, May 5, 1988, at 30.

[68] Original Manuscript, 107.

[69] Original Manuscript, 108; for extended discussion of the CIIA's activities, see Escott Reid, *supra* note 38, chs. 6 and 7.

[70] Escott Reid, *supra* note 38, at 75.

[71] "Professor J. Humphrey to Head Society," *Montreal Daily Star,* Oct. 30, 1945.

dent of the Montreal Branch of the United Nations Society.[72] He did not know then that he would soon become much more closely tied to the United Nations.

Although deeply committed to his duties at McGill, as he has been for thirty-six years, Humphrey's interests were not limited to the field of law. A francophile, and well-acquainted with French literature, law, and culture, he eagerly sought out French-Canadian nationalists. His concern about the widening cultural gulf between the French and English in Canada and at McGill in particular led him to aid in efforts to bring the first French law professor to McGill.[73] Using their Montreal apartment as a base, he and Jeanne entertained people such as André Laurendeau, editor of *L'Action Nationale*, Émile Vaillancourt, and François Albert Angers, professor at École des Hautes Études Commerciales. Fatefully, it was through his friendship with the painter Louise Gadbois that Humphrey met Henri Laugier, a former titular Professor of Medicine at the Sorbonne who had exiled himself from Vichy France during the war to come to Canada via the United States.[74] Laugier occupied a teaching position at the Université de Montréal which the Rockefeller Foundation had arranged for him. Laugier would later provide Humphrey with a rare opportunity to enter the United Nations' legal community.

The Humphreys were also actively involved with the art community in Montreal. Through friends such as the Palardys, John

[72] *United Nations News,* Oct. 1945; "United Nations Slate Named," *Montreal Daily Star,* Apr. 30, 1947. Humphrey was re-elected to this position in 1947, and was National President from 1968 to 1970.

[73] Louis Baudoin was appointed Professor of Civil Law in 1948, at the age of 78. Humphrey was also instrumental in bringing a distinguished French jurist, René Savatier, to give a series of lectures at McGill; Original Manuscript, 104-05; *A Great Adventure,* 2.

[74] *A Great Adventure* 1; Interview, May 6, 1989, at 18; "Dean Who Never Was," *supra* note 60, at 195. Henri Laugier (1888-1973), after a distinguished pre-war academic career, went to the University of Algiers as Rector in the fall of 1943 and returned to France in 1944 after the liberation. He was UN Assistant Secretary-General from 1946 to 1951. When Laugier arrived in Washington early in the war, speaking no English, a position was found for him on the recommendation of the Rockefeller Institute as a professor of physiology at the Université de Montréal. He had been a titular professor in this field at the University of Paris. Humphrey stated elsewhere that he had met Laugier through Émile Vaillancourt in Montreal (Original Manuscript, 105) and that Laugier had held the chair in psychology at the Sorbonne, before being given a post at the Université de Montréal as Professor of Medicine, in spite of his open anti-clericalism and confrontational nature; Simone Auger, "Un Canadien, peut-il fair carrière a l'ONU en 1963?," *Le Magazine de la Presse,* 9 mars 1963, at 6.

and Corinne Lyman, and Goodrich Roberts, they "got to know most of the artists in the city. . . . I was even appointed the Secretary of the Eastern Group which was organized at one enthusiastic meeting to promote their interests."[75] In addition, Humphrey was one of the incorporators and later Vice-President of the Contemporary Art Society, whose members included John Lyman, Louis Joseph Barcelan, Allan Harrison, Louis Muhlstock, Paul-Émile Borduas, Dr. Paul Dumas, and Luc Choquette.[76] Describing his friends at this time, he notes: "[I]t was a characteristic of this somewhat Bohemian group that it straddled both language groups. Not only were there both French and English Canadians, but several of the couples were mixed marriages including ourselves. . . . There were no 'two solitudes' there."[77] Nevertheless, the group remained exceptional. On his return to Montreal twenty years later, he found that the situation had changed markedly.

THE WAR YEARS

The period in which Humphrey began his teaching career was a time of grave events in international affairs. In October 1935, on the eve of the Ethiopian war, Humphrey had given a speech before the Saturday Night Club in Montreal on the League of Nations and the role it could play in the prevention of war through its mediation of the crisis resulting from Mussolini's invasion of North Africa. He stated:

If, by collective application of sanctions, the Italians can be not only curbed in their nefarious campaign, but publicly humiliated and punished as breakers of the international peace, the prestige of the League will be raised to a point that cannot easily be exaggerated, and civilization will have taken one of its greatest steps forward. On the other hand, if the League fails us in this crisis, it would be equally hard to exaggerate the extent of the step backward that civilization will take. As for the League itself, it would hardly be worth the paper on which the Covenant is written after such a defeat.[78]

Breaking decisively with F. R. Scott, David Lewis, Eugene Forsey, King Gordon, and other colleagues, Humphrey rejected the

---

[75] Original Manuscript, 101.

[76] See Christopher Varley's essay in *The Contemporary Arts Society, Montreal, 1939-1948* 96 (Edmonton: Edmonton Art Gallery, 1980).

[77] Original Manuscript, 103-3.

[78] Speech, Saturday Night Club, Oct. 17, 1935, at 1-2.

arguments made in the LSR's *Social Planning for Canada* that the
League of Nations was merely established for the defence of "principles of property." In view of Germany's and Russia's entry into
the League and despite Germany's later decision to withdraw, he
argued that the LSR's opinion, that Article 10 of the Covenant and
the Allied Powers' control of the League Council served to maintain "the status quo fixed by the Treaty of Versailles," had lost its
persuasive value. Nevertheless, he agreed that the Covenant of the
League was "essentially static in its character," and in agreement
with his friends in the LSR, continued:

peace as an ideal has been too often indissolubly bound up with the status quo as a
fact. It is not enough merely to prohibit wars of conquest and suppression [in Article 10 of the League]. An effort must be made to remove the
fundamental causes of war. War has been one of the means whereby, from
time to time, states have revised the established order. The analogy for
war in the domestic sphere is revolution, and our only safeguard against
revolution is our readiness to meet legitimate grievances by ordered
changes in the established order. We shall not have solved the problem
of peace until we can devise some ordered process whereby we can satisfy the legitimate demand for change in the international order.[79]

Article 19, which provided for the "reconsideration" of treaties
that had become "inapplicable," as well as of "international conditions whose continuance might endanger the peace of the world,"
constituted such a mechanism, though in its unamended form it
was a relatively weak, non-binding, rule of procedure. Nevertheless, this was the "first time in history, it has been recognized . . . that
grave conflicts menacing to peace may arise out of the maintenance
of what from a static point of view is legally valid law, the legitimate status quo." Humphrey correctly called for Article 19 to be
made more effective through amendment. With prescience, he
warned that "Man's fate may well depend upon whether or not
this machinery can be devised."[80] The Second World War broke
out four years later.

It was at the beginning of his third year on the McGill law faculty
that the Second World War began. Humphrey became a solid supporter of the Free French and, near the end of the war, was the
only anglophone member of a committee that tried without much
success to replace French textbooks that had been destroyed. At
the beginning of the war, however, he was, in his own words, "am-

[79] *Ibid.*, 13-14.
[80] *Ibid.*, 13.

bivalent'' about Canadian participation; he could not foresee any lasting peace without at least ''an effective system of collective security,'' if not ''some form of supranational government.''[81] If war was inevitable, he felt that it should be carried on under the auspices of the League.

When war came, Humphrey ''welcomed'' it, ''if such a word can be used with reference to such an awesome event,'' thinking that on the defeat of Germany ''a new and better international order could be created.''[82] However, he was, naturally, concerned as to Canada's role. He insisted that Canada's contribution in a second world war would only be effective if the country entered the war as a nation and of its own free choice. In 1942, during a CBC discussion between him, Hugh MacLennan, and Émile Vaillancourt, entitled ''Canadian Unity and Quebec,'' he suggested that in the pre-war period, Canada lacked a ''clear-cut personality.''[83] Canadian nationalists, he said, sought ''recognition of the independent status of Canada as a member of the international community. . .'' Independent status meant a number of things, among them the power to amend the Canadian constitution, the abolition of appeals to the Judicial Committee of the Privy Council, and Canada's right to conduct its own foreign policy. A Canadian nationalist, Humphrey was at the same time an internationalist ''and as I understood Canadian nationalism in the period between the two wars, I didn't think I was being inconsistent.''[84]

With language divisions setting the stage for political positions on conscription as well as on Canada's entry into the war, Humphrey argued that Canada needed to find its ''common national purpose.'' Such a purpose clearly included the defeat of Germany and its allies, but to allay the fears of Quebec, which obviously did not have the same emotional ties to Great Britain as the rest of the country, the common purpose needed to be phrased in accordance with a clear vision of *Canada,* not simply Canada as an

[81] Original Manuscript, 112.

[82] Interview, May 5, 1989.

[83] Transcript, CBC discussion, ''Canadian Unity and Quebec'' (Montreal: Canadian Printing and Lithographing, 1942), Nov. 29, 1942, Émile Vaillancourt, Hugh MacLennan, and John Humphrey, 16 pages, at 3 (hereafter ''Transcript, CBC''). On this event, see too Elspeth Cameron, *Hugh MacLennan, A Writer's Life,* esp. at 165-67 (Toronto: University of Toronto Press, 1981).

[84] Original Manuscript, 113; ''The Pursuit of Excellence,'' *McGill News,* Fall 1976, at 6; ''Nationalism, Freedoms and Social Justice'' (1975-76), 55 Dalhousie Review, 605, 607.

extension of Great Britain. While Vaillancourt noted that "for any country to feel a *prior* loyalty to another land makes true nation-hood impossible," Humphrey was quick to point out that loyalty to Canada and Great Britain need not be inconsistent. He agreed when Vaillancourt emphasized that to the extent that Quebec supported Canadian intervention, she did so because she believed "that England's cause is her own cause and the cause of humanity."[85]

The perceived need to establish a Canadian identity and a common national purpose resulted in Humphrey, along with Percy Corbett, taking the position that, as an assertion of Canadian autonomy in matters of foreign policy, Canada should either remain neutral in a world war involving Great Britain or enter hostilities on its own initiative. The Balfour report of 1926 and the Statute of Westminster of 1931 provided the legal framework within which a declaration of neutrality could be formulated. Corbett was of the opinion that a declaration enacted by Canada and concurred in by Great Britain, either expressly or by acquiescence, would be binding in international law.[86]

[85] "Transcript, CBC," at 7-8. Émile Vaillancourt (1889- 1968) was manager of the Montreal Tourist and Convention Bureau from 1936 to 1940. He was later Canada's ambassador to Cuba (1945-48), Yugoslavia (1948-50), and Peru (1950-55). With respect to conscription, Humphrey would say, in his Original Manuscript, 113-14:

> The country was still suffering from the divisive consequences of the imposition of conscription during the First World War. I felt so strongly about this that I wrote a letter to the Prime Minister. Quebec, I wrote, would support the war, but there must be no conscription - which was still identified as a symbol of English Canadian domination. I had a long reply to this letter from Arnold Heeney, my classmate, who was now the Prime Minister's Secretary. Heeney, however, had missed the point of my letter which he apparently interpreted as isolationist in spirit. This annoyed me. I have never been an isolationist. In my letter to the Prime Minister, I had also offered my services in any useful capacity, but no advantage was taken of this offer. The only time the government ever asked me to do anything was when, immediately after the end of hostilities in Europe, but while Canadian troops were still there, I was asked to be part of a team of lecturers who would go into the camps to help prepare them for their return to civilian life. But at the very last minute, after all the arrangements had been made and I was booked to sail from New York, the cabinet cancelled the project. I was told later that General McNaughton objected to the presence of O'Leary on the team.

[86] Such a strategy would not have been possible under the League of Nations structure as Canada would have been obliged to enter into collective sanctions designed to halt aggressor nations: "Canada and War," Transcript of "National Forum," CBC, Jan. 12, 1939 (speakers: Norman MacKenzie, University of Toronto, and Percy Corbett, McGill University), 8 pages. A great deal of the effort of Canadian diplomacy in the 1930s and 1940s lay simply in attempting to get the British and Americans to take Canada seriously as an independent nation: see John English,

For those like Humphrey who advocated "at least one week's official neutrality," there was a real danger of being perceived as disloyal to Great Britain, a most serious charge in English Canada at that time.[87] However, advocates of neutrality were not only in academia. Escott Reid recently estimated that "five of the seven senior officers in the Department of External Affairs in Ottawa: [O. D.] Skelton, [Loring] Christie, Laurent Beaudry, Hugh Keenleyside, and Scott Macdonald" held such a view at least until the outbreak of war.[88] Outrage at the number of lives needlessly lost in the First World War, revulsion against the wartime propaganda that had been accepted as truth, fear of another devastating world war, belief that the treaties terminating the First World War had been inequitable, and belief "in a balance of forces in Europe" were all factors underscoring these neutralist views.

Humphrey's position should not be taken as one of neutrality in any event. Affected by the events of the Spanish Civil War and the increasing expansionism of Germany, he was "very much pro-war." When the decision was made that Canada would enter the conflict, he was "pleased" both with MacKenzie King's decision to wait for one week after the British declaration and with President Roosevelt's recognition of Canadian neutrality during that period.[89]

Montreal soon became home to a number of refugees from many parts of Europe. Further, Montreal, and the McGill University campus in particular, replaced Geneva as the centre for the International Labour Organization in the war years. Thus the Humphreys met and entertained many international officials, including Wilfred Jenks, later Director General of the ILO. As the war wore on, Humphrey became concerned as to how the international community would be organized for peace and security in the future. Having

---

Shadow of Heaven: The Life of Lester Pearson Volume One: 1899-1948 (Toronto: Lester & Orpen Dennys, 1989).

[87] Interview, May 6, 1989, at 2-3; Escott Reid, *supra* note 38, at 91. Michiel Horn has reminded us that "Canadians expected their intellectuals to be 'useful' or 'constructive' in an auxiliary capacity, or else decorative and possibly entertaining. They did not expect them to be critical or radical. . . .When Frank Underhill came close to being dismissed . . . it was less his socialism than his 'anti-Britishism' that was at issue": Horn, *supra* note 66 at 205, 208.

[88] Escott Reid, *supra* note 38, at 124; see also 117-25.

[89] Interview, May 5, 1989, at 30-31; *The Inter-American System: A Canadian View* (Toronto: Macmillan, 1942); Escott Reid, *supra* note 38, at 153-58. See too Michael Oliver, "F. R. Scott: Quebecer," in Sandra Djwa and R. St. J. Macdonald (eds.), *On F. R. Scott* 165-77 (Montreal: McGill-Queen's University Press, 1983).

written on the Dumbarton Oaks proposals,[90] and wishing to participate in the San Francisco Conference in one capacity or another, he contacted the Department of External Affairs. Nevertheless, neither he nor Percy Corbett were placed in Canada's service, possibly because the Canadian foreign service was not yet accustomed to including academics in delegations, but perhaps also because of the views they had expressed about Canada's entry into the war.

THE "DEAN WHO NEVER WAS"

In 1945 Humphrey was involved in a controversy at McGill that still rankles half a century later. Stuart Le Mesurier was retiring as dean of the law faculty. F. R. Scott, the most senior professor, was next in line, but his outspoken views and his commitment to the CCF made him unacceptable to the Board of Governors. As Humphrey has stated, "J. W. McConnell, the owner of the *Montreal Star*, which was still in publication, and one of the wealthiest men in Canada, was a very influential Governor of the University. And he couldn't stand Frank because of Frank's socialism. Indeed, the *Star* had orders never to publish anything Frank said."[91] So Scott did not become dean of law until much later. He was not alone: many of those involved in left-wing politics in the twenties and thirties encountered similar difficulties as a result of their challenge to the establishment. The situation has been described by Escott Reid as follows:

At the beginning of November, 1937, I wrote to Underhill, 'I hope you don't get into any trouble this year with the oligarchs of Ontario, or as John Stevenson calls them, the inflated gold bugs...' Two years later, Underhill did get into trouble with the oligarchs and from 1939 to 1941, he was repeatedly threatened with dismissal from the University of Toronto....Three of his colleagues in the LSR and CCF were less fortunate. They were penalized for their left-wing views. King Gordon was dismissed in 1934 from his professorship at the United Theological College in Montreal, and Eugene Forsey and Leonard Marsh in 1941 from their lectureships at McGill University. Frank Scott was not dismissed in 1947 from the law faculty at McGill, but he was denied appointment as dean...an appointment he richly deserved. He was not made Dean until 1961. We had McCarthyism in Canada before McCarthy.[92]

[90] Humphrey, "Dumbarton Oaks at San Francisco," *The Canadian Forum* 1945, vol. XXV, no. 291, at 6-10; Interview, May 5, 1989, at 22; Interview, May 6, 1989, at 8-9.

[91] Interview, May 6, 1989, at 13; McNaught, *supra* note 66, at 424.

[92] Escott Reid, *supra* note 38, at 115, 146-48. Reid is not quite accurate on Forsey: see

F. R. Scott was thus passed over and the choice for dean was between a "downtown" lawyer and John Humphrey.

There remains a question as to the sequence of events at this stage. It is clear that Cyril James, Principal of McGill University, had discussions with Humphrey as to his possible candidacy for the deanship. Humphrey claims that an offer was extended and that he accepted it. Though he acknowledges that he did not publicly discharge any major official duties of the deanship, he is insistent on the fact that, after accepting James's offer, he did assume and discharge administrative duties as dean of the faculty before the end of the summer of 1946.[93]

News of the possible appointment spread quickly. In the minds of the Board of Governors of McGill, Humphrey possessed ideological views similar to those of F. R. Scott, or at least sympathized with them, and indeed he did.[94] In the event, two weeks after Principal Cyril James had extended what in Humphrey's mind was a firm offer, James telephoned him. The exact content of this conversation was not recorded by James in his diaries; however, as Humphrey recalls, James told him — "he didn't even invite me down to his office" — that "it would be wiser to give no further publicity to the matter until the storm blew over."[95]

Horn, *supra* note 66, at 184-85. For the full story on Underhill, see Francis, *supra* note 66.

[93] Interview, May 6, 1989, at 112-14. The McGill Archives Index of Faculty Appointments lists Humphrey as "Acting Dean of the Faculty of Law" in 1946: see Index Card on J. P. Humphrey, McGill Archives.

[94] "We were all part of the left thirties in Montreal. Indeed if we had had a McCarthy in Canada we would all have been in trouble later on": Interview, May 5, 1989, at 30; Interview, May 6, 1989, at 12-14. In 1932 Humphrey had written to his sister Ruth that "I'm like Leon Blum, to me socialism is a religion": JPH to Ruth, May 28, 1932, at 4-5. It should be remembered that Humphrey at this time had already become an outspoken critic of the politics of English language dominance in Quebec (see Humphrey's *Canadian Forum* articles "Whither Canada?" and "A Recipe for Canadian Unity," *supra* notes 43 and 44, respectively). It is possible that Humphrey's close connections with Quebec's francophone elite and his strong views on the subject of English-French relations did not sit comfortably with the Governors of McGill University at the time. See also R. A. Macdonald to RStJM, Nov. 22, 1991, at 2.

[95] JPH to RStJM, with attachment, Sept. 20, 1983; Interview, Saturday, May 6, 1989, at 13; Stanley Frost, *The Man in the Ivory Tower* (Montreal: McGill-Queen's University Press, 1991), makes no mention of the incident. See too review of Frost by Michiel Horn in *Historical Studies in Education* (forthcoming, 1992).

APPOINTMENT TO THE UNITED NATIONS

For Humphrey, the controversy over the deanship soon lost its importance. Laugier, who had left Canada at the time of the liberation of North Africa, had become Rector of the University of Algiers, then the only free French university. (In his capacity as Rector in 1944, he had awarded Humphrey an honorary doctorate.) After the liberation of France, he became Director General of Cultural Relations in the French Foreign Office. Later, he became one of the Assistant Secretaries General in the United Nations Secretariat in charge of the Department of Social Affairs, which incorporated within it the Division for Human Rights.[96]

In a telephone call to Humphrey from New York in 1946, Laugier offered him the first Directorship of the Human Rights Division. Conditional on being allowed to continue with his previously arranged holidays in the Gaspé, Humphrey accepted and thus entered a thrilling new phase of his life. In addition to his friendship with Laugier, Humphrey later attributed his own interest in the question of linguistic minorities in Canada, particularly the French in Quebec, and his bilingualism, as factors in Laugier's decision to consider him for an appointment to the United Nations. Before leaving McGill, Humphrey secured a two-year leave of absence and the University resolved the deanship problem by asking Le Mesurier to carry on.[97]

Enthusiastic about his upcoming appointment to the United Nations as Director of the Human Rights Division, Humphrey had "few, if any," qualifications for the job. When he arrived at Hunter College in New York, at the temporary headquarters of the Secretariat in August 1946, he "had very little idea of what was expected from...the Director of such a division." It was the first time such a position had been created and, as he tells it, "there was nobody from whom I could seek instructions." Laugier, "whose principal qualification in the matter was also enthusiasm," was not at Headquarters upon Humphrey's arrival.[98]

In his book, *Human Rights and the United Nations: A Great Adventure,* published eighteen years after his departure from New York,

[96] *A Great Adventure* 2; René Cassin, "Looking Back on the Universal Declaration of 1948," (1968) Rev. of Contemporary Law (No. 1) 13, at 13-14.

[97] "The Dean Who Never Was," *supra* note 60, at 196; Interview, May 6, 1989, at 13-14.

[98] *A Great Adventure* 2-3, 7; Speech, Eleanor Roosevelt Memorial Address, Collegiate Council for the United Nations, Sarah Lawrence College, June 17, 1966, 10 pages, at 2; "The Dean Who Never Was," *supra* note 60, at 196.

Humphrey describes the first twenty years of the Directorship of the Human Rights Division. His tenure there, from 1946 to 1966, spanned a period of crucial importance in the history of the organization, during which it inaugurated its law-making activities in the field of human rights, beginning with the Universal Declaration of Human Rights and ending on the eve of the adoption of the two International Covenants. His involvement in the drafting of these instruments, particularly the Universal Declaration of Human Rights, was, and remains, perhaps his most celebrated achievement and certainly a focal point for his intellectual interests and academic writings. The Human Rights Division was involved in a number of other important activities including the inauguration of a human rights "Action Programme."[99] In addition to his direct involvement with these historic events, one of Humphrey's most significant accomplishments during twenty years of service at the United Nations was the role he was able to play in keeping the United Nations' human rights program "alive when it was under attack, especially in the United Nations Secretariat."[100]

Humphrey's first task at the United Nations was to establish his Division. Though several members of his staff had already been hired by the time of his arrival, it was up to him to hire further personnel and to plan the administrative work of the Division. His first concern was to hire "some good lawyers, preferably with international experience." With Laugier's backing, he was able to "build up one of the best, although smaller, divisions in the Secretariat."[101] In fact, Laugier's assistance and counsel were in—valuable, although Humphrey's close relationship with Laugier had its disadvantages:

Things went well — perhaps too well — for me as long as he [Laugier] remained in the Secretariat. Our personal relationship was so close and

[99] B. G. Ramcharan, review of *A Great Adventure* in 23 *Canadian Yearbook of International Law* 471 (1985).

[100] "The Dean Who Never Was," *supra* note 60, 194-195.

[101] Humphrey describes the members of his staff as follows: "Intellectually, the members of the Division of Human Rights could have held their own in most groups of civil servants or academics. They were also hard-working, loyal and friendly; and they believed in the significance of what they were doing. The fact that they were of many races, nationalities, and creeds, added to their richness as a team; and such was their devotion to the United Nations that in professional matters they acted objectively without regard to the special interests of the countries from which they happened to come. When we disagreed, it was usually because of some personal or other reason such as would have divided officials in a national administration": *A Great Adventure* 7, 33-34, 96-97.

so warm that I could always depend upon his support. His departure in 1951 did more than leave a void. Not only was he no longer there with his unfailing support, but I discovered that having been so closely identified with him also had its drawbacks, for he had many enemies, and they were usually in high places. . . .Quite innocently, I inherited some of this resentment; it was, as it were, a case of guilt by association.[102]

Though initially "glamorous," work in an international organization soon began to resemble work in bureaucracies everywhere. The functioning of an international bureaucracy was found to be further complicated by cultural as well as personality conflicts, personal ambitions, and "international politics." Nevertheless, the establishment of the Division of Human Rights, which by 1959 was an office of some thirty professional officers and twenty staff from roughly twenty different countries, signalled an extremely important new era in the history of the development of international organizations and of the international law of human rights.[103]

Humphrey's enthusiasm for the human rights program was not universally shared. He soon discovered the reality of working to advance human rights in the context of increasing East-West tensions. The change of government in the United States, the departure of Mrs. Roosevelt, and the onset of McCarthyism substantially altered the mood in the United States with respect to the human rights agenda. Indeed, McCarthyism and the onset of the Cold War made work at the United Nations extremely difficult. Excerpts from Humphrey's diaries at the time show the enormous stress and drain on morale that resulted from the bringing of United Nations' personnel before the Senate Subcommittee on Internal Security.[104] In his diaries, Humphrey described a series of disturbing events as a "hate campaign against the United Nations." While speaking before the American Academy of Political and Social Science in 1947, he referred to the Division as the creation of a kind of supranational supervision of the relationship between a state and its citizens. What really upset the Americans was his reference in this speech to the human rights program as "revolutionary." "That remark," he later noted, "dogged me for the rest of my career at the United Nations' Secretariat" and formed the basis for the sus-

[102] *A Great Adventure* 7; Interview, May 6, 1989, at 17.

[103] Joseph MacSween "Hampton Man's Position in the U.N. 'Interesting but Frustrating'," *The Telegraph Journal,* Saint John, New Brunswick, Feb. 14, 1959.

[104] See A. J. Hobbins, "Human Rights Inside the United Nations: The Humphrey Diaries, 1948-1959," (1991) 4 Fontanus 143, at 156-63.

tained effort of the American Bar Association to resist the human rights program at the United Nations.[105]

Similarly, he found the Secretaries-General with whom he worked, Trygve Lie, Dag Hammarskjold, and U Thant, less than sensitive to matters of human rights.[106] He found it significant, and who in his position would not, that when, in the early years of the Secretariat, the United States accused members of the Secretariat staff of subversion, Trygve Lie, whom Humphrey never got to know intimately, failed to request advice from the Human Rights Division. Humphrey felt that "if the Universal Declaration had any meaning, it at least established standards for the organization which adopted it. . .a stronger Secretary-General would have resisted the pressures and if his position then became impossible, resigned."[107] That Laugier soon quarrelled with Lie did not improve matters.

It is of great interest to note that Humphrey found Dag

---

[105] "The Revolution in the International Law of Human Rights," (1975) 4 Human Rights 205, 209. For an illustration of the attitudes within the American Bar Association, see "Declaration on Human Rights: Canadian, American Bars Ask Delay of Action," (1948) 34 A.B.A.J. 881; Moses Moskowitz, "Is the U.N.'s Bill of Human Rights Dangerous? A Reply to President Holman," (1949) 35 A.B.A.J. 283. See also Humphrey's own diary entry of Sept. 21, 1948, where he discusses the speech of the President of the American Bar Association, Frank E. Holman: "He says that the U.N. human rights programme is an attempt to establish State socialism 'if not communism'. . .he is reported as having mentioned me personally as having admitted the 'revolutionary' character of the programme. Of course it will be revolutionary if we succeed, but there is nothing particularly revolutionary in what we have done up until now": Hobbins, *supra*, 146. According to Hobbins' research into Humphrey's diaries, Hammarskjold's attitude towards human rights had begun to alter with time. In 1957 Humphrey wrote: "It would certainly be wrong to say that he has become an enthusiastic supporter of the human rights programme, but there is very real evidence of an evolution in the right direction": Hobbins, *supra*, 165.

[106] *A Great Adventure* 3, 270, 316; Ramcharan review, *supra* note 99, at 472. Humphrey's interpretation of the alleged lack of interest of the secretaries-general in the human rights area is now coming to be widely accepted. See, for example, observations of Christine M. Cerna in (1982) 86 Am. J. Int'l L. 191-93.

[107] *A Great Adventure* 134; Roger S. Clark, review of *A Great Adventure*, (1984) 79 Am.J.Int'l.L. 195-96. Accounts of the period range from Alistair Cooke's pioneer *Generation on Trial* to Whittaker Chamber's suspect *Witness*, both of which convey the confusion and equivocation that were part of that time, to Shirley Hazzard's *Countenance of Truth* (New York: Viking, 1990), a "Counter Blast" on the secretaries-general. On Trygve Lie, see James Barros, *Trygve Lie and the Cold War* (Dekalb, IL: Northern Illinois University Press, 1989); Trygve Lie, *In the Cause of Peace* (New York: Macmillan, 1954). See too M. J. Heale, *American Anticommunism: Combatting the Enemy Within 1830-1970*, esp. at 145-91 (Baltimore and London: Johns Hopkins University Press, 1990); John Patrick Diggins, *The Proud Decades* (New York: Norton, 1988); and Lillian Hellman, *Scoundrel Time* (New York: Macmillan, 1976).

Hammarskjold, for all his enigmatic glamour, not sympathetic at all to the objectives of the Human Rights Division. Hammarskjold had wanted to reorganize the Secratariat in 1954 in such a way that the Division would have become an office rather than a separate division. In fact, Humphrey's relations with Hammarskjold were never good and were not improved by the Secretary-General's extraordinary comments to the effect that he [Hammarskjold] would like "to throw the Human Rights Covenants out of the window," because they had generated heated debate on such delicate issues as self-determination and colonialism. Humphrey was asked to make concerted efforts "to keep the human rights programme going at the slowest speed possible," instructions he says he did not follow.[108] In Humphrey's opinion it was not until 1960, when Hammarskjold made a speech in the Security Council with reference to "flagrant violations of human rights" in the Congo that, "for the first and last time," he ever showed any concern about human rights.[109] Similarly, U Thant gave "no priority" to the work of the United Nations in the field of human rights, "though in speeches prepared for him by his staff, he would come out strongly on the side of human rights."[110]

Not only had it apparently been difficult to persuade the three Secretaries-General of the significance of the human rights program, but Laugier's successors as Assistant Secretaries-General for Economic and Social Affairs were not particularly interested in the long-term development of the Division of Human Rights either, even if they had been at the beginning. In addition to constant battles over personnel and funding, Humphrey also struggled against attempts at administrative reorganization that would have moved his division to Geneva. He felt, quite rightly, that these attempts, if successful, would have moved the Division "away from the political centre" of human rights, thereby weakening the effectiveness of the program.[111] That the Human Rights Division was able to carry

---

[108] "The Dean Who Never Was," *supra* note 60, at 194-95; as to Humphrey's relations with Hammarskjold, see *A Great Adventure* 3-4, 79, 205.

[109] *A Great Adventure* 270; Clark, *supra* note 107, at 196. "Hammarskjold's attitude may have been due to American pressure, but the fact is that he never understood even the political importance of the program. I could never understand how it was he couldn't understand that human rights had political significance. I do not put Hammarskjold on the top of my list of Secretaries-General at all": Interview, July 13, 1990, at 14-15, May 6, 1989, at 16, 20, 21.

[110] *A Great Adventure* 316; Interview, May 6, 1989, at 15-16.

[111] *A Great Adventure* 47.

out its work in the face of these obstacles attests to the determination of Humphrey and his staff and their belief in the need to develop a coherent international law of human rights. The Human Rights Division, nevertheless, was moved to Geneva in 1974 under Humphrey's successor, Marc Schreiber.

FRAMEWORK OF HUMPHREY'S VIEWS ON HUMAN RIGHTS

In his article, "The International Law of Human Rights in the Middle Twentieth Century," written to celebrate the centenary of the International Law Association (ILA), Humphrey undertook a detailed examination of the development of the international law of human rights in the twentieth century.[112] In his view, the principal concerns of the international law of human rights over this period were the proper delimitation of the sphere of activities of the individual and of the collectivity, the relationship of the citizen to the state, the protection of the human being, and the definition and establishment of human dignity. Humphrey also suggested that a right of humanitarian intervention may have continued to exist even after the advent of the United Nations Charter and the General Assembly Resolution of December 21, 1965, on non-intervention by one state into the affairs of another; however, such a right, if it survived the Charter, could only be exercised by the United Nations.[113] He argued that inroads on state sovereignty had been made. The late nineteenth- and early twentieth-century saw an increased number of treaties to protect individuals against slavery, and to protect prisoners of war and workers. With the creation of the League of Nations, international law began to develop a "whole series of rules and institutions, as well as some procedures for their implementation...to protect the rights of individuals and groups." By the time of the Second World War, he said:

[I]nternational law protected the rights of aliens through their states. There may have been a right of humanitarian intervention. Slavery and the slave trade were outlawed. The League of Nations had developed a system for

---

[112] "The International Law of Human Rights in the Middle Twentieth Century" in Maarten Bos (ed.), *The Present State of International Law and Other Essays* 75 (Deventer: Kluwer, 1973).

[113] *Ibid.,* 76-78. In his preface to Richard Lillich (ed.), *Humanitarian Intervention and the United Nations* (Virginia: University of Virginia Press, 1973), Humphrey suggested that what is needed is a legal mechanism which would give the United Nations the ability to use force on humanitarian grounds in situations where there is no threat to the peace, breach of the peace, or act of aggression.

the protection of certain racial, religious and linguistic minorities. There were provisions in the Covenant of the League of Nations for the protection of the rights of the natives of colonial, and the inhabitants of mandated territories and of women and children. And the International Labour Organization had adopted an impressive number of labour conventions for the enforcement of which, it possessed elaborate procedures.[114]

It was the events of the twentieth century, particularly the atrocities committed during the Second World War, which spurred the Allied Powers to take seriously the need to protect individual rights. Later Humphrey would say that these developments in the international law of human rights were, and continue to be, "revolutionary." On the tenth anniversary of the Universal Declaration, he lamented that "the concern of our generation and of the United Nations with this question of human rights is probably more than anything else a symptom of a deep sickness in the society in which we live."[115]

CREATION OF THE UNITED NATIONS

Before considering what is perhaps Humphrey's most significant achievement — his work on the Universal Declaration of Human Rights — it is appropriate to consider the structures and politics of the newly formed United Nations. Humphrey's contribution in this domain is also of tremendous importance: he has proven to be a talented observer, raconteur, and commentator, as well as an activist administrator. His many books and articles dealing with the United Nations systems and structures provide unique, first-hand insights into critical developments of the institutions of modern international law.

The United Nations' Organization

From the outset, the United Nations' structure, as provided in

[114] *Ibid.*, 82.
[115] Speech on the Tenth Anniversary of the Universal Declaration of Human Rights, Winnipeg, Dec. 10, 1958, at 1, 5-6. For his statement on historical developments, see "The Universal Declaration of Rights," (1949) 4 Int'l J., 353-55; "Human Rights and Authority," (1970) 20 U.ofT.L.J. 412, 413; see generally, Humphrey, "The United Nations' Charter and the Universal Declaration of Human Rights," in E. Luard, *The International Protection of Human Rights* 39 (London: Thames and Hudson, 1967); "The Dean Who Never Was," *supra* note 60, at 198-99; "The United Nations Human Rights Programme," in Council for Christian Social Action of the United Church of Christ, *Social Action,* (1963) Vol. XXX, at 6 (hereafter, *Social Action*).

the Charter, included five main bodies: the General Assembly, the Security Council, the Economic and Social Council, the Trusteeship Council, and the Secretariat. ECOSOC created the Commission on Human Rights, to which was added the Commission on the Status of Women. In addition, the Commission on Human Rights created the Sub-Commission on the Prevention of Discrimination and the Protection of Minorities and the Sub-Commission on Freedom of Information and of the Press. As Humphrey described them, these institutions soon became major factors, "a vested interest...in ensuring that the United Nations would not turn from the path which it has so dramatically taken at San Francisco. Once such bodies have been set in motion, it is very hard to curb their activity and *a fortiori* to eliminate them," particularly when representatives on these subsidiary organs act in their personal capacities.[116]

Human Rights in the United Nations

In addition to peace and security, the newly created United Nations was to concern itself with economic, social, and other humanitarian issues as well as the protection of fundamental rights, which had not been mentioned in the Covenant of the League. In fact, one purpose of the United Nations was to promote human rights and fundamental freedoms, though not to protect them.[117]

While the primary concern of the drafters of the Charter had been the maintenance of peace and security, by the early 1970s the United Nations had not been able to meet the expectations of 1945 in this regard: it had shifted its focus to deal with the economic concerns of developing nations. As a result of a deepening Cold War, by 1959 the main support behind the human rights program was coming from developing countries which sought recognition of a right of self-determination for colonies and legitimacy for the struggle against racial discrimination.[118]

Returning in 1985 to his concept of the "parent of anarchy,"

---

[116] "Human Rights, The United Nations and 1968," (1968) 9 J. of Int'l Commission of Jurists 1, 3.

[117] Speech, Winnipeg, Dec. 10, 1958, at 3-4; "Human Rights, the United Nations and 1968" (1968), 9 J. of Int. Comm. of Jurists 1, at 2; "The Universal Declaration of Human Rights," (1949) 4 Int. J. 354; "The United Nations and Human Rights," (1963) *Behind the Headlines,* Canadian Institute of International Affairs, vol. XXIII, no. 1, at 26 (hereafter *Behind the Headlines*); *Social Action, supra* note 115, at 6.

[118] "The Main Functions of the United Nations in the Year 2000 A.D.," at 220; *A Great Adventure* 255; *Social Action, supra,* 6.

Humphrey saw as the "second parent of anarchy" the principle of the sovereign equality of states within the United Nations system. While equality between individuals was an "essential characteristic of democracy," the concept of equality should not, he thought, be applied to interstate relations. While equality between states was undoubtedly a basic principle of the United Nations, as reflected in the one state-one vote principle, the fact was that the use of the veto in the Security Council and the political crises in the United Nations over the years belied the reality.[119] The distribution of voting power could only be amended by a two-thirds majority plus the concurrence of the five superpowers, which meant that change would not come easily. Alternatives to the existing distribution of voting power were problematic. These included voting by demographic numbers, which would be unfair to less populated countries, such as Canada, and participation by economic contribution to the supervisory international organization, which would exclude all but a few wealthy countries from decision-making power. Clearly neither was completely satisfactory.

However, in 1945 the international community was determined to seek a framework within which peace and security could be established, while at the same time promoting human rights. The United Nations' Charter was that vehicle. Although the final draft of the Dumbarton Oaks Proposal contained only one reference to human rights, in Chapter 9, the Charter, as drafted at San Francisco, contained seven such references.[120] These additions were largely the result of lobbying efforts of non-governmental organizations which had been disappointed by the Dumbarton Proposal.[121] "It was appropriate," noted Humphrey, "that this great step should have been initiated by individuals fighting for their rights against unwilling governments."[122]

---

[119] Speech, "Two Parents of Anarchy," *supra* note 60, at 9-10; Speech "Three Parents of Anarchy," to Nova Scotia Commission on Human Rights, Apr. 18, 1988, at 7 *et seq.* Philip Alston, review of *A Great Adventure*, (1984) 6 Human Rights Quarterly 244 (hereafter, Alston).

[120] These references may be found in the Preamble, and Articles 1, 13, 55, 62, para. 2, 68, and 76. Humphrey examined them in detail in "The United Nations' Charter and the Universal Declaration of Human Rights," *supra* note 115, at 41-46; and "Human Rights and Authority," *supra* note 115, at 414-15.

[121] "The Universal Declaration of Human Rights," (1949) 4 Int'l. J. 354; "The United Nations and the Protection of Human Rights," *Report of the Iowa Commonwealth Conference on Human Rights, March 28-29, 1968*, at 29, 30 (Division of Extension and University Services: University of Iowa, Iowa City, 1968).

[122] "Human Rights and Authority," *supra* note 115, at 413.

The Chilean, Cuban, and Panamanian delegations to the San Francisco Conference urged that the Charter go even further in the protection of human rights. A later Panamanian motion to adopt its draft bill of rights was defeated at the third session of the General Assembly, "largely by the efforts of Eleanor Roosevelt, a member of the United States' delegation."[123] Article 68 of the Charter, however, permitted the establishment by the Economic and Social Council of a Commission on Human Rights. It was generally understood that this Commission would be mandated to draft an International Bill of Rights, though such a bill would not have the force of guarantees written into the Charter.[124]

The Commission on Human Rights

Soon after the creation of the United Nations, the Economic and Social Council (hereinafter "the Council") established the Commission on Human Rights pursuant to Article 68 of the Charter. In his article, "The United Nations' Commission on Human Rights and Its Parent Body," Humphrey stated that "[a]lthough the San Francisco Conference seems to have envisaged the Commission on Human Rights as a body which in the first instance. . .would draft the International Bill of Rights," the Preparatory Commission, in November-December 1945, foresaw a broader role for the Commission and included within its mandate "any matter within the field of human rights considered likely to impair the general welfare or friendly relations among nations."[125] This broad language did not survive the Council's first and second sessions. The Preparatory Commission on Human Rights, a group of nine persons acting in

[123] Eleanor Roosevelt had been a member of the United States' delegation at the First Session of the General Assembly in London. The U.S. Delegation, which included then Secretary of State, James F. Byrnes, the former Secretary of State Edward Stettinius, and Senators Tom Connally and Arthur H. Vandenberg, had relegated Roosevelt to the Third Committee of the General Assembly, which was concerned with social, humanitarian, and cultural questions and thus was assumed to be of little importance. It was to become, however, "one of the most important and productive in the United Nations"; speech, Eleanor Roosevelt, at 2; see Joseph P. Lash, *Eleanor Roosevelt: A Friend's Memoir* 296-302 (New York: Doubleday, 1964).

[124] J. P. Humphrey, "The Universal Declaration of Human Rights: Its History, Impact, and Juridical Character," in B. G. Ramcharan (ed.), *Human Rights: Thirty Years After the Universal Declaration* 21-22 (The Hague: Martinus Nijhoff, 1979); *Behind the Headlines,* at 3.

[125] "The United Nations Commission on Human Rights and Its Parent Body," in *René Cassin: Amicorum Discipulorumque Liber* III (Paris: Institut International des Droits de l'Homme, vol. 1, 1969).

their individual capacity, met from April 29 to May 20, 1946, to make recommendations to the Council regarding the functions of the definitive human rights commission. On the recommendation of the Preparatory Commission, the Council added Article 68(3) to the terms of reference to give the Commission a general competence in matters of human rights but in "language which did not have the political connotation implicit in the Preparatory Commission's recommendation." Thus the focus for debate on political aspects of questions of human rights, such as apartheid, was shifted to the General Assembly and Security Council. Nevertheless, the Commission continued to discuss such matters and still does.

The primary function of the Commission on Human Rights became the drafting of instruments on the international law of human rights, such as the Universal Declaration of Human Rights, the two Covenants, and the Convention on the Elimination of All Forms of Racial Discrimination. Humphrey argued that the Commission continued to dodge political responsibility not only with respect to matters of drafting but also with respect to periodic reports and communications alleging violations of human rights.

During Humphrey's tenure at the United Nations he thought that the Third Committee was less effective than it might have been. It was largely used by governments for political patronage appointments, with the inevitable result that a few capable people with long experience in the Committee controlled it. In addition, Committee meetings were frequent, Committee members ill prepared, and every issue on the agenda was debated at length. Nonetheless, Humphrey commented in 1965 that it was the Third Committee from which the Commission received its greatest support.

As far as the quality of membership on the Commission on Human Rights was concerned, Humphrey found it outstanding; persons of the highest calibre attended its meetings. By contrast, Dr. Ramcharan observes that today the Commission does not have the quality members it had during Humphrey's tenure.[126] The persons on the Commission are representatives of the fifty-three states which sit on the Commission; they do not speak in their individual capacities. In later years, when the emphasis shifted to matters of implementation, Humphrey suggested that the Commission on Human Rights should become an expert rather than a governmental body; he also suggested that the Commission's work would

---

[126] Ramcharan, *op. cit. supra* note 124, at 474.

have been made easier if it had had conferred on it the status of a Council within the United Nations system. This was particularly the case in light of the interplay between the Commission, the Sub-Commission, and the General Assembly during the drafting of the various human rights instruments, most of which took place without any real help from the Economic and Social Council.[127]

During the early years of the United Nations, Humphrey found that, with its concentration on economic questions, the Economic and Social Council was "unsympathetic" to the work done by the Commission, particularly as regards its drafting responsibilities. Evidence of this was provided by two later events.[128]

Sub-Commission on the Prevention of Discrimination and the Protection of Minorities

The Economic and Social Council in due course authorized the creation of three sub-commissions; one, on freedom of information, as suggested by Eleanor Roosevelt to the Preparatory Commission; a second, on the prevention of discrimination; and a third, on the protection of minorities, as proposed by the Soviet Delegation to the Economic and Social Council. The Commission then decided to limit itself to two sub-commissions: a Sub-Commission on Freedom of Information and of the Press, and a Sub-Commission on the Prevention of Discrimination and the Protection of Minorities. In his 1968 article in the *American Journal of International Law*, Humphrey examined the history and creation of this latter sub-commission composed of twelve experts (now twenty-six) acting in their individual capacities. He had observed earlier that while the Sub-Commission's members were highly gifted and dedicated people animated primarily by the purposes and principles of the United Nations, some were in fact "the instructed representatives of their governments."[129] After his retirement from the UN Secretariat, he became not only a member of this Sub-Commission but also its chairman.

No provisions for the protection of minorities were included in the United Nations Charter or the Universal Declaration of Human Rights. Apart from the formal inclusion of the protection of

---

127 "The United Nations Sub-Commission on the Prevention of Discrimination and the Protection of Minorities," (1968) 62 Am. J. Int'l L. 869, 883.
128 *Supra* note 125, at 108-09; Ramcharan, *op. cit. supra* note 124, at 474; Alston, *supra* note 119, at 224.
129 *A Great Adventure* 21, 47.

minorities in the mandate of the Sub-Commission, the United
Nations had "shown no interest in the creation of machinery for
that purpose, although it has made *ad hoc* attempts to protect particular groups which are not necessarily numerically minorities."[130]
Humphrey rightly pointed out that the two elements of the Sub-
Commission's mandate, the protection of minorities and the prevention of discrimination, while not contradictory, introduced an
element of confusion as to the direction the Sub-Commission should
take. The protection of minorities is a "disintegrative process," the
very opposite to assimilation, whose objective is to "preserve and
maintain characteristics" that the minority group values; the prevention of discrimination, in Humphrey's opinion, seeks to ensure
equality of treatment for all individuals.[131]

Though the Sub-Commission had been less than effective with
the protection of the minorities portion of its mandate,[132] its general assessment was "one of relative success," and its contribution
to the prevention of discrimination was significant. Thus in 1952,
with the blessing of the General Assembly, the Sub-Commission
began its session with "a new lease on life." The Sub-Commission
continued its studies and years later was involved in, among other
activities, the drafting of the Convention on the Elimination of All
Forms of Racial Discrimination, adopted by the General Assembly
in 1965. These activities were examined by Humphrey in the remainder of his article.

By 1968 the Sub-Commission had reached another critical point,
namely, the direction in which it should be headed: "whether its
terms of reference will, as in the past, remain keyed essentially to
the prevention of discrimination and theoretically to the protection of minorities; whether it will, in all human rights matters, become an expert body of the Commission; and whether, in light of
the political issues with which it is now required to deal, it can maintain its essential character as a body of individual experts."[133]

[130] *Ibid.*, 20; "The United Nations Sub-Commission on the Prevention of Discrimination and the Protection of Minorities," *supra* note 127, at 870, 872.

[131] "Human Rights, The United Nations and 1968," *supra* note 112, at 6-7.

[132] In 1968 Humphrey stated that the international norms for the protection of minorities were scarce, apart from the "relatively weak" Art. 27 of the International
Covenant; for his detailed explanation, see "The United Nations Sub-Commission
on the Prevention of Discrimination and the Protection of Minorities," *supra* note
127, at 873-75.

[133] *Ibid.*, 888.

Sub-Commission on the Freedom of Information and of the Press

The U.S. delegation, which had proposed the creation of a Sub-Commission on the Freedom of Information and of the Press, probably shared Humphrey's conviction that freedom of information was more than merely a fundamental right or freedom but was crucial to the guarantee of other freedoms. However, the desire to use information as an instrument of power meant that many governments controlled information for their own purposes irrespective of attempts to provide a framework for the protection of freedom of information at the international level.

The Sub-Commission on Freedom of Information and of the Press was created in 1947. Owing to its relative unpopularity with governments, as well as the assertion of members of the Western press about the absolute nature of the freedom involved, the Sub-Commission was never given a chance to develop a real programme. Nevertheless, articles on freedom of information were incorporated into the Universal Declaration of Human Rights, Article 19, and the International Covenant on Civil and Political Rights, Article 19.

The 1948 United Nations Conference on Freedom of Information, of which Humphrey was the Principal Secretary, was thought at the time to be a great success. At the proposal of the United States, France, and the United Kingdom, three draft conventions were prepared on the gathering and international transmission of news, on the institution of an international right of correction, and on freedom of information.[134] They were to be opened for signature and ratification, pending approval of the Economic and Social Council, in an effort to add to "the prestige and authority of the conventions." According to Humphrey, this was a mistake, because the states that opposed the conventions gained time in which to prevent their final adoption. In the end, it was impossible to reconcile philosophical differences between East and West, North and South. Only the convention on the Institution of an International Right of Correction entered into force. As one commentator stated:

None of the approaches — special bodies such as the Sub-Commission... rapporteurs of high expertise and qualifications (Salvador P. Lopez of the Philippines, Professor Hilding Eek of Sweden), expert studies, periodic reporting, *ad hoc* committees — could break down the political barriers. There was no careful, sustained progress such as that

---

[134] John Male, "Human Rights Was 'A Great Adventure'," review of Humphrey's *A Great Adventure* (unidentified New Zealand journal).

achieved by the group working for the prevention of discrimination, or in the programme of advisory services in human rights. As in the area of disarmament, the political will was not there. Added to which was the basic hostility of the 'Western' media of information, who apparently saw the United Nations efforts as a potential curb to their right to roam the world at will, reporting and publishing without restriction.[135]

The Sub-Commission on Freedom of Information and of the Press was dissolved by the Economic and Social Council in 1952 and its duties taken over by UNESCO, where political debate has continued over the formulation of a New World Communication Order.[136]

Thus by the late 1950s, the principal matter being actively pursued by the Sub-Commission was that of the prevention of discrimination. In later years, however, the Sub-Commission became, in effect, *the* Sub-Commission of the Commission: the laboratory where problems and delicate issues are investigated and standards and general principles formulated.[137]

Drafting the Universal Declaration of Human Rights

Humphrey's work leading up to the drafting of the Universal Declaration of Human Rights remains one of his most important contributions to the cause of human rights. It was also one of his first functions in the newly created Division of Human Rights.

The Commission on Human Rights, meeting in its first regular session on January 27, 1947 under the Chairmanship of Mrs. Roosevelt, discussed several possible forms of the international bill of rights: a non-binding General Assembly resolution, a multilateral convention binding on states ratifying it, and an amendment to the United Nations Charter. At the Commission's second session, the decision was made to create a declaration, a multilateral convention (soon knows as the Covenant and later as the Covenants after the General Assembly decided that there would be two conventions), and measures of implementation. At the first session, a non-binding General Assembly resolution was the preferred mode

---

[135] Male, *supra,* at 3; see speech, Conference on the Media, at 8.

[136] K. V. Raman, in R. St. J. Macdonald and Douglas M. Johnston (eds.), *The Structure and Process of International Law* 1027 (The Hague: Sithoff & Noordhoff, 1986).

[137] Alston, *supra* note 119, at 231; Jenks felt that these rights should not be dealt with in the international covenants as their implementation was better handled by specialized agencies such as the ILO, UNESCO and WHO: Alston, *ibid.; A Great Adventure* 141-44; Interview, May 6, at 4. See too "Review of the Work of the Sub-Commission," working paper by Mr. Theo Van Boven and Mr. Asbjorn Eido: E/CN.4/Sub.2/1989/47, July 31, 1989.

of operation.[138] It was in the light of that decision that the Secretariat draft was prepared.[139]

As is well known, the drafting process has come under scrutiny since 1947, not only to determine the intent of the drafters with respect to specific articles but also to determine the validity of the claims of authorship by those who were "present at the creation." In these circumstances, it is perhaps best to begin with a quotation describing the process of drafting by one of the Declaration's principal architects, Charles Malik:

> The genesis of each article, and each part of each article, was a dynamic process in which many minds, interests, backgrounds, legal systems and ideological persuasions played their respective roles. Also, lobbying and manoeuvering, all perfectly proper, all in conformity with the generally recognized rules of the game, never ceased behind the scenes. The complete story of how each provision actually arose can never be told, because the actual, living, dynamic process of genesis can never be recaptured or reproduced. And the claims made and published about some provisions are not altogether true, as can be shown by more thorough research into the available documents, and especially by reference to some unpublished diaries.[140]

A committee consisting of the Chairman of the Commission, Mrs. Roosevelt of the United States, the Vice-President, P. C. Chang of China, and the Rapporteur, Charles Malik of Lebanon, met at Mrs. Roosevelt's Washington Square apartment to prepare the first draft, but soon found itself without a mandate;[141] it was clear that philosophical differences between Chang and Malik would prevent them from preparing a text themselves. However, before ending its one and only meeting, the committee decided to ask Humphrey,

---

[138] Humphrey says that the Secretariat "prophetically added" that this option, the multilateral convention binding only on those states which ratified it, "might involve delays": *A Great Adventure* 22.

[139] "The Dean Who Never Was," *supra* note 60, at 196. For valuable discussion of the background see Kamleshwar Das, "Some Observations Relating to the International Bill of Human Rights," (1984) 19 Indian Y.B. Int'l Aff. 1-53; Nehemiah Robinson, *The Universal Declaration of Human Rights: Its Origin, Significance, Applications and Interpretation.* Institute of Jewish Affairs (New York: World Jewish Congress, 1958); Egon Schwelb, *Human Rights and the International Community: The Roots and Growth of the Universal Declaration of Human Rights, 1948-1963* (Chicago: Quadrangle Books, 1964); M. McDougal, H. Lasswell and L. Chen, *Human Rights and World Public Order* (New Haven: Yale University Press, 1980); and for recent stimulating analysis, see A. J. Hobbins, *supra* note 1.

[140] Charles Malik, Introduction to Frederick Nolde, *Free and Equal* 11-12 (Geneva, 1968).

[141] J. P. Humphrey, *No Distant Millenium: The International Law of Human Rights* 147 (Paris: UNESCO, 1989).

as Director of the Human Rights Division, to prepare a draft declaration.[142]

Before Humphrey could begin to draft, the Soviet Union became aware that it had been excluded from the process and promptly challenged in the Economic and Social Council the arrangements that the Human Rights Commission had made for drafting the Declaration. René Cassin also noted at this time the "symbolic omission of any European representation on the drafting committee."[143] On her own initiative, in the absence of a clear legal basis for the decision, Mrs. Roosevelt then informed the President of the Council that she was appointing a new drafting committee of eight members of the Commission: Australia, Chile, China, France, Lebanon, the United States, the United Kingdom and the Soviet Union, and that Committee met from June 9 to June 25 at Lake Success, New York.[144]

Confirming the request of the initial committee of three, the Council now requested a "documented outline" of the Bill of Rights from the Secretariat. Humphrey notes that while this request "could have been interpreted as meaning a simple list of rights. . .the so-called outline was a draft declaration."[145] The draft declaration was then prepared by him, with the help of Emile Giraud, a distinguished member of the Human Rights Division.[146]

[142] *A Great Adventure* 29. In Humphrey's words, Malik was "a Christian Lebanese who seemed to believe that St. Thomas Aquinas had had the answers to all questions," while "Chang had studied under John Dewey and called himself a pluralist": "The Dean Who Never Was," *supra* note 60, at 197. Later Malik was the President of the Economic and Social Council at the time the draft of the Universal Declaration of Human Rights was forwarded to the General Assembly; he was also the Chairman of the Third Committee presiding over 80 meetings on the consideration of the Draft Declaration; speech, "Conference on Human Rights and Religious Freedom in Europe," Venice, Feb. 4, 1988, at 1-2; "Universal Declaration," *supra* note 124, at 22-23; A. J. Hobbins, "René Cassin and the Daughter of Time: The First Draft of the Universal Declaration of Human Rights," (1989) 2 Fontanus 4, 7-27.

[143] René Cassin, "Looking Back on the Universal Declaration of 1948," (1968) 1 Rev. of Contemporary L. 13, at 15.

[144] "The Dean Who Never Was," *supra* note 60, at 197; *A Great Adventure* 29-30; "Universal Declaration," *supra* note 124, at 23; A. J. Hobbins, *supra* note 1, at 4.

[145] *A Great Adventure* 30; "Universal Declaration," *supra*, 23; Jack Cahill, "How a Canadian Drafted United Nations Rights Charter," *Toronto Star,* December 10, 1988.

[146] Émile Giraud was a distinguished internatonal lawyer in his own right, having become a professor of law at Rennes at the age of 30, and was first a member and later head of the legal section of the League of Nations from 1927 to 1946. He joined the Human Rights Division in Jan. 1947 and worked under Humphrey

The draft declaration was drawn up in the light of draft bills of rights prepared by individuals and groups, including, among others, those by Gustavo Gutierrez, H. G. Wells, Hersch Lauterpacht, the Reverend Wilfrid Parsons, S.J., Rollin McNitt, the American Law Institute (whose text had earlier been proposed by Panama), the American Association for the United Nations, the American Jewish Congress, the World Government Association, the Institut de droit international, the editors of *Free World,* and comments from the American Bar Association.[147] It is relevant to note that the majority of the drafts that Humphrey relied on were "English-speaking sources and all of them from the democratic West."[148] In the end, the Secretariat draft, not to be confused with the Secretariat Outline, the 400-page compilation of extracts from national constitutions, contained forty-eight articles which expressed a variety of civil and political rights, as well as economic, social, and cultural rights, "considered socialism by many western countries."[149] In addition to the listed rights, three basic principles were included, namely, the right of individual petition, the duty of individuals to respect the rights in the Declaration, and that the provisions of the Declaration "were to be deemed fundamental principles of international law and of the national law of each member state."[150]

The Secretariat draft, the Secretariat Outline, and a proposed draft submitted by the United Kingdom were considered by the drafting committee of eight. A working group of representatives (France, Lebanon, and the United Kingdom) was asked to "report back forthwith a logical arrangement" of the articles of the Secretariat Outline and how they should be redrafted in light of the

---

until he became deputy director of the United Nations Division for the Development and Codification of International Law: Alston, *supra* note 119, at 225-56, n. 4.

[147] *A Great Adventure* 31-32; "The Universal Declaration," *supra* note 124, at 23-24, n. 8; Alston, *supra,* 226.

[148] In S. Prakash Sinha's review of *A Great Adventure,* in (1984) 12 Int'l. J. of Legal Information 158, he expressed regret that a serious consideration of the texts of non-Western cultures was, in his opinion, neglected in the drafting process; however, see *infra* note 181.

[149] Hugh Wilson, "Human Rights Declaration: Credit Where Credit Is Due," *McGill News,* Spring 1989, at 5; A. J. Hobbins, *supra* note 1, at 4; "Human Rights and Authority," 415.

[150] *A Great Adventure* 32-33; "Human Rights and Authority," 415. Humphrey notes that, given the historical events that formed the backdrop against which the desire for a universal declaration of human rights was expressed, it is not surprising that the Declaration outlined the rights of individuals while the corresponding duties "are only mentioned once, and authority not at all."

committee's discussions and be divided between a manifesto and a convention. It was this Working Group of three which then asked the representative of France, René Cassin, to prepare a draft based on the Secretariat Outline.[151] Cassin, with the help of Émile Giraud, accomplished this task "over the week-end."[152]

The requirements of anonymity and neutrality required of an international civil servant often meant that many Secretariat proposals and drafts were given political weight and legitimacy by virtue of sponsorship by a representative or member of a particular United Nations body. For the Universal Declaration, Cassin was such a person, in his capacity as representative of France on the Working Group on the Declaration and, later, as a member of the French delegation to the Third Committee.[153] Humphrey maintains that "Cassin's draft reproduced the Secretariat draft in most of its essentials and style."[154] Nevertheless, "the belief...grew up that Cassin was the principal architect of the Declaration."[155] The whole question of authorship, particularly the claim made (mainly) on behalf of René Cassin as the *sole* author of the first draft of the Universal Declaration, remains a source of irritation to Humphrey.[156] He maintains that "the Universal Declaration had no father in the sense that Thomas Jefferson was the father of the American Declaration of Independence...literally hundreds of people...contributed to its drafting."[157] Nevertheless, Humphrey may also have

---

[151] "The Universal Declaration," *supra* note 124, at 24; *A Great Adventure* 42; A. J. Hobbins, *supra* note 1, at 5. According to Israel, Cassin was already a member of an eighteen-person committee, and was named rapporteur of that committee. It was in this capacity that he undertook the work on the declaration.

[152] J. P. Humphrey, *No Distant Millenium: The International Law of Human Rights* 149 (Paris: UNESCO, 1989) (hereafter *No Distant Millenium*).

[153] Alston, *supra* note 119, at 225, 228.

[154] *No Distant Millenium, supra* note 152, at 149.

[155] *Ibid.,* 149.

[156] Alston, *supra* note 119, at 226-228. In "René Cassin and the Daughter of Time," A. J. Hobbins examined the claims made by or on behalf of René Cassin; he wrote: "[I]t is not clear why he claimed to have authored the first draft, although several possibilities suggest themselves": *supra* note 1, at 23. According to Hobbins, Cassin's assertions as to authorship were made primarily in the 1960s "when he was over eighty. His memory was evidently faulty on details," *ibid.,* 26, n. 40. To support this theory, Hobbins refers to an article written by Cassin in 1951, soon after the drafting of the Universal Declaration. According to Hobbins, that article was "generally consistent with the events and contrary to his later recollections," *ibid.,* 23. He also points out that the later assertions by Cassin as to authorship were probably pressed as much by his friends and colleagues as by Cassin himself: *ibid.,* 26, n. 40.

[157] *Op. Cit. supra* note 152, at 149.

felt that perhaps Cassin was given a shade too much credit for his work on the early draft. Happily, however, Humphrey has, in recent years, been increasingly and prominently recognized as one of the principal drafters of the Declaration.

Cassin later described Humphrey's work as "excellent basic documentary work...which grouped methodically all the principles and themes connected with Human Rights that had already been contained in national declarations or constitutions" in addition to earlier proposals.[158] Cassin's biographer, Gérard Israel, phrased it in the following terms: "Il [Cassin] fut aidé significativement dans sa tâche par le service des droits de l'homme de l'ONU qui prit l'initiative de rassembler, en un document synoptique, les textes fondamentaux faisant partie des constitutions des pays membres au regard des droits de l'homme. Ce service interrogea également les différentes familles spirituelles et intellectuelles par le truchement de l'UNESCO, agence spécialisée de l'ONU dans l'éducation, la science et la culture."[159] Cassin later stated that since "the rational use of this work...could not be made directly in the oral debates...I was entrusted by my colleagues with drawing up a first draft upon my own responsibility."[160] However, Humphrey maintains that the Secretariat draft was much more than — indeed was something other than — a compilation of sources; he has vigorously disputed Cassin's assertion that the Secretariat draft was not capable of use in oral debate: "This statement," he says, "is patently wrong, as the record shows."[161]

When Cassin entered the Commission, he found that French as an official language of the Commission "had been virtually banished," with English being the working language. Cassin found himself in an embarassing position: he had, in his own words, "neither an assistant beside me nor experience of simultaneous interpretation...and had to pass over, simply because I had not heard

[158] René Cassin, in (1968) Rev. Contemporary L. 13, at 17-18.

[159] Gérard Israel, *René Cassin* (1887-1976): La Guerre hors la loi, avec de Gaulle, les droits de l'homme 187 (Paris: Desclée de Brouwer, 1990).

[160] René Cassin, *supra* note 158, at 18.

[161] "The Universal Declaration," *supra* note 124, at 23, n. 7. "You will remember Cassin's reference to work of the Secretariat that could not be used in oral debate. He could have been referring to the 400-page document of extracts from national constitutions but did not say so. What he actually used as the basis for his own draft was the text I had prepared under my mandate from the Committee of Three. This was of course overtaken by the mandate from ECOSOC which referred to a Secretariat Outline, but which I chose to ignore in favour of my draft": JPH to RStJM, Jan. 5, 1992, at 2.

them, certain proposals and formulations of resolutions which did not correspond to my views."[162] Perhaps this explains why Humphrey found that parts of Cassin's draft "were no more than a new French version of the official United Nations translation of the English original." Cassin had made changes in the order of certain articles; he had also combined several principles which had been dealt with separately in the Secretariat's draft or omitted other articles to be included in a later convention.

Humphrey maintains that many of Cassin's changes, in particular the order of the articles, "did not resist the test of time."[163] One such change, in Article 28 of Cassin's draft, which said that "the protection of human rights required a public force," was a truism not retained by the Drafting Committee. Cassin's Article 1, which stated that all men are brothers, and that, being endowed with reason, members of one family, they are free and possess equal dignity and rights, enunciated principles which, said Humphrey, were more philosophical than legal. Humphrey's draft had tried to avoid assertions that did not enunciate justiciable rights. He argued that these philosophical assertions created difficulties at the Commission's second session and in the Commission on the Status of Women. In his opinion, "the greatest harm that resulted from the introduction of unnecessary philosophical concepts was the needless controversy and useless debate which they invited, particularly in the General Assembly."[164]

In his recent article, "René Cassin and the Daughter of Time: The First Draft of the Universal Declaration of Human Rights," A. J. Hobbins subjected the Secretariat draft, its French translation, and the draft that Cassin authored, to careful review and assessment. He concluded that there are "significant resemblances." For those who wish to further examine the relative claims, the original manuscript has been transcribed in his article to allow for comparison of these two "first" drafts of the Universal Declaration.[165] A legislative history of the development of the provisions of the Universal Declaration is also available in the 1950s publication of the Human Rights Division, *These Rights and Freedoms,* which sets out, for each article of the Universal Declaration, the Secretariat Draft provision, the Drafting Committee version, the version of

[162] Cassin, *supra* note 158, at 15.
[163] *A Great Adventure* 43-44.
[164] "The Universal Declaration," *supra* note 124, at 25.
[165] Hobbins, *supra* note 1, at 8; see generally, *ibid.,* 8-30.

the Commission on Human Rights' second and third sessions, a summary of the General Assembly debate, and the final text of the article.

In any event, through to the spring of 1948, the Commission on Human Rights, its drafting committee, along with the Commission on the Status of Women, the Sub-Commission on Freedom of Information and of the Press, the United Nations Conference on the Freedom of Information, the Sub-Commission on the Prevention of Discrimination and the Protection of Minorities, among others, continued the drafting process. The interplay between the drafting committee and the latter Sub-Commission is demonstrated by an examination of the text of Article 36 dealing with racial, linguistic, and religious minorities. Article 36 recognized the right of minorities to establish their own schools, press, and cultural or religious institutions, but did not include a corresponding duty on governments to fund or assist these institutions. According to Humphrey:

This was not an oversight, because the text included as Article 46 of the so-called Secretariat's outline, which the drafting committee followed almost textually up to that point, stipulated that members of minorities would have the right to establish and maintain schools and other institutions 'out of an equitable proportion of any public funds available for the purpose'. . .The Sub-Commission did not strengthen the drafting committee's text, but it did refine it in one important respect: by introducing the concept that minorities, to be protected, must want differential treatment. . .Like the drafting committee, however, the Sub-Commission rejected the key requirement of financial assistance. It might have enhanced its reputation as a body of individual experts had it shown more independence; but its estimate of the political realities was nevertheless an astute one, for the General Assembly refused in 1948 to include any article on minorities in the Declaration. At the same time, the Assembly complicated. . .the future work of the Sub-Commission by nevertheless referring the whole question back to the Sub-Commission — a typical example of United Nations 'buck passing.'[166]

Thus, while no article on minorities made it into the Universal Declaration, the Sub-Commission did continue its consideration of the rights of minorities, at the request of the General Assembly.

On June 18, 1948, the Commission's draft of the Universal Declaration was adopted with twelve votes in favour and four absten-

[166] *Supra* note 127, at 873 *et seq.*

tions.[167] The draft was sent from the Economic and Social Council, which made no changes, to the Third Committee of the General Assembly, where Charles Malik was Chairman.

The Third Committee, though efficient by United Nations' standards, worked in an atmosphere "charged by the Cold War and by irrelevant incriminations." It devoted "eighty-one long meetings" to the Universal Declaration and considered "one hundred and sixty-eight resolutions containing amendments."[168] In addition, all member governments and some specialized agencies — the ILO, UNESCO, the World Health Organization — were requested to consider the draft and to offer comments and criticisms. Considerable input was also received from NGO's.[169] However, the final text of the Declaration resembled the Commission's original draft. Perhaps this was not surprising in view of the fact that "the chairman of the Third Committee and a number of other representatives, including some of the most influential, had worked on the draft in the Commission."[170]

At the voting in the Third Committee, Canada abstained. Humphrey was shocked at Canada's joining the abstainers, which included six communist countries.[171] Aware that human rights was not a priority with the Canadian delegation, he nevertheless had not thought that the government would carry its indifference to the point of abstaining in such an important vote. He believed the abstention to be the result of political pressure exerted by the American Bar Association which, having failed to change the American position, worked through the Canadian Bar Association to convince the Canadian government that the Universal Declaration incorpo-

---

[167] Byelorussia, the Soviet Union, the Ukraine, and Yugoslavia abstained.

[168] *Behind the Headlines, supra* note 117, at 4, says there were 86 meetings; "The Universal Declaration of Human Rights," (1949) 27 Can. Bar. Rev. 203 puts the number at 84; *A Great Adventure* 63-70; "The Universal Declaration," *supra* note 124, at 26. The text of the Universal Declaration was voted on as a whole and article-by-article with most articles being adopted unanimously.

[169] Humphrey noted, "It is no exaggeration therefore, to say that the Universal Declaration of Human Rights is a synthesis of the contribution of many thousands of minds": "The U.N. Charter and the Universal Declaration of Rights," in Evan Luard, *The International Protection of Human Rights* 49; "The Dean Who Never Was," *supra* note 60, at 97.

[170] "The United Nations Charter and the Universal Declaration," at 48-49; "The Universal Declaration of Human Rights," (1949) 27 Can. Bar Rev. 203-4.

[171] The countries abstaining were Byelorussia, Canada, Czechoslovakia, Poland, the Ukraine, the Soviet Union, and Yugoslavia, with Saudi Arabia and South Africa not voting: *A Great Adventure* 71.

rated too many socialist ideas.[172] Between December 6 and 10, 1948, the Canadian delegation reconsidered its position, through the intervention of Lester B. Pearson, then Secretary of State for External Affairs. Canada then voted with the majority in Plenary.[173] Humphrey comments, "I had no doubt whatsoever that this quick change in position was dictated solely by the fact that the government did not relish the company in which it found itself."[174]

The adoption of the Declaration was delayed by attempts at postponement until the Covenants were ready, and by Cuba's attempt to replace the Commission's text with that of the American Declaration of Rights and Duties of Man. On December 6, 1948, however, the Third Committee sent its report to the General Assembly and on December 10, 1948, two days before the end of the session, the General Assembly adopted the Declaration with forty-eight votes in favour, none against, and eight abstentions.[175]

The final text was not without its difficulties: "Some of the articles could have been better formulated and the document suffers from the inclusion in it of certain assertions which do not enunciate justiciable rights... there were some important omissions including the failure to include any article on the protection of minorities and to recognize any right of petition even at the national level — a right so fundamental that it is recognized even by some authoritarian countries — let alone by the United Nations."[176]

---

[172] *A Great Adventure* 78-79; "The Revolution in the International Law of Human Rights," at 205-6. See also "Declaration on Human Rights: Canadian, American Bars Ask Delay of Action," (1948) 34 A.B.A.J. 881.

[173] In his diary kept at the time, Humphrey described Canada's statement to the Plenary as "one of the worst contributions" and as a "niggardly acceptance of the Declaration." Hobbins suggests that this rather harsh criticism "show[ed] the strain Humphrey had been under and reflect[ed] the shock of Canada's earlier abstention": see Hobbins, "Human Rights Inside the United Nations," *supra* note 1, at 156, quoting a diary entry of Dec. 11, 1948. For constitutional reasons, the federal government was wary of becoming involved with questions of human rights at the international level at that point in time: see John W. Holmes, *The Shaping of Peace: Canada and the Search for World Order, 1943-1957*, at 242 (Toronto: University of Toronto Press, vol. 1, 1979).

[174] *A Great Adventure* 72; *Behind the Headlines, supra* note 117, at 4.

[175] The states abstaining included Byelorussia, Czechoslovakia, Poland, Saudi Arabia, the Ukraine, South Africa, the USSR, and Yugoslavia; *Behind the Headlines, supra*, 4.

[176] "The Universal Declaration," *supra* note 124, at 27; "The International Bill of Rights:: Scope and Implementation," (1976) 17 William & Mary L. Rev. 527, at 528-29.

Nevertheless, Humphrey was soon able to say that the Declaration "was a better document than the most sanguine could have hoped for three years ago."[177] In fact, its adoption was an extraordinary feat in light of the ideological conflict that had bedevilled the United Nations ever since San Francisco and was largely responsible for preventing the organization from carrying out many of its major functions until the late 1980s.

Criticism of the Universal Declaration from those who felt that it did not reflect the aspirations of Third World states, most of which were not in existence in 1948, is perhaps deflected by the universal values referred to in the Declaration and the involvement of the representatives of countries such as China, India, Chile, the Philippines, and Lebanon in the drafting process.[178] Humphrey himself later noted that "in its earlier and more productive years [the Human Rights Commission] was strongly influenced by liberal principles as they are recognized in the West."[179] He also observed that: "[W]ith two exceptions all the texts on which the Director worked came from English-speaking sources and all of them from the West; *but* the documentation which the Secretariat later brought together in support of his draft included texts extracted from the constitutions of many countries."[180] In his study of the influence of ethnic and linguistic structures of member states on the drafting of the Declaration, Albert Verdoodt confirms the existence of a "pan-juridical" approach; quoting from Humphrey's materials regarding a provision on the protection of minorities, Verdoodt shows how the constitutions of states from such diverse backgrounds as Byelorussia, Iraq, China, Equator, Poland, and Egypt, among many others, were consulted.[181]

177 "Universal Declaration," (1949) 4 Int'l J. 356.
178 Speech, "Education: The Ultimate Sanction of Human Rights," California State University, Long Beach, California, Nov. 8, 1985, at 10-11.
179 *Op. cit. supra* note 152, at 93.
180 *Ibid.*, 148, emphasis added.
181 Albert Verdoodt, "Influence des structures ethniques et linguistiques des pays membres des Nations Unies sur la rédaction de la Déclaration Universelle des Droits de l'Homme," in *René Cassin: Amicorum Discipulorumque Liber I: Problèmes de protection internationale des droits de l'homme* 404-16 (Paris: Éditions A. Pédone, 1969). See too Christian Tomuschat, "Human Rights in a World-Wide Framework: Some Current Issues"; Zeitschrift für ausländisches öffentliches Rechtund Völkerrecht Vol. 45 (1985), p. 547 et seq. Étienne Richard Mbaya, "L'université des droits de l'homme face à la diversité des cultures," *Proceedings of the First Annual Conference of the African Society of International and Comparative Law*, Lusaka, Jan. 30-Feb. 3) 1989. Published by the African Society of Int'l & Comp. Law, London, 1989, at 16-43.

STATUS OF THE UNIVERSAL DECLARATION[182]

Humphrey has frequently emphasized that Eleanor Roosevelt referred to the Universal Declaration as "the Magna Carta of Mankind," that Alexander Solzhenitsyn said that "its adoption was the greatest success of the United Nations," and that Pope John Paul II called it the "basic inspiration and cornerstone of the United Nations."[183] Significantly, however, the relative ease with which the Universal Declaration was adopted, as compared to the agonizing process with respect to the Covenants, is explainable chiefly on the ground that in 1948 most states took the view that the Declaration would not be a legally binding part of positive law. Though adopted as a General Assembly resolution and clearly intended to be a "common standard of achievement for all peoples and all nations," Humphrey stated in 1963, that "[i]t would be a great mistake to think that the Declaration is without legal significance."[184] From its inception, the Universal Declaration had become "not only a great catalyst of international and national legislation," but had also acquired "an authority, at least political and moral, which was second only to the Charter of the United Nations itself."[185] It had been incorporated into national legislation and constitutions and had become the subject of frequent interpretation and application by national judicial authorities.

In a speech given just six months after its adoption, Humphrey succinctly reviewed arguments as to the status of the Universal Declaration:

It has been argued and very forcibly that, since the Universal Declaration took the form of a resolution of the General Assembly, it can have no binding legal force. . . .On the other hand, it has been equally forcibly argued that the Declaration is an authentic interpretation by the General Assembly and through it by the Members of the United Nations,

---

John O'Manique, "Universal and Inalienable Rights: A Search for Foundations" (1990) 12 Human Rights Quarterly 465.

[182] For Humphrey's views, see: "The United Nations Charter and the Universal Declaration of Human Rights," at 53-55; "The Universal Declaration," *supra* note 124, at 28-37; *Behind the Headlines, supra* note 117, at 6-8.

[183] "The Dean Who Never Was," *supra* note 60, at 197.

[184] *Behind the Headlines, supra* note 117, at 6. It is reported that Humphrey "forbade any of his staff to describe the Universal Declaration as without legal authority": King Gordon to RStJM, Sept. 21, 1986, at 1.

[185] Report of the Iowa Commonwealth Conference, at 31; *Social Action, supra* note 115, at 7-8.

of the Charter provisions relating to human rights, that it confirms the principle that human rights are now a matter of international concern, and that it is even a basis for recommendation and action by the United Nations. It is also argued that the Declaration enunciates 'general principles of law recognized by civilized nations' as contemplated by Article 38 of the Statute of the International Court of Justice and is therefore a source of international law. And finally, it has been argued that whatever obligations it may impose on governments, it is certainly binding on the various organs of the United Nations as such.[186]

In addition, even by 1949 there was a "developing jurisprudence" within the United Nations with respect to human rights: the General Assembly often referred to the Declaration in its debates and in its resolutions. Humphrey has argued that this state practice was evident in the General Assembly's Declaration on the Granting of Independence to Colonial Countries and Peoples, 1514 XV, adopted in 1969, which said that states "shall observe faithfully and strictly the provisions of the Universal Declaration of Human Rights" and also in the Declaration on the Elimination of All Forms of Racial Discrimination, which included a similar statement.[187]

In 1962 the Office of Legal Affairs of the Secretariat defined the term "declaration" routinely used by the General Assembly as "a formal and solemn instrument, suitable for rare occasions when principles of great and lasting importance are being enunciated. . ." Though not legally binding, "in view of the great solemnity and significance of a declaration, it may be considered to impart, on behalf of the organ adopting it, a strong expectation that members of the international community will abide by it. . . as the expectation is gradually justified by State practice, a declaration may by custom become recognized as laying down rules binding upon States."[188] For Humphrey, the Universal Declaration has immense political and moral authority — equal to that of the Charter itself — and its impact on world opinion has been very great indeed. Having been constantly invoked and referred to inside and outside of the United Nations, he has argued that the Declaration is

[186] "The Universal Declaration of Human Rights," (1949) 4 Int'l J. 358. It will be recalled that the Universal Declaration has been used to interpret the seven references to human rights in the United Nations Charter which were left largely undefined: *A Great Adventure,* 58.

[187] Humphrey notes that all of the member states abstaining in 1948 at the adoption of the Universal Declaration except for South Africa, adopted the first of these two declarations: "Human Rights, the United Nations and 1968," at 10.

[188] UN Doc. E/Cn.4/L.610, cited in *Behind the Headlines, supra* note 117, at 6-7.

now part of the customary law of nations and thus binding on all states.[189] Whether or not the rules of the Declaration are *jus cogens,* he emphasizes that "the Declaration is, of course, more important than any convention or treaty could ever be, because a convention or treaty is only binding on those states which ratify it..."[190]

CREATION OF TWO INTERNATIONAL COVENANTS

If, as Humphrey has argued, the Universal Declaration is now part of the customary law of nations, a major justification for the creation of the covenants was that they made the obligations created by the Declaration "more precise" and provided "measures of implementation or enforcement," the latter being the "real raison d'être for the covenants." Looking back, Humphrey would have preferred a "more imaginative approach" in order to have avoided the lengthy drafting process. Such an approach would have used every possible avenue to increase the authority of the Universal Declaration, relying on the United Nations Charter's inherent powers to provide machinery for its implementation.

In 1949 Humphrey stated optimistically but accurately that "the General Assembly may be seized this year with the task of bringing to completion the project of the International Bill of Human Rights by adopting a Covenant or a Convention and measures of implementation..."[191] In its six sessions between 1949 and 1954, the Commission continued its work on the Covenant, which it had begun even before the adoption of the Universal Declaration. In fact, an incomplete draft of the Covenant had been sent to the General Assembly with the Universal Declaration in 1948. Once the Commission on Human Rights had completed the drafting process in 1954,[192] the draft covenants were sent to the Third Committee. The Third Committee then took twelve years to adopt them.

---

[189] For opposing arguments, see Sinha, *supra* note 148, at 159.

[190] C.C.I.L. proceedings, at 8-12; Report of the Iowa Conference, at 32; "Human Rights and Authority," at 414; Report of the Rapporteur, Report of the International Committee on Human Rights, in *Report of the Fifty-Third Conference Held at Buenos Aires, August 25 to August 31, 1968,* at 437 (International Law Association, 1969); "Revolution in the International Law of Human Rights," 207; "The Dean Who Never Was," *supra* note 60, at 197-98.

[191] "The Universal Declaration of Human Rights," (1949) 27 Can. Bar Rev. 204; "The Revolution in the International Law of Human Rights," 206-7.

[192] Mrs. Roosevelt's tenure as Chair of the Commission on Human Rights ended in 1950. Charles Malik replaced her as Chair for the 1951 session. When the covenants were sent to the Third Committee in 1954, the Commission was chaired by Mr. Aznai of Egypt.

The first hurdle in the drafting process was the controversial debate about the creation of one or two covenants. A state's position in this debate generally reflected its ideological viewpoint, particularly its perception of the role of government in society. For example, the representatives of Australia and the USSR on the Commission felt in 1949 that economic, social, and cultural rights should be included in a single covenant. However, after a 13:2 vote in the 1950 session of the Commission, it was decided not to include economic and social rights in a "first" covenant, thus leaving the matter of additional covenants undecided. The General Assembly decided the contrary.

The decision to create two covenants which would be completed and opened for signature simultaneously, was eventually made by the General Assembly after a series of motions, on a request from the Economic and Social Council at the behest of India, France, the United Kingdom, the United States, and Uruguay. Thus the General Assembly reversed its decision after protracted debate in the Third Committee. Humphrey notes that the General Assembly's justification for requiring different methods of implementation lay in the different nature of these two types of rights.

Economic, social, and cultural rights have been distinguished from civil and political rights by virtue of the manner in which they are considered capable of implementation. Obligations in the Covenant on Civil and Political Rights take effect from the moment of ratification; these rights, the international community decided, require immediate implementation. In contrast, economic, social, and cultural rights were considered to be program rights which could only be implemented progressively. However, as Humphrey quite rightly notes, this distinction is not as clear-cut as it appears, particularly since certain economic, social, and cultural rights, such as trade union rights, may be given immediate effect.

Yet, as has long been recognized, the possession of civil and political rights holds little meaning for individuals who do not possess adequate levels of economic, social, and cultural support. Conversely, in Humphrey's words, "[e]conomic and social rights may be a condition of social justice, but civil and political rights are a condition of freedom."[193] In attempting to implement both types of rights, a government, in order to provide necessary levels of food, shelter, and employment, may be forced to curb the en-

---

[193] "Nationalism, Freedom and Social Justice," (1975-76) 55 Dalhousie Review 605, 610.

joyment of certain civil and political rights. The possible conflict between the implementation of civil and political rights and the achievement of economic rights must consequently be addressed. That the implementation of most economic and social rights also implies the strengthening of the apparatus of government, and hence the power of the state, was probably of concern to countries who opposed the creation of a single covenant.

To foresee a possible increase in state power did not, for Humphrey, necessarily mean that one was asserting the priority of economic and social rights over civil and political rights or, worse, that "the individual can have no rights against the collectivity in which his personality is submerged."[194] At the same time Humphrey observed that while some collective rights can be easily justified, for example, medicare, "I am tempted to suggest that all collective rights are, whenever they interfere with individual rights, suspect to the extent in any event that the burden of proof should be on the majority or the authority acting in its name to show that the limitations on the exercise of personal freedoms which they entail are necessary and just."[195] He saw the challenge of the 1980s as one of discovering "how collective rights can be extended in the interest of the general welfare and greater social justice without at the same time destroying individual freedoms."[196]

Despite his acceptance of the idea that economic and social rights are program rights, the implementation of which is contingent on the availability of economic resources, Humphrey has recently suggested that debate as to the existence of second and third generation rights weakens the concept of rights as it was envisaged when, in 1948, the United Nations General Assembly adopted the Universal Declaration: "It tends to bring them down to the level of mere goals or aspirations."[197]

Though a better solution may have been to include the two types

---

[194] Humphrey suggests this argument is most often put forward by governments of totalitarian or one-party states and is made more dangerous through the combination of nationalism and "totalitarian or quasi-totalitarian socialism" to which such governments adhere, suggesting that "[t]his unholy alliance between nationalism and totalitarianism is a continuing threat not only to world peace but also to the preservation of those human rights and fundamental freedoms without which there can be no human dignity": "Nationalism, Freedom and Social Justice," 611.

[195] R. St. J. Macdonald and J. P. Humphrey (eds.), *The Practice of Freedom* xviii (Toronto: Butterworths, 1979) (hereafter *The Practice of Freedom*).

[196] "The Individual in the Eighties," 12; *The Practice of Freedom, supra*, xix.

[197] Speech, "Vème Conférence Internationale de Droit Constitutionnel," Québec, Oct. 1, 1987, at 2-3.

of rights in different parts of a single Covenant, with similar methods of implementation, it did ''not necessarily follow from the fact that methods of national application are different that systems of international control should also be different. . . a control organ, such as the Human Rights Committee. . .could rule on whether a State had failed. . .'' to use its maximum available resources towards the progressive achievement of the economic, social, and cultural rights. The compromise reached enabled certain states who were opposed in principle to the codification of economic, social, and cultural rights, to ratify the International Covenant on Civil and Political Rights.[198]

DRAFTING PROCESS

Many obstacles were encountered during the inherently difficult drafting process. Some of the articles and groups of articles were ''equal in complexity'' to the whole texts of many other treaties for which special diplomatic conferences had been convened after long preparation. As well, the work on these covenants became the context in which some of the most controversial issues in the United Nations were fought out, namely, the question of a ''colonial'' clause, the right to self-determination, and the federal states clause. Further difficulties were presented by the composition of the Third Committee and the infrequency of its meetings.[199] However, the major obstacles, as might be expected, were the suspicions of governments ''of any effort to create international machinery for the protection of human rights,'' because of their interest in protecting their sovereignty and their ''discretionary powers in their international relations.'' Humphrey concluded that these concerns were most frequent on the part of governments of countries where nationalist sentiment was the strongest.

MEASURES OF IMPLEMENTATION

In 1958 Humphrey described the first ten years of his service at the Human Rights Division as ones in which the United Nations was primarily in the normative stage of its development.[200] By 1965 he

[198] *Behind the Headlines, supra* note 117, at 10.

[199] In 1963 the Third Committee met only for three months a year and devoted only a portion of its time to the drafting of the covenants; *Social Action, supra* note 115, at 9.

[200] ''Human Rights: New Directions in the United Nations Program,'' (1958) 4 N.Y.L. Forum 391.

thought that the United Nations was nearing the completion of its standard-setting phase, a view which he reiterated in 1968.[201] His departure from the Human Rights Division coincided roughly with the completion of the initial, legislative, phase of the work of the United Nations in the domain of human rights.

He was optimistic about the creation of "effective measures of implementation" as a result of the adoption of the Convention on the Elimination of All Forms of Racial Discrimination in 1965, which was the first to incorporate a right of petition. He had envisaged "equally progressive machinery" for the two covenants, but this optimism was not well founded.

As mentioned above, the decision to create two covenants rested on the perceived nature of the rights in question and the degree of implementation that states were willing to accord to each. Both covenants incorporated a system of reporting. In a thorough examination of international measures of implementation in the Report of the ILA, Buenos Aires, Humphrey suggested that reporting had been the most successful mechanism of implementation internationally. With respect to the progressive implementation of economic, social, and cultural rights, reporting permitted the international supervisory body to consider a state's available resources in assessing the degree of progress it had achieved. Reporting also provided useful information to the international community with respect to the implementation of rights falling within either covenant.[202]

Neither covenant recognizes the right of petition for individuals or groups. The International Covenant on Civil and Political Rights relies on a weaker mechanism of implementation, the state complaint system. Under a petitioning system, an individual or group would have the right to petition the government of his state or the United Nations for the redress of grievances.[203] In a state complaint system, only state parties can launch complaints as to the failure of other states to live up to their obligations under the Covenant. In this regard, it is well known that complex relations between states often dampen their willingness to institute complaints, especially

---

[201] "The United Nations and Human Rights," (1965) Howard L.J. 373; International Law Association, *Report of the Fifty-Third Conference Held at Buenos Aires, August 25 to August 31, 1968*, at 438 (London, 1969) (hereafter ILA Report, 1968).

[202] ILA Report, 1968, *supra*, 438-39.

[203] A right to petition had been included by Humphrey in Art. 28 of the Secretariat's draft: "The Right of Petition in the United Nations," (1971) 4 Human Rights L.J. 463, 464.

when interstate relations are good.

In Humphrey's view, the International Covenant on Civil and Political Rights was generally ''a very weak system'' compared to the system of implementation under the European Convention on Human Rights. The Optional Protocol was ''only reluctantly'' adopted and many states had ''no intention whatsoever'' of accepting it. Indeed, ''[t]he machinery created by the covenant is not even as strong as that which the Commission on Human Rights had contemplated way back in 1954. It is not even as strong as the provisions, in themselves not very strong, that were put into the International Convention on the Elimination of All Forms of Racial Discrimination, which was adopted by the General Assembly in 1965.''[204]

If governments were reluctant to adopt implementation measures for civil and political rights, implementation was to be even more limited for economic, social, and cultural rights, the so-called ''program rights.'' In a process similar to the reporting required by the Covenant on Civil and Political Rights, states would report to the Economic and Social Council on the progress they had made in implementing these rights. Humphrey argued that there are those who believe that ''in the final analysis there may be more in the reporting than in the complaint system and would like to have the same type of reporting...under the two covenants.''[205]

In Humphrey's opinion, the solution to the difficulties of implementation was to recognize an individual right of petition. This avenue was not yet developed at the international level when he examined this right in his 1971 article, ''The Right of Petition in the United Nations.''[206] Despite the fact that, from the moment the United Nations was established, individuals began to address their concerns on matters of human rights to different United Nations bodies, the ''essential'' human right of petition was not incorporated into the final draft of the Universal Declaration of Human Rights. Seen as a question of implementation, both the Commission on Human Rights and the United Nations General Assembly desired to study the matter further in connection with the drafting of the Covenant on Civil and Political Rights.

It was self-interest on the part of states, and their ''fear of pub-

---

[204] Report on the Iowa Conference, 34; ILA Report, 1968, *supra* note 201, at 442-45; ''The United Nations and Human Rights,'' 374.

[205] ''The United Nations and Human Rights,'' 374.

[206] ''The Right of Petition in the United Nations,'' *supra* note 203.

lic exposure,'' that lay behind the General Assembly's initial refusal to incorporate the right of petition into the Universal Declaration as well as the Commission's decision ''not to follow the recommendation of its 1947 working group'' to create a right of petition in the covenant. Despite some movement in the General Assembly towards the recognition of a right of petition, the Commission's draft covenant of 1954 failed to include such a right.[207] However, by 1966 the Optional Protocol had been adopted by the General Assembly to give the Human Rights Committee the jurisdiction to receive and consider *individual* petitions when a state had recognized the competence of the Committee to do so. By 1991 fifty-five states-parties, more than half the number of states-parties to the Covenant, had recognized the competence of the Committee.

It is timely to recall that difficulties in establishing effective measures of implementation were compounded by the lack of initiative or by active dissuasion on the part of larger powers, including the United Kingdom and the United States.[208] Humphrey noted in 1965 that in the light of the preference of many states for implementation solely at the national level, there was no guarantee that even that system would be adopted by the General Assembly with respect to civil and political rights.

Generally, he found that while governments could agree on the standards to be set at the drafting stage of the law-making process, despite differences of interpretation of the norms agreed upon, they were, and remain, less likely to agree on mechanisms for implementation. When implementation was considered, the question of state sovereignty would inevitably arise, and ''the experience of the United Nations has been. . .that it is the governments of countries where nationalist sentiment is the strongest that have most energetically opposed the creation of effective international measures for the protection of human rights.''[209] The Cold War was further evidence of the fact that ''the chief barrier to the development of an effective world organization was the self-centred attitudes of exclusiveness and intolerance that existed in member countries.''[210] In ''Nationalism, Freedom and Social Justice'' (1975), Humphrey examined the rise of nationalism in Western Europe, beginning with the French Revolution, to emphasize the close relationship between

[207] *Ibid.*, 465, 470.
[208] *A Great Adventure* 38; Ramcharan, *op. cit. supra* note 124, at 474.
[209] ''Nationalism, Freedom and Social Justice,'' *supra* note 193, at 610.
[210] *Ibid.*, 609.

nationalism, war, and the denial of human rights. Calling nationalism the strongest, the most elemental of all political forces, he deplored the fact that "other values like fundamental human rights are sacrificed in the name of the collectivity and national aspirations." He went so far as to say that in his twenty years at the United Nations, "I experienced almost total incompatibility between even current conceptions of sovereignty and the effective rule of the international law of human rights or indeed of the effective rule of any international law. . ."[211]

RELATION OF THE INDIVIDUAL TO THE STATE

It will be remembered that the international legal order generally, and the relationship between individuals and that legal order in particular, was the subject of Humphrey's pioneering article "The Parent of Anarchy" published in 1945. It is revealing for present purposes to keep in mind that throughout his academic and professional career he has focused on this theme, on the historical development of the international law of human rights, and on the shift from a classical interstate system to a new system of world order. He has consistently underlined the role of the individual.

In considering the issue of individual freedom, Humphrey, who claims he speaks as a "liberal (with a small l)," stated that "the individual is my religion and ultimate value."[212] However, all individuals by necessity belong to collectivities. These collectivities are "the exact opposite to the individuals who comprise them and their interests very often come into conflict with those individuals."[213] A collectivity, in Humphrey's opinion, has "no organic life of its own" nor "a general will." This distinction between the individual and the collective is, moreover, extended to the differenti-

[211] Introduction, IVe Conférence Internationale de Droit Constitutionnel, "Paix, Relations internationales, Respect des droits humains," Université Laval, Faculté de droit, 1987, *Le Devoir Supplement* 23; "Two Parents of Anarchy," *supra* note 60, at 8; "The Revolution in the International Law of Human Rights," 208-9.

[212] "The Individual in the Eighties," 3. On the definition of individual Humphrey comments: "By individual, I mean a human being, a person of flesh and blood who is separate and distinct from all other individuals or any group of individuals, a person who is unique, different from any other person who ever was or will be, a person who has a body, mind, will and who knows, a soul of his own, a person who suffers when he is hurt, laughs when he is merry and rejoices when he is happy, a person who can love but who can also hate. Some of them are saints, others are worse than devils."

[213] *Ibid.*, 4.

ation between individual and collective rights, usually attributed to states. Since these two types of rights often conflict, society must address questions of priority. On this point, Humphrey repeatedly warns that ''the tendency seems increasingly to be to solve the conflict in favour of the collectivity and against the individual, to favour collective at the expense of individual rights. . .usually. . .in the name of national security, social justice or the general welfare.''[214]

On the question of the increasing power of the state and on the positive demands on the state as a welfare state, Humphrey was saying as early as 1958 that despite the nature of some positive government action, it was a ''matter of urgent necessity to establish solid barriers against excessive encroachments by the state and to preserve that residuum of individual liberty without which there can be no human dignity.''[215] The challenge in his opinion was to maintain progress with respect to economic and social development ''while preserving those essential political and civil rights which make life worth living.''[216] His opinions with respect to the student turmoil in Quebec in the late 1960s and early 1970s, discussed below, as well as the 1990 debate in Canada over the Meech Lake constitutional record, were shaped by his view of the relation between the individual, the collectivity, and human rights.

IMPLEMENTATION OUTSIDE OF THE COVENANTS

The difficulties in reaching agreement on measures of implementation and the eventual weakness of the measures drafted led the General Assembly, the Division of Human Rights, and Humphrey, as its Director, to search for mechanisms outside the covenants through which progress could be made. Humphrey's general approach may be summarized as follows. First, he believes strongly in the efficacy of public opinion as a way to pressure governments opposed to change. In his view, unless they are impelled by the force of public opinion, most governments are unlikely to — indeed they will not — take positions in the United Nations or anywhere else in favour of the creation of effective institutions for the protection of human rights. Even those governments that are the most dedicated to human rights, hesitate before agreeing to the creation of

---

[214] *Ibid.*, 6-7; *The Practice of Freedom,* xviii.

[215] Speech to Commemorate the Tenth Anniversary of the Adoption of the Universal Declaration of Human Rights, Winnipeg, Dec. 10, 1958, at 8.

[216] *Ibid.*

institutions that could curb their discretionary powers or might be used against them.[217] Thus, "the ultimate sanction of...human rights is the force of world opinion."[218] Second, he believes strongly in the importance of the role of education, by which he refers to the efforts of individuals and non-governmental organizations, in the development of human rights awareness. For example, it was the energetic lobby of voluntary organizations at the San Francisco Conference that ensured the inclusion of references to human rights in the United Nations Charter. Third, financial resources and administrative structures for research and fact-finding are, in his opinion, crucial to the effectiveness of NGO's other than those few organizations, such as Amnesty International, which possess large memberships.

With President Eisenhower's decision in 1953 not to ratify the two International Covenants, the U.S. delegation to the Commission on Human Rights proposed the creation of a three-part human rights "action programme."[219] In his article, "Human Rights: New Direction in the U.N. Program," Humphrey examined the new efforts being made at the operational level for the promotion of human rights, namely, periodic reports to the Economic and Social Council, global studies, and the advisory services in human rights.[220]

ECOSOC RESOLUTION FOR PERIODIC REPORTING

Under a 1956 resolution of ECOSOC, states were asked to report periodically on developments and progress achieved in the matter of human rights. In Humphrey's judgment, the implementation of this system of reporting was "perhaps the most important decision that the Council has ever taken in the matter of human rights," because it was the "first time that an international organization has ever asked its member states to report to it on the near totality of their relations with their own citizens, an area so intimate that it has always been considered as coming within the exclusive jurisdiction of the State and hence preserved from international

---

[217] Speech, Human Rights Day, Dec. 10, 1973, at 12-13.

[218] ILA, *Report of the Fifty-Sixth Conference Held at New Delhi, December 29, 1974 to January 4, 1975,* at 205-15 (Great Britain: International Law Association, 1976); B. G. Ramcharan, *The Concept and Present Status of the International Protection of Human Rights,* Preface, x.

[219] *A Great Adventure* 176-78; Alston, *supra* note 119, at 232-33.

[220] "Human Rights: New Directions in the U.N. Program," *supra* note 200, at 391-97.

scrutiny."[221]

While there was no legally binding obligation on states to report, many states did feel a political obligation to do so. The Secretariat prepared a summary of these reports, which was forwarded to the Commission on Human Rights which, in turn, sent "its comments, conclusions, and recommendations of an objective and general character" to the Economic and social Council. Though in 1965 the Commission had established a small committee to study the reports, and though some of its conclusions had filtered through to the Council's report, the Commission by 1963 had "not yet made any significant comments or recommendations to the Council based on these periodic reports."[222] Humphrey attributed this to "a tradition which has been built up in the Commission and which was certainly a valuable one in the early years when the Commission's functions were largely legislative, and that has been to avoid dealing with particular issues, so that the Commission has not been inclined to analyze these reports closely and to call a spade a spade or to indicate inadequacies where they may exist."[223] Thus, despite the fact that a number of states were reporting, the system of periodic reports as a whole "never worked very well in practice. . . and the reason for this was simply that most governments did not want it to work."[224]

In "The United Nations and Human Rights," published in 1965, Humphrey discussed changes to the system of periodic reporting; annual reports would be made concerning a different right every year. An additional change in 1965 was that reports were made progressive over a three-year period. A report on civil and political rights would be made in the first year, on economic, social, and cultural rights in the second, and on freedom of information in the third. Later, the reporting period was extended to once every two years, on a six-year cycle, thereby reducing the effectiveness of the reporting.[225]

[221] *Ibid.*, 392; "Human Rights, the UN and 1968," 12-13.

[222] "New Directions," 393.

[223] "The United Nations and Human Rights," 375.

[224] Speech, NGO Seminar on the Protection of Human Rights, Geneva, Sept. 8-10, 1986. Humphrey noted that "it was a rare thing all the time I was at the United Nations for either the Human Rights Commission or the Sub-Commission to discuss, much less adopt, any resolution relating to a concrete case of alleged violation of human rights": *A Great Adventure* 263; "The Revolution in the International Law of Human Rights," 212; ILA Report, 1968, *supra* note 201, at 440.

[225] *A Great Adventure* 217; *Report of the Fifty-Fifth Conference Held at New York August 21 to*

State reports were to be circulated as received from the state in question. The Sub-Commission was asked to study them in their totality and not merely refer to summaries prepared by the Secretariat. It was thought that this initial examination in the Sub-Commission by experts in their personal capacity would be conducted with fewer inhibitions than if the discussion began in the Human Rights Commission. However, the Sub-Commission, which was to send its recommendations on to the Commission, delayed its consideration of the reports and the Commission revoked its involvement with state reports the following year. Humphrey suggests that "the analysis of the reports later made by the representatives of States in the ad hoc committee which met during the 1966 session of the Commission came much nearer to the kind of thing which the Council obviously had in mind."[226] As to the ad hoc committee, he commented:

[The Secretary-General] is...to prepare an analytical summary which will include a description of the important trends revealed in the reports: difficulties encountered, methods adopted to overcome them and suggestions for possible further action. This analytical summary will be studied by the ad hoc Commission on Periodic Reports in advance of the Commission's annual session. There is no reason to believe, however, that the ad hoc Committee, even with the help of the Secretariat...will be in any better position to perform its functions than it has been in the past. The ad hoc Committe, like its parent, is a political body composed of representatives of governments and will, as in the past, base its decisions on political convenience.[227]

In these circumstances, Humphrey recommended the establishment of an independent committee of experts similar to the ILO Committee of Experts, which reviews annual reports by governments as to their implementation of conventions to which they are parties.[228] However, in 1981, the General Assembly, "on the recommendation of the Secretariat," abandoned the system of periodic reporting to the Economic and Social Council completely. It was

---

August *26, 1972*, at 572 (Great Britain: International Law Association, 1974, hereafter ILA Report, 1972); "The International Bill of Rights: Scope and Implementation," 530; "International Protection of Human Rights," CCIL, 22-23. Humphrey says that "[t]he system is now in a state of coma, if not moribund": *ibid.*, 23.

226 ILA Report, 1968, *supra* note 201, at 441.

227 *Ibid.*, 442.

228 *Ibid.*, 442; "Human Rights, the UN, and 1968," 12; ILA Report, 1972, *supra* note 225, at 574; ILA Report, 1974, *supra* note 218, at 212.

seen to be "obsolete, ineffective or of marginal usefulness," particularly in light of the systems of reporting under the two Covenants. The latter were, however, only binding on ratifying states, and, in Humphrey's opinion, this reasoning was "nonsense." He issued a vigorous call for the system of periodic reporting to be "revived" with the ILO's mechanism of reporting as a model.

"GLOBAL STUDIES"

In examining discrimination in education, the Sub-Commission on the Prevention of Discrimination and the Protection of Minorities adopted the technique of preparing global studies based on monographs on individual countries.[229] For its part, the Commission on Human Rights in 1956 began a series of studies, starting with an examination of the right of individuals to be free from arbitrary arrest, detention, and exile.[230] These studies, prepared by the Secretariat at the behest of the Sub-Commission or the Commission, were limited to the consideration of official sources and consultations with non-governmental organizations.[231] They were then forwarded to the country being considered for comments and suggestions. The purpose behind this action was to give the state an opportunity to rectify anything that might not be right in its laws or practices without too much publicity being given to the matter. From these monographs and the comments thereto, global studies were prepared by a rapporteur, in the case of the Sub-Commission, or by a committee of a number of its members, in the case of the

---

[229] *Supra* note 127, at 878-79; *Social Action, supra* note 115, at 12-13; "Human Rights: New Directions in the United Nations Program," 393-94. Mr. Charles Ammoun of Lebanon was the rapporteur for the Sub-Commission's initial study on discrimination in education. This was followed by a study on discrimination in religious rights and practices and discrimination on political rights.

[230] It also considered the right of arrested persons to communicate with those whom it is necessary for them to consult in order to insure their defence or to protect their essential interests.

[231] When studies or reports were prepared by the Secretariat, their conclusions were generally not too critical given the official nature of the studies. Often they reflected the *de jure* situation within a given country rather than the *de facto* state of affairs. This was often the result of the fact that such factual information as was available was brought to the Sub-Commission's attention by non-governmental organizations. The offer by a rapporteur to lend his name (and thus his credibility) to a Secretariat report or study permitted in many cases a greater degree of evaluation and critical analysis. Nonetheless, Humphrey felt that improvements to the "factual and critical content" of the studies would have made them more useful: "Human Rights, the UN and 1968," 12-13; ILA Report, 1968, *supra* note 201, at 453, 458.

Commission.[232] While occasionally these studies formed the basis for future conventions, resolutions, or declarations, they also provided a "unique review of the world situation with respect to the rights studied."

Various problems were associated with the system of studies undertaken by the Sub-Commission. These included lengthy preparation time, lack of resources and time available to the Secretariat for the collection of material, publication only in the language in which the country monographs had been prepared, and the relatively brief time the Sub-Commission could devote yearly to a review of these studies.[233]

ADVISORY SERVICES

In 1953 the General Assembly authorized the creation of an advisory services program in human rights. The assistance offered to states under this program was initially envisaged as assistance similar to that offered by the UN Technical Assistance Administration, namely, the provision of experts, the organization of seminars, and the grant of fellowships. However, it soon became clear that governments were reluctant to accept even this kind of assistance because they perceived it as an admission of failure insofar as the protection of human rights was concerned.[234] Accordingly, the Human Rights Division decided that the program could be salvaged if states were invited to host seminars in areas of human rights law in which they had expertise or a good record. Acting on this idea, Humphrey soon found that the Secretariat got all the invitations it wanted. In the end, the human rights seminars were the more successful part of the advisory services program, because they sought

---

[232] With respect to the procedure of writing the report, Humphrey notes that: "the Sub-Commission is at least theoretically independent of government in that its members are experts acting as individuals; and the Sub-Commission has been able to find in its own membership professionally competent and independent reporters to conduct the studies. But the members of the Commission represent governments: the technique of appointing one of its members as rapporteur was not therefore acceptable to it so its study is being undertaken by a sub-committee of four of its members": "Human Rights: New Directions in the United Nations Program," 394.

[233] In his 1968 ILA Report, Humphrey recommended that the United Nations should "publish and circulate as regular documents the country monographs prepared by the Secretariat" in all the working languages of the UN: ILA Report, 1968, *supra* note 201, at 454, 458.

[234] *A Great Adventure* 177; "The International Protection of Human Rights," CCIL, 28; *Social Action, supra* note 115, at 13.

to capitalize on the potential of education in the promotion of human rights. From 1955 until his retirement from the United Nations in 1966, Humphrey was actively involved in the development of these seminars, which were held all over the world. They included a seminar on the participation of women in public life (Bangkok, 1957), on the protection of human rights in the administration of criminal justice (The Philippines, 1958; Chile, May 1958), and on the freedom of information (New Delhi, 1962; Rome, 1964).

The object of these seminars was to provide participants and government representatives with opportunities to exchange ideas and information. No attempt was made to draft resolutions or conventions, though some seminars did produce final reports. In addition to the benefits accruing to participants and governments, Humphrey felt that the seminars publicized the United Nations human rights program and helped to create "a human rights interest...in certain sections of the community, professional and otherwise which would normally have no direct contact with the United Nations."[235]

It will be recalled that the different Secretaries-General with whom he worked, not to mention the governments with whom he dealt, were not enthusiastic about many of Humphrey's initiatives. This was particularly true of the seminar program, which met with strong opposition from Hammarskjold and even from some members of Humphrey's own division. In light of these difficulties, it is not surprising that he would later comment that "[t]he truth was...that in those years there wasn't very much the Secretariat could do to further the human rights programme apart from preparing 'studies' and organizing seminars."[236]

UNITED NATIONS HIGH COMMISSIONER FOR HUMAN RIGHTS

In 1965 both the Soviet and American delegations proposed that Humphrey's tenure as the Director of the Human Rights Division be extended by one year past the standard retirement age of sixty, a proposal that was supported by other delegations. Unfortunately, within the year Humphrey's relations with the Soviet delegation and with the Soviet bureaucrats within his Division were

---

[235] *Social Action, supra,* 14; "Human Rights: New Directions in the United Nations Program," 396; but for a perspective critical of the human rights program, see Theo van Boven, "The United Nations and Human Rights: A Critical Appraisal," (1977) 8 Bull. Peace Proposals 198, 200.

[236] *A Great Adventure* 214-15, 296.

to dissolve into acrimony over a proposal to create the office of a United Nations High Commissioner for Human Rights.[237] The background to this stimulating, and still timely, suggestion is as follows.

Under President John F. Kennedy, the United States, wishing to take an initiative with respect to human rights, suggested that the Chairman of the Human Rights Commission become a full-time international servant who would report annually on the observance of human rights in the world. Humphrey was concerned that the Human Rights Commission had no appropriate mechanism for the consideration of state reports under ECOSOC Resolution 642 B (XXVII) of 1956 on the observance of human rights, and proposed that the General Assembly appoint an independent officer to review these reports as well as advise the Commission in other areas, rather than attempting to rewrite the mandate of the Chairman, essentially a political appointee.[238] Other ideas circulating at the time included the appointment of a United Nations Ombudsman, a United Nations Attorney-General for Human Rights, who would review complaints of violations of human rights and determine which would be investigated, and the creation of an International Court of Human Rights.[239]

In 1963 a United Nations mission, described by Humphrey as a politically oriented mission of ambassadors, some of whom represented governments that had accused the Diem government in the General Assembly of violating the rights of Buddhists, was sent to Vietnam to investigate charges of persecution of the Buddhist community by the Diem government. In Humphrey's opinion, the government of South Vietnam might have preferred to have the investigation carried out by an international personality acting under the authority of the General Assembly rather than by a mission made up of ambassadors representing particular states. Humphrey's

[237] *A Great Adventure* 296-301; "A United Nations High Commissioner for Human Rights: The Birth of an Initiative," (1973) II *Canadian Yearbook of International Law* 220; "U.N. and Human Rights," 378.

[238] For a further description, see ILA Report, 1968, *supra* note 201, at 454; "A United Nations High Commissioner," 221-22; "The United Nations and Human Rights," 378; "The International Protection of Human Rights," CCIL, 21; NGO Seminar on the Protection of Human Rights, 1986, at 6.

[239] Humphrey also later recommended the establishment of a Universal Court of Human Rights or a chamber of the International Court of Justice to which individual or groups would have access: ILA Report, 1968, *supra* note 201, at 457-58; "The International Protection of Human Rights," CCIL, 21; NGO Seminar on the Protection of Human Rights, 1986, at 6.

involvement as Principal Secretary to this mission convinced him that such an inquiry would have been more useful than the United Nations mission reluctantly invited by the Diem government.

With the assassination of President Kennedy, United States' interest in the human rights program dissipated at the official level. However, the idea for a High Commissioner was inserted by Humphrey into a speech given at Columbia University by the businessman Jacob Blaustein, thereby becoming known as the Blaustein Plan. It eventually became the basis of a proposal made to the Human Rights Commission and the General Assembly by Costa Rica in 1965 and 1966 respectively. In the General Assembly, the proposal met with bitter opposition from the Soviet Union which stated that: "It was utopian to suppose that a single individual could act as an arbitrator, advisor or even judge in resolving the questions relating to human rights which would arise under various legal, philosophical or religious systems."[240]

Though Humphrey's suggestion to the United States delegation had not been made inappropriately, his relations with the Soviet delegation deteriorated once it learned that he had proposed the idea. He saw this enmity as the reason why the Soviet delegation initially opposed his election to the Sub-Commission on the Prevention of Discrimination and the Protection of Minorities upon his retirement as Director of the Human Rights Division, and also opposed his continuation on that body in 1972.

The proposal, as initially envisaged, was limited in scope. Its authors had "carefully avoided" putting anything into it that could reasonably frighten governments and prevent its adoption. By 1966 this had changed. A working group of the Human Rights Commission recommended that the High Commissioner for Human Rights be given additional powers, including the right to examine all communications alleging violations, that he be entitled to discuss them with the governments involved, and that he be empowered to evaluate developments in the implementation of human rights standards generally. As might be expected, these recommendations met with little enthusiasm in the General Assembly. Humphrey would later say that "the malady with which the patient now lies dying may therefore have been brought about by the excessive zeal of his well-wishers."[241] Though he has not abandoned

---

[240] *A Great Adventure* 298; "The United Nations and Human Rights," 378; ILA Report, 1968, *supra* note 201, at 453-54.

[241] *A Great Adventure* 300. See too R. St. J. Macdonald, "The United Nations High

his efforts to encourage the creation of the office of United Nations High Commissioner for Human Rights, realization of the idea remained remote throughout the 1970s and 1980s.

RESOLUTION 1503

By the early 1960s, previous caution about dealing with specific violations of human rights was being overtaken by the political climate in the General Assembly, which was immersed in debates over colonialism and racial discrimination. In October 1966, the General Assembly invited the Economic and Social Council and the Commission on Human Rights urgently to consider ways and means of improving the capacity of the United Nations to put a stop to violations of human rights wherever they occurred.

A small committee of the Commission studied a variety of mechanisms to improve the methods by which the Commission dealt with violations of human rights. This led the Commission to request the Sub-Commission on the Prevention of Discrimination and the Protection of Minorities to examine communications on alleged violations of human rights and to prepare a report identifying those countries where consistent patterns of gross violations of human rights were found. This, in turn, led to the adoption in 1967 by the Sub-Commission of a resolution, drafted by Humphrey, which was critical of the human rights situation in a number of African countries, as well as in Haiti and Greece. The Sub-Commission also recommended the creation of a Special Committee of Experts to examine these consistent patterns of gross violations of human rights. By 1975 Humphrey would comment that the reasons for the Commission's failure to take effective action under the above resolution lay "in the unwillingness of governments...to countenance a development which might expose their conduct to organized international scrutiny and criticism."[242] The resolution has, however, become an important device for the organization of shame against government.

Still, it was recognized that more efficient mechanisms were needed to deal with the many communications alleging human rights abuses that were reaching the United Nations. As a result, the Sub-Commission in 1967 recommended the adoption of a procedure for dealing with these communications, later institutionalized as

Commission for Human Rights," 5 *Canadian Yearbook of International Law* 84 (1967).

[242] "The Revolution in the International Law of Human Rights," 213.

ECOSOC Resolution 1503 (XLVIII) of 1970. The recommended procedure was as follows: a small working group, of which Humphrey was the first chairman, would review the communications prior to the meeting of the Sub-Commission for a minimum of ten days; where consistent patterns of human rights violations were found these would be referred to the Sub-Commission, which would then decide which situations it would draw to the Commission's attention. The Commission could then decide to study a particular situation further, with a report to the Economic and Social Council or, in appropriate cases, with the consent of the government in question, establish an ad hoc committee of experts to investigate it. Unlike the Optional Protocol, available only to nationals of states which have ratified the Protocol, Resolution 1503 is the only right of individual petition that can be used against any member state of the United Nations. As Humphrey would often emphasize, without the requirement of confidentiality the 1503 procedure would not have been adopted.[243]

That the 1503 procedure is carried out behind closed doors is a serious weakness. Humphrey maintains that confidentiality might have a useful role to play where the purpose of a complaint is to resolve a situation ''and not simply stigmatize a recalcitrant government.''[244] A further weakness is the inherently political nature of the procedure, particularly when combined with confidentiality. Humphrey was personally made aware of this years later when, at the age of eighty-five, he was actively involved in an unsuccessful 1503 complaint brought on behalf of surviving Canadian prisoners-of-war who had been held in Japanese camps during the Second World War; they sought $13.6 million dollars' compensation from the Japanese government. Convinced that there was a ''political barrier,'' Humphrey, always forward-looking, proposed that ''we should try to get the General Assembly to adopt a very short and concise Declaration on the Right of all Victims of Gross Violations [of human rights] to Compensation'' as a move towards the establishment of a convention to that effect.[245] In the result, Mr. Theo van Boven, a former director of the human rights pro-

---

[243] ILA Report, 1972, *supra* note 225, at 574-76; ''The Right of Petition,'' 473; ''The International Protection of Human Rights,'' CCIL, 24-25; ''Confidential-1503,'' UN Watch, 12 Human Rights Internet Reporter 82 (Winter 1988).

[244] NGO Seminar on the Protection of Human Rights, 1986, at 3. See the working paper on confidentiality by Chernichenko and Treat: E/CN.4/Sub.2/1989/51, Aug. 11, 1989.

[245] Interview, May 6, 1989, at 39-41.

gram, was commissioned in 1989 to prepare a study on the right
to restitution, compensation, and rehabilitation for victims of gross
violations of human rights and freedoms, with a view to exploring
the possibility of developing some basic principles and guidelines.
This was the first step on the road to a declaration, for which
Humphrey can claim some credit.[246]

It is true that the simple launching of a 1503 complaint can, indeed may, create sufficient pressure to bring about a solution to
the issue in question. Nevertheless, Humphrey continues to argue
that the 1503 procedure should be strengthened. In his article, "The
International Bill of Rights: Scope and Implementation," he stated:

Human rights cannot and should not be divorced from politics and in
a political organization like the United Nations they always will be discussed in political contexts, but there should be an opportunity in the
Organization for complaints of individuals protesting the violation of their
rights to be considered objectively on their merits, particularly if there
are gross violations following consistent patterns... [T]he Commission
is composed of politically motivated states represented by instructed
delegates; the members of any ad hoc committee of investigation set up
under the resolution would be equally politically motivated. What is needed is some judicial or quasi-judicial body, composed of independent persons acting in their personal capacity, before which individual complaints
could be brought with some hope that they would be examined fairly and
objectively.[247]

The Commission, however, has not been willing to proceed directly to make recommendations under Resolution 1503. Humphrey
continues to see some shred of hope in the fact that the Commission has studied a number of situations and "because the names
of the countries in question are known, that is itself a kind of sanction."[248]

With the establishment of measures of implementation in the
two covenants and other international instruments, such as the International Convention on the Elimination of all Forms of Racial
Discrimination of 1965, with the action program, and the 1503 complaint procedure all in place, the United Nations passed from its
initial phase of standard-setting and the promotion of human rights

[246] For details, see Gerald Utting, "The Fight for Justice," *Toronto Star,* Aug. 17, 1991,
at D-1+] *Human Rights Monitor,* Nov. 1990, Nos. 10-11, at 5.

[247] "International Bill of Rights: Scope and Implementation," 532-33.

[248] Speech, "Education: The Ultimate Sanction of Human Rights," California State
University, Long Beach, California, Nov. 8, 1985, at 18.

to the implementation phase, the phase of protecting human rights. By 1989 Humphrey, still in the vanguard, was saying that the challenge for the present generation was to improve mechanisms of implementation and "to make some of them mechanisms of enforcement and not merely of implementation."[249]

Even after his departure from the United Nations, Humphrey continued to be active in the work of the Organization. He served as Rapporteur to the United Nations Seminar on Human Rights in Jamaica (April-May 1967); he was the Vice-Chairman of the UN Seminar on Racial Discrimination in New Delhi (September 1968); and he was also a member of the United Nations Sub-Commission on the prevention of Discrimination and the Protection of Minorities, and was the Chairman of this Sub-Commission in 1970.

Humphrey served as President of the Canadian Commission on the International Year for Human Rights in 1968, and addressed the General Assembly on four different occasions, often invited by the Canadian delegation on Human Rights Day.[250] He addressed the General Assembly and representatives of Non-Governmental Organizations on December 10, 1973, the twenty fifth anniversary of the adoption of the Universal Declaration.[251] On the fortieth anniversary of the adoption of the Declaration, Humphrey, as a former Director of the Human Rights Division, in addition to attending a number of different events around the world, was invited by the Canadian government to speak at the General Assembly as part of its delegation on December 8, 1988.[252] Two days later, he spoke at the Palais de Chaillot at the invitation of French President François Mitterand.[253]

In these recent speeches Humphrey focused on themes that he has made his own, on which he has been writing and speaking for more than half a century: the history and importance of the Universal Declaration and its status as part of customary international law, the shift from classical international law to a new "world law," the need for further mechanisms of implementation and enforce-

---

[249] B. G. Ramcharan, *op. cit. supra* note 218, at xi.

[250] Interview, May 6, 1989, at 30; JPH to RStJM, Oct. 17, 1982.

[251] Bulletin, Amnesty International — Canada, Vol. 1, No. 1, Jan. 1974, at 1.

[252] Humphrey was honoured on his attendance at the Amnesty International Rock Concert held in Montreal, Quebec; Don Macdonald "Amnesty Rock Stars Salute Drafter of UN Declaration," *Ottawa Citizen*, Sept. 15, 1988; "Rights 'Father' Enjoys Rock Show," *Montreal Daily News*, Sept. 15, 1988.

[253] "How a Canadian Drafted...," Mark Abley, "Author of Rights Declaration Has His Day of Glory at the U.N.," *Montreal Gazette*, Dec. 9, 1988.

82   *Annuaire canadien de Droit international 1991*

ment, and the crucial relationship between human rights and the peace of nations.[254]

RETURN TO McGILL

On his retirement from the United Nations in 1966, Humphrey began, at the age of sixty-one, what could be regarded as his third career. Contemplating his return to Canada, he had almost agreed to go to the Université de Montréal when, as a matter of courtesy, he dropped in to McGill to see Maxwell Cohen, then Dean of the Faculty of Law. Dean Cohen persuaded him to return to McGill and immediately arranged with the Principal, Rocke Robertson, to hire him as professor of law.[255]

So, in the fall of 1966, Humphrey began teaching three courses, which in one form or another, he has continued to teach for the past quarter-century. A course entitled "Special Problems in International Law and Organization" was offered with Dean Cohen for two hours per week,[256] and "The International Protection of Human Rights" is still under his sole supervision for two hours in the first term.[257] He teaches in the second term a course on the law of international organization and another on the problems of minorities. Appointed a Professor of Economics and Political Science as well, he taught a course on International Organization in the Political Science Department until 1971, as well as the courses referred to.[258] His courses focused on institutional aspects of the protection of human rights and drew on his long experience within the United Nations. They reflected his deep commitment to "institutions, structures, procedures [and] mechanisms for generating an

[254] Speech at the United Nations General Assembly, Dec. 8, 1988. For his most recent statement see J.P. Humphrey, "Human Rights: The Necessary Conditions of Peace" 10 Int'l Relations (The David Davies Memorial Institute) 117.

[255] Interview, May 6, 1989, at 30-31; Speech, "Two Parents of Anarchy," June 4, 1985; *McGill University, Annual Report, 1965-66*, at 199.

[256] "An analytical examination of the Charter of the United Nations and a study of the development of international law and organization by and through the various organs of the United Nations and of specialized agencies": *McGill University Calendar, 1967-68*, at 17.

[257] The course description in 1967 stated: "The development of an international law on human rights by and through the United Nations, the specialized agencies and regional inter-governmental organizations": *McGill University Calendar, 1967-68*, at 17.

[258] *McGill University Calendars, 1967-68*, at 17, 52; *1968-69*, at 20, 56; *1969-70*, at 18, 23, 65; *1970-71*, at 33-34, 175.

awareness and commitment to the international human rights law agenda."[259]

On his return to McGill, Humphrey found that Canada "was a very different country from the one that I had left in 1946. Not only were we a fully independent member of the international community, but there was a new sense of national identity."[260] However, by the late 1970s he viewed the process of decentralization brought on by the growth within the country of "smaller nationalisms or provincialisms" as a threat to the future of Canada.[261] In addition, the "contrived nationalism" exemplified by Canadian content rules for radio and television programming seemed to him "a kind of cultural protectionism which can only result in national mediocrity and possibly worse."[262]

The struggle to promote and protect human rights is never over and new problems arose in this third phase of Humphrey's remarkably varied and constructive career. One of these he has labelled the "third parent of anarchy," namely, the practice of collective responsibility for violations of international law. An example of what he had in mind is the use of economic sanctions directed at collectivities or groups of individuals, measures that affect both perpetrators and victims of a particular violation of international human rights law. In these cases, innocent persons often suffer the consequences of the collective form of punishment meted out. The several conventions which recognize the responsibility of individuals for particular violations of human rights, such as genocide, remain the exception. In this connection, Humphrey reintroduces the notion of the establishment of an international court of criminal justice.[263]

A second problem with which Humphrey has long been concerned is the ever-present possibility of nuclear war, which would make all discussion of human rights irrelevant. As early as 1945 he had noted that the use of nuclear weapons at Hiroshima and

---

[259] R.A. Macdonald to RStJM, Nov. 22, 1991, at 1.
[260] Interview, May 6, 1989.
[261] "Nationalism, Freedom and Social Justice," at 607-8; Speech, *supra* note 60, at 3.
[262] "The Pursuit of Excellence," *McGill News*, Vol. 57, no. 3, 1976, at 6; Humphrey, "Le Canada est-il encore une plante si fragile que nous devons le protéger contre les ouragans qui soufflent de tous côtés?," *Le Devoir*, 2 juillet, 1975, at 5. To Humphrey, this form of Canadian nationalism "can only be counterproductive" in that these rules protect second rate Canadian productions rather than encouraging the subsidization of a cultural industry so as to make it competitive. In Humphrey's liberal view of the world, freedom of expression should be limited only by "the criterion of excellence": "Nationalism, Freedom and Social Justice," 608.
[263] Speech, "Three Parents of Anarchy," Halifax, Apr. 18, 1988.

Nagasaki provided the impetus for a ''re-examination of the principles that underlie the new international organization for the maintenance of peace and security.'' Foreshadowing the intense debate of the next thirty years, he suggested that a ''formidable'' weapons race could be avoided if nuclear weapons were not left to the monopoly of one state or a small group of states. Recognizing the danger of permitting the dissemination of nuclear information to states possessing the necessary resources to manufacture nuclear weapons, he called for the nuclear ''secret'' to be turned over to an international agency strong enough to maintain a supranational monopoly over the use of the new power as an instrument of coercion. Unfortunately, the United Nations was not yet in a position to exercise such a responsibility.

Curiously, Humphrey's position on nuclear weapons is not what one might have thought. He has suggested that the usual distinction between possession and use of nuclear arms may be counterproductive and even weaken the authority and force of international law, since there are few effective sanctions for a breach of such a law. Indeed, he asked, ''what kind of a lawyer could possibly suggest that there is any such thing as a convention binding on the nuclear powers that prohibits the possession and use of nuclear weapons?'' He found that neither state practice, *opinio juris,* or other sources of international law support the existence of such a prohibition; it is ''simply wishful thinking.'' The argument made by analogy to the prohibition on the use of certain chemical weapons ''flies in the face of the intentions of the parties to the treaties in question and of current practice and opinion.''[264]

Turning international law into soft law ''without possible sanction,'' through an attempt to establish the illegality of nuclear weapons, not only raises false hopes, but diverts attention from the resolution of issues of disarmament, the most urgent problem of our time. Disarmament, however, should not be limited to nuclear weapons; it must also include conventional weapons. To Humphrey, those who favour increases in the number of conventional weapons as a *quid pro quo* for the reduction of nuclear weapons must not forget that, in contrast to previous wars, in any major conventional war of the future the losing side will fall back on its supply of nuclear weapons even if limited in its capacity to produce them. Nuclear

[264] Speech, ''International Law and the Legality of Nuclear Weapons,'' Ottawa, June 17, 1987, at 1-2.

disarmament, though essential, must be considered in the context of conventional disarmament.

Even if this shift in emphasis were to take place at the level of political leadership, Humphrey was not optimistic about the ultimate resolution of this issue. In 1984 he said, "I do not know whether the great masses of ordinary people in the lands these leaders govern will permit them to bring this stupid arms race to a stop, because it is the virulent nationalism of the masses that breeds the animosity of peoples towards peoples, that provides the fuel as it were for the race."[265] He believes that it is at the level of education of "the masses," through the teaching of history and the underlying principles of human rights, that nationalism can best be combatted. The need to assert a broader notion of loyalty is also crucial. In his opinion, loyalty must go beyond the boundaries of the particular nation-state to embrace a wider concept of a loyalty to the world community as a whole.[266]

On the domestic level, where he has always been active, Humphrey recently argued that sections of the Meech Lake Accord threatened to weaken the government of Canada. In his view, and in the light of Canada's proximity to the United States, "it simply does not make sense to turn Canada into a weak community of communities."[267] He greatly regrets the fact that in present-day Quebec this federalist viewpoint is submerged in "the silence of Quebecers" who, while sympathetic to this vision of Canada, will only divulge this information "in private conversation."[268]

To Humphrey, who believes that human rights are vital to the protection of individual liberty and welfare, "not those of government or self-defined collectivities," the "distinct society" clause

---

[265] St. Mary's Convocation Address, May 12, 1984, at 6-7.

[266] *Ibid.*, 7-8. Note that over a half a century ago, in his speech for the Saturday Night Club, Oct. 17, 1935, Humphrey said, at 7-8:

> There is a general article, Article V, which provides that except where otherwise expressly provided in the Covenant, decisions at any meeting of the Assembly or of the Council shall require the agreement of all the members of the League represented at the meeting. Statesmen and the people they represent must, however, undergo a considerable change of heart before there is any possibility of this defect being remedied. In order for States to be willing to trust their vital interests to the decision of a majority of the members of the League a feeling of loyalty and patriotism for the international community must be substituted for the comparatively petty local and national patriotism which our teachers have told us is the greatest virtue.

[267] Speech, Bishop's College School, 8 Nov. 1989, at 7.

[268] *Ibid.*, 8.

itself presents no difficulties; "its long tradition of bilingualism" is one of the distinct features of Quebec, as well as one of the characteristics which sets Canada apart from the United States. However, he was clearly at odds with the meaning that was given to the phrase by "certain separatists and neo-separatists" in Quebec. This gave him cause for concern, particularly if the precedent of using the notwithstanding clause in the Canadian Charter of Rights to assert collective rights to the detriment of individual rights were to be followed. He emphasized, however, that opposition to such intended uses of the distinct society clause was not, in his opinion, an expression of "anti-Quebec sentiment."

The tensions over language which manifest themselves today in the aftermath of the Meech Lake Accord were also at dangerous levels in Quebec during the years of student turmoil at McGill, and within the wider "quiet revolution" of the 1960s. At that time Humphrey suggested that human rights were being threatened by a new ideology "characterized by, on the one hand, a new permissiveness and, on the other, an attack on all the forms and sources of authority."[269] In Canada, progress in human rights from his point of view was being undermined by this ideology "directed not so much against authoritarianism as against authority itself." Humphrey, who saw himself as "firmly committed to the Old Left," was uncomfortable with the views of this generation of students of the "New Left." In matters of human rights, he places himself on "the side of the great tradition...man's long struggle against authority" or rather "the oppressive authority" of kings, dictators, and in some instances democratic societies themselves. In his liberal world view, the need continually to question authority is acknowledged but must be entered into cautiously with "a level head and a sense of social responsibility." Thus he places the burden of proving that new forms of "authority" are more desirable than their predecessors on those calling for reform.

Humphrey feels that "some of the advocates of the new freedoms are really preparing...the road to fascism" where "new authority will inevitably reside in the state, not the state as we now know it in Canada, but a totalitarian state." Citing Aristotle and Hobbes, he goes on to say that human rights exist only in society "where there *is* authority," both legal and moral, but that the existence of authority without a corresponding recognition of human

---

[269] "Human Rights and Authority," 415.

rights is to be feared. The increasing authority of the state seems to be coincident with the decreasing authority of institutions such as the church, the schools, and the family. Thus the state, with its "insatiable appetite for power," is in Humphrey's opinion a threat to individual freedom; "More and more the individual stands alone, isolated, in face of the state. The individual is so weak that he must act collectively in order to protect his right as an individual. And time is running out. If we do not act now, the time may come very soon when we will no longer have even the will to act, when — like ants in an ant-hill — we will be content with our roles as simple ciphers in a collectivity."[270] To combat this, Humphrey proposed a comprehensive strategy to bring Canadian human rights standards into line with the Universal Declaration of Human Rights; the creation of a Canadian Human Rights Commission; and an expansion of the Canadian role, governmental and non-governmental, in the development of human rights awareness at the national and international level.[271]

Humphrey was given an opportunity to examine more closely the awareness of some of these rights with respect to women in Canada when, on February 2, 1968, he was appointed a member of the Royal Commission on the Status of Women in Canada. He filed a dissent to the main report in which the majority advocated a policy of affirmative action.[272] While this position may seem out of character for a human rights advocate who was active with the Commission on the Status of Women at the United Nations in previous years, it is nevertheless in keeping with his vision of the individual and his concept of discrimination. The grounds for his dissent were based on a liberal interpretation of women's equality; for him, equality must mean the removal of all forms of discrimination, including those that may be seen as forms of affirmative action, which, in his words, "would put women in a special category in the body politic."

With few exceptions, Humphrey's concept of equality is closer to the notion of formal rather than substantive equality.[273] Distinguishing between compensatory treatment ("privileges extended

---

[270] *Ibid.*, 417-19.
[271] *Ibid.*, 419-21.
[272] P.C. 1968-229, cited in *Report of the Royal Commission on the Status of Women in Canad* vii (Ottawa: Information Canada, 1970). For the majority's recommendations, see *ibid.*, 387-418; Humphrey's minority report, at 433-51.
[273] See *Andrews v. Law Society of British Columbia*, [1989] 1 S.C.R. 143, for the Supreme Court's discussion of these two notions of equality.

to make up for bad treatment in the past'') and preferential treatment (''treatment which is extended to the end that there shall be
real equality''), Humphrey considered the former an affront to the
equality of women. Thus, in his minority report, he disagreed with
those parts of the majority report which he thought extended such
special or compensatory treatment to women. One significant
recommendation which the Royal Commission made, with which
he agreed, was the creation of a federal human rights commission.
However, the proposed Status of Women Council was, in his mind,
not necessary; its advisory, consultative, and research functions could
be exercised by a human rights commission.[274]

On his second retirement from McGill in 1971, on the invitation
of the writer, then Dean of the Faculty of Law in the University
of Toronto, Humphrey spent a year in Toronto as a visiting professor.[275] Returning to Montreal in 1972, he was ''just about ready
to grow roses and so on, really retire,'' but he was stopped on
Sherbrooke Street by Dean John W. Durnford and asked why he
was not up at McGill lecturing.[276] As a result of the chance meeting, Humphrey became a part-time lecturer until 1975 and Retired
Gale Professor of Law thereafter. He taught the ''International Law
of Human Rights,'' to which a seminar on ''Problems of
International Law and Organization'' was added in 1975. He introduced a new course in 1976: ''Comparative and International
Protection of Minorities' Rights.''[277]

From 1981 to 1982, he served as a Visiting Professor at the
University of Western Ontario, where he taught, in the first term,
the introductory course in Public International Law and, in the
second term, two seminars, the International Law of Human Rights,
and the Law of International Organization. Returning to McGill
for the academic session in 1982, he continued teaching his human
rights course in addition to two seminars, one focused on international organization, the other on the protection of minority rights.[278]
His pioneering course in the law of human rights led eventually
to the current offerings in the McGill Faculty of Law of seven courses
and seminars dedicated to the subject of human rights.

[274] *Report of the Royal Commission, supra* note 272, at 418, 434-35, 437-39, 450.
[275] Speech, ''Two Parents of Anarchy,'' *supra* note 60; JPH to RStJM, Nov. 13, 1975.
[276] Interview, May 6, 1989, at 32; *McGill University Calendar, 1973-74,* at 4.
[277] *McGill University Calendars, 1973-74,* at 4; *1974-75,* at 5, 25; *1975-76,* at 4, 25; *1976-77,*
    at 23, 28.
[278] JPH to RStJM, Oct. 17, 1982.

A member of the International Law Association, Humphrey served as Rapporteur of its International Committee on Human Rights at their bi-annual conferences held in Helsinki (1966), Buenos Aires (1968), New York (1972), and New Delhi (1974). He has been an active member of the International Commission of Jurists, serving as one of two vice-presidents, attending various conferences, such as the Syracuse Conference on the Limitation and Derogation of Rights in States of Emergency, and taking part in several ICJ missions. He was one of three experts who went to Greece to inquire into the incarceration of seven lawyers who were being held incommunicado and without trial because they had been defending dissident students. In 1977 he participated in one of the ICJ's three missions to the Philippines to "study the operation of martial law from the point of view both of the legal system and of the allegations...of serious violations of human rights" under the regime of Ferdinand Marcos.[279]

A past president of Amnesty International (Canada)[280] and a past member of the Board of Directors of the International League for the Rights of Man, Humphrey has been active in the field of human rights in Canada and the world. He is a lifetime honorary member of the Canadian Council on International Law, a member of the Canadian Institute of International Affairs, and a founding father of the World Network of International Law. He played a central role in founding the Canadian Human Rights Foundation, where he served as President (1978-85), as Chairman (1985-86), and until recently as President Emeritus.[281]

In recognition of Humphrey's contribution to the development of international human rights and, in particular, his twenty years as the first Director of the Human Rights Division of the United Nations, he was appointed an Officer of the Order of Canada in 1974. He is also a member of the National Order of Quebec. In addition to his many honorary degrees, he has received numerous awards, the most significant of which is no doubt the United Nations Human Rights Prize, which he was awarded in 1988, along

[279] William Butler, John P. Humphrey and G. E. Bisson, *The Decline of Democracy in the Philippines* vii- viii (Geneva: International Commission of Jurists, 1977).

[280] Clement Trudel, "Amnestie Internationale: Y'a pas d'quoi fêter," *Le Devoir*, 11 janvier 1986; "Le juriste Humphrey sera Honoré, samedi prochain," *Le Devoir*, 25 février 1986; Susan Carson, "Sometimes Justice and Law Are Not the Same Thing," *The Montreal Star Weekend Magazine*, Feb. 9, 1974, at 12-14.

[281] Annual Report of the Canadian Human Rights Foundation, 1982-83; Interview, May 6, 1989, at 34-36.

with co-recipient, Nelson Mandela.[282] In 1988, the annual John P. Humphrey Lectureship in Human Rights was established by an anonymous donor at the McGill Law Faculty. This lectureship is "delivered annually by a person who, by word and by deed has helped advance the cause of peace and human rights, of which John Humphrey and the Universal Declaration are example and expression." Thematically, the lectureship follows the "organizational approach" to human rights law pioneered by Humphrey at McGill. In this respect, it is a tribute both to his commitment to the development of human rights law teaching at McGill, and to his outstanding contribution to the cause of human rights in general.

CONCLUDING REMARKS

John P. Humphrey has had a long and multifaceted career. He has worked as a lawyer, a law professor, and an international civil servant. He has written extensively for lawyers, and for those with no legal training; he has spoken publicly on many occasions. Running like a "golden thread" throughout his many different activities, has been his unflagging dedication to the cause of human rights.

In his early years as a professor of law, his interest in international law and organization challenged the conservative boundaries of the McGill curriculum. In later years, after his retirement from the United Nations, he brought the world of the United Nations into his classrooms. His unique insights as a participant in some of the most dramatic events in the history of international organization represent an important part of his academic and scholarly contributions. Moreover, he has written a plethora of articles on the different committees, commissions, instruments, and declarations that flourished during his time at the United Nations. His prolific writings are part scholarly analysis and part documentary history of crucial elements in the development of modern international law.

---

[282] Some of the awards include: Honorary Citizen, City of Edmonton (1964); World Jewish Congress Citation (1966); World Legal Scholar Award from World Peace through Law Centre (1973); John E. Read Medal, Canadian Council on International Law (1973); World Federalists of Canada Peace Award (1982); Saul Hays Human Rights Award, Canadian Jewish Congress (1983); Order of St. John of Jerusalem (1986); see too, Jack Cahill, "How a Canadian Drafted the United Nations Rights Charter," at D-5. In 1991, he was awarded the Medal of the Montreal Bar for outstanding contributions to the "cause of justice" and on Sept. 8, 1991, was named "Personality of the Week" by *La Presse.* See *Le Devoir,* jeudi, 5 Sept. 1991, at 6; *La Presse,* dimanche, 8 sept. 1991, at B3; *The McGill Reporter,* vol. 24, no. 1, Sept. 11, 1991, at 1.

Humphrey is perhaps best known for his significant — and courageous — contribution to the drafting of the Universal Declaration of Human Rights. He also played a key role as the first Director of the Division of Human Rights at the United Nations. In that position, which he held for twenty years, he persistently, and in the face of numerous obstacles, successfully strove to find ways and means to establish the human rights agenda within the organization and to enhance the protection of human rights around the world.

Although many of his years were spent in international spheres, Humphrey has remained deeply interested in Canada and its future. Perhaps one of the earliest and most significant indicators of this interest was his strong desire both to be bilingual and to bridge the two main language communities of Canada. From the Padlock Law, to conscription, to more current issues of national unity, he has always been outspoken about his country and its politics. Beyond that, through his many papers and speeches about international human rights and the United Nations, he has challenged Canadians to look outside their national borders to the larger human community.

Sommaire

La direction dans le droit: John P. Humphrey et le développement du droit international des droits humains

Cet article discute les premières années et la carrière de John P. Humphrey, surtout sa contribution au droit international et en particulier au développement des droits humains quand il était le premier directeur de la Division des Droits Humains des Nations Unies et quand il enseignait à McGill University. Le professeur Humphrey était auteur du brouillon de la Déclaration Universelle des Droits Humains et fondateur d'une diversité d'institutions qui s'occupent des droits humains.

Extradition in the USSR's Treaties on Legal Assistance with Non-"Socialist" States

GEORGE GINSBURGS*

F OR THE GREATER PART of the Soviet regime's diplomatic career, the idea of entering into formal engagements vis-à-vis "bourgeois" states which called for the mutual procurement of extradition services seemed outlandish. Even as late as 1987, a Soviet university textbook on international law cautioned that: "The practice of rendition of criminals encountered and encounters difficulties in those cases where states of different social types face each other, for the very concept of crime changes depending on which historically social type the given state fits. That is why cooperation between states in the sphere of struggle against criminality is possible only on those questions and in that scope which the states themselves consider suitable as far as they are concerned."[1] By then, however, the Soviet Union had already broken out of the old shell of quarantining such bilateral operations strictly to the premises of the so-called socialist community and had broadened the market to include states that did not belong to the inner sanctum. Thus, the treaty on legal assistance with Iraq, signed on June 22, 1973, contained a comprehensive package of reciprocal commitments governing inter-state rendition procedures.[2] The precedent set the tone for a string of

---

* Law School, Rutgers University, Camden, New Jersey.

[1] V. I. Menzhinskii, *Mezhdunarodnoe pravo* 317 (F. I. Kozhevnikov ed.) (Moscow, 1987, 5th ed.).

   N. T. Blatova, *Mezhdunarodnoe pravo* 283 (L. A. Modzhorian, N. T. Blatova eds.) (Moscow, 1979): "The institution of rendition occasions special difficulty when enter into relations on that score states of different socio-economic systems or states displaying vital distinctions of socio-political bases, for example, capitalist and developing countries."

[2] *Ved. SSSR* 1974 No. 19, Art. 293; *SDD*, 30, 91-100; 941 *UNTS*, 114-56.

similar ententes which the USSR concluded soon after with Greece (May 21, 1981),[3] Algeria (February 23, 1982),[4] Tunisia (June 26, 1984),[5] Cyprus (January 19, 1984),[6] and South Yemen (December 6, 1985).[7] Analogous negotiations with Ghana and Turkey are nearing completion[8] and the official media have recently revealed that the USSR and Canada are busy working on the draft of an agreement on legal assistance in civil and criminal cases.[9]

The era of glasnost and perestroika has, *inter alia*, prompted considerable discussion about the need for co-operation across the former political dividing lines to combat the rising tide of criminal phenomena endangering the existing world order. Episodes of ad hoc rendition have occurred in recent years that once would have been unthinkable, a significant pooling of law enforcement resources

---

[3] *Ved. SSSR* 1982 No. 45, Art. 839.

[4] *Ved. SSSR* 1984 No. 15, Art. 213.

[5] *Ved. SSSR* 1986 No. 48, Art. 1010.

[6] *Ved. SSSR* 1986 No. 28, Art. 525.

[7] *Ved. SSSR* 1987 No. 15, Art. 199.

[8] B. V. Kravtsov, in *Mezhdunarodnaia zhizn* 1989 No. 2, at 21. Apropos Ghana, the Soviet ambassador to Ghana in 1974-79 recounts an interesting story that bears on the topic: In Ghana, there lived around 90 Soviet citizenesses married to Ghanaians who had studied in the Soviet Union. The majority of the families were harmonious, the Soviet women quickly adapted to the unusual African conditions and traditions, learned the English language and many worked in their field of expertise. But there were also those who left their husbands and even children and engaged in prostitution. In one of the Ghanaian newspapers an item was published under the loud headline 'Russian prostitutes crowd the town of Kumasi.' In Accra, a group of Soviet citizenesses opened the 'Flamingo' bar, in fact running it as a brothel.

I informed Moscow of this and sought consent to their expulsion from Ghana, particularly so when the Ghanaian authorities did not know how to get rid of them since they were restrained by the fact that these women possessed Soviet passports. When the embassy contacted the Ghanaian authorities with a request for assistance in this matter, they reacted at once. Given that these women had not maintained ties with their husbands, the Ghanaian police suggested that they leave the confines of Ghana. True, the affair stalled because the citizenesses declared that they did not have the means to return home. Then I asked for permission to dispatch them on board Soviet vessels lying in the ports of Ghana. I got the permission. But then the captains of the ships started objecting...Nevertheless, we did manage to send off a few women that way. But many of them after bribing Ghanaian officials and even their former husbands, obtained certificates attesting that they led normal family lives, remained in Ghana and continued pursuing their ancient profession.
Iu. V. Bernov, "Iz dnevnika sovetskogo posla v Ghane," *Mezhdunarodnaia zhizn',* 1991, No. 2, at 128.

[9] *Vestnik Ministerstva Inostrannykh Del SSSR* 1990 No. 17, at 64.

has been recorded in areas dealing with specific offences posing a common threat to the international system, such as, skyjacking, drug trafficking, and terrorism, on both a bilateral and multilateral scale, and the further co-ordination of efforts by national police agencies and institutions of justice is currently being studied in a multitude of venues. The success of these bids to develop an effective mechanism of defence against pathological strains which imperil the established global fabric depends to a significant extent on getting the Soviet Union to join the venture and so its experience to date in elaborating an extradition policy versus an "alien" cast of characters could prove a useful index to what might henceforth be expected here.

Under the terms of this ensemble of agreements, the contracting parties shall upon demand (or request) surrender to one another persons located on their territory to face criminal charges or for execution of the sentence. Thus, the net is cast wide to include the nationals of the applicant state, plus foreigners and stateless persons (apatrides).[10] In connection with the rendition of these foreigners either to the state where the crime was committed or the state that suffered injury from the crime, Soviet authors commend the desirability of also notifying the country of which the *de cujus* is a citizen of the scheduled transfer.[11] The accords are silent on that point so what is at stake in this case may merely constitute an invitation to the extraditing authorities (of the USSR as well) to exercise unilateral courtesy in letting a third party know of the treatment afforded one of its citizens.[12]

Rendition is effected for acts which, pursuant to the legislation of both signatories, are considered crimes and for the commission of which the laws prescribe punishment in the shape of deprivation of freedom for not less than two years (USSR-Iraq; for more than one year—USSR v. S. Yemen, Algeria, Greece, Tunisia; for not less than one year—USSR-Cyprus) or some more severe penalty.

[10] V. Gridin, "Sotrudnichestvo v oblasti ugolovnogo prava," *Sotsialisticheskaia zakonnost* 1980, No. 6, at 62.

[11] O. E. Polents, *Mezhdunarodnoe pravo* 254 (E. A. Korovin ed.) (Moscow, 1951).

[12] Soviet scholars are aware that "the rendition of citizens of third states is regulated differently in various treaties on rendition": "In some of them there is foreseen the obligation to notify the third state, in some the further obligation to get the consent of that state to the rendition." E.g., V. I. Menzhinskii, *Kurs mezhdunarodnogo prava* 316 (F. I. Kozhevnikov ed.) (2nd ed., Moscow, 1966); *idem, ibid.,* 194 (3rd ed., Moscow, 1972); *idem, Mezhdunarodnoe pravo* 239 (F. I. Kozhevnikov ed.) (4th ed., Moscow, 1981) *idem, op. cit. supra* note 1, at 318.

Rendition in order to execute sentence takes place on the condition that the judgment has entered into force (clause omitted from the USSR-Greece and USSR-Cyprus versions which instead feature the requirement that the conviction stem from an act which, too, constitutes a crime per the legislation of both principals) and the person whose rendition is sought has been sentenced to deprivation of freedom for not less than six months (USSR v. Iraq, Tunisia; for more than six months—USSR-Greece; for not less than 1 year—USSR v. Algeria, Cyprus, S. Yemen). If several crimes were committed, the bid for extradition is valid if at least one of the crimes satisfies the criterion of extraditability (absent from the USSR-Greece and USSR-Cyprus editions).

Making extradition to stand trial contingent on meeting the "double criminality" exigency is routine procedure in international law and the Soviet Union and its partners are only following traditional usage in subscribing to that norm. While conceding that the proviso occurs widely in international practice and can be deemed generally recognized, Soviet sources admonish that the principle does not mean "mandatory identity in the designations of the crimes" and, for these purposes, the match spells nothing more than that "the act considered criminal in the requesting state constitute a crime in the requested state as well."[13] Next, the Soviet Union and its associates have opted for the newer trend in deciding what offences will be extraditable relative to cadre of these ententes. Rather than enumerating the sundry acts for which rendition could be demanded—as was once common—the contracting parties converted to the so-called rule of "minimum term of punishment" which has been gaining favor internationally because it is simple and compact. Soviet specialists pronounce their country's preference for that mode more rational because it expands the possibility of surrender and permits the rendition of criminals without complicated legal research regarding the *corpus delicti*.[14]

The time frame, it is claimed, is not set arbitrarily:

first, deprivation of freedom for a term of more than one year is assigned only for relatively serious crimes so that there are sufficient grounds for restricting the rights of the person surrendered in connection with the

[13] N. I. Marysheva, "Pravovaia pomoshch po ugolovnym delam (mezhdunarodnyi aspekt)," *Materialy po inostrannomu zakonodatelstvu i mezhdunarodnomu chastnomu pravu* 157 (Moscow, 1989, Trudy 44).

[14] *Ibid.,* 161; L. N. Galenskaia, *Mezhdunarodnaia borba s prestupnostiu* 127 (Moscow, 1972); R. M. Valeev, *Vydacha prestupnikov v sovremennom mezhdunarodnom prave* 96 (Kazan, 1976).

arrest of the criminal and his compulsory transfer to the competent organs of another state; second, in many countries, the question of rendition of criminal offenders is dealt with through court procedures which afford the possibility of contesting the decision of the court in a higher judicial instance. But such procedure prolongs the dispute over rendition for a considerable period during which the person who committed the crime may remain in custody, a prospect which is hardly justified in the event of commission of a petty crime.[15]

In any event, Soviet analysts conclude that the scheme's parameters *ratione materiae* are drawn in a way that the ensuing "cooperation on questions of rendition is unfolding on a sufficiently broad footing"[16] — not markedly unlike the range of the intra-socialist model in this province.

Finally, note that the ceiling is drastically lowered in half of the above sample where rendition is intended to allow execution of sentence. Presumably, the "discount" is warranted because less time needs to be allocated at this stage for recourse to the media of appellate relief and the concern about hardship inflicted by incarceration while filing for review seems a trifle misplaced in reference to an individual who has already been convicted and is scheduled to serve a substantial jail sentence.

In Soviet-Arab traffic, rendition does not occur if: (1) the person whose rendition is demanded is a citizen of the contracting party to which the request is addressed or a person to whom that state has granted the right of asylum; (2) the crime was committed on the territory of the contracting party that received the application; (3) criminal prosecution or execution of sentence is now barred by the legislation of the requested state because the statute of limitations has tolled or on some other lawful grounds; (4) rendition is prohibited by the law of the requested state; (5) the person whose rendition is sought is at the time when the demand for rendition is received facing investigation or trial in the requested state on that same case, or has been found guilty or acquitted of that same crime, or a decision has been entered to drop charges or this person has been punished or pardoned for the same crime; (6) or the crime incurs the filing of criminal charges under the laws of the requested state despite the fact that it was committed outside its territory.

The USSR-Greece and USSR-Cyprus provisions read a bit

---

[15] V. P. Shupilov, "Mezhdunarodnaia pravovaia pomoshch po ugolovnym delam," *Sovetskoe gosudarstvo i pravo* 87 (1974 No. 3).

[16] Marysheva, *op. cit. supra* note 13, at 162.

differently: (a) point 5 above is pared down to where rendition is foreclosed if with respect to the *de cujus*, on the territory of the requested state for the same crime there was a judgment that has acquired legal force or the proceedings in the case have been terminated; and, (b) point 6 above is deleted from the script. Both changes reduce the obstacles to rendition in the liaisons between the USSR and those two states compared with the set of hurdles that must be negotiated by the USSR and its partners from the Arab world. The latter excision results in a more consistent tone since the effect is to keep the "territorial primacy" principle intact for extradition purposes.

Since the conditions that justify refusal to perform rendition services play a crucial role in the operation of the mechanism, several component elements of the package call for closer inspection. Many states observe the injunction against extradition of their own citizens. It is not clear when the Soviet regime began to share that view. In its fledgling years, opinions among local experts split sharply. In one of the earlier pieces on this theme published in Soviet legal literature, the author mounted a spirited defence of the practice of non-rendition of one's citizens, arguing that trying them before "native" penitentiary institutions corresponded better to the strands of "native" policy of general and special prevention (i.e., deterrence) than rendition. The state, in this estimate, did not surrender its citizens owing to the same political considerations that prompted it to punish its own citizens for all or virtually all extraterritorial crimes, whereas it chose to punish foreigners for only a few of those.[17] Two years later, the compilers of an officially sponsored collection of materials on the legislation and international treaties of the USSR and union republics regarding the legal status of foreign physical and juridical persons claimed that the contrary was true of Soviet law "to which was alien the narrowly nationalistic outlook" so that it "did not bar the rendition of its own citizens, gravitating in that respect toward the Anglo-Saxon system."[18]

Since neither source cites any hard facts to back its contention, no final answer was forthcoming as to who correctly represented

[17] S. Mokrinskii, "Iuridicheskaia priroda vydachi prestupnikov i tipovaia konventsiia Soiuza SSR," *Sovetskoe pravo* 58 (1924 No. 6(12)).

[18] V. V. Egor'ev, G. N. Lashkevich, M. A. Plotkin, B. D. Rozenblium, *Zakonodatelstvo i mezhdunarodnye dogovory Soiuza SSR i soiuznykh respublik o pravovom polozhenii inostrannykh fizicheskikh i iuridicheskikh lits (Sistematizirovannye materialy s kommentariiami)* 90 (Moscow, 1926).

the Soviet position on this issue. Not long afterwards, however, the more conservative mood triumphed. As we now know, the exchange of notes between the USSR and Mongolia of February 28, 1931, concerning the mutual rendition of criminal offenders, the text of which was not released until the late sixties,[19] served notice on the Foreign Ministry of Mongolia that the Soviet partner would, *inter alia*, "not find it possible to satisfy the requests of the Government of the Mongolian People's Republic for the rendition of criminals if they had to do with citizens of the USSR. . ." If a sister regime was denied that privilege, the chances that ideological strangers would be treated any better sound extremely far-fetched. By 1951, this suspicion was fully confirmed. Apparently a consensus had been achieved that made it safe for a Soviet legal scholar to announce unequivocally that "in light of the fundamental and essential difference between the character of Soviet legislation and the legislation of capitalist states, Soviet citizens who have committed crimes against the interests of foreign states are not subject to rendition and must bear responsibility in conformity with Soviet laws."[20]

The tenor of the pronouncement does not surprise, since it coincides with the peak of the Cold War. Such dogmatic posturing has recently fallen from favor and the portrayal of relations between the Soviet Union and the non-socialist world displays greater finesse. Soviet writers currently prefer to use neutrally worded messages informing their readers that "the Soviet Union does not surrender its citizens who have committed a crime on the territory of other states to these states" and that "in these circumstances, the question is resolved by Soviet judicial organs in accordance with operative criminal legislation."[21] The change in style is welcome, of course, but the shift does not automatically spell plain sailing for extradition pursuits across the old political trenches because the intervening terrain is still heavily mined. To quote a sober assessment of the situation, "at the present time, the problem of rendition of criminals remains complicated, inasmuch as its solution is not infrequently linked with factors of a socio-political nature and

[19] *Dokumenty vneshnei politiki SSSR*, Moscow 1968, Vol. 14, 103-6; *Sovetsko-Mongolskie otnosheniia 1921-1974, dokumenty i materialy*, Vol. 1: 1921-74, at 249-52 (Moscow, 1975).
[20] Polents, *op. cit. supra* note II, at 254.
[21] I. I. Solodkin, in *Sovetskoe ugolovnoe pravo, chast obshchaia* 191 (M. D. Shargorodskii, N. A. Beliaev eds.) (Leningrad, 1960) *Idem*, in *Kurs sovetskogo ugolovnogo prava, chast obshchaia* Vol. 1, at 143 (N. A. Beliaev, M. D. Shargorodskii, eds.) (Leningrad, 1968); M. A. Gelfer, in *Sovetskoe ugolovnoe pravo, obshchaia chast* 80 (V. M. Chkhikvadze ed.) (Moscow, 1959). See, too, Marysheva, *op. cit. supra* note 13, at 162.

universally recognized international law norms on the problem of rendition do not yet exist."[22]

A further technical detail requires clarification, namely, whether the fugitive's acquisition of the citizenship of the requested state after the crime was committed but prior to submission of the extradition demand triggers the ban against the rendition of one's nationals. The impression is that such interim conversion is indeed expected to veto a bid for rendition:

On the one hand, all the material circumstances with which the law couples the inception of responsibility are determined at the moment of commission of the crime; in some cases, the very qualification of crime hinges on the existence of the foreign citizenship of the guilty person. But, on the other hand, recognition of the impossibility of denying the surrender of one's citizen only because he acquired that citizenship already after commission of the crime limits the effect of the rule of the treaties concerning the non-surrender of one's own citizens which is enunciated in general terms and does not point to the moment of acquisition of citizenship. In our opinion, there are not sufficient grounds for such a restrictive interpretation, especially so if one takes into account the equally general formulation of Art. 7 of the Law on the citizenship of the USSR.[23]

Denying rendition because the *de cujus* has been granted asylum by the requested state is common fare and, in fact, this residual remedy will normally avail even if there is no explicit caveat in the relevant entente. The Soviet Union and its present partners expressly recognize the right to grant sanctuary and that doing so precludes mutual rendition, but offer no guidelines as to how asylum might

---

[22] P. I. Savitskii, *Mezhdunarodnoe pravo* 209 (G. V. Ignatenko, D. D. Ostapenko eds.) (Moscow, 1978).

[23] Marysheva, *op. cit. supra* note 13, at 162-63. An identical thesis is propounded by Romanian scholar, R. M. Conesco, ''L'extradition dans les traités d'assistance juridique conclus par l'État socialiste Roumain avec les autres États socialistes d'Europe,'' *Revue roumaine des sciences sociales* 283 (séries de sciences juridiques, 1965, No. 2). The author cites Art. 69(5) of the corresponding treaty between Romania and Czechoslovakia which stipulates that extradition is not afforded where on the date when the request for extradition is received, the *de cujus* qualifies as a citizen of the requested contracting party, and adds: ''This specification does not exist in the other treaties, but in the absence of explicit mention the solution must, in our opinion, by medium of interpretation be the same, for it calls for acceptance as a corollary of the inadmissibility of extradition of one's own citizens.'' Art. 7 of the 1978 statute on USSR citizenship recurs as Art. 10 of the 1990 statute and simply states: ''A citizen of the USSR cannot be surrendered to a foreign state.'' *Ved. SSSR* 1978, No. 49, Art. 816 and 1990, No. 23, Art. 435. *Slovar mezhdunarodnogo prava* 48-49 (Moscow, 1986, 2nd ed.), likewise refers to Art. 7 to make the point about non-rendition of one's own citizens, without further qualification.

be practised in these circumstances. Silence thus translates into reliance on the corresponding party's policy on that count and here problems can easily arise. In the Soviet case, the difficulties stem both from the way the regime has chosen to define the contents of its own asylum package[24] and the standards it has insisted on applying to the behaviour of other states in these matters.

A local source once squarely put its finger on the distinctive flavour of the Soviet perception of the phenomenon of asylum, namely that: ''The very concept of political crime, sanctioning the right to asylum, evinces certain particularities for the reason that in Soviet law the concept of political crime possesses in the main not a national, but a social character: not an attempt against the political order of the given state, but an attempt against a designated socio-political order.''[25] The tradition of talking about asylum in ''class'' terms that stretch well beyond the fairly narrow treatment of the brand of ''political offences'' elsewhere has persisted in the Soviet repertory. Both the 1977 Constitution of the USSR (Art. 38) and the current statute on the legal status of foreign citizens in the USSR (Art. 6)[26] contemplate affording asylum on the territory of the USSR to persons ''persecuted for the defense of the workers and the cause of peace, for participation in the revolutionary and national-liberation movement, for progressive socio-political, scientific or other creative activity.'' That kind of safety net can accommodate any contingency and lets a subjective test govern the decision whether or not to give the benefits of asylum to an individual whose conduct technically runs afoul of the criminal law of a foreign state. Who does and does not get asylum in the Soviet approach, then, is in effect a matter of discretion because the qualifying indicia are so vaguely drawn.

One's sense of orientation is not improved by the glaring penchant in Soviet legal literature to pin culturally colored tags on pronouncements about rendition and asylum. What, for example, is an outside observer to think after stumbling across a paragraph stating that ''the Soviet Union adheres to the position that the rendition of criminals constitutes a lawful act in relations between states if it is employed in the interests of maintaining peace and coopera-

[24] See H.-J. Uibopuu, ''The Soviet Approach to the Right of Asylum,'' *A.W.R.-Bulletin* 152-69 (1971 No. 4).

[25] Egor'ev et al., *op. cit. supra* note 18 at 90-91.

[26] *Ved. SSSR* 1981 No. 26 Art. 836.

tion between peoples"?[27] Do these politically loaded criteria allow the Soviet apparatus to refuse rendition otherwise owed by parading a devotion to the superior values ascribed to enhancing the goals of peace and cooperation among peoples or, conversely, insist on rendition by another state even when the service is not formally due by invoking the same lofty pretext? Do the "interests of maintaining peace and cooperation among peoples" override the normal safeguards against the surrender of political offenders because a paramount desideratum is at stake and commands uncontested priority? Anything seems possible, depending on who gets to edit the script and thus control the tenor of the accompanying dialogue. Nor is one on firmer ground when Soviet lawyers proclaim that "the practice of socialist states in granting asylum is imbued with the spirit of proletarian internationalism."[28] How that spirit will affect administrative mores in cases of rendition and asylum is something only its proponents can tell and the rest of the world is left to guess at the shape the phenomenon might assume as a result of being passed through this doctrinal wringer.

This trouble is occasioned by the fact that the definition of the principle of asylum is entrusted to internal state law, meaning that it is rooted in the exercise of state sovereignty where "each state on its own and only on its own decides to whom it grants the right to asylum on its territory."[29] However, the service of the international law canon is enlisted as a prophylaxis against potential excesses by the state in its manner of procuring territorial asylum; objections are prompted by the mode of attribution of various functions to the international law medium and the choice of entries in the array of transgressions against which its injunctions are deployed.

For example, the Soviet regime has compiled an impressive track record of verbal condemnation of incidences of international terrorism. In the days when quoting Stalin on every topic was *de rigueur,* his assurance to Roy Howard of the Scripps-Howard Newspapers syndicate that "as far as we are concerned, we would never suffer a single terrorist on our territory, never mind against whom he was plotting his crime,"[30] keynoted every discussion of the subject on the pages of contemporary Soviet publications. Soviet legal scholars

---

[27] K. Ia. Chizhov, *Mezhdunarodnoe pravo* 165 (F. I. Kozhevnikov ed.), Moscow, 1957.

[28] L. N. Galenskaia, *Mezhdunarodnoe pravo* 240 (G. I. Tunkin ed.), Moscow, 1974.

[29] Iu. Iastrebova, "Institut ubezhishcha i status bezhentsev v mezhdunarodnom prave," *Sovetskoe gosudarstvo i pravo* 1990 No. 10, 130.

[30] "Beseda tovarishcha Stalina s g-nom Roi Govardom," *Bolshevik* 1936 No. 6, 4.

seized on the catechism to claim that "the Soviet Union and the countries of people's democracy consistently struggle against the granting of asylum to terrorists and war criminals" and that "Marxists always were and are consistent enemies of terrorism."[31] By contrast, the capitalist world was faulted for doing the exact opposite and engaging in wholesale abuse of the right of asylum and hiding behind its skirts to provide protection to war criminals, spies, traitors to their Motherland, fascists, saboteurs, and terrorists. Speaking at the first session of the USSR Supreme Soviet, Molotov himself charged that in France, especially, there find haven the sort of adventurers and the sort of criminal organizations that are nothing else than vipers' nests of terrorists and saboteurs. . . Obviously, this cannot be excused by the right of asylum to foreigners."[32]

After Stalin and his retainers were consigned to history, similar sentiments continued to be aired, stripped of personal credits, but still beaming the message that "the Soviet Union disapproves of terrorism—a weapon of the most reactionary groups of the imperialistic bourgeoisie for the provocation of international conflicts and the preparation of aggression—and wages battle on it."[33] Further scrubbing eventually got rid of the last of the doctrinal clichés so that now Soviet scribes are content to skip the invidious comparisons between socialist and non-socialist fare in this theatre and instead broadcast how "the institution of the right of asylum acquired a truly democratic, progressive character only in the legislation and international law practice of the Soviet Union and the other socialist states."[34] The inference is that the competition scores lower in the match and that socialist precedent sets an example on this occasion for all to follow.

The proper handling of war criminals likewise fuels controversy. In the midst of the Second World War, the Soviet government had already issued a formal statement (October 14, 1942) to the effect that "it counted on all interested states to afford each other mu-

---

[31] Polents, *op. cit. supra* note II, 254. See also N. T. Blatova, *Mezhdunarodnoe pravo* (N. T. Blatova, ed.), Moscow 1987, 324; N. T. Samartseva, *Mezhdunarodnoe pravo* (D. B. Levin, G. P. Kaliuzhnaia, eds.), 168, 170 (Moscow, 1964).

[32] *Pervaia sessiia Verkhovnogo Soveta SSSR,* Stenograficheskii otchet, 153 (Moscow, 1938).

[33] V. I. Lisovskii, *Mezhdunarodnoe pravo,* 125. (2nd ed., Moscow, 1961). In the 1970 edition, the passage has been trimmed to the bare-bones statement that "the Soviet Union disapproves of terrorism and wages battle on it." *Mezhdunarodnoe pravo,* 136. (Moscow, 1970).

[34] Chizhov, *op. cit. supra* note 27, 172. Also, Polents, 5 *op. cit. supra* note II, at 250; Lisovskii, *op. cit. supra* note 33 (1961 ed.) at 120.

tual assistance in seeking out, surrendering, prosecuting and meting out severe punishment to hitlerites and their accomplices guilty of organizing, condoning and committing crimes on occupied territories."[35] The same theme was sounded by Stalin a little more than a year later (November 6, 1943) who, in reviewing the principal post-war goals of the United Nations alliance, stressed the need "to take measures so that all fascist criminals guilty of the present war and the suffering of the peoples, no matter in what country they tried to hide, shall incur severe punishment and retribution for all the evil deeds they committed."[36] A duty to surrender war criminals was distilled, *inter alia*, from the tenor of various wartime declarations,[37] the corresponding articles of the armistice agreements with Italy, Romania, Bulgaria, Hungary, and Finland, the Four-Power declaration on the surrender of Germany of June 5, 1945, the UN General Assembly resolution of February 12, 1946, and the peace treaties with Italy, Romania, Hungary, Bulgaria, and Finland (1947). Indeed, Bulgaria, Hungary, and Romania are singled out for successfully discharging the obligations assumed in this area by the above agreements.[38]

Relying on this material, Soviet spokesmen have since waged a concerted campaign to persuade the international community that international law mandates the rendition of war criminals as a universal proposition and that failure to do so constitutes a violation of a peremptory rule of international law which must be countered.[39] It is said, for instance, that "the Soviet Union and the

[35] *Vneshniaia politika Sovetskogo Soiuza v period Otechestvennoi voiny*, 276-77 (Moscow, 1944, Vol. 1).

[36] I. V. Stalin, *O Velikoi Otechestvennoi voine Sovetskogo Soiuza*, 125 (Moscow, 1950).

[37] Declaration on the punishment for crimes committed in the course of the war of January 13, 1942, signed by Czechoslovakia, Poland, Yugoslavia, Norway, Greece, Belgium, Luxembourg, and the Free French; the Declaration on the responsibility of the hitlerites for the atrocities committed by them, published by the Moscow conference of three Ministers of October 30, 1943. See Polents, *op. cit. supra* note 11, 254-55, and Lisovskii, 5 ibid., 548-50. *Vneshniaia politika, supra* note 35, 363-64.

[38] Polents, *op. cit. supra*, note 11, at 255. See also N. A. Bazhenov, "Nerushimost printsipov Niurnberga i sotrudnichestvo gosudarstv v presledovanii natsistskikh voennykh prestupnikov," *Uroki Niurnberga*, Materialy Mezhdunarodnoi konferentsii, Moscow, November 11-13, 1986 (Doklady uchastnikov konferentsii), 11-20 (Moscow, 1988, Vol. 3); R. M. Valeev, "Niurnbergskie printsipy i voprosy vydachi lits, sovershivshikh prestupleniia protiv chelovechestva," *Ibid.*, 149-67 (Moscow, 1986, Vol. 1).

[39] The gist of the Soviet position here is that "rendition is an indispensable instrument both for the trial of already unmasked war criminals and for their detection. However, for the rendition of war criminals there must be set conditions substantially different from those which constitute the institution of rendition of crimi-

countries of people's democracy struggle against the illegal practice of the countries of the Anglo-American bloc who shelter war criminals under the guise of procuring asylum,'' in breach of the international documents that they themselves had signed.[40] In this connection, Soviet sources recognize the validity of a major departure from traditional policy of not surrendering one's own citizens in the imposition of a duty to surrender war criminals in the aftermath of the Second World War that waived this old exemption.[41] Finally, the Soviet Union and the countries of people's democracy are again praised for "stubbornly struggling against providing shelter to war criminals because their punishment represents one of the paramount conditions for preventing the recurrence of aggression."[42]

However, others did not share these convictions and no international consensus then existed that the law of nations required states to deliver "on demand" individuals suspected of having committed war crimes to their foreign accusers to stand trial in the country where the offences were perpetrated in the absence of specific extradition arrangements and on the strength alone of indications of general intent. Attitudes may subsequently have evolved in the

nals in the context of normal relations between states. The guarantees which are absolutely indispensable in normal conditions of peace time and normal relations between states cannot be applied in respect to persons who have eternally covered themselves with shame through crimes the cruelty of which does not lend itself to description.'' N. N. Polianskii, *Mezhdunarodnoe pravosudie i prestupniki voiny*, 106 (Moscow, 1945). In legal terms, this translates into the postulate that: ''The duty to surrender persons who committed crimes against humanity exists independently of the existence between states of conventions and bilateral treaties on rendition. In this finds reflection one of the particularities of the application of the institution of rendition to the given category of crimes.'' Valeev, *op. cit. supra* note 36, 157. See also Gy. Haraszti, ''The Right of Asylum,'' *Acta Juridica* 372-73 (Budapest), 1960, fasc. 3-4.

[40] Polents, *op. cit. supra* note 11, at 251, 253, 254; likewise, P. S. Romashkin, *Prestupleniia protiv mira i chelovechestva*, 256-57 (Moscow, 1967).

[41] See A. Ia. Vyshinskii, *Voprosy mezhdunarodnogo prava i mezhdunarodnoi politiki*, 370 (Moscow, 1949). In the same vein, see Valeev, *op. cit supra*, note 38, at 157: ''To persons who committed crimes against humanity likewise do not extend the principles of non-rendition of one's own citizens and political offenders.''

[42] Polents, *op. cit. supra*, note 11, at 255. On July 29, 1943, the Soviet government had already taken the initiative of instructing the Soviet envoys to Turkey and Sweden to furnish the latter with the text of the notes in which it called on the neutral countries to refuse sanctuary to war criminals and let it be known that the Soviet government would consider the granting of asylum, assistance and succor to such persons as a violation of the principles for which the United Nations were fighting. *Vneshniaia politika...*, *supra* note 35, at 348.

direction first designated by Moscow, but initially the Soviet pitch met with scepticism and rejection in many quarters and the bid to portray its opinion as the true faith attracted few converts.

Such demurrers notwithstanding, Soviet analysts pressed forward with their case, arguing that the right of asylum:

> was afforded fighters for freedom and progress evading persecution by reactionary governments. War criminals and the leading functionaries of fascism patently have nothing in common with the defenders of freedom and progress. One cannot use the concept of political offender with respect to those for whom politics are but a convenient excuse for the satisfaction of racial hatred and predatory greed, to those who in bestial fashion exterminated millions of people (the death factories at Maidanek, Hartogenbosch, Auschwitz, etc.) and committed destruction and devastation utterly unprecedented in their brutality (Lidice, Novgorod, Smolensk, Kiev, etc.). Like ancient pirates, they can only be viewed as enemies of the human race.[43]

The premise logically leads to the conclusion that "the rendition of war criminals is considered a legal obligation of all states"[44] which, Soviet legal experts take extra care to underscore, operates on a *sui generis* footing where "the presence or absence of such bilateral treaties [i.e., prescribing rendition] has no bearing in deciding the questions of surrendering war criminals inasmuch as with respect to these persons apply imperative international law norms qualifying their rendition to the interested state as a legal obligation of the state to which the demand for rendition is addressed."[45]

Testing what they preached, the Soviet authorities bombarded assorted western countries with requests for the surrender of war criminals who had found local haven, but these "legitimate demands" were rebuffed by the United States and Australia, which copied the behaviour of other "bourgeois regimes" that had opted earlier to slap a de facto embargo on such traffic with the

[43] I. P. Trainin, V. E. Grabar, N. N. Polianskii, A. N. Trainin, V. N. Durdenevskii, and D. B. Levin, "Ugolovnaia otvetstvennost prestupnikov voiny," 77 *Sotsialisticheskaia zakonnost* 1945 No. 6, 10.
See also N. T. Samartseva, *op. cit. supra* note 31, 168-69; F. I. Kozhevnikov, *Kurs mezhdunarodnogo prava* (F.I Kozhevnikov ed.), 381 (3rd ed., Moscow, 1972).

[44] N. T. Samartseva, *op. cit. supra,* note 31, 211. See also N. T. Blatova, *Mezhdunarodnoe pravo* (L. A. Modzhorian, N. T. Blatova, eds.), 277 (Moscow, 1970): "War criminals are not entitled to the right of asylum . . . that is a universally recognized rule of contemporary international law."

[45] Samartseva, *op. cit. supra,* note 31, at 212.

Soviet Union.[46]

Soviet authors sounded more positive about the compulsory quality of the obligation to surrender war criminals when writing about
members of the capitalist community than when referring to the
corollary duties of the socialist constituents here. Then, the tone
suddenly turns tentative in reporting that "the Soviet Union admits the possibility of rendition of criminals on conditions of
reciprocity, particularly war criminals and persons guilty of crimes
against peace and humanity."[47] The mode verges on the discretionary and the insertion of the mutuality clause further weakens
the original injunction, all of which stands in stark contrast with
the harsh terms of the Soviet indictment of its western opposites
for not sticking to the strict letter of the law. Time has not allayed
the antagonism and, while the Soviet style elsewhere has tended
to adapt to the niceties of today's less confrontational approach to
East-West relations, the war crimes issue continues to generate intense irritation which, even as late as 1990, could still prompt the
charge that: "The practice of granting asylum in capitalist countries is accompanied by numerous violations of generally accepted
international legal norms. After the Second World War the United
States, Great Britain and several other capitalist powers opened their
borders to Nazi war criminals, which is inconsistent with the goal
of strengthening world peace and the purposes and principles of
the United Nations."[48]

Additional candidacies have since been nominated for this special treatment. To the extent, for instance, that one is asked to believe that "in the USSR and the other socialist states, reactionaries,
war mongers, terrorists, saboteurs and kindred criminal elements
cannot enjoy the right of asylum," the clear implication is that the
rest of the world should also follow suit and routinely refuse sanctuary to this breed of outcasts. Criticism of the United States,
England, France, and other capitalist powers for affording shelter
after the Second World War to a motley collection of war criminals, traitors to the Motherland, spies, saboteurs, and plotters who
fled the USSR and other countries, reflects the same conviction

---

[46] Cf. F. I. Kozhevnikov and V. A. Romanov, *Kurs mezhdunarodnogo prava* (F. I. Kozhevnikov, ed.), 633 (2nd ed., Moscow 1966). See also D. B. Levin and G. I. Tunkin,
Mezhdunarodnoe pravo (G. I. Tunkin, ed.), Moscow 1974, 572-73.

[47] Samartseva, *op. cit. supra*, note 31, at 172. Blatova, *op. cit. supra*, note 44, at 279,
reproduces the statement with the substitution of "socialist countries" for "the
Soviet Union."

[48] *International Law*, 216 (Moscow, 1990).

that such hospitality" mocks the traditional concept of providing emergency refuge to worthy individuals by bestowing the privilege on the dregs of society.[49]

Immunity from rendition must, according to various Soviet spokesmen, likewise be denied to "deserters";[50] those guilty of crimes against peace and humanity, war crimes,[51] the crimes of genocide and apartheid;[52] and "counterrevolutionary emigres."[53] Gradually, however, attention has shifted from designated items to generic brands, with Soviet legal scholars preferring to espouse the general principle that "on the basis of sovereignty, states are not obliged to surrender criminals, with the exception of those whose crimes evince an international character and are aimed at undermining international peace and security."[54] Or, "it is prohibited to grant asylum to persons guilty of committing international crimes and, foremost, crimes against peace and war crimes"[55] (or "crimes against peace, war crimes or crimes against humanity").[56] Or, "it is commonly recognized that the right of asylum cannot be afforded . . . individuals who have committed international crimes (war criminals, etc.) . . . and persons who have committed criminal acts that run counter to the goals and principles of the United Nations."[57] Cryptic pronouncements barring asylum for "persons accused of committing international crimes"[58] also occur. Finally, UN documents are pressed into service, namely the 1948 Universal Declaration of Human Rights, which recommends that the right of asylum not avail in instances where the imputed act is "contrary to the purposes and principles of the United Nations;" and the 1967 General Assembly Declaration on territorial asylum, which calls for denying asylum to "persons concerning whom there are serious reasons to believe that they have committed crimes against peace, war crimes or crimes against humanity."

No authoritative definition of what falls under the heading of

---

[49] Samartseva, *op. cit. supra* note 31, at 168. See also Blatova, *op. cit. supra* note 44, at 276.
[50] Lisovskii, *op. cit. supra,* note 33 (1970 ed.), at 132.
[51] A. P. Movchan, *Mezhdunarodnoe pravo* (G. I. Tunkin, ed.), 345 (Moscow, 1982).
[52] Savitskii, *op. cit. supra,* note 22, at 210.
[53] Menzhinskii, *op. cit. supra,* note 12 (1981 ed.), at 237. *Idem, op. cit. supra,* note 12 (1966 ed.), at 314.
[54] Lisovskii, *op. cit. supra,* note 33 (1970 ed.), at 134. *Idem, op. cit. supra,* note 33 (1961 ed.), at 124.
[55] Merzhinskii, *op. cit. supra,* note 12 (1981 ed.), at 238.
[56] *Idem, op. cit. supra,* note 1, at 307. See also Movchan, *op. cit. supra,* note 51, at 345.
[57] Blatova, *op. cit. supra,* note 31, at 311-12.
[58] Galenskaia, *op. cit. supra,* note 28, at 239.

"international crime" exists and different slates of entries have been making the local rounds. Under the terms of the "old" international law, the duty to punish or surrender reportedly operated in cases of piracy, slavery, slave trade, trade in women and children, currency counterfeiting, illegal dissemination of drugs, dissemination of pornographic publications, and deliberate damage to underwater cables.[59] An updated sample of such major offences that must incur rendition, does not explicitly mention drug trafficking and damage to underwater cables, but goes on to name crimes against peace, war crimes, and crimes against humanity, genocide, apartheid, racial discrimination, illegal hijacking of aircraft, illegal manufacture of drugs, crimes against diplomatic agents and internationally protected persons, and exploitation of prostitution by third persons.[60]

The other circumstances entailing a refusal to grant rendition are more routine. Where the justification is that the crime was committed on the territory of the contracting party which received the application, the classical reasoning—reputedly widely followed in the international treaty repertory—assigns primacy to "the principle of extending criminal jurisdiction to all crimes committed on the territory of the given state, the principle of the territorial effect of criminal law."[61] Where denial of rendition is occasioned by the fact that criminal prosecution or execution of sentence is precluded by the legislation of the requested state because the statute of limitations has tolled or on some other lawful grounds, a couple of technical points invite a closer look. What is meant by "other lawful grounds" is never explained, except that acts of amnesty are often mentioned as one of the contingencies the authors had in mind in framing this catch-all phrase.[62] Letting the law of the requested state dictate the outcome in this situation matches the prevailing mode and also coincides with the option staked out by the Soviet regime very early in its career.[63] Doctrinal differences persist, how-

59 Menzhinskii, *op. cit. supra*, note 1, at 310.

60 Blatova, *op. cit. supra*, note 1, at 279, 282. For other recent versions and attempts to divide these phenomena into two categories -international crimes and crimes of an international nature — see I. I. Karpets, *Prestupleniia mezhdunarodnogo kharaktera* (Moscow, 1979); L. N. Galenskaia, "O poniatii mezhdunarodnogo ugolovnogo prava," *Sovetskii ezhegodnik mezhdunarodnogo prava* 1969, 247-60 (Moscow, 1970).

61 Marysheva, *op. cit. supra*, note 13, at 163.

62 *Ibid.*

63 The draft of the Model Convention of the USSR on the rendition of criminals, approved by the Council of People's Commissars on October 3, 1923, indicated

ever, with some Soviet analysts still convinced that the legislation of both principals should exercise an equal voice in the matter and others at least conceding that the requesting state has a legitimate interest in punishing the *de cujus* and cannot be satisfied when its wishes are thus thwarted. Of course, the territorial supremacy of the requested state cannot be ignored and, indeed, official policy has elected to assign priority to that claim: no one familiar with Soviet political reality will be surprised by the choice.[64]

Next, recognition that rendition cannot be afforded when prohibited by the law of the requested state sounds like a sweeping concession to any further hurdles that the domestic legislation of the respective partners places in the path of this traffic, leaving the enterprise hostage to an adequate sense of appreciation by the competent authorities that taking excessive liberties here could well wreck the whole operation. Soviet commentators shed little light on the motives behind what they correctly depict as ''the broad formulation of this essentially *renvoi* norm.'' In Soviet law, the rule against rendition of one's own citizens and in cases of asylum fixes the limits, but, as Soviet spokesmen are quick to note, ''in the countries which are the USSR's treaty partners, internal legislation may turn out to be elaborated in greater detail; it may set yet other grounds for denying rendition not envisaged in the corresponding treaty.''[65]

The idea that rendition must be refused to avoid inflicting ''double jeopardy'' — the venerable concept of *non bis idem*—is a virtual staple of the modern diplomatic canon. By offering this guarantee, the present cast merely confirms its adherence to the established code. Soviet legal writers, however, caution how the process of actual implementation may be fraught with logistical difficulties that can markedly affect the record of performance. As one of them has written, ''The designated principle may be considered universally accepted for countries of the same legal system. The extension of this principle is limited for countries where, in addition to the territorial principle, there function the effect principle and the nationality principle. It cannot always be applied in the

---

(Art. 5, Part II) that ''rendition is not effected if prior to receipt of the demand for rendition the statute of limitations on criminal prosecution or punishment of the given crime has tolled.'' The legislation of the country to which the demand was addressed controlled.

[64] E.g., Valeev, *op. cit. supra*, note 14, at 58; A. Dereviashkin, ''Materialy po mezhdunarodnomu ugolovnomu pravu,'' *Gosudarstvennyi institut po izucheniiu ugolovnoi ispravitelno-trudovoi politiki pri Prokurature Soiuza SSR*, 1934, biul, 8-9, 47.

[65] Marysheva, *op. cit. supra*, note 13, at 165.

practice of rendition between socialist and capitalist countries owing to the great diversity of criminal legislation."[66]

Finally, the Soviet-Arab branch features a reservation that ve-
toes rendition if the crime in question entails the filing of criminal
charges under the laws of the requested state despite the fact that
this crime was committed outside its territory. According to Soviet
sources, the jurisdictional scope of local criminal law is essentially
determined by territorial and personal criteria so that few opportunities will arise for invoking this clause. True, a Soviet citizen
guilty of committing a crime abroad can be prosecuted at home,
but he would be immune from rendition anyway because of the
citizenship exception. The only scenario where the problem might
occur, concerns stateless individuals located in the USSR who committed a crime abroad; they are held accountable in that case under the criminal law of the corresponding union republic and are
not exempt from extradition—producing a combination that spells
eligibility for this treatment.

Soviet legal circles have recently expressed considerable sympathy
for reforms that would sanction punishment under Soviet law for
especially dangerous acts that infringe on the bases of the Soviet
order and the person of Soviet citizens when committed by foreigners
abroad.[67] While opinions are deeply divided over the phenomenon
of universal jurisdiction—some defending it as a useful instrument
in the struggle for peace and against the worst strain of crimes, others
branding it as an imperialistic, anti-democratic ploy[68]—those who
favour testing the medium could end up winning the debate. Either
development would automatically increase the statistical probability of entitlement to such release from the commitment to procure
rendition services.

On balance, then, the language of the article dealing with this
theme strongly suggests that the parties chose to weave a loose le-

[66] Valeev, *op. cit. supra,* note 14, at 59-60. According to this source, that is why Art.
5 of the Fundamentals of criminal legislation of the USSR provides that if a citizen
of the Soviet Union who committed a crime abroad has incurred punishment
abroad, the court may commensurately lower the punishment it has pronounced
or entirely exempt the guilty person from undergoing punishment.

[67] Valeev, *op. cit. supra,* note 14, at 25; N. D. Durmanov, *Kurs sovetskogo ugolovnogo prava,*
Vol. 1, 222-23 (Moscow, 1970).

[68] *Pro,* A. A. Gertsenzon, *Ugolovnoe pravo, Chast obshchaia,* 232-33 (Moscow, 1948); I. I.
Solodkin, *Kurs sovetskogo ugolovnogo prava,* Vol. 1, 135 (Leningrad, 1968). *Anti,* M. A.
Shneider, *Sovetskoe ugolovnoe pravo, Chast obshchaia,* 46-47 (Moscow, 1955); Durmanov,
op. cit. supra, note 67, at 223.

gal fabric and leave ample room for sovereign prerogatives to shape the administrative picture, and compounded the laissez-faire bias by stretching the exemptions to the point where a fare of *ad hoc* goodwill rather than the treaty mandate holds out the best hope that the mechanism will function in a plausible manner. On the other hand, caution may be desirable and, indeed, inevitable, when first seeking rapprochement of this genre across political lines, for fear that inflated expectations may lead to extreme disillusionment before pragmatic experimentation gradually succeeds in dispelling the old suspicions and knitting a viable rapport between two very different models of civic culture.

If rendition is not effected, the requested state must so inform the other state and indicate the reasons for refusal to extradite. If the person whose extradition is being sought has been charged with, or is serving sentence for (USSR v. Greece and Cyprus), or has been sentenced for (USSR-PDRY), another crime on the territory of the requested state, rendition may be effected at the close of the proceedings or upon serving sentence or in case of pardon (release on any other legal grounds—USSR v. Greece and Cyprus). If delay in rendition results in impossibility of criminal prosecution owing to the expiration of the statute of limitations or can engender serious (USSR v. Greece and Cyprus) difficulties in the criminal prosecution of the individual whose surrender is demanded, then the requesting state can file a motivated request (request—USSR-Iraq; supplementary request—USSR-Tunisia) for temporary rendition in order to pursue criminal proceedings. The requesting state must return the person thus temporarily surrendered immediately upon termination of the preliminary or judicial proceedings without executing the sentence and no later than three months from the date of rendition (no deadline set in the Soviet-Tunisian version).

Communications concerning questions related to criminal prosecution or the extradition of offenders are carried out between the Ministry of Justice of the USSR or the Procuracy of the USSR and the Ministry of Justice of Iraq (Algeria, Tunisia, PDRY) by the diplomatic route. Decisions on these questions are made by the competent organs of the requested state on the basis of its legislation unless otherwise instructed by the language of the applicable treaty. The USSR's ententes with Greece and Cyprus only contain a general clause mandating that such traffic follow diplomatic channels and skip the rest of these logistical details.

A requisition for extradition of a person who is under investigation must be accompanied by a certified copy of a warrant of arrest listing particulars as to the circumstances of the crime and its legal definition, the text of the law defining the given crime and, if material damage occurred, particulars as to the extent of the damage that the criminal caused or intended to cause. When rendition is sought for the purpose of execution of a sentence, the requisition must be accompanied by an official copy of the sentence or other corresponding judicial ruling which has entered into final force, and the text of the law defining the crime. If the convicted person has already served a portion of the sentence, that fact shall be indicated. In all instances, the package shall include detailed information regarding the person whose surrender is claimed, particulars as to his citizenship, residence, and distinctive marks and, if possible, a photograph, save where such data can be obtained only after the offender's arrest or trial (the last proposition is replaced in the USSR's arrangements with Algeria, Tunisia, and the PDRY by a waiver of the need to procure these facts if they are recorded in the warrant of arrest or in the sentence). All the aforementioned documents must be certified by the competent authorities and authenticated on behalf of the USSR by the Ministry of Justice of the USSR or the Procuracy of the USSR and on behalf of Iraq (Algeria, Tunisia, PDRY) by the Ministry of Justice. The documents in question shall be translated into the language of the requested party (or English: USSR-Iraq); the translation must by officially authenticated (the USSR-Tunisia sample).

In the USSR's agreements with Greece and Cyprus, the wording of the matching article is slightly different. Care is taken to spell out that the application for extradition must be filed in written form. Where feasible, the offender's fingerprints should be supplied. Reference to material damage resulting from the crime talks about loss actually inflicted and omits what the perpetrator might have intended. Where rendition to serve sentence is at stake, the soliciting party must submit an authenticated copy of the sentence together with a voucher attesting that it has entered into final force. A distinctive feature of the Greek/Cyprus brand in this connection is the presence of an explicit assurance that the requesting state is not obliged to append to the request for extradition proof of guilt of the *de cujus*—which, of course, is how the matter is handled in common practice.

In the event of extradition, the requested state shall, at the behest of the other side, deliver to it any objects obtained by criminal means, as well as those objects that may be used as evidence of a crime (and the instruments of crime: USSR v. Greece, Algeria, Tunisia, PDRY). These objects are to be transferred also in cases where the offender cannot be extradited owing to death or flight or other reasons. The requested state may temporarily retain the above articles if they are required for criminal proceedings in another case being pursued on its territory. The rights of third parties to the articles remain unaffected and the property is returned to the extraditing state for transmittal to the persons entitled to it if their identity can be established (the additional business of restoring these items to their rightful owners, where these are known, is not mentioned in the Soviet-Greek and Soviet-Cypriot editions). The Soviet-Iraqi covenant alone omits to explain that the transfer of monetary sums and articles is effected in accordance with the legislation of the requested state.

If the requisition for extradition does not provide the data needed for its execution, the requested state may require that the information be procured and fix a deadline for supplying the missing facts. Upon application, this time-limit can be extended (USSR-PDRY: for valid reasons). In the USSR-Greece and USSR-Cyprus sample, the procedure is carefully spelled out: the response must be forthcoming within two months and the expiration date can be deferred for fifteen days for valid reasons. Furthermore, if the claimant state fails to observe the schedule, the detaining state may release the person taken into custody in anticipation of his rendition. This last safeguard recurs in the USSR's compacts with Algeria, Tunisia, and the PDRY (not Iraq), but only in the guise of a reference to the expiration of whatever deadline was established *ad hoc* since the relevant conventions (unlike the Greek/Cypriot specimens) do not draw up a calendar for the occasion.

Upon receiving a requisition for extradition, the requested state must immediately take steps according to its legislation to find the wanted person and, if necessary, to arrest him, save where extradition is barred. In cases admitting of no delay, a person against whom criminal proceedings have been instigated may be arrested even before receipt of a bid for extradition if the competent institution files an application for such arrest citing a warrant of arrest or a sentence that has entered into final force and if notice is given at the same time that a requisition for extradition is *en route*. The application for arrest may be remitted by telegraph or other similar means (which record the message in writing: the entire cast minus

Iraq). The requesting state must submit all documents required for extradition as soon as possible. The competent institutions of a contracting party may also arrest a person located on its territory without waiting for a corresponding application if there are grounds to conclude that he has committed on the territory of the other party a crime entailing extradition under the terms of the respective treaty. The interested side shall be notified forthwith of arrests made pursuant to or without benefit of an application or of the reasons why an application for arrest has not been complied with. Except for the Soviet Union's agreement with Iraq, the remainder of the lot take the extra precaution of letting it be known that a person arrested with or without benefit of an application to that effect may be set free if within one month (Tunisia; one month, plus a possible extension of 15 days upon proper request—Greece and Cyprus; 2 months—Algeria, PDRY) of the day when the soliciting state was notified of the arrest, no requisition for extradition has been submitted.

With the exclusion of the Soviet-Iraqi piece, the rest of the entries call for the requested state to inform its partner of its decision on each extradition claim, indicating the time and place of the slated rendition. If the requesting state does not take possession of the individual earmarked for surrender within 15 days of the date set for the transfer, the *de cujus* may be released from custody, although the time-limit may be extended at the behest of the requesting state for a maximum of 15 days (Greece/Cyprus). Vis-à-vis Algeria and S. Yemen, the release of the individual in that case is couched in a peremptory mode and no deferment is sanctioned. The Soviet-Tunisian score differs here in that the original period assigned for the transfer is left to be determined by the principals and any extension is limited to a maximum of fifteen days; the detainee must be freed if the deadline is missed; a repeat request for extradition in that event may be refused; and, if the surrender or reception of the individual scheduled for extradition cannot be effected owing to the intervention of extraordinary circumstances, the interested party so informs the other before the expiration of the set deadline and both sides then agree on a new time-table for rendition which cannot exceed fifteen days from the date when the extraordinary circumstances cease to operate. The Soviet Union's package with Algeria, Tunisia, and the PDRY also specifies that the requested state shall immediately release the arrested person if informed in writing by the requesting state that the latter is dropping its requisition for extradition.

In the Soviet-Iraqi version, an extradited person may not, without the consent of the surrendering state, be prosecuted or punished in the applicant state for an offence committed prior to extradition or some other offence which was not contemplated at the time of rendition. The clause is very poorly drafted and, despite the actual wording, must be read to mean that such prosecution or punishment is barred for any crime other than the one which incurred rendition. Indeed, the rest of the agreements more or less feature that language. The USSR-PDRY accord alone considers the manner of handling a situation where prosecution or execution of sentence is at stake for a crime committed before rendition which did not figure in the extradition dossier. The requesting state must then file a corresponding application accompanied by the usual array of documents and the state that had performed the original extradition service is at liberty to study the new bid. One is left to guess that if permission to revise the charge sheet is denied, the prisoner will be returned—but this is only a hunch since the covenant is silent on that point. By contrast, unanimity reigns on the proposition that the extradited person cannot be surrendered to a third state without the consent of the extraditing state.

However, if an extradited person is afforded the opportunity to quit the territory of the state to which he was extradited and fails to avail himself of the possibility to leave within thirty days (Iraq; one month—USSR-Greece and USSR-Cyprus; fifteen days— USSR v. Algeria, Tunisia, PDRY) after the conclusion of the criminal proceedings or, in the event of his conviction, within thirty days (Iraq; one month—USSR-Greece and USSR-Cyprus; fifteen days— USSR v. Algeria, Tunisia, PDRY) of the completion or remission of the sentence (or voluntarily returns there after having left: USSR v. Greece and Cyprus), this person may be prosecuted or punished for another crime. The grace period does not include the time during which the extradited person was unable through no fault of his own to quit the territory of the party to which he was extradited.

The Soviet-Iraqi agreement stops there in treating extradition matters per se, but the other agreements add several miscellaneous accessories. They provide that if the extradited person manages to evade criminal prosecution or serving sentence and returns to the territory of the requested state, he may at the request of the applicant state be extradited again (USSR v. Greece, Tunisia, PDRY, Cyprus; but not Algeria). The usual batch of documents need not accompany the claim in this case. If more than one state submit a requisition for the extradition of a particular individual, the requested state decides which of these requisitions should receive precedence (Greece and Cyprus; and informs the other party of its decision—Algeria, Tunisia; and informs the other party of its decision along with the reasons behind the decision—PDRY). Other than guaranteeing each treaty partner total liberty of choice in this respect, however, the language of the agreements furnishes no guide on how pride of place will be assigned in the face of competing claims. Doctrine generally tends to award priority here to the state on whose territory the extraditable offence was committed, but the present formula, as has been correctly observed, is "more elastic."[69] Be that as it may, Soviet legal scholars unanimously endorse the notion that the state on whose territory the crime was committed should get preference in such an "auction."[70] Should the fugitive be accused of committing crimes on the territory of more than one state, his rendition to the state where the worst crime occurred seems to be favoured.[71]

Finally, we have the question of transit routing, with each contracting party undertaking to visa at the request of the other transit conveyancing through its territory of persons extradited to the other party by a third state. The signatories are not obliged to permit the transit of persons whose extradition is not sanctioned pursuant to the terms of the applicable treaty. The request to permit such transit is drawn up and submitted in the same manner as a requisition for extradition. The competent authorities of the interested parties concert in each case the means, itinerary and other conditions of transit (USSR v. Greece and Cyprus). In the Soviet-Tunisian redaction, the business of affording transit services is couched in an imperative mode, that is to say, the signatories shall not fulfil requests for transit routing save where the terms set in the treaty for extradition procedures are met; otherwise, no duty

---

[69] Conesco, *op. cit. supra,* at 287.

[70] Samartseva, *op. cit. supra,* note 31, at 172; Menzhinskii, *op. cit. supra,* note 12 (1966 ed.), at 316; *idem, op. cit. supra,* note 12 (1972 ed.), at 194; *idem, op. cit. supra,* note 12 (1981 ed.), at 239; *idem, op. cit. supra,* note 1, at 318; S. V. Isakovich, *Mizhnarodno pravo* (I. I. Lukashuk, V. A. Vasilenko, eds.), 112 (Kiev, 1971); Blatova, *op. cit. supra,* note 1, at 282; *idem, op. cit. supra,* note 31, at 331; *idem, op. cit. supra,* note 44, at 279; Chizhov, *op. cit. supra,* note 27, at 165; Polents, *op. cit. supra,* note 11, at 254; *Kurs mezhdunarodnogo prava,* Vol. 3, 101 (Moscow, 1967).

[71] E.g., Lisovskii, *op. cit. supra,* note 33 (1970 ed.), at 136; *idem, op. cit. supra,* note 33 (1961 ed.), at 124.

is recognized to procure transit facilities. No reference is made either to the format and method of transmittal of the requisition for a transit permit or joint consultations designed to spell out the mechanics of the operation. No comparable arrangements are billed in the USSR-Algeria and USSR-PDRY agreements.

In Soviet legal literature, discussions of the question of the criteria governing this sort of collaboration usually boil down to recording that through-travel for these purposes is permitted "if the extradited person is not a citizen of the state through which he must proceed and if the offense committed which is grounds for demanding his extradition could likewise warrant direct extradition by the state that is letting him go through."[72]

Each contracting party (USSR v. Iraq, Algeria, PDRY) defrays all the costs incurred on its territory in connection with legal cooperation in criminal matters with the exception of those coupled with the transportation and escorting of the offender, which are charged to the party seeking extradition. The USSR, Greece, and Cyprus strike a more generous deal in that the parties agree to foot all expenses connected with the procurement of legal assistance on their respective territory, except those relating to transit transportation which are assumed by the requesting state (this is a service not contemplated in the USSR's ententes with Iraq, Algeria, PDRY). The USSR and Tunisia follow a somewhat similar practice, but limit the extraditing state's financial obligations to payment of the expenses incurred up to the moment of transfer of the extradited individual which, of course, may occur deep in its territory and presumably cause further local costs involved in conveying the *de cujus* to the border to devolve on the applicant state (whereas the USSR-Greece and USSR-Cyprus versions make it sound as though the extraditing state would assume all the relevant expenses entered on its territory regardless of who was responsible for conveying the offender out of the country). Here, too, the claimant state pays the costs of transit transportation.

In addition to this standard ensemble of extradition services, a *sui generis* arrangement for interstate rendition operates between the USSR and Finland under the auspices of the treaty of September 27, 1962, on the lease to Finland of the Soviet portion of the Saimen canal and the island of Malyi Vysotskii.[73] The agreement makes

---

[72] Menzhinskii, *op. cit. supra,* note 12 (1981 ed.) at 239-40; *idem, op. cit. supra,* note 12 (1966 ed.) at 317.

[73] *Ved. SSR* 1963 No. 36 Art. 389.

it clear that Soviet legislation and Soviet organs of authority continue to function on the leased territories with corresponding exceptions to the extent, however, that these exceptions do not affect
the interests of the USSR and its sovereignty. Finland is afforded
the right to regulate certain matters in the rented zone between
Finnish citizens and institutions according to its own legislation
pertaining to labour relations, communal, family, and commercial
and financial affairs. The list subsequently could be revised by mutual consent of the parties. In principle, the effect of Soviet criminal
law applies in the designated area, but the USSR did consent to
restrain the exercise of its powers there by conceding that "cases
of violations of the law committed in the leased territories by citizens
of Finland with respect to Finnish physical and juridical persons,
or by Finnish citizens with respect to the physical and juridical persons of third countries, or by citizens of third countries with respect
to Finnish physical and juridical persons, and not affecting the interests of the USSR and its sovereignty shall be transferred by Soviet
organs of authority for handling and resolution by the Finnish organs of authority on the territory of Finland." The entente doubtless works "to limit the competence of Soviet institutions in dealing
with criminal cases apropos foreigners, even where the latter commit a crime on the territory of the USSR."[74]

The format is unusual in that the present dispensation is purely
local in scope, whereas normally an engagement to extradite is
drawn on a national scale, and the traffic runs one way only, from
the USSR to Finland, but not *vice versa,* so that Finland owes no
reciprocal duty. Furthermore, the script mentions none of the traditional safeguards that accompany the phenomenon of extradition,
for example, tight eligibility criteria, equivalency, speciality, and
fails to indicate the procedures to be followed in order to obtain
the surrender of the *de cujus* in these circumstances. Basically, then,
what we seem to have in this instance is a decision on the part of
the Soviet regime to waive jurisdiction over offences considered to
be a "private" concern of the Finnish tenants of the assigned enclave provided these incidents do not impair the interests or
sovereignty of the USSR. The special status of the premises accounts for Moscow's willingness to compromise on the issue of the
primacy of territorial sovereignty in the discharge of criminal justice
and to treat these events as though the Soviet Union has no real

---

[74] Marysheva, *op. cit. supra,* note 13, at 148.

stake in policing disputes strictly among foreigners, although technically recorded as having occurred on territory to which the USSR retains residual title. One is tempted to portray the scheme as involving a species of *ad hoc* administrative refoulement favoring Finnish control of sundry infractions instead of deploying the elaborate routine associated with the established mode of procurement of extradition relief on the international scene in response to serious breaches of the criminal law canon.

The express bar in the core agreements between the USSR and its partners to the surrender of one's own citizens spells the need to devise an alternative solution to meet this contingency. In that vein, each signatory (USSR v. Iraq, Algeria, Tunisia, PDRY) undertakes to instigate, at the request of the other side in accordance with its legislation, the criminal pursuit of its citizens suspected of having committed on the territory of the other a crime deemed extraditable under the terms of the relevant agreement. A certificate containing information about the crime and all the available evidence must be appended to the request. The solicited party notifies the requesting party of the results of the criminal proceedings and, where a verdict is rendered, transmits a copy thereof.

By contrast, the USSR-Greece and USSR-Cyprus versions feature a general duty to prosecute one's own citizens alleged to have committed a crime on the territory of the other partner without requiring that the imputed offence qualify as extraditable. Criminal charges filed by an injured party in accordance with the laws of one signatory state with its competent institutions by the prescribed deadline are likewise valid on the territory of the other signatory state. Persons who suffered material damage owing to a crime concerning which a request to initiate criminal prosecution has been submitted may participate in the case if they have filed claims for compensation of losses. Considerably more detail is now forthcoming on how to bid for this remedy. The requisition must be put in writing and contain the designation of the requesting institution; a description of the acts constituting the crime the prosecution of which is being sought; as precise an indication as possible of the time and place of commission of the act; the text of the law of the requesting state which brands the act a crime; the name and surname of the suspect, data about his nationality, place of residence or sojourn and other vital statistics and, if possible, a sketch of the individual's physical appearance, a photograph, and fingerprints; a statement by the injured party in connection with criminal charges stemming from the complaint filed by such a person and claiming compensation for losses, where appropriate; and available information about the size of the material injury caused by the crime. Reports of the preliminary investigation and evidence in possession of the requesting state must accompany the requisition. The transfer of objects that are identified as instruments of a crime or that the criminal obtained as a result of such a crime must comply with the procedure sanctioned by the respective agreement for regulating traffic in items implicated in a crime.

The concept of prosecution of a citizen at home for a crime committed abroad, Soviet spokesmen contend, "graphically illustrates the principle of inevitability of punishment which governs relations between states in the domain of struggle against criminality."[75] A similar recourse is afforded pursuant to the terms of the Soviet Union's treaty with Finland on legal defence and legal assistance in civil, family, and criminal cases of August 11, 1978;[76] it does not, however, contemplate extradition liaisons. The entente predates its Greek and Cypriot companions by testing the policy of mandating prosecution of one's own citizens at the request of the other contracting party for committing a crime on the latter's territory without further attachments. The extraditability factor does not fit here in any case and so, once again, there is a blanket empowerment to punish a native son/daughter at the behest of the foreign partner on whose territory the offence occurred. The instructions regarding the paperwork required on this occasion served as the prototype for the matching clauses in the Greek and Cypriot entries, while the obligation assumed by the requested state to inform its partners of the measures taken upon receiving that kind of application and the upshot of the criminal prosecution and to dispatch a copy of the decision rendered in the matter recalls the Iraqi precedent. The Soviet-Finnish specimen differs from the USSR-Greece and USSR-Cyprus editions which it otherwise closely resembles in this section by eschewing all accompanying reference to the role of privately prompted criminal proceedings.

The Soviet-Finnish brand also veers away sharply from the rest (both the Arab branch and the Greek/Cypriot affiliate) in imposing an array of stringent external conditions on the operation of this piece of equipment. Thus, the services must be denied if their

[75] *Ibid.*, 169.
[76] *Ved. SSR* 1980 No. 34 Art. 690.

procurement might harm the sovereignty or security or run counter to the fundamental principles of legislation of the requested state;
the act charged is not recognized as a crime by the legislation of
the requested state; prosecution for the act charged is barred under the legislation of the requested state because the statute of limitations had lapsed, owing to an act of amnesty or on some other
valid grounds. In addition, a bid for that sort of assistance may
be refused when a decision has been made on the territory of the
requested state apropos that particular offence not to file charges
or to drop the charges, or a verdict was rendered, or, if in connection with the crime, preliminary investigation is in progress or the
case is being heard before a court on the territory of the requested
state.

The rationale for inserting these safeguards lies in the bare logistics of having to compensate for the absence of extradition provisions in the Soviet-Finnish treaty. In the Arab agreements, for
instance, analogous injunctions are brought into play by the simple expedient of hitching this stage of the drill to the extraditability quotient and allowing the hurdles set up on that track to control
this routine as well. Ultimately, then, the USSR's arrangements
with Greece and Cyprus emerge as the most liberal in the lot on
that score in that, if read literally, the respective texts bind the interested parties to prosecute their own citizens for committing a
crime on the other partner's territory at the latter's request without
option. Accounts by Soviet spokesmen tend to confirm the impression of the sweeping scope of the undertaking by pointing out, *inter
alia,* that:

the duty to engage in criminal pursuit is extended to any act which is
considered a crime...the question is resolved relating to indictment upon
the complaint of an injured party. If, for instance, at stake are criminal
cases which are instituted in the USSR per the complaint of the injured
party (Art. 27 of the Code of Criminal Procedure of the RSFSR)—cases
of slander, insult, battery, the question then arises whether it is sufficient
for criminal prosecution in the foreign state that a complaint was filed
by the injured person with a Soviet court. In accordance with the treaties,
criminal charges pressed by the injured party pursuant to the laws of one
state in its competent organs by the prescribed deadline are valid also
on the territory of the other contracting state...the matter is resolved
of hearing a civil suit in a case in connection with which the question
is raised of waging prosecution. Persons filing claims for compensation
of damage caused by the crime are joined to the cases.

In several respects, the line dividing socialist from non-socialist practices here has been blurred vis-à-vis Greece and Cyprus— creating a degree of intimacy between the USSR and these two countries that had previously seemed suitable only for intramural commerce. The rapprochement is, in fact, hailed as a positive sign:

The obligation to prosecute envisaged in the designated treaties [i.e., between the USSR and its socialist mates]: (1) independently of extradition; (2) with respect to any crime; (3) even in those cases where in the requested state the given act is not criminally punishable—attests to trust in the practice of the institutions of justice of the contracting states, the new level of development of legal assistance in criminal matters. Such a form of regulation ought also to be espoused in the other treaties of the USSR on legal assistance, added to which, in our opinion, there is no impediment to the inclusion of a number of the rules discussed in the treaties of the USSR with non-socialist countries as well. In the treaty of the USSR with Greece many of them can already be found (Arts. 35-36, 54), in particular, the obligation is contemplated of pursuing criminal prosecution in regard to any crimes and not only those which entail extradition. Close to them are the norms of Art. 26 of the treaty of the USSR with Finland on legal defense and legal assistance.[77]

The procedural picture, too, looks clearer. It should be noted, however, that this kind of prosecution "on assignment" occurs solely upon receipt of a corresponding request which "makes this genre of legal assistance resemble the performance of requisitions in criminal cases." To be sure, the kinship with extradition is also very strong; that dependency is openly acknowledged in the language of the Arab quartet. The manner of preparing and submitting a requisition for such prosecution gets proper attention in the Finnish, Greek, and Cypriot samples. As distinct from a demand for extradition where proof need not be furnished, a requisition seeking "proxy" prosecution must supply the materials of the inquiry and preliminary investigation and the evidence in possession of the agency which submits the application, along with whatever objects pertain to the case. The purpose of notifying the requesting agency of the final results of the proceedings and sending it a copy of the verdict is to keep the authorities informed and to put an end to any local proceedings still afoot, that is, if charges were filed, they must be dropped and, if charges have not yet been filed, the competent authorities are forthwith stopped from doing so.[78]

[77] Marysheva, *op. cit. supra*, note 13, at 172.

[78] *Ibid.*, 169, 171-72.

Unlike the other agreements, the Soviet-Finnish pact had hitherto not dealt with the mode of implementation of the proposed scheme of cooperation in the realm of criminal justice. The schedule is familiar. For example, legal assistance is afforded through diplomatic channels—a fixture of the Soviet record of dealings with non-socialist partners. An annexed protocol further spells out that: only the organs of the USSR procuracy and the public prosecutor of Finland are entitled to contact each other with demands to instigate criminal prosecution and, in Finland, criminal prosecution for crimes committed abroad is initiated on orders of the Chancellor of Justice.

Finally, the Soviet Union's agreements with Greece and Cyprus increase the range of the "prosecution on assignment" medium by importing an artifact whose employment so far had been restricted to the inner precincts of the socialist community, namely, the technique governing "transfer of prosecution." The relevant clause directs that, where the accused at the time of the dispatch of the requisition to initiate criminal proceedings is being held in custody on the territory of the contracting party from which the request emanates, the *de cujus* is to be conveyed to the territory of the other party (Greece; transferred to the competent organs on the territory of the other party—Cyprus). This method of passage is practised when a citizen of one state commits a crime on the territory of the other during a temporary sojourn there, say, while on a tourist trip. By past routine and, in particular, the principle of territoriality, the offender ought in this case to be convicted and serve sentence in the state where the crime was committed, unless he managed in the meantime to leave and (probably) return home. Currently, the incident is handled differently: if, for example, a Greek citizen should commit a crime during a stay in the USSR, the Soviet authorities file criminal charges against the individual and then transfer the applicable materials and the accused to the Greek organs of criminal prosecution. As has correctly been observed, "transfer of prosecution is an obvious departure from the principle of territoriality in favor of realizing the principle of responsibility per the criterion of the citizenship of the person committing the crime. It presumes a definite allocation, coordination of jurisdiction between states."[79]

At the close of the proceedings in the state that assumed the bur-

[79] L. Gardocki, "Mezhdunarodnoe sotrudnichestvo po ugolovnym delam,"

den of prosecution, the transferring state must consider the criminal convicted and recognize that its organs are barred from staging a new round of proceedings in the case. The detour is not afforded crimes against the state, especially grave crimes, for example, murder and robbery, because they strike a major social chord. The desiderata of social deterrence supposedly also militate against transfer of prosecution. Furthermore, these cases tend to be complicated from an evidentiary point of view and letting them be tried abroad can easily create difficulties in establishing the truth. Equally inexpedient is resort to this proxy when several suspects are involved who are nationals of different states, when the act counts as a crime only where it was committed, and when the criminal code of the state of which the wrongdoer is a citizen does not brand the act a crime. Hence, the new pipeline has primarily operated as a means of funnelling abroad a grab bag of cases of petty infractions and the track record of the judicial and investigatory organs of the socialist states to date attests that

frequently the demands to initiate criminal prosecution are dispatched in accordance with the treaties not only in cases of impossibility of filing charges against the guilty person owing to his stay in another country, but also in those cases where the crime does not represent a major social danger, does not infringe on the social and state order. In the latter instances, often all the materials regarding the foreigner along with a demand that criminal charges be filed against him are dispatched to the country of which he is a national.[80]

Liaisons between the Soviet Union and its Greek and Cypriot partners in this sector can safely be expected to evolve on the same modest scale and procure comparable relief from fairly minor strains of irritation.

Sotsialisticheskaia zakonnost 1979 No. 6, 61-2. See also M. Plachta, "Transfer of Proceedings and Transfer of Prisoners: New Instruments of Cooperation in Criminal Matters among the Socialist Countries of Eastern Europe," 2, Conn. J. Int'l L., 311-43 (1988).

[80] A. I. Bastrykin, "Vozbuzhdenie ugolovnogo presledovaniia po dogovoram o pravovoi pomoshchi mezhdu sotsialisticheskimi gosudarstvami," *Vestnik Leningradskogo universiteta* (1984), No. 17, vyp. 3, 84. The size of the traffic generated by the transfer of prosecution assignments may be quite significant. See L. N. Galenskaia, S. V. Kuzmin, "Sovremennye tendentsii razvitiia dogovornogo sotrudnichestva gosudarstv v borbe s prestupnostiu," *Sovetskii ezhegodnik mezhdunarodnogo prava 1986,* 323 (Moscow, 1987), citing L. Gardocki, *Zagadnienia internacjonalizacy odpowiedzialnosci karneza presestwe popelnione za granica,* 38-39 (Warsaw, 1979).

On the plus side, the message is that: "The institution of transfer of criminal prosecution will be utilized as relations between the socialist countries develop, especially in conditions of expansion of tourism and mutual contacts. The distinguishing characteristic of this institution lies in that the person who committed the crime is brought to trial and, what is particularly important, serves sentence back in his own country."[81] Again, the prospect between the USSR and the non-socialist constituency in this theatre can be painted in analogous colours.

The negative column contains some entries as well. Formally speaking, the principle of legality is slighted because prosecution is pursued, but in a foreign venue. The "export" can also cause hardship to the injured party who is left behind; deploying evidence is apt to encounter difficulties since the case is heard far from the scene of the crime which is quite inconvenient whenever knowledge of the physical setting, language, and so forth, is important to an understanding of the circumstances. The proof gathered by the organs of the transferring state cannot be sufficient for rendering a decision because of the adverse effect of the rule mandating reliance on first-hand sources—a quality forfeited in cross-frontier commuting. Thus, in some criminal cases, the option of transfer of prosecution may well turn out to be inadvisable and unjustified, notwithstanding its feasibility as regards the assignment and execution of punishment. Adoption of the institution of execution of the sentence of another state in criminal cases could solve many of these problems, even though that procedure faces its own technical hurdles that would have to be surmounted before the mechanism might be expected to operate at an optimal level.

A few miscellaneous accessories must still be catalogued to complete the stock-taking. For example, the Soviet-Iraqi agreement calls on each contracting party to notify the other of the sentences (each sentence—USSR v. Algeria, Tunisia) pronounced by their courts on the latter's citizens and entered into final force, to wit, data concerning the convicted person, the court that pronounced sentence, the date when sentence was pronounced, the nature of the crime, and the punishment imposed (plus, if possible, the furnishing on request of a set of fingerprints of the convicted person: USSR-Tunisia). In the Soviet-Greek and Soviet-Cypriot ententes, the for-

---

[81] Gardocki, *op. cit. supra,* note 79.

mula is abbreviated to recording that the parties shall annually exchange information on sentences pronounced by their courts on citizens of the other country and entered into final force. In the Finnish and Tunisian cases, the signatories also agree to supply each other on request, data on sentences that have entered into final force pronounced by the courts of the requested state regarding persons who face criminal charges on the territory of the requesting state. The USSR and Greece and Cyprus, too, arrange to share the contents of their respective files on individuals with a criminal record awaiting arraignment on the territory of the other partner and to inform one another of the results of criminal prosecution of persons concerning whom a request to instigate criminal prosecution had been received and those who had been extradited (dispatching upon request a copy of the sentence that had entered into final force). The result of criminal proceedings against extradited individuals must likewise be communicated to the surrendering state according to the terms of the USSR-PDRY covenant.

Documents that are duly issued or authenticated on the territory of one party by a competent organ are accepted on the territory of the other in accordance with its legislation (Iraq, Algeria; are accepted on the territory of the other without legalization—Tunisia, PDRY). The official documents of one party enjoy on the territory of the other in accordance with its legislation the probative value of official documents (Iraq, Algeria, PDRY). In the USSR-Finland version, documents transmitted by the contracting parties to each other in connection with the procurement of legal assistance are accepted without legalization; the USSR-Greece version adds that official documents issued on the territory of one party in connection with the procurement of legal assistance are also recognized as official documents on the territory of the other party. The USSR and Cyprus opt for a more elaborate script whereby documents issued or witnessed in due form and stamped with the official seal of the competent state institution or official person of one contracting party are said not to require on the territory of the other partner any sort of validation. The waiver extends to signatures on documents and signatures notarized in accordance with the regulations of the respective party. As for documents that are considered official documents on the territory of one party, they are afforded the probative value of official documents on the territory of the other as well.

In the treaties special care is taken to provide for adequate access to the contents of the legal portfolios of the interested parties. Thus, the Soviet Union and Iraq provide that their Ministries of Justice will trade information upon request regarding current or past home legislation and exchange delegations and experience on legal questions (delegations omitted in the Algerian and PDRY samples; both delegations and experience replaced by practice of application of current or past home legislation in the Tunisian text). Vis-à-vis Finland, Greece, and Cyprus, the related package of services includes traffic in information between the respective Ministries of Justice concerning current or past home legislation and judicial practice on legal questions marked for processing pursuant to the agreement.

The Soviet Union and Iraq treaty spells out that all questions encountered in the course of interpretation and implementation of the agreement must be resolved by their Ministries of Justice or settled by a protocol. The USSR and Cyprus and Finland further state that the provisions of the agreement do not affect the rights and duties of the signatories stemming from other international agreements into which they had entered before the present treaty went into effect.

Ad hoc brands of extradition are not an uncommon phenomenon in the annals of international diplomacy. The Soviet regime, too, has resorted to it on several occasions both seeking and extending the favor, on the premise that "'states have always felt that they had the right to surrender any criminal,'"[82] although the duty to do so arose only pursuant to specific treaty engagements. Even at a time when the Soviet Union had no extradition treaties with other states, it was said to follow a policy of "'not refusing individual requests for the extradition of criminals insofar as the state originating the request guaranteed the USSR reciprocity in such cases.'"[83] A similar rationale animated, for instance, the crafting of the law

---

[82] S. B. Krylov, *Mezhdunarodnoe pravo* (V.N. Durdenevskii and, S. B. Krylov, eds.), 426 (Moscow, 1947).

[83] *Ibid.,* 427. Cf. Samartseva, *op. cit. supra,* note 31, at 172: "The Soviet Union visas the possibility of surrendering criminals on condition of reciprocity, in particular, war criminals and persons guilty of crimes against peace and humanity." See also Blatova, *op. cit. supra,* note 44, at 279: "The socialist countries visa the possibility of surrendering criminals on conditions of reciprocity, in particular, war criminals and persons guilty of crimes against peace and humanity." See also Chizhov, *op. cit. supra,* note 27, at 164: "The Soviet Union does not deny the possibility and advisability of international cooperation in the realm of struggle against criminality."

of November 21, 1929,[84] by virtue of which any Soviet official abroad
who refused to come home when summoned by the authorities could
be declared an outlaw, but was not stripped of his Soviet citizenship: "In this manner, the possibility was retained of demanding
the surrender of the person refusing to come back if, in addition
to a political act, he had committed an act regarded as criminal."[85]
The stratagem makes good technical sense, except that the motives
are suspect.

The rare pre-war examples of ad hoc extradition cast the Soviet
brass in the worst possible light. An eyewitness account recalls a
rash of suicides by Persian inmates in the GULAG system during
the late thirties. What happened was that:

one day on Moscow's order all persons of Persian descent were arrested
in Astrakhan. Among them were two categories: those who had lived in
Russia before the revolution; and those who in 1929 after the uprising
against Reza Shah had fled from Persia to the USSR. Virtually no investigation took place and one day all of them got the decision of the special
secret police tribunal. Those who had lived in Russia before the revolution received ten years, and those who in 1929 had fled to the USSR—
compulsory deportation to their native land, which meant the death
penalty back home. They would gladly have sat out ten years in the USSR
and their friends, instead of ten years, would have gladly gone to Persia.
But the cruelty was carefully planned. And those who did not want to
be decapitated in Persia took their own life in the Soviet prison.[86]

Just as vile is a second episode that involved a secret deal between
the Nazi and Soviet regimes soon after the conclusion of the
Molotov-Ribbentrop pact in 1939. Germans and former Austrians
who had found sanctuary in the USSR were rounded up by the
NKVD and handed over to the Gestapo,[87] despite the fact that they
had previously been granted political asylum in the Soviet Union
and fully qualified as political refugees who, even according to Soviet
legal literature, should have enjoyed all the rights associated with
that status, including absolute guarantees against extradition, transfer or expulsion to the state from which they had fled.[88] Estimates

---

[84] *SZ SSSR* 1929 No. 76 Art. 732.

[85] V. Durdenevskii, "Zakon o grazhdanstve Soiuza Sovetskikh Sotsialisticheskikh
Respublik," *Problemy sotsialisticheskogo prava* (1938), No. 6, 63.

[86] *Detstvo v tiurme, Memuary Petra Iakira,* 59-60 (Munich, 1972).

[87] A. Weissberg, *The Accused,* translated by E. Fitzgerald, 502 (New York, 1951).

[88] *Inter alia,* L. N. Galenskaia, *Pravo ubezhishcha, Mezhdunarodnopravovye voprosy,* 42, 65,

of the number of victims of this operation vary from ''some 600 German Communists, most of them Jews,''[89] turned over to the Gestapo at Brest-Litovsk to over 1,000.[90] In today's climate of re-evaluation of many aspects of the country's historical past, this blank spot has also started to attract the critical attention of both local scholars and the mass media, where the incident has recently been denounced as ''one of the most shameful moments of Stalin's game with Berlin.''[91]

As the Second World War drew to a close, bids to punish war criminals and repatriate refugees and displaced persons generated substantial traffic which in many ways reminded one of the mechanics of rendition. Thus, in December 1944, the Soviet government, with the consent of its British and American allies, announced its willingness to accede to a request from Bulgaria to hand over eleven persons accused as war criminals.[92] Similarly, in 1950 the Soviet official news agency reported that ''971 Japanese war prisoners who had perpetrated grave crimes against the Chinese people...were being put at the disposal of the Central People's Government of the

79, 83 (Moscow, 1968); *Iuridicheskii slovar* (P. I. Kudriavtsev, ed.), Vol. 2 (2nd ed., Moscow, 1956), 196.

[89] *New York Times Book Review,* November 18, 1990, at 46.

[90] D. S. Davidovich, ''Tragicheskie stranitsy istorii KPG,'' *Novaia i noveishaia istoriia* (1990), No. 4, 225, referring to figures circulating in the West. A. S. Iakushevskii, ''Sovetsko-Germanskii dogovor o nenapadenii: vzgliad cherez gody,'' *Voprosy istorii KPSS* (1988), No. 8, 91, strikes a strange note in a cursory reference to how ''Discontent was engendered among the anti-fascists living in the USSR also by the individual unfriendly acts of the Soviet leadership toward some of them. In the beginning of 1940, a few groups of German and Austrian anti-fascists who had suffered repression in the thirties and were undergoing investigation or confinement in the USSR were transferred to the German authorities. What is especially unfortunate is that in a majority of cases this was done against the will of those being transferred,'' citing W. Leonhard, *Der Schock des Hitler-Stalin-Paktes*, 66-68, 79-84 (Freiburg, 1986).

[91] *Pravda,* April 30, 1989. According to a recent exposé, co-operation between Germany and the Soviet Union resulting in the deportation of certain prisoners from the USSR began as early as 1937. ''Among the deportees are 'specialists,' political emigrés (quite often the German authorities had no idea that these people were in the USSR) and people who had lived in Russia for decades. They had one thing in common — all were arrested...Prior to 1939, a deportee was issued a passport, although with a short-term visa. There was a chance to run away en route since there is no common border with Germany.'' After 1939, direct handing over was practised. I. Shcherbakova, ''NKVD and Gestapo: Partners by Vocation,'' *Moscow News* (1991), No. 22, at 16.

[92] *Soviet Foreign Policy during the Patriotic War: Documents and Materials,* A. Rothstein tr., Vol. 2, 198 (London, 1945).

Chinese People's Republic.''[93] The problem with the repatriation campaign was that its practice frequently entailed physical duress to compel sizable elements of the refugee and displaced persons population stranded abroad to accept evacuation to their homeland, generally under a misguided impression that those who refused passage back home were right to be afraid of punishment for treason or collaboration with the enemy.[94] The irony, of course, is that although the great majority of these unfortunates were guilty only of having fallen into German hands and surviving the ordeal, they were in fact treated by the Stalin regime as criminals once they were restored to Soviet jurisdiction. Judging, then, by the lot that befell the returnees, the transfers really did amount to a wholesale rendition of ''offenders''—as their western custodians professed to believe to excuse the compulsory measures employed to ship these people home and the Soviet apparatus claimed they were in consigning them to long stretches in the penitentiary system.

A thin line separated the two tracks and the distinction was often ignored by those in charge for the sake of convenience and to achieve their goal of promptly getting most of these uprooted souls resettled where they supposedly belonged. Certainly, that is the impression left by a press account published years later which credited Franz Josef of Liechtenstein with having at the time led his country ''in resisting Soviet demands to extradite about 500 Russians, including Grand Duke Vladimir Cyrillovich, heir to the throne of All the Russias, who had sought shelter in Liechtenstein.''[95]

Nothing comparable in scale marks the record of Soviet relations with the outside world in the intervening period. Even so, cases occasionally do crop up and a random sampling will at least serve to shed light on what sort of matters are at stake here. Thus, we know of an unsuccessful effort in 1962-63 by the Soviet consular branch in India to obtain the surrender of V. S. Tarasov, a mem-

---

[93] *Vneshniaia politika Sovetskogo Soiuza*, 1950 god, 154-55 (Moscow, 1953); *Izvestiia*, April 22, 1950.

[94] "A War Mystery: Return of Reluctant Prisoners to Soviet," *New York Times*, February 24, 1980, at 34; M. R. Elliott, *Pawns of Yalta: Soviet Refugees and America's Role in their Repatriation* (Urbana-Chicago-London, 1982). A precedent had already been set with the treatment accorded 90 servicemen who fell into Japanese hands in the course of border clashes in the Far East and were repatriated in 1940. Each received 10 years in strict regime labour camps which nobody was expected to survive. Post-Second World War returnees uniformly got 6 years at hard labour. V. Gritsenko, "Togda vse byli prestupnikami. Dazhe loshadi," *Izvestiia*, August 9, 1991.

[95] *New York Times*, November 15, 1989, at B28.

ber of the crew of a Soviet merchant vessel, on a theft charge after he had jumped ship in the port of Calcutta and applied for political asylum in the United States.[96] By contrast, in 1978, a Soviet political dissident and former prisoner, Bogdan Klimchuk, managed to cross the Iranian frontier, but was returned by the Shah's regime to the Soviet Union and tossed into prison.[97] In a 1989 story about improved conditions on the Sino-Soviet border, military spokesmen on the Soviet side of the frontier talked of relaxed border duty owing, *inter alia,* to the infrequency of entry/exit violations in either direction and a tested trust in the "Chinese comrades" to give back any Russian who decided to dart next door.[98]

Recently, the United States government deported two accused war criminals, Fedor Fedorenko and Karl Linnas, to the USSR whereas, pursuant to an entente with Finland, the latter is expected to return to the USSR "all Soviet citizens who are caught on Finnish territory while attempting to escape" and routinely does so.[99] In the latest burst of good will, the Soviet Union surrendered to the United States a certain Felix Kolbovskii, occasioning the following remarks by the USSR Deputy Minister of Internal Affairs, V. Trushin:

Instances of surrender of foreign criminals in our practice have up to now been an extremely rare occurrence. However, judging by everything, the situation is noticeably changing. The question of Kolbovskii was decided in just a few days. Through Interpol channels, we were contacted with a request for his surrender only last week. We were remitted the necessary documents, including papers confirming that a warrant for the arrest of Felix Kolbovskii, citizen of the United States, had been issued, signed by the district judge of the city of St. Louis. Kolbovskii is accused of commercial fraud and misrepresentation.

[96] J. N. Saxena, "Extradition of a Soviet Sailor," 4, Am. J. Int'l. L., 883-88 (1963).

[97] *New York Times,* February 19, 1986, at A2, and N. Sharansky, "Rights Parley — or Sham?" *ibid.,* January 22, 1989, at 25.

[98] *New York Times,* April 30, 1989, at 18. Per the Sino-Soviet Joint communique of May 19, 1991, both sides agreed "to promote exchanges and cooperation in the legal sphere, and work out and conclude an accord on judicial assistance in handling civil and criminal cases. The responsible organs of the PRC and the USSR will coordinate in the fight against organized crime, international terrorism, drug trafficking, smuggling and other criminal activities. The forms and methods of cooperation in this respect will be discussed on separate occasions." *Pravda,* May 20, 1991, and 21 *Beijing Review,* 1991, at 17-19.

[99] *Ten Years Later: Violations of the Helsinki Accords, August* 1985, A Helsinki Watch Report, 186, 279 (New York, 1985).

Armed with a permanent visa, the suspect had visited the Soviet Union regularly. His possession of the special entry permit, which few people are privileged to have, was explained by the fact that Kolbovskii headed a joint project operating in the USSR and his entrepreneurial activities on the local scene had already attracted the attention of the KGB, which had no difficulty pinpointing his whereabouts in Moscow. "After concerting with the USSR Procuracy, he was quickly arrested and handed over to officials in the U.S. embassy."

The story has a sequel "The festive mood was somewhat spoiled by a letter of thanks received from the US embassy. Rather by its ending. Expressing their gratitude to the Soviet Interpol agents' contribution to the struggle against international crime, the diplomats said, nevertheless, that the US authorities still could not guarantee Soviets the extradition of requested Soviet citizens in the absence of a bilateral agreement." Notwithstanding the caveat, such favours have been returned. Thus, an inquiry was received from the United States concerning the identity of a certain Soviet citizen of Armenian origin who was detained on charges of illegally entering the country from Mexico. Officials in Moscow established that the man had four previous convictions in the USSR. Since he was in possession of a Soviet passport, the Americans shipped him back to the USSR.

Other countries, too, have adjusted their policy in this department. One individual who stole a million rubles in the USSR fled to the FRG and settled there. The Soviet government asked for his surrender and, despite the absence of an appropriate treaty, the FRG honored the request. A sailor who jumped ship in Australia with a big sum of foreign currency whose provenance he could not explain was scheduled to be flown to Singapore where the local police would put him on board a Soviet aircraft for the last leg of the journey home. Meantime, a Frenchman accused of large-scale swindling was taken into custody in Kaunas and escorted back to France to stand trial with his accomplices.[100]

Though random and piecemeal, these operations help create an

[100] *Izvestiia*, March 13, 1991. V. Kiselyov, "The Gentlemen from Interpol Live in a Computerized Paradise South-East of Moscow but Catch Criminals with Bare Hands," *Moscow News* (1991), No. 31, p. 15; A. Liutyi, "Ostap Bender pozavidoval by," *Pravda*, April 6, 1991; A. Sakhnin, "Na teplokhod ne vernulsia...," *ibid.*, March 15, 1990; Iu. Kovalenko, "Ot Interpola ne skroeshsia dazhe v Kaunase," *Izvestiia*, July 15, 1991.

atmosphere of mutual understanding that, until suitable agreements are concluded, at least makes it possible to interdict some of the more egregious violations of the law staged across state borders and sow the kind of trust that paves the way for more formal rapport. The volume of extradition so far has not been large, but chances are good that the pace will soon pick up. The Soviet Union's present push to engineer a rapprochement with the rest of the world community has also produced expressions of interest in pooling resources to combat the incidence of major social pathologies that now threaten the welfare and stability of the existing world order. A string of treaties, declarations, communiqués, and reports of diplomatic talks records a commitment by the respective parties effectively to cooperate in the fight against organized crimes and illegal drug-trafficking, terrorism, and air piracy.[101] Policing these phenomena will undoubt-

[101] E.g., Soviet-Argentinian declaration of October 25, 1990, *Izvestiia*, October 26, 1990. Soviet-South Korean declaration of December 14, 1990, *Izvestiia*, December 15, 1990. Treaty between the USSR and the FRG of November 9, 1990, *Pravda*, November 10, 1990, and *Vestnik Ministerstva Inostrannykh Del SSSR* 1989 No. 9, 25, and 1990 No. 4, 35; *Report on the USSR*, 1991, No. 22, p. 37, *Pravda*, Aug. 12, 1991. The Netherlands: *Vestnik* 1989 No. 9, 26. Treaty between the USSR and Italy of November 18, 1990, *Pravda*, November 19, 1990, and *Vestnik* 1989 No. 10, 38, and *Izvestiia*, April 24, 1990. Treaty between the USSR and France of October 29, 1990, *Pravda*, October 30, 1990, and *Vestnik* 1989 No. 5, 25. Soviet-Spanish Political Declaration of October 27, 1990, *Pravda*, October 28, 1990, and *Soviet News* 1990 No. 6550, 363, 366, and *Vestnik*, 1990 No. 13, 76, and No. 18, 40-41; Treaty of Friendship and Cooperation of July 9, 1991, *Pravda*, *Izvestiia*, July 13, 1991. United States: *New York Times*, April 7, 1989, at A6; *Report on the USSR* 1989 No. 40, 35; *Vestnik* 1989 No. 24, 76; "Professionals Talking Shop, KGB and CIA: A Joint Answer to Terrorism?," *New Times* 1989 No. 43, 34-35; *Soviet News* 1989 No. 6457, 5; *Izvestiia*, October 3, 1989, December 3, 1990, February 2, 1990, and May 20, 1990; *Chelovek i zakon* 1990 No. 1, 77-80. Great Britain: *New York Times*, May 1, 1988, at 25. Canada: *Pravda*, April 20, 1990. Joint Soviet-Norwegian Statement of June 5, 1991, *Pravda*, *Izvestiia*, June 7, 1991. Joint Soviet-Mexican Declaration of July 4, 1991, *Pravda*, *Izvestiia*, July 6, 1991, mentioning the signature of an agreement on cooperation in the struggle against trafficking in drugs and psychotropic substances and their use. A similar agreement was signed with Turkey in 1990, *Mezhdunarodnaia zhizn',* 1991, No. 8, p. 158. In May 1991, it was announced that the USSR Minister of Internal Affairs and the state secretary of the German Interior Ministry had signed an agreement intended to increase co-operation in fighting organized crime, the narcotics trade, illegal arms dealing, the trade in human beings, illicit gambling, fraud, blackmail, and economic crime, *Report on the USSR*, 1991, No. 22, p. 37. See, also the section on "condemning terrorism" in the Final document of the Vienna meeting of the Conference on Security and Cooperation in Europe, January 1989, and the letter to the UN Secretary-General from the representatives of Bulgaria, Hungary, the GDR, Poland, Romania, the USSR, and Czechoslovakia of July 23, 1987, on measures to prevent international terrorism, *Vestnik* 1988 No. 10, 18-19. For a sampling of recent Soviet pronouncements on the need for closer international cooperation in dealing with these matters, *Vestnik* 1989 No. 1, 55-56,

edly require in the long run closer ties between the institutions of justice of the states concerned and the procurement of extradition relief is one of the more potent weapons in that arsenal.

Similar pressures are felt at the more prosaic level where bids to contain the less serious types of criminal conduct today often cannot succeed without the collaboration of the competent agencies of the affected states. For instance, the gradual vindication of democratic values in the USSR and in those states formerly within its orbit must lead, *inter alia,* to a radical relaxation of controls over the free movement of people, goods, and services across national frontiers. Yet, as Soviet spokesmen are quick to point out, it is precisely this quality of enhanced mobility that contributes to "internationalizing" the scope of criminality and renders imperative widespread collaboration between the law enforcement departments of different states in an effort to quarantine the epidemic. Paradoxically, then, improvements in the local political climate are apt to increase the need for mutual reliance in police and judicial affairs.

In fact, the Soviet press has already sounded the alarm, circulating stories about the marked increase in the Soviet mafia's involvement in car theft rings, burglaries and robberies, prostitution, smuggling, and drug-trafficking in Sweden and Finland.[102] These growing international links have prompted the Moscow CID to call for greater cooperation with other countries to stem the menace. Here is just one example of the kind of development that is causing serious concern in responsible branches of the Soviet legal apparatus:

According to the CID, members of Moscow's mafia have begun running illicit gambling operations in Warsaw and other East European capitals.

And they say there is now a "Polish Connection" in the increased number of foreign cars now making their appearance on the streets of Moscow.

Seventy percent of them have been stolen in Germany and other West European countries and driven by Polish thieves to the border with the USSR, where they are handed over to their Soviet counterparts. From there they end up in Moscow, where they fetch sky-high prices.

Soviet and other European police forces have been powerless up until recently to combat the gangs, because there were no agreements on police cooperation between the countries concerned.

---

and No. 9, 38, and 1990 No. 4, 45; *Soviet News* 1989 No. 6492, 303.

[102] Iu. Kuznetsov, "Prestupniki na eksport," 5 *Pravda,* February 8, 1991.

But the picture is likely to change as the USSR, which recently joined Interpol, becomes fully integrated into the organization.[103]

After the police have done their share, the respective organs of justice will have their work cut out for them, singly and in concert. Moreover, membership in Interpol is bound to encourage older constituents to favour the idea of forging further institutional liaisons with the USSR in this province and agreements sanctioning reciprocal extradition of criminal offenders may well prove attractive. Indeed, a major first step was taken in this direction in 1990 *with the conclusion of an agreement between the USSR and Finland on the reciprocal transfer of persons sentenced to deprivation of freedom in order to undergo punishment.*[104]

Even in simpler terms, the removal of some of the barriers to travel to and from the USSR can have a substantial impact on crime statistics involving Soviet citizens abroad and foreigners visiting the USSR. The mass media has drawn attention to the sizable number of Soviet citizens who, in a hunt for quick profits in other lands, have run afoul of local currency and visa regulations, and have preyed on both hosts and fellow guests and been victimized by their own countrymen. Many have ended up in jail and the same fate awaits others unless measures are soon taken to control the flow and screen out the undesirable elements.[105] Should prophylactic measures fail, both extradition and transfer of prosecution remedies will have to be brought into play to check a situation that plainly has the potential to mushroom.

Wider reliance on extradition in the USSR's relations with regimes hitherto classified as non-socialist means that some adaptations will have to be made in the original models that were intended, respectively, to service the socialist and non-socialist states. While the technical details of the prospective overhaul are hard to pin down at this early stage of the process, general speculation on what they

---

[103] *Soviet Weekly,* January 31, 1991, at 4.

[104] To that effect, see A. Krivopalov, "Nashi syshchiki na rodine Sh. Kholmsa," *Izvestiia,* April 9, 1991, who correctly observes that at the moment the cupboard is bare here. "Dvesti piatdesiat dogovorov," *Mezhdunarodnaia Zhizn',* 1991, No. 8, 158.

[105] Cf. E. Vostrukhov, "Za reshetkoi, Reportazh o sovetskikh turistakh, okazavshikhsia v iugoslavskoi tiurme," *Izvestiia,* March 11, 1991. See also J. Tagliabue, "Smugglers Overrun Germany's Border with East," *New York Times,* February 18, 1991, at 3; R. Borecki, "Russians Are Coming!: A New International Mafia Born from the Economic Chaos of Socialism," *New Times,* 1991, No. 26, at 24-25; "Spekulianty odoleli," *Izvestiia,* July 18, 1991.

might be does not sound implausible. Thus, Moscow's current accent on the goal of de-ideologization of the political scene has had the effect of stripping the old code of socialist mores of its magical properties, in the sense that the special virtues once attributed to intra-socialist culture are no longer treated as a value monopolized by the members of the community and automatically barred from being shared with partners on the opposite side of the doctrinal fence. As a result, the door is now open for a convergence of the two rival prototypes towards a common middle ground where they may be expected to acquire an assortment of each other's more desirable characteristics and shed many of the more egregious differences.

The non-socialist script will probably be rewritten in such a way as to ease the tougher tests designed to defend sovereign priorities. Lowering the hurdles which today leave the heart of the operation at the mercy of either state by allowing broad latitude in exercising unilateral option to invoke domestic legal and policy criteria for determining how relevant treaty norms shall be interpreted and implemented, is a minimal first step. Conversely, various articles of faith which radically affected the mechanics of procurement of legal assistance among socialist states will have to be abandoned.[106] The pious pronouncements that safeguards against infringements on the sovereign rights and national security cares of the member states were redundant in the cozy surroundings of the socialist family, no longer fit the more aloof attitude certain to prevail in this midst once the divorce is consummated. As the appetite for civic diversity asserts itself, the participants are bound to launch experiments with their own models of legislation and inevitably chances will increase that significant divergence from the local legal canon will be invoked to deny legal relief that until recently had been afforded routinely because the very existence of these asymmetries was officially disavowed in the cloistered socialist world. In short, the exceptions of *ordre public* and incompatibility of legal paraphernalia shall doubtless be restored to the books from which they had been expunged to suit the dictates of dogma. The staple exemptions of political offence and asylum which on occasion spare the host state the obligation to perform legal assistance services otherwise owed the requesting state, are also sure to be reactivated. The

---

[106] See the author's "The Soviet Union and International Co-operation in Legal Matters: Criminal Law — The Current Phase," Int'l Comp. L. Qu. (1970) Part 4, at 626-70.

kind of presumed consensus that had obliterated these concepts in the spirit of communion of the socialist congregation cannot escape a realistic assessment and fresh appreciation of their role in the context of normal secular relations between sovereign peers.

Random pieces of evidence have already surfaced indicating that this reappraisal may be afoot in response to ad hoc incidents posing a practical challenge to the status quo. For instance, on September 24, 1989, an independent Hungarian daily, *Mai Nap,* carried a story of a Soviet citizen of Hungarian nationality who had asked for political asylum in Hungary. In June 1990, the Polish news agency PAP reported that two Soviet citizens had now applied for political asylum in Poland: one was a Belorussian man resisting military conscription on religious grounds and the other was a Lithuanian woman whose motives were not identified. By the same token, the old assumption that if one socialist state granted asylum to a fugitive from the "class enemy," the rest would forthwith extend commensurate immunity to the common victim has recently flunked its first test: Edward Lee Howard, a CIA agent who had defected to the Soviet Union, was expelled from Hungary in November 1989 after persistent prodding by American authorities and is thought to have returned to Soviet sanctuary.[107] Nor have the winds of change bypassed the Soviet Union. Erich Honecker, the ex-boss of East Germany, has been granted shelter in the Soviet Union and all requests from the German government for his return have so far been rebuffed. Similarly, Bulgaria has decided to ask the Soviet Union to extradite a Bulgarian Interior Ministry general linked to the death of an exile dissident, Georgi Markov, in London in 1978, but it remains "unclear whether the Soviet authorities will cooperate with General Todorov's extradition."[108] The "rescue" episodes could well set a precedent, if any significance attaches to the following published account:

Soviet Foreign Ministry spokesman Vitalii Churkin told reporters that former Communist officials in Eastern Europe were being persecuted for holding views at variance with the present official line and that the USSR would consider their requests for political asylum on a case-by-case basis...Churkin also said that "witch hunts" were being conducted against

---

[107] *Report on the USSR,* June 29, 1990 at 33; *New York Times,* December 1, 1989, at A5.

[108] E.g., N. Zholkver, "The Honecker Affair," *New Times,* 1991, No. 5 at 24-25; *Report on the USSR,* 1991, No. 23, at 40; A. Ostalskii, "E. Khonekker dolzhen byt nemedlenno vozvrashchen v Germaniiu," *Izvestiia,* Sept. 6, 1991. For the Todorov case, see *New York Times,* July 22, 1991, at A2.

these people in the press and in courtrooms.[109]

On the other hand, the precipitous decline in the public role of the Communist party machine has cast a pall on the attractiveness of the Soviet Union as a retirement home for these foreign legionnaires. Honecker himself is said to be considering settling elsewhere and Markus Wolf, the East German spymaster, has forsaken the Soviet Union to return to Germany, where he may yet stand trial.[110]

These healthy signs of reversion to independent decision making by the region's successor regimes should, if reason triumphs, clear the decks of political ballast, without jettisoning the valuable cargo of equipment designed to promote functional collaboration among the countries concerned to restrain a predicted surge of pathological phenomena undesired by all parties regardless of the current complexion of the respective civic cultures. The bid to renovate the premises will pay an extra dividend inasmuch as whatever rapport solidifies in the wake of the impending alterations should sufficiently resemble the non-socialist scheme, and vice versa, to produce a uniform gauge in place of the broad and narrow tracks previously operated for the benefit of the split constituencies.[111]

What still looms as a major imponderable is the potential impact of the latest constitutional crisis in the USSR on the central government's ability to fulfil its international engagements. The previously monolithic apparatus of the procuracy which is entrusted with extradition matters, has been noticeably weakened by the centrifugal forces now plaguing the Soviet Union and, in particular, by the eruption of secessionist movements which have sought to assemble their own judicial apparatus, including a procuratorial branch insulated from Moscow's control.[112] The Baltic republics

[109] *Report on the USSR* 1991 No. 14 at 35. See also "Seeking Political Asylum: Who Can Expect to Be Granted Political Asylum in the Soviet Union?," *New Times*, 1987 No. 41, at 27.

[110] K. Isakov, "Patient of Ward 603," *New Times*, 1991, No. 23, at 32-3; *New York Times*, October 18, 1991, at A6.

[111] Thus, mentioning that the Soviet Union has 20 or so treaties envisaging the extradition of criminals, a Soviet parliamentary deputy has noted that "they were all drawn up differently and in some instances one procedure is contemplated, and in others something else." What was badly needed here was standardization, along the lines of the model treaty prepared by the UN Committee for the Supression of Crime and the Treatment of Criminals. *Pravda*, September 19, 1990.

[112] For the parlous situation on the law enforcement front, see the item cited in the previous footnote; V. Kozhemiako's interview with V. P. Barannikov, Minister of Internal Affairs of the USSR, *Pravda*, Sept. 26, 1991; V. Maleev's interview with

are a case in point. Thus, the federal procuracy's capacity to deliver the goods destined for international legal assistance commerce may well be hamstrung in some instances by these internal conflicts about who is entitled to exercise which powers. It is too early to tell what future shape the USSR will take. The federation may crumble, in which case the question will arise whether its international treaties lapse forthwith or, alternatively, which successor entity or combination of entities might opt to preserve the preceding arrangements. Or the federation may be converted into a confederation in which a designated central institution will administer the foreign treaties repertory in concert with competent organs of the component units, entailing the necessity of prior agreement for the performance of an international service that requires local input. Or, of course, there may still be an attempt to restore strong central authority on the older model, in which case the uncertainty of who would be in charge of minding the treaty store would be dispelled.

Meanwhile, the situation in the Soviet Union has turned so chaotic that one gets the sense that all these alternatives are being tried concurrently. In the wake of the failed coup, Mr. Gorbachev warned the national Congress that problems of law enforcement were among the top priorities that demanded coordinated action, that is, a renovated union frame.[113] As far as possible, federal law agencies have attempted to conduct business as usual, including the pursuit of international contacts; for example, while the conspirators were being rounded up, an agreement on co-operation was signed in Havana between the USSR procurator offices and the Procurator General of Cuba.[114] Behind the scenes, though, the central police apparatus was already looking for ways to preserve its effectiveness by striking bargains with insurgent republican leaders.[115] For instance, in 1990 an agreement was signed between the government of the Estonian republic and the USSR Ministry of Internal Affairs on mutual relations in the sphere of activity of organs of internal affairs; it sought to ensure co-operation between the respective police branches in order to overcome the constitutional crisis which had undermined the central organization's ability to carry out its duties

---

V. Kravtsev, Procurator General of the USSR, "Zakon vne zakona," *Ekonomika i zhizn',* 1990, No. 47, p. 9; A. Reinieks (First Deputy of the Procurator of the Latvian SSR) "Dve prokuratury — dva zakona," *Pravda,* December 27, 1990.

[113] *New York Times,* September 4, 1991, at A1.

[114] *Izvestiia,* August 27, 1991.

[115] *Izvestiia,* August 2, 1990; *Moscow News,* 1991, No. 5, at 7.

on the territory of certain independence-minded republics. The need was admitted for similar arrangements with other republics and the venture was dubbed a Soviet "Interpol" designed to pool federal and republican resources in repressing criminal operations that spilled over both international and interrepublican borders. The Minister responsible for this "deal," V. Bakatin, was soon dismissed from his post and criticized by his opponents precisely for his role in this affair. After the failed putsch, he re-emerged as the new head of the KGB and let it be known that "of all the things I didn't manage to do as minister, my greatest regret is not finishing this important task," namely, to push through similar agreements with Lithuania, Latvia, Moldova, Russia, Uzbekistan et al. In his opinion, the compromise had allowed the MVD "to go on working as before" at the small price of the parties recognizing each other instead of one bidding to dominate the other.

Of course, after the coup that kind of *modus vivendi* no longer fitted the changed conditions. Instead, the Prime Minister of Estonia and the Minister of Internal Affairs of the USSR recently signed an agreement concerning the struggle against crime; under its terms the Union committed itself to return fugitive offenders to Estonia and to supply the Estonian police with weapons and all necessary equipment.[116]

The weakening of the Union regime has also spurred the republics both to enter into direct contacts with each other and, in a sign of the republics' resurgent sovereignty, to debut on the international arena. In July 1991, the RSFSR and Uzbek ministers of justice signed an agreement on mutual legal assistance and the exchange of information. "This is the first agreement of its kind. The RSFSR will sign similar agreements soon with other republics."[117] By the autumn of that year, the Russian republic was launching its own diplomatic overtures abroad and, symptomatically, its inaugural entente with France featured a protocol on the development of cooperation in the field of law and law enforcement activity.[118]

A significant by-product of these phenomena is the genesis in interrepublican traffic of early examples of other international law practices to accompany their treaty and diplomatic enfranchisement. The picture even includes an appeal for political asylum in Russia

[116] *Izvestiia*, September 14, 1991.

[117] *Report on the USSR*, 1991, No. 31, at 48.

[118] *Izvestiia*, September 26, 1991.

by a people's deputy from Kazakhstan[119]— not perhaps a good omen of how democratic culture is faring in some regions of the former union, but a clear indication that at present power lies in the various constituent entities of the late federation and not in Moscow.

Yet, the deep concern on the part of all to preserve and strengthen the available defences against the onslaught of crime is also unmistakable. Whether by medium of state succession or otherwise, the existing treaties on extradition have an excellent chance of surviving the current turmoil and, in fact, of attracting further increments as a remodeled Soviet Union or its heirs move into the political mainstream and shed old prejudices against joining the rest of the international community in a concerted endeavour to curb the epidemic of crime.

Sommaire

Les traités do coopération judiciaire en matière d'extradition conclus entre l'URSS et les États non ''socialistes''

Les ententes formelles qui ont été conclues entre l'URSS et les pays non "socialistes" et qui prévoient l'échange de services en matière d'extradition sont plutôt une nouveauté en droit international soviétique. Dans cet article, l'auteur analyse les dispositions de tels traités et il les compare avec les conventions conclues en ce domaine entre pays socialistes, afin de déterminer les considérations politiques qui ont influencé le contenu de ces deux types d'accords. Il examine aussi la pratique de l'extradition ad hoc en tant que moyen auxiliaire de coopération entre États dans le cadre de la lutte contre le crime. L'auteur analyse si les changements survenus sur le plan constitutionnel en URSS auront un effet sur la volonté et la capacité du pays ou des régimes successeurs de s'acquitter des obligations qui ont déjà été contractées. Enfin, il souligne que les leaders de la perestroika et de l'après-perestroika de l'ex-URSS souhaitent de plus en plus se joindre au reste de la communauté internationale dans sa lutte contre certains crimes qui menacent le bien-être, la stabilité et la sécurité de toute l'humanité, soit le terrorisme, le traffic des stupéfiants, la prise d'otages, les violations graves des droits de la personne, etc. La réduction des tensions idéologiques entre les États de l'ex-URSS et les pays ayant un credo politique différent facilite la mise en commun des ressources en ce domaine, mise en commun qui auparavant était soit rejetée, soit réduite au plus strict minimum en raison des préjugés doctrinaux qui prévalaient alors de part et d'autre. Il est donc possible aujourd'hui d'espérer qu'un tel rapprochement permettra une lutte plus efficace contre un ennemi commun.

---

[119] *Ibid.,* September 24, 1991.

Réflexions sur la validité des opérations entreprises contre l'Iraq en regard de la Charte des Nations Unies et du droit canadien

YVES LE BOUTHILLIER* ET MICHEL MORIN**

INTRODUCTION

LE 2 AOÛT 1990, les forces armées iraquiennes envahissaient l'État du Koweït, au mépris des règles les plus fondamentales du droit international. Le même jour, le Conseil de sécurité de l'Organisation des Nations Unies condamnait cette invasion, exigeant le retrait des forces de l'Iraq ainsi que le rétablissement du *statu quo ante*.[1] Le 6 août, le Conseil décrétait qu'un embargo économique serait imposé, dans le but de suspendre tout échange commercial avec l'Iraq.[2] Un comité composé de tous les membres du Conseil fut chargé d'examiner les rapports du secrétaire général et de solliciter les infor-

---

* Professeur, Section de common law, Université d'Ottawa.

** Professeur, Section droit civil, Université d'Ottawa.
   Les auteurs tiennent à remercier les collègues qui ont accepté de lire et de commenter leurs manuscrits respectifs. Hélène Laporte a révisé le texte de la première partie, avec sa minutie et son efficacité habituelle. Richard Goulet a assuré un appui assidu à Yves LeBouthillier en qualité d'assistant à la recherche; Denis Boivin, Pierre Dessureault et Sarkis Seraydarian ont effectué bénévolement des recherches. A tous nos remerciements pour leur précieuse collaboration. Deux personnes ont inspiré et soutenu notre décision d'intenter une action Harry Mussom, qui s'est dépensé sans compter pour le mouvement pacifiste, et Jay Hammond, qui a accepté d'être demandeur avec nous, afin de représenter les étudiants susceptibles d'être directement touchés par le conflit. Les auteurs profitent de cette occasion pour leur rendre hommage.

---

[1] Résolution 660 (1990) du 2 août 1990, aux points 2 et 3.

[2] Résolution 661 (1990) du 6 août 1990.

mations requises sur l'application de cette résolution.[3] Le 9 août, à la suite d'une proclamation de l'Iraq décrétant une ''fusion totale et irréversible'' avec le Koweït, le Conseil déclarait que l'annexion du Koweït n'avait ''aucun fondement juridique'' et était ''nulle et non avenue.''[4]

Le 18 août 1990 débutait un autre épisode peu édifiant: certains membres du personnel diplomatique en poste au Koweït ou en Iraq étaient pris en otage. Le Conseil exigeait ce même jour que l'Iraq rapporte les décrets imposant la fermeture des missions diplomatiques ou consulaires au Koweït et retirant l'immunité accordée au personnel de ces missions. Il exigeait également que l'Iraq autorise et facilite le départ du Koweït et de l'Iraq des nationaux d'États tiers, en plus de ne prendre aucune mesure de nature à compromettre leur santé ou leur sécurité.[5] Ces otages seront éventuellement relâchés vers la fin du mois de novembre 1990, mettant ainsi un terme à une autre violation flagrante du droit international.

Le 25 août 1990, pour donner suite à sa décision d'imposer un embargo économique, le Conseil autorisait l'interception de navires, dans les termes qui suivent:

1. *Demande* aux États membres qui coopèrent avec le Gouvernement koweïtien et déploient des forces navales dans la région de prendre des mesures qui soient en rapport avec les circonstances du moment selon qu'il sera nécessaire, sous l'autorité du Conseil de sécurité, pour arrêter tous les navires marchands qui arrivent ou qui partent afin d'inspecter leur cargaison et de s'assurer de leur destination et de faire appliquer strictement les dispositions de la résolution 661 (1990) relatives aux transports maritimes . . .
4. *Demande en outre* aux États concernés de coordonner les actions qu'ils prendront en application des paragraphes qui précèdent, en faisant appel en tant que de besoin aux mécanismes du Comité d'État-major et, après des consultations avec le Secrétaire général, de présenter des rapports au Conseil de sécurité et à son comité créé par la résolution 661 (1990), pour faciliter la surveillance de l'application de ladite résolution.[6]

Seules les interventions visant des navires étaient autorisées par cette résolution. De plus, ces opérations devaient se dérouler sous l'au-

---

[3] *Id.,* point 6.

[4] Résolution 662 (1990) du 9 août 1990.

[5] Résolution 664 (1990) du 18 août 1990. Le Conseil réitérera cette prise de position Résolution 667 (1990) du 16 septembre 1990, Résolution 674 (1990) du 29 octobre 1990.

[6] Résolution 665 (1990) du 25 août 1990.

torité du Conseil de sécurité. Ce dernier a d'ailleurs continué à contrôler l'application des sanctions économiques. Par sa résolution 666,[7] il affirma être le seul organisme habilité à déterminer si des "considérations humanitaires" devaient s'appliquer dans le cas des denrées alimentaires, cette exception ayant été prévue par la résolution 661 du 6 août 1990, celle-là même qui imposait l'embargo. Le Comité créé par cette résolution fut chargé d'examiner cette question, tout comme celle des demandes d'aide présentées conformément à l'article 50 de *la Charte des Nations Unies.*[8] Le Conseil a réaffirmé enfin que l'embargo s'appliquait aux aéronefs.[9]

C'est dans ce contexte qu'il convient d'examiner la résolution 678 du 29 novembre 1990, dont la partie pertinente se lit comme suit:

2. *Autorise* les États qui coopérent avec le Gouvernement koweïtien, si au 15 janvier 1991 l'Iraq n'a pas pleinement appliqué les résolutions susmentionnées conformément au paragraphe 1 ci-dessus, à user de tous les moyens nécessaires pour faire respecter et appliquer la résolution 660 (1990) et toutes les résolutions pertinentes ultérieures et pour rétablir la paix et la sécurité internationales dans la région.[10]

Ainsi, après le 15 janvier 1991, les États Membres devenaient les seuls juges des "moyens nécessaires" devant être employés pour contraindre l'Iraq à se retirer du Koweït "et pour rétablir la paix et la sécurité internationales dans la région." Le Conseil en était réduit à jouer le rôle d'un spectateur impuissant assistant aux opérations d'une coalition de pays. Aucun mécanisme de coordination et de contrôle des opérations militaires n'a été mis en place.

Si les objectifs poursuivis par les résolutions résumées ci-dessus étaient conformes à la *Charte des Nations Unies,* il en va différemment de la résolution 678, qui vide de leur substance les dispositions relatives au rétablissement de la paix et de la sécurité internationales. Cette résolution permet en effet aux États membres d'entreprendre des opérations militaires que le Conseil ne peut ni empêcher, ni contrôler. Par le fait même, cet organe n'est plus en mesure de jouer

---

[7] Adoptée le 13 septembre 1990.

[8] Résolution 669 (1990) du 24 septembre 1990. L'article 50 de la *Charte des Nations Unies* se lit comme suit "Si un État est l'objet de mesures préventives ou coercitives prises par le Conseil de sécurité, tout autre État, qu'il soit ou non Membre des Nations Unies, s'il se trouve en présence de difficultés économiques particulières dues à l'exécution desdites mesures, a le droit de consulter le Conseil de sécurité au sujet de la solution de ces difficultés."

[9] Résolution 670 (1990) du Conseil de sécurité.

[10] Résolution 678 (1990) du 29 novembre 1990.

le rôle qui lui est dévolu par la *Charte des Nations Unies*. Cette abdication de ses fonctions est incompatible avec l'objectif énoncé par le préambule de la Charte, soit ''accepter des principes et instituer des méthodes garantissant qu'il ne sera pas fait usage de la force des armes, sauf dans l'intérêt commun.'' Un tel résultat ne peut être autorisé par la *Charte des Nations Unies*.

On connaî t la suite des événements. Le 16 janvier 1991, une coalition de pays entreprenait un série de bombardements systématiques en Iraq et au Koweït, avec un degré de précision fort difficile à évaluer, tout comme le nombre de victimes civiles et militaires.[11] Pour sa part, l'Iraq dirigeait certains de ses missiles contre l'État d'Israël, qui n'était pas directement impliqué dans le conflit; fort heureusement, ces attaques firent très peu de victimes. Le 22 février 1991, malgré le progrès notable des négociations diplomatiques, le président des États-Unis d'Amérique adressait un autre ultimatum à l'Iraq, exigeant que le retrait de ses troupes débute dès le lendemain à midi, heure de Washington (!). Le 24 février, l'offensive terrestre était lancée; elle prit fin le 28 février.[12] Le 2 mars 1991, le Conseil

---

[11] Le 15 mars 1991, le chef d'état-major des forces aériennes américaines a déclaré lors d'une conférence de presse que 88 500 tonnes de projectiles en tout genre avaient été larguées pendant l'offensive aérienne. De ce nombre, seulement 6 250 tonnes (7 %) étaient guidées au laser, qui auraient atteint leurs cibles dans environ 90 % des cas. Par contre, selon une source anonyme oeuvrant au Pentagone cité par le *Washington Post,* les bombes ordinaires ne touchent leur objectif que dans 25 % des cas. En combinant ces statistiques, on peut affirmer que 70 % des projectiles largués ont raté leurs cibles (*Facts on File, 1991,* Rand McNally and Co., p. 215). La précision ''chirurgicale'' des bombardements fut observée principalement à Bagdad, sans doute parce que les médias y étaient présents. Le 19 février, le sous-ministre iranien des affaires étrangères affirmait que 20 000 civils étaient décédés et que 60 000 personnes avaient été blessées par suite des bombardements (*id.,* p. 105). Dès le 11 février, le Croissant rouge iraquien parlait de 6 à 7 000 décès; pour sa part, le commandant de la guérilla kurde estimait que 3 000 civils étaient décédés dans les districts kurdes (*id.,* p. 91). Signalons enfin que l'ensevelissement sous le sable de milliers de soldats iraquiens sous des tranchées relève de la boucherie pure et simple, non de la ''chirurugie'' (voir les dépêches des agences de presse citées par le quotidien *La Presse,* 13 septembre 1991, p. A-1). On notera qu'au Koweî t, l'invasion iraquienne fit quelques centaines de victimes *Facts on File, 1990,* Rand McNally and Co., p. 565, R. W. APPLE Jr., ''Naked Aggression,'' *New York Times,* 3 août 1990, p. A-1. Quelques milliers de personnes sont mortes durant l'occupation; plusieurs personnes furent torturées (Noam CHOMSKY, ''Aftermaths Voices from Below,'' *Z Magazine,* octobre 1991, vol 4, no. 10, pp. 19, 22).

[12] En juin 1991, la *Defense Intelligence Agency* estimait que 100 000 militaires iraquiens avaient péri durant le conflit; il y aurait eu 300 000 blessés (*Facts on file, op. cit. supra* note 11, p. 417). Les quatres journées de combats terrestres firent des victimes autant chez les militaires iraquiens battant en retraite que chez les civils évacuant les zones de combat. Une route engorgée au nord de Koweî t City fut

de sécurité fixait ses exigences pour un cessez-le-feu.[13] Celles-ci étaient immédiatement acceptées par l'Iraq. Le lendemain, le cessez-le-feu était conclu entre les représentants des forces coalisées et ceux de l'armée iraquienne.

Le 5 avril 1991, le Conseil de sécurité énonçait les conditions d'un cessez-le-feu permanent, qui furent acceptées par l'Iraq, non sans protestations.[14] Le même jour, le Conseil "condamne la répression

---

surnommée la "route de la mort" en raison du bombardement systématique qui s'y déroula (*id.*, p. 215).

[13] Résolution 686 (1991). Le Conseil exigeait que l'Iraq revienne sur les mesures prises en vue d'annexer le Koweît, reconnaisse qu'il était responsable des dommages subis du fait de l'invasion de ce pays, libère les détenus ressortissants de pays étrangers ou rende leurs dépouilles mortelles, et restitue les biens koweïtiens saisis lors de l'occupation. De plus, l'Iraq devait mettre fin aux actes d'hostilité, donner accès aux prisonniers de guerre ou rendre les dépouilles mortelles des membres de la coalition, en plus de fournir les éléments d'information permettant de localiser les explosifs ou les armes chimiques situés au Koweît ou dans la zone occupée par la coalition.

[14] Résolution 687 (1991). La résolution crée une zone démilitarisée s'étendant sur dix kilomètres à l'intérieur de l'Iraq et sur cinq kilomètres à l'intérieur du Koweît, à partir de la frontière reconnue par un accord de 1963. Cette zone doit être surveillée par un groupe d'observateurs, après quoi les forces de la coalition se retireront complètement de l'Iraq. La résolution "décide" en outre que l'Iraq "doit accepter" (!) la destruction ou l'enlèvement d'armes chimiques et biologiques, ainsi que des missiles ayant une portée de plus de 150 kilomètres. Le Secrétaire général des Nations Unies est chargé de soumettre un plan prévoyant la création d'une Commission spéciale. Celle-ci sera autorisée à procéder à des inspections en territoire iraquien, puis à se faire remettre des armes chimiques ou biologiques et à superviser la destruction de missiles. De façon similaire, le Directeur de l'Agence internationale de l'énergie atomique et la Commission spéciale doivent s'assurer de la destruction ou de l'enlèvement des matériaux pouvant servir à la fabrication d'armes nucléaires. Enfin, un fonds de compensation est créé, financé à même un pourcentage de la valeur des exportations de pétrole en provenance de l'Iraq, l'embargo économique étant levé pour ce produit. Ici encore, le Secrétaire général est chargé de préparer un texte déterminant le fonctionnement du fonds. La résolution se termine en déclarant qu'après l'acceptation inconditionnelle par l'Iraq de ces conditions, un cessez-le-feu "en bonne et due forme" entrera en vigueur. L'acceptation ayant été signifiée au Conseil, il faut en conclure que le cessez-le-feu est en vigueur.

Le 9 avril 1991, le Conseil acceptait le rapport du Secrétaire général concernant le groupe d'observateurs, baptisé *Mission d'observation des Nations Unies pour l'Iraq et le Koweît*. Le Conseil affirmait que le mandat de ce groupe serait réexaminé tous les six mois, afin de déterminer s'il devait être maintenu (Résolution 689 (1991)). Le 20 mai. le Conseil approuvait la création du Fonds de compensation, selon les modalités proposées par le Secrétaire général (Résolution 692 (1991)). Le 15 août 1991, le Conseil décrétait que 30 % des revenus générés par l'exportation de pétrole iraquien devrait être versé au Fonds de compensation (Résolution 705 (1991). Il autorisait également l'Iraq à exporter du pétrole pendant six mois, à condition que les sommes déboursées par les acheteurs soient intégralement versées

des populations civiles iraquiennes y compris dans les zones de peuplement kurdes," "exige" que l'Iraq "mette fin sans délai à cette répression" et exprime "l'espoir qu'un large dialogue" s'instaure "en vue d'assurer le respect" des droits de la personne en Iraq. Le Conseil "insiste" également pour que l'Iraq autorise l'accès immédiat des organisations humanitaires internationales aux personnes en détresse.[15]

Du côté canadien, les forces armées ont pris part aux opérations militaires autorisées par le Conseil de sécurité des Nations Unies. Leur implication résultait du décret TR/90-III,[16] qui mettait en service actif[17] les forces canadiennes régulières ainsi que les forces de

---

dans un "compte-séquestre" administré par le Secrétaire de l'Organisation. Cet argent devait alors servir à acquérir des produits alimentaires et des médicaments, selon des modalités devant être déterminées par le Secrétaire général; leur distribution devait également se dérouler sous la supervision de l'Organisation. En date du II octobre, les résolutions 707, 712 et 715 (1991) ont complété les précédentes. A propos de l'indemnisation et du contrôle des exportations, Pierre-Marie DUPUY écrit "[le Conseil] constitue ainsi unilatéralement des situations juridiques opposables à tous, au nom d'une conception indubitablement extensive des compétences qu'il possède en matière de rétablissement et de maintien de la paix. Le problème constitutionnel ainsi posé est alors de savoir si le relai du chapitre VII par le relais de l'elliptique article 25 suffit à couvrir une gamme aussi vaste de décisions" "Après la guerre du Golfe...," (1991) 95 *R.G.D.I.P.* 621, 626.

[15] Résolution 688 (1991).

[16] (1990) 124 *Gaz. Can.* II, 4199.

[17] En consultant les dictionnaires, on constate que l'expression "service actif" signifie "être sous les drapeaux," c'est-à-dire servir dans l'armée. Dans le contexte de la *Loi sur la défense nationale,* L.R.C. (1985), c. N-5, il est cependant possible d'être membre des Forces Canadiennes sans être en service actif. Ainsi, les membres de la "force régulière" sont enrôlés pour un "service continu et à plein temps" (art. 15 (1)); ils (ou elles) peuvent cependant être placés en "service actif" (art. 31)). De même, les membres de la "force de réserve" "ne sont pas en service continu et à plein temps," sauf lorsqu'ils sont en service actif (art. 16 (3)). Cette expression signifie donc aller au combat ou être envoyé dans une zone où des hostilités risquent de se produire. Cette interprétation est confirmée par une version antérieure de la *Loi sur la défense nationale,* (S.R.C. 1927, c. 132)

2. En la présente loi, à moins que le context ne s'y oppose, l'expression
(a) "circonstances critiques," "évènement soudain," et "temps critique" signifie guerre, invasion, émeute ou insurection, réelles ou appréhendées...
(c) "en activité" ou "sous les drapeaux" ou "service actif," appliqué à quiconque doit le service militaire, veut dire qu'il est enrôlé, engagé, désigné par le sort ou appelé à l'activité ou au service dans une circonstance critique, ou qu'il est de service, ou a été appelé au service, pour prêter main-forte aux autorités civiles;
(d) "en service" ou "au service" veut dire convoqué pour l'exécution de services militaires autres que ceux spécifiés comme service [actif]; 22....
2. La troupe permanente est disponible en tout temps pour le service général.

réserve. Ce décret fut adopté le 26 septembre 1990, à l'époque où
seul l'embargo maritime était en vigueur. Il autorisait la participation des militaires canadiens en ces termes:

Et attendu qu'il paraît opportun au Canada de participer à toute action
prise en vertu des résolutions 661 et 665 et de prendre toute action qui
peut s'avérer indiquée, conformément à la Charte des Nations Unies.

À ces causes, sur avis conforme du ministre de la Défense nationale
et en vertu de l'alinéa 31 (1) b) de la Loi sur la défense nationale, il plaît
à Son excellence le Gouverneur général en conseil de mettre en service
actif à l'étranger les militaires suivants qui font partie de l'effort militaire
multinational dans la Péninsule arabique et ses environs ou qui lui servent de soutien immédiat. . .

Ainsi, la participation aux opérations destinées à faire respecter
les sanctions économiques était autorisée par ce décret. Il en allait
de même pour toute action subséquente entreprise ''conformément
à la Charte des Nations Unies.'' L'article 31 (1) b) de la *Loi sur la
défense nationale,*[18] sur lequel le décret TR/90-11 est expressément fondé,
permet d'ailleurs de mettre les forces canadiennes en service actif
dans l'hypothèse suivante:

(b) soit en conséquence d'une action entreprise par le Canada aux termes
de la Charte des Nations Unies, du Traité de l'Atlantique-Nord ou de
tout autre instrument semblable pour la défense collective que le Canada
peut souscrire.

Là encore, les forces canadiennes peuvent prendre part aux seules
opérations qui respectent la *Charte des Nations Unies*. Nous avons déjà
mentionné qu'à notre avis, la résolution 678 ne rencontre pas cette
exigence. Il s'ensuit que si les forces canadiennes pouvaient valide-

---

64. Le gouverneur en conseil peut mettre la milice. . .en service actif. . .en quelque moment que ce soit où il paraît à propos de le faire en raison de circonstances critiques.

73. Lorsqu'un officier ou soldat est tué au service actif, ou meurt de blessures
reçues ou de maladies contractées au service actif, à l'exercice ou à l'instruc-
tion, ou pendant qu'il est en service, il est pourvu au soulagement de sa veuve
et de sa famille, à même le Trésor public, suivant l'échelle prévue.

Dans l'article 2 (d), nous avons substitué ''service actif'' à l'expression ''service
d'activité'' pour tenir compte du fait qu'une seule expression est utilisée tout au
long de la version anglaise, soit *on active service* (voir art. 2 (g) et 2 (h)). La version
française compte pas moins de quatres expressions (service actif, sous les drapeaux,
en activité, service d'activité). Nous croyons que l'article 73 montre bien que le
service actif se déroule en zone de combat, puisu'il ne désigne ni l'entraînement,
ni le service ordinaire.

18 L.R.C. (1985), c. N-5, telle que modifiée: L.R.C. (1985), c. 31 (1er supp.), art. 60,
Ann. I, art. 14, en vigueur le 2 octobre 1986: (1986) 120 *Gaz. Can.* II, 4379.

ment participer à l'arraisonnement et à l'inspection des navires dans le Golfe Persique, il n'en va pas de même pour les opérations militaires dirigées contre l'Iraq et découlant de la résolution 678. Dans la mesure où ces opérations violaient la *Charte des Nations Unies*, elles contrevenaient par le fait même à la *Loi sur la défense nationale*. Il convient cependant de signaler que les forces canadiennes présentes sur les lieux étaient peu considérables.

Le 29 janvier 1991, les auteurs de cet article ont intenté une action déclaratoire en Cour fédérale, invoquant les arguments présentés ci-dessus. Les conclusions priaient la Cour de déclarer que "les forces canadiennes doivent s'abstenir de participer aux opérations entreprises par suite de l'adoption de la résolution 678 du Conseil de sécurité, en particulier les opérations se déroulant sur le territoire de l'État de l'Iraq ou du Koweït ou dans l'espace aérien de ces États." La suite des événements ayant rendu la question théorique, nous avons consenti à la radiation de l'action. Le texte qui suit examine les diverses questions que la Cour aurait dû trancher. Dans un premier temps, la résolution 678 du Conseil de sécurité sera examinée à la lumière de la *Charte des Nations Unies*. Dans un second temps, il deviendra nécessaire de déterminer si les questions posées ci-dessus auraient pu être examinées par les tribunaux canadiens.

I. L'INVALIDITÉ D'UNE RÉSOLUTION AUTORISANT UN USAGE NON
   CONTRÔLÉ DE LA FORCE

Les premières quarante-cinq années d'existence du Conseil de sécurité ont été marquées par la confrontation entre l'Union soviétique et les États-Unis. L'accord des cinq membres permanents étant nécessaire pour assurer son fonctionnement efficace,[19] le Conseil était condamné à l'inaction tant que durait la guerre froide. Ce n'est pas par hasard que la seule fois où le Conseil a été en mesure de consentir à l'usage de la force pour repousser une agression, l'Union soviétique était absente.[20]

À la suite de l'écroulement du mur de Berlin, les espoirs étaient

---

[19] Le paragraphe 27(3) de la Charte des NU confère un droit de veto aux cinq membres permanents du Conseil de sécurité sur toute question non procédurale. Ces membres permanents sont la Chine, les États-Unis, la France, le Royaume-Uni et l'URSS.

[20] En 1950, suite à l'invasion de la Corée du sud par la Corée du nord, le Conseil de sécurité avait adopté une série de résolutions permettant l'usage de la force pour repousser cette agression. Ces résolutions avaient été adoptées malgré l'absence de l'Union soviétique qui, à l'époque, refusait de participer aux réunions

grands que la nouvelle coopération est-ouest se reflète au sein du Conseil. Dans ce contexte, l'agression du Koweït par l'Irak représentait un défi inattendu et déterminant pour l'orientation future de cet organe. L'activité fébrile du Conseil durant la crise, culminant avec l'adoption de la résolution 678 autorisant l'usage de la force contre l'Irak, a été qualifiée de véritable renaissance. Certains ont même écrit qu'enfin, le Conseil fonctionnait comme il était originellement prévu.[21]

Pourtant, nous verrons que dans les faits, le Conseil n'a pas exercé le contrôle souhaité par les auteurs de la Charte et que c'est une coalition d'États, dominée par les États-Unis, qui a été autorisée par la résolution 678 à occuper l'espace militaire (A). Dans un deuxième temps, nous nous interrogerons sur la légalité de la résolution 678 en regard de la Charte (B). Si nous sommes véritablement à l'aube d'un nouvel ordre fondé sur le respect du droit international, il est essentiel que des organes aussi importants que le Conseil de sécurité nous montrent la voie par un respect scrupuleux de sa propre Charte.

A. L'ABDICATION DU CONSEIL DE SÉCURITÉ AU PROFIT DE LA COALITION

Aux termes de la *Charte des Nations Unies,* le Conseil de sécurité joue un rôle primordial dans le maintien de la paix et la sécurité internationales. Il convient donc d'examiner attentivement le mécanisme élaboré par les auteurs de la Charte (1). Dans un deuxième temps, nous verrons les failles de la résolution 678, qui permettait à une coalition d'États échappant au contrôle du Conseil de diriger les opérations militaires dans le Golfe (2).

1. *Le rôle du Conseil de sécurité dans le maintien de la paix et de la sécurité internationales*

Plus que tout autre instrument qui l'ont précédée, la Charte repose sur le concept de sécurité collective pour le maintien de la paix et de la sécurité internationales. Tous les États membres acceptent

---

du Conseil pour protester contre l'exclusion de la Chine populaire. Sur cette affaire, voir *infra* note 77.

[21] B. RUSSETT et J. S. SUTTERLIN, ''The U.N. in a New World Order,'' (1991) 70:2 *Foreign Affairs* 69, 75: ''The Gulf action became possible because the permanent members of the Security Council cooperated on a matter of peace and security in the way originally foreseen when the United Nations was founded.''

qu'ultimement, leur sécurité individuelle repose sur une action commune entreprise contre l'État qui transgresse l'ordre établi. Ce principe est d'ailleurs clairement énoncé dès le préambule[22] et le premier article de la Charte.[23]

L'adhésion des États au concept de sécurité collective a nécessité la création de l'Organisation des Nations Unies,[24] au sein de laquelle le Conseil de sécurité a la responsabilité de mettre en application le principe décrit ci-dessus.[25] L'autorité dévolue à cet organe est l'un des aspects novateurs de la Charte.[26] Alors qu'en matière de maintien de la paix le Conseil de la Société des Nations pouvait uniquement faire des recommandations aux États,[27] le Conseil de sécurité peut prendre des décisions et les imposer aux membres des Nations Unies.[28] De même, contrairement au Pacte de la Société, la Charte met sur pied un dispositif militaire placé sous le contrôle du Conseil.[29] Ces dispositions indiquent clairement une intention de créer un système centralisé permettant à

[22] Le préambule de la Charte des NU déclare: ''NOUS, PEUPLES DES NATIONS UNIES, résolus à préserver les générations futures du fléau de la guerre qui deux fois en l'espace d'une vie humaine a infligé à l'humanité d'indicibles souffrances...ET A CES FINS à unir nos forces pour maintenir la paix et la sécurité internationales, à accepter des principes et instituer des méthodes garantissant qu'il ne sera pas fait usage de la force des armes, sauf dans l'intérêt commun...''

[23] Paragraphe 1(1) de la Charte des NU: ''Les buts des Nations Unies sont les suivants: Maintenir la paix et la sécurité internationales et à cette fin: prendre des mesures collectives efficaces en vue de prévenir et d'écarter les menaces à la paix et de réprimer tout acte d'agression ou autre rupture de la paix.''

[24] Y. DINSTEIN, *War, Aggression and Self-Defense* (1989?), p. 254: ''Collective security postulates the institutionalization of the lawful use of force in the international community. What is required is a multilateral treaty, whereby contracting parties create an international agency vested with the power to employ force against aggressors (and perhaps other law-breakers).''

[25] Article 24 de la Charte des NU: ''Afin d'assurer l'action rapide et efficace de l'Organisation, ses Membres confèrent au Conseil de sécurité la responsabilité principale du maintien de la paix et de la sécurité internationales et reconnaissent qu'en s'acquittant des devoirs que lui impose cette responsabilité le Conseil agit en leur nom.''

[26] R. B. RUSSELL, *United Nations Experience with Military Forces: Political and Legal Aspects* (1964), p. 7.

[27] Article 16 du Pacte de la SDN.

[28] Article 25 de la Charte des NU: ''Les Membres de l'Organisation conviennent d'accepter et d'appliquer les décisions du Conseil de sécurité conformément à la présente Charte'': *voir Avis sur la Namibie,* arrêt C.I.J. Recueil, 1971, p. 16.

[29] Article 42 à 48 de la Charte des NU.

l'Organisation d'intervenir dans les conflits menaçant l'ordre international.[30]

La compétence du Conseil est précisée au chapitre VII de la Charte, aux articles 39 à 51. En vertu de l'article 39, le Conseil peut décider qu'il existe des conditions nécessitant le recours à la sécurité collective. Il peut s'agir d'une menace contre la paix, d'une rupture de la paix ou d'un acte d'agression. Le Conseil peut alors prendre les mesures qui lui paraissent justifiées pour maintenir ou rétablir la paix et la sécurité internationales.[31] Il peut aussi décider quels États auront à mettre en oeuvre ces mesures.[32] Enfin, son action prend préséance sur la souveraineté traditionnelle des États. À titre d'exemple, l'adoption de mesures par le Conseil met fin au droit de légitime défense d'un État.[33]

Les mesures que peut adopter le Conseil sont de deux ordres: les mesures non militaires imposées en vertu de l'article 41[34] et les mesures militaires imposées aux termes de l'article 42 de la Charte. Le Conseil peut recourir à ces dernières mesures si, à son avis, les mesures non militaires se sont révélées insuffisantes. Il peut également prendre immédiatement des mesures militaires s'il estime que les autres types de mesures seraient inadéquates.

L'article 43 de la Charte a pour objet d'assurer au Conseil une capacité d'intervention militaire. À cette fin, les États membres devaient s'engager à mettre à la disposition du Conseil, sur son invitation et conformément à des accords spéciaux, des contingents nationaux.[35] La conclusion d'accords est requise pour déterminer

---

[30] G. FISCHER, "Article 42," dans J.-P. Cot et A. Pellet (dir.), *La Charte des Nations Unies* (1985), pp. 705-16, 706.

[31] Article 39 de la Charte des NU: "Le Conseil de sécurité constate l'existence d'une menace contre la paix, d'une rupture de la paix ou d'un acte d'agression et fait des recommandations ou décide quelles mesures seront prises conformément aux Articles 41 et 42 pour maintenir ou rétablir la paix et la sécurité internationales."

[32] Paragraphe 48(1) de la Charte des NU: "Les mesures nécessaires à l'exécution des décisions du Conseil de sécurité pour le maintien de la paix et de la séurité internationales sont prises par tous les membres des Nations Unies ou certains d'entre eux, selon l'appréciation du Conseil."

[33] Article 51 de la Charte des NU: "Aucune disposition de la présente Charte ne porte atteinte au droit naturel de légitime défense... jusqu'à ce que le Conseil de sécurité ait pris les mesures nécessaires pour maintenir la paix et la sécurité internationales."

[34] L'article 41 de la Charte des NU stipule que ces mesures "peuvent comprendre l'interruption complète ou partielle des relations économiques et des communications ferroviaires, maritimes, aériennes, postales, télégraphiques, radio-électriques et des autres moyens de communications, ainsi que la rupture des relations diplomatiques."

[35] Paragraphe 43(1) de la Charte des NU.

les effectifs et la nature de ces forces, leur degré de préparation et leur emplacement général, ainsi que la nature de l'équipement et de l'assistance à fournir.[36] Pour ce qui est du contrôle, la Charte indique clairement que les forces mises à la disposition du Conseil sont placées sous la direction stratégique d'un comité d'état-major, composé des chefs d'état-major des cinq membres permanents du Conseil de sécurité.[37] Évidemment, ce comité d'état-major est lui-même soumis au contrôle du Conseil,[38] qui a également la responsabilité générale d'élaborer les plans pour l'emploi de toute force armée.[39] Quant à la question du commandement des forces sur le terrain, la Charte prévoit qu'elle sera réglée ultérieurement.[40]

Le chapitre VIII de la Charte complète le chapitre VII, en ajoutant une dimension régionale au mécanisme de sécurité collective. En vertu de l'article 53, le Conseil de sécurité peut utiliser un organisme régional pour l'application des mesures militaires décrétées sous son autorité. Il peut également autoriser le recours aux mesures décidées par des organismes régionaux. Ainsi, même dans le cadre d'opérations régionales auxquelles prennent part un nombre limité d'États, le Conseil continue de jouer un rôle prépondérant. Lorsqu'il délègue l'exécution de mesures coercitives, sa responsabilité demeure néanmoins entière. C'est à lui qu'il incombe de juger de la nécessité des mesures prises, au fur et à mesure de leur application. L'article 54 confirme ce rôle omniprésent du Conseil: ''Le Conseil de sécurité doit, en tout temps, être tenu pleinement au courant de toute action entreprise ou envisagée en vertu d'accords régionaux ou par des organismes régionaux, pour le maintien de la paix et de la sécurité internationale.''

En plus de la délégation limitée de pouvoirs de nature coercitive, prévue aux articles 53 et 54, le Conseil peut aussi déléguer certaines de ses fonctions au secrétaire général en vertu de l'article 98 ou à des organes subsidiaires aux termes de l'article 29.[41] Mis

---

[36] Paragraphe 43(2) de la Charte des NU.

[37] Article 47 de la Charte des NU.

[38] Le modèle de force internationale de l'article 43 se situe entre deux autres considérés à San Francisco: (1) une armée permanente des Nations Unies sous le contrôle exclusif de celles-ci; (2) des contingents nationaux à la disposition du Conseil de sécurité, mais demeurant en tout temps sous le contrôle de leur armée nationale respective. *Voir* le rapport de J. PAUL-BONCOUR, Comité III, UNCIO, vol. XII, 589.

[39] Article 46 de la Charte des NU.

[40] Paragraphe 47(3) de la Charte des NU.

[41] Dans l'avis consultatif *Certaines Dépenses des Nations Unies,* arrêt C.I.J. Recueil, 1962,

à part ces articles, aucune disposition de la Charte ne permet au Conseil de sécurité de déléguer sa responsabilité en matière de maintien de la paix et de la sécurité internationales.

Malheureusement, le système complexe de sécurité collective envisagé par les rédacteurs de la Charte achoppe dès les premières années d'existence de l'Organisation. Les cinq membres permanents du Conseil ne peuvent s'entendre, en 1947, sur la teneur des accords envisagés à l'article 43.[42] À ce jour, ceux-ci n'ont toujours pas été conclus; jusqu'à la crise du Golfe, le rôle du comité d'état-major a été négligeable.[43] De plus, la majorité des personnes écrivant sur le sujet sont d'avis qu'en l'absence de tels accords, un État n'a pas l'obligation de mettre des troupes à la disposition du Conseil, même si celui-ci lui en fait la demande pour répondre à une urgence.[44]

Bien que les rédacteurs de la Charte aient fait preuve d'un optimisme certain en prévoyant la conclusion rapide de ces accords, ils ont dû prévoir une disposition transitoire. Il s'agit de l'article 106, dont l'objet est de permettre à l'Organisation de répondre efficacement aux menaces à la paix. Cet article oblige les cinq États détenant un siège permanent au Conseil de sécurité à se concerter entre eux "en vue d'entreprendre en commun, au nom des Nations Unies, toute action qui pourrait être nécessaire pour maintenir la paix et la sécurité internationales." S'ils agissent alors au nom de l'Organisation, c'est en leur qualité d'États victorieux à l'issue de la Deuxième Guerre mondiale, non à titre de membres permanents du Conseil de sécurité. Libérés de la régle du veto du Conseil, ils sont en échange astreints à celle de l'unanimité. Une action prise conjointement par ces cinq États cesse d'être une action des Nations Unies aussitôt que l'un d'eux juge approprié d'y mettre fin.[45]

151, la Cour déclare à la p. 177: "La Charte ne défend pas au Conseil de sécurité d'agir au moyen des instruments de son choix: au terme de l'article 29 il 'peut créer des organes subsidiaires qu'il juge nécessaires à l'exercice de ses fonctions'; en vertu de l'article 98 il peut charger le Secrétaire général de d'autres fonctions."

[42] *Voir Rapport du Comité d'état-major,* Doc. off. C.S., 1947, supp. no 1.

[43] *Voir* S. D. BAILEY, *The Procedure of the UN Security Council* (1975), p. 211.

[44] D. BOWETT, *Self-Defense in International Law* (1958), p. 205; O. SCHACHTER, "United Nations Law in the Gulf Conflict" (1991) 85 *A.J.I.L.* 452, 464-65; J. STONE, *Legal Controls of International Conflict* (2e éd., 1954); C. CHAUMONT, "Nations Unies et neutralité," (1956) 89 *R.C.A.D.I.* 1, 39-40; F. SEYERSTED, "United Nations Forces: Some Legal Problems," (1961) 37 *B.Y.I.L.* 462.

[45] L'article 107 prévoit que ces mêmes États peuvent entreprendre ou autoriser une

Il existe donc une différence fondamentale entre une action entreprise sous l'autorité de l'article 106 et une action du Conseil de
sécurité entreprise sous l'égide du chapitre VII de la Charte. Dans
le premier cas, le désistement d'un des cinq États met fin à l'action de l'Organisation. Par contre, une opération autorisée par le
Conseil de sécurité se poursuivra tant et aussi longtemps que le
Conseil refuse d'y mettre fin. Compte tenu du fait que les membres
permanents ont un droit de veto, l'opposition d'un seul d'entre eux
entraîne la continuation indéfinie des hostilités. Pour cette raison,
une action autorisée par le Conseil de sécurité est beaucoup plus
lourde de conséquences. Elle pourrait se poursuivre au nom des
Nations Unies même si le consensus initial au sein du Conseil n'existe plus.

Évidemment, le respect intégral du dispositif prévu au chapitre
VII de la Charte rend ce genre d'abus plus improbable. Par le biais
du comité d'état-major, les cinq membres permanents conservent
un contrôle collectif sur les opérations militaires. Ils n'ont alors guère
d'autres choix que de s'entendre, à défaut de quoi ils mettent en
péril les opérations qu'ils ont décidé d'entreprendre.

Par conséquent, le systéme de sécurité collective, mis en place
par les chapitres VII et VIII de la Charte et l'article 106, exige que
les cinq membres permanents agissent de concert et qu'ils contrô-
lent ensemble une action coercitive. Pourtant, avant le déclenchement de la guerrre du Golfe, ces cinq membres avaient été incapables
de s'entendre sur la conclusion d'accords en vertu de l'article 43
ou sur une action conjointe en vertu de l'article 106.[46]

2. *L'absence de contrôle du Conseil de sécurité sur les opérations militaires de la coalition*

Avec la fin de la guerre froide et la nouvelle unanimité des
membres permanents au Conseil, la communauté internationale
était en droit de s'attendre à ce que, suite à l'épuisement des moyens
pacifiques de réglement pris en réponse à l'agression du Koweït

action contre les États ennemis de la deuxième guerre. Bien que le libellé de cet
article soit moins explicite que celui de l'article 106 sur la nécessité d'une action
conjointe, les pays de l'Ouest ont soutenu que "l'article en question ne conférait
aux grandes puissances qu'un droit d'intervention collectif et indivisible." *Voir* V.
Y. GHEBALI, "Article 107," dans J.-P. Cot et A. Pellet (dir.), *La Charte des Nations
Unies* (1985), pp. 1409-16, 1415.

[46] E. JIMENEZ DE ARECHEGA, *Voting and the Handling of Disputes in the Security Council*
(1950), p. 175.; S. KHARE, *The Use of Force under the U.N. Charter*, (1985), p. 187.

par l'Irak, l'Organisation des Nations Unies coordonne une véritable opération de sécurité collective. Ceci aurait marqué d'une empreinte indélébile le nouvel ordre mondial auquel faisait fréquemment allusion le président américain.[48] En l'absence d'accords conclus en vertu de l'article 43, le Conseil aurait pu constituer une armée internationale ou encore invoquer l'article 106. Dans le premier cas, le Conseil aurait demandé aux États de fournir, sur une base volontaire, des troupes pour faire partie d'une force armée soumise à son contrôle. Dans le passé, notamment en ce qui a trait aux opérations de maintien de la paix,[49] l'Organisation a su, à l'occasion, mobiliser sous sa gouverne les resources de plusieurs États pour atteindre ses objectifs. Dans l'alternative, les cinq membres permanents auraient pu diriger une opération conjointe en vertu de l'article 106 et inviter d'autres États à y participer.[50]

La démarche initiale du Conseil laissait espérer qu'on aurait enfin recours au systéme de sécurité collective envisagé par la Charte. À la suite de l'adoption de la résolution 661, qui imposait à l'Irak un régime de sanctions non militaires des plus sévères, les États-Unis ont unilatéralement arraisonné des navires irakiens, afin d'assurer le respect des sanctions décrétées.[51] Cette action, qualifiée par Washington d'acte compatible avec la légitime défense collective du Koweït,[52] a suscité les protestations de certains membres du Conseil de sécurité ainsi que du secrétaire général. À leur avis, ce genre d'action devait être autorisé par le Conseil, conformément aux

---

[47] Plusieurs auteurs ont critiqué l'usage de la force contre l'Iraq comme étant précipité et par conséquent contraire à l'obligation de règlement pacifique des différends. Voir B. H. WESTON, "Security Council Resolution 678 and Persian Gulf Decision Making: Precarious Legitimacy," (1991) 85 *A.J.I.L.* 516, 521; R. FALK, "La force au mépris du droit: les Nations Unies sous la coupe de Washington," dans *Le Monde Diplomatique*, février 1991, p. 3.

[48] Sur le nouvel ordre international, *voir*, entre autres, le commentaire de C. LAYNE, "Why the Gulf War Was Not in the National Interest," dans *The Atlantic Monthly*, juillet 1991, p. 55.

[49] Sur les opérations de maintien de la paix, *voir*, entre autres, D. BOWETT, *United Nations Forces* (1964); J. BALLALOUD, *L'ONU et les opérations de maintien de la paix* (1971).

[50] Notons toutefois que certains auteurs, invoquant le caractère transitoire de l'article 106, ont soutenu que cet article était possiblement désuet. D. BOWETT, *ibid.*, à la p. 277; H. KELSEN, *The Law of the United Nations (with supplement)*, (1966), p. 976; J. W. HALDERMAN, "Legal Basis for United Nations Armed Forces," (1962) 56 *A.J.I.L.* 971, 985.

[51] M. R. GORDON, "Bush Orders Navy to Halt All Shipments of Iraq's Oil and Almost All Its Imports," dans *N.Y. Times*, August 13, 1990, at A-1, col. 4.

[52] P. LEWIS, "Security Council's Rare Unity May Be Threatened over U.S. Warships in the Gulf," dans *N.Y. Times*, 11 août 1991, p. A-1.

mécanismes prévus par la Charte.[53] Ployant sous les pressions de la communauté internationale, Washington a proposé l'adoption de la résolution 665. Par cette résolution le Conseil limitait et contrôlait le recours à la force navale.[54] On y stipule que toutes les actions prises par les États présents dans le Golfe le sont ''sous l'autorité du Conseil de sécurité.'' On ne permet aux États d'agir que pour des fins trés précises: ''arrêter tous les navires marchands qui arrivent ou qui partent afin d'inspecter leur cargaison et de s'assurer de leur destination et de faire appliquer strictement les dispositions de la résolution 661 (1990) relatives aux transports maritimes.'' De plus, le Conseil demande ''aux États concernés de coordonner les actions qu'ils prendront en application des paragraphes qui précédent, en faisant appel en tant que de besoin aux mécanismes du Comité d'État-major...Enfin, le Conseil demande également à ces États ''de présenter des rapports au Conseil de sécurité [après des consultations avec le secrétaire général...pour faciliter la surveillance de l'application de ladite résolution.''

Par contre, le temps venu d'autoriser une attaque armée contre l'Irak, le Conseil de sécurité a laissé le champ libre à une coalition d'États, faisant ainsi écho à la déclaration de George Bush: ''we will not go in with one hand tied behind our back.''[56] Le rôle du Conseil dans le maintien de la paix était alors tout à fait nominal. Il n'a exercé aucun contrôle sur le déroulement des opérations; com-

---

[53] E. SCIOLINO, ''Putting Teeth in an Embargo: How U.S. Convinced the U.N.,'' *N.Y. Times*, 30 août 1991, p. A-1 et A-15 où sont rapportés les faits suivants: ''But by Monday Aug. 13, several members of the Security Council were asserting in a closed meeting that an impatient American President was imposing a blockade, calling it something else, using a questionable legal formula to justify it and doing it without telling anybody. The diplomats, led by Yves Fortier, Canada's representative, argued that the Security Council should instead take a step-by-step approach under the Charter's Article 42, which provides for blockades and other military actions but only with explicit Security Council approval...'' M. Fortier a également fait la déclaration suivante: ''I said that these are uncharted waters, that there are no precedents, so why not play it as the framers of the Charter had envisioned it?''; voir aussi L. C. GREEN, ''Iraq, the U.N. and the Law,'' (1991) 29 *Alb. L.R.* 560, aux pp. 567-68.

[54] M. CHEMILLIER-GENDREAU, ''Que vienne enfin le règne de la loi internationale,'' dans *Le Monde diplomatique*, janvier 1991, p. 18.

[55] Cette référence au Conseil de sécurité contredit ceux qui avaient prononcé cet organe défunt (voir KHARE, *op. cit. supra*, note 46, à la p. 144) ou qui prétendaient qu'on ne pouvait y faire appel en l'absence des accords prévus à l'article 43 (voir M. CADIEUX, dans C.I.J., *Avis consultatif sur certaines dépenses des Nations Unies, Mémoires, plaidoyers et documents*, 1962, p. 302).

[56] Facts on File, 1990, *op. cit. supra*, note 11, à la p. 901.

me à l'époque de la guerre de Corée, les États-Unis ont refusé de placer leurs forces sous contrôle international.[57] Alors que la résolution autorisait des actions autrement plus lourdes de conséquences que celles permises par la résolution 665, les États n'avaient aucune obligation de déposer des rapports sur leurs actions. Il leur suffisait simplement de tenir le Conseil régulièrement informé.

Une telle conduite constitue indéniablement une abdication du Conseil de sécurité, comme l'écrivait récemment Burns Weston.[58] Nous verrons ci-dessous que cette abdication est totale, puisque la résolution 678 n'exige pas que le Conseil précise davantage les objectifs à atteindre, la nature des opérations ou le type d'armement utilisé. Le Conseil n'est pas non plus en mesure d'évaluer la proportionnalité des actions entreprises, ni de décider du déclenchement ou de la durée du conflit armé.[59]

En ce qui concerne les objectifs à atteindre, la marge de manoeuvre qu'offrait le texte de la résolution 678 ne pouvait être plus large. En effet, le Conseil de sécurité ne se limitait pas à demander que soit fait usage de tous les moyens nécessaires "pour faire appliquer la résolution 660 (1990) et toutes les résolutions pertinentes ultérieures," mais aussi "pour rétablir la paix et la sécurité internationales dans la région." Au sujet de la généralité de cet objectif, Oscar Schachter écrit: "This aim appeared to leave room for almost any action by the Security Council that might reason-

---

[57] B. ANDELMAN, "UN Envoy Suggests Soviets Could 'Take Out' Iraqi Leaders," dans *The Sun Times of Canada*, 23 janvier 1991, p. 1. On y rapporte les propos suivants de l'ambassadeur canadien aux Nations Unies M. Yves Fortier: "Canada would have preferred a United Nations command (in the Persian Gulf)...the U.S. would have none of it. Colonel Pickering said, 'No way. We are providing 70 per cent of the hardware, we will have the majority of the body bags. We will not submit to a U.N. command.' "; voir aussi L. C. GREEN, *op. cit. supra*, note 55, à la p. 574. Sur le refus des américains de tout contrôle de l'ONU dans le conflit de Corée, voir RUSSELL, *op. cit. supra*, note 26; L. M. GOODRICH et A. P. SIMONS, *The United Nations and the Maintenance of International Peace and Security* (1955), p. 455.

[58] B. H. WESTON, *op. cit. supra*, note 47, à la p. 526.

[59] Le secrétaire général Javier Perez de Cuellar a lui-même confirmé par les commentaires suivants la mise au rancart de son organisation: "Les hostilités ont été autorisées par le Conseil de sécurité. Ce n'est pas une guerre des Nations Unies. Il n'y a pas de 'casques bleus' ni le drapeau de l'ONU, et je suis seulement informé du déroulement de la guerre par les rapports des alliés. On ne peut pas dire que les Nations Unies soient responsables de cette guerre. Cela dit, c'est une guerre légale dans le sens où elle a été autorisée par le Conseil de sécurité. L'ampleur de cette guerre c'est une toute autre affaire." Ces propos ont été rapportés par A. BASSIR-POUR, "La guerre du golfe: un entretien avec M. Perez de Cuellar," dans *Le Monde*, 9 février 1991, p. 6.

ably be related to ensuring continued peace and security in the Gulf region.''[60]

Ce n'est pas le Conseil de sécurité, comme le prétend Schachter, mais bien la coalition qui était en mesure de décider quels devaient être les objectifs de la résolution 678 et comment ils devaient être atteints. La coalition pouvait se fixer n'importe quel objectif et prendre toute action qu'elle jugeait nécessaire. Toute tentative de restreindre l'ampleur de ses activités aurait pu faire l'objet d'un veto de la part des membres permanents actifs au sein de la coalition.[61] Par conséquent, la coalition pouvait, sans qu'on puisse la contredire, décider que les objectifs de la résolution consistaient en réalité à: obtenir le retrait des troupes irakiennes du Koweït;[62] anéantir la menace militaire que pose l'Irak pour la région;[63] et renverser Saddam Hussein.[64] Avec un objectif aussi vague, il était à craindre que le consensus au sein du Conseil de sécurité ne se désagrège avec le temps.[65]

La coalition dispose de la même marge de manoeuvre quant au type d'actions entreprises, puisque le Conseil n'a imposé aucune limite concernant les moyens à prendre pour atteindre ses objectifs. En fait, la résolution 678 ne prévoyait aucune restriction sur le type d'armement ou sur la nature des opérations permises.[66]

[60] O. SCHACHTER, *op. cit. supra*, note 44, à la p. 467; B. H. WESTON, *op. cit. supra*, note 47, à la p. 525.

[61] C. WARBRICK, ''Current Developments in Public International Law: The Invasion of Kuwait by Iraq,'' (1991) 40 *I.C.L.Q.* 482, 491.

[62] C. J. SABEC, ''The Security Council Comes of Age: An Analysis of the International Legal Response to the Iraqi Invasion of Kuwait,'' (1991) 21 *Ga. J. Int'l & Comp. L.* 63, 99.

[63] E. V. ROSTOW, ''Until What? Enforcement Action or Collective Self-Defense?'', (1991) 85 *A.J.I.L.* 506, 514.

[64] A. PYRICH, ''Recent Developments: United Nations Authorisations of Use of Force,'' (1991) 32 *Harvard I. L. J.* 265, 269.

[65] D. W. GREIG, ''Self-Defense and the Security Council: What Does Article 51 Require?'', (1991) 40 *I.C.L.Q.* 366, 398; K. BOUSTANY, ''La guerre du Golfe et le système d'intervention armée de l'ONU,'' (1990) 28 *A.C.D.I.* 379, 392-93. Un tel désaccord peut même avoir des conséquences inattendues et désastreuses, comme l'a démontré l'intervention de la Chine dans le conflit de Corée, suite à la décision des États-Unis de franchir le 38e parallèle. Sur cette question voir I. F. STONE, *The Hidden History of the Korean War* (1952), p. 137; RUSSELL, *op. cit. supra*, note 26, à la p. 36.

[66] Le secrétaire général des Nations Unis a d'ailleurs reconnu les problèmes d'interprétation que posent des termes tels ''tous les moyens nécessaires'' en affirmant que: ''La résolution 678, malheureusement ou heureusement, cela dépend de quel côté on se place, est très vague. Le texte permet tous les moyens nécessaires. D'un

Analysant le conflit de Corée, Derek Bowett écrit: "one can envisage certain action which would have gone beyond the necessities and the purposes of the United Nations action: for example, the wholesale destruction of every major town in North Korea by an all-out aerial attack."[67]

On peut se demander en quoi l'attaque de la coalition contre l'Irak diffère de l'hypothèse posée par Bowett. Pour Jean Salmon, l'assaut aérien contre l'Irak va au-délà de la résolution 678: "Tout d'abord au nom des nécessités de la guerre les bombardements en Irak s'étendent à toute l'infrastructure du pays: ministères, communications, routes et ponts, industries, ressources énergétiques, complexes chimiques, centrales nucléaires (pourtant surveillées par l'A.I.E.A.). En quoi ces diverses cibles sont-elles conformes à l'exécution des résolutions du Conseil de sécurité concernant la libération du Koweït?"[68]

De fait la détermination de la proportionnalité entre les objectifs à atteindre et les moyens à prendre est laissée à l'appréciation de chaque membre de la coalition,[69] sans que le Conseil ne fixe aucune limite sur les dommages pouvant être infligés.[70] On sait que plusieurs critères servent à évaluer si une action a respecté la règle de proportionnalité. L'un de ces critères est le nombre de victimes. Schachter écrit: "Thus, when defensive action is greatly in excess of the provocation, as measured by relative casualties or scale of weaponry, international opinion will more readily condemn such defense as illegally disproportionate. Some of the Security Council decisions that declared that the use of force be illegal reprisal rather than legitimate defense noted the much higher number of casualties resulting from the defense in relation to those caused by an earlier attack."[71]

En l'espèce, la disproportion entre les pertes irakiennes et les

point de vue humain, la perte d'une vie est toujours de trop. Mais je suis contraint par les règles," dans *Le Monde, supra* note 59.

[67] D. BOWETT, *op. cit. supra,* note 49, à la p. 55.

[68] J. SALMON, "Droit international, politique et idéologie dans la guerre du Golfe," dans Centre de droit international U.L.B., *Entre les lignes: Le droit international et la guerre du Golfe* (1991), pp. 4-12, 11.

[69] C. WARBRICK, *op. cit. supra,* note 61, à la p. 491.

[70] R. FALK, *op. cit. supra,* note 47.

[71] O. SCHACHTER, "The Right of States to Use Armed Force," (1984) 82 *Michigan Law Review* 1619, 1637; *voir aussi* D. BOWETT, "Reprisals Involving Recourse to Armed Force," (1972) 66 *A.J.I.L.* 1, 33-36.

pertes alliées, incluant celles du Koweït, est beaucoup plus grande
que toute disparité mentionnée dans les résolutions auxquelles
Schacter fait allusion.[72] En supposant qu'une telle conduite soit contraire aux règles du droit international régissant les conflits armés,[73]
le Conseil de sécurité, en autorisant l'usage de la force sans en contrôler la mise en oeuvre, s'empêche de sanctionner tout membre
permanent qui serait responsable d'une telle action.

Le Conseil a aussi abdiqué tout contrôle sur le déclenchement
et la durée des hostilités. En fixant d'avance une date à partir de
laquelle la force peut être utilisée par la coalition, le Conseil n'est
plus l'autorité qui décide si la force doit être utilisée, et le cas échéant,
à partir de quel moment. Il permet ainsi à un membre permanent
d'empêcher que cette date soit repoussée, même si un réglement
pacifique semble imminent. Le Conseil n'a pas davantage prévu
de durée maximale à l'exercice de la force, au terme de laquelle
la coalition doit présenter une demande de renouvellement de son
mandat. Pourtant, dès la fin des hostilités, les résolutions du Conseil concernant le cessez-le-feu, la réparation des dommages subis
et le désarmement de l'Iraq contenaient des restrictions de cette

[72] M. ALBERT, N. CHOMSKY et S. SHALOM, "A Post-War Teach-In," avril (1991) *Z Magazine* 43, 57; voir aussi *supra,* notes 11 et 12.

[73] L'application du concept de proportionnalité dans le cadre d'un conflit armé sou-
lève de nombreuses questions comme en témoigne le commentaire suivant: "For
it is clear that sometimes the course which will result in the fewest lives lost may
involve killing innocents. Such was alleged to be the case in the atomic bombing
of Hiroshima and Nagasaki, which was justified in part by appeal to the quantitative principle. The quantitative principle requires modification, however, before
it can plausibly be thought to be actually held by nations...it might require accepting a greater loss of life on one's side if by so doing one could achieve fewer
deaths overall, and few nations would accept such an exchange. A qualified quantitative principle would assert that one ought to pursue those war policies consistent with eventual victory that will result in fewest lives lost on one's own side.
Now it is clear that the quantitative principle even in this modified sense may conflict with the principle of innocence...," R. L. HOLMES, *On War and Morality*
(1989), p. 105; voir aussi R. W. TUCKER "Justice and the War," (1991) 25 *The
National Interest* 108, aux pp. 111-12: "In the conduct of the Gulf War, the issue of
proportionality also arose as a result of the huge disparity in combatant casualties
suffered by the respective sides. Is proportionnality violated when a belligerent
takes a multitude of the enemy's lives in order to save, or simply not to put at
risk, a few of his own? That this was done in the recent war is clear. In doing so,
military commanders invoked the plea of military necessity as justification for their
actions. Given the indeterminate character of military necessity, the appeal to it
often appeared plausible. Even so, there are surely limits, ill-defined though they
may be, to the number of enemy lives that may justifiably be taken to avoid risk-
ing however small a number of one's own. At some point, the imperious claims
of military necessity must yield to the claims of humanity."

nature, qui sont également courantes pour les opérations de maintien de la paix.[74]

La résolution 678, en plus de ne prévoir aucune limite précise, a *de facto* légitimé toute action prise au nom du Conseil, puisqu'un membre permanent pouvait utiliser son droit de veto et empêcher toute condamnation de son comportement. Lorsqu'un membre permanent se fonde sur une telle résolution et décide de donner préséance à ses intérêts nationaux, c'est l'ensemble de l'organisation qui s'en trouve discréditée.[75] C'est d'ailleurs précisément pour empêcher cette situation que la Charte prévoit un mécanisme de sécurité collective. Pourtant, à deux reprises, le Conseil a ignoré ce mécanisme au profit de quelques États: la première fois lors de la guerre de Corée et la deuxième fois, lors de la guerre du Golfe.

Après la guerre de Corée, Derek Bowett écrit:

> However difficult it may be for the political organs of the United Nations to agree upon and formulate a continuing policy, it is considered that there is extraordinary danger in the proposal to entrust any United Nations operation involving the use of force in the name of the United Nations to a limited group of States. This would be tantamount, virtually, to an abdication by the United Nations of its responsibility in favour of a grouping of States, generally regional in character, which could then, in the name of the United Nations (and with all the moral and even financial backing which that implies) pursue a policy unacceptable to the collectivity of States.[76]

Si le contexte de la guerre froide était l'une des principales motivations pour ne pas placer les opérations en Corée sous le contrôle du Conseil de sécurité,[77] les mêmes difficultés n'existaient pas lors

---

[74] Voir *supra*, note 14; au sujet des opérations de maintien de la paix, voir M. AKEHURST, *A Modern Introduction to International Law* (4e éd., 1982) aux pp. 193 à 195.

[75] K. BOUSTANY, *op. cit. supra*, note 65, aux pp. 392 et 398; A. PYRICH, *op. cit. supra*, note 64, à la p. 272; B. RUSSETT et J. S. SUTTERLIN, *op. cit. supra*, note 21, aux pp. 76-77.

[76] D. BOWETT, *op. cit. supra*, note 49, à la p. 215.

[77] Certains ont vu dans l'action du Conseil lors de la crise du Golfe une analogie avec l'affaire de la Corée. Cette affaire a débuté le 25 juin 1950 lorsque les troupes de la Corée du Nord ont envahi le territoire de la Corée du sud. Le Conseil de sécurité a réagi promptement en adoptant, entre le 25 juin et le 7 juillet, trois résolutions dont les points saillants étaient: (1) une invitation aux autorités de la Corée du nord "à retirer immédiatement leurs forces armées" (résolution du 25 juin), (2) une recommandation aux Etats membres "d'apporter à la République de Corée toute l'aide nécessaire pour repousser les assaillants et rétablir dans cette région la paix et la sécurité internationales" (résolution du 27 juin) et (3) une recommandation aux États membres de placer leurs forces militaires "à la disposition d'un commandement unifié sous l'autorité des États-Unis" à qui il appartiendra de

du conflit dans le Golfe.

Ayant exposé les graves problèmes découlant de l'attitude du Conseil de sécurité dans cette affaire, il nous reste à examiner la résolution 678 sur le plan de la légalité. Plusieurs personnes écrivant sur le sujet ont conclu que la résolution était conforme à la Charte,[78] bien que certaines aient mis en doute sa légitimité[79] ou noté

désigner "le commandant en chef de ses forces" (résolution du 7 juillet). Plusieurs auteurs ont disputé la valeur de précédent de cette affaire comme opération de sécurité collective. Les critiques sont de trois ordres: (1) le Conseil a adopté ces résolutions malgré l'absence de l'Union soviétique alors que le paragraphe 27(3) de la Charte requière le vote positif de tous les membres permanents pour des questions de cette importance. Notons toutefois que dans l'*Avis sur la Namibie, supra* note 28 la Cour internationale de justice a indiqué qu'une pratique soutenue au sein du Conseil de sécurité démontrait qu'une abstention n'empêchait pas l'adoption d'une résolution. La Cour écrit à la p. 22: "pour empêcher l'adoption d'une résolution exigeant l'unanimité des membres permanents, une membre permanent doit émettre un vote négatif." (2) Le Conseil de sécurité a recommandé l'usage de la force alors qu'en vertu des articles 39 et 42 il ne peut que décider d'user de la force. Sur cette question voir *infra*, note 121. (3) Le Conseil a été, contrairement à l'article 42, complètement évincé au profit des États-Unis pour toutes les questions ayant trait au contrôle des opérations. M. VIRALLY, *L'Organisation mondiale* (1972), à la p. 474 a qualifié l'opération "d'habillage juridique." Voir également M. C. ALIBERT, *Du droit de se faire justice dans la société internationale depuis 1945* (1983), p. 68; R. VAYRYNEN, "The United Nations and the Resolution of International Conflicts," (1985) xx *Cooperation and Conflict* 141, 151. Pour certains auteurs il s'agirait d'une opération de légitime défense collective dirigée par les États-Unies plutôt que d'une opération des Nations Unies: voir M. AKEHURST, *op. cit. supra*, note 74, p. 224; H. KELSEN, *op. cit. supra*, note 50, aux pp. 936-37; J. STONE, *op. cit. supra*, note 44, p. 232. Devant tant d'incertitude face à la nature juridique des opérations de Corée il est difficile d'y voir un précédent utile. Ainsi J. L. KUNZ, "Sanctions in International Law," (1960) 54 *A.J.I.L.* 324 écrit à la p. 341: "the armed action in Korea was not, in a strict legal sense, an enforcement action by the United Nations; it is also probable that this action will not constitute a precedent, but remain rather an isolated event." De même on ne peut possiblement argumenter que la seule pratique du Conseil dans l'affaire de Corée suffit en soi pour modifier la Charte. Sur cette question R. HIGGINS, "The Court of the European Communities," (1961) 37 *B.Y.I.L.*, écrit à la p. 322: "the text of the charter of an international organization may be modified or extended by its operation in practice. How far such practice, if not embodied in a formal amendment, is legally binding is an interesting question. It might be difficult to maintain that because the Security Council had followed a certain practice on two or three occasions, such practice should constitute a binding precedent." Notons enfin que dans l'affaire de Corée le Conseil de sécurité a éventuellement transféré la question à l'Assemblée générale par le biais de la résolution "l'Union pour la paix," une résolution en soi très controversée. Evidemment, le fait que l'Assemblée générale ait été saisie de la question ne réglait en rien l'incertitude juridique entourant les résolutions antérieures du Conseil.

[78] O. SCHACHTER, *op. cit. supra*, note 44; E. V. ROSTOW, *op. cit. supra*, note 63; C. J. SABEC, *op. cit. supra*, note 62; L. C. GREEN, *op. cit. supra*, note 53.

[79] B. H. WESTON, *op. cit. supra*, note 47; E. ROBERT, "La licéité des sanctions

"l'anomalie" que constitue le manque de contrôle exercé par le Conseil.[80] Enfin, d'autres ont dénoncé à la fois l'invalidité et l'absence de légitimité de cette résolution.[81] Parmi celles-ci, Richard Falk écrit: "l'ONU se devait de contrôler la définition des buts de guerre et des moyens de les atteindre. Le Conseil de sécurité n'a en rien d'autorité pour déléguer ce type de responsabilités à un ou plusieurs de ses membres, et sa légitimité par rapport à l'ensemble des membres de l'Organisation est sérieusement remise en question."[82]

Dans la section qui suit, nous nous employons à démontrer que l'abdication du Conseil de sécurité au profit de la coalition ne trouve aucune justification dans la Charte.

B. L'ABSENCE DE FONDEMENT JURIDIQUE DE LA RÉSOLUTION 678

Le chapitre VII de la Charte est l'unique autorité invoquée par le Conseil de sécurité pour justifier l'adoption de la résolution 678. Celle-ci, nous l'avons vu, traite à la fois du droit à la légitime défense et du système de sécurité collective. Par conséquent, nous examinerons successivement pourquoi la résolution 678 ne peut se justifier ni en vertu du premier (1) ni en vertu du second (2).

1. *La résolution 678 ne permet pas la légitime défense collective*

L'article 51 de la Charte prévoit qu'un État victime d'une agression armée conserve son droit de légitime défense individuelle ou collective jusqu'à ce que le Conseil de Sécurité ait pris les mesures nécessaires pour maintenir la paix et la sécurité internationales. Les États-Unis[83] et à un moindre degré, le Royaume Uni[84] ont

---

des Nations Unies contre l'Iraq," dans *Centre de droit international U.L.B., Entre les lignes: Le droit international et la guerre du Golfe* (1991), pp. 25-33.

[80] P.-M. DUPUY, "Après la guerre du Golfe...," *op. cit., supra,* note 14, p. 624; C. ROUSSEAU, "Chronique des faits internationaux," (1991) 95 *R.G.D.I.P.* 439, 470; C. J. SABEC, *op. cit. supra,* note 62.

[81] R. FALK, *op. cit. supra,* note 47; M. CHEMILLIER-GENDREAU, "Le droit confisqué par la politique," dans *L'Événement européen,* mars 1991, p. 95.

[82] R. FALK, *ibid.*

[83] P. LEWIS, *op. cit. supra,* note 52.

[84] C. WARBRICK, *op. cit. supra,* note 61, aux pp. 487 et 491: "The government has resisted the view that once the Security Council had taken measures under Resolution 661, the right of self-defence had terminated in accordance with Article 51. On the other hand, after the passage of Resolution 678, it has sometimes used a different formula, describing action as having been taken 'under the authority of

prétendu que les nombreuses résolutions adoptées par le Conseil pour résoudre la crise du Golfe n'avaient pas pour effet de suspendre le droit de légitime défense collective. L'existence de ce droit expliquerait alors pourquoi la coalition, et non le Conseil, a orchestré l'effort militaire dans le Golfe. Par conséquent, il importe de déterminer si, par ses actions, le Conseil a mis fin, temporairement du moins, à ce droit. En effet, seule la préservation de ce droit nous permettrait de concilier les termes de la Charte avec l'absence de contrôle du Conseil sur les opérations armées dirigées contre l'Irak ((a) ci-dessous).

En admettant que le droit de légitime défense collective ait été suspendu jusqu'à l'adoption de la résolution 678, peut-on prétendre que celle-ci a rétabli ce droit? À notre avis, c'est le libellé même de la résolution 678 qui permet d'écarter cette conclusion ((b) ci-dessous).

(a) L'adoption de ''mesures nécessaires'' par le Conseil de sécurité a suspendu le droit de légitime défense collective

Nous sommes d'avis qu'en décidant d'imposer des sanctions non militaires à l'Irak par sa résolution 661, le Conseil prenait ''des mesures nécessaires pour maintenir la paix et la sécurité internationales,'' conformément à l'article 51 de la Charte. En recourant à ces mesures, le Conseil a mis fin au droit de légitime défense collective des États membres de la coalition. Comme nous l'avons mentionné auparavant, certains États soutiennent, toutefois, une position contraire.[85] Il est donc nécessaire d'examiner en détail le pouvoir que l'article 51 accorde au Conseil et le libellé des résolutions pertinentes.

Dans un premier temps, on peut se demander qui, du Conseil de sécurité ou du pays agressé, détient la compétence de décider si les ''mesures nécessaires'' ont été prises. Certains auteurs affirment qu'il appartient seul à l'État agressé de faire cette détermination.[86] D'autres suggèrent que cette question est à la fois du ressort

[the] UN Security Council Resolution'. . .The British governement has taken the view that its military action has been both an exercise of the right of collective self-defence and action under the authority of the Security Council, as time has passed, giving emphasis to the second position.''

[85] *Ibid.;* P. LEWIS, *op. cit. supra,* note 52.

[86] L. M. GOODRICH et E. HAMBRO, *Charter of the United Nations* (2e éd., 1949), p. 300.

de l'État victime et du Conseil de sécurité.[87] Toutefois, la majorité des auteurs accordent ce pouvoir uniquement au Conseil de sécurité.[88] Ce dernier point de vue nous semble plus conforme à la lettre et à l'esprit de la Charte, qui accorde au Conseil un rôle de premier plan pour toute question relative au maintien de la paix.

Deuxièmement, on peut s'interroger sur la signification de l'expression ''mesures nécessaires.'' De quel type de mesures s'agit-il? Pour nos fins, il suffit de suggérer qu'une lecture des articles 39, 41, 42 et 51 démontre que les mesures envisagées par les articles 41 et 42 sont clairement visées par l'article 51.[89]

Pour ceux et celles qui favorisaient une marge de manoeuvre des plus large pour la coalition, les mesures nécessaires pour mettre fin au droit de légitime défense collective n'étaient rien de moins que le rétablissement de la situation telle qu'elle existait avant l'agression du Koweït par l'Irak.[90] Toutefois, cette interprétation ne trouve aucune justification dans la Charte, laquelle permet au Conseil, lorsqu'il décide ''des mesures nécessaires,'' d'opter pour une approche graduelle. Le Conseil peut d'abord prendre des sanctions non militaires. C'est seulement lorsqu'il estime que ces mesures se sont révélées ''inadéquates,'' qu'il peut, en vertu de l'article 42, entreprendre des opérations armées.[91] En d'autres termes, si l'on

---

[87] D. BOWETT, *op. cit. supra,* note 44, à la p. 196; E. V. ROSTOW, *op. cit. supra,* note 63, à la p. 512.

[88] Y. DINSTEIN, *op. cit. supra,* note 24 aux pp. 196-97; C. H. M. WALDOCK, ''The Regulation of the Use of Force by Individual States in International Law,'' (1952-II) 81 *R.C.A.D.I.* 451, 495-96; J. STONE, *op. cit. supra,* note 44, à la p. 244; V. P. NANDA, ''The Iraqi Invasion of Kuwiait: The U.N. Response,'' (1991) 15 *S. Ill. U.L.J.* 431, 450; M. E. O'CONNELL, ''Enforcing the Prohibition on the Use of Force: The U.N.'s Response to Iraq's Invasion of Kuwait,'' (1991) 15 *S. Ill. U.L.J.* 453, 477; R. HIGGINS, ''The Legal Limits to the Use of Force by Sovereign States: United Nations Practice,'' (1961) 37 *B.Y.I.L.* 269, 304; J. N. SINGH, *Use of Force under International Law* (1984), p. 25; H. KELSEN, ''Collective Security and Collective Self-Defense under the Charter of the United Nations,'' (1948), 42 *A.J.I.L.* 783,793.

[89] Kelsen écrit: ''It may be doubted whether the Security Council under Article 51 can take enforcement measures other than those provided for in Articles 39, 41 and 52,'' H. KELSEN, *op. cit. supra,* note 50, à la p. 931. A savoir si le seul fait de saisir le Conseil de sécurité d'une question est suffisant ou si le Conseil doit décider d'une mesure de nature positive, voir D. BOWETT, *op. cit. supra,* note 44, à la p. 196; S. KHARE, *op. cit. supra,* note 46, à la p. 79; J. CASTENEDA, *Legal Effects of United Nations Resolutions* (1969), p. 211; J. N. SINGH, *ibid.,* à la p. 24.

[90] C. WARBRICK, *op. cit. supra,* note 61, aux pp. 487-88; E. V. ROSTOW, *op. cit. supra* note 63, à la p. 511.

[91] Article 42 de la Charte des N.U.: ''Si le Conseil estime que les mesures prévues

permet à certains États d'avoir recours à la force au nom de la légitime défense collective, avant même que le Conseil ne décide que la force est "nécessaire," on élimine par le fait même toute la discrétion conférée au Conseil par l'article 42. De plus, il est essentiel d'interpréter les termes "mesures nécessaires" à la lumière de la mission première du Conseil qui consiste à "maintenir la paix et la sécurité internationales," par opposition à la réparation du tort subi par l'État agressé.[92] Que cela soit souhaité et ultimement atteint par les mesures prises par le Conseil ne change en rien la mission première du Conseil.

Si l'imposition de sanctions en vertu de l'article 41 mettait fin au droit de légitime défense individuelle et collective, comment expliquer qu'on ait fait référence à ce droit dans le préambule de la résolution 661?[93] De prime abord, cette affirmation du droit de légitime défense collective paraî t inutile, à moins que le Conseil n'ait voulu par ce moyen marquer son approbation des actes pris par le Koweït avant l'intervention active du Conseil.

L'économie de l'article 51 suspend ce droit de légitime défense dès la prise de mesures par le Conseil. Par contre, si la résolution 661 avait prévu un délai avant la mise en oeuvre de ces mesures, la mention du droit à la légitime défense aurait pu être interprétée comme un simple rappel de l'existence de ce droit. Celui-ci aurait pris fin à l'expiration du délai fixé.

Certains sont pourtant d'avis qu'il faut y voir une indication du droit du Koweït et de ses alliés de se prévaloir du droit de légitime défense, malgré la décision du Conseil d'imposer des sanctions non

à l'article 41 seraient inadéquates ou qu'elles se sont révélées telles, il peut entreprendre...toute action qu'il juge nécessaire.''

[92] A ce sujet, *voir* D. W. GREIG, *op. cit. supra,* note 65, à la p. 390; D. BOWETT, *op. cit. supra,* note 44, à la p. 197; Y. DINSTEIN, *op. cit. supra,* note 24, à la p. 196.

[93] Quant au pourquoi de cette référence au droit de légitime défense dans la résolution 661, certains y voient un exemple typique du droit au service de la politique étrangère des États comme le révèle le passage suivant: "In a newspaper commentary, it was suggested that the inclusion of this paragraph, though 'innocuous at first sight,' was the result of a 'brilliant legal stratagem' on the part of the United States. For several decades the interpretation of Article 51 had been that the right of self-defence was thought to be suspended when the Security Council took appropriate action...The inclusion of a reaffirmation of Article 51, however, would theoretically allow one to argue that the right was again recognized, despite the Security Council's actions, and provided the United States with a concrete, albeit technical, argument in favour of unilateral action." Wells, "Kuwait Request Brings a New Word into International Law," *The Independent,* Aug. 14, 1990, Foreign News §, at 9,'' dans S. J. SABEC, *supra,* note 62, à la p. 98.

militaires à l'Irak.[94] On pourrait tout aussi bien en conclure que le Conseil a jugé utile de faire allusion à la légitime défense, précisément pour indiquer qu'il adoptait les mesures dans le cadre de l'article 51.

De plus, la formulation de la résolution 678 confirme clairement qu'avant son adoption, le droit des États de recourir à la force était suspendu. En effet, le Conseil y "décide" d'offrir à l'Irak l'opportunité de se conformer à ses résolutions avant le 15 janvier 1991. Dans ces circonstances, il est impensable qu'un membre de la coalition eût pu, sans contrevenir à une décision du Conseil, faire usage de la force avant la date prescrite. En outre, le fait que libellé de la résolution "autorise" les États à recourir à la force démontre bien qu'aucune mesure coercitive ne pouvait être prise sans l'accord du Conseil. En effet, dans la Charte, l'emploi de ce terme signifie que l'accord du Conseil est nécessaire pour recourir à ce type de mesures. Ainsi, l'article 53 de la Charte prévoit qu'"aucune action coercitive ne sera entreprise en vertu d'accords régionaux ou par des organismes régionaux sans *l'autorisation* du Conseil de sécurité..." (nous mettons en italiques).

Accepter l'existence parallèle du droit de légitime défense collective et de sanctions économiques décidées par le Conseil, signifierait que les membres permanents et leurs alliés conserveraient, malgré leur participation aux actions du Conseil, la liberté d'agir à leur guise pour régler un conflit. Dans de telles conditions, le Conseil, contrairement au rôle central que lui confère la Charte dans le maintien de la paix, ne se verra que très rarement confier le plein contrôle pour résoudre une crise. Par conséquent, une interprétation plus conforme à l'esprit de la Charte nécessite qu'on octroie au Conseil le contrôle exclusif des actions de nature coercitives.[95]

[94] E. V. ROSTOW, *op. cit. supra,* note 63, aux pp. 511-12; O. SCHACHTER, *op. cit. supra,* note 44, aux pp. 457-59; *contra* L. C. GREEN, *op. cit. supra,* note 53, aux pp. 565-66.

[95] T. FRANCK, "UN Police Action in Lieu of War: 'The Old Order Changeth','' (1991) 85 *A.J.I.L.* 63, 64: "A new-style, UN authorized police action functioning alongside a traditional sovereign exercise of war powers is conceptually and operationally untenable, the more so when states seeking the freedom to act unilaterally have forces committed alongside others in a Security police action. As a textual matter, it is obvious on its face that the Charter, in creating the new police power, intended to establish an exclusive alternative to the old war system. The old system was retained only as a fallback, available when the new system could not be made to work; not, as some U.S. hawks argue, as an equal alternative, to be chosen at the sole discretion of the members."

(b) La résolution 678 n'a pas fait renaître le droit de légitime défense collective

Si la résolution 661 ne fait qu'une référence furtive à la légitime défense collective, la résolution 678 n'en contient aucune. Tout au plus, cette résolution "rappelle et réaffirme" toutes les résolutions antérieures du Conseil, incluant la résolution 661. Si l'action autorisée par la résolution 678 se fondait sur la légitime défense, celle-ci y serait sûrement mentionnée expressément, surtout en raison de la division qui régnait au sein du Conseil quant au droit d'un État d'agir unilatéralement contre l'Irak.[96]

De plus, le mandat accordé à la coalition, aussi ambigu qu'il puisse être, dépasse largement l'exercice du droit de légitime défense. Tel que mentionné précédemment, il s'agit non seulement de forcer l'Irak à se conformer à toutes les résolutions antérieures du Conseil, mais aussi de "rétablir la paix et la sécurité dans la région."[97] De même, il n'est pas certain que tous les États membres de la coalition aient un droit de légitime défense collective.[98] Par conséquent,

---

[96] *N.Y. Times, supra* note 53.

[97] Contra E. V. ROSTOW, *op. cit. supra,* note 63, qui écrit à la p. 514: "But the Security Council resolutions also contemplate 'measures to restore international peace and security in the area.' The phrase is not a rhetorical flourish. It has always been an essential ingredient of the law of self-defense." S'il est vrai que l'objectif de rétablir la paix et la sécurité internationales est souvent entremêlé avec la légitime défense, il a aussi une portée beaucoup plus large. *Voir* D. W. GREIG, *op. cit. supra,* note 65, à la p. 390; D. BOWETT, *op. cit. supra,* note 44, à la p. 197; Y. DINSTEIN, *op. cit. supra,* note 24, à la p. 196; J. N. SINGH, *op. cit. supra,* note 88, à la p. 31. Notons que dans le conflit de Corée, le Conseil a utilisé une terminologie visant à restreindre la portée de ces termes. Alors que dans une résolution adopté le 27 juin 1950 le Conseil "recommande aux membres des Nations Unies d'apporter à la République de Corée toute l'aide nécessaire pour repousser les assaillants et rétablir dans cette région la paix et la sécurité," dans une autre résolution adoptée le 7 juillet, le Conseil "se félicite de l'appui rapide et vigoureux que les gouvernements...ont apporté...en vue d'aider la République de Corée à se défendre contre la dite attaque armée et *ainsi* de rétablir la paix et la sécurité internationales dans la région" (nous soulignons). Cette dernière résolution recommandait aux divers États ayant répondu à l'appel du Conseil de placer leurs forces sous un commandement unifié désigné par les États-Unis. Sur l'affaire de Corée voir *supra,* note 77.

[98] Derek Bowett affirme que seuls les États dont les intérêts sont, pour des raisons de proximité géographique ou de dépendance politique ou économique, gravement influencés par l'agression d'un État tiers, peuvent prétendre à un droit à la légitime défense collective. Voir D. BOWETT, *op. cit. supra,* note 49, aux pp. 32, 34 et 303; voir aussi S. KHARE, *op. cit. supra,* note 46, à la p. 174; H. KELSEN, *op. cit. supra,* note 50, à la p. 792; *contra* I. BROWNLIE, *International Law and the Use of Force by States* (1963), p. 330; C. H. M. WALDOCK, *op. cit. supra,* note 88, à la

leur participation à l'operation armée, même à la demande du pays victime de l'agression, ne pourrait être ''autorisée'' qu'à titre de mesures coercitives découlant du système de sécurité collective prévu par la Charte.[99]

Le contexte de l'adoption de la résolution 678 nous laisse également songeur. Le fait qu'il s'agisse de permettre l'usage de la force plus de cinq mois après qu'un État ait été conquis et alors que les négociations et les sanctions non militaires auraient pu se poursuivre ne dénote pas une opération typique de légitime défense.[100]

Enfin, affirmer que la résolution 678 n'est qu'une autorisation de recourir à la légitime défense collective semble contraire au libellé de l'article 51 et au rôle confié au Conseil de sécurité pour la mise en oeuvre de la sécurité collective. Les mesures mentionnées à l'ar-

p. 504; J. M. SINGH, *op. cit. supra,* note 88, à la p. 12; O. SCHACHTER, *op. cit supra,* note 71, aux pp. 1638-39; voir également D. W. GREIG, *op. cit. supra,* note 65, aux pp. 373-75 ainsi que J. COMBACAU, ''The Exception of Self-Defense in U.N. Practice'' dans A. Cassese (éd.), *The Current Legal Regulation of the Use of Force* (1986), pp. 9, 31 pour une discussion éclairée sur le sujet; commentant la référence au droit de légitime défense collective dans le préambule de la résolution 661, Schachter, *op. cit. supra,* note 71, écrit à la p. 457: ''In affirming the applicability of collective self-defense in the gulf situation, the Council recognized (again by implication) that third states had the right to use force to aid Kuwait, even though those states had not been attacked and no treaty or other special links with Kuwait. The point has some importance because earlier legal commentary by respected scholars such as Bowett and Kelsen had suggested a contrary position. The Council's affirmation supports the position that any state may come to the aid of a state that has been illegally attacked.'' Pourtant, nous ne voyons pas très bien en quoi la référence au droit de légitime défense collective par le Conseil tranche en faveur d'une interprétation large de ce droit. Dans la résolution 661, le Conseil n'a fait que reprendre une partie du libellé de l'article 51 de la Charte sans émettre aucune opinion sur la portée de cet article et, en particulier, sur les États qui pouvaient l'invoquer suite à l'agression par l'Irak.

[99] De la même façon, tel que mentionné précédemment, le Conseil peut, en vertu de l'article 53, ''autoriser'' des mesures coercitives par des organismes régionaux.

[100] A ce sujet B. H. WESTON, *op. cit supra,* note 47, écrit aux pp. 520 et 521: ''delegated collective self-defense actions involving the use of force still would be justified only on the basis of overwhelming necessity, including the absence of other means and time for deliberation, as reflected in both traditional international law and post-Charter theory and practice. Other means and time for deliberation arguably being present both on November 29, 1990, when Resolution 678 was adopted and, more importantly, on January 16, 1991, when it was acted upon...it is by no means clear that a Security Council intent upon uncompromised freedom of action would be wise to cite Article 51 as authority for its delegation of war-making powers against Iraq.'' Notons également que dès novembre 1990, le secrétaire général des Nations Unies déclarait que le droit à la légitime défense individuelle et collective du Koweî t avait pris fin dû à l'absence de résistance armée par cet État. Voir *Washington Post,* 9 novembre 1990, p. A30, col. 5.

ticle 51, vraisemblablement celles décrites aux articles 41 et 42, doivent justement se substituer à une action de légitime défense.[101] De plus, alors que le Conseil de sécurité a lui-même été créé pour remédier à ce qu'on percevait être les lacunes du droit de légitime défense,[102] il serait pour le moins curieux, qu'ayant pris des mesures pour résoudre le conflit, on en vienne à en conclure qu'en définitive son action n'a fait que rétablir ce droit. Comme l'a si bien dit Stone: ''In the final resort Article 51 is a provision of the Charter whose invocation must ever testify to the breakdown of the Charter.''[103]

2. *La résolution 678 n'est pas conforme au système de sécurité collective prévu par la Charte*

Si la résolution 678 met en marche une opération de sécurité collective, elle doit nécessairememt avoir pour fondement un pouvoir exprès ou implicite du Conseil. Pourtant elle n'entre pas dans les paramètres des quelques dispositions pertinentes de la Charte: les articles 42 (a ci-dessous) et 39 (b ci-dessous). Elle n'est pas davantage la manifestation d'un pouvoir implicite, mais plutôt d'une abdication: c (i) ci-dessous. Subsidiairement, même si on pouvait considérer qu'elle représente un exercice de pouvoir par le Conseil, cet exercice serait contraire aux buts même de l'Organisation: c (ii) ci-dessous).

(a) La résolution 678 n'est pas autorisée par l'article 42

Quiconque se prête à un examen sommaire du chapitre VII de la Charte est naturellement porté à conclure qu'une action militaire autorisée par le Conseil de sécurité, postérieurement à l'imposition de sanctions économiques, a pour fondement l'article 42. Après tout, ne s'agit-il pas là de la chronologie d'actions que la Charte envisage lorsqu'il y a agression? Une telle analyse présuppose nécessairement que l'article 42 est en vigueur. Toutefois, puisque la Charte semble lier la mise en oeuvre de l'article 42 à la conclusion des accords prévus à l'article 43. Ainsi, l'article 106 stipule:

En attendant l'entrée en vigueur des accords spéciaux mentionnés à l'article 43, qui, de l'avis du Conseil de sécurité, lui permettront de com-

---

[101] H. KELSEN, *op. cit. supra*, note 89.

[102] D. BOWETT, *op. cit. supra*, note 49, à la p. 305.

[103] J. STONE, *op. cit. supra*, note 44, à la p. 273.

mencer à assumer les responsabilités lui incombant en application de l'article 42, les parties à la Déclaration des Quatre Nations signée à Moscou le 30 octobre 1943 et la France se concerteront entre elles...

Puisqu'aucun accord n'a encore été signé entre le Conseil de sécurité et les États membres, plusieurs auteurs affirment que le Conseil ne peut justifier un usage de la force sur la base de l'article 42.[104] D'ailleurs, lors des débats au Conseil de sécurité pendant la crise de Corée, le représentant anglais a déclaré:

Si la Charte était entièrement entrée en vigueur et si l'accord prévu à l'article 43 de la Charte avait été conclu, nous aurions évidemment agi différemment, et l'action à entreprendre par le Conseil de sécurité pour repousser l'attaque armée aurait indubitablement été fondée sur l'article 42. Mais, étant donné la situation, nous ne pouvons naturellement agir qu'en vertu de l'article 39, qui autorise le Conseil de sécurité à recommander les mesures qui peuvent être prises pour rétablir la paix et la sécurité internationales.[105]

Cependant, d'autres auteurs soutiennent que le Conseil serait tout à fait libre d'invoquer l'article 42 sans avoir à utiliser les forces spécifiquement prévues par l'article 43. En plus de noter le caractère transitoire de l'article 106,[106] ces auteurs avancent que rien dans l'article 42 n'empêche le Conseil de demander aux États de mettre volontairement à sa disposition des contingents nationaux.[107] Cet argument trouve un certain support dans l'énoncé suivant de la Cour Internationale de Justice: "On ne peut pas dire que la Charte ait laissé le Conseil de sécurité impuissant en face d'une situation

---

[104] B. H. WESTON, *op. cit. supra*, note 47, à la p. 519; J. M. SINGH, *op. cit. supra*, note 88, à la p. 80; J. CASTENEDA, *op. cit. supra*, note 89, aux pp. 265-68; K. BOUSTANY, *op. cit. supra*, note 65, p. 386.

[105] Doc. off. C.S., 476e séance, p. 3, (1950).

[106] D. BOWETT, *op. cit. supra*, note 49, à la p. 277; O. SCHACHTER, *op. cit. supra*, note 44, à la p. 464; voir, par contre, la résolution 2734 (XXV) du 16 décembre 1970 de l'Assemblée générale dans laquelle l'Assemblée "recommande que le Conseil de sécurité prenne des mesures pour faciliter la conclusion des accords envisagés à l'article 43 de la Charte en vue de développer pleinement sa capacité d'agir pour imposer le respect de ses décisions, comme le prévoit le chapitre VII de la Charte."

[107] O. SCHACHTER, "The Place of Law in the United Nations," dans EAGLETON ET SWIFT (éd.), 1950 Annual Review of United Nations Affairs (1951), 205, 221; J. FISHER, *op. cit. supra*, note 30, aux pp. 710-13; M. AKEHURST, *op. cit. supra*, note 74 à la p. 185; F. SEYERSTED, *op. cit. supra*, note 44, aux pp. 438-39; J. ANDRESSY, "Uniting for Peace," (1956) 50 *A.J.I.L.* 563, 470; A. CHAYES,

d'urgence, en l'absence d'accords conclus en vertu de l'article 43."[108]

Même si on devait conclure des paragraphes précédents que l'article 42 est en vigueur, encore faut-il établir que l'"autorisation" du Conseil équivaut à une décision par celui-ci d'user de la force.[109] Une telle interprétation est suspecte, puisqu'il est clair que c'est aux États membres de la coalition et non au Conseil que revient ultimement cette décision.[110] Évidemment, aucune interprétation n'est nécessaire si l'on adopte le point de vue soutenu par quelques auteurs, selon lequel l'article 42 permet au Conseil d'agir par décision, autorisation ou recommandation. Ainsi Schachter écrit: "But even if Article 42 allows for mandatory 'action,' this should embrace the lesser power to recommend or authorize action. It does not make sense to require a mandatory decision where a recommendation or authorization would suffice to achieve the desired action."[111]

Afin de poursuivre notre analyse de la légalité de la résolution 678 au regard de l'article 42, nous allons supposer non seulement que cet article est en vigueur, mais qu'il permet aussi au Conseil de sécurité d'autoriser les États à prendre des mesures militaires. Comme corollaire à son pouvoir d'autorisation, le Conseil aura évidemment la capacité de restreindre le champ d'action des États. Par exemple, en se référant à la fois à l'article 42 et à l'article 48,[112]

"The Use of Force in the Persian Gulf," dans L. Fisler Damrosch et D. J. Scheffer (éd.), *Law and Force in the New International Order* (1991), 3, 5; D. BOWETT, *op. cit. supra*, note 49, à la p. 277 est d'avis que le Conseil de sécurité pourrait recommander, par le biais de l'article 39 et en se référant à l'article 42, la mise sur pied d'une force armée des Nations Unies. Sur la validité de recommandations fondées sur la partie VII, voir *infra*.

[108] Avis consultatif *Certaines dépenses des Nations Unies, supra*, note 41, à la p. 167.

[109] Le libellé de l'article 42 ne semble pas permettre au Conseil d'agir par recommandation. Pour une discussion sur ce sujet, voir J. FISCHER, *op. cit. supra*, note 30, aux pp. 710 et 714. Voir aussi J. W. HALDERMAN, "Some Legal Aspects of Sanctions in the Rhodesian Case," (1968) 17 *I.C.L.Q.* 672, 685.

[110] *Contra* B. H. WESTON, *op. cit. supra*, note 47, à la p. 521 qui écrit: "In any event, as if to reject the Korean comparison expressly, the Security Council, in Resolution 678, made an authorization (or decision), not a recommendation"; voir aussi A. C. AREND, "International Law and the Recourse to Force: A Shift in Paradigms" (1990) 27 *Stan. J.I.L.* 1, 40.

[111] O. SCHACHTER, *op. cit. supra*, note 44, à la p. 462; A. CHAYES, *op. cit. supra*, note 107, à la p. 5.

[112] *Supra*, note 32.

le Conseil pourrait sûrement décider de ne permettre l'usage de la force qu'aux États qui accepteraient de se placer sous son contrôle.[113] À l'opposé, on peut se demander si le Conseil peut donner carte blanche aux États et leur permettre d'user de la force pour le maintien de la paix. Certains auteurs insistent sur la large marge de manoeuvre que confère le texte de l'article 42. Schachter en conclut qu'une résolution du Conseil de sécurité autorisant la coalition à recourir à la légitime défense collective constituerait une "action" aux termes de l'article 42. Il explique: "The word 'action' does not have to mean that those armed forces are under the control or command of the Council. That such command and control was contemplated under other articles of chapter VII should not be read in Article 42."[114]

Pourtant, on ne voit pas en vertu de quel principe on devrait interpréter l'article 42 sans tenir compte des autres articles du chapitre VII. En effet, comment faire abstraction de l'article 46 qui, comme l'indique son libellé, n'est aucunement tributaire de la conclusion des accords de l'article 43: "Les plans pour l'emploi de la force armée sont établis par le Conseil de Sécurité avec l'aide

---

[113] D. H. BOWETT, *op. cit. supra*, note 49, à la p. 33, ne semble pas penser que le Conseil puisse prendre des "décisions" significatives malgré l'absence d'accords sous l'article 43. Ainsi il écrit: "In any event, why should not the Council, especially when agreements under article 43 are lacking, act by way of recommendation rather than decision?"

[114] O. SCHACHTER, *op. cit. supra*, note 44, à la p. 462; L. C. GREEN, *op. cit. supra*, note 53, à la page 575; F. SEYERSTED, *op. cit. supra*, note 44, analysant l'article 42, affirme à la p. 439: "It does not even appear to exclude a force composed of national contingents under national command, such as the force actually employed in Korea"; voir aussi M. AKEHURST, *op. cit. supra*, note 74, à la p. 184; dans leur commentaire sur l'article 42, L. M. GOODRICH & E. HAMBRO, *op. cit. supra*, note 86, à la p. 310 écrivent: "there is nothing in Article 42, as it stands, which would prevent the establishment and use of an international armed force under Security Council direction." Les auteurs n'évoquent pas la possibilité que l'article 42 puisse servir de fondement à des forces dirigées par des États. A savoir si l'opération de Corée peut reposer sur l'article 42, notons le commentaire suivant de G. FISCHER, *op. cit. supra*, note 30, à la p. 714: "les organes de l'ONU ont nié qu'il s'agissait dans l'affaire de la Corée d'un recours à l'article 42 [Répertoire ONU, supplément n° 3, vol. II, 1971, pp. 340-41] et personne n'a soutenu une thèse différente." A notre connaissance, seul S. KHARE, *op. cit. supra*, note 46, aux pp. 144-45, émet sans réserve l'opinion que l'action du Conseil en Corée avait pour fondement l'article 42 (p. 144-145). Notons aussi que plusieurs auteurs dont V. P. NANDA, *op. cit. supra*, note 88, à la p. 449, et P. M. DUPUY, *op. cit. supra*, note 14, à la p. 624 ont émis l'opinion que la résolution 678 n'avait pas pour base l'article 42.

du Comité d'État-major."[115]

Cette interprétation ne signifie pas que le Conseil doit diriger les opérations militaires sur le terrain. Il lui appartient, cependant, à tout le moins, de définir le type d'opérations à y être entreprises. D'ailleurs, cette interprétation est confirmée par l'article 42, en vertu duquel le Conseil peut décider "toute action qu'il juge nécessaire. . . .Cette action peut comprendre des démonstrations, des mesures de blocus et d'autres opérations exécutées par des forces aériennes, navales ou terrestres de membres des Nations Unies."

Le Conseil doit donc faire un choix stratégique parmi ces diverses options. D'ailleurs à deux occasions dans le passé le Conseil a permis un usage limité de la force. Il s'agit en premier lieu de la résolution 665;[116] en second lieu, en 1966, alors que le Conseil a permis au Royaume-Uni de recourir à la force navale contre des navires transportant du pétrole destiné à la Rhodésie. Commentant cette affaire, un auteur écrit:

From the angle of the United Nations Charter it is hardly possible to regard the deployment of H.M.S. *Berwick* and its armed boarding party, which compelled the *Manuela* to alter course away from Beira, as other than the use of armed force. But the conditions of its use had been closely circumscribed, and the force involved was minimal. . .it is obviously desirable, and closer to the purposes of the Charter, that the use of force by or through the United Nations itself should be as far as possible restricted in time and place to what is necessary to maintain or restore peace.[117]

Enfin, débordant largement le cadre du chapitre VII, nous expliquerons plus loin comment une autorisation d'utiliser la force sans le contrôle du Conseil et sans garantie qu'il puisse la révoquer, nous

---

[115] M. CHEMILLIER-GENDREAU, *op. cit. supra*, note 81, à la p. 99; K. BOUSTANY, *op. cit. supra*, note 65, à la p. 389.

[116] *Supra*, note 54.

[117] J. E. S. FAWCETT, "Security Council Resolutions on Rhodesia," (1965-66) 41 *B.Y.I.L.* 103, 119. Notons que cet auteur réfute la thèse voulant que cette résolution repose sur l'article 42 pour des raisons que nous exposons dans la citation correspondant à la note 127. Soulignons également que lors des débats au Conseil de sécurité sur l'opportunité de permettre au Royaume-Uni d'user de la force contre la Rhodésie, certains États ont fait valoir qu'en tant que puissance administrante le Royaume-Uni n'avait pas besoin de l'autorisation ou l'approbation du Conseil pour agir. Voir en particulier C S, 21e année, 1285e séance; voir aussi J. COMBACAU, *Le pouvoir de sanction de l'ONU*, (1974) aux pp. 26 à 28 pour une discussion intéressante du fondement juridique de cette affaire.

apparaît contraire aux buts mêmes de la Charte.[118]

(b) La résolution 678 n'est pas autorisée par l'article 39

Durant la crise du Golfe, le précédent coréen a souvent été invoqué pour justifier l'action du Conseil de sécurité. Comme nous l'avons vu ci-dessus, lors de cette affaire, le Conseil a adopté une résolution recommandant aux États de mettre leurs troupes à la disposition d'un commandement unifié, désigné par les États-Unis d'Amérique. Le représentant britannique a déclaré que cette résolution était basée sur l'article 39.[119] Certains auteurs ont depuis accepté la thèse britannique.[120] Par contre, plusieurs rejettent cette explication; ils sont d'avis que les seules recommandations visées par l'article 39 sont celles relatives au règlement pacifique des différends et que l'emploi de mesures coercitives doit faire l'objet d'une décision du Conseil.[121] Tout en concordant avec le libellé de l'article 39,[122] ce point de vue reflète le délicat compromis qu'on retrouve aux chapitres VI et VII de la Charte. Dans le chapitre VI, les États insistent pour garder intacte leur souveraineté et limitent le rôle du Conseil et de l'Assemblée générale à la formulation de recommandations dénuées de force obligatoire. Par contre, au chapitre VII, les États, durement éprouvés par deux conflits mondiaux en l'espace d'une génération,[123] consentent à ce que le Conseil décide de mesures coercitives obligatoires pour suppléer à ses recommandations pour le règlement pacifique de différends.[124] De toute façon, même si le Conseil pouvait recommander l'emploi de mesures coercitives, on ne peut qualifier la résolution 678 de simple recommandation.[125]

---

[118] Voir *infra* la section intitulée: la résolution 678 est contraire aux objectifs de la Charte.

[119] *Supra,* note 105.

[120] D. BOWETT, *op. cit. supra,* note 49, à la p. 32; J. W. HALDERMAN, *op. cit. supra,* note 109, à la p. 688.

[121] B. H. WESTON, *op. cit. supra,* note 47, à la p. 521; P. GUGGENHEIM, *Traité de droit international public,* Tome II, (1954), p. 270; H. KELSEN, *op. cit. supra,* note 50, aux pp. 932-933; J. STONE, *op. cit. supra,* note 44, à la p. 230.

[122] *Supra,* note 31.

[123] Voir le préambule de la Charte des N.U.

[124] R. B. RUSSELL et J. E. MUTHER, *A History of the United Nations Charter* (1958), p. 458 et aux pp. 669-70.

[125] A. PYRICH, *op. cit. supra,* note 64, à la p. 269; voir aussi B. H. WESTON, *op. cit. supra,* note 110; *contra* E. V. ROSTOW, *op. cit. supra,* note 63, à la p. 509.

Comme nous le mentionnons auparavant, en 1966 le Conseil de sécurité avait accordé au Royaume-Uni l'autorisation de recourir à la force navale contre des navires à destination de la Rhodésie.[126] Le commentaire que fait J. Fawcett sur la question nous semble tout à fait pertinent: "What in fact is missing in the Charter is an express power of the Security Council to authorize action, a power beyond recommendation, but falling short of a decision covered by Article 25. In placing the naval action in the framework of the Charter, the choice lies between Articles 39 and 42, but there are serious difficulties with either, and the conclusion may perhaps be that it was anomalous, and outside the Charter."[127]

En supposant que les articles 39 et 42 ne confèrent pas de pouvoir d'autorisation, il y a cependant lieu de considérer si les pouvoirs implicites du Conseil de sécurité ne lui permettent pas d'agir ainsi.

(c) La résolution 678 ne repose pas sur les pouvoirs implicites du Conseil de sécurité

(i) Le Conseil a abdiqué son pouvoir

Il n'y a aucun doute que les pouvoirs que possède une organisation internationale ne sont pas restreints à ceux que mentionne expressément sa charte constitutive.[128] Ainsi, dans un passage bien connu de l'affaire *Réparation des dommages subis,* la Cour internationale de justice déclare:

Selon le droit international, l'Organisation [des Nations Unies] doit être considérée comme possédant ces pouvoirs qui, s'ils ne sont pas expressément énoncés dans la Charte, sont, par une conséquence nécessaire, conférés à l'Organisation en tant qu'essentiels à l'exercice des fonctions de celle-ci. Ce principe de droit a été appliqué à l'Organisation internationale du Travail par la Cour permanente de Justice internationale dans son Avis consultatif n13, du 23 juillet 1926 (Série B, n 13, p. 18), et il doit l'être aux Nations Unies.[129]

Depuis, la Cour a fréquemment validé les actions prises par l'Assemblée générale et le Conseil de sécurité, en faisant appel à la no-

---

[126] Sur cette question voir *supra,* note 117.

[127] FAWCETT, *ibid.,* à la p. 100.

[128] H. G. SCHERMERS, *International Institutional Law,* volume 1 (1972), p. 155.

[129] Arrêt C.I.J. Recueil, 1949, p. 174, 182.

tion de pouvoirs implicites.[130]

En principe, rien ne semble s'opposer à la reconnaissance d'un pouvoir implicite du Conseil de sécurité d'autoriser des actions en son nom. De fait, nous avons vu que l'article 53 prévoit expressément que le Conseil peut autoriser des organismes régionaux à prendre des mesures coercitives. Toutefois, le simple fait d'autoriser une action ne signifie pas que le Conseil en perd le contrôle ultime. Au contraire, comme l'écrit Edem Kodjo, au sujet de l'article 53: "Au total, il nous apparaît difficile, quasiment impossible, que le Conseil de sécurité donne le blanc-seing à une organisation régionale dans ce domaine. S'il accorde son autorisation, il est obligé de suivre les opérations jusqu'à leur terme afin qu'elles ne s'écartent pas des normes prescrites par la Charte."[131] Par conséquent, par analogie avec l'article 53, il n'y a pas de doute que le Conseil a le pouvoir implicite d'autoriser l'usage de la force, s'il en contrôle en tout temps l'application.

Toutefois, nous avons vu que la résolution 678 n'est autre chose qu'un blanc seing donné à la coalition, puisque toute nouvelle résolution peut faire l'objet d'un veto par un seul membre permanent. Dans ces conditions, le Conseil n'exerce aucun pouvoir implicite; il abdique plutôt ses responsabilités au profit de quelques États membres. Une telle conduite est contraire aux principes généraux applicables aux organisations internationales. Traitant des limites au pouvoir de délégation des organisations internationales, Schermers écrit: "There are two limits to this power of delegation: (1) no more powers may be delegated than the organ itself possesses...(2) Responsibility may not normally be transferred...."[132]

Comme le souligne le même auteur dans son ouvrage,[133] une décision de la Cour de justice des communautés européennes, l'affaire *Meroni,* illustre bien ces concepts. Dans cette affaire, la Cour insiste sur les limites au transfert d'un pouvoir discrétionnaire. Selon la Cour, "la délégation d'un pouvoir discrétionnaire, en le confiant à des autorités différentes de celles qui ont été établies par le Traité pour en assurer et en contrôler l'exercice dans le cadre de leurs attributions respectives, porterait atteinte à cette garantie [que

---

[130] *Voir* entre autre *Effet de jugements du tribunal administratif des Nations Unies accordant indemnité,* arrêt C.I.J. Recueil, 1954, p. 47; *Certaines Dépenses des Nations Unies, supra,* note 41; *Avis sur la Namibie, supra,* note 28.

[131] E. KODJO, "Article 53," dans J.-P. Cot et A. Pellet (dir.), *La Charte des Nations Unies* (1985), pp. 815-29, 824.

[132] H. G. SCHERMERS, *op. cit. supra, note* 128, à la p. 152.

[133] *Ibid.*

représente] l'équilibre des pouvoirs, caractéristique de la structure institutionnelle de la Communauté."[134]

De la même façon, les États membres ayant expressément "conféré au Conseil de sécurité la responsabilité principale du maintien de la paix et de la sécurité internationales,"[135] celui-ci ne peut abdiquer un pouvoir aussi crucial au profit d'une coalition d'États sans porter gravement atteinte au système édifié dans la Charte.[136]

---

[134] CJCE 13 juin 1958 *Meroni*, aff. 9/56, rec. 1958, p. ii, 44. Dans cette affaire, la Haute Autorité de la Communauté Européenne du Charbon et de l'Acier avait délégué un de ses pouvoirs à deux institutions privées. La Cour, avant de conclure à l'invalidité de cette délégation, énonce les principes suivants aux pp. 43-44: "attendu que les conséquences résultant d'une délégation de pouvoirs sont très différentes suivant qu'elle vise des pouvoirs d'exécution nettement délimités et dont l'usage, de ce fait, est susceptible d'un contrôle rigoureux aux regards de critères fixés par l'autorité délégante, ou un pouvoir discrétionnaire, impliquant une large liberté d'appréciation, susceptible de traduire par l'usage qui en est fait une véritable politique économique; attendu qu'une délégation du premier type n'est pas susceptible de modifier sensiblement les conséquences qu'entraîne l'exercice des pouvoirs qu'elle affecte, alors qu'une délégation du second type, en substituant les choix de l'autorité délégataire à ceux de l'autorité délégante, opère un véritable déplacement de responsabilité. . .' '; voir aussi *CJCE* 17 décembre 1970 Koster, aff. 2270, avec 1970, p. 1161. Certains arrêts de la Cour internationale de justice semblent reprendre les mêmes principes. Dans *Demande de réformation du jugement n° 158* du Tribunal administratif des Nations Unies, arrêt C.I.J., Recueil, 1973, 1666, à la p. 174, la Cour, discutant du pouvoir reconnu à l'Assemblée générale d'autoriser les organes de l'ONU à demander un avis consultatif (paragraphe 96(2)), a pris soin de préciser que "l'Assemblée générale ne délègue pas son propre pouvoir de demander un avis consultatif" lorsqu'elle "crée un organe subsidiaire chargé d'attributions particulières et doté du pouvoir de solliciter un avis consultatif dans l'exercice de ses attributions." De même, elle s'assure, à la p. 173, du fait que le Comité créé par l'Assemblée, composé des membres de l'Assemblée, est bien un organe de l'ONU au sens de l'article 96(2). Il semble donc que dans l'esprit de la Cour, le pouvoir de déléguer n'est pas absolu. Voir aussi *Effet de jugements du tribunal administratif des Nations Unies accordant indemnité*, arrêt C.I.J. Recueil, 1954, p. 47 où la Cour a jugé que l'Assemblée générale était liée par les décisions d'un tribunal administratif qu'elle avait créé. Toutefois, la Cour indique, à la p. 61, qu' ' "En créant le tribunal administratif, l'Assemblée générale ne déléguait pas l'exercice de ses propres fonctions; elle exerçait un pouvoir qu'elle tenait de la Charte: celui de réglementer les rapports avec le personnel." Enfin, voir par analogie l'avis consultatif *Compatibilité de certains décrets-lois Dantzikois avec la constitution de la ville libre*, 1936, C.P.J.I., série A/B, n° 65, où une loi décrétait que les actes "contraires au sentiment populaire sain" constitueraient un crime. La Cour permanente, à la p. 56, considère qu'une telle mesure transfère "au juge une importante fonction que la Constitution a voulu réserver à la loi en raison de sa nature intrinsèque et dans le but de placer la liberté individuelle à l'abri de toute atteinte arbitraire de la part de la Puissance publique."

[135] *Supra*, note 25.

[136] C'est aussi l'opinion de H. G. SCHERMERS, *op. cit. supra*, note 128, qui écrit à la p. 154: "It may be legal if the Security Council of the UN, with the support of the permanent members, were to transfer power to an organ in which no right

Malgré cela, certains auteurs affirment que la décision de la Cour dans l'affaire des *Dépenses* permet de conclure que la résolution 678 peut reposer sur les pouvoirs implicites du Conseil de sécurité.[137] Cette affaire concernait les opérations de maintien de la paix en Egypte et au Congo. Malgré le fait qu'aucun article de la Charte ne prévoyait ce type d'opération, la Cour en a confirmé la légalité en se fondant sur les pouvoirs implicites de l'Organisation. Toutefois, à l'opposé de ce qui s'est passé lors de la guerre du Golfe, c'est l'Organisation elle-même qui prenait les mesures et contrôlait ces opérations de maintien de la paix.[138] Notons également que la Cour a jugé que les mesures prises lors de ces opérations n'incluaient pas des mesures de type coercitif prévues par le chapitre VII

of veto would be applicable. The permanent members would then voluntarily renounce their special position. Even in this case the legality of the delegation could be questioned, however, if it were not expressly provided for in the Charter, since it may well be in the interest of the other Members of the UN for the five permanent members of the Security Council to bear full responsibility for all functions attributed to it.''

[137] O. SCHACHTER, *op. cit. supra*, note 44, à la p. 461; pour B. H. WESTON, *op. cit. supra*, note 49, les pouvoirs implicites du Conseil sont également la seule base juridique possible pour la résolution 678. Ainsi il écrit, à la p. 522: ''Thus, with Resolution 678 evidencing no explicit or clearly implicit authorization in the text of chapter VII, its travaux préparatoires or pertinent state practice, one is left to conclude that the Security Council created an entirely new precedent, seemingly on the basis of some assumed penumbra of powers available to the Council under chapter VII — an 'Article 42 1/2' authorization, as some UN watchers have called it.''; D. BOWETT, *op. cit. supra*, note 49, à la p. 34, avait auparavant justifié l'opération de la Corée sur la même base.

[138] B. RUSSETT et J. S. SUTTERLIN, *op. cit. supra*, note 21, à la p. 72, décrivent ainsi le système de contrôle de ce type d'opérations: ''a commander of the U.N. force is appointed by the secretary general after the peacekeeping operation has been authorized by the Security Council for a defined mission. Troop contingents provided by member states serve under their national officer — a batallion commander, for example — who in turn receives orders from the U.N. force commander. The U.N. force commander reports to the secretary general from whom he receives operational guidance. The secretary general reports to the Security Council and obtains its concurrence if any change in the peacekeeping mission is contemplated.'' Sur le contrôle du secrétaire général en Égypte, D. BOWETT, *op. cit. supra*, note 49, écrit, à la p. 104: ''whatever the breath of the field in which he could operate, legally his powers were circumscribed by the terms of his authority given by the General Assembly, whose powers are founded in the Charter and the 'Uniting for Peace' Resolution; there could not be a total delegation of the Assembly's powers to the secretary general.'' Dans l'affaire des *Dépenses*, la Cour conclut à la légalité des actions du secrétaire général au Congo, parce qu'à plusieurs occasions le Conseil et l'Assemblée générale avaient approuvé sa conduite. Toutefois, la Cour reconnaît implicitement qu'il peut se présenter des situations où il pourrait y avoir usurpation. Voir *supra*, note 41, à la p. 177.

de la Charte.[139]

Deuxièmement, si la Cour fait référence aux pouvoirs implicites de l'Organisation, c'est précisément pour étendre la compétence de l'Organisation aux dépens de la liberté d'agir des États.[140] Il serait pour le moins curieux que le même concept de "pouvoirs implicites" servent maintenant à accroître la liberté d'action de quelques États, en leur permettant d'agir à leur guise au nom de l'Organisation.[141]

Quant à l'énoncé de la Cour, "On ne peut pas dire que la Charte ait laissé le Conseil de sécurité impuissant en face d'une situation d'urgence, en l'absence d'accords conclus en vertu de l'article 43,"[142] Katia Boustiany a bien raison d'écrire que

> Même en admettant que le blocage des dispositions pertinentes dudit Chapitre VII. . . ne dépouille pas de manière absolue le Conseil de Sécurité des moyens requis pour maintenir ou rétablir la paix et la sécurité internationales, il n'en demeure pas moins que le recours à la contrainte armée contre un État ne constitue une prérogative du Conseil de Sécurité que lorsqu'il décide d'agir lui-même en vertu des pouvoirs que les États lui ont confiés à cet effet.[143]

Nous avons vu ci-dessus que d'autres solutions auraient permis au Conseil d'agir par l'entremise des États en conservant une certaine forme de contrôle sur leurs opérations. Il ne lui était donc pas nécessaire de s'effacer entièrement devant la coalition.

[139] Avis consultatif *Certaines Dépenses des Nations Unies, supra,* note 41, p. 177.

[140] *Id.,* pp. 167-68: "Il est naturel d'accorder le premier rang à la paix et la sécurité internationales, car les autres buts ne peuvent être atteints que si cette condition fondamentale est acquise. . .Sauf dans la mesure où ils ont confié à l'Organisation la mission d'atteindre ces buts communs, les États membres conservent leur liberté d'action. Mais lorsque l'Organisation prend des mesures dont on peut dire à juste titre qu'elles sont appropriées à l'accomplissement des buts déclarés des Nations Unies, il est à présumer que cette action ne dépasse pas les pouvoirs de l'Organisation."

[141] D'ailleurs, dès l'affaire des *Réparation des dommages subis au service des Nations Unies, supra,* note 129, la Cour avait insisté, à la p. 183, sur la nécessité de pouvoirs implicites pour justement assurer l'indépendance de l'Organisation vis-à-vis des États: "Tant afin d'assurer l'exercice efficace et indépendant de ses fonctions que pour procurer à ses agents un appui effectif, l'Organisation doit leur fournir une protection appropriée. . .Afin de garantir l'indépendance de l'agent et, en conséquence, l'action indépendante de l'Organisation elle-même, il est essentiel que l'agent, dans l'exercice de ses fonctions, n'ait pas besoin de compter sur une autre protection que celle de l'organisation. . ."

[142] *Supra,* note 41, à la p. 167.

[143] K. BOUSTANY, *op. cit. supra,* note 65, à la p. 389.

(ii) La résolution 678 est contraire aux objectifs de la Charte

Dans l'affaire *Certaines Dépenses des Nations Unies,* la Cour précise qu'une organisation internationale ne peut exercer que les pouvoirs compatibles avec les buts qu'elle poursuit. Examinant la relation entre les buts et les pouvoirs de l'Organisation, la Cour déclare:

Certes ses buts sont très vastes, mais ils ne sont pas illimités, non plus que les pouvoirs conférés pour les atteindre. Sauf dans la mesure où ils ont confié à l'Organisation la mission d'atteindre ces buts communs, les États membres conservent leur liberté d'action. Mais lorsque l'Organisation prend des mesures dont on peut dire à juste titre qu'elles sont appropriées à l'accomplissement des buts déclarés des Nations Unies, il est à présumer que cette action ne dépassse pas les pouvoirs de l'Organisation.[144]

À supposer que l'autorisation de la résolution 678 constitue l'exercice d'un pouvoir du Conseil de sécurité, encore faut-il qu'elle soit ''appropriée'' à l'accomplissement des buts de l'Organisation, et en particulier celui énoncé à l'article 1(1) de la Charte:

Maintenir la paix et la sécurité internationales et à cette fin: prendre des mesures collectives efficaces en vue de prévenir et d'écarter les menaces à la paix et de réprimer tout acte d'agression...

Le libellé de l'article 1(1) indique clairement que ce sont les ''mesures collectives'' qui sont appropriés pour maintenir la paix. Que peut-on entendre par ces termes? Pour Kelsen, ces ''mesures'' sont celles prévues au chapitre VII de la Charte.[145] D'autres auteurs signalent la difficulté d'interpréter des termes aussi vagues.[146] Toutefois, pour nos fins, il suffira de démontrer pourquoi certaines mesures ne sont pas visées par l'article 1.

On peut au départ convenir qu'il ne s'agit pas de mesures de légitime défense, car les États ont créé une organisation dans le but de substituer l'action concertée au droit traditionnel de légitime défense, qui est un droit d'exception.[147] De même, nous croyons qu'il faut exclure toute mesure sur laquelle l'organisation n'exerce

---

[144] *Supra* note 41, à la p. 168.

[145] H. KELSEN, *op. cit. supra,* note 50, aux pp. 14 et 970.

[146] C. F. AMERASHINGHE, ''The Charter Travaux Préparatoires and United Nations' Powers to Use Armed Forces,'' (1966) 4 *C.Y.I.L.* 81, 99.

[147] J. STONE, *supra,* note 44, à la p. 264: ''It is perfectly true that the first purpose of Article 1, paragraph 1, is concerned with collective measures for removing threats

pas de contrôle. Une telle interprétation est certainement compatible avec le préambule de la Charte, où les États membres s'engagent "à accepter les principes et instituer des *méthodes* garantissant
qu'il ne sera pas fait usage de la force des armes, sauf dans l'intérêt commun."[148] Seul un contrôle de l'usage de la force, exercé
par l'Organisation, offre une telle garantie.[149] Le fait que la méthode
spécifiquement prévue par les rédacteurs de la Charte n'a toujours
pas fonctionné n'élimine pas pour autant la nécessité de ce contrôle.

En autorisant les États présents dans le Golfe à user de "tous
les moyens nécessaires," le Conseil laissait à chacun de ces États
la liberté d'agir à sa guise plutôt que de mettre en place "des mesures
collectives efficaces en vue de prévenir et d'écarter les menaces à
la paix et de réprimer tout acte d'agression." De fait, donner carte
blanche à autant d'États peut même constituer une menace poten-
tielle à la paix, étant donné leurs intérêts nationaux respectifs, souvent divergents. Dans ces conditions, la résolution 678 ne contient
aucune exigence qui puisse s'apparenter à une "méthode" garantissant que la force sera utilisée uniquement "dans l'intérêt
commun."

CONCLUSION DE LA PARTIE I

Même si le Conseil de sécurité a voulu fonder la légitimité de
la résolution 678 sur le chapitre VII, à première vue cette résolution ne correspond à aucune des dispositions de ce chapitre.

Certains ont prétendu que cette résolution reposait sur le droit

---

to the peace, and the suppression of acts of aggression; and it is true also that
Article 51 uses the term 'collective' in its reservation of the inherent right of self-
defense against armed attack. And other affinities may also be pointed out on
the merely verbal level. Yet on any level but that of a mere play on words it is
clear that the two provisions are at poles as distant from each other as order is
from chaos, as modern England from England of the War of the Roses, as a society from a leaderless robber band struggling among themselves for dominance,
as the administration of justice from a duel; in short as ordered living from the
anarchic struggle to survive." Voir aussi H. KELSEN, *op. cit. supra*, note 50, à
la p. 922: "The framers of the Charter did not anticipate that the system of collective security laid down in the Charter will not work at all, and they certainly
did not intend collective self-defence as a substitue for collective security."

[148] Sur la valeur du préambule comme guide d'interprétation, voir J.-P. COT et A.
PELLET, *La Charte des Nations Unies*, (1985), aux pp. 5 et 6; voir aussi la plaidoirie
de la Norvège dans l'affaire *Certaines dépenses des Nations Unies, supra*, note 55, à la
p. 360.

[149] *Contra* J. N. SINGH, *op. cit. supra*, note 88, aux pp. 122-23.

de légitime défense collective. Pourtant la Charte prévoit qu'il s'agit là seulement d'un droit temporaire, en attendant l'intervention du Conseil. Comme nous l'avons vu, ce droit a pris fin au plus tard le 6 août 1990, lorsque le Conseil a adopté des mesures non militaires contre l'Irak. Ni le libellé de la résolution 678 ni le contexte de son adoption ne nous permettent de conclure qu'en autorisant l'usage de la force, le Conseil entendait rétablir le droit de légitime défense, ce qui aurait constitué une démarche sans précédent.

Les articles relatifs au système de sécurité collective ainsi que les pouvoirs implicites que pourraient invoquer le Conseil ne semblent pas davantage applicables pour un nombre de raisons explicitées ci-dessus. Toutes convergent vers une seule conclusion: la fonction du Conseil de sécurité, en tant qu'organe politique, est d'agir au nom de la communauté internationale, pour maintenir la paix et la sécurité internationales, et non de légitimer les actions d'États aspirant au rôle de policier mondial. En effet, le Conseil doit être le cerveau du système de sécurité collective mis en place par la Charte. Avec la résolution 678, il se contente de transférer l'initiative à qui veut bien la prendre. En se prêtant à ce genre d'exercice, il laisse à quelques États, depuis leurs capitales respectives et en fonction de leurs intérêts propres, la responsabilité de décider de la destinée de ce monde.

II. L'ILLÉGALITÉ DE LA PARTICIPATION CANADIENNE AUX OPÉRATIONS MILITAIRES QUI NE RESPECTENT PAS LA CHARTE DES NATIONS UNIES

Les problèmes considérables résultant de l'approche permissive privilégiée par le Conseil de sécurité ont été exposés ci-dessus. Ces difficultés nous amènent à conclure que la résolution 678 viole la *Charte des Nations Unies*. Quelles sont les conséquences de cette situation dans l'ordre interne canadien? L'article 31 (1) b) de la *Loi sur la défense nationale* envisage uniquement la participation des forces canadiennes aux opérations entreprises "aux termes de la Charte des Nations Unies." L'historique de cette disposition montre que le législateur a entendu restreindre la très large marge de manoeuvre conférée par le passé au gouvernement, éliminant du même coup certaines prérogatives reconnues à la Couronne par la common law (A). Les tribunaux doivent donc s'assurer du respect de cette loi, même s'ils sont ainsi confrontés à des controverses politiques ou à une décision prise par un organisme international (B). Reste à savoir qui peut soulever une telle question: les militaires sont-ils les seuls à pouvoir agir? Nous verrons que la jurisprudence récente reconnaî t à certains citoyens ou citoyennes la qualité pour agir dans l'intérêt public (C).

A. LA SUPPRESSION D'UNE PRÉROGATIVE DE LA COURONNE

Les prérogatives de la Couronne reconnues par la common law sont fréquemment invoquées pour souligner que le gouvernement détient certains pouvoirs discrétionnaires en matière de défense. Une présentation sommaire de ces pouvoirs (1) permettra de mettre en évidence l'importance des termes choisis par le législateur (2). Cette analyse permet de conclure que les prérogatives de la Couronne en ce domaine ont été éliminées par la législation (3).

I. *Déclaration de guerre et commandement des forces armées*

En common law, la Couronne peut exercer un certain nombre de pouvoirs pour défendre les intérêts du Royaume. L'un d'entre eux consiste à déclarer la guerre.[150] Il importe toutefois de préciser la signification de ces termes. Une déclaration de guerre annonce officiellement le déclenchement des hostilités. Elle met un terme aux relations commerciales entre les belligérants.[151] Elle peut résulter d'une notification par voie diplomatique, ou d'actes d'agression.[152] Lorsque ceci se produit, les contrats conclus avec un résident du pays ennemi deviennent contraires à l'ordre public. Ceci permet à la Couronne de saisir les biens échangés en raison de la conclusion de ces contrats.[153] En outre, un étranger de nationalité ennemie ne peut plus intenter une action devant les tribunaux canadiens.[154]

---

[150] *Renvoi: Résolution pour modifier la Constitution*, [1981] 1 R.C.S. 754, 877. En principe, la Couronne fédérale jouit, dans son domaine de compétence, des mêmes prérogatives que la Couronne en Angleterre: *R. c. Bank of Nova Scotia*, (1886) 11 R.C.S. 1, 10 et 18.

[151] *Janson c. Driefontein Consolidated Mines*, [1902] A.C. 484 (Ch. des L.).

[152] *Id.; The Teutonian*, (1872) 4 L.R.P.C. 171; 17 E.R. 366, 370.

[153] *Janson c. Driefontein Consolidated Mines*, loc. cit., supra, note 151, p. 499 (Lord Davey).

[154] *Id.; Daimler Co. Ltd c. Continental Tire and Rubber Co. (Great Britain) Ltd.*, [1916] 2 A.C. 307 (Ch. des L.); *Viola c. Mackenzie, Brown and Co.*, (1915) 24 B.R. 31; *Canadian Stewart Co. c. Perik and Price Brothers*, (1915) 25 B.R. 158; *Fabry c. Finlay*, (1916) 32 D.L.R. 673 (C.A.Q.); *Ragusz c. Harbour Commissioners of Montreal*, (1916) 18 R.P. 98, 30 D.L.R. 662 (C.A.Q.); *De Kozarijouk c. B. and A. Asbestos Co.*, (1914) 16 R.P. 213 (C.S.); *Guseta c. Laing*, (1915) 48 C.S. 427; *Dangler c. Hollinger Gold Mines*, (1915) 23 D.L.R. 384 (C.S. Ont.); *Luczyckic. Spanish River Pulp and Paper Mills Co.*, (1915) 25 D.L.R. 198 (H.C. Ont.); *Newman c. Bradshaw*, (1916) 28 D.L.R. 769 (C.S.C.-B); *Lampel c. Burger*, (1917)

En Angleterre, les tribunaux ont affirmé que la déclaration attribue à la Couronne des prérogatives de temps de guerre, telle que la saisie de navires appartenant à l'ennemi, ou de marchandises transportées par un navire britannique pour le compte d'une personne ennemie.[155] La Couronne peut même réquisitionner des biens appartenant à ses sujets, si elle le juge nécessaire pour mener à bien ses opérations militaires. Elle doit toutefois indemniser leur propriétaire.[156]

Ces quelques précisions permettent de mieux cerner le rôle d'une déclaration de guerre. Celle-ci attribue une série de pouvoirs exceptionnels à la Couronne, visant principalement les conséquences de la guerre au plan matériel. La conclusion d'un traité de paix met fin à l'état de guerre ainsi qu'aux pouvoirs exceptionnels qui en résultent;[157] il s'agit là encore d'une prérogative. Cependant, ces pouvoirs discrétionnaires ne concernent pas les forces armées. Ils ont uniquement des conséquences civiles. Signalons qu'en 1991, aucun pays n'a déclaré la guerre à l'Iraq, parce qu'une coalition de pays prétendait agir sous l'égide des Nations Unies.

En Angleterre, les pouvoirs de commandement dévolus à l'exécutif ne semblent pas être accrus par la déclaration de guerre.[158] En effet, le déploiement et la conduite des forces armées est déjà une prérogative de la Couronne en temps de paix.[159] Sa Majesté peut cependant requérir de ses sujets qu'ils prennent les armes afin de repousser une invasion.[160] À l'inverse, lorsque les hostilités se

---

40 O.L.R. 165 (C. de l'É.); *Lutha c. Halycznk*, (1918) 14 O.W.N. 219 (C. de l'É.); *Crenidas c. B.C. Electric Railway*, [1919] 2 W.W.R. 549 (C.S.C-B.).

[155]   *The Roumanian*, [1916] 1 A.C. 125 (C.J.C.P.).

[156]   *Burmah Oil Co. c. Lord Advocate*, [1965] A.C. 75 (ch. des L.).

[157]   Dans l'arrêt *Secretary of State of Canada c. Alien Property Custodian for the United States of America*, [1931] R.C.S. 170, le juge Duff déclare qu'un traité de paix produit des effets juridiques indépendamment de toute législation (p. 198). Si cette affirmation est incontestable pour la cessation de l'état de guerre et ses conséquences, il n'en va pas de même pour les dispositions du traité concernant les droits privés, qui requièrent l'intervention du législateur pour être reconnues en droit interne: *Bitter c. Secretary of State of Canada*, [1944] R. C. de l'É. 61, 76-77; *Civilian War Claimant Association Ltd c. The King*, [1932] A.C. 14 (ch. des L.).

[158]   La conduite de la guerre relève cependant de la Couronne, qui doit disposer des pouvoirs nécessaires pour ce faire: *Burmah Oil Co. c. Lord Advocate, loc. cit. supra*, note 156, p. 100 (Lord Reid), p. 145-46 (Lord Pearce), p. 166 (Lord Upjohn).

[159]   *Chandler c. D.P.P.*, [1964] A.C. 763.

[160]   *Burmah Oil Co. c. Lord Advocate, loc. cit. supra*, note 156, p. 122; *Broadfoot's* case, (1743) Fost 154, 168 E.R. 76, 78.

déroulent à l'extérieur du pays, la Couronne ne peut conscrire les civils sans y être autorisée par une loi du Parlement.[161]

Au Royaume-Uni, la décision d'expédier des militaires à l'étranger dans une zone de combat est donc prise par la Couronne. Il n'existe pas de loi portant sur ce sujet.[162] Il en va de même pour la participation aux opérations de maintien de la paix des Nations Unies.[163] La situation est tout autre au Canada, puisque le législateur a édicté des régles régissant la ''mise en service actif.'' La Couronne y est bien libre de déclarer la guerre, c'est-à-dire d'annoncer officiellement le déclenchement des hostilités. Pour mettre son projet à exécution et expédier des militaires au combat, elle doit toutefois se conformer à la *Loi sur la défense nationale.* Il convient donc d'examiner celle-ci.

2. *L'intervention du législateur*

À l'heure actuelle, l'article 31 (1) de la *Loi sur la défense nationale* se lit comme suit:[164]

31. (1) Le gouverneur en conseil peut mettre en service actif les Forces canadiennes ou tout élément constitutif, unité ou autre élément de ces forces, ou l'un de leurs officiers ou militaires de rang, n'importe où au Canada ou à l'étranger quand il estime opportun de le faire:

(a) soit pour la défense du Canada, en raison d'un état d'urgence

(b) soit en conséquence d'une action entreprise par le Canada aux termes de la Charte des Nations Unies, du Traité de l'Atlantique Nord ou de tout autre instrument semblable pour la défense collective que le Canada peut souscrire.

Il existe donc deux motifs pouvant être invoqués par le gouverneur en conseil. L'alinéa 31 (1) a) lui permet de mettre les forces canadiennes en service actif ''lorsqu'il le juge opportun...a) pour la défense du Canada, en raison d'un état d'urgence.'' Aux termes de l'article 2, l'expression ''état d'urgence'' signifie ''Guerre, invasion, émeute ou insurrection, réelle ou appréhendée.'' Cette défi-

[161] *Broadfoot's* case, note précédente, en obiter; la situation est différente dans le cas des marins.

[162] *Nissan c. A.G. of England,* [1970] A.C. 179 (Ch. des L.), particulièrement 229 (Lord Pearce). Voir également en Cour d'appel, [1968] 1 Q.B. 286, 340 (Lord Denning), ainsi que le commentaire de D. R. GILMOUR, ''British Forces Abroad and the Responsibility for Their Actions,'' [1970] *Public Law* 120, 141-142.

[163] *Nissan c. A.G. of England, loc. cit. supra,* note 162 (Ch. des L.).

[164] *Loc. cit. supra,* note 18. Sur la signification de l'expression ''service actif,'' voir *supra* note 17.

nition date de l'adoption de la loi, en 1950, quoique l'expression "circonstance critique" ait alors été employée.[165] Elle était également contenue dans l'*Acte concernant la Milice et la Défense de la Puissance du Canada*, édicté en 1868.[166] Lors des deux derniers conflits mondiaux, l'armée de métier a été expédiée à l'étranger aux termes d'une disposition législative semblable.[167]

On sait qu'en droit constitutionnel canadien, les tribunaux ont systématiquement refusé de remettre en question les décisions du gouvernement portant sur la durée d'un état d'urgence[168] ou sur son existence.[169] Il s'agissait dans ces arrêts de l'application de la *Loi sur les mesures de guerre*;[170] les mêmes principes semblent devoir s'appliquer à la *Loi sur la défense nationale*, qui définit en termes presque identiques l'expression "état d'urgence."[171] C'est dire que l'article 31 (1) a) confère un pouvoir d'appréciation extrêmement large au gouverneur en conseil, que les tribunaux refuseraient probablement de contrôler.

On pourrait cependant prétendre que l'expression "pour la défense du Canada" limite quelque peu la marge de manoeuvre du gouvernement. Il faut toutefois rappeler qu'il est possible d'envoyer des militaires "à l'étranger" en raison d'une guerre "réelle ou appréhendée." Pour cette raison, la "défense du Canada" peut fort bien autoriser une participation militaire aux hostilités se déroulant à l'extérieur du pays.[172] Est-il néanmoins possible de sou-

---

[165] *Loi sur la défense nationale*, S.C. 1950, c. 43, art. 2.

[166] S.C. 1868, c. 40, art. 61.

[167] *Acte de la milice*, S.C. 1904, c. 23, art. 70; S.R.C. 1906, c. 41, art. 69; S.R.C. 1927, c. 132, art. 64. Voir, à titre d'illustration, (1914-15) 48 *Gaz. Can.*, 675; 746; 815; 832; 839; 840; 951; 1291; 1448; (1939-40) 73 *Gaz. Can.*, 1246; 1247; 1319; 1555; 1918; 2414.

[168] *Fort Frances Pulp and Power Co. Ltd* c. *Manitoba Free Press Co. Ltd*, [1923] A.C. 695; *Co-operative Committee on Japanese Canadians* c. *A.G. of Canada*, [1947] A.C. 87; *Renvoi relatif à la validité des Règlements sur les baux en temps de guerre*, [1950] R.C.S. 124; *Renvoi concernant la Loi anti-inflation*, [1976] 2 R.C.S. 373.

[169] *Gagnon* c. *La Reine*, [1971] C.A. 454, 460.

[170] L.R.C. (1985), c. W-2.

[171] La *Loi sur les mesures de guerre*, art. 2 et 3, conférait des pouvoirs réglementaires très étendus "en raison de l'existence réelle ou appréhendée de l'état de guerre, d'invasion ou d'insurrection." L'état d'urgence est défini de la même façon par l'article 2 de la *Loi sur la défense nationale*. La *Loi sur les mesures de guerre* a été abrogée par la *Loi sur les mesures d'urgences*, L.R.C. (1985), c. 22 (4e supp.), art. 80.

[172] On retrouve cette conception du terme "défense" dans un obiter de la Chambre des Lords: "The Crown clearly considered that the sending of troops was justified to protect the realm by stopping a conflagration which might have serious consequences to the safety of this country if it was allowed to spread. Of that matter the Crown is the judge." *A. G.* c. *Nissan*, *loc. cit. supra*, note 157, p. 229 (Lord Pearce); voir aussi p. 237, D-E (Lord Pearson).

tenir que seuls les intérêts du Canada doivent être menacés et qu'il n'est pas possible de prêter main-forte à un pays en détresse? Compte tenu du caractère extensible de la notion de "'défense'" et de la jurisprudence citée ci-dessus, il nous semble que si les tribunaux étaient saisis de la question, ils refuseraient de substituer leur opinion à celle du gouvernement.[173] Cette analyse permet de conclure qu'après la Seconde Guerre mondiale, le gouvernement canadien aurait pu participer aux opérations militaires entreprises par les Nations Unies. Il lui suffisait d'invoquer la disposition correspondant à l'article 31 (1) a) de la *Loi sur la défense nationale* actuelle.

C'est dans ce contexte qu'il convient de s'interroger sur l'origine de l'article 31 (1) b). Ce paragraphe a été ajouté à *Loi sur la défense nationale* en 1950, quelques mois après l'adoption de cette dernière loi.[174] Lorsqu'il est invoqué, seules les opérations conformes aux traités qu'il mentionne justifient la mise en service actif des forces canadiennes. La référence à la *Charte des Nations Unies* plutôt qu'aux résolutions du Conseil de sécurité est également significative. Lorsque le législateur entend simplement se conformer aux décisions du Conseil, il sait le dire clairement.[175]

La citation de la *Charte des Nations Unies* n'est pas anodine: elle résulte du fait qu'à l'époque de la guerre de Corée, le Conseil de sécurité était paralysé et l'Assemblée générale des Nations Unies avait pris la relève.[176] Le législateur désirait que le Canada puisse

---

[173] En Angleterre, la Chambre des Lords a été saisie d'une affaire où des manifestants avaient bloqué l'accès à un aéroport militaire, dans le but de diffuser leur opposition à la possession d'armes nucléaires: *Chandler* c. *D.P.P.*, *loc. cit. supra*, note 159. Ils furent accusés de s'être approché d'un endroit "prohibé" dans un dessein contraire aux intérêts ou à la sûreté de l'État. Les accusés prétendaient que le fait de chercher à convaincre le public de renoncer aux armes nucléaires ne pouvait être considéré comme un dessein contraire aux intérêts ou à la sûreté de l'État. La Chambre des Lords rejeta cet argument, estimant que l'intention de bloquer l'accès à l'aéroport constituait le dessein prohibé par la loi en cause. Les Lords ajoutent qu'il n'est pas possible d'inviter le jury ou le juge à déterminer si la renonciation aux armes nucléaires serait dans l'intérêt de l'État, parce qu'il s'agit d'une question d'opinion individuelle qui ne peut être tranchée par les tribunaux. Les juges s'appuient également sur le fait que l'armement des forces armées est une prérogative de la Couronne. De façon similaire, au Canada, les tribunaux refuseraient vraisemblablement d'évaluer ce qui est nécessaire pour "la défense" du pays.

[174] *Loi concernant les forces canadiennes*, S.C. 1950-51, c. 2, art. 4.

[175] La *Loi sur les Nations Unies*, L.R.C. (1985), c. U-2, autorise le gouverneur en conseil à mettre en oeuvre une mesure du Conseil de sécurité décrétée "en conformité avec l'article 41 de la Charte des Nations Unies" (soit l'imposition de sanctions économiques).

[176] Sur l'invasion de la Corée du Sud, voir *supra*, note 77. La *Loi concernant les forces*

participer à toute action découlant de la *Charte des Nations Unies.* Il
faut en conclure qu'il entendait que la Charte elle-même soit respectée. Dans le cas contraire, il lui aurait suffi de mentionner les actions entreprises à la suite de l'adoption d'une résolution du Conseil
ou de l'Assemblée générale.

Qu'en est-il de l'expression "lorsqu'il le juge opportun" contenue dans le paragraphe introductif de l'article 31 (1)? Certes, ces
mots soulignent le fait que le gouverneur en conseil jouit d'une
discrétion très large, tout particulièrement lorsqu'il s'agit de déterminer si un état d'urgence existe. Dans cette hypothèse, sa discrétion n'est pas limitée par la loi et peut difficilement être révisée
par les tribunaux. Cette expression du législateur ne permet cependant pas au pouvoir exécutif de décider souverainement si la *Charte
des Nations Unies* a été respectée. Le législateur a tout simplement
précisé qu'il n'entendait pas imposer au gouverneur en conseil l'obligation de prendre part aux opérations entreprises par les Nations
Unies. Si le gouvernement décide d'agir, l'opération à laquelle le
Canada participe doit être conforme à la *Charte.*

Une dernière question se pose. Au cours d'un débat judiciaire,
le gouvernement pourrait-il prétendre que sa décision est justifiée
parce qu'il aurait pu invoquer une situation d'urgence, même s'il
ne l'a pas fait? On peut se demander s'il est possible de justifier
l'exercice d'un pouvoir délégué par une disposition qui n'a pas été
invoquée lors de la décision contestée.[177] Le problème se pose

canadiennes, loc. cit. supra, note 174, fut sanctionnée le 9 septembre 1950. En
Chambre, le ministre de la défense nationale a tenté d'expliquer la modification
de la disposition concernant la mise en service actif des forces armées. A son avis,
l'occupation d'une partie du territoire de la Corée du Sud ne constituait pas une
"invasion" et la réaction des Nations Unies ne pouvait être qualifiée de guerre.
Pour cette raison, le ministre considérait qu'il n'existait pas de "circonstance critique" au sens de la *Loi sur la défense nationale* de l'époque: *Débats de la Chambre des
communes,* Troisième session, Vingt-et-unième législature, 1950, p. 455, 507 et 518.
Par ailleurs, la modification de 1950 avait également pour but d'offrir aux militaires
participant aux opérations se déroulant en Corée les prestations accordées aux
anciens combattants des deux conflits mondiaux. Rappelons en terminant sur
ce point que les débats parlementaires ne peuvent servir à interpréter une loi.
Par contre, ils peuvent être utilisés dans le but d'identifier la difficulté à laquelle
le législateur entendait remédier: Pierre-André C O TÉ, *Interprétation des lois,* 2e édition, Éditions Yvon Blais Inc, 1990, p. 402-418. De tout ceci, il faut conclure que
le législateur entendait fournir un fondement aux opérations de Corée sans qu'il
soit nécessaire de décréter l'existence de "circonstances critiques." Le fondement
retenu, la *Charte des Nations Unies,* s'impose alors à l'exécutif.

[177] L'arrêt *Pugsley* c. *Garson,* (1922) 50 N.B.R. 414 (C.A.), affirme que le gouvernement
n'est pas obligé de mentionner la loi qui l'autorise à agir (p. 424). Évidemment,

différemment dans le cas des situations d'urgence.[178] Celles-ci autorisent le pouvoir fédéral à suspendre temporairement le partage des compétences législatives effectué par la *Loi constitutionnelle de 1867*.[179] Pour ce faire, les juges doivent pouvoir conclure que le Parlement faisait face à un état d'urgence.[180] Une telle décision ne peut être prise lorsque la loi a été adoptée sans faire état d'une situation de crise.

De même, l'exercice des pouvoirs qui étaient jadis conférés par la *Loi sur les mesures de guerre*[181] présupposait l'existence d'un état d'urgence. Le gouvernement ne pouvait adopter un décret énonçant que cette situation avait pris fin, en édictant du même souffle de nouvelles règles. Ce faisant, il prétendait exercer des pouvoirs qu'il ne détenait plus.[182] Décréter l'état d'urgence est donc une décision

cette loi doit être portée à l'attention des tribunaux par la suite et avoir été invoquée à bon escient.

[178] Voir, entre autres, les décisions citées *supra*, note 168.

[179] 30-31 Vict., R.-U., c. 3.

[180] La majorité des juges s'entendent sur ce principe dans le *Renvoi concernant la Loi anti-inflation, loc. cit.*, *supra*, note 168: voir p. 422 (le juge Laskin); p. 438 (le juge Ritchie); pp. 463-66 (le juge Beetz).

[181] *Loc. cit supra*, note 170; la *Loi sur les mesures d'urgence*, L.R.C. (1985), c. 22 (4e supp.), ne s'applique pas davantage que l'article 31 (1) (a) de la *Loi sur la défense nationale*, L.R.C. (1985), c. N-5, pour la même raison: le gouvernement n'a adopté aucun décret contenant une ''déclaration de situation de crise'' au sens de l'article 57 de la *Loi sur les mesures d'urgence*. Seule la partie IV de cette dernière loi est pertinente pour nos fins. Le gouvernement aurait certes pu déclarer ''qu'il existe un état de guerre justifiant en l'occurrence des mesures extraordinaires à titre temporaire'' (art. 38). Ces dernières sont définies ainsi: ''toute mesure'' que le gouverneur en conseil ''croit, pour des motifs raisonnables, fondée ou opportune pour faire face à la crise'' (art. 40 (1)). Toutefois, elles ne peuvent avoir pour effet d'''obliger des personnes à servir dans les Forces canadiennes'' (art. 40 (2)). Ce dernier alinéa vise la conscription de civils et n'exclut pas la mise en service actif de l'armée de métier. On voit cependant mal pourquoi le gouvernement utiliserait la *Loi sur les mesures d'urgence*. En effet, une ''déclaration de situation de crise'' doit être ratifiée par le Parlement, sans quoi elle est abrogée (art. 50 (7)). Elle cesse d'avoir effet après cent vingt jours, sauf si elle est prorogée par le gouvernement (art. 43 (1)). La prorogation doit également être approuvée par le Parlement (art. 60). Pour sa part, l'article 32 de la *Loi sur la défense nationale* exige simplement que le Parlement siège ou soit convoqué. Aucun autre mécanisme de contrôle n'est prévu; le gouvernement n'a donc aucun intérêt à invoquer la *Loi sur les mesures d'urgences*, puisque l'article 31 (1) (a) de la *Loi sur la défense nationale* lui permet déjà d'agir en temps de crise, sans que sa décision ait un caractère temporaire.

[182] *In re Price Brothers and Co. and Board of Commerce of Canada*, (1919-20) 60 R.C.S. 265. Cet arrêt a été implicitement renversé par l'arrêt *Fort Frances Pulp and Power Co. c. Manitoba Free Press Co., loc. cit. supra*, note 168. Le Conseil privé semble cependant prêt à reconnaî tre que le texte du décret doit être examiné pour déterminer

lourde de conséquences. Une situation de crise ne se présume pas. Dire qu'il faut prendre part aux opérations militaires entreprises par les Nations Unies est une chose. Dire qu'il existe un état d'urgence en est une autre, beaucoup plus grave du point de vue politique, juridique et constitutionnel. Il serait tout à fait inacceptable qu'un juge déclare *a posteriori* qu'une telle situation existait, sans que le gouvernment ait eu à répondre de sa décision devant l'opinion publique. Les alinéas (a) et (b) de l'article 31 (1) de la *Loi sur la défense nationale* sont donc conceptuellement distincts; ils doivent le demeurer.

3. *Les conséquences de la législation*

L'article 15 de la *Loi constitutionnelle de 1867* réaffirme l'existence d'une prérogative de la Couronne concernant les forces armées:

À la Reine continuera d'être et est par la présente attribué le commandement en chef des milices de terre et de mer et de toutes les forces militaires et navales en Canada.

On sait que le gouverneur général administre le gouvernement du Canada au nom de la Reine (art. 10) et qu'il doit agir de l'avis du Conseil privé (art. 13). C'est donc lui (ou elle) qui est responsable du commandement des forces canadiennes. Cette prérogative peut cependant être restreinte par une loi fédérale.[183] C'est précisément ce que fait l'article 31 de la *Loi sur la défense nationale:* la décision de mettre les forces canadiennes en service actif doit être prise par le gouverneur général en conseil. Si l'alinéa (1) b) est invoqué, l'action militaire en cause doit être entreprise aux termes des traités

---

s'il y a véritablement urgence dans l'esprit du gouvernement. En l'espèce, il conclut que la situation de crise pouvait fort bien subsister pour la réglementation de certains produits seulement: voir pp. 706-8.

[183] L'article 44 de la *Loi constitutionnelle de 1982* permet au Parlement fédéral de modifier par une simple loi les dispositions de la Constitution relatives au pouvoir exécutif fédéral, sous réserve des articles 41 et 42. Seule la charge de la Reine et du gouverneur général pourrait être affectée dans l'hypothèse que nous envisageons (art. 41 a)). Nous croyons cependant que la charge du gouverneur général comprend uniquement les fonctions essentielles au parlementarisme, telles que le pouvoir de nomination et de destitution au Conseil privé, la prorogation et la dissolution de la Chambre des communes, ainsi que la sanction des lois. Pour cette raison, rien n'empêche le Parlement de légiférer en matière de défense nationale, par exemple en prévoyant qu'il devra approuver au préalable une déclaration de guerre ou la nomination du chef d'état-major des forces canadiennes. Le Parlement peut d'ailleurs légiférer sur "La milice, le service militaire et le service naval, et la défense du Pays": *Loi constitutionnelle de 1867*, (art. 91 7).

qui y sont mentionnés. Enfin, l'article 32 dispose que dans l'hypothèse où le Parlement est ajourné ou prorogé le jour de l'adoption du décret, il doit recommencer à siéger dans les dix jours.

Peut-on néanmoins soutenir que la prérogative coexiste avec la *Loi sur la défense nationale?* Une telle approche a été clairement rejetée par un arrêt de la Chambre des lords, *A.G. c. De Keyser's Royal Hotel.*[184] Au cours de la Première Guerre mondiale, la Couronne avait réquisitionné un hôtel pour des membres des forces armées. Certaines lois britanniques lui permettaient d'agir ainsi, mais en lui imposant l'obligation d'indemniser le propriétaire des biens réquisitionnés. Le procureur général prétendit alors qu'une prérogative de la Couronne lui permettait de réquisitionner des biens en temps de guerre sans payer d'indemnité. Cet argument a été rejeté en termes très clairs. Les motifs de lord Atkinson nous semblent représentatifs de l'opinion de tous les lords:[185]

It is quite obvious that it would be useless and meaningless for the Legislature to impose restrictions and limitations upon, and to attach conditions to, the exercise by the Crown of the powers conferred by a statute, if the Crown were free at its pleasure to disregard those provisions, and by virtue of its prerogative do the very thing the statutes empowered it to do. One cannot in the construction of a statute attribute to the Legislature (in the absence of compelling words) an intention so absurd. It

---

[184] [1920] A.C. 508.

[185] *Id.,* 539-40. Voir 526 (Lord Dunedin), 554 (Lord Moulton), 561-62 (Lord Summer) et 575-76 (Lord Parmoor). Cet arrêt a été cité par des tribunaux canadiens appliquant le principe contenu dans les passages cités ci-dessus: *The King c. Zornes,* [1923] R.C.S. 257, 266 (le juge Anglin); *In re Silver: A.G. for Canada c. A.G. for Quebec,* [1929] R.C.S. 557, 566 (le juge Mignault), arrêt renversé par la suite sans citer l'affaire *De Keyser Royal Hotel* ([1932] A.C. 514); *Canadian Pacific Railway Co. c. City of Winnipeg,* [1952] 1 R.C.S. 424, 450 (le juge Kellock); *R. c. Nisbet Shipping Co.,* [1953] 1 R.C.S. 480, 503 (le juge Locke), dissidence confirmée par la suite, [1955] 4 D.L.R. 1, 4 (C.J.C.P.); *Oakfield Developments (Toronto) Ltd c. Ministre du revenu national,* [1969] 2 R.C. de l'E. 149, 160, conf. sans commentaires sur ce point, [1971] R.C.S. 1032; *A.G. of Newfoundland c. Churchill Falls (Labrador) Co.,* (1984) 49 Nfld & P.E.I.R 181, 243 (C.S.), conf. sans commentaires sur ce point (1985) 56 Nfld & P.E.I.R (C.A.) et [1988] 1 R.C.S. 1085; *Deputy Sheriff of Calgary c. Walter's Trucking Service Ltd,* (1965) 50 D.L.R. (2d) 711, 712 et 719 (C.A. Alb.). Dans un arrêt unanime, la Cour suprême a cité une autre partie de l'arrêt *De Keyser's,* celle où les juges refusent de présumer que le législateur a entendu s'approprier des biens sans indemniser leur propriétaire: *Manitoba Fisheries Ltd c. La Reine,* [1979] 1 R.C.S. 101, 109. Il semble donc évident que cet arrêt est reçu en droit canadien. Au sujet de l'effet d'une loi sur une prérogative de la Couronne, le lecteur ou la lectrice pourra consulter les arrêts suivants: *R. c. Bank of Nova Scotia, loc. cit. supra,* note 150, p. 18; *Association des employés du Gouvernement de la Nouvelle-Écosse c. Commission de la Fonction publique de la Nouvelle-Écosse,* [1981] 1 R.C.S. 211, 222-223.

was suggested that when a statute is passed empowering the Crown to do a certain thing which it might theretofore have done by virtue of its prerogative, the prerogative is merged in the statute. I confess I do not think the word 'merged' is happily chosen. I should prefer to say that when such a statute, expressing the will and intention of the King and of the three estates of the realm, is passed, it abridges the Royal Prerogative while it is in force to this extent: that the Crown can only do the particular thing under and in accordance with the statutory provisions, and that its prerogative power to do that thing is in abeyance.

La *Loi sur la défense nationale* énonce les règles à suivre pour mettre les forces canadiennes en service actif. Au Canada, avant l'arrêt *De Keyser's Royal Hotel,* quelques juges ont exprimé des doutes sur l'existence d'une prérogative concernant la mise en service actif des forces armées ou la conscription de civils, puisque ces questions faisaient l'objet de dispositions législatives précises.[186] Dans le cas de l'article 31 (1), il est manifeste que la prérogative a été remplacée par une loi fédérale.[187] Pour s'en convaincre, supposons que le gouverneur général mette les troupes en service actif alors que le Parlement ne siège pas. Cette situation fait l'objet de l'article 32 de la *Loi sur la défense nationale.* Peut-on imaginer un seul instant que la prérogative royale permette de passer outre à cet article?

---

[186] Parlant de l'article 69 de l'*Acte de la la milice,* S.R.C. 1906, c. 41, le juge Stuart écrit: "s. 69...is the only statutory authority for the sending of any troops out of Canada": *Calgary Brewing and Malting Co.* c. *McManus,* (1916) 10 W.W.R. 969 (C.A. Alb.). L'arrêt *Re Lewis,* (1918) 41 D.L.R. 1 (C.A. Alb.) concernait des règlements adoptés en vertu de la *Loi des mesures de guerre,* 1914, S.C. 1914, 2e sess., c. 2, qui supprimaient les exemptions prévues par une loi imposant la conscription, la *Loi du service militaire, 1917,* S.C. 1917, c. 19. Le juge Beck écrit: "in addition to statute it was hesitatingly suggested, though not seriously argued, that the order might be supported as an exercise of the Royal Prerogative. It is impossible, in my opinion, to sustain the order on any such ground. There is, undoubtedly, a considerable field in which the Royal prerogative can still be exercised...but I can see no portion of that field which would include such a case as this, in which the statute expressly places the jurisdiction to make orders in the constitutional tribunal of the governor in Council" (p. 16). Ces propos nous semblent s'appliquer parfaitement à l'article 31 (1) de la *Loi sur la défense nationale.* L'arrêt *Lewis* a été désavoué par la suite par la Cour suprême, pour d'autres motifs: *In re Gray,* (1918) 57 R.C.S. 150.

[187] Voir en ce sens Paul LORDON, *Crown Law,* Butterworths 1990, pp. 81-82. La ministre de la justice fédérale a soutenu en Chambre que le gouvernement exerçait une prérogative de la Couronne en ordonnant aux forces armées de prendre part à des opérations militaires: *Débats de la chambre des communes,* 2e session, 34e Législature, vol. 131, No 271, le mardi 15 janvier 1991, p. 17072. Ce pouvoir est bien de nature discrétionnaire, mais il ne fait plus partie des prérogatives de la Couronne, puisqu'il est circonscrit par une loi.

Une telle position est indéfendable dans un système de souveraineté parlementaire: la prérogative royale se compose exclusivement des pouvoirs ou des droits qui n'ont pas été limités ou supprimés par la législation. Dès qu'une loi entre clairement en conflit avec la prérogative, cette dernière doit s'effacer.[188]

L'article 31 (1) b) de la *Loi sur la défense nationale* limite le pouvoir discrétionnaire dont jouissait par le passé le gouverneur en conseil. Il autorise l'envoi de militaires à l'étranger dans le but de participer à une action qui respecte les termes de la *Charte des Nations Unies*. Cette condition essentielle est inconciliable avec le pouvoir absolu dont jouit la Couronne en Angleterre. Même dans l'hypothèse où l'article 31 (1) a) est invoqué, le gouvernement doit décréter qu'il existe un état d'urgence. L'article 32 l'oblige alors à répondre de sa décision devant le Parlement. Les tribunaux canadiens sont pour leur part obligés de s'assurer que l'exécutif respecte les lois du pays. Une action militaire qui viole la *Charte des Nations Unies* est par le fait même illégale, et il ne saurait être question de prérogative dans ce cas. Seule une règle de droit interdisant aux tribunaux de se pencher sur des questions de défense nationale ou de politique pourrait constituer un obstacle à un recours fondé sur l'article 31 (1) b) de la *Loi sur la défense nationale*.

B. LE RÔLE DES TRIBUNAUX CANADIENS

Par le passé, les tribunaux ont examiné sans sourciller les conventions internationales ou les traités intégrés à la législation fédérale, imposant du même coup au gouvernement l'obligation de les respecter (1). Le fait qu'une décision émane d'une organisation internationale pourrait pousser les tribunaux à ne pas contredire celle-ci; il faudra donc examiner les décisions traitant de cette question (2). Certaines règles jurisprudentielles d'origine étrangère pourraient également être invoquées pour inciter les juges à adopter une attitude différente. Il faudra donc se demander si ces principes sont reçus en droit canadien (3).

1. *Les tribunaux et la législation intégrant une convention internationale*

[188] René DUSSAULT, Louis BORGEAT, *Traité de droit administratif,* 2e édition, tome I, Presses de l'Université Laval, 1984, pp. 67-68; Peter HOGG, *Constitutional Law of Canada,* 2nd ed., Carswell, 1985, pp. 10-11; P. LORDON, *op. cit. supra,* note 187, pp. 65-67; *Thomson c. Canada (Sous-ministre de l'Agriculture),* C.S. Can., no. 22020, le 13 février 1992, p. 10 de la version française des notes du juge Cory.

Le Parlement fédéral a édicté de nombreuses lois renvoyant à une convention internationale. Les tribunaux canadiens ont eu à interpréter ces lois et ils ont analysé le traité ou la convention en cause comme une disposition législative ordinaire.[189] Tout récemment, la Cour suprême du Canada se penchait sur le rôle d'un tribunal administratif chargé d'appliquer une loi mettant en oeuvre une convention internationale. Elle en venait à la conclusion qu'un tel organisme n'agissait pas de façon déraisonnable en confrontant la convention internationale à la loi pour découvrir si cette dernière est ambiguë.[190] *A fortiori,* les tribunaux ordinaires peuvent agir de la sorte.[191] En somme, lorsqu'une loi renvoie expressément à une convention internationale, les tribunaux considèrent que cette dernière fait partie de la législation. Ils interprètent ses dispositions lorsque le besoin s'en fait sentir.

Par ailleurs, les tribunaux canadiens ont toujours exigé que les pouvoirs conférés par une loi à une autorité administrative soient exercés dans le respect le plus strict des dispositions législatives pertinentes. Il s'ensuit que les pouvoirs octroyés par les termes d'une convention intégrée à une loi fédérale doivent être exercés conformément à la teneur de cette convention. Deux arrêts de la Cour

[189] Mentionnons à titre d'exemple la *Convention de Vienne sur les relations diplomatiques, intégrée par la Loi sur les privilèges et immunités diplomatiques et consulaires,* L.R.C. (1985), c. P-22, qui fut interprétée par la Cour d'appel de l'Ontario dans *R. c. Palacios,* (1984) 1 O.A.C. 356; la Convention de Varsovie, intégrée par la *Loi sur le transport aérien,* S.R.C. 1952, c. 45, et interprétée par la Cour suprême dans *Ludecke c. Lignes aériennes Canadien Pacifique Ltée,* [1979] 2 R.C.S. 63 et *Compagnie Montréal Trust c. Lignes aériennes Canadien Pacifique Ltée,* [1977] 2 R.C.S. 793; la Convention de Berne, intégrée par la *Loi concernant le droit d'auteur,* S.R.C. 1952, c. 42 et interprétée par la Cour suprême dans *Durand et Cie c. La Patrie Publishing Co. Ltd,* [1960] R.C.S. 649; le Traité de Paix de 1919, repris par la *Loi des traités de paix,* 1919, S.C. 1919, c. 30 et interprété (entre autres) par la Cour suprême dans *Secretary of State of Canada c. Nietzke,* (1921) 62 R.C.S. 262; la Convention d'octobre 1818, conclue entre le Roi Georges III et les Etats[Unis d'Amérique, intégrée par l'*Acte concernant la pêche par les navires étrangers,* S.R.C. 1886, c. 94, interprétée par la Cour suprême dans *The Ship "Frederick Gerring Jr." c. The Queen,* (1897) 27 R.C.S. 271. Le texte de la convention n'est pas toujours reproduit dans la loi; il suffit qu'elle soit citée pour que les tribunaux l'interprètent. Le Parlement peut même prévoir qu'un traité particulier prévaudra sur la législation fédérale. Si tel est le cas, les tribunaux appliqueront le traité de préférence à la loi fédérale, par exemple en matière d'extradition (*République d'Italie c. Piperno,* [1982] 1 R.C.S. 320, 324; *R. c. Parisien,* [1988] 1 R.C.S. 950, 958; *Les États-Unis d'Amérique c. Allard,* [1991] 1R.C.S. 861, 865, ou de droit fiscal (*R. c. Melford developments Inc.,* [1982] 2 R.C.S. 504, 513-14).

[190] *National Corn Growers Association c. Canada (Tribunal canadien des importations),* [1990] 2 R.C.S. 1324, 1371 (le juge Gonthier, au nom des quatres juges majoritaires).

[191] *Id.,* 1348 (la juge Wilson, au nom des trois juges minoritaires).

suprême du Canada reconnaissent clairement ce principe. Le premier, *Chateau-Gai Wines Ltd c. Institut national des appellations d'origine des vins et eaux-de-vie,*[192] concernait la *Loi sur l'Arrangement commercial Canada-France, 1933.*[193] Le texte de cet "Arrangement" était annexé à la loi. Aux termes de l'article 2 de cette Annexe, les appellations de lieu d'origine des vins et des eaux-de-vie devaient être "enregistrées...dans les services compétents" de l'une des Hautes parties contractantes pour être protégées dans ce pays.

En l'espèce, l'appellation avait été portée au registre des marques de commerce du Canada. L'appelante soutenait que cet enregistrement n'était pas autorisé par la législation canadienne. Le juge Pigeon, qui s'exprime au nom des juges majoritaires, rejette cet argument, étant d'avis que la loi de 1933 avait modifié implicitement les lois en vigueur.[194] Il prend cependant soin de s'assurer que l'enregistrement a eu lieu et qu'il ne protège pas une expression tombée dans le domaine public, une exception prévue par l'article 2 de l'Annexe. Dissident, le juge Laskin, alors juge puîné, s'exprime ainsi, au nom de trois de ses collègues:

> Il est vrai que le gouvernement canadien a joué un rôle dans l'enregistrement dans le registre des marques de commerce mais, s'il ne s'agissait pas d'un enregistrement dans les services compétents selon le sens de l'art. II, je ne vois pas comment les intimées peuvent dégager de l'intervention du gouvernement canadien quelque appui à leur prétention. Il n'appartient pas au gouvernement canadien ni à aucune autre autorité administrative qui est du ressort de celui-ci de décider du caractère régulier d'une cause d'action fondée sur une loi, à moins que cette loi ne spécifie clairement que le gouvernement ou l'autorité administrative a ce pouvoir d'appréciation. Autrement, les cours ont le droit et le devoir de décider du caractère régulier de semblable condition. C'est le cas de la présente espèce. Selon les termes de l'article II, le mot 'Champagne'...ne sera protégé que lorsqu'il aura été enregistré dans les 'services compétents.'[195]

Le juge Laskin conclut que le fonctionnaire responsable du registre n'est pas un service compétent au sens de l'"Arrangement." Il est cependant clair que les juges de la Cour suprême s'entendent sur le principe en cause: une condition énoncée dans un traité annexé à une loi doit être respectée. Dans le cas contraire, les droits

---

[192] [1975] 1 R.C.S. 190.

[193] S.C. 1933, c. 31.

[194] *Loc. cit. supra,* note 192, p. 205.

[195] *Id.,* 220.

qui en résultent n'auront pas pris naissance et ne seront pas reconnus par les tribunaux. Cette idée se dégage encore plus nettement de l'opinion majoritaire, qui examine les effets d'une directive expédiée par la Direction des aliments et drogues, recommandant aux producteurs d'utiliser l'appellation "Canadian Champagne," pour éviter de créer une "impression erronée." Le juge Pigeon déclare à ce propos: "Je ne vois pas comment cette décision administrative pourrait avoir une valeur juridique quelconque à l'encontre de la loi de 1933. . . . Dès que l'on vient à la conclusion que l'effet de l''Arrangement' sanctionné par cette loi est d'ordonner que les appellations d'origine enregistrées soient protégées au Canada, *aucune autorité administrative ne peut valablement en ordonner autrement.*"[196]

Il est donc clair que le gouvernement canadien, comme tout autre organisme administratif,[197] doit se conformer aux règles énoncées par une convention internationale qui a été expressément intégrée à une loi fédérale.

L'arrêt *Secretary of State of Canada* c. *Alien Property Custodian for the United States of America*[198] applique également ce principe. Il s'agissait dans cette affaire d'interpréter l'*Arrêté du Traité de paix, Allemagne, 1920,* édicté aux termes de la *Loi des Traités de paix, 1919.*[199] Après un considérant rappelant la signature du Traité de Versailles le 28 juin 1919, l'article un de cette loi autorisait le gouverneur en conseil à

---

[196] *Id.,* p. 209; nous mettons en italiques.

[197] Dans l'arrêt *Capital Cities Communications Inc.* c. *Conseil de la Radio-Télévision canadienne,* [1978] 1 R.C.S. 141, le juge Pigeon, dissident, écrit (p. 189):
    en ce qui concerne l'appel de la décision du Conseil, il convient de prendre connaissance d'office du fait que, en vertu de la Convention, les appelantes ont un droit juridiquement protégé à l'utilisation des canaux qui leur sont attribués pour la diffusion d'émissions dans une région qui s'étend en-deçà des frontières canadiennes. En conséquence, le Conseil ne pouvait à bon droit autoriser une interférence avec ces droits, en violation de la Convention signée par le Canada.
    Les juges majoritaires estiment que la Convention ne s'applique pas aux opérations qui sont à l'origine du litige (p. 175). Le juge en chef Laskin précise cependant (p. 173):
    Rien n'indique que le Conseil tire un pouvoir quelconque de la Convention ni que la Convention, en elle-même, limite le pouvoir de contrôle conféré au Conseil par la *Loi sur la radiodiffusion* . . . Les seules conséquences intérieures ou internes possibles viendraient de l'application d'une législation donnant à la Convention un effet juridique au Canada.
    Là encore, il est clair qu'un organisme administratif est contraint de respecter une convention à laquelle réfère sa loi habilitante.

[198] *Loc. cit. supra,* note 157.

[199] S.C. 1919, c. 30.

édicter les décrets "nécessaires pour la mise en vigueur desdits traités." L'Arrêté précité réglait le sort des biens appartenant à l'ennemi et confisqués durant la guerre.

Le litige concernait des actions de compagnies canadiennes ou des titres au porteur émis au Canada. Ces valeurs mobilières pouvaient être transférées par simple endossement; en 1917, elles étaient détenues à New York par des nationaux allemands. Elles avaient été attribuées au curateur canadien par des décisions de diverses cours supérieures, rendues en octobre 1919. Quelques mois plus tôt, le *Alien Property Custodian* des États-Unis d'Amérique avait cependant obtenu la possession des certificats ou des titres en question. Le curateur canadien a donc intenté une action contre le curateur américain afin d'être déclaré propriétaire de ces titres ou de ces actions; il a été débouté en Cour de l'Échiquier.

En Cour suprême, le juge Lamont s'exprime au nom de deux de ses collègues. Il affirme que l'article 297 d) du *Traité de Versailles* ainsi que l'annexe s'y rapportant ont confirmé la validité des mesures de confiscation prises par les Hautes parties contractantes.[200] Interprétant l'Arrêté précité, le juge Lamont conclut que les valeurs mobilières en question n'appartenaient plus à des nationaux ennemis lors de leur attribution au curateur canadien, puisqu'à cette date elles avaient déjà été confisquées par le curateur américain. La première confiscation, survenue aux États-Unis, était donc la seule dont les tribunaux canadiens devaient tenir compte. Le juge Duff, qui a reçu l'appui du juge Newcombe, résout le litige de façon plus globale. Il affirme que la portée du décret édicté par le gouvernment doit être circonscrite par l'objectif poursuivi par le législateur, soit la mise en application du Traité de Versailles.[201] Celui-ci reconnaissant expressément la validité des mesures de confiscation prises par les pays alliés, le décret ne pouvait être interprété de manière à rendre ces mesures inopérantes au Canada.

Ainsi, une convention internationale à laquelle renvoie une loi possède la même autorité que celle-ci. Par le passé, les tribunaux canadiens ont clairement fait savoir que le gouvernement était tenu de respecter scrupuleusement les termes d'une telle convention. Seule la nature très particulière de la *Charte des Nations Unies* pourrait les inciter à modifier leur approche. Dans ce contexte, il est nécessaire d'étudier les décisions où les tribunaux ont été confrontés aux décisions d'organisations internationales.

[200] *Loc. cit. supra,* note 157, p. 177.
[201] *Id.,* pp. 196-97.

2. *Les tribunaux et les organisations internationales*

Il convient de se demander si les tribunaux canadiens ont adopté une attitude de déférence à l'égard des décisions prises par des organisations internationales. Il n'en est rien; au contraire, ils ont refusé d'accepter l'interprétation de conventions retenue par les organismes compétents au plan international. Dans une affaire portant sur le droit des employés du secteur public de faire la grève,[202] le juge de première instance conclut que certaines conventions ne protègent pas ce droit,[203] malgré une série ininterrompue de décisions à l'effet contraire, rendues par des comités relevant de l'Organisation internationale du travail.[204] Dans cet arrêt, les tribunaux canadiens se sentent libres d'interpréter à leur façon les conventions internationales. À notre connaissance, il n'existe pas d'arrêts où ils se sont déclarés liés par l'interprétation des organismes compétents au plan international.

Plus généralement, lorsqu'une convention internationale intégrée à une loi fédérale habilite un organe à prendre une décision, les tribunaux canadiens vérifieront si les termes de cette convention ont été respectés avant de donner effet à la décision. L'affaire *R. c. Wedge*[205] illustre cette proposition. Il s'agissait en l'espèce d'une accusation d'avoir violé la réglementation concernant la pêche du flétan, adoptée sous l'autorité de la *Loi sur la convention relative à la pêche du flétan dans le Pacifique septentrional, 1937.*[206] Cette loi reproduisait en Annexe une convention conclue avec les États-Unis d'Amérique pour les fins précitées, en plus d'attribuer certains pouvoirs de mise en oeuvre au gouverneur en conseil.[207]

La convention attribuait également certains pouvoirs à la Commission internationale des pêcheries. Étudiant la méthode utilisée pour fixer la date de clôture de la saison de pêche, le juge Fisher affirme: ''I agree that the International Fisheries Commission must exercise its powers strictly within the limits and in the manner

---

[202] *Alberta Union of Provincial Employees* c. *The Queen*, (1980) 120 D.L.R. (3d) 590 (B.R. Alb.).

[203] *Id.*, pp. 595 et 620-22. La Cour d'appel de l'Alberta endossa cette opinion (1982) 130 D.L.R. (3d) 191) et l'autorisation de se pourvoir fut refusée ([1981] 2 R.C.S. v); voir cependant la dissidence du juge en chef Dickson dans le *Renvoi relatif à la Public Service Employees Relations Act (Alb.)*, [1987] 1 R.C.S. 313, qui accepte l'interprétation du droit international retenue par les organes compétents.

[204] Voir sur ce sujet le commentaire de Michael BENDEL, (1981) 13 *Ott. L.R.* 169.

[205] [1939] 4 D.L.R. 323 (C.S.C.-B.).

[206] S.C. 1937, c. 36.

[207] *Loc. cit. supra*, note 205, p. 337.

prescribed by the said Act and Convention.'' À son avis, toutes les exigences pertinentes avaient cependant été respectées par la Commission.

L'affaire *Burnell* c. *Commission mixte internationale*[208] illustre ce même principe. Il s'agissait en l'espèce d'un résident canadien dont la propriété avait été endommagée par une élévation du niveau de l'eau du fleuve Saint-Laurent. Cette élévation avait été approuvée par la Commission mixte internationale, autorisée à régler le niveau de l'eau par la *Loi du Traité des eaux limitrophes internationales*[209] ainsi que par le traité annexé à cette loi. Le demandeur intenta une action en Cour fédérale; il poursuivait la Commission en dommages. Saisi d'une demande de radiation de l'action, le juge en chef adjoint Thurlow laisse entendre que l'inobservation d'une disposition du Traité pourrait constituer une cause d'action.[210] La demande a toutefois été rejetée, au motif que la commission n'avait pas la capacité d'être poursuivie en justice.

Une dernière décision montre bien que les tribunaux vérifient fréquemment si une autorité internationale agit conformément à la convention qui lui confère des pouvoirs. L'affaire *United Nations* c. *Canada Asiatic Lines Ltd*[211] concernait une action intentée par l'Organisation des Nations Unies. Une loi fédérale avait conféré la personnalité juridique à cette organisation: *Loi sur les privilèges et immunités des Nations Unies.*[212] La défenderesse soutenait cependant que le secrétaire général des Nations Unies n'était pas habilité à mandater les procureurs qui avaient intenté l'action. La loi fédérale précitée ne réglait pas cette question, même si la convention qui y était annexée décrétait que l'Organisation avait la capacité d'ester en justice (Article premier). Pour résoudre le problème, le juge Smith fait appel à la Charte des Nations Unies, plus précisément à l'article 97.[213] Ceci lui permet de conclure que le secrétaire général est autorisé à poser des actes d'administration comme celui qui était contesté en l'espèce. On peut donc affirmer qu'une initiative non autorisée par la Charte des Nations Unies aurait été déclarée invalide par les tribunaux canadiens.

Lorsqu'une convention intégrée à une loi fédérale habilite une

[208] [1977] 1 C.F. 269 (s.p.i.).
[209] S.R.C. 1970, c. I-20.
[210] *Loc. cit. supra,* note 208, p. 273.
[211] [1954] R.P. 158 (C.S.).
[212] S.C. 1947, c. 69, devenue L.R.C. (1985), c. P-23.
[213] Et non pas l'art. 970 (voir p. 160 de la décision).

organisation à agir, les tribunaux refusent de donner effet aux décisions qui ne respectent pas cette convention. Il convient cependant de se demander si l'existence d'un recours dans l'ordre
international est susceptible de modifier leur attitude. Plus précisément, la possibilité de demander à la Cour internationale de justice
un avis consultatif portant sur une "question juridique" exclut-
elle la compétence des tribunaux canadiens? Ce recours n'est ouvert
qu'à l'Assemblée générale ou au Conseil de sécurité des
Nations Unies.[214] Dans l'hypothèse que nous étudions, on voit mal
le Conseil demander un avis sur la légalité de ses propres décisions;
en pratique, seule l'Assemblée générale est susceptible d'agir en
ce sens. Il est clair qu'un simple individu ne peut s'adresser à la
Cour.[215]

Dans ce contexte, deux attitudes peuvent être adoptées. La
première consiste à s'incliner devant la volonté du Conseil et de
l'Assemblée générale, en refusant de remettre en question leurs décisions, même si celles-ci constituent une condition préalable à l'application de la *Loi sur la défense nationale*. Une telle position serait
cependant totalement nouvelle; elle serait justifiée par le fait que
le Conseil et l'Assemblée sont des organismes politiques sur la scène
internationale. L'autre attitude consiste à affirmer que l'existence
d'un recours éventuel devant la Cour internationale de justice ne
saurait être opposée au citoyen ou à la citoyenne canadienne qui
conteste la légalité d'une décision du gouverneur en conseil.

Certes, dans l'hypothèse où la résolution du Conseil de sécurité
serait déclarée invalide par les tribunaux canadiens, une décision
contradictoire pourrait être rendue par la Cour internationale de
justice. Une telle situation ne serait pas nouvelle, puisque les
tribunaux canadiens refusent de tenir compte des conventions internationales qui ne sont pas reprises par la législation interne,[216]

---

[214] *Charte des Nations Unies,* art. 96 1. L'article 12 interdit à l'Assemblée de formuler
une recommandation concernant un différend ou une question dont le Conseil
est saisi conformément à la *Charte*. L'Assemblée peut toutefois discuter de cette
question ou des pouvoirs du Conseil sans formuler de recommandation (art. 10).
De même, elle peut demander à la Cour internationale de justice de déterminer
l'étendue des pouvoirs du Conseil; ceci ne constitue pas une recommandation.
Il est intéressant de se demander si le renvoi à cette Cour constitue une décision
importante devant être prise à la majorité des deux tiers (art. 18 2.).

[215] *Statut de la Cour internationale de justice,* art. 34 1: "Seuls les États ont qualité pour
se présenter devant la Cour."

[216] Voir Claude Emmanuelli, *Droit international public,* t. 1, Wilson et Lafleur, Montréal, 1990, nos. 193-201, pp. 79-85 et les autorités qui y sont citées.

ainsi que des décisions rendues par des organisations internationales.[217] On voit mal pourquoi ils se préoccuperaient soudainement du fait que leur décision peut être contraire aux règles de droit international.

Au surplus, la participation aux opérations militaires du Conseil s'est faite sur une base volontaire. Ainsi, la résolution 678 se contente d'"'autoriser'" les pays qui le désirent à "user de... moyens nécessaires.'' De plus, le Conseil demande ''à tous les États concernés d'apporter l'appui voulu aux mesures'' qu'il vient d'autoriser. Cette formulation n'impose cependant aucune obligation précise, puisqu'elle ne définit ni les États concernés, ni le type d'appui envisagé. De façon plus générale, les dispositions du chapitre VII de la *Charte des Nations Unies* concernant l'emploi de la force n'ont pas un caractère obligatoire pour les pays tiers. Il se contente de prévoir la conclusion d'accords préalables, qui obligent l'État signataire à mettre des forces armées à la disposition du Conseil.[218] Ces accords doivent être ratifiés selon les règles constitutionnelles propres de cet État.[219] Ainsi, un État dont la constitution prohiberait les forces armées ne pourrait conclure d'accord. Il ne violerait pas pour autant la *Charte.* De même, les tribunaux canadiens pourraient déclarer que les opérations militaires autorisées par le Conseil contreviennent à la *Charte.* La résolution 678 n'imposant aucune obligation, le Canada pourrait parfaitement cesser de participer aux opérations qui en découlent.[220] Ce faisant, il respecterait un document beaucoup plus fondamental dans l'ordre international, la *Charte des Nations Unies* elle-même.

À notre avis, une procédure dans l'ordre international qui n'est pas accessible au simple citoyen canadien ne saurait le priver de son droit de saisir les tribunaux de la légalité d'une décision. Pour s'en convaincre, il convient d'examiner l'arrêt *Vérificateur général du Canada* c. *Ministre de l'Énergie, des mines et des ressources,* rendu par la Cour suprême du Canada. Le vérificateur général du Canada est habilité à ''prendre connaissance librement de tout renseignement

[217] Voir *supra,* note 202.
[218] *Charte des Nations Unies,* art. 43.
[219] *Id.,* art. 43 3.
[220] La situation pourrait être différente si le Canada avait conclu un accord par lequel il s'engageait à founir des forces armées. Même dans cette hypothèse, on peut soutenir que les tribunaux ont toujours apprécié souverainement si les lois canadiennes étaient respectées, sans se préoccuper des répercussions de leurs décisions sur la scène internationale.
[221] [1989] 2 R.C.S. 49.

se rapportant à l'exercice de ses fonctions; à cette fin, il peut exiger que les fonctionnaires fédéraux lui fournissent tous renseignements, rapports et explications dont il a besoin.''[222] En l'espèce, ce préposé du Parlement avait demandé à voir les documents consultés par le cabinet en vue de faire l'acquisition de sociétés pétrolières, ce qui lui avait été refusé. Il a alors présenté à la Cour fédérale une requête en *mandamus* et en injonction permanente. La division de première instance lui a donné gain de cause, mais cette décision a été renversée par la Cour d'appel et par la Cour suprême.

Le juge en chef Dickson a rédigé l'opinion de la Cour. À son avis, la solution du litige résulte de l'article 7 (1) b) de la *Loi sur le vérificateur général*.[223] Cette disposition prévoit que le vérificateur général doit préparer "un rapport annuel dans lequel... il indique s'il a reçu, dans l'exercice de ses activités, tous les renseignements et éclaircissements réclamés." Il s'agirait là d'un recours approprié, de nature politique, se substituant aux recours judiciaires.[224] Le juge en chef insiste cependant sur le fait que le vérificateur général est un préposé du Parlement et qu'il s'agit en l'espèce d'un différend opposant le pouvoir législatif et le pouvoir exécutif.[225] Il signale également, et il s'agit à notre avis d'une considération déterminante, que le Règlement de la Chambre des communes ne permet pas aux députés d'avoir accès aux documents réclamés par le vérificateur général.[226] Il conclut que le rapport prévu par l'article 7 (1) b) constitue le seul recours face à un refus de fournir des documents.

Le juge en chef prend bien soin de qualifier de fondamental le droit de recourir aux tribunaux. Seule l'existence d'un substitut approprié permet de conclure que les cours de justice n'ont plus compétence.[227] En l'espèce, une citoyenne canadienne ne dispose d'aucun recours qui puisse remplacer une action intentée au Canada. Les tribunaux ont donc l'obligation de statuer sur une demande où la violation d'une loi canadienne est dénoncée.

Dans le domaine des relations internationales, une autre doctrine particulière pourrait être invoquée pour empêcher les tribunaux nationaux d'examiner les résolutions du Conseil de sécurité. Il s'agit des actes de gouvernement (*Acts of State*), qui ac-

---

[222] *Loi sur le vérificateur général*, L.R.C. (1985), c. A-17, art. 13 (1).

[223] *Id.*

[224] *Loc. cit. supra*, note 221, p. 95.

[225] *Id.*, 103.

[226] *Id.*, 109.

[227] Voir *supra* note 224.

cordent en Angleterre une large marge de manoeuvre à l'exécutif. Les actes de gouvernement sont posés par la Couronne à l'occasion de ses relations avec d'autres États ou avec leurs nationaux.[228] Il pourra s'agir, par exemple, de la conclusion d'un traité, d'une déclaration de guerre ou de l'acquisition d'un territoire par cession. Ils découlent de l'exercice d'un pouvoir discrétionnaire et ne peuvent pour cette raison être remis en cause par les tribunaux. Un auteur affirme même que seule la prérogative de la Couronne peut expliquer leur existence.[229]

Les actes de gouvernement existent parce qu'à l'extérieur du Royaume-Uni, aucune règle de droit britannique ne régit les relations entre la Couronne et les États étrangers ou leurs nationaux. Pour cette raison, les tribunaux britanniques ne peuvent être saisis de litiges concernant ces questions.[230] La même solution prévaut lorsqu'un acte interne d'un État étranger leur est soumis: il ne saurait être question de discuter en Grande-Bretagne de la validité d'un tel acte.[231] La Couronne ne peut invoquer cette doctrine lorsque ses préposés commettent un acte dommageable à l'intérieur du Royaume-Uni. L'étranger résidant au Royaume-Uni ou le sujet britannique lésés dans de telles circonstances peuvent s'adresser aux tribunaux.[232] Pour reprendre les termes du comité judiciaire: "Because between Her Majesty and one of her subjects there can be no such thing as an act of State.''[233]

Cette considération nous semble déterminante: les sujets britanniques peuvent toujours recourir aux voies de justice pour faire constater une violation de la loi ou une atteinte à leurs droits, si celle-ci s'est produite à l'intérieur des limites du Royaume-Uni.[234] Le fait qu'il s'agisse de relations internationales n'y change rien. Ce principe vaut tout autant, sinon plus, au Canada, où la doctrine des actes de gouvernement ne semble pas avoir connu la même for-

---

[228] Voir *Nissan* c. *A.G.*, [1970] A.C. 179.

[229] D. R. GILMOUR, ''British Forces Abroad and the Responsibility for Their Actions,'' [1970] *Public Law* 120, 143-46.

[230] *Nissan* c. *A.G.*, [1970] A.C. 179, 212 F-G (Lord Reid); 216 et 218 (Lord Morris of Borth-y-Guest); 231 (Lord Wilberforce); 239-40 (Lord Pearson).

[231] *Carr* c. *Fracis Time and Co.*, [1902] A.C. 176 (Ch. des L.).

[232] *Johnstone* c. *Pedlar*, [1921] 2 A.C. 262 (Ch. des L.).

[233] *Walker* c. *Baird*, [1892] A.C. 491, 494 (C.J.C.P., pourvoi en provenance de Terre-Neuve). Voir également *Johnstone* c. *Pedlar*, [1921] 2 A.C. 262 (Ch. des L.), 272 (Vicomte Finlay); 281 (Lord Atkinson); 295 (Lord Phillimore).

[234] La question des droits d'un sujet britannique lésé par des actes de la Couronne ou de ses préposés qui sont commis à l'étranger reste entière: *Nissan* c. *A.G., loc. cit. supra*, note 225.

tune qu'en Angleterre.[235]

Peut-on néanmoins soutenir qu'une résolution du Conseil de sécurité équivaut à un acte de gouvernement? Deux objections permettent d'écarter immédiatement une telle proposition. En premier lieu, les Nations Unies ne sont pas assimilées à un État souverain.[236] La notion d'acte de gouvernement ne concerne donc pas les organisations internationales. En second lieu, lorsque le législateur prévoit qu'une convention produira des effets, les tribunaux ont l'obligation de s'assurer que les dispositions de la loi nationale sont respectées. Les actes de gouvernement ne portent pas atteinte au droit du citoyen ou de la citoyenne de s'opposer à la violation des règles en vigueur dans son pays. De ce point de vue, même si les relations avec les Nations Unies étaient qualifiées d'actes de gouvernement, la *Loi sur la défense nationale* devrait être respectée par le gouvernement canadien. Le principe de la souveraineté parlementaire s'applique ici. Est-il néanmoins possible d'affirmer que les tribunaux devraient refuser de se prononcer sur des questions controversées mettant en cause la politique extérieure du gouvernement? C'est la question qu'il faut maintenant examiner.

3. *Les questions politiques*

La doctrine des questions politiques a été élaborée aux États-Unis. Elle repose sur des principes constitutionnels qui n'ont pas cours au Canada.[237] L'arrêt *Operation Dismantle Inc. c. La Reine* a permis à la Cour suprême, unanime sur ce point, d'examiner cette

---

[235] L'opinion des trois juges dissidents dans *Calder* c. *P.G. de la Colombie-Britannique*, [1973] R.C.S. 313, examine rapidement cette question. Le juge Hall écrit: ''L[a *ratio*] des arrêts sur lesquels s'est fondée la Cour d'appel est qu'[un tribunal national] ne peut réviser l'acte de gouvernement si, ce faisant, la Cour se trouverait à appliquer un traité entre deux états souverains'' (p. 405; traduction modifiée pour les termes entre crochets). Il conclut que cette doctrine ne s'applique pas au titre autochtone, qui découle de la common law ainsi que de la *Proclamation royale* de 1763:
> En appliquant la doctrine de l'acte de gouvernement, la Cour d'appel a complètement omis de tenir compte du fondement de la doctrine, simple reconnaissance de la prérogative du Souverain d'acquérir des territoires d'une façon qui ne peut être contestée par la suite devant un tribunal [national]. (p. 406)
Voir également une allusion à cette doctrine dans *Capital Cities Communications Inc.* c. *Conseil de la Radio-Télédiffusion canadienne, loc. cit. supra*, note 197, p. 182 (le juge Pigeon, dissident).

[236] *Nissan* c. *A.G., loc. cit. supra*, note 230, p. 214 (Lord Reid); p. 222 (Lord Morris of Borth-y-Guest; p. 223 (Lord Pearce); p. 237 (Lord Wilberforce); p. 241 (Lord Pearson).

[237] *Operation Dismantle Inc.* c. *La Reine*, [1985] 1 R.C.S. 441, 468-69 (la juge Wilson).

question. Le juge Dickson, à l'époque juge puîné, écrit: ''Je ne doute pas que les tribunaux soient fondés à connaî tre de différends d'une nature politique ou mettant en cause la politique étrangère.''[238] Ces propos ne sont aucunement limités aux questions constitutionnelles. Dans l'arrêt *Finlay* c. *Canada (Ministre des finances),*[239] le juge Le Dain fait référence à l'arrêt précité. Au nom d'un banc unanime comprenant le juge en chef Dickson et la juge Wilson, il affirme:

> Suivant mon interprétation, les propos du juge Wilson, auxquels le juge Dickson (maintenant juge en chef) a souscrit sur la question de la justiciabilité, affirment que lorsqu'est en cause un litige que les tribunaux peuvent trancher, ceux-ci ne devraient pas refuser de statuer au motif qu'à cause de ces incidences ou de son contexte politique, il vaudrait mieux en laisser l'examen et le règlement au législatif ou à l'exécutif. Cela, bien entendu, fut dit dans le contexte de l'obligation judiciaire de statuer en matière constitutionnelle en vertu de la *Charte,* mais j'estime que cela s'applique également à un litige non constitutionnel portant sur les limites d'un pouvoir conféré par la loi. Il y aura indubitablement des cas où la question du respect provincial des conditions d'un partage des frais avec le fédéral soulèvera des points qui ne relèvent pas de la compétence des tribunaux, mais les points litigieux particuliers concernant l'inexécution provinciale que soulève la déclaration de l'intimé sont des points de droit dont les tribunaux peuvent manifestement être saisis.[240]

---

[238] *Id.,* 459; voir également les propos de la juge Wilson, approuvés ''pour l'essentiel'' par le juge Dickson: ''si on nous demande de décider si un acte spécifique de l'Exécutif porte atteinte aux droits des citoyens, non seulement est-il approprié que nous répondions à la question, mais c'est notre devoir en vertu de la *Charte* d'y répondre'' (p. 472). En matière d'extradition, la Cour a réaffirmé que la discrétion dont jouit l'Exécutif ne saurait être opposée à la *Charte canadienne des droits et libertés: Canada* c. *Schmidt,* [1987] 1 R.C.S. 500, 521 et 532; *Argentine* c. *Mello* [1987] 1 R.C.S. 536, 558; *États-Unis d'Amérique* c. *Cotroni,* [1989] 1 R.C.S. 1469, 1511 (dissidence de la juge Wilson); *Kindler* c. *Canada (Ministre de la Justice),* J.E. 91-1495 (C.S.C.), notes du juge McLachlin, p. 10 de la version française. Il est vrai qu'en procédant à l'analyse des questions juridiques en cause, les juges soulignent fréquemment que ''[l]'exécutif a des connaissances beaucoup plus grandes que la Cour dans le domaine des relations extérieures'' *(ibid.).* Néanmoins, ils vérifient toujours si la loi ou la constitution ont été respectées.

[239] [1986] 2 R.C.S. 607.

[240] *Id.,* 633. Voir *Guérin* c. *La Reine,* [1984] 2 R.C.S. 335, 350-52 et 385, où la Cour écarte la notion de ''fiducie politique''et reconnaît que l'article 18 de la *Loi sur les indiens,* S.R.C. 1954, c. 149, autorise un bande indienne à recourir aux tribunaux lorsque l'entente qu'elle a conclue avec le gouvernement fédéral en cédant ses terres n'a pas été respectée. Dans le *Renvoi relatif au Régime d'assistance publique du Canada (C.-B.),* [1991] 2 R.C.S. 525 le procureur général du Canada a prétendu que la question posée par le renvoi était de nature politique et que la Cour devait refuser

À notre avis, la conformité de la résolution 678 avec la *Charte des Nations Unies* est un point de droit dont un tribunal peut manifestement être saisi, pour reprendre la formule du juge Le Dain. De plus, cette question ne nécessite aucune preuve particulière.[241] Rien ne s'oppose à ce qu'elle soit tranchée par un tribunal canadien.

L'article 32 de la *Loi sur la défense nationale* pourrait cependant être invoqué pour inciter les juges à ne pas remettre en cause la décision de l'exécutif. Cette disposition prévoit que le Parlement doit siéger lors de la mise en service actif des forces armées, ou être convoqué dans un délai de dix jours. Cette exigence a manifestement pour but de permettre qu'un débat politique ait lieu, même si aucune autre condition n'est imposée. Une résolution de la Chambre des communes "réaffirmant son appui aux Nations Unies pour mettre fin à l'agression du Koweït par l'Irak" a d'ailleurs été adoptée le 22 janvier 1991, après le déclenchement des attaques aériennes.[242]

d'y répondre. Le juge Sopinka déclare alors qu'une question peut présenter "un aspect suffisamment juridique pour justifier qu'une cour y réponde," parce que cette décision "servira à résoudre une controverse, ou bien. . .aura quelque autre valeur pratique" (p. 546). Dans l'arrêt *Chandler* c. *D.P.P., loc. cit. supra*, note 159, le vicomte Radcliffe, après avoir affirmé que les tribunaux ne pouvaient déterminer si le déploiement d'armes nucléaires était contraire aux intérêts d l'État, précise: "It is not debarred from doing so merely because the issue is what is ordinarily known as 'political.' Such issues may present themselves in courts of law if they take a triable form" (p. 798). De même, Lord Devlin rappelle que les tribunaux ne révisent pas les décisions impliquant des choix politiques, prises dans l'exercice d'un pouvoir discrétionnaire, que celui-ci soit conféré par la prérogative ou par une loi. Il ajoute cependant: "The courts will not review the proper exercise of discretionary powers but they will intervene to correct excess or abuse" (p. 810).

[241] Dans *Operation Dismantle Inc.* c. *La Reine, loc. cit. supra*, note 237, les appelants tentaient d'empêcher les essais de missiles de croisière auxquels devait procéder le gouvernement américain en Alberta. Ils affirmaient que ces expériences auraient pour effet d'intensifier la course aux armements et d'accroître les risques d'une guerre nucléaire, ce qui aurait porté atteinte à leur droit à la vie et à la sécurité de la personne (*Charte canadienne des droits et libertés*, art. 7). Le juge Dickson écrit (p. 454): "toutes ces allégations ont pour prémisse des suppositions et des hypothèses sur la manière dont des nations indépendantes et souveraines, agissant dans une arène internationale radicalement incertaine, où les circonstances changent continuellement, réagiront à la décision du gouvernement canadien d'autoriser les essais du missile de croisière. . . En bref, il n'est tout simplement pas possible pour une cour de justice, même avec les meilleures preuves disponibles, de faire autre chose que de spéculer sur la possibilité que la décision du cabinet fédéral de procéder aux essais du missile de croisière accroisse le danger de guerre nucléaire." Aucun problème de cette nature ne se pose lorsqu'il faut déterminer si une résolution du Conseil de sécurité respecte la *Charte des Nations Unies*.

[242] Chambre des Communes, Deuxième session, 34e législature, *Procès-Verbaux*, le mardi 22 janvier 1991, 17h, p. 2592. Les arguments présentés dans cet article avaient déjà

Il convient alors de se demander si cette procédure parlementaire prive les tribunaux de leur compétence.

Un problème semblable s'est posé lors de la Première Guerre mondiale. La *Loi du service militaire, 1917*[243] exemptait certaines catégories de personnes de la conscription, tout en préservant expressément[244] les pouvoirs conférés au gouverneur en conseil par la *Loi des mesures de guerre, 1914.*[245] En avril 1918, deux règlements, adoptés sous l'autorité de cette dernière loi, suppriment les exemptions prévues par la loi de 1917. Ces règlements ont été approuvés par une résolution du Sénat et de la Chambre des communes. Saisie d'un litige portant sur cette question, la Cour suprême du Canada déclare les règlements valides, en s'appuyant sur le fait que la loi de 1917 déclarait ne pas restreindre les pouvoirs résultant de la *Loi des mesures de guerre, 1914.*[246] Quatre juges sur six affirment cependant que l'adoption d'une résolution ne saurait avoir d'influence sur la validité du règlement.[247]

La Cour d'appel de l'Alberta avait été saisie auparavant de la même question; elle était parvenue à un résultat opposé à celui de la Cour suprême. Quatre juges sur cinq avaient eux aussi refusé de tenir compte d'une résolution des Chambres du Parlement.[248] Le juge Stuart a bien saisi l'énormité de la proposition contraire: ''The Courts, I am sure, would never dream of paying attention to a mere resolution of parliament declaring that in its opinion a certain section, say, of the Bank Act, meant so and so. This is the principle upon which the court would undoubtedly act in time of peace and, as Viscount Reading said, the same principle must be applied in time of war.''[249]

La *Loi des mesures de guerre, 1914* ne prévoyait cependant pas la convocation du Parlement, comme le fait l'article 32 de la *Loi sur la*

été utilisés par les partis d'opposition lors des débats en Chambre, notamment le 28 novembre 1990, la veille de l'adoption de la résolution 678 du conseil de sécurité, ainsi que du 15 au 22 janvier 1991, lors des débats sur la résolution citée ci-dessus.

[243] S.C. 1917, c. 19.

[244] *Id.,* art. 13 (5).

[245] S.C. 1914, 2e sess., c. 2.

[246] *In re Gray,* (1918) 57 R.C.S. 150.

[247] *Id.,* 164 (le juge Idington, dissident, avec l'appui du juge Brodeur); 183 (le juge Anglin, avec l'appui du juge Davies).

[248] *Re Lewis,* (1918) 41 D.L.R. 1 (C.A. Alb.), 13 (le juge Start); 15 (le juge Beck); 19 (le juge Simmons); 20-21 (le juge Hyndman).

[249] *Id.,* 13-14.

défense nationale. Faut-il y voir une intention du Parlement d'exclure tout autre forme de recours judiciaire? La réponse à cette question dépend de l'interprétation de l'arrêt *Vérificateur général du Canada* c. *Ministre de l'Énergie, des mines et des ressources,* résumé ci-dessus.[250] Après avoir lu cette décision, il est possible de soutenir que l'article 32 de la *Loi sur la défense nationale* constitue un recours de nature politique, puisqu'il permet aux députés et aux sénateurs d'interroger les membres du gouvernement ayant recommandé la mise en service actif des forces armées. Il convient cependant de noter qu'aucune procédure précise n'est prévue, mise à part la convocation du Parlement qui a été ajourné ou prorogé. Lorsque le législateur souhaite obtenir l'approbation des députés pour qu'une décision du gouverneur en conseil soit exécutoire, il sait s'en exprimer en termes clairs.[251]

Le simple fait que le Parlement siège ne saurait constituer un "recours," encore moins un recours approprié. Dans l'arrêt cité ci-dessus, le juge en chef Dickson prend soin de souligner que les tribunaux doivent évaluer soigneusement le recours prévu par la loi afin de déterminer s'il est adéquat et si l'on peut conclure que le législateur a implicitement décrété qu'il serait exclusif.[252] Il affirme de plus "qu'en temps normal (c'est-à-dire dans une poursuite intentée par un citoyen), un recours politique ne satisferait pas au critère de l'adéquation...." Enfin, sa conclusion contient une mise en garde qui s'applique parfaitement au cas qui nous intéresse: "L'analyse en l'espèce ne doit pas non plus être interprétée comme une atteinte au principe fondamental selon lequel les tribunaux ne doivent pas refuser volontiers d'accorder les recours nécessaires quant à des droits reconnus par les lois du Canada."[254]

Ce "principe fondamental" nous semble beaucoup trop important pour être contrecarré par la simple obligation de convoquer le Parlement. À notre avis, l'article 32 de la *Loi sur la défense nationale* ne saurait constituer un substitut aux recours judiciaires. De même, la doctrine des questions politiques ou l'adoption d'une résolution approuvant la décision du gouverneur en conseil n'ont aucune portée sur un litige impliquant le respect de la *Loi sur la défense nationale.*

[250] *Loc. cit. supra,* note 221.
[251] *Loi sur les mesures d'urgence,* L.R.C. (1985), c. 22 (4e supp.), art. 57 à 63.
[252] *Loc. cit. supra,* note 21, pp. 95-96.
[253] *Id.,* 97.
[254] *Id.,* 110.

Ainsi, les tribunaux saisis d'une telle question aurait l'obligation d'y répondre. Reste à savoir si un membre du public aurait un intérêt suffisant pour agir en ce sens.

C. LA QUALITÉ POUR AGIR

Seuls les militaires sont directement concernés par la décision du gouverneur général de mettre les forces armées en service actif. En principe, ce sont eux qui ont l'intérêt voulu pour agir en justice. Les règles de droit judiciaire applicables aux actions d'intérêt privé ont cependant été considérablement assouplies dans le cas des recours de droit public (1). La situation particulière des militaires doit être prise en considération (2), afin de montrer que de simples citoyens, par exemple deux professeurs de droit, doivent être autorisés à agir dans l'intérêt public (3).

1. *La qualité pour agir dans l'intérêt public*

Les conditions de recevabilité d'une action en justice ont été mises de côté dans l'hypothèse où une question de droit constitutionnel importante risquait de ne pouvoir être soumise aux tribunaux.[255] L'arrêt *Ministre de la justice du Canada* c. *Borowski*[256] a étendu cette nouvelle approche aux contestations fondées sur la *Déclaration canadienne des droits*.[257] L'opinion majoritaire, rédigée par le juge Martland, formule ainsi le critère à appliquer:

Selon mon interprétation, ces arrêts décident que pour établir l'intérêt pour agir à titre de demandeur dans une poursuite visant à déclarer qu'une loi est invalide, si cette question se pose sérieusement, il suffit qu'une personne démontre qu'elle est directement touchée ou qu'elle a, à titre de citoyen, un intérêt véritable quant à la validité de la loi, et qu'il

---

[255] *Thorson* c. *Procureur général du Canada,* [1975] 1 R.C.S. 138; *Nova Scotia Board of Censors* c. *MacNeil,* [1976] 2 R.C.S. 265.

[256] [1981] 2 R.C.S. 575. Pour des applications subséquentes en droit constitutionnel, voir *Dumont* c. *Canada (Procureur général),* [1990] 1 R.C.S. 279, ainsi que l'opinion dissidente du juge O'Sullivan, (1988) 52 D.L.R. (4th) 25 (C.A. Man.); *Energy Probe* c. *Canada (A. G.),* (1989) 58 D.L.R. (4th) 513 (C.A. Ont.), autorisation de se pourvoir en Cour suprême refusée, [1989] 2 R.C.S. ix; *Conseil Canadien des Églises* c. *Canada (Ministre de l'Emploi et de l'Immigration),* C.S.C. 21946, le 23 janvier 1992. Au Québec, ces règles permettent même à une association sans but lucratif de plaider au nom de ses membres: *Conseil du patronat du Québec* c. *Procureur général du Québec,* C.S.C. 21097, le 6 décembre 1991, approuvant la dissidence du juge Chouinard, [1988] R.J.Q. 1516.

[257] L.R.C. (1985), App. III.

n'y a pas d'autre manière raisonnable et efficace de soumettre la question à la cour.[258]

L'arrêt *Finlay* c. *Ministre des finances du Canada*[259] allait franchir un pas de plus et rendre ce critère applicable au contentieux administratif. M. Finlay était prestataire de l'aide sociale au Manitoba. Le montant qui lui était versé à chaque mois avait été réduit pour rembourser un trop perçu antérieur, conformément à la loi manitobaine pertinente. Or le gouvernement fédéral défrayait une partie substantielle des coûts afférents au programme d'aide sociale manitobain, conformément au *Régime d'assistance publique du Canada* en vigueur à cette époque.[260] Ce Régime prévoyait la conclusion d'une entente entre le gouvernement fédéral et le gouvernement du Manitoba et autorisait le versement de la contribution fédérale si les conditions énoncées dans l'entente étaient respectées.

En l'espèce, la province du Manitoba s'était engagée à fournir une aide assurant un minimum vital aux prestataires. M. Finlay alléguait que les déductions imposées conformément à la loi manitobaine contrevenaient à cette entente. Il demandait à la Cour fédérale d'enjoindre le ministre des Finances de cesser les paiements. Le gouvernement fédéral a présenté une requête pour faire radier l'action, alléguant que M. Finlay n'avait pas qualité pour agir. Acueillie en première instance, la requête a été rejetée en Cour d'appel fédérale.

En Cour suprême, le juge Le Dain conclut en premier lieu que M. Finlay n'a pas qualité pour demander la cessation des paiements,

---

[258] *Loc. cit. supra,* note 256, p. 598. Une doctrine abondante commente cette évolution, tant du point de vue du droit constitutionnel que de celui du droit administratif. Après l'arrêt *Borowski,* voir Pierre VERGE, "La recevabilité de l'action d'intérêt public," (1983) 24 *C. de D.* 177; David J. MULLAN et Andrew J. RO-MAN, *"Minister of Justice of Canada* v. *Borowski:* The Extent of the Citizen's Right to Litigate the Lawfulness of Government Action," (1984) 4 *Rec. Ann. de Wind. d'Acc. à la Just.* 303; Janice T. TOKAR, "Administrative Law: Locus Standi in Judicial Proceedings," (1984-85) 14 *Man. L.J.* 209; Thomas A. CROMWELL, *Locus Standi: A Commentary on the Law of Standing in Canada,* Carswell, 1986; Thomas A. CROMWELL, "From Trilogy to Quartet: *Minister of Finance of Canada* v. *Finlay,*" (1987) 7 *Rec. Ann. de Wind. d'Acc. à la Just.* 103; William BOGART, "Understanding Standing, Chapter IV: *Minister of Finance of Canada* v. *Finlay,*" (1988) 10 *Sup. Ct. L. R.* 377; Fabien GÉLINAS, "Le *locus standi* et les actions d'intérêt public et la *relator action:* l'empire de la common law en droit québécois," (1988) 29 *C. de D.* 657; William BOGART, "The Lessons of Liberalized Standing?," (1989) 27 *Osgoode H. L. J.* 195.

[259] [1986] 2 R.C.S. 607.

[260] S.R.C. 1970, c. C-1.

puisqu'il est impossible de déterminer l'effet d'un tel jugement sur le gouvernement manitobain et sa législature. Le "lien" entre la situation personnelle de M. Finlay et les conclusions recherchées serait trop lâche pour que M. Finlay se qualifie personnellement.[261] M. Finlay doit donc être autorisé à représenter le public en général, ou à tout le moins, une catégorie particulière du public, celle des personnes dans le besoin.[262]

Le juge Le Dain déclare ensuite que les critères développés en droit constitutionnel doivent dorénavant s'appliquer aux contestations portant sur le "pouvoir que confère la loi de faire des dépenses publiques ou quelque autre action administrative."[263] Il emploiera subséquemment l'expression "limites d'un pouvoir conféré par la loi"[264] ou "action en jugement déclaratoire portant qu'une autorité administrative a agi sans pouvoir légal."[265] Le litige auquel nous nous intéressons dans ce texte entre clairement dans cette catégorie d'action. Il ne reste plus qu'à se demander s'il est nécessaire de reconnaître la qualité pour agir à un simple citoyen, parce qu'il n'existe pas d'autre moyens raisonnables et efficaces de saisir un tribunal de la question en litige.[266]

2. *La situation des militaires*

En principe, les militaires sont les seules personnes directement concernées par la décision de mettre les forces canadiennes en service actif. Il faut donc se demander s'ils sont en mesure d'intenter une action en justice portant sur les questions examinées précédemment. Une difficulté majeure se présente cependant, qui n'existait pas dans

---

[261] *Loc. cit. supra*, note 259, pp. 623-24.

[262] *Ibid.*

[263] *Id.*, 630-31. Ce principe sera appliqué à plusieurs reprises *Association of Stop Construction of Rafferty Project Inc.* c. *Swan*, (1988) 68 Sask R. 52 (B.R.); *B.C. Fed. of Labour* c. *Workers Compensation Board of British Columbia*, (1988) 27 B.C.L.R. (2d) 175 (C.S.C.-B.); *Elizabeth Fry Society* c. *Saskatchewan Legal Aid Commission*, (1989) 56 D.L.R. (4th) 96 (C.A. Sask.) et (1988) 67 Sask. R. 63 (B.R.); *Greater Victoria Concerned Citizens Association* c. *Provincial Capital Commission*, (1990) 46 Admin. L. R. 74 (C.S.C.-B.); *Bury* c. *Saskatchewan Government Insurance Corp.*, [1991] 1 W.W.R. 47 (B.R. Sask.); *Vanier* c. *Côté*, [1991] R.J.Q. 1083, 1086 (C.S.). Pour la jurisprudent antérieure, voir T. CROMWELL, *op. cit. supra*, note 258, p. 140 à 146. Voir également *Pearce* c. *Pappenfus*, (1982) 19 Sask R. 243 (B.R. Sask.); *Jeffrey* c. *Université de Moncton*, (1985) 62 R.N.-B. 410 (B.R.).

[264] *Loc. cit. supra*, note 259, p. 632.

[265] *Id.*, 636.

[266] *Id.*, 633.

les arrêts de la Cour suprême portant sur la qualité pour agir. Certaines dispositions de la *Loi sur la défense nationale* peuvent en effet être interprétées de manière à interdire aux militaires de discréditer dans l'opinion publique les forces canadiennes. Si tel est le cas, il n'est évidemment pas raisonnable d'obliger un militaire à enfreindre la loi... pour faire respecter la loi.

L'article 93 de la *Loi sur la défense nationale*[267] réprime tout "comportement cruel ou déshonorant," alors que l'article 94 déclare coupable d'une infraction celui qui "tient des propos traî tres ou déloyaux à l'égard de Sa Majesté." La peine maximale imposée est de cinq ans d'emprisonnement dans le premier cas, de sept ans dans le second. Enfin, l'article 129 prévoit la "destitution ignominieuse" pour tout "acte, comportement ou négligence préjudiciable au bon ordre et à la discipline."

Ces infractions ne visent que les militaires,[268] qui sont jugés par des officiers.[269] Elles peuvent être interprétées de manière à s'appliquer à un recours en justice mettant en cause la légalité des opérations militaires entreprises par les forces canadiennes. Évidemment, on peut soutenir qu'une loi ne devrait jamais être interprétée de façon à priver un citoyen ou une citoyenne de son droit de recourir aux tribunaux. L'obligation de loyauté imposée aux membres des forces armées peut cependant être plus considérable que celle qui est imposée aux civils.[270] Affirmer qu'une loi a été violée ne serait peut-être pas qualifié d'action "déloyale." Par contre, le fait d'intenter l'action en justice décrite ci-dessus est forcément "préjudiciable au maintien du bon ordre et de la discipline."

Certains jugements rendus durant la Seconde Guerre Mondiale montrent bien que le risque de condamnation n'est pas négligeable. La décision *R. c. Coffin*[271] concernait un professeur ayant tenu des propos pacifistes dans sa salle de cours. Il a été accusé d'avoir fait des déclarations préjudiciables à la sûreté de l'État. La disposition en question mentionnait dans le même paragraphe les pro-

---

[267] L.R.C. (1985), c. N-5.

[268] *Loi sur la défense nationale*, L.R.C. (1985), c. N-5, art. 60 et 2, "code de discipline militaire."

[269] *Id.*, art. 166 à 176; "infraction d'ordre militaire," art. 2.

[270] Sur la nature particulière de la relation entre un militaire et Sa Majesté, voir *Cooke* c. *The King*, [1929] R. C. de l'É. 20; *McArthur* c. *The King*, [1943] R.C. de l'É. 77; *R.* c. *Généreux*, C.S.C., no. 22103, le 13 février 1992, pp. 31-34 des notes du juge en chef.

[271] [1940] 2 W.W.R. 592 (Police Court).

pos préjudiciables à l'effort de guerre (*efficient prosecution of the war*). Le magistrat s'exprime ainsi:

if any and all persons under any and all circumstances were to be permitted both publicly and privately to state the views which the accused has stated and if a considerable number of people accepted those views there would be in Canada a public opinion divided on the question of prosecuting this war. If opinion were divided the national war effort would be weakened. These Regulations are based upon the premise that the safety of the state depends upon the war being won, for which the united effort of all people is essential. The advocacy of the historic position of the Quakers in these matters, statements which weaken the courage and resolution of any Canadian — all of these is prohibited by those regulations.[272]

En substituant le mot ''militaire'' au mot ''canadien,'' ce passage implique qu'un militaire contestant la légalité de la mise en service actif agit de façon ''déloyale'' ou ''préjudiciable au bon ordre ou à la discipline.'' Toujours durant la Seconde Guerre Mondiale, un individu avait écrit une lettre, inspirée par sa religion, où il affirmait qu'il était inacceptable de saluer le drapeau national ou de se lever pendant l'hymne national. Il a été déclaré coupable d'avoir fait une déclaration susceptible de susciter du mécontentement à l'égard de Sa Majesté.[273]

Ces décisions ne seraient sans doute pas rendues de nos jours, en raison de l'avènement de la *Charte canadienne des droits et libertés*. Il n'en reste pas moins qu'un débat sérieux pourrait s'engager sur ces questions. Dans ces conditions, il nous semble irréaliste de demander à un militaire de s'exposer à des poursuites fondées sur des infractions pouvant impliquer la destitution ''ignominieuse'' de l'armée, une décision contre laquelle il est sans doute fort difficile de se pourvoir.

D'autre part, les *Ordonnances et Règlements royaux applicables aux forces canadiennes*[274] restreignent les droits des militaires. Ainsi, il leur est interdit de déclarer ou de faire quoique ce soit qui, après avoir été révélé, serait susceptible de jeter le discrédit sur les membres des forces canadiennes (art. 19.14 (2) a)). Les militaires ne peuvent agir de sorte que les personnes placées sous leur commandement soient insatisfaites de leurs affectations (art. 19.14 (2) b)). De plus, ils doi-

[272] *Id.*, 602-3.

[273] *R. c. Clark*, [1941] 3 W.W.R. 228 (Police Court, Man.).

[274] Inédits.

vent obtenir une autorisation avant de "communiquer [leur] opinion
sur un sujet militaire quelconque à des personnes non autorisées
à [les] recevoir..." (art. 19.36 c)); la même règle s'applique à la
préparation d'un document portant "sur un sujet militaire" et qui
doit "être communiqué au public de vive voix ou autrement" (art.
19.36 e)).

En principe, toute communication avec les média qui concerne
les Forces canadiennes doit émaner du ministre ou de son représentant (art. 19.375). Nous avons vu que l'art. 19.14 vise des comporte-
ments dont la révélation éventuelle est considérée préjudiciable à
l'armée. Pour sa part, l'art. 19.36 e) vise la préparation d'un document portant sur un sujet militaire, qui doit être communiqué au
public. Il est possible que le fait d'intenter une action risquant de
susciter un débat public entre dans cette catégorie, auquel cas il
est nécessaire d'obtenir une autorisation avant de déposer la procédure. Dans l'ensemble, le règlement semble interdire aux militaires
de contester la décision de mettre les forces canadiennes en service
actif, puisqu'une telle initiative attirera inévitablement l'attention
du public.

En dernier lieu, il faut noter qu'un militaire en service actif dans
le Golfe Persique n'est pas raisonnablement en mesure de communiquer de façon continue avec un avocat ou de venir témoigner au
Canada. L'instance risque de plus d'être interrompue s'il décède
au combat, une possibilité qu'il ne faut certainement pas exclure.
À notre avis, compte tenu de toutes ces difficultés, les tribunaux
n'ont d'autre choix que de reconnaître à certains civils la qualité
pour agir dans l'intérêt public. Il n'existe pas d'autres moyens
raisonnables de leur soumettre la question en litige. Les arrêts de
la Cour suprême cités ci-dessus n'exigent pas qu'aucune personne
ne soit en mesure de contester la loi. Il suffit qu'il soit "peu probable que le groupe le plus directement touché conteste la loi."[275]

3. *Les citoyens concernés*

---

[275] *Conseil canadien des Églises* c. *La Reine,* [1990] 2 C.F. 534, 553 (C.A.F.). La Cour suprême
a renversé cette décision récement en raison du fait que plusieurs demandeurs
du statut de réfugié avaient effectivement contesté la loi en question (*Conseil canadien des Églises* c. *Canada (Ministre de l'emploi et de l'immigration,* no. 21946, le 23 janvier
1992, p. 22 de la version française des notes du juge Cory). Le critère demeure
toutefois inchangé: est-il nécessaire de reconnaître à un citoyen ou à une citoyenne
la qualité pour agir dans l'intérêt public afin que les tribunaux puissent être saisis de la question?

L'arrêt *Finlay* c. *Ministre des Finances du Canada*[276] énonce un certain nombre de conditions concernant le citoyen autorisé à intenter une action d'intérêt public. Outre le fait qu'une questions sérieuse doit être soulevée, le représentant doit avoir un ''intérêt véritable'' dans ce litige. Il ne doit pas s'agir d'un trouble-fête (*busybody*).[277] Ces restrictions ont été critiquées; on leur a reproché de permettre aux juges d'écarter les contestations qui leur déplaisent sans justifier leur décision.[278] De plus, à ce jour, elles ne semblent pas avoir été utilisées par la jurisprudence.

Dans l'hypothèse qui nous intéresse, il nous semble indéniable qu'une question sérieuse est posée. Reste à savoir ce qui constitue un ''intérêt véritable.'' Faut-il s'inspirer des deux protagonistes des arrêts de la Cour suprême (MM. Thorson et Borowski)? Faut-il avoir mené une campagne publique pendant de nombreuses années, en tentant de ne pas payer ses impôts et en prenant la parole sur toutes les tribunes? Faut-il être un pacifiste à tout crin, participer à toutes les manifestations et signer toutes les pétitions? On voit mal ce que cette exigence ajouterait au débat judiciaire.

À l'instar de la doctrine,[279] nous croyons que le simple fait d'intenter une action en justice et d'encourir les frais considérables qui en résultent démontre un intérêt véritable envers les questions en litige. Il semble que la Cour suprême soit préoccupée par la présentation de questions ''futiles'' et par la dissipation des ressources judicaires.[280] Il suffit donc qu'un plaideur soit sérieux et déterminé pour qu'il ne soit pas qualifié de ''trouble-fête'' (*busybody*), ce terme désignant vraisemblablement les personnes qui intentent des actions de façon intempestive. Il ne saurait en aucun cas s'appliquer aux demandeurs qui posent des questions difficiles aux tribunaux.

CONCLUSION DE LA PARTIE II

Les prohibitions contenues dans la *Loi sur la défense nationale* ainsi que dans les *Ordonnances et Règlements royaux applicables aux forces canadiennes* font en sorte qu'une militaire n'est pas raisonnablement en mesure de contester la décision du gouverneur en conseil de mettre

---

[276] *Loc. cit. supra*, note 259.

[277] *Id.*, 633.

[278] D. J. MULLAN et A.J. ROMAN, *loc. cit. supra*, note 258, pp. 311-25; T.A. CROMWELL, *loc. cit.* (1987), *supra*, note 258, p. 112; W. BOGART, *loc. cit.* (1988), *supra*, note 258, pp. 39-94.

[279] Voir *supra*, note 258.

[280] *Finlay* c. *Ministre des finances du Canada, loc. cit. supra*, note 259, p. 633.

les forces canadiennes en service actif. Il est donc nécessaire d'autoriser un citoyen ou une citoyenne à agir dans l'intérêt public, afin que les tribunaux canadiens puissent déterminer si la *Loi sur la défense nationale* a été respectée. Celle-ci renvoie à la *Charte des Nations Unies*, qui a créé la Cour internationale de justice. L'Assemblée générale des Nations Unies peut certes demander un avis consultatif à cette Cour; ceci ne saurait cependant priver un citoyen ou une citoyenne de son droit de contester la validité d'un acte posé par le gouvernement canadien. Si tel était le cas, l'exécutif serait libre de violer une loi canadienne pour le seul motif que l'Assemblée générale des Nations Unies ou le Conseil de sécurité refusent de saisir la Cour. Une telle situation serait contraire aux principes fondamentaux du système juridique canadien.

Le Parlement a autorisé les opérations militaires conformes à la *Charte des Nations Unies*. Dans ces conditions, les tribunaux doivent interpréter celle-ci. Ils ont agi ainsi par le passé, lorsqu'ils étaient confrontés aux conventions internationales intégrées à une loi fédérale. Il serait regrettable qu'ils changent soudainement d'attitude. Le prestige des Nations Unies aurait alors donné carte blanche au gouvernement canadien, dans un domaine où le contrôle de la légalité revêt une importance capitale.

CONCLUSION GÉNÉRALE

Dans les pages qui précèdent, nous avons tenté de montrer que le Conseil doit en tout temps contrôler le déroulement des opérations militaires entreprises par les Nations Unies. Est-ce là sombrer dans le juridisme? Nous ne le croyons pas. Cet argument juridique correspond très exactement au problème politique ressenti lors de la guerre du Golfe. L'absence de responsabilité des belligérants face à la communauté internationale autorisait tous les abus. La nécessité d'une concertation aurait certainement favorisé un certaine retenue lors des raids aériens et accru les chances de succès des négociations qui se déroulèrent subséquemment, immédiatement avant le début de l'offensive terrestre. Dans l'hypothèse où celles-ci eussent abouti, un nombre considérable de vies humaines auraient été épargnées.

À l'heure actuelle, le droit international autorise l'emploi de la force, mais uniquement en dernier recours. L'approche privilégiée par la *Charte des Nations Unies* consiste à donner au Conseil de sécurité le pouvoir de décider si l'usage de la force est nécessaire, en définissant le type de mesures qui doivent être prises. Certains soutiendront qu'en 1991, les membres permanents devraient plutôt avoir la possibilité de mettre sur pied une coalition qui soit libre d'agir à sa guise sur le plan militaire. Si tel est le cas, il est parfaitement inutile de se draper de l'autorité des Nations Unies; le retrait pur et simple de cette institution serait préférable au galvaudage des principes qui sont censés guider sa conduite. Ainsi, dans le contexte de la guerre du Golfe, le recours à la thèse de la légitime défense collective vide de toute substance les dispositions de la Charte concernant le Conseil de sécurité.

L'inefficacité du Conseil de sécurité constitue certainement l'un des grands problèmes de l'ordre international actuel: lorsqu'il n'est pas paralysé par l'exercice du droit de veto, cet organisme renonce à exercer son rôle et se contente de légitimer l'usage de la force. Dans ces conditions, l'adoption de la résolution 678 constitue un précédent fort regrettable pour les Nations Unies. À l'avenir, les États membres auront tout intérêt à demander au Conseil l'autorisation de prendre des mesures collectives sur lesquelles aucun contrôle n'est exercé. Le droit de veto que détiennent les membres permanents accentue d'ailleurs cette réticence des États à se laisser diriger par le Conseil. En attendant une éventuelle modification de la Charte, on ne peut qu'être inquiet devant la prééminence économique et militaire acquise récemment par les États-Unis d'Amérique, qui ont littéralement les moyens d'acheter les votes des membres du Conseil de sécurité.[281]

Du côté canadien, le large pouvoir discrétionnaire conféré au gouvernement pose assurément problème. Aucune disposition législative ne permet aux parlementaires de déterminer s'il est opportun de recourir aux armes. Dans certains milieux, on semble croire qu'il existe toujours une prérogative de la Couronne en ce domaine. Cette affirmation est techniquement inexacte, mais elle traduit une certaine réalité. La *Loi sur la défense nationale* n'offre aucun mécanisme permettant de renverser la décision du gouvernement. Seule la référence expresse à la *Charte des Nations Unies* nous a permis de développer un argument juridique. Évidemment, cette référence aurait pu être modifiée facilement. En déposant un tel projet de loi, le gouvernement aurait cependant reconnu qu'il existait des doutes sérieux sur la légalité des opérations entreprises.

La doctrine des questions politiques refait régulièrement surface

---

[281] Voir B. H. WESTON, *op. cit. supra*, note 47, aux pp. 523 à 525.

au Canada, malgré son rejet systématique par les juges. Là encore, cette perception est juridiquement fausse, mais correspond à une attitude assez répandue. Sans être devin, on peut facilement prévoir que plusieurs juges hésiteraient à remettre en question la légalité d'une opération entreprise par une coalition de pays et fondée sur une résolution du Conseil de sécurité. Pourtant, cette hésitation traduit simplement l'importance de l'enjeu: des vies humaines, en particulier celles de militaires canadiens. À notre avis, il eut été inconcevable que les tribunaux laissent subsister un doute sur la question en refusant de se prononcer.

Une page d'histoire vient d'être tournée. Le nouvel ordre mondial reste encore à définir, mais les événements de la guerre du Golfe ne laissent guère présager une transformation radicale du monde où nous vivons.

Summary

Reflections on the Validity of the Operations against Iraq in Light of the Charter of the United Nations and Canadian Law

On November 30, 1990, Resolution 678 of the Security Council purported to authorize the use of force in the Persian Gulf. It was acted upon by a coalition of States during the first months of 1991. At the end of January, the authors filed an action in the trial division of the Federal Court. In their statement of claim, they alleged that the Canadian government was acting in violation of section 31(1)(b) of the National Defence Act, which authorizes military action undertaken pursuant to the United Nations Charter. In the authors' opinion, Resolution 678 was contrary to the United Nations Charter, and thus Canadian Forces could not rely upon the National Defence Act to take military action in the Gulf. The action was discontinued as hostilities ended before the case could be heard. This article presents the arguments the authors intended to raise in court.

In Part I the authors argue that Resolution 678 cannot be justified by any of the Charter provisions, either as a measure of collective self-defence or as an example of the collective security system envisaged by the provisions of chapter VII of the Charter. Neither can the theory of implicit powers be invoked, since Resolution 678 amounts to a total abdication of power by the Security Council and, moreover, cannot be reconciled with the stated purposes of the United Nations.

In Part II the authors address the jurisdiction of Canadian courts to deal with the matter. They first explain how the royal prerogative relating to the armed forces has been displaced by statute. They then demonstrate that Canadian courts have always held it to be within their jurisdiction to interpret conventions referred to in a statute, and that nothing in this case warrants derogation from this well-established rule. Finally, the authors deal with the question of standing.

The Environment and the
Law of Conventional Warfare

L. C. GREEN*

IN RECENT YEARS, with increasing concern for the ecology and the environment, and with threats about holes in the ozone layer and the danger of the "greenhouse effect," public pressure has been exerting itself to ensure that steps be taken on an official level to reduce the dangers to the extent that may be feasible. Not only has this resulted in official and unofficial conferences comprising a variety of experts, but there has been widespread concern as to the effect of military operations with both conventional and unconventional weapons. Governments have responded to this pressure, to some extent as a result of the adoption by the General Assembly[1] of a convention prohibiting military or other hostile use of the atmosphere. When Iraq, during the Gulf War, occasioned a major oil spill in the Gulf by sabotaging Kuwaiti oilfields causing massive maritime pollution; there were numerous calls for the prosecution of those responsible for having committed what were described as environmental war crimes. Before it is possible to assess the validity of these accusations, it is necessary to see to what extent the customary or conventional international law of armed conflict recognizes such a crime; the extent to which Iraq might be bound thereby; and whether or not the Iraqi actions constituted breaches of this law or might have been otherwise justifiable.

In accordance with customary international law, damage caused should be proportionate to the end to be achieved and it has been accepted since classical times that warlike activities should not be

---

* LL.B., LL.D., F.R.S.C., University Professor, Honorary Professor of Law, University of Alberta. Paper prepared at request of Department of External Affairs for presentation at the Conference of Experts on the Use of the Environment as a Tool of Conventional Warfare, Ottawa, July 9-12, 1991. The views expressed are those of the writer alone and do not necessarily reflect those of the Department.

---

[1] 1168 UNTS 151.

directed at non-combatants. It has always been accepted that some collateral civilian damage is probably inevitable, but belligerents have been expected to try to keep this to a minimum. Even the Old Testament provides that the Israelites, when attacking cities, were not to "destroy the trees thereof by wielding an axe against them; for thou mayest eat of them, but thou shalt not cut them down; for is the tree of the field man, that it should be besieged by thee?"[2]

Josephus went so far as to state that the ban on destruction was extensive enough to forbid setting fire to enemy land or destroying beasts of labour.[3]

In the Middle Ages, there were military codes clearly recognizing that civilian resources did not constitute legitimate military objectives. For example, Maximilian II, about 1570, decreed that "none shall thieve any plough or mill or baking oven or any thing which serves the needs of the community whether it be from friend or foe. . . nor shall he willingly cause wine or grain or flour to leak away or to spoil or come to any harm on pain of corporal punisment."[4] And in 1690, a further decree provided that "he who dare in foreign countries to set ablaze or demolish hospitals or schools or baking ovens or to despoil a smithy or ploughs or farm implements in a township or hamlet shall be punished as a bloody villain."[5] Further, during the Seven Years' War, Friedrich of Prussia warned his forces that "particular care shall be taken to avoid any damage to wooded areas, homes, fields and gardens, fruit, fruit trees, barns and all property belonging to estate owners and farmers."[6] It is clear from these extracts that the European law of war was restricted to preserving those items that were essential to the civilian population and for the future.[7]

The first modern codification of the laws regulating the conduct of the armed forces during conflict is in the Lieber Code of 1863, which was aimed at the behaviour of American forces in the Civil

---

[2] Deuteronomy 20.19.

[3] Roberts, "Judaic Sources of and Views on the Laws of War," 37 Naval Law Rev. 221, 231 (1988).

[4] *Artikel auf Teutsche Landsknechte*, Art. 53.

[5] *Kriegsvölkerrecht: Leitfaden für den Unterrecht* (The International Law of Warfare, Instructional Outlines) Part 7, para. 3 (German Forces Publications ZDv 15/10, 1961).

[6] Churfürstlich Brandenburgisches Kriegsrecht, Art. 59 (1960). Both these quotations come from Corpus Juris Militaris Kriegsrecht und Artikels Brieffe (Johann Friedrich Schukzen, ed., 1693).

[7] General Orders No. 100 by President Lincoln, in Schindler and Toman, *The Laws of Armed Conflicts* 3 (1988).

War. This was expressive of generally accepted rules at the time and served as a model for a number of other national codes,[8] and, ultimately, to some extent, Hague Convention II of 1899 and IV of 1907.[9]

The Lieber Code laid down a number of provisions for the protection of the civilian population but allowed starvation where necessary to secure a faster subjugation of the enemy. Private property was to be respected, but unlike the earlier codes mentioned, there was no specific preservation of the means of sustenance or the future ability of enemy territory to maintain a population. On the other hand, the Code did reiterate that the prime objectives of a force are members of the opposing armed force and the destruction of those objects that are of military significance. As for the Hague Conventions, the annexed Regulations provide for the protection of private property and requisitions against payment for military purposes. Again, there is no reference to any obligation to protect agricultural or similar resources, although Article 22 makes it clear that "the right of belligerents to adopt means of injuring the enemy is not unlimited." The only indication of what this limitation means in a general sense is to be found in the Martens Clause embodied in the Preamble:

Until a more complete code of the laws of war has been issued, the High Contracting Parties deem it expedient to declare that, in cases not included in the Regulations . . . the inhabitants and the belligerents remain under the protection and the rule of the principles of the law of nations, as they result from the usages established among civilized peoples, from the laws of humanity, and the dictates of the public conscience.

It may be argued that "the laws of humanity and the dictates of the public conscience" extend to the general protection of the civil population including its means of sustenance, and that this means that a belligerent must ensure that his activities do not in any way unreasonably interfere with the future well-being of the civilian population of the enemy.

Before discussing other specific treaties relating to armed conflict, one must look at developments concerning protection of the environment in order to ascertain whether any general rule of customary or treaty law has been established that can be said to apply at all times in both peace and war. In this connection, it should

[8] Holland, *The Law of War on Land* 71-72 (1908).

[9] Schindler and Toman, *op. cit. supra* note 7, at 63.

be borne in mind that the fact that some states have enacted legislation to protect their own environment, does not amount to evidence of any *opinio juris* or a general principle of law recognized by civilized nations in the manner in which that term is used in Article 38 of the Statute of the International Court of Justice. Similarly, the fact that the International Court of Justice or other international tribunals have made reference to issues of pollution does not mean that there is any rule of customary international law of a general character with regard to environmental pollution.[10]

The first major attempt to deal with environmental protection in a general manner on the international level was the 1948 United Nations Convention on the Law of the High Seas.[11] By Article 24 states are required to draw up regulations to prevent pollution by the discharge of oil from ships or pipelines and by Article 25 to take measures to prevent pollution of the seas from the dumping of radioactive waste. The United Nations Convention on the Law of the Sea, 1982[12] is wider than this. Article 1 defines ''marine pollution'' as: ''the introduction by man, directly or indirectly, of substances or energy into the marine environment, including estuaries, which result in such deleterious effects as harm to living resources and marine life, hazards to human health, hindrance to marine activities, including fishing and other legitimate uses of the sea, impairment of quality for use of sea water and reduction of amenities.'' The Article also defines ''dumping'' as: ''any deliberate disposal of wastes or other matter from vessels, aircraft, platforms or other man-made structures at sea [and] any deliberate disposal of vessels, aircraft, platforms or other man-made structures at sea; [but it does not include] the disposal of wastes or other matters incidental to, or derived from the normal operation of vessels, aircraft, platforms or other man-made structures at sea and their equipment. . . [nor does it include] placement of matter for a purpose other than the mere disposal thereof. . . .''

Perhaps more important than these provisions are Articles 192 and 194 concerning the protection and preservation of the marine environment. Article 192 imposes a general obligation to ''protect and preserve'' the environment, and 194 obliges ''States [to] take

[10] See, e.g., *Trail Smelter Arbitration* (1938/1941), UN Rep. Int'l Arb. Awards 1905. See also Schafer, ''The Relationship between the International Laws of Armed Conflict and Environmental Protection,'' 19 Calif. Western Int'l L.J. 287, 296-97 (1989).

[11] 450 UNTS 11.

[12] 21 Int'l Leg. Mat. 1261.

all measures necessary to ensure that activities under their jurisdiction or control are so conducted as not to cause damage by pollution to other States and their environment, and that pollution arising from incidents or activities under their jurisdiction or control does not spread beyond the areas where they exercise sovereign rights. . . .'' Moreover, they are "obliged to minimize to the fullest possible extent the release of toxic, harmful or noxious substances, especially those which are persistent, from land-based sources, from or through the atmosphere. . . .''

The only other Articles of the Convention to which reference need be made are: Article 235, imposes responsibility for fulfilling international obligations concerning protection and preservation of the marine environment and imposing liability "in accordance with international law," a provision that reiterates that in Article 139 which imposes responsibility to ensure compliance and responsibility for damage, even though caused by states themselves; and those relating to the freedom of the seas in general.

Article 87 merely confirms the established rule of international law that the high seas are open to all states, while Article 88 specifically provides that "the high seas shall be reserved for peaceful purposes." This implies that not even the normal activities of maritime warfare would be compatible with the obligations imposed by the 1982 Convention if conducted outside the territorial sea of the belligerents. However, the Convention has not yet entered into force and — of major significance — while the Convention is *lex generalis,* the law of war is *lex specialis* and, to the extent that its provisions are contrary to those of the *lex generalis,* they prevail.

Other international instruments seeking to regulate pollution of the environment are not strictly relevant, for they relate to particular types of pollution, for example, that caused by shipping, including nuclear-powered vessels. From the point of view of armed conflict, there is a series of treaty articles and United Nations resolutions against damage caused by nuclear testing or discharges.

Of special interest in the law of armed conflict is the 1976 Convention on the Prohibition of Military or Any Other Hostile Use of Environmental Modification Techniques.[13] This is not really concerned with methods of warfare that may have a deleterious effect upon the environment, for it defines "environmental techniques" as "any technique for changing — through the deliberate manipu-

---

[13] 1108 UNTS 151.

lation of natural processes — the dynamics, composition or structure of the Earth, including its biota, lithosphere, hydrosphere and
atmosphere, or of outer space." This suggests that means and
methods of warfare that adversely affect the environment, even if
that is foreseen, would not, subject to any other restriction, be contrary to the law of armed conflict insofar as it concerns these means
and methods of warfare. Against this is the fact that a belligerent's
right to employ means to injure his enemy is not unlimited and,
therefore, the right to resort to such measures is subject to the rule
on proportionality[14] and to the limitation on injury to civilians and
civilian objects. In addition, the damage resulting from the "environmental modification" must be "widespread, longlasting or
severe."

The international instrument that seeks to protect the environment during armed conflict is Protocol I of 1977 Additional to the
Geneva Conventions of August 12, 1949, and relating to the Protection of Victims of International Armed Conflicts.[15] Article 35
extends the scope of the 1976 Convention, since it prohibits the employment of "methods or means of warfare which are intended,
or may be expected, to cause widespread, long-term *and* severe
damage to the natural environment." Article 55 carries the restriction further: "Care shall be taken in warfare to protect the natural
environment against widespread, long-term and severe damage.
This protection includes a prohibition of the use of methods or
means of warfare which are intended or may be expected to cause
such damage to the environment and thereby to prejudice the health
or survival of the civilian population."

Since it was well established that oilspills from tankers could result
in massive environmental damage, it is perhaps surprising that the
draftsmen of the Protocol, when referring to works and in
stallations containing dangerous forces, made no reference to the
danger potential in the destruction of oilfields or wells. Article 56
of the Protocol protects from attack those works or installations
containing dangerous forces — dams, dykes, and nuclear elec-
trical generating installations — attack upon which "may cause
the release of dangerous forces and consequent severe losses
among the civilian population." The essential difference between
the Convention and the Protocol is that in the former the effects

---

[14] See, e.g., Fenrick, "The Rule of Proportionality and Protocol In Conventional
Warfare," 98 Mil.L.R. 91 (1982).
[15] Schindler and Toman, *op. cit. supra* note 7, at 621.

must be "widespread, longlasting or severe," while in the Protocol they must be cumulative.

According to the leading commentary on the Protocol, Articles 35 and 55 "will not impose any significant limitation on combatants waging conventional warfare. It seems primarily directed to high level policy decision makers and would affect such unconventional means of warfare as the massive use of herbicides or chemical agents which could produce widespread long-term and severe damage to the natural environment."[16] The writers of this commentary mention only unconventional means of warfare as the type of weapon envisaged by the Protocol and this term is normally understood to refer to nuclear, chemical, and bacteriological weapons. In fact, the limitation of the Protocol — and thus of all its restrictive provisions — is made clear in the introduction to the draft put forward by the International Committee of the Red Cross in 1973: "Problems relating to atomic, bacteriological and chemical warfare are subjects of international agreements or negotiations by governments, and in submitting these draft Protocols the ICRC does not intend to broach these problems. It should be borne in mind that the Red Cross as a whole at several International Red Cross Conferences has clearly made known its condemnation of weapons of mass destruction and has urged governments to reach agreements for banning their use."[17] Moreover, the three leading nuclear powers present at the Conference — the Soviet Union, the United Kingdom, and the United States — made it clear that they did not consider the Protocol as having any impact on these weapons; India was the only participant that went on record as expressing its opposition to this view.

In addition to treaties seeking to regulate specific sources of pollution or to limit environmental damage during conflict, there are numerous declarations aimed at condemning environmental pollution as such. If these were as compulsive as they are sometimes claimed to be, rules on environmental protection might be considered to constitute *jus cogens*[18] operative in both peace and war. The most significant of these instruments is the Declaration on the Human Environment adopted by the United Nations Stockholm Conference in 1972.[19] The Conference adopted a number of

[16] Bothe, Partsch, and Solf, *New Rules for Victims of Armed Conflicts* 348 (1982).
[17] *Ibid.*, 188-89.
[18] See, e.g., Hannikainen, *Peremptory Norms (Jus Cogens) in International Law* (1988).
[19] II Int'l Leg. Mat. 1416.

Principles, only a few of which are relevant:

Principle 2. The natural resources of the earth including the air, water, land, flora and fauna and especially representative samples of natural ecosystems must be safeguarded for the benefit of present and future generations through careful planning and management as appropriate.

Principle 5. The nonrenewable resources of the earth must be employed in such a way as to guard against the danger of their future exhaustion and to ensure that benefits from such employment are shared by all mankind.

Principle 6. The discharge of toxic substances or of other substances and the release of heat, in such quantities or concentrations as to exceed the capacity of the environment to render them harmless must be halted in order to ensure that serious or irreversible damage is not inflicted upon ecosystems . . . .

Principle 7. States shall take all possible steps to prevent pollution of the seas by substances that are liable to create hazards to human health, to harm living rsources and marine life, to damage amenities or to interfere with other legitimate uses of the sea.

Principle 21. States have, in accordance with the Charter of the United Nations and the principles of international law, the sovereign right to exploit their own resources pursuant to their own environmental policies, and the responsibility to ensure that activities within their jurisdiction or control do not cause damage to the environment of other States or to areas beyond the limits of national jurisdiction.

Principle 22. States shall cooperate to develop further the international law regarding liability and compensation for the victims of pollution and other environmental damage caused by activities within the jurisdiction or control of such States to areas beyond their jurisdiction.

Principle 26. Man and his environment must be spared the effects of nuclear weapons and all other means of mass destruction. States must strive to reach prompt agreement, in the relevant international organs, on the elimination and complete destruction of such weapons.

These Principles are directed to imposing obligations upon states to ensure that, in exercising their sovereign right to exploit their resources as they will, they do not adversely affect the environment permanently and do nothing to harm the environment of neighbouring states. Equally significant is the fact that the only reference made to the environment in wartime relates to the damage likely to result from the use of nuclear and other weapons of mass destruction. There is no reference to the harm to the environment likely to be caused by conventional weapons, by the fuels used in mechanical warfare, by destruction likely to result from abandoned

and non-recyclable or non-reusable material, or by the release of
smoke or other deleterious matter, unless the use of the latter is
already illegal under some other rule relating to armed conflict.

Perhaps even more important than any of these reservations is
the fact that, even though the Declaration was adopted by accla-
mation at a United Nations Conference, it does not amount to a
legally binding document. It is not a treaty, has not been registered
as such with the United Nations Secretariat, and does not even enjoy
the status of a General Assembly Resolution which, in any case,
would lack any legally binding authority. The mere fact that the
instrument is entitled ''Declaration'' does not give it any special
status. As the legal department of the United Nations Secretariat
pointed out in 1962:

> In view of the greater solemnity and significance of a declaration, it may
> be considered to import, on behalf of the organ adopting it, a strong ex-
> pectation that Members of the international community will abide by it.
> Consequently, in so far as the expectation is gradually justified by State
> practice, a declaration may by custom become recognized as laying down
> rules binding upon States. In conclusion, it may be said that in United
> Nations practice, a declaration is a solemn instrument resorted to only
> in very rare cases relating to matters of major and lasting importance
> and where maximum compliance is expected.[20]

The Stockholm Declaration was adopted before the adoption of
Protocol I and the states participating in the Geneva Conference
at which the Protocol was adopted, were aware of its existence; the
majority of them had participated at Stockholm. Nevertheless, other
than the references to environmental protection already noted above,
it can hardly be said that the existence of the Stockholm Declaration on the Human Environment had any effect upon what was
adopted in 1977. Similarly, little has happened since to suggest that
state action in this matter has been sufficient to ensure that ''[this]
declaration [has] by custom become recognized as laying down rules
binding upon States.'' This is important in view of the fact that,
in its Draft Declaration on State Responsibility, the International
Law Commission in Article 19(3)(d) listed as an international crime
''a serious breach of an international obligation of essential importance for the safeguarding and preservation of the human environment, such as those prohibiting massive pollution of the atmosphere

---

[20] Doc. E/CN.4/L 610, Apr. 2, 1962, c. Schermers, *International Institutional Law*, Vol. II,
at 500.

or of the seas."[21] Once again it must be pointed out that this document lacks any legal significance, even though it may amount to the *opinio juris* of the members of the Commission and, as yet, there is no indication that it is likely to be embodied into any international obligation of the type envisaged.[22]

As is clear from the above, other than what appears in the Convention forbidding environmental modification and in Protocol I, there is no treaty provision specifically directed against environmental weapons or conventional weapons adversely affecting the stability of the environment by pollution. Insofar as customary law is concerned, therefore, it has to be considered whether such effects are already forbidden by what is generally known as the laws and customs of war, especially in the light of the Martens Clause.

As has been mentioned, in every war — and the Gulf war is no exception — there is inevitably a certain amount of environmental pollution. Where the Gulf war is concerned, this was particularly likely to occur in view of the intensive destruction of military hardware of every kind after the Coalition aerial attacks, and this was compounded by the damage done to oil installations and tankers, both of which in modern technological and mechanical warfare are legitimate military targets, regardless of any intentional destruction on the part of the Iraqi authorities directed against Kuwaiti installations.

When it became likely, in light of the massive aerial offensive, that the Coalition forces would launch a land or sea attack, or perhaps both simultaneously against occupied Kuwait or Iraq, the latter released a vast oil spill from the Kuwaiti oilfields into the Gulf and set fire to some hundreds of Kuwaiti oilwells and installations. The oil flowing into the Gulf destroyed much of the natural water-life and moved southwards along the coast of Saudi Arabia, one of the states contributing forces to the Coalition. It was anticipated that this would adversely affect Saudi desalination equipment and, thus, the drinking water of the civilian population. As to the fires, it was generally believed the smoke and chemicals discharged into the atmosphere would have a deleterious pollutive effect, which was likely to be widespread, longlasting, and severe, and therefore contrary to both the Environmental Modification Convention and Protocol I.

---

[21] Yearbook of the I.L.C., 1979, Vol II, pt. 2, at 91.
[22] For critical analysis of this aspect of the draft, see Green, "New Trends in International Criminal Law," II Israel Y.B. Human Rights 3, 27 *et seq.* (1981).

Under the 1976 Convention, as indicated above, "environmental modification techniques" involve deliberate manipulation of natural processes; however, there is no evidence to suggest that this is what Iraq was in fact doing. Moreover, Iraq has not ratified the Convention, so that its provisions are not binding on it in any way. Since only about one-third of the members of the United Nations have ratified this Convention, it cannot be argued that it has established anything in the nature of general or universal international law. With regard to the Protocol, the same arguments apply even more emphatically. In this case, neither Iraq nor the United States nor the United Kingdom has ratified it and, to whatever extent some of the provisions of that instrument may be said to constitute principles of customary law now written into treaty form, this cannot be said of the provisions relating to environmental protection. Further, the original fears that the damage to the environment resulting from the spill would be widespread and longlasting appear to have been somewhat exaggerated. It has been reported that

the world's largest oil spill has devastated Saudi Arabia's northeast coast [but] large areas of the Gulf may have had a lucky escape. A combination of hot sunshine and slow moving currents could have protected much of the waterway from up to six million barrels of oil which poured into the sea from damaged Iraqi, Kuwaiti, and Saudi installations and tankers. Environmentalists believe the Gulf's high salinity made the oil float on the surface, leaving it to evaporate under the blazing sun. Fifty to seventy per cent of the oil would have disappeared in 24 hours as its lighter constituents evaporated.[23]

Again, in assessing any Iraqi liability for breaches of the law of armed conflict, had the Convention been operative, one must not ignore the Iraqi claim that the spill was generated in order to frustrate a possible marine invasion. This action would not be in breach of the Convention and, if true, would probably constitute a reasonable means of warfare on Iraq's part. However, it would also be necessary for Iraq to show that its action did not result in disproportionate civilian damage and that the destruction of the Saudi desalination equipment could not have been foreseen or was a reasonable collateral damage incidental to the defensive action undertaken.

As to the smoke generated by the fires intentionally set to the wells and installations, it would first be necessary to estimate how

---

[23] *The Times* (London), May 8, 1991; Jan. 15, 1992; see also, Homer-Dixon, "It's Not the End of the World," *Globe and Mail* (Toronto), May 30, 1991.

much of this smoke was caused by these fires as distinct from that resulting from Coalition bombing of similar installations. In addition, it should not be overlooked that, traditionally, smoke has been an accepted means of warfare providing protective cover for advancing or retreating forces. However, the latter type of smoke has been of a temporary character, whereas the smoke generated by these fires will persist at least as long as the fires continue. Furthermore, the traditional smoke has been local in character, while this has entered the atmosphere and, being windborne, will travel beyond the geographic limits of the war zones. In this case, too, Iraq may argue that the purpose of the fires was twofold. In the first place it may contend that the destruction of the wells was intended to deny their availability to the mechanized units of the Coalition, for, as such, they would amount to legitimate military objectives,[24] even within the terms of Article 52 of Protocol I had they been applicable; that article provides that "military objectives are limited to those objects which by their nature, location, purpose or use make an effective contribution to military action and whose total or partial destruction, capture[25] or neutralization, in the circumstances ruling at the time, offers a definite military advantage." This definition is not so very different from that to be found in Spaight's *War Rights on Land* published in 1911: "War matériel and army supplies generally; *property situated in the anticipated field of battle* or in the zone of actual fighting...are...subject to destruction."[26] Nor does it deviate substantially from Article 23(g) of the Hague Regulations of 1907 which forbids the destruction or seizure of the enemy's property *"unless such destruction or seizure be imperatively demanded by the necessities of war."*

In the light of the Nuremberg Tribunal's holding that the Regulations had hardened into rules of customary law,[27] there would seem to be little doubt that oil installations of every kind are in fact legitimate military objectives open to destruction by any belligerent. Nevertheless, it is now well-established that even military objectives should only be destroyed if the military advantage to be gained

---

[24] U.S. Dept. of the Air Force, Doc. AFP 110-31, Nov. 19, 1976, *International Law: The Conduct of Armed Conflict and Air Operations,* lists "petroleum facilities" as legitimate targets for attack: 5-18, n. 23.

[25] See, e.g., the judgment of Whyatt, C.J., Singapore, in *N.V. de Bataafsche Petroleum Maatschappij* v. *The War Damage Commission (Singapore Oil Stocks case)* (1956), 23 I.L.R. 810.

[26] See p. 128.

[27] H.M.S.O., Cmd. 6964 (1964), at 65; 41 Am. J. Int'l L. 172, 248-49 (1947).

so outweighs the collateral civilian damage as to render this proportionate, however severe it may be.

Second, Iraq could argue that the smoke generated in this fashion was nothing other than an extensive use of the smoke cover normally provided by traditional smoke producers, and that it was intended to provide cover for its own forces, as well as obscuring the vision of attacking mechanized and other forces, whether on land or in the air. Any tribunal established to try Iraqi officials for having generated such extensive smoke cover would perhaps be hard put to deny this Iraqi contention, although it would be open to that tribunal to hold, on the basis of the evidence before it, that the amount generated and its persistence were disproportionate to the military end sought and that the longterm effect exceeded this end, particularly in view of the early termination of hostilities as a result of Iraq's acceptance of truce terms dictated to it by the Security Council.

It is apparent that there is no clear treaty provision that Iraq's use of these methods, even though they resulted in environmental pollution, amounted to a breach of the written law of international armed conflict. It therefore is necessary to ascertain whether, in accordance with the customary rules relating to the conduct of armed conflict, the measures against the oil wells and installations were, in fact, directed in their consequences more at the civilian population not only of Kuwait or Saudi Arabia, both of which were adverse parties, but also, by their persistence and the penetration of the atmosphere, against the interests of neutrals whose rights were affected adversely far beyond what was reasonably tolerable in accordance with the law of armed conflict.

Regardless of the facts outlined above, it is also now well-established in customary law that the means and methods of warfare that belligerents choose to employ is not an unrestricted right. Moreover, it is also generally accepted that the weapons employed should not cause unnecessary harm or suffering, that is to say, damage not necessary to the achievement of a definite military advantage — and this is merely another way of giving expression to the principle of proportionality.

Whether the Iraqi actions with regard to the destruction of the oil installations would fall into the class of activities that are regarded as illegal in the sense just indicated depends on a careful analysis of the facts and an assessment of the extent to which the actions may be justifiable on the basis of military necessity.[28] This is a matter for judicial determination in the light of expert military and scientific evidence, and is a decision that should be made by neutral judges rather than by those chosen from among representatives of the powers making up the Coalition.

The fact that there seems to be no clear law with regard to environmental war crimes or the use, as distinct from the modification, of the environment as a conventional weapon other than what may be drawn from a somewhat liberal interpretation of customary law, raises the question of what may be done in the future to fill this lacuna.

The chances of securing the adoption of a new treaty dealing specifically with this issue are somewhat remote. The drafting of such a treaty would probably take years, and a further lengthy period would ensue before sufficient ratifications or accessions, including those of the powers most likely to endanger the environment, could be secured. Moreover, without the introduction of punitive clauses and the means whereby punishment could be inflicted, a treaty might well be little more than a paper tiger in the face of any state determined to go its own way. In the absence of such provisions, breach of the treaty by a party would carry only the normal consequances of treaty breach,[29] which do not include criminal prosecution. Further, the drafting of the treaty would itself raise innumerable problems in view of the difficulty of securing agreement as to what constitute legitimate objectives in an era of mechanized warfare as well as determining what amounts to 'longlasting' or 'severe' damage beyond that which is tolerably sustainable — a problem that would undoubtedly occasion inumerable differences of opinion among the scientific experts.

Perhaps the solution to this problem lies in the United Nations General Assembly or even the Security Council charging the International Law Commission, as a matter of urgency, to take up this issue in the same way as it did the Principles of International Law Recognized by the Charter of the Nuremberg Tribunal, calling upon such expert evidence, both scientific and military, as might assist it in this task. It would then be necessary for the Security

---

[28] For a discussion of military necessity, see the trial of Gen. Rendulic, *Hostages* case (1948), 8 UN Trials of War Criminals 34, 68-69.

[29] See, e.g., McNair, *The Law of Treaties*, Part VI (1961); see also Vienna Convention on the Law of Treaties, 1969, 1155 UNTS 331.

under Chapter VII of the Charter relating to potential threats to the peace, breaches of the peace, and acts of aggression, to adopt a Resolution which, in accordance with Article 24 of the Charter, would be binding upon all members, condemning the use of weaponry inimical to the environment and contrary to the principles adopted by the Commission. These principles and the resolution based thereon would, of course, have to declare that the rules in question constituted part of the customary rules of warfare, so that breaching them would amount to war crimes and would be punishable.

Whatever rules are established, it remains true that they will only be effective if states abide by them and if states are prepared to prosecute violators, as they would war criminals, that is to say, in the absence of an international criminal court, to prosecute before their own military tribunals those persons regardless of rank or position against whom there was prima facie evidence of their responsibility for having resorted to methods contrary to the rules.

Sommaire

L'environnement et le droit de la guerre classique

Déjà, dans l'Ancien testament, les guerres menées par les Israéliens faisaient l'objet de restrictions en matière d'environnement. Ainsi, les armées étaient autorisées à s'emparer des récoltes pour se nourrir, mais il leur était interdit de détruire les arbres et les ressources agricoles afin de ne pas priver les générations futures. La plupart des codes militaires, qui ont été adoptés au cours de la période féodale, renferment des dispositions similaires qui interdisent aux armées de s'attaquer au bétail, à l'outillage agricole ou alimentaire. Par ailleurs, le code Lieber, première codification moderne du droit de la guerre à l'intention des armées sur le terrain, autorisait la privation des denrées alimentaires destinées à la population civile comme acte de guerre légitime. Toutefois, quand les puissances se sont réunies à La Haye en 1899 et an 1907 pour élaborer ce qui est aujourd'hui considéré comme les principes fondamentaux du droit des conflits armés, à savoir le Règlement annexé à la Convention IV de La Haye de 1907, elles ont déclaré que les moyens utilisés à des fins de guerre n'étaient pas illimités, que les maux de la guerre doivent être réduits autant que les nécessités militaires le permettent et que "les populations et les belligérants restent sous la sauvegarde et sous l'empire des principes du droit des gens, tels qu'ils résultent des usages établis entre nations civilisées, des lois de l'humanité et des exigences de la conscience publique." Il n'y avait donc rien qui visait directement la protection de l'environnement au sens large du terme. Il est rapidement devenu établi, toutefois, qu'en temps de guerre, les belligérants ne devaient s'attaquer qu'aux objectifs militaires et ce, conformément au principe de proportionnalité en veillant à ne pas causer de dommages incidents excessifs compte tenu des fins militaires recherchées.

Ce n'est qu'en 1958, dans le cadre de la Convention de Genève sur la haute mer, que les préoccupations à l'égard de la protection de l'environnement ont abouti à des demandes en faveur de la prise de mesures contre la pollution marine. Celles-ci ont également été cristallisées dans la Convention des Nations Unies sur le droit de la mer de 1982, laquelle proclame que la haute mer est ouverte à tous et qu'elle "est affectée à des fins pacifiques." Ce traité est, toutefois, lex generalis *tandis que le droit des conflits armés est* lex specialis; *or vu que cette dernière n'est pas expressément écartée, les belligérants peuvent toujours faire la guerre sur la mer malgré les dangers de pollution.*

Le premier traité qui a visé les effets de opérations militaires sur l'environnement est la Convention de 1976 sur l'interdiction d'utiliser des tecnhiques de modification de l'environnement; toutefois celle-ci n'interdit que les techniques de modification de l'environnement ayant des "effets étendus, durables ou *graves." Le Protocole I de 1977, additionnel aux Conventions de Genève de 1949, est allé un plus loin. Toutefois, il n'avait pas une portée générale et n'interdisait seulement que l'utilisation des "méthodes ou moyens de guerre qui sont conçus pour causer, ou dont on peut s'attendre qu'ils causeront, des dommages étendus, durables* et *graves à l'environnement." Le protocole I de 1977 prévoyait en outre "l'interdiction d'utiliser des méthodes ou moyens de guerre conçus pour causer ou dont on peut s'attendre qu'ils causent de tels dommages à l'environnement naturel et compromettront, de ce fait, la santé ou la survie de la population." Les dommages causés à la nature, aux oiseaux ou à la faune, n'ayant pas un caractère indispensable pour la population civile, ne semblent pas visés par cette interdiction. Par conséquent, les dommages causés par les incendies des puits de pétrole ou les déversements de pétrole dans le golfe aux cours des opérations militaires Koweït-Iraq, dans la mesure où ils touchaient le bétail, ne contrevenaient pas au Protocole. De toute façon, il faut remarquer que le Protocole n'avait pas été ratifié par l'Iraq, le R.-U. et les É.U., et par conséquent ne s'appliquait pas à ces opérations militaires. Malgré l'appui de la population et les résolutions des Nations Unies concernant la protection de l'environnement, on ne peut pas conclure que ces dispositions équivalent à des règles de droit countumier ou de* jus cogens. *De plus, les justifications de l'Iraq en ce qui concerne la destruction du pétrole, matériel nécessaire à la guerre moderne — le fait de priver la Coalition de cette ressource, le recours à la fumée comme écran protecteur, etc. — semblent représenter des motifs suffisants pour faire valoir que les dommages causés à l'environnement, qui se sont avérés beaucoup moins graves ou durables qu'il avait été initialement prévu, n'étaient pas disproportionnés et que les mesures de destruction prises n'étaient pas illégales. Il serait donc difficile de soutenir que de telles mesures prises par l'Iraq constituaient une contravention à la loi ou des crimes de guerre.*

Legal Aspects of Targeting
in the Law of Naval Warfare

W. J. FENRICK*

A T THE OXFORD SESSION of August 9, 1913, the Institute of International law adopted a Manual of the Laws of Naval War,
which has since become known as the Oxford Manual.[1] The Oxford Manual was intended to provide a contemporary restatement
of the law of naval warfare. Political, legal, and technological developments since 1913 have, not surprisingly, rendered the Oxford
Manual obsolete. A comparison of older texts on the law of the
sea, such as the 1943 edition of Higgins and Colombos, *The International law of the Sea*, with a contemporary text, such as the 1983
edition of Churchill and Lowe, *The Law of the Sea*, indicates one overwhelming difference between them. The older texts are divided into
two parts, each of roughly equal length, concerned with the law
of the sea in time of peace and the law of the sea in time of war.
The newer texts focus almost exclusively on the law of the sea in
time of peace; most of them totally ignore the law of the sea in time
of war or the law of naval warfare. Even a scholar such as the late
D. P. O'Connell, who adopted a traditional approach to law of the
sea matters and was quite knowledgeable about naval affairs, devoted
less than ten percent of the space in his two volume treatise on *The
International Law of the Sea* to the law of naval warfare.

There are a number of reasons for the decline of interest in the

---

* Commander W. J. Fenrick, Director of International Law, Department of National
Defence, Ottawa. The views expressed herein are those of the writer and do not
necessarily reflect either the policy or the opinion of the Canadian government.
This article is based on a report on *Military Objectives in the Law of Naval Warfare* prepared by the writer for the Round Table of Experts on International Humanitarian Law Applicable to Armed Conflicts at Sea for the November 10-14, 1989,
Meeting in Bochum, Germany, and used as the basis for discussions at the meeting.

[1] The Oxford Manual and an article commenting on it are contained in N. Ronzitti,
ed., *The Law of Naval Warfare* 277-341 (London, 1988).

law of naval warfare. First there is the appalling history of the two world wars with respect to the law of war. Then there is a general acceptance that aggressive war is illegal, although the end result of this acceptance appears to be that states continue to fight each other in the exercise of their right of self-defence but without a declaration of war. There is also a lack of familiarity in the academic legal community with modern naval technology and strategy, and, perhaps, a feeling in the academic legal community that work concerning the law of the sea in time of armed conflict is somewhat sordid and futile. Even if one concedes the legitimacy of some of these concerns, a coherent and practicable body of law for application during armed conflict can provide some marginal humanitarian benefit. Law is most important when it is most under strain.

There is a need at present for serious discourse between qualified academic lawyers and practitioners concerning the desirable parameters for the body of law to regulate armed conflict at sea. The law of armed conflict is not a body of law designed to pander to persons of a bellicose disposition; it is what might be called a second level barrier to barbarism. If attempts to avoid an armed conflict fail, then the conflict should be conducted in accordance with certain rules. Although the time is ripe for discussion of both what the law is and how it should evolve, it is far too early to begin serious thinking about a diplomatic conference to codify and develop the law. A new *Oxford Manual of the Laws of Naval Warfare* is needed, and scholars and practitioners have been meeting in an Annual Round Table of Experts on International Humanitarian Law Applicable to Armed Conflicts at Sea, in San Remo in 1987, Madrid in 1988, Bochum in 1989, Toulon in 1990, and Bergen in 1991 with the object of producing such a manual.

The purpose of this article is to contribute to the debate on the central legal issue of targeting. A few preliminary comments are essential. While the law of naval warfare has been developed for a different environment from that of land warfare or air warfare, the three fundamental principles of the law of armed conflict referred to in Resolution 2444 (XXIII) of the United Nations General Assembly and unanimously adopted on December 19, 1968 also form the basis for it, namely that: the right of belligerents to adopt means of injuring the enemy is not unlimited; it is prohibited to launch attacks against the civilian population as such; and distinctions must be made between combatants and non-combatants, the latter to be spared as much as possible. One cannot assume, however, that the concepts or contents of the law of land or air warfare are automatically transferable to the law of naval warfare. In particular, naval warfare normally has an economic aspect and, as a result, frequently impinges on the commercial activities of the subjects of neutral states. The extent of the belligerent right to interfere with neutral commerce is an extremely important aspect of any sustained international conflict with a significant naval element. Furthermore, the treaty law concerning naval warfare, except for the 1949 Geneva Second Convention on the wounded, sick, and shipwrecked, and the 1936 London Submarine Protocol (the continued validity of which is a topic of frequent discussion), is pre-First World War law. As a result, the current law of naval warfare cannot be found exclusively in treaty texts.

An analysis and assessment of state practice in naval warfare during the two World Wars and in the post-1945 period is an essential element of any attempt to state the current law. Regrettably, no one has done the necessarily detailed historical analysis of this practice, although scholars could arrive at a reasonably sound impression of state practice by reviewing naval histories and periodicals. In any event researchers must assess state practice as well as analyze its content; the fact that a deed was done and went unpunished does not necessarily make it legally acceptable. For example, the crew of the US submarine, Wahoo, apparently massacred thousands of survivors of a Japanese troop transport in early 1943 and the US commanding officer, who reported the incident, was decorated for it.[2] This action is no more acceptable than the killing of survivors of the Greek ship Peleus, for which members of a German submarine crew were convicted on war crimes charges.[3]

Declared wars are extremely rare in the UN Charter era. It has been suggested that, in the absence of a state of war, a state engaged in an international armed conflict has no entitlement to exercise belligerent rights such as seizing enemy merchant vessels or board, search, and seize neutral merchant vessels. Some thoughtful work supports this suggestion,[4] but war is a question of fact and

---

[2] C. Blair, *Silent Victory*, Vol. I, at 352-60 (Philadelphia, 1975).

[3] *The Peleus Trial* (1945), 1 L.R.T.W.C. 1-21.

[4] Proponents of this approach include E. Lauterpacht, "The Legal Irrelevance of the 'State of War',"(1968) Am. Soc. Int'l L. Proc. 38; D. P. O'Connell, *The Influence of Law on Seapower* (1975); and C. Greenwood, "The Relationship between *Jus ad Bellum* and *Jus in Bello*," 9 Rev. Int. Studies 221 (1983), "The Concept of War in Modern International Law," 36 Int'l and Comp. L.Q. 283 (1987), and

the application of the laws of war must be conditioned on fact if coherence is to be achieved. All of the law of war, including those portions of the law of naval warfare affecting neutral shipping, has a prohibitive as well as a permissive character. In the words of the late Richard Baxter, "For the purposes of an economic blockade having an impact on neutrals, it is assumed that the belligerent would resort to the use of violence against neutrals if such conduct were necessary in order to overcome the enemy. The law thus protects those neutrals by keeping coercion within the permissible limits established."[5] The UN Charter does not constitute an insurmountable barrier prohibiting the invocation of belligerent rights against non-participants to an international armed conflict. Similarly, although the scale or intensity of an armed conflict may provide sound reasons for making more or less restrictive targeting decisions, to use such a factor as a determinant for the legality of targeting criteria would be unwise. There would be a natural tendency for a state to view any conflict in which it was involved as a general war justifying very liberal targeting criteria while conflicts in which it was not involved would be limited wars requiring a restrictive approach to targeting.

The scope of this article is confined to a discussion of military objectives, that is, objects that may be attacked on, under, or above the water, but not objects or persons on land. The first half will deal with the principle of distinction and the concept of the military objective; the state of the law before World War I; a summary of developments up to the Geneva Conventions of 1949, including state practice, treaty law, case law, and juridical writings; and a brief review of state practice since 1949, including national law of naval warfare manuals. The remainder of the article will deal with the following topics: the potential relevance of the Protocol I definition of military objective to the law of naval warfare; vessels and aircraft that may not be attacked; vessels that clearly may be attacked; the merchant ship as target; and the problem of target identification, including a brief discussion of ruses and perfidy in the modern law of naval warfare. The article will conclude with a summary attempt to restate the law concerning military objectives in naval warfare.

"Self-Defence and the Conduct of International Armed Conflict," in Y. Dinstein and M. Tabory, eds., *International Law in a Time of Perplexity* 273 (1989).

[5] R. R. Baxter, "The Definition of War," 16 Rev. Égypt. de droit Int'l 10 (1960).

THE PRINCIPLE OF DISTINCTION AND THE CONCEPT OF
THE MILITARY OBJECTIVE

If a law of armed conflict purporting to regulate the conduct of military operations is to exist, an essential element of this law, no matter how inchoate, is the principle of distinction, also referred to as the principle of identification. That law is premised upon a requirement to distinguish between objects or persons that may be attacked and those that may not be attacked. The increasing percentage of civilian casualties relative to total casualties in contemporary conflicts has led some writers to suggest that the principle of distinction has become blurred, but this could not be viewed as a positive development. The principle of distinction is a fundamental aspect of the law of naval warfare, although it has not been explicitly addressed in any treaty on the subject.

The major contemporary treaty on law of armed conflict is the 1977 Additional Protocol I to the 1949 Geneva Conventions relating to the Protection of Victims of International Armed Conflicts, ratified by Canada on November 20, 1990.[6] As a matter of convenience, of Additional Protocol I is not applicable to attacks directed against objects on, under, or over the seas, Article 48 of that document may be used as a statement of the principle of distinction: "48. In order to ensure respect for and protection of the civilian population and civilian objects, the Parties to the conflict shall at all times distinguish between the civilian population and combatants and between civilian objects and military objectives and accordingly shall direct their operations only against military objectives."

It is necessary, however, to go further and explore the meaning of the term "military objective." "Military objective" is defined in Additional Protocol I and the relevance of that definition to naval warfare will be discussed later in this article. It suffices to note here that military objectives are not confined to warships and to naval auxiliary vessels operating in support of a nation's armed forces; depending on the circumstances, they may include privately owned vessels manned by civilian crews and flying the flags of states that are not involved in the conflict.

Conceptually, one may explain the meaning of "military objective" in the law of naval warfare by a variety of means: a general definition of military objective; a list of objects constituting mili-

---

[6] C.T.S. 1991/2.

tary objectives; a general definition and a list or; the converse of the above indicating objects exempt from attack.

No treaty contains a general definition of military objective for the law of naval warfare. As will be seen later, some treaties contain lists from which one might derive categories of vessels that are exempt from attack. Unfortunately, some of these lists are obsolete or unclear. For example, the 1936 London Submarine Protocol[7] indicates that a merchant vessel may not be sunk on sight, but it does not contain a detailed discussion of the term, "merchant vessel." As a result, states engaged in an armed conflict occasionally indulge in creative reclassification or "our side has merchant vessels which are exempt from attack while theirs has naval auxiliaries which we can sink on sight." A more rigorous approach to definition is perhaps desirable. As another example, Article 4 of the Hague Convention XI of 1907[8] indicates that vessels charged with religious, scientific, or philanthropic missions are exempt from capture and, presumably, attack. Does this mean that modern marine scientific research vessels, which may gather information of considerable military significance, may not be attacked?

A variety of approaches has been suggested to address the problem of the military objective in modern naval warfare. It is quite understandable that naval officers faced with making targeting decisions would prefer "bright line" rules that draw easily identifiable distinctions between permissible and impermissible objects of attack. Unfortunately, just as reality in the form of the irregular combatant makes bright line rules difficult to draw in the law of land warfare, so reality in the form of the merchant ship which may or may not be providing support for the belligerent war effort makes bright line rules difficult to draw in the law of naval warfare. The existence of a refractory reality does not mean that one abandons the search for bright line rules. It does mean, however, that the search may be difficult.

Some writers have proposed a zonal approach whereby, once appropriate measures have been taken to warn all concerned that presence in an area is dangerous, and to give ships and aircraft in the area time to leave it, a belligerent may presume anything in the area without permission to be there is a legitimate military objective. This approach facilitates the making of targeting decisions but it is certainly not a part of existing law, although state

---

[7] Ronzitti, *op. cit. supra* note 1, at 349.
[8] *Ibid.*, 173.

practice in recent conflicts indicates that some customary law standards for exclusion zones may be emerging.[9]

THE LAW BEFORE THE FIRST WORLD WAR

The pre-1914 law concerning targeting at sea may be summarized as follows:[10] (a) Enemy warships and naval auxiliaries could be attacked on sight outside neutral territorial seas. (b) Enemy merchant vessels could be captured outside neutral territories and could be attacked if they resisted visit, search, or capture (which they were legally entitled to do). Enemy merchant vessels being convoyed by enemy warships were deemed to be resisting visit, search, or capture and could be attacked on sight, as could enemy merchant ships taking a direct part in hostilities. Other enemy merchant vessels had to be given an opportunity to comply with a request for visit, search, or capture before they could be attacked. Although there was some opposition, the weight of authority favoured the view that defensive armament did not change the status of merchant vessels.[11] Captured enemy merchant vessels could be destroyed for reasons of military necessity, provided that the passengers, crew, and ship's papers were first placed in a position of safety. (c) Neutral merchant vessels could be stopped and searched outside neutral territorial seas. Neutral merchant vessels could be captured if they breached or attempted to breach a validly declared blockade or if

[9] The zonal issue has been discussed in several recent articles, including F. C. Leiner, "Maritime Security Zones Prohibited Yet Perpetuated," 24 Va. J. Int'l. L. 967-92 (1983-84); J. Gilliland, "Submarines and Targets Suggestions for New Codified Rules of Submarine Warfare," 73 Georgetown L. J. (1985) 975-1005; Weiss, "Problems of Submarine Warfare Under International Law," 22 Intra. L. Rev. of N.Y. 136 (1966-67); and W. J. Fenrick, "The Exclusion Zone Device in the Law of Naval Warfare," 24 *Canadian Yearbook of International Law* 91-126 (1986). None of these articles suggest that every object in a zone should be subject to attack although Weiss adopts the most robust approach to targeting. The zonal issue was the subject of heated discussion at the 1990 Toulon Round Table meeting. Eventually, however, all participants appeared to accept the view that a party to a conflict cannot gain any additional legal rights by establishing zones that might adversely affect the legitimate uses of defined areas of the sea.

[10] This summary is based on a similar summary in L. Doswald-Beck, "The International Law of Naval Armed Conflicts The Need for Reform," 7 It.Y.I.L. 251-82, at 252-4 (1986-87), which, in turn is derived from the 1909 London Declaration concerning the Laws of Naval War, Ronzitti, *op. cit. supra* note 1, at 223, and the 1913 Oxford Manual.

[11] A. Pearce Higgins, "Defensively Armed Merchant Ships," in his *Studies in International Law and Relations* 239-95 (1928).

they carried goods liable to capture as absolute or conditional contraband. Neutral merchant vessels being convoyed by enemy warships were deemed to be resisting visit and seach and could be
attacked on sight. As a general statement, neutral merchant vessels being convoyed by neutral warships were exempt from search,
but the convoy commander had an obligation to ensure that neutral merchant vessels in the convoy were not carrying contraband
or breaching a blockade.[12] Neutral merchant vessels not being convoyed had to be given an opportunity to comply with a request for
visit and search before they could be attacked. There was some question concerning whether or not captured neutral merchant vessels
could be destroyed in any circumstances. It was, however, generally agreed that the passengers, crew, and ship's papers had to be
placed in a position of safety before the vessel was destroyed. (d)
In accordance with Article 46 of the 1909 Declaration of London,
neutral merchant vessels which performed the following types of
un-neutral service, were to be treated in the same way as if they
were enemy merchant vessels: (1) taking a direct part in hostilities;
(2) operating under the orders or control of an agent placed on board
by the enemy government; (3) operating in the exclusive employment of the enemy government; and (4) transporting enemy troops
or transmitting intelligence to the enemy. Both enemy and neutral
merchant vessels taking a direct part in hostilities could be attacked
without warning. However, the meaning of the expression "taking a direct part in hostilities" was not further elaborated upon;
it clearly included vessels that are firing at the other side. What else
did it include? The Report prepared by the Drafting Committee
for the 1909 Declaration clearly envisages that the vessels included
in categories (ii), (iii), and (iv) above could not be attacked on sight.[13]
(e) Neutral or belligerent vessels in the following categories were
exempt from attack or capture so long as they did not take any part
in hostilities: coastal fishing vessels; small boats employed in local
trade; vessels charged with religious, scientific, or philanthropic missions; and hospital ships.[14] (f) As a matter of customary law, shipwrecked persons in the water or in life boats were not legitimate

---

[12] Art. 61 and 62 of 1909 London Declaration.
[13] "The General Report presented to the Naval Conference on behalf of its Drafting
Committee" 61-161, at 124-25, in A. Cohen, *The Declaration of London* (London, 1911).
[14] Art. 3 and 4 of 1907 Hague Convention XI Relative to Certain Restrictions with
Regard to the Exercise of the Right of Capture in Naval War, in Ronzitti, *op. cit.*
supra note 1, at 177.

targets. (g) As a matter of customary law, for reasons buried in history but probably related to weapons technology of days gone by, it was a permissible ruse of war for enemy merchant vessels to fly false colours and to disguise themselves as neutral vessels or as merchant vessels. The only qualification was that a warship must cease using false colours before it started firing. This use of false flags was inconsistent with the practice in land warfare.

DEVELOPMENTS UP TO GENEVA CONVENTIONS OF 1949

Both World Wars I and II tended to become total wars and, as each war progressed, methods of warfare that were generally viewed as abhorrent at the beginning of the conflicts, became common practice by their end. Prior to the First World War, the idea that merchant ships should be sunk on sight was rejected as totally unacceptable; by 1917, Germany commenced an unrestricted submarine warfare campaign which almost brought Britain to its knees. The Second World War began where the First World War left off. By October 1939, Germany was once again waging unrestricted submarine warfare in certain areas. As the war progressed, Britain waged an unrestricted submarine warfare campaign in the Skagerrak and the United States waged an extremely successful unrestricted submarine warfare campaign against Japan in the Pacific. Furthermore, both Axis and Allied Powers also used aircraft in anti-shipping campaigns in various areas during the war. If anything, aircraft were even less able than submarines to perform the traditional roles of visit, search, and removal of crew and passengers prior to sinking merchant vessels. By the end of the Second World War, because of the use of aircraft and submarines to destroy commerce, cynics might have summarized naval targeting rules as follows: don't sink hospital ships or clearly marked neutral vessels uninvolved in the conflict and don't attack shipwrecked survivors or their lifeboats. Even these minimal rules were occasionally infringed, but no state publicly indicated that this infringement was a desirable policy. The British jurist, H.A. Smith, writing in the immediate aftermath of the Second World War, argued that in a general war there was no such thing as a belligerent private merchant vessel, as all these vessels would be controlled by the state and used purely to further the war effort. In his view, all enemy merchant vessels were legitimate military objectives in a general war and could be attacked on sight.[15]

Although the use of submarines and aircraft to sink merchant
vessels on sight was inconsistent with the pre-1914 law of naval
warfare, there were militarily important reasons for doing so. As
the World Wars tended towards totality, merchant shipping was incorporated into the belligerent war effort, and it was reasonable
to conclude that, in general, merchant vessels did not travel to and
from belligerent states unless they carried cargoes that would either
improve the ability of a belligerent to make war or provide revenue
to bolster the belligerent's war economy. As the submarine was a
small vessel and, with the exception of torpedoes, weakly armed,
it was not able to perform the traditional tasks of visit and search
of merchant vessels once the opposing belligerent began to arm merchant vessels and to order them to act aggressively in self-defence
by ramming. Further, the British tactic of using Q-Ships, warships
disguised as merchant vessels which would attempt to lure submarines within range of their weapons and then disclose their identity and attack, did not provide an incentive for submarines to comply
with traditional practices.

A variety of attempts were made in the period between the World
Wars to enforce and to develop the law of naval warfare. A small
number of war crimes trials involving German accused were held
before German courts in Leipzig following the German defeat. Two
of these cases raised issues concerning the law and naval warfare.
In the *Dover Castle* case the accused, the commanding officer of a
German submarine, was charged with torpedoing the British hospital ship, *Dover Castle,* and with sinking her with exceptional brutali-
ty. The accused conceded that he knew the *Dover Castle* was a hospital
ship and that he sank her deliberately, although he also argued that
he allowed one and a half hours to elapse before firing a second
torpedo to finish sinking the ship so that the sick and wounded could
be saved. He introduced certain documents in his defence in which
the German government of the day announced that only certain
British hospital ships would be respected in future because it was
believed the others were being used for warlike purposes. The accused argued that he had attacked the *Dover Castle* in compliance
with superior orders made because of German concerns that
the privileged status of allied hospital ships was being abused.

[15] H. A. Smith, *The Crisis in the Law of Nations* 60-62 (1947).

He was acquitted on the basis of these superior orders.[16]

In the *Llandovery Castle* case, two officers of a German submarine crew were tried for offences arising out of the sinking of the British hospital ship, *Llandovery Castle*. The commanding officer of the submarine, who could not be located at the time of trial, decided on his own initiative to sink the hospital ship because he was convinced, erroneously, that it was carrying troops and munitions. After the sinking, it became obvious that the *Llandovery Castle* was an innocent vessel and, in order to cover up evidence of his offence, the submarine captain ordered his crew to massacre the survivors; he also swore the crew to secrecy concerning the event and falsified his logbook and charts. The court found that the two accused crew members participated in the the massacre and cover up in compliance with superior orders given by the captain. In this case however superior orders were not considered to be a defence because "the firing on the boats was an offence against the law of nations" and "the killing of defenceless shipwrecked people is an act in the highest degree contrary to ethical principles."[17]

During the interwar period, a number of attempts were made by Britain to abolish submarines, notably at the Washington Conference of 1921-22 and the London Conference of 1930, but on all such occasions Britain was blocked by France, which argued that submarines were useful vessels of war, particularly for weaker powers, although they should be required to follow the same rules as surface vessels.[18] A set of rules for submarine warfare was developed at the London Naval Conference and inserted as Part IV, Article 22 , in the 1930 London Treaty for the Limitation and Reduction of Naval Armaments[19] and reaffirmed in a 1936 Procès-Verbal (the London Protocol of 1936).[20] The rules are as follows:

(1) In their action with regard to merchant ships, submarines must conform to the rules of international law to which surface vessels are subject. (2) In particular, except in the case of persistent refusal to stop on being duly summoned, or of active resistance to visit or search, a warship, whether surface vessel or submarine, may not sink or render incapable of navigation a merchant vessel without having first placed passengers,

---

[16] *The Dover Castle Case,* 16 Am. J. Int'l L. 704-8 (1922).

[17] *The Llandovery Castle Case, ibid.,* 708-23.

[18] W. T. Mallison, *Studies in the Law of Naval Warfare Submarines in General and Limited Wars* 36-47 (Washington, 1968).

[19] Ronzitti, *op. cit. supra* note 1, at 348.

[20] *Ibid,* 352.

crew and ship's papers in a place of safety. For this purpose the ship's boats are not regarded as a place of safety unless the safety of the passengers and crew is assured, in the existing sea and weather conditions, by the proximity of land, or the presence of another vessel which is in a position to take them on board.

The proper interpretation of the above rules is by no means clear, but some assistance can be derived from the Report of the Committee of Jurists which prepared the text of the 1930 London Treaty. The report stated in part that "The Committee wish to place it on record that the expression "merchant vessel," where it is employed in the declaration, is not to be understood as including a merchant vessel which is at the moment participating in hostilities in such a manner as to cause her to lose her right to the immunities of a merchant vessel."[21] Unfortunately, the Committee did not go on to explain the meaning of "participating in hostilities."

A major piece of scholarly work with a number of innovative ideas is the Draft Convention, with comment, on the Rights and Duties of Neutral States in Naval and Aerial War, prepared by the Research in International Law of the Harvard Law School and published in the Supplement Section to the July 1939 issue of the *American Journal of International Law*. The drafters of the Convention made the following suggestions: (a) Enemy armed merchant ships should be treated as warships (Articles 2, 19, 28, 32-39, 55). (b) Belligerents should forbid their merchant vessels to display the flag of a neutral state, or otherwise to represent themselves to be neutral vessels (Article 20). (c) Belligerent submarines, aircraft, and surface vessels must comply with the London Submarine Protocol Rules in their action with regard to unarmed merchant vessels (Article 54). (d) A belligerent may treat as an enemy warship neutral vessels exclusively engaged in transporting enemy troops or taking a direct part in hostilities on the side of the enemy (Article 65). (e) A belligerent may establish a blockade zone within fifty miles of enemy controlled coasts (Article 1, 69). (f) Neutral vessels engaged in trade with other neutrals or in trade with one belligerent agreed to by both belligerents should be specially certified and elaborately identified by means of lights, paint, and special markings (Articles 41-48). (g) These neutral vessels may be convoyed by neutral warships which are also specially identified (Articles 43, 44). An obvious purpose of the Draft Convention was to reduce the possibility of a neutral United States

---

[21] *Documents of the London Naval Conference, 1930*, at 443 (London, 1930).

being involved in future foreign wars as had occurred in the First World War. It may, however, contain some ideas that are usable today.

Naval warfare issues were raised in a number of war crimes trials following the Second World War. Admirals Doenitz and Raeder were tried, together with the other German major war criminals before the International Military Tribunal (IMT) at Nuremberg for, among other things, war crimes on the high seas, in particular, with waging unrestricted submarine warfare contrary to the London Protocol of 1936. Flottenrichter Otto Kranzbuhler, Admiral Doenitz's lawyer, conducted a particularly skilful defence on the submarine warfare charges.

Concerning belligerent merchant vessels, Kranzbuhler focused on the ambiguity of the concept "merchant ship" and the uncertainty connected with the words "active resistance" in the London Protocol. Bearing in mind that ships sailing in enemy convoy were usually deemed to be engaged in "active resistance," he argued that all armed merchantmen should also be deemed to be engaged in active resistance, as arming served the same purpose as a naval escort and as it was not possible to distinguish between defensive and offensive weapons. He stated it thus:

And this very same common sense demands also that the armed merchantman be held just as guilty of forcible resistance as the convoyed ship. Let us take an extreme instance in order to make the matter quite clear. An unarmed merchant ship of 20,000 tons and a speed of 20 knots, which is convoyed by a trawler with, let us say, 2 guns and a speed of 15 knots, may be sunk without warning, because it has placed itself under the protection of the trawler and thereby made itself guilty of active resistance. If, however, this same merchant ship does not have the protection of the trawler and instead the 2 guns, or even 4 or 6 of them, are placed on its decks, thus enabling it to use its full speed, should it in this case not be deemed just as guilty of offering active resistance as before? Such a deduction really seems to me against all common sense. In the opinion of the Prosecution the submarine would first have to give the merchant ship, which is far superior to it in fighting power, the order to stop and then wait until the merchant ship fires its first broadside at the submarine. Only then would it have the right to use its own weapons. Since, however, a single artillery hit is nearly always fatal to a submarine but as a rule does very little harm to a merchant ship, the result would be the almost certain destruction of the submarine.[22]

[22] *Trial of the Major War Criminals Before the International Military Tribunal Nuremberg, 14 November*

He went on to argue:

However, another factor of greater general importance, and also of greater danger to the submarines, was the order to report every enemy ship in sight, giving its type and location. This report was destined, so said the order, to facilitate taking advantage of an opportunity which might never recur, to destroy the enemy by naval or air forces. This is an unequivocal utilization of all merchant vessels for military intelligence service with intent directly to injure the enemy. If one considers the fact that according to the hospital ship agreement even the immunity of hospital ships ceases if they relay military information of this type, then one need have no doubts about the consequences of such behaviour on the part of a commercial vessel. Any craft putting out to sea with the order and intention of using every opportunity that occurs to send military reports about the enemy to its own naval and air forces is taking part in hostilities during the entire course of its voyage and, according to the fore-mentioned report of 1930 of the committee of jurists, has no right to be considered a merchant vessel. Any different conception would not do justice to the immediate danger which a wireless report involves for the vessel reported and which subjects it, often within a few minutes, to attack by enemy aircraft.[23]

Concerning enemy merchant vessels, he concluded:

All of the admiralty's directives, taken together, show that British merchant vessels, from the very first day of the war, closely co-operated with the British navy in combating the enemy's naval forces. They were part of the military communications network of the British naval and air forces and their armament of guns and depth charges, the practical training in manipulation of the weapons, and the orders relative to their use, were actions taken by the British Navy.

We consider it out of the question that a merchant fleet in this manner destined and utilized for combat should count among the vessels entitled to the protection of the London Protocol against sinking without warning. On the basis of this conception and in connection with the arming of all enemy merchant vessels, which was rapidly being completed, an order was issued on 17 October, 1939 to attack all enemy merchant ships without warning.[24]

The IMT did, of course, accept Kranzbuhler's argument concerning belligerent merchant vessels and, although it held Doenitz not guilty for his conduct of submarine warfare only against ''British armed merchant ships,'' in the context of its judgment, it actually exoner-

---

1945 - 1 October 1946 (Nuremberg, 1948) (hereinafter IMT), Vol XVIII, at 319.

[23] *Ibid.*, 323.

[24] *Ibid.*, 323.

ated Doenitz from responsibility for attacks on all belligerent merchant vessels because of the general belligerent practice of incorporating all such vessels into the war effort. Kranzbuhler's
arguments were less successful where neutral vessels were concerned.
His first argument was that all vessels, including neutral vessels,
which sailed blacked-out in the "war area," an undefined term,
were subject to attack. He said:

Examining the question of blacked-out vessels from the legal standpoint,
Vanselow, the well-known expert on the law governing naval warfare,
makes the following remark: "In war a blacked-out vessel must in case
of doubt be considered as an enemy warship. A neutral as well as an enemy merchant vessel navigating without light voluntarily renounces during the hours of darkness all claim to immunity from attack without being
stopped." I furthermore refer to Churchill's declaration, made in the
House of Commons, on 8 May 1940, concerning the action of British submarines in the Jutland area. Since the beginning of April they had orders to attack all German vessels without warning during the daytime, and
all vessels, and thus all neutrals, as well, at night. This amounts to recognition of the legal standpoint as presented. It even goes beyond the German order, insofar as neutral merchant vessels navigating with all lights
on were sunk without warning in these waters. In view of the clear legal
aspect it would hardly have been necessary to give an express warning
to neutral shipping against suspicious or hostile conduct. Nevertheless,
the Naval Operations Staff saw to it that this was done.[25]

The second danger to neutral shipping was what Kranzbuhler
referred to as "zones of operations" and what have since been
referred to as "exclusion zones." He argued that the fact that these
zones were not referred to in the London Protocol did not mean
they were not permissible. They constituted a normal part of state
practice and it was open to the IMT to find that they were legally
permissible subject to certain criteria of reasonableness. Technology compelled changes in the 19th century law.[26] The IMT did not
accept Kranzbuhler's arguments concerning operational or exclusion zones and found Doenitz's orders to sink neutral ships without
warning in these zones a violation of the Protocol. It then went on
to announce that no sentence would be assessed on the ground of
breaches of the Protocol by either Doenitz or Raeder because of
similar practices by the Allied Powers,[27] the only known successful

[25] *Ibid.*, 327.

[26] *Ibid.*, 329-30.

[27] XXII IMT, 557-60.

use of the *tu quoque* plea in a war crimes trial. The IMT's condemnation of exclusion zones notwithstanding, they have been used in a number of recent conflicts.

Assessing the impact of the IMT judgment on the scope and applicability of the London Protocol is not a simple task. Professor O'Connell attempted to cut the Gordian knot by arguing: "The truth is that the requirements of the London Protocol are to be observed only in the situation where the submarine can act with minimal risk on the surface. Since that situation is now an ideal hardly ever in practice to be realized, one is compelled to draw from the Doenitz trial the conclusion that submarine operations in time of war are today governed by no legal text, and that no more than lipservice is being paid in naval documents to the London Protocol."[28] There is some basis for arguing that the London Protocol was drafted in favour of surface naval powers, particularly Great Britain, as a fall back position after efforts to outlaw the employment of submarines to destroy commerce had failed and as an attempt to neutralize the effectiveness of the submarine in that role. The Protocol is virtually unworkable in a general war between naval powers where one side has a substantial preponderance in surface naval strength, because it does not confer substantially equal benefits on both sides. The practical effectiveness of the law of war in a particular conflict is conditional upon, among other factors, a crude reciprocity and a rough equivalence of benefits.

The key to a workable interpretation of the London Protocol lies in determining the proper meaning of the undefined term "merchant vessel" in that document. In a general war, the true merchant vessel is rarely to be found because the belligerent states normally assume such a degree of control over their own vessels and neutral vessels engaged in trading with them as to convert them into *de facto* naval auxiliaries. As *de facto* naval auxiliaries, they should be subject to the same treatment as *de jure* naval auxiliaries, that is, they may be sunk on sight outside of neutral waters. Even in a general war, however, there may be genuine neutral traffic which is entitled to proceed unmolested. For example, in the Second World War, before the USSR declared war on Japan in 1945, there was significant neutral merchant traffic to and from the Pacific coast

---

[28] D. P. O'Connell, "International Law and Contemporary Naval Operations," 44 B.Y.I.L. 18-85, at 52 (1970). A. Vanvoukos, *Termination of Treaties in International Law* 271-73 (Oxford, 1985), contends that the London Protocol is no longer binding but his only authorities are the Doenitz decision and the views of O'Connell.

of the USSR which passed through the Pacific War Zone declared by the U.S. and was not molested by USN submarines. In a war more limited than that of the Second World War, for example Korea or the Falklands, many merchant vessels, even those of the contending parties, will be engaged in normal trade quite unconnected with the war effort; they would clearly not be *de facto* naval auxiliaries and would thus be entitled to all of the benefits of the London Protocol. Naval warfare issues occasionally arose in other war crimes trials.

There is an indication in the proceedings of the International Military Tribunal for the Far East that on occasion Japanese submarines massacred survivors in compliance with superior orders.[29] Also, Lieutenant Commander Moehle, an officer formerly commanding a U-boat flotilla at Kiel, was tried and convicted for ordering the commanding officers of U-boats to destroy ships and their crews.[30] In the *Von Ruchteshell* trial,[31] a former commander of German surface raiders was found guilty of continuing to fire at merchant ships after they had indicated their surrender, and of sinking enemy merchant vessels without making any provision for the safety of survivors. This case also raised the issue of whether or not it was legitimate for a surface raider to attack a merchant ship without warning and, by implication, it held that no war crime was committed by such attacks when the merchant ship was incorporated into the enemy war effort by being armed or by having wireless communications. After the Doenitz case, the next most famous case is probably the *Peleus* trial,[32] which forms the basis for Gwyn Griffin's novel, *Operational Necessity*. The Peleus was a Greek ship torpedoed in mid-Atlantic in March, 1944, by a German submarine. After the ship sank, all but three survivors were killed by machine gun fire or hand grenades. The captain of the submarine and four crew members were tried by a British military court in Hamburg in 1945. The report of the case contains the following comment concerning the defence of operational necessity:

The Commander of the U-boat did not plead that he had acted on superior orders. His defence was that he thought that the floating rafts were a danger to him, first, because they would show an aeroplane the exact

[29] Mallison, *op. cit. supra* note 18, at 142-43.

[30] *Moehle Trial* (1946), 9 L.R.T.W.C. 75-82.

[31] *Von Ruchteschell Trial* (1947), 9 L.R.T.W.C. 82-90.

[32] Peleus Trial, *op. cit. supra* note 3.

spot of the sinking, and secondly, because rafts at that time of the war could be provided with modern signalling communications. The position of U-boats was very precarious, particularly in that part of the Atlantic where the incident occurred. Eck, therefore, thought his measure justified. It was clear to him that, as a result of his shooting at the rafts, the survivors would die. The Judge Advocate ruled that the question whether or not any belligerent is entitled to kill an unarmed person for the purpose of saving his own life did not arise in the present case. It may be, he said, that circumstances would arise in which such a killing might be justified. On the facts which had emerged in the present case, however, the Judge Advocate asked the Court whether or not it thought that the shooting with a machine gun at substantial pieces of wreckage and rafts would be an effective way of destroying every trace of the sinking. A submarine commander who was really and primarily concerned with saving his crew and his boat would have removed himself and his boat at the highest possible speed at the earliest possible moment for the greatest possible distance.[33]

The court found all of the accused guilty. The Captain and two crew members were executed. One crew member was sentenced to life imprisonment and the last received fifteen years imprisonment. Perhaps partly as a result of aversion to the state practice in the two World Wars and its impact on the pre-1914 law of naval warfare, relatively little attention was paid to the development of the law of naval warfare in the immediate post-war period. The Second Geneva Convention of 1949[34] is the only post-war treaty specifically devoted to warfare in the maritime environment. From a targeting perspective, this Convention re-emphasized that hospital ships are exempt from attack or capture (Articles 22, 24, 25), added medical transports (Article 30), medical aircraft (Article 39), and small coastal rescue craft (Article 27) to the exempt category, and provided additional details indicating how exempt vessels are to be marked (Article 43).

State Practice since 1949

Although armed conflicts have been all too common since the Second World War, there has been relatively little violence at sea during these conflicts. The major international conflicts involving substantial naval warfare were the Korean conflict, the Vietnam conflict, the various Arab-Israeli conflicts, the Indo-Pakistani conflicts of 1965 and 1971, the Falklands conflict, the Iran-Iraq conflict, and

[33] *Ibid.*, 15.
[34] Ronzitti, *op. cit. supra* note 1, at 503.

the recent Gulf conflict. The naval campaign in the Korean war was essentially confined to the area off the Korean coast. No attacks were made on UN sea lines of communication and it does not appear to have been necessary to convoy merchant vessels approaching the area of operations. For all practical purposes, even the carrier striking forces conducting operations against the North Koreans and Chinese operated from a high sea sanctuary. Target selection was relatively limited as there were no unrestricted attacks on neutral shipping, or apparently any attacks at all on neutral vessels. North Korean fishing vessels were, however, seized and destroyed and the anti-fishing campaign appears to have been an extension beyond previous practice. It must, however, be conceded that Canadian and other contraband lists in the Second World War specified food as conditional contraband.[35] Except for the close blockade of the North Korean coast, the traditional panoply of economic warfare measures was not utilized. Although all other naval weapons were used, neither nuclear weapons nor submarines in the commerce destruction role were used during the conflict.

Substantial efforts were made by the United States to limit the scope of the naval campaign during the Vietnam conflict. For all practical purposes, combat operations were confined to the internal waters, territorial seas, and contiguous zones off Vietnam, although, once again, USN carriers conducted combat operations from within a *de facto* high seas sanctuary. No attacks were made on the sea lines of communication of the United States or its allies but some anti-submarine warfare precautions were taken when valuable vessels, such as troop carriers, approached the area of operations.[36] Although operations were conducted by warships against military objectives on the North Vietnamese coast and against water borne logistics craft throughout the conflict, prior to 1972 no attempt was made to interfere with the shipping of non-participants and substantial efforts were devoted to ensuring that North Vietnamese coastal fishermen could continue to ply their trade.[37] When a blockade of sorts was established in 1972, the blockade was enforced by mines laid in claimed North Vietnamese waters. Non-participant shipping was not interfered with on the high seas at any time although, during the blockade, a notification line was established to warn such shipping away from mined areas. This ap-

[35] R. W. Tucker, *The Law of War and Neutrality at Sea* 267 (Washington, 1955).
[36] D. P. O'Connell, *The Influence of Law on Sea Power* 110 (Manchester, 1975).
[37] O'Connell, *op. cit. supra* note 28, at 34-35.

proach placed the onus on non-participants. If they entered the mined area, they exposed themselves to the risk of being mined. As in Korea, no nuclear weapons or submarines in the commerce destruction role were used. It appears, however, that USN forces also exercised substantially greater restraint in using other weapons as a result of stringent rules of engagement.[38]

In both the Korea and Vietnam conflicts, American sea control of the area of operations and of the relevant lines of communication was undisputed. In the several Arab-Israeli conflicts, sea control was disputed but of debatable relevance. The navies involved were small coastal forces although, as they acquired missile boats in the 1960's, they were strong enough to pose an identifiable threat within short distances from their respective coasts. Except for the 1948-49 War of Independence when the minuscule navies of the participants hardly deserved the name, the conflicts were brief and sea control, which requires time to have an impact on the land struggle, was not considered important by the participants. Apart from the limitations imposed by lack of naval strength, there is little indication of restraint in the naval conflict. There is evidence from Israeli sources, unconfirmed elsewhere, that Egypt used submarines to attack neutral shipping without warning in the Yom Kippur conflict.[39] Egypt exploited its favourable geographic position by closing the Suez Canal to Israeli traffic and by seizing all goods destined for or exported from Israel which came within Egyptian territory as absolute contraband. In so doing it applied its own version of the general war law of contraband and failed to resuscitate the traditional differentiation between absolute contraband, conditional contraband, and free goods, a differentiation that one might consider particularly useful for policy reasons in limited conflicts. Further, Egyptian actions were taken in a time of ostensible peace and in the face of a contrary Security Council Resolution.[40] In the Yom Kippur conflict, Egypt purported to establish a long distance blockade at Bab el Mandeb which was more akin to the British blockades in the two World Wars than to the close blockades off Korea and Vietnam. There is no indication Israel fought a more restrained naval campaign than its opponents. It merely lacked as

---

[38] "Selected United States Rules of Engagement, Vietnam era," 14 Syracuse J. Int'l L. and Comm. 795-828 (1988).

[39] C. Herzog, *The War of Atonement* 263-64 (Jerusalem, 1975).

[40] T. D. Brown, "World War Prize Law Applied in a Limited War Situation Egyptian Restrictions on Neutral Shipping with Israel," 50 Minn. L. Rev. 849-73 (1966).

favourable a geographic position. Certainly neither side recognized the existence of "sanctuaries" similar to those which existed in the Korea and Vietnam conflicts. The sole indication of restraints if found in the discussion in the UN Security Council following the sinking of the Israeli destroyer *Eilat* in 1967; it provides some minimal support for the argument that limited naval conflicts should be restrained to the territorial seas of the participants.[41]

During both the 1965 and 1971 Indo-Pakistan conflicts, there was a substantial degree of interference with commercial intercourse between the respective belligerents and third states. In these conflicts, both India and Pakistan issued contraband lists. In the 1965 conflict, a considerable number of ships and their cargo were captured by Pakistan. Most of the ships were in Pakistan ports at the time of capture. In a decision of October 28, 1965, the High Court of Dacca condemned 50 ships and their cargoes in prize.[42] Professor von Heinegg has summarized the impact of the 1971 conflict as follows:

During the 1971 war with Pakistan India captured 3 Pakistani merchant vessels whereas Pakistan seemingly was not able to interfere with Indian merchant shipping at all. However, neutral merchant shipping was affected by measures of both belligerents. In darkness neutral ships were not allowed to approach the Pakistani coast less than 75 nautical miles. Neutral ships in Pakistani ports were damaged by Indian attacks. On December 4, 1971, India declared a blockade of Eastern Pakistan. Neutral ships were allowed to leave the blocaded area within a period of 24 hours. When it became evident that the markings and names of many ships had been changed the Indian navy stopped, visited and diverted neutral ships to Calcutta if they carried cargo of military significance. On December 10, 1971, the Indian government announced that neutral ships were given a period of grace until the morning of December 12 in order to leave the port of Karachi and Pakistani territorial waters. Pakistan and India boarded and searched about 115 neutral ships.[43]

In the Falklands conflict, Argentina and Great Britain repeatedly stressed their desires to limit the conflict. Argentina took precautions to minimize British casualties in its invasion of the Falklands

[41] O'Connell, *op. cit. supra* note 28, at 28-29.

[42] Printed in ILM 46 (1970), 472.

[43] W. H. von Heinegg, "Visit Search, Diversion and Capture — Conditions of Applicability," unpublished Introductory Report prepared for the Round Table of Experts on International Humanitarian Law Applicable to Armed Conflicts at Sea, Bergen, 20-24 September 1991.

and it returned the small British garrison to Great Britain once the invasion was completed. Britain emphasized that its objective was to secure withdrawal of Argentine forces from the islands with minimal casualties on both sides. Both sides established a variety of exclusion zones to minimize the impact of the conflict on non-participants and on each other. Nevertheless, because of the geographic location of the Falkland Islands, and because of the inherent mobility of warships and military aircraft, the conflict involved a brief but intense naval struggle which of necessity occurred on the high seas, which spilled over outside of the proclaimed exclusion zones, and which had a small but identifiable impact on non-participants. The British naval task force could not operate from a high seas sanctuary akin to that utilized by American forces off Korea and Vietnam because the Argentine navy and air force possessed sufficient striking power to attack it. The conflict could not be limited to the territorial seas of the participants because of Argentine strike capability and because the disputed territory was in the middle of an ocean. The conflict could not be limited to the relatively confined area of the British Total Exclusion Zone and the ''defensive bubble'' because warships and military aircraft are inherently mobile and, as in the case of the General Belgrano, they pose a threat to the opposing party wherever they may be located. Distance does not neutralize the threat, it merely increases the amount of the time available to counter it.[44]

The Iran-Iraq conflict, which finally ended in 1988, provides a contrast with the brief and conspicuously limited Falklands conflict. The fighting in the case of the Falklands occurred in an isolated area of the South Atlantic, away from heavily travelled shipping lanes and, for all practical purposes, only involving vessels that were either warships or engaged in direct support of one of the belligerents. In the Iran-Iraq conflict, fighting occurred in the restricted area of the Persian Gulf, one of the world's most important shipping lanes. Neither Iran nor Iraq were major naval powers but both, as a result of oil profits, were equipped with modern combat aircraft at the beginning of the conflict and Iran also had a number of small gunboats. Iran is the only state located on the entire length of the eastern coast of the Gulf (635 nautical miles) while Iraq had a mere ten mile coast at the northern end of the Gulf. Iranian bomb

---

[44] W. J. Fenrick, ''Legal Aspects of the Falklands Naval Conflict,'' 1 Canadian Forces JAG Journal 29-50 (1985).

attacks closed down the two Iraqi oil terminals in the Persian Gulf
and blocked access to all three of Iraq's commercial ports at the
start of the conflict. No commercial shipping sailed to or from Iraq
during the conflict, although it is reasonable to presume that some
of the ships visiting the ports of Iraq's neighbours in the Persian
Gulf carried goods that were eventually transported overland to Iraq.
The Iran-Iraq conflict was a major conflict. For the only time since
the Second World War, deliberate and sustained operations were
carried out against merchant ships. Generally speaking, prior to
March 1984, Iraq attacked all vessels in a proclaimed exclusion zone
at the northern end of the Gulf. From March 1984 until the end
of the conflict, Iraq switched the focus of its anti-shipping campaign in an effort to attack the weak link in Iran's war economy
and to arouse world interest in the conflict; it directed most of its
attacks against tankers, most of them neutral and unconvoyed, sailing to or from Kharg Island, the very heavily defended main Iranian oil terminal, located towards the northern end of the Persian
Gulf. All of these attacks were delivered by shore-based aircraft and
almost all involved the use of air launched missiles. Iraq appears
to have devoted minimal effort to obtaining visual identification
of the target before missile launch, with the result that accidents,
such as the Iraqi attack on the USS Stark, did occur.

On the other hand, Iran did not attack commercial shipping until
Iraq commenced its anti-tanker campaign in 1984. Since there was
no sea traffic with Iraq, Iran attacked neutral merchant shipping
destined to and from neutral ports in the Gulf, presumably in an
effort to persuade Iraq's financial backers, the other Gulf states,
to dissuade Iraq from its campaign against the Kharg Island tankers.
Iran's attacks on merchant shipping were less numerous than those
of Iraq and, in general, less costly in lives and property damage
because they were conducted with rockets instead of missiles.[45] In
addition, Iran devoted more effort to target identification than did
Iraq. It did not, however, conduct its attacks in declared exclusion
zones and some of them were carried out in neutral territorial waters.
One author summarized the maritime aspects of the conflict as
follows:

Throughout the eight year course of the Gulf War, Iran and Iraq have

---

[45] During the conflict, Iraq attacked 322 ships and Iran attacked 221 ships. R.
O'Rourke, "Gulf Ops," United States Naval Institute Proceedings 1989 Naval
Review Issue, 42, at 43.

attacked more than 400 commercial vessels, almost all of which were neutral State flagships. Over 200 merchant seamen have lost their lives because of these attacks. In material terms, the attacks have resulted in excess of 40 million dead weight tons of damaged shipping. Thirty-one of the attacked merchants were sunk, and another 50 declared total losses. For 1987 alone, the strikes against commercial shipping numbered 178, with a resulting death toll of 108. In relative terms, by the end of 1987, write-off losses in the Gulf War stood at nearly half the tonnage of merchant shipping sent to the bottom in World War II. In all, ships flying the flags of more than 30 different countries, including each of the permanent members of the United Nations Security Council, have been subjected to attacks.[46]

The same author observed, however, that despite the relative intensity of the tanker war, only about 1% of the ship voyages were attacked.[47] A particularly unusual aspect of the Iran-Iraq conflict was the involvement of US naval ships to protect neutral rights in its final stages. This involvement culminated in the tragic incident in which the USS *Vincennes* shot down an Iranian Airbus with the loss of all on board when the Airbus was erroneously identified as an Iranian fighter demonstrating hostile intent.[48]

The recent conflict in the Gulf precipitated by the Iraqi invasion of Kuwait on August 2, 1990 and terminated in early April, 1991 by the Iraqi National Assembly decision to accept the provisions of Security Council Resolution 687 (1991) of April 8, 1991,[49] had a substantial naval aspect. Iraq has a very small navy; the Coalition forces had overwhelming naval superiority and, once the fight-

[46] F. V. Russo, "Neutrality at Sea in Transition State Practice in the Gulf War as Emerging International Customary Law," 19 Ocean Devel. and Int'l L. 381-99, at 381 (1988).

[47] *Ibid.*, 397.

[48] The most detailed account of the Airbus Incident is the ICAO Report with many attachments contained in ICAO Document C-WP18708 of November 7, 1988. It is difficult to get an adequate grip on the facts of the naval side of the Gulf War but the U.S. Naval Institute Proceedings for the past few years contain several useful articles. The Gulf War was a topic for discussion at two panels of the 1988 Am. Soc. Int'l L. Meeting and at a Conference at Syracuse University, but the proceedings have not yet been published. In addition to Russo, *op. cit. supra* note 46, see M. Jenkins, "Air attacks on Neutral Shipping in the Persian Gulf The Legality of the Iraqi Exclusion Zone and Iranian Reprisals," 8 Boston Coll. Int'l and Comp. L.R. 517-49 (1985); "Conference Report The Persian/Arabian Gulf Tanker War," 19 Ocean Devel. and Int'l L.299-321 (1988); D. B. Biller, "Policing the Persian Gulf," 11 Loy-L.A. Int'l and Comp. L.J. 171-205 (1989); and R. Wolfrum, "Reflagging and Escort Operation in the Persian Gulf An International Law Perspective," 29 Va. J. Int'l L. 387-99 (1989).

[49] Int'l Leg. Mat 847 (1991).

ing started, rapidly established air superiority. Consequently, the
Iraqi navy was effectively neutralized early in the conflict and
Coalition warships and merchant ships were not attacked by Iraqi
warships or military aircraft, although some ships were damaged
by Iraqi mines. From a law of naval warfare perspective, the most
significant issues were generated by the oil spill in the Persian
Gulf and by the Coalition naval forces engaged in the Maritime
Interdiction Force (MIF) which implemented the economic
sanctions mandated by Security Council Resolution 661 (1990) of
August 6, 1990.[50]

Iraq outraged the international community when it caused major
oil spills in the Persian Gulf in late January, 1991 by opening the
oil valves at the Sea Island Terminal near Kuwait City and subsequently the oil valves at its offshore terminal at Amin Al-Bakr.
Although the damage caused by this intentional oil spill was substantial, it would have served a military purpose to some extent
if Coalition forces had attempted an amphibious landing at Kuwait
City, as the oil would have significantly impeded ship movements.
Damage caused by the deliberate Iraqi oil spill was inadvertently
exacerbated when Coalition air forces, attempting to close the valves
by bombing, caused some further spillage. Further, the Persian Gulf
is an area that has been polluted by oil spills on many occasions
in the past. Without attempting to condone Iraqi actions in causing a deliberate oil spill in the Gulf, these actions were substantially different in kind and in environmental effect from the wanton
destruction of Kuwaiti oil fields on land by Iraqi forces.

On August 2, 1990, the Security Council adopted Resolution 660
(1990)[51] which condemned the Iraqi invasion of Kuwait. On August
6, 1990, it adopted Resolution 661 (1990)[52] which imposed economic sanctions prohibiting imports or exports from Iraq or Kuwait.
In Resolution 665 (1990),[53] adopted on August 25, 1990, the Security
Council called "upon those Member States cooperating with the
Government of Kuwait which are deploying maritime forces to the
area to use such measures commensurate to the specific circumstances as may be necessary under the authority of the Security
Council to halt all inward and outward maritime shipping in order to inspect and verify their cargoes and destinations and to en-

[50] Int'l Leg. Mat. 1325 (1990).
[51] *Ibid.*
[52] *Ibid.*
[53] *Ibid.*, 1329.

sure strict implementation of the provisions related to such shipping laid down in Resolution 661 (1990). . . ." The resolution provided
the legal basis for establishing the Maritime Interdiction Force
(MIF) which operated primarily in the Red Sea and in and near
the Persian Gulf. Resolution 666 (1990),[54] adopted on September
13, 1990, provided for the possible importation of foodstuffs in
humanitarian circumstances, and Resolution 670 (1990),[55] adopted on Sepember 25, 1990, confirmed that Resolution 661 (1990) applied to all means of transport, including aircraft. Canada deployed
three warships, the destroyers HMCS *Athabaskan,* HMCS *Terra Nova,*
and the supply ship HMCS *Protecteur,* to participate in the MIF operation. The Canadian warships, together with their helicopters, carried out 1,877 of 7,645 (24.6 per cent) of the interceptions or hailing
of suspect vessels during the interdiction effort up to the close of
hostilities. Because the Coalition forces possessed overwhelming
naval superiority and demonstrated the capability and willingness
to use force to prevent vessels travelling to or from Iraq, the use
of deadly force was not required. Warning shots were occasionally
fired and armed boardings were occasionally required. No one was
killed during the successful MIF operation and no ships were sunk.[56]

Fortunately, one need not rely exclusively on what states have
done in armed conflict to determine state practice or the positions
states have adopted on current issues in the law of naval warfare.
A review of current manuals on this law is also helpful. These manuals do not constitute law in themselves but they are evidence of state
practice and they may contain persuasive statements of law. The
specific manuals available to the writer were: a. for the French Navy,
Armed Forces Official Bulletin No. 102-3 *Maritime Law-Instructions
on the Application of International Law in Case of War* (1st ed. 1965) b. for
the Australian Navy, ABR5179 — *Manual of the Law of the Sea* (1987),
c. for the Canadian Navy, *Canadian Forces Law of Armed Conflict Manual
(Second Draft)* (1984), d. for the United States Navy, NWP9, (Rev
A), *The Commander's Handbook on the Law of Naval Operations (1989)* and
*Annotated Supplement to the Commander's Handbook on the Law of Naval Oper-
ations* (1989), and e. for the German Navy, ZDV 152 — *Humanitarian
Law in Armed Conflicts — Manual —* (Draft) (January 1991). The Armed
Forces of the United Kingdom are also thought to be prepar-

[54] *Ibid.,* 1330.

[55] *Ibid.,* 1334.

[56] T. Delery, "Away, the Boarding Party," United States Naval Institute Proceedings 1991 Naval Review Issue, 65-71.

ing a Tri-Service Manual.

Most of the manuals perused have what might be referred to as an English-language bias. The United States Navy materials are particularly influential because of the place of the USN among the world's navies, because of the number of well-qualified international lawyers employed by the USN, and because of what might be referred to as a process of intellectual technology transfer. Navies that are less well equipped with international lawyers adopt USN arguments and statements of the law because they are unable to dedicate the resources necessary to conduct independent assessments.

The Relevance of Additional Protocol I

The precise impact of Additional Protocol I of 1977 on the conduct of naval operations is still a topic of some debate.[57] It clearly has a substantial impact on operations on and over land areas, including naval shore bombardment and the operations of naval aircraft over land areas. Different parts and sections of Protocol I have different fields of application. Article 1 indicates that the Protocol is to apply in international armed conflicts and Article 1(4) expands the definition of these conflicts. Part II, concerned with the wounded, sick, and shipwrecked, clearly applies to all land, sea, and air operations in international armed conflicts. Part III, concerned with methods and means of warfare, and combatant and prisoner of war status, and Part IV, concerned with protection of the civilian population, present greater problems. It is suggested that Section 1 of Part III, concerned with methods and means of warfare, applies to all land, sea, and air operations; the reasons for this opinion are that Article 35(1) simply refers to ''any armed conflict'' and Article 39(3), referring to the misuse of flags and uniforms, specifically indicates that there is no intention to change the recognized rules concerning the use of false flags in naval warfare. The exclusion clause in Article 39(3) would not have been necessary if the section did not apply to naval warfare. The only provision in this section that might add to the existing law of naval warfare and have an impact on targeting is Article 35(3) which states that

---

[57] E. Rauch, *The Protocol Additional to the Geneva Conventions for the Protection of Victims of International Armed Conflicts and the United Nations Convention on the Law of the Sea Repercussions on the Law of Naval Warfare* (Berlin, 1984), and ''Proceedings of the Committee for the Protection of Human Life in Armed Conflicts on Law of Naval Warfare at 1985 Conference in Garmisch — Partenkirchen,'' 26 Military Law and Law of War Review 9-181 (1987).

"It is prohibited to employ methods or means of warfare which are intended, or may be expected, to cause widespread, long term and severe damage to the natural environment." The means of warfare generally used in the naval milieu, namely torpedoes, guns, and missiles, are not means which normally have a substantial adverse environmental impact. This provision, then, is aimed at such methods of war as environmental modification techniques. Oil tankers were attacked and sunk during World War II and during the Iran-Iraq conflict. And during the Falklands conflict, the Argentine cruiser General Belgrano was sunk by the nuclear powered British submarine, HMS Conqueror. No one has suggested it was permissible for Conqueror to sink General Belgrano but not permissible for General Belgrano to sink Conqueror because of the potential adverse environmental impact.

Although the major parties in the recently concluded Gulf war, Iraq, the USA, the United Kingdom, and France, are not parties to Additional Protocol I, there has been some discussion about the applicability of the standard set in Article 35(3) to the oil spill in the Gulf. The precise meaning of the terms "widespread, long term and severe" in Article 35(3) is not yet generally agreed upon, but these terms undoubtedly are meant to impose a very high threshold of applicability. In particular, the expression "long term" appears to mean "measured in decades."[58] The discussion at the Conference of Experts on the Use of the Environment as a Tool of Conventional Warfare, cosponsored by the United Nations and by the government of Canada and held in Ottawa on July 9-12, 1991, indicated that there was widespread agreement that the Iraqi oil spill did not meet the "long term" criterion in Article 35(3). Assuming that view is correct, it is unlikely that the sinking of super tankers or of nuclear powered vessels would violate Article 35(3).

Part IV, Section I of Protocol I (Articles 48-67), which is concerned with the protection of the civilian population, has a more limited field of application. Article 49(3) provides: "3. The provisions of this Section apply to any land, air or sea warfare which may affect the civilian population, individual civilians or civilian objects on land. They further apply to all attacks from the sea or from the air against objectives on land but do not otherwise affect the rules of international law applicable in armed conflict at sea

---

[58] International Committee of the Red Cross, *Commentary on the Additional Protocols* 410-20 (Geneva, 1987) and M. Bothe, K. Partsch, & W. Solf, *New Rules for Victims of Armed Conflict* 198 and 342-48 (Boston, 1982).

or in the air.'' The proper interpretation of this paragraph is contentious. It is clear that Part IV, Section I, regulates naval shore
bombardment by means of ships or aircraft. The question is what
is the meaning of the expression ''may affect'' in the article? Attacks directed against objects on or under the seas would not normally directly affect the civilian population on land. The one article
in the section that might have an impact, after a fashion, on naval
targeting is Article 54 which prohibits starvation of civilians as a
method of warfare. This provision may require reconsideration of
traditional commerce interdiction measures such as blockade and
contraband. Article 54(1) would prohibit a naval blockade to prevent the import of foodstuffs in order to hasten the end of an armed
conflict through starvation of the civilian population. Furthermore,
objects indispensable to the survival of the civilian population must
not be declared or treated as absolute contraband. Foodstuffs and
drinking water must not be treated as conditional contraband even
if they are used by the enemy in direct support of military aciton,
provided that their seizure and condemnation may leave the civilian
population with such inadequate supplies as to cause its starvation
or force its movement. A blockading nation is not compelled by
Article 54 to allow a blockaded nation to replenish foodstuffs when
the blockaded nation has sufficient stocks but is using them for other
warlike purposes such as making explosives. As a result, it may be
necessary for parties to Protocol I to exempt from attack ships known
to be carrying exclusively objects indispensable to the survival of
the civilian population even if such ships breach a blockade or are
so unwise as to refuse to stop for visit and search. As indicated earlier, during the Persian Gulf conflict, Security Council Resolution
666 (1990) provided for the possible importation by Iraq of foodstuffs for humanitarian reasons.

   Although most of Part IV, Section I, of Protocol I is not, strictly
speaking, applicable to the targeting of objects on, over, or under
the seas, it does contain some concepts and texts that might eventually be considered suitable for incorporation in the law of naval
warfare. In particular, Article 52 defines the term ''military objective'' and Articles 51 and 57 embed the principle of proportionality
in treaty law. Article 52(2) states: ''2. Attacks shall be limited strictly
to military objectives. Insofar as objects are concerned, military
objectives are limited to those objects which by their nature, location, purpose or use make an effective contribution to military ac-

tion and whose total or partial destruction, capture or neutralization, in the circumstances ruling at the time; offers a definite military advantage." If one considers it desirable to have a general definition as part of any provision concerning military objectives in the law of naval warfare, it may well be that this definition in Protocol I is suitable for the purpose. One of the leading commentaries on the Protocols discusses the definition in the following terms:

Military objectives are those objects which by their nature, location, purpose or use:
a) make an effective contribution to military action, and
b) whose total or partial destruction, capture or neutralizaiton, in the circumstances ruling at the time, offers a definite military advantage. . . .

2.4.2   The objects classified as military objectives under this definition include much more than strictly military objects such as military vehicles, weapons, munitions, stores of fuel and fortifications. Provided the objects meet the two-pronged test, under the circumstances ruling at the time (not at some hypothetical future time), military objectives include activities providing administrative and logistical support to military operations such as transportation and communications systems, railroads, airfields and port facilities and industries of fundamental importance for the conduct of the armed conflict. . . .

2.4.3   Military objectives must make an "effective contribution to military action." This does not require a direct connection with combat operation. . . . Thus a civilian object may become a military objective and thereby lose its immunity from deliberate attack through use which is only indirectly related to combat action, but which nevertheless provides an effective contribution to the military phase of a Party's overall war effort. . . .

Enemy Vessels and Aircraft Exempt from Capture or Destruction
    A review of French, Australian, Canadian, German, and American manuals or draft manuals reveals a high degree of consensus on this topic.[60] As the listing in the USN Commander's Handbook is the most comprehensive and most recent, its paragraph 8.2.3. is quoted here for illustrative purposes:

Certain classes of enemy vessels and aircraft are exempt under the law of naval warfare from capture and destruction provided they are innocently employed in their exempt category. These specially protected ves-

---

[60] French Manual, Art. 20-23; Australian, para. 823; Canadian, paras. 718-19; German, paras. 1034-36; and U.S.A., para. 8.2.3.

sels and aircraft must not take part in the hostilities, must not hamper
the movement of combatants, must submit to identification and inspection procedures, and may be ordered out of harm's way. These specifically exempt vessels and aircraft include:

1. Vessels and aircraft designated for and engaged in the exchange of
   prisoners (cartel vessels).
2. Properly designated and marked hospital ships, medical transports,
   and known medical aircraft.
3. Vessels charged with religious, non-military scientific, or philanthropic
   missions. (Vessels engaged in the collection of scientific data of potential military application are not exempt.)
4. Vessels and aircraft guaranteed safe conduct by prior arrangement between the belligerents.
5. Small coastal (not deep-sea) fishing vessels and small boats engaged
   in local coastal trade. Such vessels and boats are subject to the regulations of a belligerent naval commander operating in the area.
6. Civilian passenger vessels at sea and civil airliners in flight are subject to capture but are exempt from destruction. Although enemy lines
   of communication are generally legitimate military targets in modern
   warfare, civilian passenger vessels at sea, and civil airliners in flight
   are exempt from destruction, unless at the time of the encounter they
   are being utilized by the enemy for a military purpose (e.g. transporting troops or military cargo) or refuse to respond to the directions of
   the intercepting warship or military aircraft. Such passenger vessels
   in port and airliners on the ground are not protected from destruction.
   If an exempt enemy vessel or aircraft assists the enemy's military effort in any manner, it may be captured or destroyed. Refusal to provide immediate identification upon demand is ordinarily sufficient legal
   justification for capture or destruction. All nations have a legal obligation not to take advantage of the harmless character of exempt vessels and aircraft in order to use them for military purposes while
   preserving their innocent appearance. For example, the utilization by
   North Vietnam of innocent appearing small coastal fishing boats as
   logistic craft in support of military operations during the Vietnam Conflict was in violation of this obligation.

The only type of vessel that should be added to the list in the
Handbook is small coastal rescue craft which are entitled to protection from attack or capture under Article 27 of the Geneva Convention of 1949. There is no treaty provision providing similar
protection to larger rescue vessels of the type which occasionally
accompanied convoys during the World War II. The USN materials are the only ones reviewed that explicitly state that civilian
passenger vessels at sea and civil airliners in flight are subject
to capture but are exempt from destruction. A footnote to the

subparagraph on this topic in the USN Annotated Supplement to
NWP9 (Rev A) states in part: "The rule prohibiting destruction
of civilian passenger vessels at sea and civilian airliners in flight
which have become military objectives is premised upon the assessment that the inevitable death of the large number of civilians
normally carried in them would, in the circumstances described
in the text of paragraph 6, be clearly disproportionate to whatever
military advantage that might be expected from attacking such vessels or aircraft. The rule denying protection from destruction to
passenger vessels in port and airliners on the ground assumes they
are not carrying passengers at the time of attack."

The USN provision concerning civilian passenger vessels and
civilian airliners is eminently sensible and also provides some support for the argument that the concepts of a general definition of
the military objective and the rule of proportionality should be incorporated into the law of naval warfare. The history of naval warfare
indicates that it is occasionally necessary to state the obvious. For
this reason, it is also desirable that any list of prohibited targets
include ships and aircraft that have clearly surrendered and shipwrecked personnel in the water or on life boats or rafts.

Enemy Vessels and Aircraft that May be Attacked at All Times
   All of the manuals reviewed indicated that attacks may be directed
against enemy warships, naval or military auxiliary vessels, and military aircraft at any time anywhere outside neutral territorial seas.[61]
These attacks may be exercised without warning and without regard
to the safety of the enemy crew. It was suggested during the Falklands conflict that the action of the United Kingdom in sinking
the Argentine Cruiser General Belgrano outside of proclaimed exclusion zones was unfair. There is no international legal requirement to confine attacks against warships, auxiliary vessels, or
military aircraft to particular zones once an armed conflict occurs,
except for the general obligation not to fight in neutral waters. None
of the manuals consulted have attempted to define "naval or military auxiliary vessel." A British author has suggested that a naval
auxiliary is a vessel engaged at the relevant time in direct support
of enemy warships, whether or not it is formally incorporated
in the belligerent fleet and whether or not it is in company with

[61] French Manual, Art. 1; Australian, para. 818; Canadian, para. 715; German, para.
1021 and U.S.A., para. 8.2.1.

enemy warships.[62]

The Merchant Ship as Target

The central issue concerning targeting in the law of naval warfare is, when may a merchant ship be a legitimate military objective? A rough definition of merchant vessel is any cargo carrying vessel, publicly or privately owned, flying the flag of a belligerent or neutral state. As indicated above, under the pre-1914 law merchant ships, enemy or neutral, could only be attacked on sight when they took a direct part in hostilities or when they were being convoyed by enemy warships, as they were then deemed to be resisting visit and search. In all other cases they had to be ordered to submit to visit and search and then refuse to comply with the order before they could be attacked, even if they were armed for defensive purposes. The pre-1914 law and its reaffirmation in the 1936 London Submarine Protocol notwithstanding, neutral and belligerent merchant ships unconvoyed by enemy warships or aircraft were attacked on sight by submarines, aircraft, and on occasion, surface warships in both World Wars. Further, unconvoyed neutral and belligerent merchant ships were attacked by aircraft and surface warships in the Iran-Iraq war. The only case in which individuals were charged with war crimes, including the attacking of merchant ships without warning, is the trial of Doenitz and Raeder before the International Military Tribunal at Nuremberg. As said above, they were both acquitted of the charges insofar as belligerent merchant vessels were concerned, convicted insofar as neutral merchant vessels were concerned, but awarded no sentence on the charge because of similar Allied practices. In the *Peleus Trial*, the accused were charged jointly with:

Committing a war crime in that you in the Atlantic Ocean on the night of 13/14th March, 1944, when Captain and members of the crew of Unterseeboot 852 which had sunk the steamship "Peleus" in violation of the laws and usages of war were concerned in the killing of members of the crew of the said steamship, Allied nationals, by firing and throwing grenades at them.

It was submitted on behalf of the Defence that the charge may be read in two different ways, according to which the phrase "in violation of the laws and usages of war" could qualify either the word "sunk" or the word "concerned," and what followed it.

[62] G. Schwarzenberger, *International Law*, Vol. II — *The Law of Armed Conflict* 379 (London, 1968).

It was made clear at the outset by the Prosecution that the phrase ''in violation of the laws and usages of war'' qualified the words that follow it, and not the words that precede it, or in other words, that the prisoners were not accused of having violated the laws and usages of war by sinking the merchantman, but only by firing and throwing grenades on the survivors of the sunken ship.[63]

It is more difficult to state a generally agreed view of the existing law concerning the treatment of merchant vessels in an international armed conflict than it is to state a similar view of the pre-First World War law. Prior to that war, the normal practice was to capture enemy merchant vessels and neutral merchant vessels subject to capture because capture conferred economic benefits on the captors and because the capturing vessel was not normally exposing itself to substantial risks by so doing. Modern technology, in particular the invention of the aircraft, the submarine, modern means of detection, modern means of communication, and modern long-range weapons such as missiles, have rendered the seas a much more dangerous environment for warships. Today, capturing a vessel, unless the capturing power has a substantial maritime superiority, below the surface, on the surface, and in the air, is often not a practical measure of war. Furthermore, providing an opportunity for the crew of a merchant vessel to abandon ship before the merchant vessel is attacked is often not a practical measure of war. It has been suggested by at least one writer, Louise Doswald-Beck, that the traditional law is simply unsuitable for modern conditions and that it should be re-thought using the broad basic principles of military necessity, humanity, and good faith. In particular, she suggests that the traditional practice of stop, search, and capture is the exception in modern naval warfare.[64] In practice, a military objective is a ship which will be attacked and may be destroyed. For this reason it is desirable to confine the classification of military objectives as narrowly as possible. Certainly, in any attempt to state the law, it must be borne in mind that the crews of merchant vessels, although they may be treated as prisoners of war upon capture, are civilians and that there is an obligation, which pervades the law of armed conflict, to spare the civilian population insofar as that is practicable.

Under pre-First World War law, any merchant vessel could be

---

[63] Peleus Trial, *op. cit. supra* note 3, at 2.

[64] Doswald-Beck, *op. cit. supra* note 10, at 276-82.

attacked without warning if it sailed under convoy of enemy warships or if it engaged in acts of war on behalf of the enemy and
enemy merchant vessels could be attacked if they were offensively
armed. Intelligence gathering for the enemy by neutral merchant
vessels rendered them subject to capture. (Enemy merchant vessels outside of neutral waters were always subject to capture in any
event). A number of the modern manuals on the law of naval
warfare, the United States (paragraphs 8.2.2.2, 8.3.1 and 8.4), the
French (Article 2) the German (paragraph 1025), and the Australian
(paragraph 822 and Chapter 10), consider intelligence gathering as
equivalent to engaging in acts of war on behalf of the enemy. The
United States (paragraphs 8.2.2.2, 8.3.1, 8.4 and 7.5.1), German
(paragraph 1025), and Australian (paragraph 822 and Chapter 10)
manuals also indicate that any merchant vessel acting as a naval
or military auxiliary of the enemy's armed forces is subject to attack without warning. In addition, the German Manual (paragraph
1025) and the United States Manual (paragraphs 8.2.2.2, 8.3.1, and
8.4) indicate that armed enemy merchant ships are subject to attack without warning. The rationale for this latter position is that,
with modern weapons, it is impossible to determine whether the
armament on merchant ships is to be used offensively or merely
defensively. There is a strong probability that a modern consensus
could be achieved on the following propositions: During an international armed conflict: 1. Any merchant vessel may be attacked:
(a) if it engages in acts of war on behalf of the enemy; (b) if it acts
as an auxiliary to the enemy's armed forces (c) if it is incorporated
into or assists the enemy's intelligence system; or (d) if it sails under convoy of enemy warships or military aircraft. 2. Any enemy
merchant vessel may be attacked: (a) if it is armed to an extent that
it could inflict significant damage to a warship; or (b) it refuses an
order to stop or actively resists visit, search, or capture. 3. A neutral merchant vessel may be attacked if it is believed on reasonable
grounds that the vessel is carrying contraband or breaching a blockade and, after prior warning, the vessel intentionally and clearly
refuses to stop or resists visit, search, and capture. 4. Passenger vessels when engaged in carrying civilian passengers at sea, may not
be attacked. 5. Neutral or belligerent vessels in the following
categories are exempt from attack or capture so long as they do
not take any part in hostilities: coastal fishing vessels, small boats
employed in local trade, hospital ships, medical transports, and ves-

sels charged with religious, philanthropic, or non-military scientific missions.

A central question remains, namely, when, if ever, may enemy or neutral merchant vessels which do not meet the criteria listed in the preceding paragraph, be attacked on sight during an international armed conflict? Does the answer to this question depend on the answers to such questions as whether or not a declared war exists, what the scale of the conflict is, whether the location of the vessel is inside or outside a particular zone, what the function of the vessel is, or whether the vessel flies the flag of a belligerent or neutral state. It is suggested that whether or not a declared war exists, what the scale of the conflict is, and whether the location of the vessel is inside or outside a particular zone are all irrelevant issues. The relevance of the flag the merchant vessel is entitled to fly as an absolute criterion for targeting decisions is also debatable. In *Amerada Hess* v. *Argentina Republic,* the owners of the Liberian tanker *Hercules* sought damages from Argentina for a bombing attack on the *Hercules* during the Falklands conflict which occurred outside the exclusion zones proclaimed by Argentina and the United Kingdom. The United States Court of Appeal (Second Circuit), which seems to have relied primarily on peace time law of the sea treaties although it did conduct a cursory review of older law of naval warfare treaties, held that neutral ships had a right of free passage on the high seas, saying: ''In short, it is beyond controversy that attacking a neutral ship in international waters, without proper cause for suspicion or investigation, violates international law. Indeed, the relative paucity of cases litigating this customary rule of international law underscores the longstanding nature of this aspect of freedom of the high seas. Where the attacker has refused to compensate the neutral, such action is analogous to piracy, one of the earliest recognized violations of international law. See 4 W. Blackstone, *Commentaries* 68, 72. Argentina has cited no contrary authority.''[65]

The Supreme Court of the United States reversed the decision of the Court of Appeal, but on grounds unrelated to that court's finding concerning the legality of the attack on the Hercules.[66] The Court of Appeal appears to have held the opinion that any attack

[65] *Amerada Hess* v. *Argentina Republic,* US Court of Appeals (2nd Circuit) 1987, 79 I.L.R. 10.
[66] United States Supreme Court Decision in *Argentina Republic* v. *Amerada Hess Shipping Corp et al.,* 28 Int'l Leg. Mat. 382 (1989).

on a neutral merchant vessel without a prior request for visit and search would be unlawful. It is suggested that this opinion is erroneous, although it may well be that the actual attack on the *Hercules* was unlawful as it was not providing any support to the United Kingdom in the war.

The primary legal criterion for determining whether or not a merchant vessel is a legitimate military objective should be a functional one based on the task the merchant vessel is employed on at the time the targeting decision is made. Of course, decision makers may, for political reasons such as a desire to limit a conflict, decide that neutral merchant vessels may not be attacked even when they are employed on tasks that otherwise would make them legitimate military objectives.

As indicated earlier, during the Iran-Iraq conflict, Iraq attacked tankers, most of them neutral, unconvoyed, and unincorporated in the Iranian intelligence system, but engaged in exporting oil from Iran to support the Iranian war economy. Iran attacked neutral ships engaged in exporting or importing goods, including oil, to neutral Gulf states, some of which were engaged in providing economic support to the Iraqi war effort. Some merchant vessels which do not meet the generally agreed criteria listed earlier (engaging in acts of war, acting as an auxiliary, incorporated in the intelligence system, or being convoyed) may nevertheless constitute legitimate military objectives. If this is so, how are their tasks to be described? Furthermore, would or should the actions of Iraq or Iran be legitimate under a modern restatement of the law of naval warfare?

The current manual of the United States Navy suggests (paragraphs 8.2.2.2, 8.3.1, and 8.4) that enemy merchant ships may be attacked and destroyed without warning if they are integrated into the enemy's ''war-fighting/war-sustaining effort'' and compliance with the 1936 London Protocol would subject the attacking force to imminent danger or otherwise preclude mission accomplishment. The Annotation to this provision states that ''Although the term 'war-sustaining' is not subject to precise definition, 'effort' that indirectly but effectively supports and sustains the belligerent's warfighting capability properly falls within the scope of the term.'' Another Annotation (to paragraph 7.4) provides as examples ''imports of raw materials used for the production of armaments and exports of products the proceeds of which are used by the belligerent to purchase arms and armaments." It then goes on to provide (paragraph 7.5.2) that neutral merchant vessels acquire the character of enemy merchant vessels and are liable to the same treatment when they "operate directly under enemy control, orders, charter, employment, or direction." On the not unreasonable assumption that the neutral tankers carrying Iranian oil exports were operating under Iranian charter or control and sailing in an area where it would not be practicable for Iraqi forces to comply with the 1936 London Protocol, the attacks of Iraqi forces on neutral tankers would have been lawful under the criteria in the USN Manual. On the other hand, the Iranian actions would not have been lawful because there was not a sufficient linkage between the tasks carried out by the neutral vessels it attacked and the Iraqi "war-fighting/war sustaining effort."

Although the influence of the views expressed in the USN Manual are difficult to overestimate, it must not be presumed that a simple comparison of activities in the Iran-Iraq war with the criteria listed in the USN Manual will provide a generally accepted assessment of legality. Professor Kalshoven,[67] among others, has suggested that criteria such as the "contribution to the war effort" or integration into the "war-fighting/war-sustaining effort" are too broad and, potentially, allow a belligerent too much latitude for classifying maritime commerce with his enemy as a legitimate military objective. At the 1989 Round Table at Bochum in the Federal Republic of Germany concerned with the Military Objective and the Principle of Distinction in the Law of Naval Warfare, a draft document was produced which suggested that perhaps the appropriate phrase to describe a residual category of merchant vessels that are legitimate military objectives, would be merchant vessels that "make an effective contribution to military action" by, for example, carrying military materials. Although this phrase also leaves some scope for interpretation, it would appear that, if the effective contribution referred to must be reasonably direct, attacks on neutral merchant vessels carrying exports might be illegitimate.

TARGET IDENTIFICATION, RUSES, AND PERFIDY

One of the major problems in modern naval warfare conducted

---

[67] F. Kalshoven, *Comments for Bochum Meeting,* unpublished, at 7-8, and F. Kalshoven, *Enemy Merchant Vessels as Legitimate Military Objectives,* unpublished comments for 1990 Newport Meeting, at 6-8.

with current technology is target identification. Simply put, there is an imbalance between the technology for seeing and the technology for killing. The Naval commanders have weapons available to them which they can use to attack targets beyond visual range (BVR) or even over the horizon (OTH), where it is difficult or impossible to confirm that the target is a legitimate military objective. They have an interest in ensuring that the object attacked is a legitimate military objective and also that it is not one of their own side's ships or aircraft (the Blue on Blue problem) or a ship or aircraft otherwise exempt from attack. Blue on Blue attacks are in fact quite common in modern conflicts; aircraft, in particular, are frequently shot down by their own side. These incidents occur because on scene commanders are concerned about the protection of their own units and believe that waiting until they have positive visual identification of potential targets will place their units at too great a risk; they must make targeting decisions on an assessment of probabilities. The commanding officer of the USS *Vincennes* ordered that Iran Air Flight 655 be shot down in the Persian Gulf on July 3, 1988, because he believed, erroneously but on the basis of a less than reckless assessment of the facts provided to him, that the aircraft was an Iranian F-14 which would attack his ship before it came within range for accurate visual identification.

The current law concerning ruses of war and perfidy in a naval setting is fairly straightforward but, in the light of the current state of weapons technology, one might question whether certain aspects of it, in particular the false flag rule, are not anachronistic and harmful to the underlying principles of the law of armed conflict.

Ruses of war are permitted. They are acts that are intended to mislead an adversary and induce him to act recklessly, but they infringe no rule of international law applicable to armed conflict and are not perfidious because they do not invite the confidence of an adversary with respect to protection under that law. Examples of ruses are the use of camouflage, deceptions, utilization of enemy codes, passwords, and countersigns. The fog of war has not been completely dissipated by modern technology; it is still possible to deceive the enemy concerning the identity and location of naval units even in the era of radar and reconnaissance satellites.

Under the customary international law of naval warfare, it is permissible for a belligerent warship to fly false colours and disguise its outward appearance in other ways in order to deceive the enemy into believing the vessel is of neutral nationality or is other than a warship. However, it is unlawful for a warship to go into action without first showing its true colours; use of neutral flags, insignia, or uniforms during an actual armed engagement at sea is forbidden. Merchant vessels are also permitted to practise this deception but they thereby run the risk of capture, damage, or even destruction. Belligerent military aircraft are not permitted to wear false markings in order to deceive the enemy.

Although ruses of war are permitted, perfidy is prohibited. Perfidy is defined in Article 37 (1) of Additional Protocol I as follows: "Acts inviting the confidence of an adversary to lead him to believe that he is entitled to, or is obliged to accord, protection under the rules of international law applicable in armed conflict, with intent to betray that confidence, shall constitute perfidy." Article 38 goes on to state: "1. It is prohibited to make improper use of the distinctive emblem of the red cross, red crescent or red lion and sun or of other emblems, signs or signals provided for by the Conventions or by this Protocol. It is also prohibited to misuse deliberately in an armed conflict other internationally recognized protective emblems, signs or signals, including the flag of truce, and the protective emblem of cultural property. 2. It is prohibited to make use of distinctive emblem of the United Nations, except as authorized by that Organization." Article 39 (2), however, indicates the Protocol does not alter the traditional rules of international law concerning the use of flags in the conduct of armed conflict at sea.

It is unlikely that targeting decisions in a high technology naval conflict would be made at ranges where the colour of a flag flown by a ship would be a relevant consideration. One might, however, question the current desirability of a rule that encourages the disguising of warships to simulate ships which might not be legitimate objects of attack. It is one thing to say that warships need not be required to take positive measures to indicate their location and status as warships; it is another to suggest that "feigning noncombatant status" still is a desirable practice.

The identification issue has been addressed by the ICRC and other organizations in an effort to ensure that medical transports and other ships and aircraft entitled to protection under the Geneva Conventions and the Additional Protocols are properly identified before they are subjected to the risk of attack.[68]

---

[68] P. Eberlin, "The Identification of Medical Aircraft in Periods of Armed Conflict," (1982) I.R.R.C. 202-15; "Identification of Hospital Ships and Ships Protected by the Geneva Conventions of 12 August 1949," (1982) I.R.R.C. 315-28; "Revision

One recent development in the general area of identification is Resolution 18 of the World Administrative Radio Conference for the Mobile Services, Geneva, 1983.[69] This resolution establishes procedures for identifying "ships and aircraft of states not parties to an armed conflict." Ships and aircraft using these procedures may, however, assume that they are entitled to protection when in fact they are not. The fact that a ship or aircraft is registered in a state not party to an armed conflict does not, by itself, mean that it is not a legitimate military objective. Furthermore, under the law as it exists at present, one might question whether or not ships or aircraft, including warships and military aircraft, of states engaged in an armed conflict would violate the law of armed conflict if they used Resolution 18 procedures. Would such an act be perfidious or a lawful ruse of war?

It is clear that the identification issue is ripe for reconsideration. This reconsideration, however, would not be a simple task. It is relatively easy for states to agree not to abuse protective signs for a small number of immune objects, such as hospital ships and medical transports. It may be much more difficult to reach agreement to consider warships disguised as neutral ships or as merchant vessels, and belligerent merchant vessels disguised as neutral vessels, as engaging in perfidious acts, because states at war may gain substantial military benefits from these practices.

SUMMARY RESTATEMENT

The principle of distinction is a fundamental principle of the law of naval warfare. If naval commanders are to comply with it, they must be provided with definitions, lists, or criteria which enable them to differentiate between objects that may be attacked and those that may not be attacked. The concept of the military objective is a legal device that will assist commanders to make these differentiations in a manner that assigns proper weight to both military necessity and humanitarian considerations. An explanation of the concept of the military objective which includes both   a   general   definition

of Annex I to Protocol I Regulations Concerning Identification," (1983) I.R.R.C. 22-27; "The Protection of Rescue Craft in Periods of Armed Conflict," (1985) I.R.R.C. 140-52; "Underwater Acoustic Identification of Hospital Ships," (1988) 28 I.R.R.C. 505-18.
69 "Amendments to the Radio Regulations Concerning Medical Means of Transport and Neutral Means of Transport," (1984) 24 I.R.R.C. 50-59.

and a list of objects constituting military objectives, would appear to be the most helpful approach for naval commanders. The general definition should include the criteria to be met by any object for it to be a legitimate military objective. The list should illustrate the general definition.

No treaty in force at present provides a general definition of the military objective in the law of naval warfare. The definition contained in Article 52 (2) of Protocol I is usable in naval warfare, although, generally speaking, one might pay less heed to the factor of "location" in naval warfare than in land warfare. That definition is: "military objectives are limited to those objects which by their nature, location, purpose or use make an effective contribution to military action and whose total or partial destruction, capture or neutralization, in the circumstances ruling at the time, offers a definite military advantage." Enemy warships, military aircraft, and naval or military auxiliary vessels come with this definition and may be attacked at any time anywhere beyond the territorial seas of states not involved in the conflict. An auxiliary vessel is a vessel providing direct support for the enemy armed forces, for example, by carrying troops or acting as a replenishment vessel; it need not be formally incorporated in the enemy fleet, in company with enemy warships, or owned by or under the exclusive control of its armed forces.

A merchant vessel may be roughly defined as a cargo carrying vessel, publicly or privately owned, flying the flag of a belligerent or neutral state. Some merchant vessels are legitimate military objectives; others are not. The test to determine whether or not one is a legitimate military objective should be a functional test: what is it doing and to what extent is it either directly participating in hositilities or contributing to the enemy war effort?[70]

Any merchant vessel may be attacked without warning and destroyed when it engages in acts of war on behalf of the enemy such as laying mines, minesweeping, cutting undersea cables, visiting neutral merchant ships or attacking merchant ships on one's own side; acts as a de facto auxiliary to an enemy's armed forces, for example, by carrying troops or acting as a replenishment vessel;

[70] The near classic discussion of the functional approach to the merchant ship as military objective is Mallison, *op. cit. supra* note 18, particularly at 97-149. A thoughtful application of the Mallison approach to the Persian Gulf conflict is made by Russo, *op. cit. supra* note 46.

is incorporated into, or assists in any way, the intelligence system of the enemy's armed forces; sails under convoy of enemy warships or military aircraft; or makes an effective contribution to enemy military action, for example, by carrying military materials.

In addition, enemy merchant vessels may be attacked without warning when, for other reasons, they constitute a military objective within the terms of the generic definition. They may be attacked without warning when they are armed; the old concept of defensively armed merchant vessels is an anachronism. Further, they may be attacked, after prior warning, for actively resisting visit, search, or capture or wilfully and persistently refusing to stop after being duly summoned.

Neutral merchant vessels, which are believed on reasonable grounds to be carrying contraband or attempting to breach a blockade, may be attacked, after prior warning, for actively resisting visit, search or capture, or wilfully and persistently refusing to stop after being duly summoned, and then only after all other practicable means of stopping the vessel concerned have failed.

Vessels that are not referred to above and do not constitute legitimate military objectives within the meaning of the general definition, clearly should not be attacked. Ideally, it should not be necessary to draft a list of vessels and aircraft exempt from attack, as that category should simply include the vast number of ships uninvolved in the conflict. For greater clarity, however, and because some of the listed categories of vessels and aircraft are entitled to special protection as a result of treaties, and because the exemption is from capture as well as attack, it is useful to provide a list of enemy vessels and aircraft exempt from capture and destruction. These specifically exempt vessels and aircraft include: vessels and aircraft designated for and engaged in the exchange of prisoners (cartel vessels), because of the agreement of the parties; hospital ships, coastal rescue craft, medical transports, and known medical aircraft, because of the Geneva Conventions of 1949; vessels charged with religious, non-military scientific, or philanthropic missions, because of Hague Convention XI of 1907 (vessels engaged in the collection of scientific data of potential military application are not exempt); vessels and aircraft guaranteed safe conduct by prior arrangement between the belligerents; small coastal (not deep-sea) fishing vessels and small boats engaged in local coastal trade, because of the Hague Convention XI of 1907; these vessels and boats are, however, subject to the regulations of a belligerent naval commander operating in the area; vessels engaged exclusively in the carriage of goods, normally foodstuffs, indispensable to the survival of the civilian population (for parties to Protocol I only).

In addition, sea-going rescue craft, civilian passenger vessels at sea, and civil airliners in flight are subject to capture but exempt from attack because attacks directed against them would cause disproportionate damage to humanitarian interests. Passenger vessels and civil airliners may, however, be attacked if, at the time of the encounter, they are being used by the enemy for a military purpose, such as transporting troops or military cargo, or if they refuse to respond to the directions of an intercepting warship or military aircraft. The shipwrecked are not legitimate objects of attack whether they are in the water, in lifeboats, or on rafts.

Target identification constitutes one of the major problems for the naval commander in modern warfare. The problem is caused by an imbalance between the technology for killing and the technology for seeing, but it is exacerbated by legal developments in forums unfamiliar with the law of armed conflict, such as Resolution 18 of Mobile WARC 83. The general issue of identification would appear to be particularly ripe for re-examination in forums familiar with the law of armed conflict. Whether or not a targeting decision is right or wrong when measured against an absolute standard, the potential criminal liability of the commander must be determined on the basis of the facts as he understood them to be and by determining whether his actions were intentional, reckless, or merely imperfect, as most human actions are.[71]

Sommaire

Aspects juridiques du choix des objectifs et des moyens de traitement en droit de la guerre maritime

Il est nécessaire de reformuler le droit de la guerre maritime en tenant compte des préoccupations actuelles, de la technologie moderne et de la pratique des États. Les traités

---

[71] People can also rise above legal standards. The writer occasionally lectures on the law of naval warfare at the Canadian Forces Maritime Warfare Centre in Halifax. One of the attendees at a recent lecture was a Canadian naval officer who was with the Canadian destroyers which deployed to the Persian Gulf. He stated that the hardest decisions he had to make during the period of hositilities were, repeatedly, to decide not to fire at potential targets when he had the autority to engage them because, in his professional judgment, these ships or aircraft did not pose a genuine threat to the ships he was required to protect. Fortunately, his judgment was always correct.

existants en ce domaine sont désuets. L'auteur souhaite donc la tenue prochaine d'une conférence internationale de codification consacrée à ce droit. Une des questions fondamentales du droit de la guerre maritime réside dans le choix des objectifs qui peuvent être légitimement attaqués. L'article passe en revue le droit existant, la pratique des États pendant les conflits récents et le droit interne relatif aux conflits armés. Il laisse entendre qu'une reformulation du droit actuel devrait réaffirmer le principe de distinction en renfermer une définition générale du terme "objectif militaire" fondée sur la définition incluse dans le Protocole additionnel I de 1977. Il souligne également les catégories de navires qui sont des objectifs légitimes et ceux qui ne devraient pas faire l'objet d'attaques. En outre, il se demande si la marine marchande devrait être un objectif légitime et dans quelles circonstances.

Visit, Search, Diversion, and Capture in Naval Warfare: Part I, The Traditional Law

WOLFF HEINTSCHEL VON HEINEGG*

SINCE 1945 MEASURES OF ECONOMIC WARFARE AT SEA have played a much less important role than during the two world wars. The war between Iran and Iraq has shown a tendency of belligerents to neglect measures of economic warfare and to turn to a policy of unrestricted sinking. Still, if a party to a conflict is able to interfere with the enemy's commerce without resort to the use of armed force, it will certainly endeavour to take all measures of economic warfare provided by traditional law. Since traditional law to a great extent dates back to the beginning of the twentieth century or even to 1856, the question arises whether in modern armed conflicts at sea these rules are still applicable. This question poses itself not only because advances in technology have had an impact on naval warfare but also because the law concerning naval operations, expecially the law on measures of economic warfare, may have been altered by state practice after 1945 and by the progressive development of international law as such.

In order to establish what the present status of the law concerning economic warfare at sea is, the present article gives an overview of the traditional law of visit, search, diversion, and capture. "Traditional law" here denotes all those rules that up to 1954 were adopted in international conventions[1] or developed by state practice. Treatment of crews and passengers as well as requisitions and

---

* Institut für Friedenssicherungsrecht und Humanitares Völkerrecht, Ruhr-Universität Bochum.

---

[1] Hence, the 1949 Geneva Conventions as well as the 1954 Convention for the Protection of Cultural Property in the Event of Armed Conflict are dealt with here under the heading of "traditional law."

angary will not be dealt with. A subsequent article in the next volume of this *Yearbook* will be devoted to an examination of state practice since 1945 and will also deal with the question whether and to what extent certain principles and rules of (general) international law have had an impact on the traditional law as developed by state practice.

I SHORT HISTORICAL SURVEY

The beginning of the traditional law of naval warfare can be fixed to the date of the Paris Declaration of 1856. This, however, does not mean that prior to that date there was no regulation of measures of economic warfare at sea. Until the twelfth century, war at sea, whether belligerent measures were directed against the enemy or against subjects of "non-enemies," was conducted without legal restrictions.[2] Or, as put by Nys: "Durant les premiers siècles du moyen âge, la guerre maritime ne fut que piratérie."[3] Ships and goods were protected to a certain extent only in case of an alliance or of some other kind of treaty obligation.

The concept of neutrality was for the first time acknowledged in 1164[4] and subsequently in the famous *consolato del mare*.[5] However, the inviolability of neutral property was not extended to enemy goods on board neutral ships or to enemy ships carrying neutral goods.copy This rule, according to which neutral goods were exempt from capture anywhere on the high seas, can be traced back to 1221 and was

---

[2] See, *inter alia*, H. Wehberg, "Das Seekriegsrecht," in Stier-Somlo (ed.), *Handbuch des Völkerrechts* Vol. 5, at 15 (Berlin-Stuttgart-Leipzig, 1915).

[3] E. Nys, *Les origines du droit international*, 211 (Paris, 1894).

[4] Pardessus (*Collection des lois maritimes*, Vol. II, at cxxii (Paris, 1826)) mentions the following precedent occurring in that year: During the war between Pisa and Genova Pisa captured a Saracen ship that allegedly was carrying goods belonging to a citizen of Genova. The Sultan of Egypt complained of the capture by maintaining that the goods belonged to one of his subjects (it is interesting to note that the Sultan did not advance a violation of his flag). Pisa, after determining the Saracen ownership, released the ship.

[5] With regard to the *consolato del mare*, E. Nys (*op. cit. supra* note 3, at 232) correctly remarks: "Le consulat de la mer n'est pas un code des lois maritimes rédigé et publié par l'autorité législative d'un ou de plusieurs États; c'est une collection de coutumes de la mer appliquées par la cour consulaire de Barcelone et on peut le considérer comme résumant les usages maritimes admis dans les différentes riveraines de la Méditerranée."

[6] In all these cases the cargo was paid. In case of enemy ships, the captor, having taken the cargo to a port of his country, usually claimed payment for the journey. The neutral owner of the cargo could also purchase the ship. See H. Wehberg, *supra* note 2, at 18.

also embodied in the *consolato del mare* of 1370. Until 1856, the date of the Paris Declaration, it remained unchanged.

Because of the increasing arms trade between belligerents and neutrals, the law of contraband soon began to develop. Either belligerent states unilaterally condemned neutral ships and goods that were considered contraband or they agreed to prohibit their subjects to engage in contraband trade.[7] The carriage of contraband did not in every case involve the condemnation of the ship and her cargo. According to a French ordinance of 1584, condemnation of contraband was lawful only if full compensation was paid. By a French ordinance of 1681 the condemnation of the ship as well as of her cargo that was not contraband was prohibited.[8]

In the sixteenth century, belligerents interfered with all transports destined for besieged places. Whereas in the beginning blockade was confined to fortified sea towns, belligerents later applied that method to parts of the coast in order to exclude any trade connections.[9] In those days, when there were no rules exempting enemy property from capture and condemnation, exclusively neutrals were affected by contraband regulations and by declarations of blockade. The purpose of such measures was, however, to harm the enemy and not to harm neutrals. Hence it was generally acknowledged that neutrals had to be informed about those measures in advance. After the distinction between enemy and neutral property had become accepted, it was necessary to introduce the right of visit and search which to a certain extent was also laid down in the *consolato del mare.*[10]

Whereas the partial exemption of neutrals from belligerent measures had thus become part of at least generally accepted customs, enemy property for a long time remained unprotected.[11] At the same time, states began to fight piracy, which made it necessary to distinguish between pirates on the one hand and those who were entitled to capture and to other prize measures on the other hand.

[7] *Ibid.*, 19.

[8] Wheaton, *Histoire des progrès du droit des gens en Europe*, 82 (1841).

[9] C. Dupuis, *Le droit de la guerre maritime d'après les doctrines anglaises contemporaines*, 180 (Paris, 1899).

[10] E. Nys, *op. cit. supra* note 3, at 230.

[11] E.g., according to Article 41 of the Magna Charta, with the outbreak of war enemy merchantmen are to be imprisoned and their goods are to be confiscated without payment of compensation. Later, however, according to the Statute of Staples merchantmen of importance for trade relations were given 40 days of grace to leave the country.

Accordingly, the exercise of measures of prize law was made subject to prior authorization — usually in the form of letters of reprisal and letters of marque. These were accompanied by certain control measures which were necessary in order to ensure that, for example, capture was exercised properly. Booty remained with the captor or buccaneer, who distributed it among his officers and crews. The legal portion of the sovereign gradually decreased and was then abolished altogether.[12]

The procedural and material principles of the law of prize laid down in the *consolato del mare* were originally developed by the Mediterranean towns and were then taken over by Northern and Western European powers, first by The Netherlands in their war against the Hanse in 1438, then, for example, by England and Sweden (Treaties of 1661 and 1666) and by England and Denmark (Treaty of 1670). With the increasing importance of sea power, however, those principles were soon adapted to the changed conditions. By the famous Ordonnance de la Marine of 1681 France with regard to states not having concluded special treaties on the matter unilaterally asserted the right to capture all goods on enemy ships and all ships carrying enemy cargo.[13] The Netherlands and Portugal, both very dependent on their sea trade, succeeded in mitigating those rules by entering into special agreements according to which enemy goods on board neutral ships were exempt from capture. Capture of neutral goods on board enemy ships were, however, subject to capture. Hence, the flag became decisive for establishing whether a ship and her cargo were exempt from capture or not.[14]

Since neither the rules of the *consolato del mare* nor the French rules or those laid down in treaties to which, for example, The Netherlands was a party, became generally accepted there was a considerable uncertainty about the law on the matter. On the other hand, since the fourteenth century sea traffic and trade had become that important that the great shipping companies had their merchant ships accompanied by warships.[15] In the seventeenth century especially Queen Christine of Sweden and then The Netherlands

---

[12] In England it was abolished by the Prize Act of 1708, in France by the Ordinance of 1756.

[13] This is the so-called French doctrine of hostile infection: "La robe d'ennemi confisque la robe de l'ami."

[14] See Wehberg, *supra* note 2, at 23.

[15] See E. Nys, *op. cit. supra* note 3, at 231.

introduced the convoy system for their respective merchantmen. The warships were ordered not to tolerate any visit and search of the merchant ships they accompanied. Their presence was considered as sufficient proof for the belligerent cruiser that the cargo was of an innocent character.[16]

For the development of the right of visit and search Article 17 of the 1659 Pyrenean Treaty between France and Spain played a decisive role because that provision influenced the law until the beginning of the twentieth century. The contents of the notion of contraband underwent a number of changes. Whereas France had a restrictive position with regard to booty, the contraband lists of the French ordinances of 1543 and 1584 as well as of the Ordonnance Touchant la Marine of 1681 comprised only ammunition. In a number of treaties, including the Pyrenean Treaty, that definition was also adopted. According to the Treaty of Utrecht, a number of articles, such as metals and material for ship repairs, were expressly excluded from the rules on contraband. In some bilateral treaties the parties even agreed on a comprehensive freedom of trade.[17] However, England continued to capture foodstuffs, sails, and metals as contraband.[18] Owing to the teachings of Hugo Grotius, who had introduced the distinction between absolute and conditional contraband, gradually other articles than weapons and ammunition were considered contraband.

Despite the influence those treaties may have had on the traditional law, the parties did not always adhere to them. For example, France, in her ordinance of 1744, abolished the principle "free ship, free goods." The same was true with regard to England, which applied that principle only to ships of those states that had concluded special agreements on the subject-matter. The contraband lists were extended considerably and comprised articles exempted by the Treaty of Utrecht.

Hence, until the nineteenth century there was no established and settled body of the law concerning measures of economic warfare at sea because the era of "armed neutralities" did not contribute to the emergence of generally accepted rules.[19] It was not before 1856 that states multilaterally agreed on certain rules that may be

---

[16] H. Wehberg, *supra* note 2, at 24.

[17] E.g., in the 1642 Treaty between England and Portugal and in the 1661 Treaty between Portugal and The Netherlands.

[18] E.g., in the 1625 Treaty of Southampton between England and The Netherlands.

[19] See the overview by K. H. Bernsten, *Das Seekriegsrecht*, 7 (Berlin, 1911).

considered the starting point of traditional law. Despite the importance of the Paris Declaration, this date is not absolute in the sense
that an examination of the traditional law could start from it leaving out of consideration the practice of states prior to 1856.

II TRADITIONAL LAW OF VISIT, SEARCH, DIVERSION, AND CAPTURE

Annihilation of the enemy's commerce being one of the great
aims of naval warfare,[20] the traditional law provides a set of measures of economic warfare that enable belligerents to achieve this
task. Accordingly, all merchant vessels, whether enemy or neutral,
may be stopped and searched or diverted into port. Private property
of the enemy, both ships and goods, found at sea outside neutral
territorial waters is liable to capture except when protected by some
customary or conventional rule of international law.[21] The right
to capture neutral merchant vessels and neutral goods, however,
is conferred on a belligerent in certain exceptional situations only.[22]
Therefore, a distinction has to be made between enemy ships and
goods on the one hand and neutral ships and goods on the other
hand. Certain measures of economic warfare are in conformity with
international law only when the ship or goods affected have enemy
character.[23]

A ENEMY CHARACTER OF VESSELS (AIRCRAFT) AND GOODS

Before elaborating on the traditional rules and principles governing the determination of enemy or neutral character of ships and
goods, one should consider two important aspects. First, these rules
are without prejudice to the traditional law of neutrality *stricto sensu;*
as will be seen, they only justify the conclusion that a ship or certain
goods may or may not be considered to be of enemy character.
Second, there was and presumably still is a principal difference between what may be considered the (traditional) Anglo-American

---

[20] C.J. Colombos, *The International Law of the Sea*, para. 594 (5th ed., London, 1962);
F. Berber, *Lehrbuch des Völkerrechts, Vol. II,* 183, 191 (Munich 1969); Oppen-
heim/Lauterpacht, *International Law,* Vol. II, at 458 (7th ed., London, 1952). See also
Lord Palmerston's speech to the House of Commons on March 17, 1862, Hansard
(Commons), 3rd Series, Vol. 165, coll. 1693-99; D. Steinicke, *Wirtschaftskrieg und Seekrieg*
(Hamburg, 1970).

[21] R.W. Tucker, *The Law of War and Neutrality at Sea,* 74 (Washington, 1957); Colombos,
supra, para. 599; Berber, *supra,* 194.

[22] See *infra* pp. 00-00.

[23] See, *inter alia,* Tucker, *op. cit. supra* note 21, at 75.

approach[24] for determining enemy character and the (traditional) continental European[25] approach. This difference stems from the fact that according to Anglo-American doctrine,[26] in contrast to the continental-European doctrine,[27] with the outbreak of war any intercourse with the enemy automatically becomes illegal.

General Rule

According to British prize law[28] and practice, the commercial domicile[29] of a merchant determines his hostile or neutral character independently of his origin, descent, place of birth, or nationality:[30] "where the protection and power are, there is the subjection. . ."[31] The names of enemy persons are included in so-called "black lists." Neutral and even British merchants having their domicile in enemy territory[32] are thus considered neutral and not hostile only "in the event of their clearly establishing and manifesting by their

[24] For a general overview see G. H. L. Fridman, *Enemy Status,* in 4 Int'l & Comp. L. Q. 613-28 (1955).

[25] Berber, *op. cit. supra* note 20, at 200.

[26] See, e.g. Oppenheim/Lauterpacht, *op. cit. supra* note 20, at 319.

[27] See, e.g., Berber, *op. cit. supra* note 20, at 204.

[28] Trading with the Enemy Act, 1914, 4 and 5 Geo. V, c. 87, and Trading with the Enemy, 1939, 2 and 3 Geo. V, c. 89.

[29] Whereas J. W. Garner, *International Law and the World War,* Vol. I, at 61 (London, 1929), speaks of "domicile" Oppenheim/Lauterpacht *op. cit. supra* note 20, at 272 assumes that enemy character is acquired "by being domiciled" in an enemy country. According to McNair, *Legal Effects of War,* 40 (3rd ed., Cambridge, 1948), "enemy" is "a person of any or no nationality voluntarily resident or present and carrying on business in territory owned or occupied by an enemy power. . . ."

[30] The Privy Council in the *Kara Deniz,* ([1922] B. & C.P.C. 1070) decided that property belonging to a neutral subject ought to be condemned as the owner had, by trading in Turkey, acquired a hostile commercial domicile there.
    The Trading with the Enemy Act of 1939 defines "enemy" as "any individual resident in enemy territory, any individual or body of persons (whether corporate or unincorporated) carrying on business in enemy territory or in any other place, if and so long as the body is controlled by a person who, under this section, is an enemy, and any body of persons constituted or incorporated in, or under the laws of, a State at war with His Majesty, but does not include any individual by reason only that he is an enemy subject."

[31] Sir James Marriott, *Le Théodore, Hay and Marriott,* 258, 261.

[32] "Enemy territory" under section 15 of the Trading with the Enemy Act of 1939 means "any area which is under the sovereignty of, or in occupation of, a Power with which His Majesty is at war not being an area in the occupation of His Majesty or of a Power allied with His Majesty."

acts an intention to leave the hostile country for the purpose of settling in a neutral country or in the Queen's Dominions."[33] With regard to corporations, the principles of the *Daimler* case[34] are of significance; accordingly, associations controlled by the enemy, even though not incorporated in an enemy territory, are deemed to be enemy if they are under the control of a person resident or carrying on business in enemy territory.[35]

The United States trading with the enemy legislation[36] more or less follows the same patterns by defining "enemy" as any person resident within the territory of any nation with which the United States is at war, or resident outside the United States and doing business within such territory, and enemy subjects, wherever resident or wherever doing business, whom the United States President by proclamation includes within the term "enemy."[37] Although the United States had strongly opposed the introduction of black lists by Great Britain,[38] it adopted that system when a belligerent.[39] As to the enemy character of corporations and the different tests applied to them, corporations are deemed to be enemies if they are incorporated under enemy law, do business in an enemy country, are controlled by enemy subjects,[40] or are proclaimed as enemies by the government.[41] However, non-enemy shareholders

---

[33] McNair, *International Law Opinions*, Vol. III, at 27 (Cambridge, 1956).

[34] *Daimler Co.* v. *Consolidated Tyre and Rubber Co.*, [1916] 2 A.C. 307 (H.L.). Note, however, that originally the so-called control theory had been rejected by the House of Lords.

[35] C.J. Colombos, *op. cit. supra* note 20, para. 631.

[36] Trading with the Enemy Act of October 6, 1917, in 12 Am. J. Int'l L. suppl., 27 (1918), and Trading with the Enemy Act of December 18, 1941.

[37] In 1948 section 39 was amended (Public Law No. 896) and the nationality principle for the "policy of non-return" was introduced. cf. *Guessefeld* v. *McGrath* (1952), 19 AILC 325.

[38] Berber, *op. cit. supra* note 20, at 201; Tansill, *America Goes to War* 535 et seq. (1938).

[39] On January 12, 1945, the American "black list" comprised 14,543 names; see J. Stone, *Legal Control of International Conflicts* 452 (1954).

[40] Originally the United States Trading with the Enemy Act, 1917, did not include the control test (see also *Schulz Co.* v. *Raines & Co.* (1917, 15 AILC 215; *Behn, Meyer & Co.* v. *Miller* (1925), AILC 275). However, the United States Supreme Court did apply it, arguing that some changes in section 5(b) of the Act effected by the first War Powers Act, 1941, were intended to introduce it (*Clark* v. *Uebersee Finanz-Korporation*, 332 U.S. 480 (1947); *Kaufmann* v. *Société Internationale* (1952), 19 AILC 473).

[41] Cf. *Society for the Propagation of the Gospel* v. *The Town of New Haven* (1823), 19 AILC 41; *Janson* v. *Driefontein* (1902), 4 BILC 693); J. M. Mössner, "Enemies and Enemy Subjects," in: R. Bernhardt (ed.), *Encyclopedia of Public International Law*, Instalment 3, at 163-67, 163 (1982) (cited hereafter as EPIL).

are not affected.[42]

Under the control test, which was applied by the Mixed Arbitral Tribunals after the First World War as well as by the majority of states in the Second World War, a corporation not registered under enemy law or doing business in enemy countries is nevertheless to be treated as an enemy corporation if controlled by enemies. The person controlling the corporation must be an enemy and have effective control.[43]

On the other hand, the continental European doctrine — at least in the early twentieth century — adhered to the principle of nationality as long as individuals were concerned.[44] With regard to corporations, the German Ordinance of January 15, 1940,[45] for example, applies the theory of control.

At the Hague Peace Conferences of 1899 and 1907 the term "enemy" was used exclusively as referring to the adversary state.[46] Article 16 of Hague Convention V, which was not ratified by Great Britain and hence not applicable in the First World War, defines neutrals as nationals of a state not party to the war. Owing to the different notions in the national legislation of states, however, no generally accepted concept developed in international law. Since at the Hague the attempt to reach agreement with regard to neutral persons failed because of a British reservation to Hague Convention IV, states are under no restriction in determining the enemy character of persons by different tests and may choose the test that they consider most suitable for their needs.[47] This view was shared by the Institut de Droit International. According to Article 51, paragraph 3, of the 1913 Oxford Manual, "each State must declare, not later than the outbreak of hostilities, whether the enemy or neutral character of the owner of the goods is determined by his place of

---

[42] 343 U.S. 156 (1952).

[43] *Parfums Tosca* case, Ann. Dig., Vol. 9, at 557; *Aeroxon* case, 20 ILR 615 (1955).

[44] Berber, *op. cit. supra* note 20, at 200; M. Domke, "Feindbegriff," in K. Strupp/ H.-J. Schlochauer, *Wörterbuch des Völkerrechts,* Vol. I, at 509 (2nd ed., Berlin, 1960) (cited as hereafter WVR I). At the beginning of the Second World War, the German Ordinance of January 15, 1940, as well as the French Ordinance of September 1, 1939, combined the principle of nationality with the principle of domicile.

[45] RGBl. 1940 I, at 191; 12, para. 1, states: "wenn das Unternehmen unmittelbar oder mittelbar unter mazgebendem feindlichen Einfluigers steht."

[46] Cf. Regulations on Land Warfare, annexed to Convention IV, Arts. 2, 4, 42, 45; Convention VI, Arts. 2, 3, 4; Convention IX, Art. 2; Convention XI, Art. 5. The approach of referring to the belligerent party as such dates back to Hugo Grotius: see his *De jure belli ac pacis,* Liber III, Caput III, 1.

[47] J. M. Mössner, "Enemies and Enemy Subjects," in EPIL 3, at 163-67, 165.

residence or his nationality."[48]

Enemy Character of Merchant Vessels (and Aircraft)

As the Privy Council stated in *The Unitas,* "prima facie, the flying of an enemy flag in wartime is conclusive of the nationality of a ship."[49] This is the generally accepted rule, which accordingly is also laid down in Article 57, paragraph 1, of the 1909 London Declaration,[50] in Article 51, paragraph 1, of the 1913 Oxford Manual,[51] and, for example, in Article 6, paragraph 1, of the German Prize Ordinance of 1939.[52]

Under international law each state may determine for itself the conditions on which it will grant its nationality to a merchant ship.[53] According to the United States Supreme Court, this is "perhaps the most venerable and universal rule of maritime law."[54] The flag, however, is only one piece of evidence of a ship's nationality; it does not absolutely prove it unless accompanied by the ship's papers showing the regular registration of the ship in one of the ports of her flag State.[55] Hence, for example, British prize courts were entitled, in circumstances justifying suspicion that the flag and papers had been assumed for the purpose of disguising the real character of the vessel, to inquire closely into its real ownership and effective control.[56] If the vessel belongs — partly — to enemy persons, the entitlement to fly a neutral flag according to the laws of the flag state does not exempt it from condemnation.

[48] AIDI, Vol. 26 (1913), pp. 64-72; reprinted in N. Ronzitti (ed.), *The Law of Naval Warfare,* 278-328 (Dordrecht/Boston/London, 1988).
[49] Privy Council, *The Unitas,* [1950] A.C. 536, 552, 558. See also U.S. Supreme Court, *Lauritzen v. Lauritzen,* 345 U.S. 571 (1953); Berber, *op. cit. supra* note 20, at 201; Tucker, *op. cit. supra* note 21, at 76.
[50] Declaration concerning the Laws of Naval Warfare, signed at London, February 26, 1909; Text in 3 Am. J. Int'l L., Suppl., 179-220 (1909), and in Ronzitti (ed.), *op. cit. supra* note 48, at 224-56.
[51] AIDI, Vol. 26 (1913), 64-72.
[52] RGBl, 1939, I, at 1585; see also C. C. Hyde, *International Law,* Vol. 3, at 2075 (2nd ed., Boston, 1945).
[53] The Hague Permanent Court of Arbitration, Arbitral Award of August 8, 1905, in *The Muscat Dhows* case. See also G. Breuer, "Flaggenrecht, Internationales," in WVR I, 532.
[54] U.S. Supreme Court, *Lauritzen v. Lauritzen,* 345 U.S. 571 (1953).
[55] Tucker, *op. cit. supra* note 21, at 76; Berber, *op. cit. supra* note 20 at 203; Colombos, *op. cit. supra* note 20, para. 310.
[56] Colombos, *supra,* para. 604. See also *The St. Tudno,* [1916] P. 271 (Sir Samuel Evans).
[57] H. Pflüger, "Die 'feindliche Eigenschaft' von Schiff und Ladung in der englischen Prisenrechtsprechung des Weltkriegs," (Hamburg, 1929).

Article 6 of the 1939 German Prize Ordinance emphasizes the entitlement to fly a certain flag. Only if a ship is not entitled to fly the flag is its neutral or enemy character determined by the nationality of its owner. When the character of a ship cannot be clearly established, it is presumed to be of enemy character (Article 6, paragraph 2).

With regard to transfer to a neutral flag, Articles 55 and 56 of the 1909 London Declaration distinguish between a transfer effected before and a transfer effected after the outbreak of hostilities.[58] According to Article 55, the former is valid unless it is proved that the transfer was made in order to evade the consequences to which an enemy vessel as such is exposed. There is, however, a rebuttable presumption that the transfer is void, if the transfer to a neutral flag has taken place less than sixty days before the outbreak of hostilities and if the bill of sale is not on board the ship. If the transfer to a neutral flag was effected more than thirty days before the outbreak of hostilities there is an absolute presumption that it is valid if it is unconditional, complete, and in conformity with the laws of the countries concerned, and if its effect is such that neither the control of, nor the profits arising from the employment of, the vessel remain in the same hands as before the transfer.[59] According to Article 56, the transfer of an enemy vessel to a neutral flag, effected after the outbreak of hostilities, is void unless it is proved that the transfer was not made in order to evade the consequences to which an enemy ship is exposed. There is, however, an absolute presumption that such a transfer is void[60] (1) if the transfer has been made during a voyage or in a blockaded port; (2) if a right to repurchase or recover the vessel is reserved to the vendor; and (3) if the requirements of the municipal law governing the right to fly the flag under which the vessel is sailing have not been fulfilled. Thus, the burden of proof falls on the belligerent in respect of transfers prior to the outbreak of war, and on the neutral in respect of transfers made subsequently.[61]

Article 7, paragraph 1, of the German Prize Ordinance of 1939 considers any transfer to a neutral flag void if the transfer was made

---

[58] Hyde, *op. cit. supra* note 52, Vol. 3, at 2079.

[59] Similar rules are laid down in Art. 52 of the 1913 Oxford Manual.

[60] See also Art. 52 of the 1913 Oxford Manual.

[61] Cf. the British report of March 1, 1909, cited in F. Kalshoven, "Commentary on the 1909 London Declaration," in N. Ronzitti (ed.), *op. cit. supra* note 48, at 257-75, 267.

in view of the conditions of war. Insofar as this formulation is concerned, there is no considerable difference from the 1909 London Declaration. This is also true with regard to the presumption laid down in Article 7, paragraph 2. According to this rule, a transfer is presumed to have been made in view of the conditions of war (1) if made after the law of prize has taken effect, and (2) if effected within sixty days before that date and if (a) the bill of sale is not on board, or (b) the transfer is not unconditional or not complete, or (c) the disposition over, and the profits arising from the employment of, the vessel remain in the same hands as before the transfer.

A similar but probably more flexible approach underlies the rule that Great Britain applied: property transferred from an enemy to a neutral must be *bona fide* and absolutely transferred; there must be a sale divesting the enemy of all further interest in it, and anything tending to continue this interest vitiates a contract of this description altogether.[62] A similar view was taken by the U.S. Department of State, in a Memorandum of August 7, 1914,[63] stating that "[a] neutral has a perfect right to purchase the merchant vessels of belligerents during a state of war, when such purchase is bona fide, without defeasance, reservation of a title or interest and intended to convey and perfect a permanent title to the purchaser." France's practice was to refuse to recognize the validity of any transfer made in time of war. Transfers made prior to the outbreak of hostilities were generally treated as valid if carried out in accordance with the municipal laws. In 1912, however, Articles 55 and 56 of the 1909 London Declaration were incorporated into Article 13 of the Instructions of December 19, 1912.[64]

Hence, with regard to the traditional law governing the determination of enemy character of ships, there is general agreement that every ship is vested with the nationality of the state whose flag it is flying. There are, however, differences with regard to cases of suspicion, especially if there has been a transfer from a belligerent to a neutral flag. The provisions of the 1909 London Declaration, which may be considered an attempt to compromise differences in state practice, did not successfully contribute to the establish-

---

[62] Colombos, *op. cit. supra* note 20, para. 609; see also Lord Stowell in *The Sechs Geschwister*, [1801] 4 C. Rob. 100.

[63] U.S. Dept. of State, Memorandum of August 7, 1914, Congressional Record, August 11, 1914, at 14758; see also Tucker, *op. cit. supra* note 21, at 78.

[64] In the case of *The Dacia*, the French Court of Prize in its decision of August 5, 1915 applied Art. 56 of the London Declaration: 22 Rev. gén. [1915].

ment of a generally accepted rule of international law.[65]

Enemy Character of Goods

The enemy character of goods found on board enemy merchant vessels is determined by the neutral or enemy character of the owner. With regard to this old rule, which is laid down in Article 58 of the 1909 London Declaration, the above stated differences between the Anglo-American and the continental European approach for determining the enemy character of persons become decisive.[66] The London Conference failed to resolve this controversy.[67] Whereas in Anglo-American law and jurisprudence the enemy character of goods is ascertained by the domicile of their owner,[68] according to the German Prize Ordinance of 1939 it depends on the nationality of the owner (Article 8, paragraph 1), the domicile being decisive only in cases where the owner is a stateless person or a corporation.

In the absence of proof, goods found on board enemy merchant vessels are presumed to be enemy goods: ''Robe d'ennemi confisque robe d'ami.'' This rebuttable presumption dates back to Hugo Grotius.[69] It is laid down in Article 59 of the 1909 London Declaration and was applied by the prize courts during the two world wars.[70] Thus, it is incumbent upon the neutral claimant to establish that the cargo carried in the enemy ship belongs to him.

In state practice the question whether or not ownership in the goods has passed is determined by the municipal law of the parties involved or in accordance with the municipal law of the captor, if the goods were sold prior to the outbreak of, and without anticipa-

---

[65] Berber, *op. cit. supra* note 20, at 193 f.; Tucker, *op. cit. supra* note 21, at 80 et seq..

[66] See Tucker, *supra*, 81; Hyde, *op. cit. supra* note 52, at 2085; F. Kalshoven, ''Commentary on the 1909 London Declaration,'' in Ronzitti (ed.), *op. cit. supra* note 48, at 257-75, 267.

[67] See Tucker, *supra*, 81; Kalshoven, *supra*, 267; G. Schramm, *Das Prisenrecht* 127 (Berlin, 1913).

[68] Colombos, *op. cit. supra* note 20, para. 605. E.g., in *The Roumanian*, [1915] 1 Ll.P.C. 191 (Sir Samuel Evans), held that goods may be confiscated even when on board British ships.

[69] Hugo Grotius, *op. cit. supra* note 46, Caput VI, VI.: ''Quare quod dici solet, hostiles censeri res in hostium navibus repertas, non ita accipi debet quasi certa sit juris gentium lex, sed ut praesumtionem quandam indicet, quae tamen validis in contrarium probationibus possit elidi.''

[70] Colombos, *op. cit. supra* note 20, para. 616. Note, however, that according to Art. 8, para. 2, of the German Prize Ordinance of 1939, the presumption seems to apply to goods found on board neutral merchant vessels as well, since it only refers to goods in general and not to goods found on board enemy merchant vessels.

tion of, hostilities.[71] With regard to the transfer of goods made after the outbreak of war or in contemplation of hostilities, the rule laid down in Article 60, paragraph 1, of the 1909 London Declaration comes into operation.[72] Accordingly, enemy goods on board an enemy vessel retain their enemy character until they reach their destination, notwithstanding any transfer effected after the outbreak of hostilities while the goods are being forwarded.[73] They retain their neutral character only if, prior to capture, a former neutral owner exercises, on the bankruptcy of an existing enemy owner, a recognized legal right to recover the goods (Article 60, paragraph 2, of the London Declaration).

British and American courts have always disregarded mortgages, liens, or any other special rights "created by contracts or dealings between individuals."[74] Or, as Sir Samuel Evans put it: "upon the authorities, upon principle and upon grounds of convenience and practice, claims based on liens, mortgages, insurance or any other security, must be rejected."[75] The only exceptions relate to liens for civil salvage and general average, in which cases the prize courts enjoy jurisdiction to reward salvors on the ground that they are questions of the laws of nations and materially different from mariners' contracts.[76]

B VISIT, SEARCH, AND DIVERSION

Visit and Search

Being directed against the enemy's commerce, it is in the nature of naval warfare that neutral merchant shipping is affected by the prohibition of carrying contraband and by the institution of a blockade.[77] The means to control and enforce these measures is conveyed upon the belligerents by the right of stopping, visiting, and searching all merchant ships[78] in those areas of the sea where

[71] Tucker, *op. cit. supra* note 21, at 85.
[72] See also *ibid.*, 86.
[73] The same applies according to Art. 9 of the 1939 German Prize Ordinance.
[74] Cf. Privy Council, *The Odessa*, [1916] 1 A.C. 145.
[75] *The Marie Glaeser*, [1914] P. 218.
[76] Colombos, *op. cit. supra* note 20, para. 606; H. Krüger, "Salvage," in WVR III, 156; see also *The Two Friends*, [1799] 1 C. Rob. 271; *The Prins Knud*, [1942] A.C. 667 (P.C.).
[77] The present article will not deal with this method. Contraband is being dealt with *infra* pp. 317-18.
[78] It is an incontestable right of the lawfully commissioned cruisers of a belligerent nation to visit and search all merchant vessels, "whatever be the ships, whatever be the cargoes, whatever be the destinations" (Lord Stowell in *The Maria*, [1799]

the law of naval warfare applies. Among those international lawyers publishing on the traditional law, there is almost unanimous
agreement that the right to exercise control over all merchant vessels arises from the fact that states refuse to undertake any responsibility for trade in which their subjects engage.[79] The belligerent,
being left to protect himself against all intervention in war by neutral merchants and shipowners to his disadvantage, is considered
to be defending himself by the right of visit and search.[80]
   It is important to emphasize that, despite President Wilson's
speech of January 8, 1918,[81] until the end of the Second World War,
the freedom of the high seas never did constitute an obstacle to the
right of visit and search (and capture) in times of war.[82] It was generally agreed that the freedom of navigation was subject to other rules
of international law. Traditionally, these other applicable rules included belligerent rights in wartime, such as the traditional belligerent rights of visit and search (and capture).[83] On the other hand,
the right of visit and search was not generally[84] considered unlimited

---

1 C. Rob. 340, 360). Visit and search is not an independent right but "a right growing
out of, and ancillary to, the greater right of capture" (Chief Justice Marshall in
The Nereide [1815], 9 Cranch. 388, 427). See also U. Scheuner, "Durchsuchung von
Schiffen," in WVR I, 407.

[79] Hyde, *op. cit. supra* note 52, at 1958; Colombos, *op. cit. supra* note 20, para. 866;
Tucker, *op. cit. supra* note 21, at 332; *Oppenheim/Lauterpacht, op. cit. supra* note 20, at
848; Ch. Rousseau, *Le droit des conflits armés,* 318.

[80] Schramm, *op. cit. supra* note 67, at 298; Colombos, *supra,* para. 866.

[81] "Absolute freedom of navigation upon the seas, outside territorial waters, alike
in peace and in war, except as the seas may be closed in whole or in part by international action for the enforcement of international covenants"; cf. Arnold-Forster,
The New Freedom of the Seas 72-73 (1942).

[82] "it is a fundamental principle of international maritime law that, *except* by special
convention or in *time of war,* interference by a cruiser with a foreign vessel pursuing a lawful avocation on the high seas is unwarranted and illegal and constitutes
a violation of the sovereignty of the country whose flag the vessel flies." (Anglo-
American Claims Commission, cases of *The Jessie, The Thomas F. Bayard,* and *The
Pescawha,* Nielsen Report (1926), at 479-80 (emphasis added)).

[83] See *inter alia* O. Rojahn, "Ships, Visit and Search," in EPIL 4, at 224-26; R. Ott-
müller, *Die Anwendung von Seekriegsrecht in militärischen Konflikten seit 1945* 35 (Hamburg,
1978). Even Hugo Grotius, who is considered to be the staunchest supporter of
the freedom of navigation, seems indirectly to have accepted certain limitations
if an activity on the high seas is harmful or dangerous to another: "Et si quic-
quam prohibere posset, puta, piscaturam, qua dici quodammodo potest pisces ex-
hauriri, at navigationem non potest, per quam mari nihil perit." (Mare liberum,
Caput V.) "Unde cum navigatio nemini possit esse nociva nisi ipsi naviganti, par
est ut nemini possit, aut debeat impediri, ne in re sua natura libera, sibique ne-
mine noxia navigantium libertatem impediat. . ." (*ibid.,* Caput VII).

[84] See Oppenheim/Lauterpacht, *op. cit. supra* note 20, at 849; it is maintained that

but subject to considerations of proportionality, for example, as laid down in Article 2, no. 86, of the French instructions of December 19, 1912. "Toutefois, suivant les circonstances, notamment suivant les parages où vous vous trouverez, où suivant l'éloignement du théâtre des opérations, il peut arriver que vous ayez des motifs de supposer que la visite ne peut entraîner aucune saisie. Dans ce cas, l'exercice du droit de visite peut n'être qu'une vexation inutile dont il est préférable de s'abstenir."

Entitlement to Exercise the Right of Visit and Search

According to the traditional law, during war — and since an armistice does not terminate a war, during its existence[85] — visit and search may be performed by duly commissioned warships and by military aircraft.[86] A submarine, being a public vessel of war, is entitled to exercise the right of visit and search of merchant vessels subject, however, to the fundamental condition that it should observe strictly all the rules laid down for surface warships.[87] Military aircraft are also entitled to exercise the right of visit and search.[88] For practical reasons, in most cases an aircraft can only divert ships into port. Under the conditions of modern warfare at sea, however, visit and search can very effectively be exercised by helicopters.

Ships that May Be Visited and Searched

In principle, all merchant ships, whether enemy or neutral, may be stopped, visited and, if the examination of the ship's papers has left the officer unsatisfied about the character of the ship and its

---

"whether the part of the open sea in which a belligerent man-of-war meets with a neutral merchantman is near or far away from that part of the world where hostilities are actually taking place makes no difference, so long as there is suspicion against the vessel."

[85] See inter alia Colombos, *op. cit. supra* note 20, para. 868; Oppenheim/Lauterpacht, *supra*, 546.

[86] Lord Stowell in *The Maria,* [1799] 1 C. Rob. 340, 360; Tucker, *op. cit. supra* note 21, at 333; Colombos, *supra*, para. 866; Oppenheim/Lauterpacht, *op. cit. supra* note 20, at 848; see also the provisions laid down in Hague Convention VII relating to the Conversion of Merchant Ships into Warships. Privateering had officially been abolished by the Paris Declaration respecting Maritime Law of April 16, 1856.

[87] Cf. Colombos, *supra*, para. 868; see also U. Scheuner, "Durchsuchung von Schiffen," in WVR I, at 407-08. The equation of submarines with surface warships follows from the 1936 London Procès-Verbal relating to the rules of submarine warfare set forth in Part IV of the Treaty of London of April 22, 1930 (173 LNTS 353-57; printed in Ronzitti, *op cit. supra* note 48, at 352.

[88] Hyde, *op. cit. supra* note 52, at 1971; Scheuner, *supra,* 407-8.

cargo, searched. With regard to neutral warships and other public vessels operating in the service of the neutral's armed forces, however, there is general agreement that they are exempt from visit and search.[89] Even though all enemy merchant vessels are *prima facie* liable to capture, the procedure of visit and search also applies to them, first, because belligerents are obliged, before they apply force for the purpose of capturing them, to call upon these ships to stop and to submit to search and second, because, even though the ship may be an enemy ship, it may belong to a class that is immune from capture.[90]

Whereas neutral merchant ships travelling alone may be visited and searched in any case,[91] different rules apply if they travel under convoy.[92] Two situations have to be kept apart. Neutral merchant vessels under the convoy of a belligerent warship are subject to the same treatment as enemy merchant ships; travelling under enemy convoy is held to be sufficient evidence of forcible resistance to the right of stoppage, visit, search, and capture which involves in all cases the condemnation of the vessel.[93] With regard to neutral merchant vessels under neutral convoy, there had been a tendency to exempt them from search.[94] However, when on July 7, 1916,

[89] Cf. art. 32 of the 1913 Oxford Manual; Tucker, *op. cit. supra* note 21, at 334; Colombos, *op. cit. supra* note 20, para. 870; Oppenheim/Lauterpacht, *op. cit. supra* note 20, at 849.

[90] Colombos, *supra,* para. 883. With regard to the classes of protected enemy ships, see *infra* pp. 311-14.

[91] In the 1913 arbitration between France and Italy in the case of *The Carthage* (Award of the Arbitral Tribunal of the Permanent Court of Arbitration at The Hague in the *Case of the French Mail Steamer Carthage,* Am. J. Int'l L., 623-29 (1913); RIAA, Vol. II, at 449-61), the arbitral tribunal held: "d'après les principes universellement admis, un bâtiment de guerre belligérant a, en thèse générale et sans conditions particulières, le droit d'arrêter en pleine mer un navire de commerce neutre et de procéder à la visite pour s'assurer s'il observe les règles sur la neutralité, spécialement au point de vue de la contrebande."

[92] For a general overview, see R. Stödter, *Flottengeleit im Seekrieg* (Hamburg, 1936), and R. Stödter, "Convoy," in EPIL 3, at 128-30.

[93] Art. 63 of the 1909 London Declaration. See also Lord Stowell in *The Maria,* [1799] 1 C. Rob. 340; the decision of the U.S. German Mixed Claims Commission, United States, *Garland Steamship Corp., and Others* v. *Germany* (1924), 7 RIAA 73; *The Motano,* 7 RIAA 83; Berber, *op. cit. supra* note 20, at 195; Stödter, *supra,* 63.

[94] Especially during the eighteenth century by states adopting a position of armed neutrality. The Greco-German Mixed Arbitral Tribunal, in the *Kyriakides* case, Recueil des décisions des Tribunaux Mixtes, Vol. 8, at 349, 351 (1929), held, that in cases where neutral merchant ships wish to protect themselves against submarines, they should appeal to their own government in order to obtain a convoy for their flag, and it was said that this was a measure of protection expressly indi-

Great Britain renounced the Declaration of London, it announced that it would henceforth observe the historic and admitted law of nations. Therefore, British prize courts maintained the position that neutral merchant ships under neutral convoy are subject to the right of visit and search. Moreover, in the case of *The Maria*[95] and of *The Elsebe,*[96] the principle was reaffirmed that resistance by the convoying men-of-war is considered as implying the resistance of the convoyed merchant vessels, even if the latter do not in fact resist visit and search. Hence, the rules laid down in Articles 61 and 62 of the 1909 London Declaration, in Article 56 of the Harvard Draft on Rights and Duties of Neutral States in Naval and Aerial War,[97] as well as, for example, in Article 34 of the 1939 German Prize Ordinance, have not become incorporated into the generally accepted body of international law. It thus remained an unsettled matter in state practice whether or not the right of visit and search may be exercised upon neutral merchant vessels under convoy of neutral warships of the same nationality.[98]

Resistance to Visit and Search

On the one hand, enemy merchant ships have an uncontested right to resist capture and, since these are the first stages in the capture of such ships, to resist visit, search, and approach.[99] On the other hand, an enemy merchant ship that refuses or opposes visit by force must take the consequences of its action. By the traditional law, a deliberate and continued resistance to search is followed by the legal consequence of the condemnation (and even destruction)[100] of the vessel and its cargo.[101]

---

cated by art. 61 of the Declaration of London. See also Scheuner, *supra* note 87, at 408; Schramm, *op. cit. supra* note 67, at 300.

[95] [1799] 1 C. Rob. 340.

[96] [1804] 5 C. Rob. 174.

[97] 33 Am. J. Int'l L., Suppl., 166-817 (1939).

[98] This view is taken, e.g., by Berber, *op. cit. supra* note 20, at 195; Colombos, *op. cit. supra* note 20, para. 873; and R. Stödter, "Convoy," in EPIL 3, at 129. However, M. M. Whiteman, *Digest of International Law*, Vol. 11, at p. 37 (1968), takes the view that "the right of a neutral state to convoy its merchant vessels is generally recognized in international law."

[99] Oppenheim/Lauterpacht, *op. cit. supra* note 20, at 467.

[100] This follows from the 1936 London Procès-Verbal.

[101] Pierce Higgins, *Defensively Armed Merchant Ships*, 25; Colombos, *op. cit. supra* note 20, para. 884; Schönborn, "Der Widerstand feindlicher Handelsschiffe gegen Visitationen und Aufbringung," in AöR 1918, at 161; W. Kaak, *Der gewaltsame Widerstand feindlicher Handelsschiffe gegen prisenrechtliche Maznahmen,* (Kiel, 1952).

Neutral merchant vessels are under an obligation to submit without resistance to visit and search.[102] If they attempt flight, the warship is entitled to employ sufficient force to stop them. It follows from Article 63 of the 1909 London Declaration and from state practice that mere flight does not involve the capture of the vessel, though it may be considered sufficiently suspicious to cause the commander of the warship to detain it.[103] Forcible resistance on the part of a neutral merchant ship to visit and search is an act of hostility and renders it liable to capture and even destruction.[104]

Search in Port/Diversion and Navicerts

Because of the increased size of vessels, visit and search on the high seas and, because of ingenious arrangements that were made to disguise their true nature, the determination of enemy or contraband character of cargoes became increasingly difficult in the two world wars. In addition, warships exercising the right of visit and search on the high seas were exposed to submarine and aircraft attacks. For these reasons,[105] the British and Allied Powers claimed that search at sea, except in rare cases, was impossible and that the diversion and detention in port for the purpose of search was in reality less a new right than an adaptation of existing rights to modern conditions of commerce and navigation.[106] Despite initial, especially American,[107] protests against the diversion and search-

---

[102] Berber, *op. cit. supra* note 20, at 194 f.; Y. Dinstein, "Neutrality in Sea Warfare," in EPIL 4, at 19-28, 24.

[103] See *inter alia The Maria* [1799] 1 C. Rob. 340.

[104] Berber, *op. cit. supra* note 20, at 195; Oppenheim/Lauterpacht, *op. cit. supra* note 20, at 856.

[105] Tucker, *op. cit. supra* note 21, at 340, believes that "the substantial and compelling reason for diversion was that little or no evidence to support a case of seizure — let alone for later condemnation — could be worked up by restricting attention to the ship's papers and to the nature of the cargo carried. In the vast majority of instances where vessels were encountered bound for a neutral port, and carrying cargo to be delivered to a neutral consignee, the ship's papers themselves furnished no real assurance of the ultimate destination of the cargo. Instead, the evidence necessary to justify seizure normally could come only from external sources. Not infrequently, this information was collected prior to the act of visit. More often, however, it could be gathered only after a vessel had been diverted to a belligerent contraband control base."

[106] J. Wolf, "Ships, Diverting and Ordering into Port," in EPIL 4, at 223-24; U. Scheuner, "Kursanweisung," in WVR II, at 385; Colombos, *op. cit. supra* note 20, para. 887. With regard to state practice during the world wars, see *ibid.*, paras. 889 et seq.

[107] At the beginning of the First World War, the United States, then a neutral, protested against the British practice of diverting neutral vessels into port for search.

ing of ships in port, this practice soon was adopted in the prize rules of a considerable number of states.[108] For example, the German Oberprisenhof in *The Star* and *The Bertha Elisabeth* dismissed an application for compensation based on groundless diversion of neutral merchant vessels.[109] It may be added that, despite statements to the contrary,[110] the practice of diversion being based on the traditional right of visit and search, there were no substantial limitations on its exercise. Hence, "the difference between the indiscriminate diversion of merchant vessels and diversion in circumstances (usually derived from external sources) held to create sufficient reason to justify search is surely one bordering on sophistry."[111]

On the one hand, diversion and detention entail a considerable financial loss for the neutral vessel diverted from its course. On the other hand, belligerents are confronted with the choice of "either to permit goods to enter neutral ports, part of which are certainly destined to find their way into enemy hands, or to impose rigid controls upon such commerce at the risk of interfering on occasion with what is undeniably legitimate neutral trade."[112] This dilemma was partially resolved by Great Britain and its allies by the introduction of an alternative system, which is considered "the most promising method by which friction between neutrals and belligerents could be avoided,"[113] namely the system of "navicerts."[114]

In a letter dated November 7, 1914, the State Department claimed that "search should be made on the high seas at the time of the visit and . . . the conclusion of the search should rest upon the evidence found in the ship and investigation and not upon circumstances ascertained from external sources." See the exchange of notes between Great Britain and the United States in 9 Am. J. Int'l L., Spec. Suppl., 55 (1915); 10 Am. J. Int'l L., Spec. Suppl., 73 (1916).

[108] Wolf, *supra* note 106; Tucker, *op. cit. supra* note 21, at 340; see also *The Zamora*, [1916] 2 A.C. 77 (P.C.); *The Attiki*, Ann. Dig., Vol. 12 (1943-45), at 473; Arts. 60-63 of the 1939 German Prize Ordinance; Art. 2 of the British Prize Rules of 1939; Art. 107 of the French Prize Rules of 1934; Art. 182 of the Italian Prize Rules of 1938.

[109] *Entscheidungen des Oberprisenhofs*, Bd. 1, at 52, 55.

[110] Even British authors have steadily maintained that diversion must not be undertaken indiscriminately. In *The Bernisse* and *The Elve*, [1921] 458, the Privy Council made clear that under certain circumstances diversion could be held to be unjustified. In *The Mim* (Ann. Dig. (1947), Case No. 134, at 311), the British Prize Court held that "in the absence of reasonable suspicion the ship must be allowed to proceed."

[111] Tucker, *op. cit. supra* note 21, at 341.

[112] *Ibid.*, 280.

[113] Colombos, *op. cit. supra* note 20, para. 898.

[114] See H. Ritchie, *The "Navicert" System during the World War* (1938); J. V. Lovitt, "The Allied Blockade," II Dept. of State Bull. 597 (1944); G. G. Fitzmaurice, "Some

The possession of this certificate facilitates the passage of the cargoes concerned; especially delays for further inquiries are eliminated.[115] The same system was adopted by Great Britain during the Second World War,[116] but, from August 1, 1942, the navicert system was linked to the "ship's warrants" scheme.[117] Thus, the navicert system, which was originally offered as a convenience to a neutral shipper as an alternative to the delays incident to contraband detention, "developed into a complete control of neutral trade. No import of a commodity would be navicerted if it exceeded the quota or if either the consignor or consignee were objectionable. Even the 'end use' within the neutral country was controlled if desirable. Exports were similarly rigidly controlled."[118] At the beginning of the Second World War, Germany introduced a system analogous to the British navicert system, but without the far-reaching controls connected with ship navicerts and ship's warrants.[119]

The advantages of such a system of certificates, however, is limited to the belligerent issuing them and the neutral accepting them. With regard to the other belligerent power, the possession of navicerts by a neutral merchantman gives the former sufficient ground for suspecting the latter of being involved in the war effort of the adversary or of rendering unneutral assistance.[120] At the beginning of the Second World War, neutral governments such as Switzerland, Sweden, The Netherlands, and Belgium opposed reintroduction

---

Aspects of Modern Contraband Control and the Law of Prize,'' in 22 BYIL 83 (1945); D. Steinicke, *Kriegsbedingte Risiken der neutralen Seeschiffahrt,* (Hamburg, 1968); D. Steinicke, *Das Navicertsystem* (Hamburg, 1966).

[115] Tucker, *op. cit. supra* note 21, at 280.

[116] Great Britain introduced it in November 1939. The British Order in Council of July 31, 1940, declared that goods that were not covered by a valid navicert would be liable to seizure.

[117] R. Stödter, "Safe-Conduct and Safe Passage," in EPIL 4, at 193-96, 194.

[118] Lovitt, *supra* note 114, at 601.

[119] D. Steinicke, *Das Navicertsystem* 277; Stödter, *supra* note 117, at 195.

[120] When in the First World War Germany issued safe-conducts for ships, the ships having accepted German control were considered by the United States to have lost their neutral character. According to a French decree of August 27, 1918 (Journal officiel, August 8, 1918, at 613) and an Italian decree of October 10, 1918 (Gazetta ufficiale, November 25, 1918, No. 277), neutral vessels that placed themselves under enemy control were considered, in the absence of proof to the contrary, to be navigating in the interest of the enemy and were liable to capture and condemnation. The German Supreme Prize Tribunal in *The Ole Wegger* (Ann. Dig., Vol. 12 (1943-45), at 532) decided that the acceptance of a British ship's warrant constituted subjection of a vessel to the enemy's control and therefore unneutral assistance.

of the certificate system and prohibited their subjects from submitting to investigations by foreign authorities.[121] Hence it is doubtful whether the certificate system can be regarded as part of the generally accepted rules of international law.[122] Similar, or even stronger, doubts exist about a procedure according to which a neutral state should issue certificates covering cargoes on board ships of their nationality.[123]

Improper Exercise of the Right of Search and Diversion

Any search, diversion, or detention must be of the shortest possible duration.[124] In cases of unreasonable diversion, undue delay, or unnecessary interference with the ship's voyage, compensation should be awarded by the prize court. The same applies to an unreasonable delay in the institution of prize proceedings. However, the fact that the claimants have suffered inconvenience does not by itself afford a valid claim for damages.[125]

C CAPTURE/SEIZURE AND CONDEMNATION OF ENEMY VESSELS (AIRCRAFT) AND GOODS ON BOARD THESE VESSELS (AIRCRAFT)

It is a well-established principle[126] of traditional law that, in those areas of the sea where belligerent measures may be taken, enemy property, whether vessels or goods, is liable to capture[127] and, subject to a decision of a prize court, to condemnation.[128] Private

---

[121] Stödter, *supra* note 119.

[122] See, *inter alia*, P. C. Jessup (reporter), "Rights and Duties of Neutral States in Naval and Aerial War," 33 Am. J. Int'l L., Suppl., 166-793, at 514 (1939); Tucker, *op. cit. supra* note 21, at 282; D. Steinicke, *Das Navicertsystem*, 101, and *Kriegsbedingte Risiken* 12.

[123] See Colombos, *op. cit. supra* note 20, para. 899, referring *inter alia* to the Havana Convention of February 20, 1928, on Maritime Neutrality (135 LNTS 188-216; reprinted in Ronzitti (ed.), *op. cit. supra* note 48, at 771-78).

[124] Scheuner, *supra* note 87, at 407; Colombos, *supra*, para. 893.

[125] Colombos, *supra*, paras. 893, 894.

[126] See, *inter alia*, Hyde, *op. cit. supra* note 52, at 2074.

[127] Capture has to be distinguished from the right of angary (see Oppenheim/ Lauterpacht, *op. cit. supra* note 20, at 759; R. Lagoni, "Angary, Right of," in R. Bernhardt [ed.], EPIL 3, at 18 et seq.) and from requisitions (see Colombos, *op. cit. supra* note 20 paras. 617).

[128] D. Steinicke, *Handelsschiffahrt und Prisenrecht* (Hamburg, 1973), gives an excellent overview of treaties, national legislation, and instructions on the treatment of merchant vessels in time of war.

property at sea is not immune from confiscation during a war.[129] Since, according to the traditional law, an armistice does not terminate a war, the right of capture may also be exercised after agreement of an armistice.[130] Since the middle of the eighteenth century, there had been a strong movement in favour of what may be characterized as the principle of the immunity of private property at sea aiming at the abolition of the right of capture.[131] Among the supporters of that position were the Institut de Droit International (sessions of 1875, 1877, 1878) and the Inter Parliamentary Union (15th conference in Berlin, 16th conference in Brussels). Their main argument was that, war being a legal relationship between states, belligerent measures may not be taken against the peaceful population and private property. Some states incorporated the principle of inviolability· of private property in their national legislation or in bilateral treaties.[132] At the Hague Peace Conference of 1907, the United States delegation declared that "the private property of all citizens or subjects of the signatory Powers, with the exception of contraband of war shall be exempt from capture or seizure on the sea by the armed vessels or by the military forces of any of the said signatory Powers. But nothing herein contained shall extend exemption from seizure to vessels and their cargoes which may attempt to enter a port blockaded by the naval forces of any of the said Powers."[133] Great Britain opposed the American proposal strongly. At the sixth ses-

---

[129] Colombos, *op. cit. supra* note 20, para. 589; Tucker, *op. cit. supra* note 21, at 74; Lord Stowell in *Le Louis*, [1817] 2 Dods, 210-43; see also the cases of *The Jessie*, *The Thomas F. Bayard*, and *The Pescawha*, decided by the Anglo-American Claims Commission, Nielsen Report (1926), at 479-80.

[130] Berber, *op. cit. supra* note 20, at 193.

[131] See, *inter alia*, Abbé Bonnot de Mably, *Le droit public de l'Europe fondé sur les traités* (Paris, 1748).

[132] E.g., treaty between Brazil and Uruguay of October 21, 1851; Costa Rica and Colombia of June 11, 1856; United States and Prussia of September 10, 1785; United States and Italy of February 26, 1871; art. 211 of the Italian Codice per la marina mercantile of June 25, 1865 and of October 24, 1877 (subject to reciprocity).

According to Berber *op. cit. supra* note 20, at 206, private enemy property was not affected in the French-German War (1870/71), the Chinese-Japanese War (1894), or in the Spanish-American War (1898).

[133] Official Records, Vol. III, at 1141; Tucker, *op. cit. supra* note 21, at 74. A statement to the same effect was made in the American memorandum of June 30, 1899, to the 1899 Hague Peace Conference (printed in Th. Niemeyer, *Urkundenbuch zum Seekriegsrecht*, Vol. I, at 152 (Berlin, 1913). The U.S.A. held this position from the end of the eighteenth until the beginning of the twentieth century; see, e.g., Treaty of Amity and Commerce between Prussia and the U.S. of September 10, 1785; Italo-American Treaty of Commerce and Navigation of February 26, 1871.

306 Annuaire canadien de Droit international 1991

sion of Committee IV on July 17, 1907, the British delegate, Sir Ernest Satow, explained the British point of view as follows:

il n'est pas inutile de rappeler que l'abolition du droit de capture entraîne nécessairement l'abolition du blocus commercial. Car l'une et l'autre mesure ont pour but d'entraver le mouvement commercial de l'adversaire, et de le priver, dans la mesure du possible, des fournitures qui lui sont indispensables pour le maintien de la vie économique. D'un autre côté, comme l'ont fait remarquer plus d'un des Délégués à la Conférence, tant que le terme 'contrebande de guerre' ne sera pas strictement limité aux articles qui par leur nature même peuvent immédiatement être utilisés dans un but militaire, et tant que chaque Puissance individuellement se croit autorisée à comprendre sous cette rubrique toute sorte de vivres et de matières brutes servant aux industries pacifiques, rien ne sera plus facile que de donner à l'exception une étendue aussi large qu'à la règle. Il est donc évident que la proposition d'exempter de la capture et de la confiscation les navires marchands belligérants et leurs cargaisons, n'est qu'une équivoque capable seulement d'égarer l'opinion publique mal instruite.[134]

The majority of delegates shared this viewpoint[135] and the American and similar proposals failed in the final vote. It may be added that, when belligerents, the United States availed itself of all the rights claimed by Great Britain insofar as they were necessary to the successful conduct of their naval operations.[136] Hence, despite efforts to oppose the practice, especially the British practice of capture, the naval powers were not willing to relinquish a practice as old as naval warfare itself.[137] The right of capture remained a recognized principle of the law of naval warfare since its exercise was generally considered a ''necessarium ad finem belli.''[138]

[134] Official Records, Vol. III, at 183.

[135] Besides Great Britain, France, Russia, Japan, Spain, Portugal, Mexico, Colombia, and Panama voted against abolition.

[136] Colombos, op. cit. supra note 20, para. 592. Moreover, the U.S., during the Civil War, had made a notable extension of the doctrine of ''continuous voyage'' to contraband and even asserted its application to blockade.

[137] See also Hyde, op. cit. supra note 52, at 2061.

[138] G. Schramm, op. cit. supra note 67, 105; Oppenheim/Lauterpacht, op. cit. supra note 20, at 462. Colombos, op. cit. supra note 20, para. 594, states: ''By accepting the inviolability of enemy property *before a properly organized international society is created for the permanent peace in future,* Great Britain and the United States would be abandoning the most formidable weapon secured to them by their naval superiority'' (emphasis added).

Enemy Vessels (Aircraft) and Goods on Board Enemy Vessels (Aircraft)

According to the traditional law, enemy vessels (whether warships or merchant ships,[139] and irrespective of the nature of their cargo and their destination) and their cargo are liable to capture if not specially protected.[140] Whereas enemy cargo on board enemy merchant ships can always be seized and captured as prize,[141] neutral cargo on board enemy merchant vessels can be seized only if it is contraband,[142] if the vessel is a blockade runner,[143] if it travels in convoy, or actively resists visit and search.[144]

Capture of a vessel is complete when the prize is under the control of the captor.[145] The property, however, does not pass to the captor until the prize has been condemned by a prize court of the captor.[146] The lawfulness of the act of capture is, not dependent upon later condemnation by a prize court, which constitutes a valid and complete title. On the capture of an enemy warship and of an enemy public ship, both not prizes *stricto sensu*,[147] the property passes

---

[139] Private yachts, passenger ships, and even wrecks are also liable to capture; K. Terfloth, *Das Seebeuterecht an gesunkenen Schiffen* (Bonn, 1955).

[140] Tucker, *op. cit. supra* note 21, at 74; Oppenheim/Lauterpacht, *op. cit. supra* note 20, at 462; G. Schramm, *op. cit. supra* note 67, 305 et seq.; Pierce Higgins, "Ships of War as Prize," in 4 BYIL 103 (1925); Y. Dinstein, "The Laws of War at Sea," in Isr. YBHR, 1980, at 40; Art. 33 of the 1913 Oxford Manual.

[141] Oppenheim/Lauterpacht, *supra,* 476.

[142] Contraband is being dealt with *infra, pp.* 317-18.

[143] Art. 21 of the 1909 London Declaration.

[144] Art. 63 of the 1909 London Declaration.

[145] See, e.g., Arts. 64 et seq. of the 1939 German Prize Ordinance; Colombos, *op. cit. supra* note 20, para. 903; Oppenheim/Lauterpacht, *op. cit. supra* note 20, at 474. Note that capture differs from other acts, such as those amounting to no more than diversion into port for search. The distinguishing criterion is the intent of the belligerent. See also Tucker, *op. cit. supra* note 21, at 344. A prize is lost (a) when it escapes through being rescued by its own crew, (b) when the captor intentionally abandons it, or (c) when it is recaptured: see Oppenheim/Lauterpacht, *supra,* 494.

[146] Oppenheim/Lauterpacht, *supra,* 474; Berber, *op. cit. supra* note 20, at 195 ff.; McNair, *op. cit. supra* note 29, at 72; Art. 112 of the 1913 Oxford Manual; U.S. District Court for the Western District of Washington, *The Wilhelmina,* 78, F. Suppl. 57 (1948).

[147] According to Story (*Notes on the Principles and Practice of Prize Courts* 28 (1854, ed. by F. T. Pratt), prize extends "to all captures made on the sea jure belli; to all captures in foreign ports and harbours; to all captures made on land by naval forces and upon surrenders to naval forces either solely or by joint operations with land

at once to the captor.[148] With regard to all other cases, it is a "well-recognised rule that a prize must be brought into a convenient port for adjudication. The propriety or rather the necessity of acting upon this rule is based . . .on the principle that the property of private persons must not be converted without due process of law."[149] If the capture of a vessel "is not upheld by the prize court, or if the prize is released without any judgement given, the parties interested have the right to compensation, unless there were good reasons for capturing the vessel."[150]

In principle, captured enemy merchant ships[151] must be taken into port in order to be adjudicated upon. When circumstances render this course impossible, however, the prize may be destroyed.[152] According to British practice,[153] the captor is allowed to destroy a prize when it is in such a condition as prevents her from being sent to any port for adjudication, and when the capturing vessel is unable to spare a prize crew to navigate the prize into such a port.[154]

In state practice as well as in legal writings, there had been a tendency to allow destruction in nearly every case.[155] Indeed, it may be argued that, according to the wording of the 1936 London Procès-Verbal relating to the Rules of Submarine Warfare,[156] the destruc-

---

forces; and this, whether the property so captured be goods or mere choses in action; to captures made in rivers, ports and harbours of the captor's own country, to money received as a ransom or commutation on a capitulation to naval forces alone or jointly with land forces."

[148] Oppenheim/Lauterpacht, *op. cit. supra* note 20, at 474; W. G. Downey, Jr., "Captured Enemy Property, Booty of War and Seized Enemy Property," 44 Am. J. Int'l L. 488 (1950); Colombos, *op. cit. supra* note 20, para. 930. The same applies to goods on board such vessels if it is property of the enemy state. Private property on board such ships is subject to the law of prize.

[149] Colombos, *supra,* para. 925; see also P. Guttinger, "Réflexions sur la jurisprudence des prises maritimes de la Seconde Guerre Mondiale," 25 RGDIP 54 (1975).

[150] Art. 64 of the 1909 London Declaration.

[151] The cases in which an enemy merchant ship may be considered a legitimate military objective and may consequently be sunk on sight or after prior warning are not dealt with here.

[152] Since a judgment of a prize court finally transfers a captured vessel to the captor, it is evident that after transfer the captured vessel as well as her cargo may be destroyed: Oppenheim/Lauterpacht, *op. cit. supra* note 20, at 487.

[153] *The Acteon* (1815), 2 Dod. 48; *The Felicity* (1819), 2 Dod. 381; *The Valeria,* [1921] 1 A.C. 477; *The Stoer* [1916] 5 Ll. P.C. 18.

[154] Oppenheim/Lauterpacht, *op. cit. supra* note 20, at 487 ff.

[155] See the examples given, *ibid.,* 487.

[156] Procès-Verbal relating to the Rules of Submarine Warfare Set Forth in Part IV of the Treaty of London of April 22, 1930, signed at London, November 6, 1936: Text in 173 LNTS 353 (1936).

tion of merchant ships can be considered legal only if passengers, crew, and ship's papers have been placed in a place of safety. Beside general considerations of proportionality there are, however, many reasons why the destruction of merchant ships should be limited. In this regard, under the traditional law, only in a very few instances can the capturing warship be considered a place of safety. Moreover, enemy merchant vessels may be carrying neutral cargo which cannot be classified as contraband. Accordingly, Article 104 of the 1913 Oxford Manual provides that

> Belligerents are not permitted to destroy seized enemy ships, except in so far as they are subject to confiscation and because of exceptional necessity, that is, when the safety of the captor ship or the success of the war operations in which it is at that time engaged, demands it.
>
> Before the vessel is destroyed all persons on board must be placed in safety, and all the ship's papers and other documents which the parties interested consider relevant for the purpose of deciding on the validity of the capture must be taken on board the war-ship. The same rule shall hold, as far as possible, for the goods.[157]

For these reasons destruction of enemy merchant vessels must be treated as an exceptional measure and must be limited in the narrowest way.[158] Hence, mere reference to military exigencies does not suffice to justify the destruction. In any event, a prize court has to adjudicate whether the destruction was lawful.[159] If the destruction was illegal its owner has a right to compensation according to the principle of *restitutio in integrum*.[160]

With regard to captures of and by aircraft, the same rules are valid unless for practical reasons different considerations apply.[161] According to Article 55 of the Hague Air Warfare Rules, captured aircraft and their cargoes shall be made the subject of prize proceedings in order that neutral claims may be determined. Whereas the German Prize Ordinance of 1939 applies only to vessels, the

---

[157] Oxford Manual of Naval Warfare, adopted by the Institut de Droit International on August 9, 1913, AIDI 26 (1913), at 641 (printed in: Ronzitti [ed.], *op. cit. supra* note 48, at 277.).

[158] Colombos, *op. cit. supra* note 20, paras. 909 f.; Oppenheim/Lauterpacht, *op. cit. supra* note 20, at 487.

[159] Oppenheim/Lauterpacht, *supra*, 488.

[160] In its award of October 13, 1922, the Hague Permanent Court of Arbitration, 17 Am. J. Int'l L. 363, 392 (1923), ruled that "just compensation implies a complete restitution of the status quo ante based not upon future gains...but upon the loss of profits of the...owners as compared with other owners of similar property."

[161] Tucker, *op. cit. supra* note 21, at 108; Oppenheim/Lauterpacht, *op. cit. supra* note 20, at 496, 873.

British Prize Act of 1939 as well as the Italian War Regulations of
1938 declare the law of prize to apply also in relation to aircraft
and goods carried therein.

Enemy Vessels (Aircraft) and Goods Exempt from Capture and Condemnation

Enemy Vessels in Port at the Outbreak of Hostilities

In approximately the mid-nineteenth century, enemy merchant
ships, in an opposing enemy port on the outbreak of war were granted a period of grace during which they were allowed to depart freely.[162] The same applied to vessels that entered an enemy port and
had departed their last port in ignorance of the outbreak of hostilities.[163] There was, however, no legal duty to grant a period of grace.[164]
Rather it was left to the discretion of the belligerents, and the practice
of states differed to a considerable extent.[165]

The Second Hague Peace Conference was to settle this question.[166] At the conference, there was strong opposition by Great
Britain, France, Japan, and Argentina against fixing an obligatory
period of grace. Thus, in this regard the practice of states did not
reflect a binding rule of customary law nor did it contribute to the
formulation of a binding rule of treaty law. In Article 1 of Hague
Convention VI, the contracting parties only agree that "it is desirable" that these ships be granted an unmolested departure from
an enemy port. Under Articles 2 and 3 of the Convention, only two
categories of ships are exempt from confiscation; they may, however,

[162] It is reported that in the Crimean War (1854) for the first time France and Great
Britain granted a period of grace to Russian vessels in their respective ports. According to a British Order in Council, "any Russian merchant vessel which prior
to the date of this Order shall have sailed from any foreign port bound for any
port or place in Her Majesty's dominions, shall be permitted to enter such port
or place and to discharge her cargo, and afterwards forthwith to depart without
molestation, and any such vessel, if met at sea by any of Her Majesty's ships,
shall be permitted to continue her voyage to any port not blockaded."

[163] G. Schramm, *op. cit. supra* note 67, 129.

[164] Hence, the period was called "indult," "délai de faveur," "days of grace," "Gunst-
frist." See also Oppenheim/Lauterpacht, *op. cit. supra* note 20, at 479; L. Kotzsch,
"Indult," in WVR II, 19.

[165] Whereas, e.g., Prussia on June 21, 1866, granted a period of 6 weeks for Austrian
merchant vessels, and France at the beginning of the Franco-German War of 1870/71
granted a period of 30 days. In the Spanish-American War, Spain granted 5 days,
and at the outbreak of the Russo-Japanese War, Russia granted a period of 48
hours. See also Hyde, *op. cit. supra* note 52, at 2045.

[166] Hyde, *supra,* 2048.

either be detained, without payment of compensation though subject to restoration at the conclusion of hostilities, or requisitioned,
on payment of compensation. The categories are: merchant ships
unable, owing to circumstances of *force majeure,* to leave the enemy
port within the period contemplated in Article 1, or not allowed
to leave, and enemy merchant vessels which left their last port of
departure before the commencement of the war, and are encountered on the high seas while still ignorant of the outbreak of hostilities. These rules do not apply to merchant ships whose build shows
that they are intended for conversion into warships (Article 5).[167]

A large number of states failed to ratify Hague Convention VI;
Germany and Russia attached reservations.[168] During the First
World War, the practice of states parties to the Convention was far
from uniform.[169] After Great Britain and France had denounced
the Convention,[170] it became clear that in the Second World War
states considered themselves not bound by the rules laid down therein or by a similar rule of customary law.[171]

Categories of Protected Enemy Vessels

The legal aspects of the special protection of enemy vessels from
destruction according to conventional and customary law being
based on the same considerations,[172] it suffices to list those categories
of enemy vessels that — under the traditional law, are also exempt

[167] Similar rules are laid down in arts. 36 et seq. of the 1913 Oxford Manual.

[168] The list of signatures, ratifications, and accessions and the reservations of Germany
and Russia are printed in Ronzitti, *op. cit. supra* note 48, at 93.

[169] See, e.g., the decision of the Privy Council in *The Achaia,* [1916] 2 A.C. 198, *The
Belgia,* [1916] 2 A.C. 183 and *The Gutenfels,* [1916] 2 A.C. 112. A review of First World
War practice is given by A.P. Higgins, ''Enemy Ships in Port at the Outbreak
of War,'' in 3 BYIL 55-78 (1923-24); and by Kotzsch, *supra* note 164, at 19. See also
Hyde, *op. cit. supra* note 52, at 3, 2049 et. seq.

[170] Great Britain denounced the Convention in 1925, France in 1939.

[171] Berber, *op. cit. supra* note 20, at 193; S. W. D. Rowson, ''Prize Law during the
Second World War,'' in 24 BYIL 160 (1947); A. de Guttry, ''Commentary on the
1907 Hague Convention VI,'' in Ronzitti (ed.), *op. cit. supra* note 48, at 102. Lord
Merriman in *The Pomona* held that in absence of reciprocal agreement there was
no rule of international law exempting from condemnation enemy ships found
in a belligerent's port at the outbreak of hostilities: Ann. Dig. (1941-42), Case No.
159, at 509-14. Germany formally adhered to Hague Convention VI subject to
reciprocity.

[172] For an assessment of the current legal situation, see W. Heintschel v. Heinegg
(ed.), *The Military Objective and the Principle of Distinction in the Law of Naval Warfare:
Collected Papers and Proceedings,* Bochum, FRG, November 1989.

from capture.[173] It is emphasized, however, that the special protection of these vessels ceases as soon as they take any part whatever in hostilities:[174]

— vessels used exclusively for fishing along the coast;[175]
— small boats engaged in local trade;[176]
— vessels charged with religious, scientific, or philanthropic missions;[177]
— vessels exclusively engaged in the transfer of cultural property;[178]
— cartel vessels, that is, vessels designated for and engaged in the exchange of prisoners or acting as bearers of a flag of truce;[179]
— vessels furnished with a safe conduct or a licence;[180]
— vessels transporting equipment exclusively intended for the treatment of wounded and sick members of armed forces or for the prevention of disease, provided that the particulars regarding their voyage have been notified to the adverse power and approved

---

173 Passenger ships, which according to the traditional law are considered merchant vessels, are not exempt from capture. However, as the case of *The Athenia* shows, in the Second World War there at least existed a prohibition of sinking without prior warning: see K. Zemanek, "The Athenia," in EPIL 3, at 41.

174 See, *inter alia*, Art. 3, para. 2, and Art. 8 of Hague Convention XI.

175 Art. 3, Hague Convention XI, relative to Certain Restrictions with Regard to the Exercise of the Right of Capture in Naval War. Perhaps the most important decision on that issue is the one by the U.S. Supreme Court in *The Paquete Habana*, 175 U.S. 677 (1900). See also Oppenheim/Lauterpacht, *op. cit. supra* note 20, at 477; Hyde, *op. cit. supra* note 42, at 2053; D. P. O'Connell, *The International Law of the Sea*, Vol. II, at 1122. In the case of *The Berlin*, 7 Ll.P.C. 544 (1921), the Privy Council, while in principle acknowledging the special protection of such vessels, held that *The Berlin* "by reason of her size, equipment, and voyage,...was a deepsea fishing vessel engaged in a commercial enterprise which formed part of the trade of the enemy country, and, as such could be and was properly captured as prize of war."

176 Hague Convention XI, Art. 3. See also I. A. Shearer, "Commentary on Hague Convention XI," in Ronzitti (ed.), *op. cit. supra* note 48, at 186; Tucker, *op. cit. supra* note 21, at 96; G. Schramm, *op. cit. supra* note 67, 143.

177 Hague Convention XI, Art. 4. See also Hyde, *op. cit. supra* note 52, at 2056; Tucker, *supra*, 96; A. Schüle, "Schiffe mit humanitären Zwecken," in WVR III, 209.

178 Art. 14, para. 1 (b), of the 1954 Convention for the Protection of Cultural Property in the Event of Armed Conflict. See also L. V. Prott, "Commentary," in Ronzitti (ed.), *op. cit. supra* note 48, at 585.

179 See, *inter alia*, O'Connell, *op. cit. supra* note 175, at 1123; Oppenheim/Lauterpacht, *op. cit. supra* note 20, at 538, 541; Colombos, *op. cit. supra* note 20, paras. 660; Art. 45 of the 1913 Oxford Manual.

180 That was expressly acknowledged by the Privy Council in the case of *The Bathori*. See also R. Stödter, "Geleit," in WVR I, 639; Oppenheim/Lauterpacht, *supra*, 536; Art. 48 of the 1913 Oxford Manual. This, of course, only applies with regard to the belligerent having issued them.

by the latter;[181]

— vessels transporting consignments of medical and hospital stores and objects necessary for religious worship intended only for civilians;[182]

— vessels transporting consignments of foodstuffs, medical supplies and clothing of an occupied territory, as long as they comply with the conditions laid down by the occupying power;[183] and

— hospital ships, including their lifeboats, and coastal rescue craft.[184]

With regard to the exemption of enemy mail ships from capture, Article 9 of the Anglo-French Postal Treaty of 1890 provided: "En cas de guerre entre les deux nations, les paquebots des deux administrations continueront leur navigation sans obstacle ni molestation jusqu'à notification de la rupture des communications postales faite par l'un des deux gouvernements, auquel cas il leur sera permis de retourner librement et sous protection spéciale dans leurs ports respectifs." Such treaty obligations[185] occurred in isolated cases only and thus did not become embodied in customary international law.[186] Under Hague Convention XI, enemy mail ships are also not specially protected.[187]

Notwithstanding a few incidents to the contrary,[188] the same is true with regard to enemy merchant vessels that fall into the power of a belligerent because of *force majeure,* through shipwreck, or by being compelled to put into enemy port.[189]

As long as aircraft serve the same functions as the vessels listed above, they are equally protected.[190] The protection of these vessels and aircraft ceases as soon as a belligerent uses them for military purposes or if they do not comply with the conditions for their protection either agreed upon by the parties to the conflict or laid

---

[181] Art. 38, Geneva Convention II.

[182] Art. 23, para. 1, Geneva Convention IV.

[183] Art. 59, Geneva Convention IV.

[184] Arts. 22 et seq., Geneva Convention II. See also J. C. Mossop, "Hospital Ships in the Second World War," in 26BYIL 398 (1949); A. Schüle, "Lazarettschiffe," in WVR II, 408.

[185] Similar rules were laid down in the Postal Treaty between Great Britain and Denmark of 1846.

[186] G. Schramm, *op. cit. supra* note 67, 149; Oppenheim/Lauterpacht, *op. cit. supra* note 20, at 480.

[187] See also Art. 53, para. 2, of the 1913 Oxford Manual.

[188] E.g., in 1799 the Prussian merchant *Diana* which because of distress was compelled to put into Dunkerque, was released by the French prize court.

[189] Art. 34 of the 1913 Oxford Manual; Oppenheim/Lauterpacht, *op. cit. supra* note 20, at 479; G. Schramm, *op. cit. supra* note 67, 151.

[190] See, *inter alia,* Tucker, *op. cit. supra* note 21, at 96; Art. 39, Geneva Convention II.

down by one of the parties unilaterally.[191] The special protection from capture does not exempt these ships and aircraft from visit, search, and diversion.[192]

Categories of Goods and Articles Exempt from Capture

Under the traditional law the following goods and articles found on board enemy vessels are exempt from capture and confiscation either by conventional or by customary law:

— neutral goods, unless contraband or found on board a vessel actively resisting visit and search or guilty of breach of blockade;[193]
— personal belongings of crew members and passengers of captured vessels;[194]
— equipment exclusively intended for the treatment of wounded and sick members of armed forces or for the prevention of disease, provided that the particulars regarding their voyage have been notified to the adverse power and approved by the latter;[195]
— instruments and other material essential for the performance of the duties of relief societies;[196]
— cultural property;[197]
— postal correspondence and information material of and for a national Information Bureaux and the Central Information Agency;[198]
— consignments of medical and hospital stores and objects necessary for religious worship intended only for civilians;[199]
— consignments of foodstuffs, medical supplies and clothing for an occupied territory, as long as in compliance with the conditions laid down by the occupying power;[200] and
— to a certain extent, postal correspondence, whatever its official or private character, unless destined for or proceeding from a

---

[191] See, e.g., Art. 34, Geneva Convention II; Art. 3, para. 2, Hague Convention XI.
[192] See, e.g., Art. 31, Geneva Convention II.
[193] 1856 Paris Declaration; Arts. 21 and 63 of the 1909 London Declaration and *infra*, p. 322-27.
[194] Art. 29 of the London Declaration; see, e.g., Colombos, *op. cit. supra* note 20, para. 685.
[195] Art. 38, Geneva Convention II; see also Art. 29 of the London Declaration.
[196] This follows from the fact that otherwise the special status of such societies would be meaningless.
[197] Protected by the 1954 Convention for the Protection of Cultural Property in the Event of Armed Conflict.
[198] Arts. 74 and 122 *et seq.* Geneva Convention III.
[199] Art. 23, para. 1, Geneva Convention IV.
[200] Art. 59, Geneva Convention IV.

blockaded port.[201]

Whereas most of the categories listed above may be considered to reflect customary law with regard to the limited protection of postal correspondence, it needs to be emphasized that Article 1 of Hague Convention XI is neither declaratory of a pre-existing rule of customary international law nor did it afterwards contribute to the development of a rule of customary law to this effect.[202] Prior to the conclusion of Hague Convention XI, despite some treaties to the contrary,[203] no general rule existed granting postal correspondence special exemption from capture and the events of the two World Wars have reduced the significance of these provisions almost to a vanishing point.[204] In opposition to neutrals claiming a wide interpretation of the notion ''postal correspondence,'' both world wars provide abundant evidence that belligerents are not prepared, in any event, to exempt mails from the application of contraband.[205]

CAPTURE/SEIZURE AND CONDEMNATION OF NEUTRAL VESSELS (AIRCRAFT) AND GOODS FOUND ON BOARD SUCH VESSELS (AIRCRAFT)

The concept of neutrality, its development, its characteristics, and its kinds have, during the ages, undergone considerable changes.[206] It is often difficult, not only for these reasons, to establish whether a state is neutral *stricto sensu* or whether it takes some intermediate position. Even though one cannot evade the question of neutrality altogether,[207] in the context of capture it will suffice to characterize all those merchant vessels to be neutral which, according to the traditional rules stated above,[208] may not be considered enemy.

Capture of Neutral Merchant Vessels

Enemy merchant (and other) vessels are captured for the purpose

---

[201] Art. 1, Hague Convention XI.
[202] See, *inter alia,* Hyde, *op. cit. supra* note 42, at 1974.
[203] See the examples given by Colombos, *op. cit. supra* note 20, para. 666.
[204] Tucker, *op. cit. supra* note 21, at 90.
[205] *Ibid.,* 94; U. Scheuner, ''Beuterecht im Seekrieg,'' in WVR I, 199.
[206] Oppenheim/Lauterpacht, *op. cit. supra* note 20, at 623; Tucker, *op. cit. supra* note 21, at 165; U. Scheuner, ''Neutralitätsrechte und -pflichten im Seekrieg,'' in WVR II, 601; Berber, *op. cit. supra* note 20, at 210.
[207] Rights and duties of neutral states, as distinguished from neutral nationals and neutral ships, are not dealt with here. However, aspects of neutrality and non-belligerency will be dealt with *infra.*
[208] *Supra.*

of appropriating them in exercise of what may be called the right of booty. In principle, neutral merchant vessels may not be captured, condemned, or destroyed,[209] but they and their (neutral or enemy) cargo may be captured in four exceptional cases: carriage of contraband; refusal and active resistance to visit and search; unneutral service; and breach of blockade.[210] Hence, capture of neutral merchant vessels and their cargo may be considered a legal reaction of a belligerent to certain behaviour of the neutral merchantman[211] which, it may be added, does not in any event constitute a violation of international law.[212]

As in the case of enemy merchant ships, the legality of capture of neutral merchant vessels is not dependent upon later condemnation by a prize court. It suffices if the captor can establish that ''at the moment of seizure circumstances were such as to warrant suspicion of enemy character, whether of vessel or of cargo, or of the performance of acts held to constitute contraband carriage, blockade breach, or unneutral service.''[213] The seizure of neutral vessels and neutral cargo does not serve to effect transfer of title in favour of the captor, but only places him in temporary possession of the property. The final decision on whether there is sufficient cause for confiscating the vessel and cargo lies with the competent prize court alone. The captor, therefore, is obliged to take all reasonable measures in order to preserve the vessel and its cargo intact and to take it into the nearest port without undue delay (Article 48 of the 1909 London Declaration). However, according to Article 49 of the London Declaration, ''[a]s an exception, a neutral vessel which has been captured by a belligerent warship, and which would be liable to condemnation, may be destroyed if the observance of Article 48 would involve danger to the safety of the warship or to the success of the operations in which

---

[209] See, *inter alia*, Hyde, *op. cit. supra* note 52, at 2041.

[210] Breach of blockade is not dealt with here.

[211] The question whether a belligerent may capture and condemn neutral merchant vessels by way of reprisal in response to violations of the neutral flag state's duty of impartiality will not be dealt with here. In this regard see Tucker, *op. cit. supra* note 21, at 252. The position taken here is that a belligerent may not assert the law of reprisals in order to justify actions against neutral merchant vessels and their cargo because of prior violations of the laws of war by the adversary.

[212] See *infra;* Berber, *op. cit. supra* note 20, at 223; Tucker, *supra*, 253.

[213] Tucker, *ibid.*, 346.

she is engaged at the time.''[214] Of course, before destruction all persons on board and all the ship's papers and documents must be placed in safety (Article 50 of the London Declaration).

Carriage of Contraband

Neutral merchant vessels engaged in the carriage of contraband, or reasonably suspected of being so engaged, are liable to seizure[215] and, under certain conditions, may be condemned. Whereas some states place emphasis upon the knowledge of the owner or master of the vessel, others consider the proportion of contraband carried by the vessel to be decisive.[216] The Declaration of London reflects the latter practice in Article 40; it provides that ''[a] vessel carrying contraband may be condemned if the contraband, reckoned either by value, weight, volume, or freight, forms more than half the cargo.'' In view of the differing practice it is doubtful whether this rule, by the end of the Second World War, ''succeeded in obtaining widespread acceptance.''[217]

Even though the penalty for the carriage of contraband is the condemnation of the goods and of the neutral merchant vessel,[218] it is not considered a violation of international law for a neutral to engage in contraband trade, for a neutral state is under no duty

---

[214] The German Oberprisenhof in *The Medea* (Entscheidungen des Oberprisenhofs Bd. 1 (1918), at 131) held that destruction of neutral merchant vessels may be exercised if in accordance with Art. 49 of the London Declaration.

[215] See Art. 37 of the London Declaration; Tucker, *op. cit. supra* note 21, at 276; Hyde, *op. cit. supra* note 52, at 2160; Oppenheim/Lauterpacht, *op. cit. supra* note 20, at 826. However, a ''vessel may not be captured on the ground that she has carried contraband on a previous occasion if such carriage is in point of fact at an end'' (Art. 38 of the London Declaration). With regard to the question which articles constitute contraband, see *supra*.

[216] The former position was taken by Anglo-American doctrine and practice (see, *inter alia*, Privy Council, *The Sidi Ifni*, [1945] 1 Ll.P.C. (2nd) 200, 204; *The Ringende Jacob* [1798] 1 C. Rob. 89), the latter by continental European countries (see, *inter alia*, the decision of the German Oberprisenhof in *The Björn*, Entscheidungssammlung Bd. 1, at 152).

[217] This view is also taken by Tucker, *op. cit. supra* note 21, at 277. Note, however, that Hyde *op. cit. supra* note 52, at 2160, obviously takes a different position. In the case of *The Berkelstrom*, the Netherlands government took the view that neutral prizes may not be destroyed because the 1909 London Declaration had remained unratified. In that case the proportion of contraband carried by the vessel played a decisive role, too.

[218] See *supra*.

to prohibit it.[219] Hence, the right of a belligerent to capture and condemn contraband goods and vessels carrying such goods does not correspond with a legal duty on behalf of neutral merchantmen to refrain from such an activity. It is simply a case of two conflicting rights with the belligerent right of capture prevailing over the neutral's right of carrying contraband: "It is no transgression of the limits of a neutral's duty, but merely the exercise of a hazardous right, in the course of which he may come into conflict with the rights of the belligerent and be worsted."[220]

According to the "rule of 1756," neutral vessels engaged in trade that is closed in time of peace, are liable to the same treatment as enemy merchant vessels, since they are incorporated into the enemy's merchant fleet.[221] During the preparations for the 1909 London Conference, only Great Britain and Germany referred to the treatment of these ships.[222] The conference did not deal with this problem. Thus, the "case where a neutral vessel is engaged in trade which is closed in time of peace" remains outside the scope of the 1909 London Declaration (Article 57, paragraph 2) as well as of the generally accepted body of customary international law.

Resistance to Visit and Search

Forcible resistance on the part of a neutral merchant ship to visit and search is an act of hostility and renders it liable to capture and involves in all cases its condemnation.[223] According to the wording

---

[219] See, *inter alia,* Hyde, *op. cit. supra* note 52, at 2307 ff. According to Art. 7 of the 1907 Hague Convention XIII concerning the Rights and Duties of Neutral Powers in Naval War, "a neutral Power is not bound to prevent the export or transit, for the use of either belligerent, of arms, ammunition, or, in general, of anything which could be of use to an army or fleet." Only the supply of war materials by a neutral Power itself is prohibited (Art. 6). However, according to the Washington Rules of 1871 which were adopted for the Court of Arbitration in the case of *The Alabama* "[a] neutral Government is bound. . .to exercise due diligence in its own ports and waters, and, as to all persons within its jurisdiction, to prevent any violation of the foregoing obligations and duties."

[220] *The Kronprinsessin Margareta,* [1921] 1 A.C. 754. Lord Summer in *The Prins der Nederlande,* [1921] 1 A.C. 760, put it as follows: "Neutrals who carry contraband do not break the law of nations; they run a risk for adequate gain, and, if they are caught, take the consequences. If they know what they are doing, those consequences may be very serious; if they do not, they may get off merely with some inconvenience or delay; this must suffice them."

[221] Colombos, *op. cit. supra* note 20, para. 940.

[222] G. Schramm, *op. cit. supra* note 67, 160.

[223] Art. 63 of the London Declaration; O. Rojahn, "Ships, Visit and Search," in

of the 1936 London Procès-Verbal, in the case of persistent refusal to stop on being duly summoned, or of active resistance to visit and search, a neutral merchant ship may even be sunk without a further warning. The International Military Tribunal in its judgment on Dönitz[224] took the view that the 1936 London Procès-Verbal is also applicable to ships flying the flag of a neutral/non-belligerent state. If one considers the 1936 London Protocol to be a treaty containing rules of naval warfare applicable to the belligerent parties only, one may doubt this point of view.[225] Such a restriction does not imply that a belligerent would be left without any legal means to react to active resistance to visit and search, for in such a case the neutral merchant vessel violates an international obligation and may not assert the right of freedom of navigation which is subject to the belligerents' right of visit and search. It is, however, important to note that "the law on the sinking of vessels is naturally much more stringent in the case of neutral ships which must not be destroyed. If the vessel is destroyed owing to unavoidable causes, full compensation must be paid by the captor to the neutral shipowner."[226]

Unneutral Service

It is a well-established right of belligerents to prevent neutral vessels from transporting troops[227] or from transmitting information for the adversary.[228] Nevertheless, for a considerable period of time, there were no separate rules on these and similar acts of assistance

---

EPIL 4, at 224; Hyde, *op. cit. supra* note 52, at 1981; Oppenheim/Lauterpacht, *op. cit. supra* note 20, at 856.

[224] Der Prozez gegen die Hauptkriegsverbrecher vor dem Internationalen Militär-gerichtshof, Band I, Nuremberg, 1947, at 350, 352.

[225] Of course, one could argue that if the destruction of enemy merchant vessels is restricted to exceptional cases, in any event the same must be true with regard to neutral merchant vessels. This does not mean, however, that reference to the 1936 London Protocol is indispensable.

[226] Colombos, *op. cit. supra* note 20, para. 918.

[227] That was already acknowledged in the treaties concluded between The Netherlands, Sweden, and France in 1614 and between The Netherlands and the Hanse in 1615.

[228] At the beginning of the Crimean War (1854), the transmission of information was equated to carriage of contraband. At the beginning of the Civil War (1861), a similar position was taken by Great Britain, France, and Spain in their respective declarations of neutrality. See also Art. 8 of the Italian Ordinance of June 20, 1866; the French Instructions of July 25, 1870; Art. 10 para. 7 of the Spanish Instructions of April 24, 1898, and Art. 15 of the U.S. Instructions to Blockading Vessels and Cruisers of June 20, 1898.

by neutral vessels. Rather, transport of troops and transmission of information were dealt with under the heading of contraband or "contrebande par analogie."[229] Moreover, state practice with regard to "unneutral assistance/service" and the consequences of such acts for neutral vessels and their cargo were far from uniform.[230]

During the first meeting of Committee IV of the Hague Peace Conference on June 24, 1907, Great Britain made the following proposal:

Il y a deux catégories de vaisseaux de guerre:
A. Vaisseaux de combat;
B. Vaisseaux auxiliaires.
A. . . .
B. Sera compris dans le terme 'vaisseau auxiliaire': Toute navire marchand, soit belligérant soit neutre, qui sera employé au transport de marins, de munitions de guerre, combustibles, vivres, eau ou toute autre espèce de munitions navales, ou qui sera destiné à l'exécution de réparations ou chargé du port de dépêches ou de la transmission d'information si le dit navire est obligé de se conformer aux ordres de marche à lui communiqué soit directement soit indirectement, par la flotte belligérante. Sera de même compris dans la définition tout navire employé au transport de troupes militaires.[231]

This proposal started from the assumption that assistance to a belligerent by neutral merchant vessels constituted a violation of the laws of neutrality. For this reason it met strong opposition by the Dutch and the United States delegations. At the thirteenth meeting of Committee IV, the British proposal was withdrawn.[232] Hence, none of the 1907 Hague Conventions contributed to a clarification of the questions involved.

At the London Naval Conference, however, the delegates were,

---

[229] Italian Prize Ordinance of June 20, 1866; Russian Prize Ordinance of February 14, 1904, and Japanese Prize Ordinance of 1904.

[230] See, *inter alia*, G. Schramm, *op. cit. supra* note 67, 253.

[231] Official Records, Vol. III, at 1135.

[232] At that meeting Lord Reay made the following statement: "La définition soumise à la Conférence du vaisseau auxiliaire par la Délégation britannique visait l'assistance hostile et une infraction aux obligations des neutres. La question de l'assistance hostile, aussi connue sous le nom de 'non neutral service' n'ayant pas été étudiée, ne se trouvant pas au programme de la Conférence, nous sommes d'avis que la discussion serait prématurée et qu'elle pourra être incluse dans le programme d'une Conférence ultérieure après avoir subi un examen sérieux de la part des Gouvernements représentés à la Conférence. Je suis autorisé par mon Gouvernement à retirer la définition du vaisseau auxiliaire. Le Droit international existant sera applicable à l'assistance hostile."

able to agree on Articles 45-47 dealing with "unneutral service."[233] According to Article 45, a neutral vessel is liable to the same treatment as a neutral vessel liable to condemnation for carriage of contraband. "If she is on a voyage especially undertaken with a view to the transport of individual passengers who are embodied in the armed forces of the enemy, or with a view to the transmission of intelligence in the interest of the enemy," or "If, to the knowledge of either the owner, the charterer, or the master, she is transporting a military detachment of the enemy, or one or more persons who, in the course of the voyage, directly assist the operations of the enemy." According to Article 46, a neutral vessel is liable to the same treatment as an enemy merchant vessel "if she takes direct part in the hostilities; if she is under the orders or control of an agent placed on board by the enemy Government; if she is in the exclusive employment of the enemy Government; if she is exclusively engaged at the time either in the transport of enemy troops or in the transmission of intelligence in the interest of the enemy."

Even though the Italian Prize Instructions of October 13, 1911, and the French instructions of December 19, 1912, to a considerable extent adopted the provisions of the London Declaration on unneutral service, at least by the end of the Second World War, they do not anymore serve as a general indication of the existing law. In state practice the scope of unneutral service has expanded and the consequences for those performing this service have become more rigourous.[234] In view of the variety of acts included within the category of unneutral service, no generally accepted and comprehensive rules have evolved. Despite these difficulties, with regard to the following acts there seems to exist agreement that they may be considered unneutral service by a neutral merchant vessel (as well as by a neutral aircraft):[235] direct participation in the military operations of a belligerent;[236] acting in any capacity as a naval

---

[233] This heading is a bad translation from the French "De l'assistance hostile," for hostile assistance does not imply a violation of the laws of neutrality.

[234] Tucker, *op. cit. supra* note 21, at 319.

[235] Apart from the 1923 Hague Rules of Aerial Warfare which simply provide that "a neutral private aircraft is liable to capture if it is engaged in unneutral service" (Art. 53 c), there is no codification on this issue whatsoever. Nevertheless, it may be assumed that the rules on unneutral service also apply to neutral aircraft.

[236] With regard to Part IV of the 1930 London Naval Treaty, the Committee of Experts emphasized that "the expression 'merchant vessel,' where it is employed in the declaration, is not to be understood as including a merchant vessel which is at the moment participating in hostilities in such a manner as to cause her to

or military auxiliary to a belligerent's armed forces;[237] travelling under convoy of a belligerent warship;[238] operating directly under the control, orders, charter, employment, or direction of a belligerent government;[239] acceptance of a safe-conduct pass, ship's warrant or navicert of one of the belligerents;[240] carriage of enemy persons;[241] and carriage of dispatches.[242]

The first three of these acts render neutral vessels in any case liable to capture and, if necessary, to attack and destruction on sight.[243] The fourth and fifth acts do not justify destruction, they do, however, give sufficient ground for capture and the same treatment as enemy merchant vessels. Acts falling within the sixth and seventh categories may result in the liability of the vessel to capture.[244]

Cargo on Board Neutral Merchant Vessels

All goods on board neutral merchant vessels, whether enemy or neutral, are in principle exempt from capture. This follows from the 1856 Paris Declaration respecting Maritime Law. There are, however, exceptions to the rule.

Neutral Merchant Vessels Forcibly Resisting Visit and Search

With regard to cargo on board a neutral vessel which forcibly

---

lose her right to the immunities of a merchant vessel" (Documents of the London Naval Conference 1930, London, 1930, at 443).

[237] This includes transmission of intelligence to the enemy. See, *inter alia*, W. T. Mallison, *Studies in the Law of Naval Warfare: Submarines in General and Limited Wars*, 122; Oppenheim/Lauterpacht, *op. cit. supra* note 20, at 837.

[238] Supra, oo; see also R. Stödter, Flottengeleit, and "Convoy," in EPIL 3, at 128-130; M. Donner, "Armed Merchant Ships and Convoys," in D. Fleck (ed.), *The Gladisch Committee on the Law of Naval Warfare*, 26.

[239] Oppenheim/Lauterpacht, *op. cit. supra* note 20, at 839; Tucker, *op. cit. supra* note 21, at 322.

[240] See *supra*, oo.

[241] Oppenheim/Lauterpacht, *supra* 833. In the case of *The Friendship*, [1807] 6 C. Rob. 420, the High Court of Admiralty condemned *The Friendship* because it was considered to be a "vessel engaged in the immediate military service of the enemy."

[242] Hyde, *op. cit. supra* note 52, at 2174; Tucker, *op. cit. supra* note 21, at 330.

[243] Tucker, *supra*, 320; Oppenheim/Lauterpacht, *op. cit. supra* note 20, at 833.

[244] Tucker, *supra*, 325. However, as shown in the case of *The Asama Maru*, belligerents regularly confine themselves to removing enemy persons from the neutral vessel; see also *The Manouba*, Martens, N.R.G. Vol. 8, at 170; H. W. Briggs, "Removal of Enemy Persons from Neutral Vessels on the High Seas," in 34 Am. J. Int'l L. 249 (1940); U. Scheuner, "Die Wegnahme feindlicher Staatsangehöriger von neutralen Schiffen," in ZVR 24 (1941), 411.

resists visit and search, Article 63 of the 1909 London Declaration provides that the cargo is liable to be treated in the same way as that carried by an enemy ship if it belongs to the shipowner. State practice on this question is not uniform. This cargo is generally condemned by British prize courts,[245] not always by American.[246] According to Articles 12 and 37, paragraph 2, of the 1939 German Prize Ordinance, neutral cargo belonging to the master or owner of a vessel that offers forcible resistance, is subject to condemnation.

Contraband

Enemy goods on board neutral merchant vessels and neutral goods on board enemy and neutral vessels may be captured only if — leaving aside the cases of blockade,[247] of unneutral service[248] and of resistance to visit and search[249] — they constitute contraband.[250]

To constitute an article as contraband of war, two elements are necessary: it must be susceptible of belligerent use and it must be (directly or indirectly) destined to the enemy.[251] Whereas there is general agreement about the validity of this definition,[252] there has always been controversy about what goods belong to the class of contraband.[253] The same is true with regard to the distinction between three categories of articles which dates back to Hugo Grotius: absolute contraband, conditional contraband, and free goods.[254] These three categories underlie the rules laid down in the 1909

---

[245] *The Maria*, [1799] 1 C. Rob. 340, 374; *The Elsebe*, [1804] 5 C. Rob. 174.

[246] However, in *The Nereide*, (1815) 9 Cranch. 388, 441, Mr. Justice Story took the English view.

[247] Blockade is not being dealt with here.

[248] Unneutral service is being dealt with *supra*, 319-22.

[249] See *supra*.

[250] See, *inter alia*, Hyde, *op. cit. supra* note 52, at 2163; U. Scheuner, "Konterbanderecht," in WVR II, 290.

[251] U. Scheuner, *ibid.;* Tucker, *op. cit. supra* note 21, at 263; Colombos, *op. cit. supra* note 20, para. 706.

[252] Colombos *ibid.* The Declaration of Paris of 1856 uses the term without attempting to define it.

[253] Even though a number of bilateral treaties had been concluded in order to fix what articles belonged to which category, they, because of their differing content, did not contribute to a clarification.

[254] Hugo Grotius, *op. cit. supra* note 46, Caput I, V: "Sunt enim res quae in bello tantum usum habent, ut arma: sunt quae in bello nullum habent usum, ut quae voluptati inserviunt: sunt quae et in bello et extra bellum usum habent, ut pecuniae, commeatus, naves, et quae navibus adsunt. . . . In tertio illo genere usus ancipitis distinguendus erit belli status."

London Declaration, which was the first and only attempt of states to agree on this disputed subject.[255] The rules of the London Declaration on contraband expressly refer only to goods on board neutral ships, but they also apply to neutral goods on board enemy vessels. According to Article 39 of this Declaration, contraband goods are liable to condemnation. This rule also applies to goods that belong to the owner of contraband and are on board the same vessel (Article 42). As already mentioned, the London Declaration distinguishes three categories, namely absolute contraband (Article 22), conditional contraband (Article 24), and free goods (Articles 28 and 29).

Absolute contraband comprises all articles exclusively used for war, and conditional contraband comprises articles that are susceptible of use for purposes of peace as well. The London Declaration enumerates those articles that constitute absolute contraband and those that constitute conditional contraband. Only if a belligerent wishes to add certain articles to one of those lists is he obliged to notify a contraband list to the other parties. He may, however, not deviate from the basic definition of absolute or conditional contraband. With regard to those articles that according to Articles 28 and 29 may not be declared contraband of war (*inter alia* rubber and metallic ores), states felt unable to exempt them from capture.[256]

Absolute contraband is liable to capture if it is shown to be destined to territory belonging to or occupied by the enemy, or to the armed forces of the enemy (Article 30). It is immaterial whether the carriage of the goods is direct or entails transshipment or a subsequent transport by land.[257] Therefore, in Article 30 the doctrine of continuous voyage is expressly acknowledged as far as absolute contraband is concerned. Continuous voyage does not refer to the vessel but to the goods in question; the decisive factor is not the direct destination but the ultimate or final destination of the goods.[258]

Conditional contraband is liable to capture only if it is destined for the use of the armed forces or of a government department of the enemy state (Article 33).[259] It is not sufficient that the goods

[255] See also the overview given by Hyde, *op. cit. supra* note 52, at 2099.

[256] J. W. Garner, "Violations of Maritime Law by the Allied Powers during the World War," 25 Am. J. Int'l L. 33 (1931).

[257] Cases in which proof of the destination is complete are laid down in Art. 31.

[258] See also the commentary by Renault in the *Rapport général présenté à la Conférence Navale au nom du Comité de Rédaction.*

[259] According to Art. 34, this destination is presumed to exist if the goods are

in question are destined for territory belonging to or occupied by the enemy. The doctrine of continuous voyage does not apply to conditional contraband. This follows from Article 35 according to which conditional contraband is not liable to capture, except when found on board a vessel bound for territory belonging to or occupied by the enemy, or for the armed forces of the enemy.[260] Conditional contraband, if shown to be destined for the use of the armed forces or of a government department of the enemy state, is liable to capture only if the enemy country is a landlocked state (Article 36).

The London Declaration remained unratified and the practice of states during the two world wars[261] showed that it was impossible to settle once and for all the question on which goods are to be considered contraband.[262] In state practice the distinction between absolute and conditional contraband, though formally retained, was soon abolished and the rules originally designed to apply to absolute contraband alone were also applied to those categories which, in the London Declaration, were classified as conditional contraband. On August 27, 1914, Great Britain dismissed a further unmodified application of the London Declaration and, after gradually extending the list of absolute contraband, by an Order in Council of April 13, 1916, repealed the provision distinguishing absolute and conditional contraband. France, Germany, and others followed suit. All raw materials,[263] foodstuffs,[264] fuels of any kind, money,

---

consigned to enemy authorities, or to a contractor established in the enemy country who, as a matter of common knowledge, supplies articles of this kind to the enemy. A similar rebuttable presumption arises if the goods are consigned to a fortified place belonging to the enemy, or other place serving as a base for the armed forces of the enemy.

[260] See also the commentary by Renault, *supra* note 258.

[261] J. H. W. Verzijl, *Le droit des prises de la Grande Guerre* (Leyden, 1924); M. M. Whiteman, *Digest of International Law*, Vol. 1, c. 32 (Washington, 1968); A. Gervais, "Le droit des prises maritimes dans la seconde guerre mondiale. La jurisprudence française (britannique, italienne, allemande) des prises maritimes dans la seconde guerre mondiale," in RGDIP 1948, at 82-161; 1949, at 201-74; 1950, at 251-316; 1951, at 481-546. Parties to the Balkan wars of 1912/13 more or less adhered to its rules, even though, in the case of *The Carthage*, coal and foodstuffs were considered contraband: see Scheuner, "Konterbanderecht," in WVR II, 291.

[262] Oppenheim/Lauterpacht, *op. cit. supra* note 20, at 801.

[263] British High Court of Justice, *The Alwaki* [1940] P. 215.

[264] See, *inter alia*, the judgement of February 1, 1918, of the Privy Council in *The Louisiana*, [1918] 7 Ll.P.C. 410; [1918] A.C. 461. In *The Kim and Other Vessels*, [1915] P. 367, it was declared: "Apart altogether from the special adaptability of these cargoes

and gold were considered absolute contraband.[265] Even though, for example, France[266] and Italy[267] in the aftermath of the First World War, adhered to the distinction between absolute and conditional contraband and restricted absolute contraband to war material in the Second World War, almost all goods were included in lists of absolute contraband.[268] This practice was justified by the doctrine laid down by Hall that "contraband must vary with the circumstances of particular cases, and that in considering the inclusion of articles in the lists, the mind must chiefly be fixed upon the characteristics of essentiality of the articles to the prosecution of the war."[269] In view of the totality of the Second World War, the British Prize Court in *The Alwaki and Other Vessels* declared, in condemning foodstuffs held to be destined to Germany, that "there is the clearest possible evidence of German decrees which . . . impose Government control on all these articles and prescribe that they are automatically seized at the moment of crossing the frontier or. . . at the moment of coming into the customs house."[270]

Neither did states subscribe to an exclusive application of the doctrine of continuous voyage to absolute contraband.[271] Even in 1900 Great Britain had maintained that articles ultimately destined for the enemy were contraband, although the vessels carrying them were bound for a neutral port.[272] In view of the fact that during

(i.e. foodstuffs) for the armed forces, and the highly probable inference that they were destined for the forces, even assuming that they were indiscriminately distributed between the military and civilian population, a very large proportion would necessarily be used by the military forces." With regard to the controversy on foodstuffs, see Hyde, *op. cit. supra* note 52, at 2108.

[265] Scheuner, "Konterbanderecht," in WVR II, 291.

[266] Arts. 40-60 of the French Instructions of March 8, 1934.

[267] Arts. 159-67 of the Italian Legge della Guerra of July 8, 1938.

[268] E.g., the list of articles of absolute contraband announced by Great Britain on September 4, 1939, comprises *inter alia* coin, bullion, currency, evidence of debt; also metal, materials, dies, plates, machinery, or other articles necessary or convenient for their manufacture. The 1939 German Prize Ordinance included a list of articles of absolute contraband similar to that of the London Declaration. However, on September 12, 1939, a new list (RGBl. 1939 I, 1585) was published, which was to a great extent identical with the British list of September 4.

[269] Colombos, *op. cit. supra* note 20, para. 776, referring to Hall, 781.

[270] Ann. Dig., (1938-40), Case No. 223, at 586.

[271] See the examples given by Hyde, *op. cit. supra* note 52, at 2130, and by Oppenheim/Lauterpacht, *op. cit. supra* note 20, at 816, 821.

[272] Cases of the German vessels *Bundesrath, Herzog* and *General,* Parl. Papers, Africa, No. 1 (1900).

the world wars direct carriage of contraband was the exception rather than the rule, it soon became accepted that goods documented to neutral ports and consigned to persons in neutral territory are nevertheless liable to seizure if it can be shown that the ostensible neutral destination serves only as an intermediate point for further transit, whether by land, sea, or air, to an enemy.[273] According to Articles 24 of the 1939 German Prize Ordinance, goods included in lists of conditional contraband destined to a neutral port were not considered contraband only if reciprocity was ensured. Enemy destination was presumed when there was a connection between the neutral port and territories belonging to or occupied by the enemy. Especially when goods were consigned "to order," or when the ship's papers were missing or not in order, reasonable suspicion of transshipment was sufficient to consider the goods in question contraband.[274] The same was true if either the consignee was suspected of trading with the enemy[275] or if the quantity of goods destined for a neutral port exceeded the state's normal import requirements.[276] In all these cases the inference of an ultimate enemy destination could be displaced only by a positive showing that the goods in question had an innocent destination.[277]

The right to seize and condemn certain goods could, according to the so-called doctrine of infection, be extended to articles not constituting contraband, if found on board the vessel carrying contraband and if belonging to the same owner.[278] This rule was also laid down in Article 42 of the 1909 London Declaration. However, after it had become evident that this treaty would not enter into force, the continuing validity of the doctrine of infection became a matter of dispute.[279]

---

[273] H. W. Briggs, *The Doctrine of Continuous Voyage* (1926); Tucker, *op. cit. supra* note 21, at 270; Scheuner, "Konterbanderecht," in WVR II, 291. See also the cases of *The Kim* [1915] P. 215, and *The Louisiana* [1918] A.C. 461.

[274] Privy Council, *The Monte Contes,* [1944] Ac. 6.

[275] British High Court of Justice, *The Charles Racine,* [1944] 1 Ll.P.C. (2nd), 187.

[276] Privy Council, *The Stjernblad,* [1918] 6 Li.P.C. 101.

[277] Tucker, *op. cit. supra* note 21, at 273.

[278] *The Sarah Christina,* [1799] 1 C. Rob. 237; *The Eleonora Wilhelmina,* [1807] 6 C. Rob. 331; *The Kim,* [1915] P 215; U.S. Supreme Court in *Carrington* v. *Merchants' Insurance Co.* (1834) 8 Peters, 495; *The Peterhoff* (1866), 5 Wall. 28.

[279] E.g., the French Prize Court in *The Frederick VIII* (Journal Officiel of May 19, 1922, at 5277) stated that such goods were protected by the rules laid down in the 1856 Paris Declaration. Lord Merriman in *The Hakozaki Maru* considered the doctrine of infection to be "highly artificial." See also Tucker, *op. cit. supra* note 21, at 276, fn. 29.

III CONCLUDING REMARKS ON THE TRADITIONAL LAW

At the time of the drafting of the 1909 London Declaration, it was already a matter of dispute which of its provisions reflected customary law and which had to be considered to be new rules.[280] The Declaration certainly contains a considerable number of rules that, at least in substance, correspond with the generally recognized principles of international law of those days. Hence, in the First World War several belligerents adjusted their conduct to these rules. During the Second World War, "major parts of the law of prize came to be distorted beyond recognition"[281] and the insufficiency of the 1909 London Declaration for restricting the conduct of belligerents became evident. Prize courts in numerous decisions acknowledged the extension of belligerent rights to capture private property at sea by means of an extensive presumption of enemy destination, the doctrine of continuous voyage, and by the abolition of the distinction between absolute and conditional contraband.[282] The right of capture to a great extent was exercised in ports taken by military operations from land.[283] In view of a number of precedents of the First World War,[284] no legal objections were made.

State practice during the Second World War, therefore, probably contributed to a certain qualitative change of the law. Whether this is the case has to be verified by scrutinizing the practice of states after 1945. As will be seen, in post-Second World War conflicts, the law of prize did not play as decisive a role as before. Only in two conflicts was prize law *stricto sensu* applied. Thus, it is of importance to look beyond the actual behaviour of states during armed conflicts at sea and to take into consideration evidence of *opinio iuris* derived from military manuals. Finally, the question arises to what extent certain well-established principles and rules of international law have had, or are in the process of having, a bearing on the legality of belligerent measures of economic warfare.

---

[280] See, *inter alia*, F. Kalshoven, "Commentary on the 1909 London Declaration," in Ronzitti (ed.), *op. cit. supra* note 48, at 269.

[281] *Ibid.*, 272.

[282] See M. M. Whiteman, *Digest of International Law*, Vol. 10, at 797 (Washington, 1968).

[283] Hyde, *op. cit. supra* note 52, at 1965.

[284] Among those precedents, the most prominent are: *The Roumanian*, [1914] 1 B.& C.P.C. 75, 356; *Ten Bales of Silk at Port Said*, [1916] 1 B.& C.P.C. 247.

Sommaire

Droit de visite, fouille, déroutement et capture.
Partie I: Le droit traditionnel

Bien que les belligérants aient eu tendance depuis 1945 à ne pas recourir à la guerre maritime économique et à opter plutôt pour une politique de torpillage sans restriction, il est encore pertinent d'examiner les mesures relevant de la guerre maritime économique qui sont acceptables en vertu du droit international traditionnel et de se demander si ces règles s'appliquent à la guerre maritime moderne.

Afin d'établir ce qu'est le droit positif de la guerre maritime économique, la première partie de cet article donne un aperçu du droit traditionnel relatif à la visite, la fouille, le déroutement et la capture. On entend ici par "droit traditionnel" les règles qui ont été adoptées dans le cadre d'ententes internationales ou élaborées grâce à la pratique des États jusqu'en 1954. Le traitement des équipages et des passagers ainsi que la réquisition et l'angarie ne sont pas abordés. La pratique des États depuis 1945 sera examinée dans la deuxième partie de cet article qui paraîtra dans le prochain volume de l'Annuaire.*

*These questions will be considered in Part II of this study, entitled "State Practice since the Second World War," to be published in Volume XXX of this *Yearbook*.

Notes and Comments /
Notes et commentaires

L'examen des rapports périodiques du Canada
en application du Pacte international relatif
aux droits économiques, sociaux et culturels

S I L'ÉTAT CANADIEN A MIS UN CERTAIN TEMPS à devenir partie au *Pacte* *international relatif aux les droits éconmiques, sociaux et culturels*,[1] il lui a été permis d'élaborer des formules originales de préparation et de présentation de ses rapports périodiques,[2] qui ont notamment été utilisées pour le Pacte sur les droits économiques.[3] Les rapports de l'État canadien se sont par ailleurs avérés la source du dialogue entre les représentants canadiens et les organes chargés de l'application du Pacte sur les droits économiques institués par le

---

[1] (1976) 993 R.T.N.U. 13, [1976] R.T. Can. n° 46 [ci-après dénommée le Pacte sur les droits économiques ou le Pacte]. Le Pacte sur les droits économiques a été adopté par l'Assemblée générale des Nations Unies le 16 décembre 1966 et est entré en vigueur le 3 janvier 1976. Le dépôt de l'instrument d'adhésion du Canada au Pacte sur les droits économiques a eu lieu le 19 mai 1976 et, en vertu de son article 35, le Pacte est entré en vigueur pour le Canada le 19 août 1976.

[2] V. à ce sujet D. TURP, "La préparation et la présentation des rapports du Canada en application des traités relatifs aux droits et libertés," (1986) 24 *A.C.D.I.* 161 et en particulier l'article 8 des Modalités et mécanismes pour la mise en oeuvre du Pacte international relatif aux droits économiques, sociaux et culturels, du Pacte international relatif aux droits civils et politiques ainsi que le Protocole facultatif se rapportant à ce dernier, reproduit dans J.-Y. MORIN, F. RIGALDIES et D. TURP, *Droit international public: notes et documents*, Montréal, Les Éditions Thémis, 1988, pp. 384-85 [ci-après dénommés Modalités et mécanismes].

[3] *Id.*, aux pp. 191-193 et 201-6.

Conseil économique et social des Nations Unies.

À cet égard, il importe de rappeler que le Pacte sur les droits économiques établit un mécanisme unique de contrôle systématique en vertu de laquelle les États doivent rendre compte de leur respect des normes contenues dans le Pacte par la soumission de rapports périodiques au Conseil économique et social.[4] Le devoir des États à l'égard de ce contrôle est formulé au paragraphe 16 § 1 du Pacte, qui stipule que les États parties s'engagent à présenter des rapports sur les mesures qu'ils auront adoptées et sur les progrès qu'ils auront accomplis en vue d'assurer le respect des droits reconnus dans le Pacte.

Pour assumer les responsabilités à l'égard de ces rapports, dont l'alinéa 16 § 2 (a) du Pacte lui confie en outre ''l'examen,'' le Conseil économique et social définit, conformément au paragraphe 17 § 1, un programme en vertu duquel les États doivent présenter leurs rapports. C'est par la résolution 1988,[5] adoptée quelque cinq mois après l'entrée en vigueur du Pacte, que le Conseil arrête un programme suivant lequel les États sont invités à présenter leurs rapports en trois étapes biennales, d'abord sur les articles 6 à 9, ensuite sur les articles 10 à 12 et enfin sur les articles 13 à 15. Aux fins de procéder à l'examen de ces rapports, le Conseil économique et social fait appel à des organes subsidiaires qui se voient confier la tâche d'examiner les rapports.

La collaboration du Canada aux fins de l'établissement d'un dialogue avec ces organes subsidiaires est acquise dès l'origine et se traduit par l'envoi de délégués de haut niveau et de compétence reconnue. Mais cette volonté de collaboration n'engendre pas nécessairement un dialogue utile avec les groupes de session du Conseil économique et social chargés d'examiner les rapports, composés d'abord de représentants gouvernementaux[6] et ultérieurement

---

[4] Pour une description de ce mécanisme, v. E. SCHWELB, ''Some Aspects of the Implementation of the International Covenant on Economic, Social and Cultural Rights,'' (1968) 1 *R.D.H.* 263. V. aussi P. HARVEY, ''Monitoring Mechanisms for International Agreements Respecting Economic and Social Human Rights,'' (1987) 12 *Yale J. Int'l L.* 396 ainsi que les communications et rapports présentés à l'occasion d'un symposium sur la mise en oeuvre du Pacte international relatif aux droits économiques, sociaux et culturels, reproduits dans (1987) 9 *H.R.Q.* 121-267.

[5] C.E.S. Rés. 1988, Doc. off. C.E.S., 60e session, supp. n° 1, p. 11, Doc. NU E/5850 (1976).

[6] *Id.,* al. 9 (a). V. aussi C.E.S. Rés. 1978/10, Doc. off. C.E.S. 33e session, supp. n° 1, p. 36, Doc. NU E/1978/78 (1978)[ci-après denommé le Groupe de représentants gouvernementaux ou Groupe de représentants].

d'experts gouvernementaux,[7] mais qui seront remplacés par un Comité des droits économiques, sociaux et culturels,[8] lequel s'efforcera d'entreprendre un dialogue réel avec les délégués canadiens.[9] L'objet du présent commentaire est d'analyser la participation canadienne à ce dialogue et d'évaluer la qualité de cette participation, de même que l'effectivité du contrôle exercé par les organes d'application du Pacte sur l'État canadien. À cet égard, l'on peut suggérer que les groupes de travail de session invités à examiner les trois rapports initiaux du Canada le font de façon fort superficielle (I), alors que le Comité des droits économiques, sociaux et culturels se prête à un examen nettement plus critique du deuxième rapport du Canada en application des articles 6 à 9 du Pacte (II).

I. L'EXAMEN SUPERFICIEL DES RAPPORTS PÉRIODIQUES DU CANADA PAR LES GROUPES DE TRAVAIL DE SESSION

Dans le cas de l'examen par le Groupe de travail de session du *Rapport initial du Canada relatif aux articles 6 à 9 du Pacte sur les droits économiques*,[10] l'État canadien s'efforce de faire une présentation détaillée de son premier rapport en application de ce traité, en confiant toutefois cette présentation à une délégation de quatre personnes, une seule d'entre elles émanant d'un gouvernement provincial. Effectuant seul la présentation générale du rapport, le représentant de la mission permanente du Canada auprès des Nations Unies à New York, M. Morden, considéré par le groupe comme l'observateur du Canada,[11] rappelle l'attention scrupuleuse consacrée par le Canada à l'application des deux Pactes dans le cadre du système con-

---

[7] C.E.S. Rés. 1981/158, Doc. off. C.E.S. 1981, supp. nᵒ 1, p. 56, Doc. NU E/1981/81 (1981) [ci-après dénommé le Groupe d'experts gouvernementaux ou Groupe d'experts].

[8] C.E.S. Rés. 1985/17, Doc. off. C.E.S. 1985, supp. nᵒ 1, p. 15, Doc. NU E/1985/85 (1985) [ci-après dénommé le Comité des droits économiques ou Comité].

[9] Pour une évaluation générale de la qualité du contrôle des organes de surveillance du Pacte sur les droits économiques, v. D. TURP, "Le contrôle du respect du Pacte international relatif aux droits économiques, sociaux et culturels," dans *Le droit international au service de la paix, de la justice et du développement: Mélanges Michel Virally*, Paris, Pedone, 1991, p. 465. V. aussi les commentaires de F. SUDRE, *Droit international et européen des droits de l'homme*, Paris, P.U.F., 1989, pp. 279-80 et T. BUERGENTHAL et A. KISS, *La protection internationale des droits de l'Homme*, Kehl, Éditions N. P. Engel, 1991, pp. 28-32.

[10] Doc. NU E/1978/8/Add. 32 (1978).

[11] Il est intéressant de noter que la terminologie utilisée par le Groupe de travail diffère de celle utilisée par le Comité des droits de l'Homme où l'on qualifie les membres des délégations de représentants plutôt que d'observateurs.

stitutionnel du Canada. Il décrit le processus complexe de consultation à laquelle une telle application donne lieu, ce qui explique, selon lui, l'impossibilité pour l'État canadien de respecter les dates limites fixées par le Conseil pour la présentation des rapports.

L'observateur du Canada fait par ailleurs une présentation des renseignements contenus au rapport. Il n'élabore guère sur l'application par les juridictions du Canada des articles 1 à 5 du Pacte, rappelant seulement que celles-ci souscrivent aux principes y énoncés. Avant de procéder à l'étude systématique des données contenues au rapport sur les articles 6 à 9, le délégué canadien évoque "l'une des principales innovations intéressant les quatre articles traités dans le rapport, la Charte canadienne des droits et libertés mise au point récemment grâce à une coopération à tous les niveaux du gouvernement, qui codifie et étend les droits existants et en introduit de nouveaux dans la Constitution."[12] Le délégué canadien ne met toutefois pas l'accent sur les dispositions qui ont un intérêt particulier pour la mise en oeuvre du Pacte sur les droits économiques, tels les articles 15 et 28 relatifs aux droits à l'égalité, mais aussi à l'article 36 relatif à la péréquation et aux inégalités économiques régionales.[13] Mais dans cette présentation générale, l'observateur canadien évoque la législation en matière de discrimination et réfère aux organes et mécanismes créés pour assurer le respect des normes d'égalité, et notamment les commissions indépendantes de droits de la personne et des médiateurs.

Le porte-parole de la délégation canadienne poursuit ensuite sa présentation en résumant les données du rapport relatives aux articles 6 à 9. Sur l'article 6, M. Morden insiste sur l'adoption de multiples programmes et mesures administratives pour favoriser l'application du droit au travail. Il met en outre l'accent sur le fait que le gouvernement fédéral et du Québec ont, en ce qui concerne l'article 7 du Pacte, promulgué des lois assurant un salaire égal pour un travail égal. Un développement plus important est consacré à l'article 8 sur les droits syndicaux et est complété par un renvoi aux rapports bisannuels du Canada à l'O.I.T. au sujet de la Convention no 87. Enfin, sur l'article 9, l'observateur du Canada décrit les divers programmes de soins de santé, les régimes de sécurité sociale et la vaste gamme des services sociaux "visant à réduire, supprimer ou prévenir les causes ou les effets de la pauvreté, de

---

[12] Doc. NU E/1982/WG.1/SR.1, p. 7, par. 40 (1982).

[13] L'article 36 sera mentionné pendant l'examen du Rapport sur les articles 10 à 12: v. E/1984/WG.1/SR.6, p. 3. par. 9.

l'abandon des enfants ou du recours à l'assistance sociale."[14]

Cette présentation du rapport du Canada est suivie d'un dialogue entre les membres du groupe de travail de session et les autres délégués canadiens, qui ne permet pas un examen véritablement minutieux de la mise en oeuvre des articles 6 à 9 du Pacte par l'État canadien. Ainsi, une seule séance, d'une durée de moins de deux heures, est consacrée à l'examen du rapport et seuls 8 des 18 membres du Groupe de travail de session participent au dialogue, un observateur de l'Organisation internationale du travail prenant aussi la parole à la fin de la séance. Au plan substantif, les commentaires et questions des membres ne portent véritablement que sur les mesures fédérales de mise en oeuvre et les données provinciales, pourtant si importantes en la matière et occupant l'essentiel du rapport, sont dans l'ensemble ignorées.[16]

Au-delà des remarques sur la qualité du rapport du Canada, de son caractère complet, voire même sur son excellence,[17] les membres du groupe n'approfondissent guère les questions plus difficiles de mise en oeuvre. Des questions sont posées sur le rôle et la possibilité du gouvernement fédéral et du Comité permanent en regard de la mise en oeuvre du Pacte sur les droits économiques, sur les types de relations patronales-ouvrières, les licenciements injustes et le versement adéquat des prestations de sécurité sociale. Toutefois, les représentants des États d'Europe de l'Est se font quant à eux plus critiques. Ainsi, le représentant de la Bulgarie constate que le rapport comprend des données qui datent de 1977, sans toutefois mentionner, comme il aurait pu le faire, que la présentation orale du rapport devait être l'occasion de mettre à jour de telles données. Il ajoute "qu'il ne suffit pas que le droit au travail soit reconnu par la loi, mais qu'il doit être mis en pratique, étant frappé à cet égard par la grande disparité entre la rénumération annuelle moyenne des hommes et des femmes."[18] Le représentant soviétique déplore quant à lui le taux très faible de syndicalisation et s'inquiète de la situation des Indiens du Canada.[19] Il reprend à son compte les remarques sur la disparité des salaires des hommes et

[14] Doc. NU E/1982/WG.1/SR.1, p. 10, par. 52 (1982).
[15] V. par exemple la question posée par le représentant gouvernemental Alafi, qui demande dans quelle mesure un employé peut bénéficier de la protection des autorités fédérales: v. *id.*, p. 4, par. 13 (1982).
[16] *Id.*, p. 2, par. 1 (AKAO) et p.4, par. 11 (VEITIA).
[17] *Id.*, p. 2, par. 3 (BORCHARD).
[18] *Id.*, p. 3, par. 8 (MRATCHKOV).
[19] *Id.*, p. 5, par. 16 et 18 (SOFINSKY).

des femmes,[20] comme le fera aussi le représentant de la Biélorussie.[21]

Les réponses des observateurs du Canada sont en règle générale satisfaisantes. Deux des quatre observateurs du Canada sont chargés de répondre aux questions et le font d'ailleurs immédiatement après les interventions des membres du groupe. Certaines réponses demeurent incomplètes et des promesses sont faites de fournir dès que possible des précisions sur la ventilation numérique des relations patronales-ouvrières demandée par le membre ouest-allemand du groupe[22] ou le système complexe de prestations de services sociaux.[23] Une autre observatrice du Canada complète parfois les réponses et manifeste d'ailleurs une certaine franchise lorsqu'elle admet que le public est moins informé, dans certains domaines comme la création d'emploi, des multiples programmes et de l'aide dont il peut disposer. Elle manifeste la même franchise lorsqu'elle dit que le Canada est ''sérieusement préoccupé par la disparité entre les rémunérations moyennes des hommes et des femmes'' et que seules deux provinces ''appliquent les principes d'égalité de rémunération pour un travail égal préconisé par l'O.I.T.''[24] Cependant, elle est prise à partie pour une réponse donnée au représentant soviétique sur le niveau de syndicalisation, que ce dernier n'accepte guère, ne ''compren[ant] pas comment la prédominance de petites entreprises explique ce niveau sur le faible niveau de syndicalisation,''[25] une réponse que l'observatrice du Canada tiendra d'ailleurs à rectifier ultérieurement.[26]

Ce premier examen d'un rapport canadien en application du Pacte sur les droits économiques est décevant et tend à démontrer les lacunes du contrôle systématique exercé par un Groupe de travail de session formé de représentants gouvernementaux. Ces lacunes ne seront d'ailleurs que partiellement comblées par l'examen du rapport initial du Canada sur les articles 10 à 12.

Présenté en avril 1985 à un Groupe de travail de session composé d'experts gouvernementaux cette fois, ce deuxième rapport ne connaît pas un sort beaucoup plus intéressant que le précédent. En effet, non seulement le temps consacré à l'examen du rapport sur les articles 10 à 12 n'est-il à peine plus important, mais les

[20] *Id.*, p. 5, par. 17.
[21] *Id.*, p. 6, par. 26 (MARDOVICH).
[22] *Id.*, p. 2, par. 4 (NOLAN).
[23] *Id.*, p. 3, par. 6.
[24] *Id.*, p. 6, par. 22 (DAY).
[25] *Id.*, p. 6, par. 23 (SOFINSKY).
[26] *Id.*, p. 6, par. 24 (DAY).

membres du Groupe ne disposent pas d'un temps suffisant pour lire le rapport, comme le souligne l'expert bulgare Mitrev, qui prie instamment le Secrétariat de veiller à l'avenir à ce que des "rapports aussi volumineux soient diffusés suffisamment à l'avance pour permettre aux membres du Groupe de travail de les étudier à fond."[27] Ceci a notamment comme conséquence que la lecture des parties provinciales du rapport n'a guère été possible, comme l'avoue la présidente du groupe qui regrette "de ne pas être en mesure de traiter des parties du rapport concernant l'application du Pacte dans chacune des provinces."[28] Cette situation est d'ailleurs aggravée en raison de l'incompréhension persistante du système fédéral canadien et du partage des responsabilités constitutionnelles en matière de droits de la personne. Elle se traduit par la remarque de l'expert soviétique qui trouve "surprenant qu'un cinquième seulement du rapport fournisse des renseignements sur l'action au niveau fédéral et que les quatre cinquièmes restants contiennent des renseignements provenant des provinces"[29] et celle de l'expert bulgare pour qui le rapport du Canada pose des difficultés au plan conceptuel.[30] Ceci se reflète aussi dans les questions posées qui concernent presqu'exclusivement les mesures fédérales de mise en oeuvre.[31]

Ces questions constitutionnelles ont pourtant été clairement exposées lors de l'examen du rapport précédent, mais aussi par le représentant permanent du Canada auprès des Nations Unies dans sa présentation générale du rapport. Celui-ci dirige d'ailleurs une imposante délégation de 11 personnes, incluant 4 représentants provinciaux, et mentionne d'ailleurs à nouveau l'existence des Modalités et mécanismes et celle d'un Comité permament, qui s'est avéré selon lui "un instrument utile à même d'assurer une collaboration étroite entre le gouvernement fédéral et les gouvernements des provinces et territoires pour ce qui est d'appliquer les pactes et de répondre à d'autres obligations dans le domaine des droits de l'Homme, y compris l'établissement des rapports au titre des Pactes."[32]

Cette présentation générale n'a par ailleurs qu'un intérêt réduit, car les données du rapport concernant les articles 10, 11 et 12 sont

---

[27] Doc. N.U. E/1984/WG.1/SR.4, p. 6, par. 28 (MITREV).

[28] *Id.,* p. 10, par. 50 (BENDIX).

[29] *Id.,* p. 4, par. 18 (SVIRIDOV).

[30] *Id.,* p. 6, par. 29 (MITREV).

[31] *Id.,* p. 3, par. 11 (KORDS).

[32] *Id.,* p. 2, par. 2 (PELLETIER).

exposées très succinctement et ne font l'objet d'aucune mise à jour. Le rappel par le représentant permanent de l'entrée en vigueur de la *Charte canadienne des droits et libertés* revêt également un intérêt moindre, d'autant que la Charte n'est pas située dans la perspective de la garantie qu'elle pourrait offrir en matière de droits économiques, sociaux et culturels. La référence au rôle des organisations non gouvernementales est plus originale et la reconnaissance que des progrès sont encore à faire pour atteindre l'idéal auquel tend le Pacte terminent la présentation générale du rapport sur une note d'une franchise certaine.

Les experts gouvernementaux, qui participent à l'examen du rapport sur les articles 10 à 12, sont tous nouveaux et n'ont pas été présents lors de l'examen du rapport précédent, ce qui explique leur ignorance du système constitutionnel canadien. Leurs commentaires et questions sont d'une généralité parfois déconcertante et ne contribuent guère à clarifier la situation relative à la mise en oeuvre du Pacte ou aux lacunes d'icelle.

En dépit de certaines incongruités,[33] les remarques de l'expert soviétique ne sont toutefois pas dénuées d'intérêt et portent à nouveau sur la discrimination, la situation particulière des peuples autochtones en regard de la Charte canadienne ainsi que les problèmes découlant de discrimination entre les provinces qui pourrait résulter de l'article 6 de cette Charte sur la liberté de circulation. Celui-ci demande d'ailleurs aux représentants canadiens des statistiques concernant le chômage au Canada, citant de sa propre initiative le bulletin mensuel de la statistique de l'ONU. Il souhaite également obtenir des données précises sur le nombre de familles et d'individus se trouvant au-dessous du seuil de la pauvreté, le nombre de personnes âgées pouvant être considérées comme pauvres, sur le nombre de personnes sans logis au Canada et enfin sur le nombre de personnes souffrant de maladies mentales. Ce sont donc des problèmes concrets de mise en oeuvre du Pacte qui intéressent l'expert soviétique et qui lui font exiger des autorités canadiennes la présentation d'informations qui tendront à démontrer la mise en oeuvre encore déficiente des droits économiques et sociaux consacrés aux articles 10 à 12.[34]

Reprenant certains thèmes évoqués par son collègue soviétique, l'expert bulgare n'hésite pas à signaler, quant à lui, le manque de

---

[33] V. cette curieuse remarque selon laquelle le Canada n'aurait qu'une constitution depuis deux ans: id., p. 4, par. 17 (SVIRIDOV).
[34] *Id.*, p. 4-6, par. 19-27.

précisions des données du rapport sur la Commission canadienne des droits de la personne et les recours qui peuvent être intentés devant cette commission.[35] Il s'interroge aussi sur les conditions devant être remplies pour bénéficier des prestations de maternité et s'intéresse à la portée d'une décision de la Cour suprême du Canada. Il demande aussi des renseignements très précis sur la protection des mineurs délinquants et démontre avoir fait une lecture fort attentive et critique du rapport du Canada. L'experte danoise, qui assume la présidence du Comité, pose quant à elle un nombre important de questions et demande des compléments d'information. Comme l'expert bulgare, elle s'inquiète de la teneur des règles relatives à l'âge minimum auquel on peut être reconnu coupable au Canada d'un délit prévu au Code criminel.[36]

Les remarques de ces trois seuls membres ne sauraient suffire pour que nous concluions à un effort utile de contrôle systématique du Groupe de travail de session d'experts gouvernementaux. Mais, la délégation canadienne ne prend pas pour autant l'exercice à la légère. Les réponses préparées par les membres de la délégation et les données présentées par ceux-ci lors d'une séance subséquente d'examen sont empreintes de sérieux et prouvent la volonté de l'État fédératif canadien de participer de façon dynamique à ce contrôle. D'ailleurs, six membres de la délégation sont mis à contribution pour répondre aux questions soulevées par les membres du groupe de session.

Ainsi, le représentant du Secrétariat d'État du Canada reprend pour les membres du groupe les enseignements sur le partage des compétences en matière de droits de la personne et décrit avec précision les mécanismes fédéraux-provinciaux auxquels il est fait appel dans ce processus de mise en oeuvre des traités internationaux relatifs aux droits de la personne. Il donne également des précisions sur la portée de l'enchâssement des droits ancestraux ou issus de traités des peuples autochtones dans la *Charte canadienne des droits et libertés,* sur les questions d'incorporation des Pactes dans la législation interne et de la relation entre le Pacte sur les droits économiques et la Charte. Il fait enfin allusion à l'utilisation des paiements de péréquation pour assurer le développement économique et social et mentionne l'inclusion dans la *Loi constitutionnelle de 1982* d'une disposition à cet effet, en l'occurrence l'article 36. Ce

---

[35] *Id.,* p. 7, par. 30 (MITREV). V. aussi *id.,* p. 8, par. 38 (TEXIER) et p. 8, par. 40 (BEN HAMIDA).

[36] *Id.,* p. 9, par. 47 (BENDIX).

représentant ne se gêne pas par ailleurs pour corriger l'expert soviétique et lui rappeler que la première Constitution du Canada date de 1867 et qu'une terminologie plus appropriée aurait pu être utilisée par cet expert lorsqu'il fut fait allusion à la structure politique du Canada.[37]

Des réponses fort detaillées sont par ailleurs données à la question relative à la protection des mineurs délinquants. La déléguée provenant du ministère des Affaires extérieures saisit cette occasion pour informer les membres du groupe que la *Loi sur les jeunes délinquants* a été remplacée par la *Loi sur les jeunes contrevenants,* cette dernière visant à assurer un meilleur respect des droits des mineurs.[38] Sans doute, cette information aurait-elle dû être mentionnée dans la présentation générale du rapport, ce qui aurait eu pour effet de lever l'incertitude qui régnait sur l'état du droit canadien en la matière.

Sur la compétence de la Commission canadienne des droits de la personne, cette même déléguée donne des éclaircissements et des précisions utiles sur le pouvoir de porter plainte devant la Commission canadienne. Elle mentionne également la possibilité de faire des communications analogues aux commissions provinciales de droits de la personne,[39] ce qui fournit l'occasion au délégué québécois d'expliquer brièvement les rôles et responsabilités de la Commission des droits de la personne du Québec et de glisser un mot sur le rang hiérarchique de la Charte québécoise parmi les lois du Québec.[40]

D'autres modifications législatives, destinées à éliminer des pratiques discriminatoires à l'égard des femmes, sont mentionnées durant cette période de réponses aux questions, tandis que d'autres délégués sont mandatés pour répondre à des questions diverses sur l'emploi, le droit à un niveau de vie suffisant, au divorce et au logement.

En définitive, les membres de la délégation canadienne s'efforcent de répondre systématiquement aux questions posées par les membres du Groupe et offrent, dans la grande majorité des cas, des réponses précises et détaillées. Dans l'intervention liminaire de la délégation, le représentant du Secrétariat d'État du Canada et président du Comité permanent termine en mentionnant que le

[37] Doc. NU E/1984/WG.1/SR.6, p. 4, par. 10 (RAYNER).
[38] *Id.,* p. 4 , par. 12 (SWORDS).
[39] *Id.,* p. 4 , par. 13.
[40] *Id.,* pp. 4-5 , par. 15 (BERGERON).

gouvernement "étudierait avec attention les observations faites par les membres et chercherait à donner l'information additionnelle requise dans son prochain rapport."[41]

La présentation du dernier rapport dans le cadre du premier cycle de rapports relatifs au Pacte sur les droits économiques et relatif aux articles 13 à 15[42] donne lieu à une amélioration sensible des procédures d'examen du Groupe de session d'experts gouvernementaux et à un dialogue nettement plus constructif. Ainsi, les membres du Groupe consacrent un temps nettement plus important à l'examen du rapport relatif aux articles 13 à 15. Comme nous en informe le *Rapport de la délégation canadienne,*[43] qui est le premier document de la sorte préparé après l'examen d'un rapport périodique du Canada, près de quatre heures, réparties sur trois séances, ont été nécessaires pour le discours d'ouverture, les commentaires et les questions des membres du groupe et les réponses des délégués.

Non seulement n'a-t-on pas, comme par le passé, étudié de façon trop expéditive le rapport, mais au surplus le rapport paraît avoir été lu de façon approfondie et intéressée, car il suscite des questions de la part de neuf des dix-huit experts dont la pertinence et l'intérêt sont incontestables.

Sans doute, la qualité accrue de l'examen résulte-t-elle aussi de la participation toujours aussi intéressée de la délégation du Canada à l'examen du rapport. Même si la délégation est plus modeste et ne compte que six membres, quatre délégués fédéraux et deux délégués provinciaux, elle est composée de personnes qui ont déjà participé à des séances antérieures d'examen du Pacte sur les droits économiques et qui connaissent les exigences du contrôle systématique. La délégation est rehaussée en statut par la présence du représentant permanent du Canada auprès des Nations Unies, Stephen Lewis. Celui-ci prononce d'ailleurs un remarquable discours d'ouverture, pendant lequel il présente le rapport à partir d'un texte préparé à son intention par les membres de la délégation, dont il ponctue la lecture de remarques sur des leçons de son expérience personnelle en matière de protection des droits de la personne.

---

[41] *Id.,* p. 4, par. 10 (RAYNER).

[42] E/1982/3/Add. 34 (1982).

[43] *Examen du rapport du Canada aux Nations Unies sur les articles 13 à 15 du Pacte international relatif aux droits économiques, sociaux et culturels,* New York, 22-24 avril 1986, Doc. n° 312-3-1, mai 1986 [ci-après dénommé Rapport de délégation (art. 13 à 15)].

Ce discours d'ouverture a par ailleurs une portée fort générale et aborde à nouveau les questions de fédéralisme et de droit constitutionnel, déjà évoquées lors de la présentation des rapports précédents.[44] Comme auparavant, les mesures tendant à mettre en oeuvre les droits visés par le rapport sont exposées de façon plutôt générale, mais une nouvelle pratique est inaugurée, celle de faire état de quelques faits nouveaux pour mettre à jour l'information comprise dans le rapport. C'est ainsi que l'ambassadeur Lewis révise les données contenues au rapport et informe les membres du groupe des réformes législatives et les programmes nouveaux adoptés notamment par le gouvernement fédéral, la province d'Ontario et le territoire du Yukon.[45]

Ces remarques sont suivies des interventions des experts gouvernementaux, parmi lesquels l'on retrouve l'un de ceux qui avait siégé lors de l'examen du rapport sur les articles 6 à 9 et deux autres qui avaient participé à l'examen du rapport sur les articles 10 à 12 du Canada. Cette nouvelle continuité dans le membership se reflète d'ailleurs dans les commentaires et questions de ces membres qui tendent à porter sur des questions de fond plutôt que sur des questions de nature procédurale, sans que ne soit ignoré cette fois le rôle des provinces dans la mise en oeuvre du Pacte sur les droits économiques.

Ainsi, les experts bulgare, français et espagnol s'intéressent-ils à des questions plus controversées, telles l'enseignement public et privé, la discrimination à l'égard des personnes handicapées, la participation des femmes et d'autochtones aux divers niveaux d'enseignement. Les autres experts posent des questions de nature diverse, dans l'ensemble fort pertinentes et qui donnent l'occasion aux délégués canadiens de donner des informations supplémentaires sur la mise en oeuvre des droits culturels dans l'État fédératif canadien.

Préparée collectivement,[46] la réplique de la délégation canadienne donne lieu à des interventions de l'ensemble de ses membres.[47] Les habituelles précisions d'ordre constitutionnel et administratif sont apportées par un délégué fédéral et une déléguée provinciale.[48] Cette

---

[44] Doc. NU E/1986/WG.1/SR. 13, p. 2, par. 3-7.

[45] *Id.*, p. 3, par. 7.

[46] V. au sujet des travaux de préparation de cette réplique, le Rapport de délégation (art. 13 à 15), p. 6.

[47] Doc. NU E/1986/WG1/SR.15, p. 7, par. 37-38 (SIROIS).

[48] *Id.*, p. 7, par. 39 (EWART).

dernière déléguée donne également un nombre important d'informations sur les droits culturels tels qu'interprétés et appliqués en Ontario et rapporte par ailleurs la position de autochtones au Canada, qui ne sont pas considérés, selon elle, ''comme une minorité culturelle mais comme un peuple distinct dont le rôle est unique au Canada.''[49] Le délégué du Québec répond aux questions relatives au droit à l'éducation et donne d'ailleurs d'instructifs compléments statistiques en la matière.[50] Le représentant du Secrétariat d'État met à jour quant à lui les données statistiques sur la recherche scientifique et sur le taux d'analphabétisme, et notamment celui régnant dans les territoires et chez les populations autochtones.[51]

Des réponses fort détaillées sont par ailleurs présentées par le délégué provenant du ministère de la Justice du Canada et directeur de la section des droits de la personne de ce même ministère. C'est ainsi que ce délégué fédéral aborde des questions telles la syndicalisation des fonctionnaires et la confidentialité des données, mais aussi les questions de discrimination et de liberté d'expression telles qu'elles peuvent se poser dans l'application des droits reconnus aux articles 13 à 15 du Pacte sur les droits économiques. Il annonce par ailleurs que de nouvelles dispositions relatives à l'obscénité ont été ajoutées au Code criminel et complètent des informations données par les autres membres de la délégation sur les populations autochtones et aux responsabilités du gouvernement fédéral dans le domaine de l'enseignement.[52] La dernière intervention est celle du délégué du ministère des Affaires extérieures du Canada, J. Gaudreau, qui réaffirme, comme paraissait le souhaiter le membre tunisien du Groupe d'experts, M. Ben Hamida, l'adhésion du Canada au nouvel ordre de l'information et énumère les mesures concrètes prises par le Canada pour contribuer à l'emergence de ce nouvel ordre.[53]

À la fin de ce premier cycle de présentation et d'examen des rapports initiaux du Canada en application du Pacte international relatif aux droits économiques, sociaux et culturels, il est permis de constater que l'État canadien a participé de façon dynamique au processus de contrôle systématique du Pacte et qu'il a constamment voulu assurer la présence dans ses délégations de personna-

[49] *Id.,* p. 8, par. 47.
[50] *Id.,* pp. 9-10, par. 49-53.
[51] Doc. NU E/1986/WG.1/SR.16, pp. 2-3, par. 3-4 (SIROIS).
[52] *Id.,* pp. 3-6, par. 8-17 (LOW).
[53] *Id.,* p. 6, par. 18 (GAUDREAU).

lités prestigieuses et compétentes, tout en tentant d'assurer une continuité dans la composition des délégations. L'amélioration des méthodes de travail des délégations a été perceptible, tant au plan de la présentation générale des rapports, qui a donné lieu à la préparation préalable d'un discours d'ouverture qu'en regard des réponses aux questions dont la préparation a fait l'objet d'une réflexion collective. De plus, au lendemain de l'examen du dernier rapport de ce premier cycle, le rapport initial sur les articles 13 à 15, le Secrétariat d'État du Canada établit un rapport de la délégation du Canada sur l'examen de rapport qui contient une évaluation générale de l'examen du rapport[54] ainsi que des recommandations relatives au suivi de cet examen.[55]

L'analyse des séances d'examen des rapports initiaux du Canada permet par ailleurs de noter une amélioration sensible des travaux de contrôle effectué par les organes chargés de l'application du Pacte sur les droits économiques. Entre l'examen du rapport initial du Canada sur les articles 6 à 9 par un groupe de représentants gouvernementaux et celui intéressant les articles 10 à 12 et 13 à 15 effectué par des groupes d'experts gouvernementaux, il y a une évolution caractérisée par une analyse plus approfondie des rapports du Canada et la formulation de questions d'une pertinence et d'un intérêt plus évidents. La continuité relative dans le membership des groupes d'experts gouvernementaux qui analysent les deuxième et troisième rapports initiaux du Canada a certes favorisé un tel approfondissment.

Mais les rapports établis par les groupes de travail de représentants ou d'experts gouvernementaux à la suite de leurs sessions d'examen des rapports des États ne révèlent toutefois aucune évolution significative. On ne peut y retrouver ni observation additionnelle ni évaluation des mesures de mise en oeuvre du Pacte sur les droits économiques, les rapports se contentant de références aux dates de présentation et aux cotes des trois rapports canadiens.[56] Mais l'émergence du Comité sur les droits économiques, sociaux et culturels vient modifier toutefois les pratiques d'examen des rapports

---

[54] Rapport de délégation (art. 13 à 15), pp. 6-7.

[55] *Id.,* p. 7.

[56] V. le *Rapport du Groupe de travail de session chargé d'étudier l'application du Pacte international relatif aux droits économiques, sociaux et culturels,* Doc. NU E/1982/56, p. 5, par. 14; *Rapport du Groupe de travail de session chargé d'étudier l'application du Pacte international relatif aux droits économiques, sociaux et culturels,* Doc. NU E/1984/83, p. 7, par. 14; *Rapport du Groupe de travail de session d'experts gouvernementaux chargé d'étudier l'application du Pacte international relatif aux droits économiques, sociaux et culturels,* Doc. NU E/1986/49.

périodiques en application du Pacte sur les droits économiques.

II. L'EXAMEN CRITIQUE DES RAPPORTS PÉRIODIQUES DU CANADA PAR LE
COMITÉ DES DROITS ÉCONOMIQUES, SOCIAUX ET CULTURELS

La création en 1986 du Comité des droits économiques, sociaux et culturels,[57] organe d'experts indépendants dont la composition et les pouvoirs sont dorénavant comparables à ceux du Comité des droits de l'Homme, contribuera davantage encore à l'amélioration du contrôle systématique du Pacte sur les droits économiques, comme en fera foi l'examen par le nouveau Comité du deuxième *Rapport du Canada sur l'application des articles* 6 à 9 du Pacte sur les droits économiques.[58]

En effet, le Comité qui devait examiner le rapport du Canada lors de sa première session en 1988,[59] mais qui en reporta l'examen en 1989, consacra deux séances entières et près de quatre heures à l'examen de ce rapport, dépassant le temps qu'elle avait d'ailleurs au préalable alloué pour un tel examen. D'autres mesures permettent de constater l'amélioration, telles la préparation par un groupe de travail pré-session du Comité d'une liste de questions qui est transmise au gouvernement canadien avant la date d'examen du rapport[60] ainsi que la rencontre informelle entre les président et secrétaire du Comité avec certains membres de la délégation canadienne.[61]

Ces mesures du Comité allaient faciliter les tâches de la délégation canadienne, qui avaient aussi pris un soin important dans la préparation de la séance d'examen du rapport et de sa première participation aux travaux du Comité des droits économiques,

---

[57] C.E.S. Rés. 1985/17, Doc. off. C.E.S. 1985, supp. n° 1, p. 15, Doc. NU E/1985/ (1985). V. au sujet du contexte qui a mené à la création du Comité, P. ALSTON, "Out of the Abyss: The Challenges Confronting the New U.N. Committee on Economic, Social and Cultural Rights," (1987) 9 *H.R.Q.* 331.

[58] Doc. NU E/1984/7/Add. 28.

[59] Sur les travaux de cette première session et notamment sur la révision des procédures d'examen des rapports périodiques par le nouveau Comité, v. P. ALSTON et B. SIMMA, "First Session of the U.N. Committee on Economic, Social and Cultural Rights," (1987) 81 *A.J.I.L.* 747, aux pp. 753-54.

[60] Sur cette innovation procédurale et d'autres mesures destinées à améliorer le caractère constructif du dialogue avec les États parties, v. P. ALSTON et B. SIMMA, "Second Session of the U.N. Committee on Economic, Social and Cultural Rights," (1988) 82 *A.J.I.L.* 603, aux pp. 611-12.

[61] Voir à ce sujet *Examen du rapport du Canada aux Nations Unies sur les articles 6 à 9 du Pacte international relatif aux droits économiques, sociaux et culturels*, Genève, 10 et 13 février 1989, sans date [ci-après dénommé Rapport de délégation (art. 6 à 9)].

sociaux et culturels. Ainsi, les membres de la délégation avaient été choisis à la suite de consultation préalable avec les représentants officiels au Comité permanent des fonctionnaires sur les droits de la personne. Le Secrétariat d'État avait aussi coordonné les préparatifs de l'examen du rapport et résumait ultérieurement ses démarches de coordination de la façon suivante:

[Le Secrétariat d'État] a invité les représentants officiels au Comité permanent des fonctionnaires des droits de la personne à soumettre des suggestions pour le contenu du discours d'ouverture, des informations concernant les développements survenus depuis la soumission des rapports, ainsi que des éléments de réponse aux questions susceptibles d'être soulevées au cours de l'examen du rapport. Outre les ministères représentés dans la délégation, certains ministères fédéraux ont aussi été invités à fournir des informations, dont le ministère des Affaires indiennes et du Nord canadien et le ministère de la Santé et du Bien-être social.

L'ébauche du discours d'ouverture a été préparée par le Secrétariat d'État en consultation avec les membres de la délégation. L'ébauche à été transmise à la mission du Canada à Genève au cours de la semaine précédant la date prévue pour l'examen du rapport.

Des consultations ont également eu lieu au Canada concernant des documents soumis au Comité des droits économiques, sociaux et culturels par l'Organisation internationale du Travail et par le Conseil des Quatre points cardinaux, une organisation non gouvernementale accréditée auprès des Nations Unies. Le ministère du Travail du Canada s'est chargé de recueillir les informations nécessaires dans le premier cas, en consultation avec les provinces concernées; le ministère des Affaires indiennes et du Nord canadien s'est chargé de préparer des notes concernant le document du Conseil des Quatre points cardinaux qui portait sur la situation des autochtones au Canada, et en particulier les Micmacs de la Nouvelle-Écosse....

Afin que les membres de la délégation aient à leur disposition du matériel pouvant les aider à préparer les réponses aux questions, le Secrétariat d'État a recueilli des documents pertinents qui ont ensuite été transmis à la mission du Canada à Genève par le ministère des Affaires extérieures.[62]

À ces multiples démarches préparatoires s'ajoutait aussi une rencontre préalable de certains membres désignés de la délégation présents à la réunion du Comité permanent des fonctionnaires chargés des droits de la personne des 17 et 18 janvier 1989. Les cinq délégués fédéraux et deux délégués provinciaux qui formaient selon l'un des membres du Comité sur les droits économiques une

[62] Rapport de délégation (art 6 à 9), pp. 2-3.

délegation de très haut niveau, se retrouvent quelques semaines plus tard à Genève avec les autres membres de la délégation, ainsi qu'avec le représentant permanent du Canada auprès de l'Office des Nations Unies à Genève, qui jouera un rôle actif dans la préparation de la séance d'examen du rapport ainsi que dans le choix des réponses à apporter au Comité. La délégation se réunit d'ailleurs à trois reprises avant l'examen du rapport pour terminer la rédaction du discours d'ouverture, répartir les tâches au sein de la délégation et examiner les questions soumises à l'avance par le Comité.[63]

Confiée au représentant permanent, la présentation du deuxième rapport du Canada au titre des articles 6 à 9 sera bien reçue par les membres du Comité. S'agissant d'un nouveau Comité, le chef de la délégation canadienne considère utile de décrire à nouveau certains éléments de la structure fédérale du Canada et de rappeler les rôles respectifs des gouvernements féderal, provinciaux et territoriaux en matière de droits de la personne et de mise en oeuvre des traités. Le représentant canadien donne par ailleurs des informations sur la diffusion du rapport au Canada et souligne notamment que celui-ci est mis à la disposition des personnes intéressées aux droits de la personne, ''ces mesures sembl[a]nt aller dans le sens des suggestions du Comité concernant les consultations avec les organisations non-gouvernementales.''[64]

L'intérêt de la présentation réside également dans le fait que les statistiques contenues dans le rapport, qui reflètent la situation qui prévalait au moment de la rédaction du rapport en 1987, sont mises à jour en décembre 1988. Il est également fait état dans la présentation des nouveaux programmes sur l'équité en matière d'emploi, l'équité salariale, la protection de la loi contre le harcèlement au travail, en particulier le harcèlement sexuel, l'élargissement de la protection de la loi fondée sur la déficience mentale, les mesures visant à abolir la retraite obligatoire, l'adoption de nouvelles mesures de sécurité et d'hygiène du travail et les accords de sécurité sociale conclus par le gouvernement du Canada et celui du Québec avec différents pays.[65]

Le représentant permanent du Canada signale encore que de nombreuses modifications législatives ont été apportées aux lois pour rendre celles-ci conformes à la *Charte canadienne des droits et libertés* et mentionne de plus que cette dernière, ainsi que les chartes et la

---

[63] *Id.*, p. 3.
[64] Doc. NU E/C.12/1989/SR. 8, p. 2, par. 4.
[65] *Id.*, p. 3 , par. 6.

législation provinciales sur les droits de la personne, ont parfois été interprétées à la lumière des dispositions du Pacte sur les droits économiques, dans le cas notamment de l'article 8 sur les droits syndicaux.[66] Il mentionne aussi certains devéloppements récents en regard de nouveaux problèmes tels l'usage de tests de dépistage du sida et l'usage de la drogue au travail et l'emploi de personnes handicapées, abordés dans le cadre de la cinquième conférence des ministres chargés des droits de la personne en septembre 1988.[67]

Enfin, le porte-parole principal de la délégation cherche même à aborder la question de l'impact de l'Accord de libre-échange canado-américain, entré en vigueur le 1er janvier 1989, sur les droits reconnus aux articles 6 à 9 du Pacte et soutient que cet accord "ne limite pas la capacité qu'ont les différents gouvernements du Canada de mettre au point des programmes sociaux appropriés et de protéger ceux qui existent déjà," ni "n'affecte...les législations du travail fédérales et provinciales."[68]

Ce discours d'ouverture initie d'ailleurs un dialogue auquel participeront 14 des 18 membres du Comité, ce qui démontre l'intérêt accru que suscite le rapport et surtout le désir des experts d'exercer un contrôle nettement plus systématique. Après une série des questions fort pertinentes posées par l'expert de nationalité française[69] et une demande d'observations sur le cas des Indiens Micmacs de Nouvelle-Écosse par l'expert d'origine mexicaine,[70] qui n'hésite d'ailleurs pas à faire appel à l'information diffusée par le Conseil des Quatre points cardinaux, le rapport du Canada fait l'objet d'une attaque assez virulente de la part de l'expert australien,[71] que l'experte espagnole cherchera à qualifier de critiques constructives.[72]

Il est ainsi fait reproche à la délégation canadienne de laisser croire qu'un examen de la législation soit vraiment révélateur de la situation prévalant au Canada, les lois étant "si nombreuses que quelques lignes sur chaque sujet n'aideront guère le gouvernement fédéral ou les gouvernements provinciaux à déterminer dans quelle

[66] *Id.*, p. 4 , par. 10.
[67] *Id.*, p. 3 , par. 14.
[68] *Id.*, p. 5 , par. 16.
[69] *Id.*, p. 5, par. 19 à 26 (TEXIER).
[70] *Id.*, p. 5, par. 27 (WIMER ZAMBRANO).
[71] *Id.*, pp. 6-7, par. 29 à 34 (ALSTON). V. aussi les remarques de M. MRACHKOV, *id.*, p. 7 , par. 35.
[72] *Id.*, p. 8, par. 40 (JIMENEZ BUTRAGUENO).

mesure ils respectent le Pacte.''[73] L'expert australien demande par
ailleurs à la délégation canadienne de l'éclairer sur la légitimité des
droits économiques et sociaux reconnus dans les articles 6 à 9 ainsi
que sur la jurisprudence canadienne relative à certains de ces droits,
et notamment sur celle dans laquelle le texte même du Pacte ou
des conventions de l'O.I.T. a été invoqué. Il demande également
un complément d'information sur la situation des groupes plus vul-
nérables et défavorisés et souhaite voir la délégation commenter
les informations contenues dans le document du Conseil des Quatre
points cardinaux.[74]

À l'égard des autoctones, il est aussi intéressant de constater que
l'expert équatorien fait référence au rapport initial du Canada sur
les articles 6 à 9 et demande à la délégation d'informer le Comité
sur l'issue des négociations avec les peuples autochtones auxquels
il a été fait allusion dans le précédent rapport.[75] Les questions relatives aux autochtones préoccupent également l'expert péruvien, qui
n'hésite pas non plus à soulever le cas des Micmacs de Nouvelle-
Écosse,[76] comme le fait aussi l'expert sénégalais, lequel aborde au
surplus la délicate question de l'application pratique au Canada
l'article premier du Pacte sur les droits économiques consacrant
le droit des peuples à disposer d'eux-mêmes.[77]

Plusieurs autres problèmes sont soumis à l'attention de la delé-
gation canadienne pendant la période de commentaires et questions réservée aux membres du Comité. Ainsi, des compléments
d'information sont demandés sur le chômage, les programmes de
formation professionnelle, le départ volontaire à la retraite, le con-
gé de maternité, le régime des pensions, l'égalité d'accès aux emplois du secteur privé pour les femmes, la possibilité pour les
étrangers et réfugiés de bénéficier des droits reconnus aux articles
6 à 9 du Pacte et le niveau de syndicalisation et les heures de travail. L'observateur de l'Organisation internationale du travail in-
tervient quant à lui en dernier lieu et souligne plusieurs mesures
positives prises par le Canada en application des conventions de
l'O.I.T. et relatives aux droits économiques et sociaux des articles
6 à 9 du Pacte, répondant ainsi à certains questions des membres

[73] *Id.*, p. 6, par. 31 (ALSTON).

[74] *Id.*, p. 7, par. 34.

[75] *Id.*, p. 7, par. 37 (MARCHAN ROMERO).

[76] *Id.*, p. 9, par. 47-48 (ALVAREZ VITA).

[77] *Id.*, p. 10, par. 57 (KONATE).

du Comité.[78]

On constate ainsi que les membres du Comité adoptent une attitude critique à l'égard du rapport canadien et veulent que le dialogue avec le Comité révèle davantage les problèmes concrets d'application du Pacte sur les droits économiques. Ils ne passent ainsi rien sous silence et obligent la délégation canadienne à rendre compte des multiples aspects de la mise en oeuvre des articles 6 à 9 du Pacte, imposant un travail très lourd aux délégués canadiens de façon à ce qu'un fructueux dialogue puisse suivre cette première séance.

Pour accomplir cette tâche herculéenne, les membres de la délégation canadienne se réuniront à trois reprises pour discuter d'abord de la préparation de réponses et pour évaluer ensuite les projets de réponse qu'ils ont formulé.[79]

L'examen des réponses formulées par les membres de la délégation canadienne révèle un souci particulier de satisfaire les multiples demandes du Comité et d'apporter des réponses précises et détaillées aux questions posées. Le plus critique des membres du Comité commentera d'ailleurs les efforts de la délégation en des termes fort élogieux:

M. Alston dit que le gouvernement canadien s'est admirablement acquitté de l'obligation essentielle qui incombe à tous les États parties au Pacte qui est d'assurer l'application des dispositions du Pacte sur son territoire et de faire rapport à ce sujet en toute bonne foi au Comité. Il remercie vivement la délégation canadienne d'avoir répondu en détail à toutes les questions qui lui ont été posées, notamment à celles concernant les populations autochtones, et d'avoir bien voulu transmettre au Comité des documents émanant de sources non gouvernementales.[80]

Précédées par des observations générales du représentant permanent du Canada, qui prend d'ailleurs acte de certains reproches adressés au Canada et promet à cet égard de recommander aux autorités canadiennes de tenir compte de ces observations du Comité dans l'établissement des prochains rapports,[81] les réponses offertes par les divers membres de la délégation paraissent en effet fort adéquates. Elles sont exhaustives, s'appuient sur des statistiques

[78] *Id.*, p. 11, par. 59 (DAO).

[79] Rapport de délégation (art. 6 à 9), p. 5.

[80] Doc. NU E/C.12/1989/SR. 11, p. 18, par. 72.

[81] *Id.*, p. 2, par. 5 (DE MONTIGNY MARCHAND).

ou de la jurisprudence récentes[82] et révèlent non seulement la compétence personnelle des membres de la délégation, mais aussi leur excellent niveau de préparation. Les membres de la délégation répondent d'ailleurs à la fois aux questions écrites présentées au préalable ainsi qu'aux questions orales des membres, et ne sentent que très rarement le besoin de promettre l'inclusion de renseignements plus précis dans le rapport subséquent.[83]

Si de nombreuses réponses mériteraient d'être mentionnées et démontreraient l'excellence de la réplique de la délégation canadienne, il nous appartient ici de signaler celles qui participent de façon particulièrement constructive au dialogue entre la délégation canadienne et les membres du nouveau Comité. Ainsi, dans un remarquable exposé sur les questions reliées au droit au travail, la déléguée Caron souligne la position adoptée par le Canada à l'égard du droit de grève et l'attitude de coopération qu'il a notamment eue lorsque des plaintes de violation de la liberté syndicale ont été portées à l'attention du Canada par l'OIT.[84] La déléguée du Nouveau-Brunswick donne quant à elle d'utiles précisions sur le harcèlement sexuel et les allocations de chômage,[85] alors que le délégué québécois fait particulièrement référence aux mesures adoptées par le Québec dans le domaine de la formation des adultes, les heures de travail, la retraite obligatoire, n'esquivant d'ailleurs pas la question de l'expert français sur la question de la réduction du personnel de la fonction publique du Québec.[86]

L'intervention du directeur de la section des droits de la personne du ministère de la Justice est également d'un intérêt certain. Ainsi, celui-ci répond aux questions d'ordre constitutionnel, à celles portant sur la *Charte canadienne des droits et libertés* et sa jurisprudence d'application ainsi qu'aux inquiétudes exprimées par les membres du Comité sur les problèmes des peuples autochtones. Il mentionne à cet égard l'influence décisive qu'a eue la constata-

---

[82] Ainsi, l'on cite en réponse à des questions de l'expert allemand Simma relative à la discrimination l'affaire *McKinney v. University of Guelph*, [1989] 1 R.C.S. 193, qui a été décidée un mois plus tôt par la Cour suprême du Canada: *id.*, p. 14, par. 43 (LOW).

[83] V. toutefois les engagements de présenter, dans le prochain rapport, "un peu plus de jurisprudence" sur la santé et l'hygiène au travail: Doc. NU E/C.12/SR. 11/p. 5, par. 15 (CARON). V. aussi les précisions que la même déléguée s'engage à donner sur la question du délai requis pour que le droit à l'emploi soit garanti: *id.*, p. 17, par. 70 (CARON).

[84] *Id.*, p. 7-8, par. 22 (CARON).

[85] *Id.*, p. 8, par. 23 (COMEAU-GODIN).

[86] *Id.*, pp. 8-9, par. 25-26 (LAFLEUR).

tion du Comité des droits de l'Homme dans l'affaire *Lovelace* sur les changements législatifs intervenus pour éliminer la discrimination à l'égard des femmes autochtones, mais invoque l'examen en cours de ces questions par le Comité des droits de l'Homme pour ne pas discuter des problèmes des Micmacs évoqués par plusieurs membres du Comité.[87] Il profite par ailleurs de la réference faite par l'expert Konate au droit à l'autodétermination pour affirmer, ce qui n'avait pu être fait dans le cadre de l'examen des rapports initial et complémentaire relatifs au Pacte sur les droits civils, que ''la notion d'autodétermination ne peut être interprétée comme autorisant des agissements de nature à porter atteinte à l'intégrité territoriale ou à l'unité politique ou à la cohérence d'un État souverain et indépendant comme le Canada.''[88] Il ajoute que l'''autodétermination supposant une séparation géographique et une autonomie politique et économique absolue, ce n'est pas une notion que l'on peut retenir dans le contexte canadien, pour essayer de trouver des solutions pratiques aux vrais problèmes qui se posent.''[89]

La période réservée aux observations des membres du Comité ne donne lieu à de rares commentaires, comme si les réponses détaillées avaient intimidé les membres du Comité et les avait réduit au silence. L'expert chypriote posera une question, qu'il n'était pas approprié, selon le président, de formuler à ce stade des travaux,[90] à laquelle la déléguée du ministère du Travail du Canada voudra toutefois répondre, ce qui lui permettra d'ajouter quelques commentaires sur l'exercice du droit de grève et la question des licenciements arbitraires.[91] Seul l'expert australien réagira aux réponses formulées par les membres de la délégation canadienne pour manifester son désaccord avec l'interprétation formulée par le délégué fédéral sur la portée du droit à l'autodétermination, regrettant que le gouvernement canadien ''persiste à considérer que l'autodétermination suppose nécessairement une séparation géographique'' et continue d'appuyer ''une conception anachronique de l'autodétermination.''[92]

Par contraste avec les rapports des groupes de représentants et

[87] *Id.*, p. 15, par. 53 (LOW).
[88] *Id.*, p. 15, par. 52.
[89] Ibid.
[90] *Id.*, p. 17, par, 67 (SPARSIS).
[91] *Id.*, p. 17, par. 68-70 (CARON).
[92] *Id.*, p. 18, par. 72 (ALSTON).

d'experts gouvernementaux, le rapport du Comité sur les droits économiques, sociaux et culturels contiendra un excellent résumé analytique des interventions faites pendant la séance d'examen du rapport canadien. Y seront repris des éléments du discours d'ouverture, suivis de considérations générales, alors que les extraits du dialogue entre les membres du Comité et de la délégation canadienne seront reproduits en fonction de l'article concerné. Pour compléter son résumé analytique, le Comité présente des "Observations finales," qui reprennent les commentaires conclusifs des membres du Comité et tiennent lieu d'évaluation générale du deuxième rapport périodique sur les articles 6 à 9 du Pacte sur les droits économiques et de sa présentation par la la délégation canadienne. Les membres du Comité s'exprimeront ainsi:

> Concluant à l'examen du rapport, les membres du Comité ont renouvelé leurs remerciements à la délégation canadienne pour avoir répondu de façon très précise à nombre de questions posées. Ils ont noté par ailleurs que, s'il était particulièrement difficile aux États fédéraux de s'acquitter, en matière d'établissement de rapports de leurs obligations de façon satisfaisante pour chacun des territoires et provinces qui les constituaient, il importait néanmoins que les difficultés rencontrées fussent décrites en détail dans le rapport, qui devait en outre préciser dans quelle mesure les droits pertinents n'étaient pas appliqués. Ils ont toutefois ajouté que des parties du rapport du Canada consistaient pour beaucoup en une énumération des dispositions législatives applicables, ce qui ne permettait pas au Comité de tirer des conclusions détaillées sur la façon dont l'État partie se conformait au Pacte.[93]

Si ces observations finales ne portent que sur les normes de présentation des rapports et leur contenu, elles ne sont pas négligeables pour autant en ce qu'elles révèlent ainsi l'intention du Comité de procéder à une évaluation individuelle des rapports et de faire porter à terme les observations finales sur des questions de fond et les lacunes de la mise en oeuvre du Pacte sur les droits économiques. Au cours de la session durant laquelle le rapport du Canada fait l'objet d'un examen, le Comité a cherché à signaler de telles lacunes[94] et n'hésitera sans doute pas à faire à l'égard du Canada lorsque celui-ci présentera son prochain rapport périodique sur les

---

[93] *Rapport du Comité des droits économiques, sociaux et culturels sur les travaux de sa première session*, Doc. NU E/1989/22, E/C. 12/1989/5, p. 29, par. 112.

[94] V. les observations finales relatives aux rapports de la France, *id.*, p. 41, par. 160 et du Rwanda, p. 47, par. 190.

articles 10 à 15 du Pacte sur les droits économiques.[95]

Lorsque l'on fait le bilan de l'examen des quatre premiers rapports soumis par l'État fédératif canadien en application du Pacte international relatif aux droits économiques, sociaux et culturels, il y a lieu de souligner les efforts importants consentis par les autorités canadiennes pour donner une signification réelle au contrôle systématique du Pacte. Après s'être doté d'un appareil de coopération institutionnelle et intergouvernementale, dont la création découlait directement de l'adhésion du Canada aux Pactes, l'État canadien a immédiatement mis celui-ci au service de contrôle international et a préparé des rapports d'une qualité indéniable, qu'une habile présentation a de surcroît permis d'enrichir.

La participation dynamique et intéressée des membres des délégations canadiennes au dialogue avec les membres des groupes de travail de session et du Comité des droits économiques, sociaux et culturels a valu des éloges nombreux à l'État canadien, mais a surtout rendu celui-ci conscients des lourdes responsabilités qui incombaient au Canada dans le processus de mise en oeuvre du Pacte sur les droits économiques. Cette responsabilité doit être assumée avec une compétence accrue en raison de la volonté du Comité des droits économiques, sociaux et culturels d'effectuer une surveillance de plus en plus efficace[96] de l'importance grandissante qui est conférée aux droits économiques, sociaux et culturels à l'échelle inter-

[95] Le Canada a transmis aux Nations Unies le 11 octobre 1991 son *Deuxième rapport du Canada sur les articles 10 à 15*, Direction des droits de la personne, Multiculturalisme et citoyenneté Canada, Ottawa 1991 et celui-ci devrait faire l'objet d'un examen lors de la septième session du Comité des droits de l'Homme en 1992. La préparation de ce rapport, qui était attendu le 30 juin 1990, a été effectuée en application de dispositions transitoires relatives à l'achèvement des premier et deuxième cycles de présentation des rapports, qui prévoient le regroupement en un seul rapport des deuxièmes rapports périodiques du Canada sur les articles 10 à 12 et 13 à 15. En vertu de la résolution 1988/4 du 24 mai 1988 du Conseil économique et social, les rapports périodiques subséquents seront des rapports d'ensemble sur les articles 1 à 15 du Pacte et devront être présentés tous les cinq ans.

[96] Il est d'ailleurs intéressant de noter à cet égard que le Comité des droits économiques, sociaux et culturels discute actuellement de la possibilité de rédiger un Protocole facultatif au Pacte sur les droits économiques destiné à lui permettre d'examiner des communications individuelles concernant des violations au Pacte: v. à ce sujet M. CRAVEN et C. DOMMEN, ''Making Room for Substance: Fifth Session of the Committee on Economic, Social and Cultural Rights,'' (1991)9 *N.Q.H.R.* 83, à la p. 91.

nationale, tant à l'O.N.U.[97] que dans ses institutions spécialisées.[98] La possibilité réelle que le Canada puisse assumer, du fait de sa récente admission à l'Organisation des États américains, de nouvelles obligations en la matière au niveau régional[99] ainsi que la proposition d'inclure une charte des droits sociaux dans la Constitution du Canada[100] sont des raisons additionnelles qui militent en faveur d'une sensibilité accrue du Canada et sa participation de plus en plus intéressée à l'élaboration et la mise en oeuvre des droits économiques, sociaux et culturels.

DANIEL TURP
Faculté de droit, Université de Montréal

Summary

The Periodic Reports Submitted by Canada under the International Covenant on Economic, Social and Cultural Rights

The author examines how periodic reports submitted by Canada under the International Covenant of Economic, Social and Cultural Rights are studied. He shows that the study of Canadian reports by the sessional working groups of the Economic and Social Council of the United Nations has been very superficial, although the creation of the Committee on Economic, Social and Cultural Rights has considerably changed how Canadian reports are evaluated. This new committee has shown itself to be much more critical of the measures taken by Canada to implement its obligations under the Economic Rights Covenant. The author emphasizes the general good quality of Canada's reporting and stresses that Canada should maintain a constructive dialogue with the committee in light of the increasing importance of these rights at the universal, regional, and national levels.

[97] V. les travaux du rapporteur de la Sous-Commission de la lutte contre les mesures discriminatoires et de la protection des minorités et notamment le rapport sur la *Réalisation des droits économiques, sociaux et culturels*, Doc. NU E/CN. 4/Sub. 2/1990/19 (1990), dont les principaux éléments sont résumés dans R. BRODY, M. CONVERY et D. WEISSBRODT, "The 42nd Session of the Sub-Commission on Prevention of Discrimination and Protection of Minorities," (1991) 13 *H.R.Q.* 261, aux pp. 282-83. V. aussi A. EIDE, "Realization of Social and Economic Rights and the Minimum Threshold Approach," (1989) 10 *H.R.L.J.* 35.

[98] V. inter alia J.-P. LAVIEC, "La protection des droits économiques et sociaux de l'Homme par l'Organisation internationale du Travail," (1991) 3 *R.U.D.H.* 61.

[99] V. au sujet des progrès réalisés en matière de droits économiques, sociaux et culturels dans le cadre américain, A. A. CANÇADO TRINDADE, "La protection des droits économiques, sociaux et culturels: évolutions et tendances actuelles, particulièrement à l'échelle régionale," (1990) 94 *R.G.D.I.P.* 913, aux pp. 927-40.

[100] V. la proposition formulée par le premier ministre de l'Ontario d'inclure dans la Constitution du Canada d'une charte des droits sociaux: v. *Une charte sociale canadienne: la consolidation de nos valeurs communes*, document de travail, Ministère des Affaires Intergovernementales, Toronto, Ontario, septembre 1991. V. aussi les propositions pour l'inclusion de tels droits dans une Constitution du Québec J.-Y. MORIN, "Pour une nouvelle Constitution du Québec," (1985) 30 *R. de D. McGill* 171, aux pp. 197-200 et "La Constitution d'un Québec souverain," *Le Devoir*, 18 décembre 1991, p. B-8.

The Canadian Laws Offshore Application Act: The Legislative Incorporation of Rights over the Continental Shelf

INTRODUCTION

THE CANADIAN LAWS OFFSHORE APPLICATION ACT received royal assent on December 17, 1990 and entered into force by order on February 4, 1991.[1] The Act represents a major effort by parliament to bring Canadian law into line with the modern law of the sea through the application of federal and provincial legislation to the continental shelf. Departing from the ad hoc approach that has characterized Canadian legislation applicable to the shelf up to now, the legislation is a first step towards a comprehensive legal regime for the offshore.

The Act creates a general framework for the application of all laws to the shelf, and fills some important gaps, particularly in relation to the extraterritorial application of the Criminal Code. With its entry into force, the whole body of federal legislation applies to the internal waters, territorial sea and to "marine installations or structures" that are "attached" to the continental shelf. In addition, the Governor in Council is authorized to apply federal laws in or above the shelf, or to any part of it, by regulations. Provincial and territorial laws can be extended to offshore areas outside the boundaries of any province or territory through the technique

---

[1] The legislation was first introduced as Bill C-104 in April 1986 by the Honourable John Crosbie, when he was Minister of Justice and Attorney General of Canada. It died on the order paper at the end of the first session of the 33rd Parliament and, because of other legislative and governmental priorities, did not get reintroduced until the second session of the 34th Parliament in October 1989, as Bill C-39, and was not adopted until the fall of 1990. The Act entered into force by order on February 4, 1991, and it appears as chapter 44 of the Statutes of Canada, 1990.

of incorporation by reference.

I. Background

The impetus for the new legislation, apart from the increased jurisdiction accorded coastal states by international law, was the positive result from the federal perspective of the 1984 *Hibernia Reference*.[2] In that decision, the Supreme Court of Canada paved the way for comprehensive federal legislation on the shelf by disposing of the case of Newfoundland, the province with perhaps the strongest claim to jurisdiction over the offshore. Until 1984, there had been considerable uncertainty as to which level of government could control offshore oil and gas development. Although the situation on the west coast was resolved in 1967 with the *B.C. Offshore Reference*,[3] on the Atlantic coast, oil and gas exploratory permits continued to be issued by both federal and provincial authorities until the decision of the Supreme Court of Canada. As a result of the jurisdictional conflict, neither level of government took the logical step of enacting comprehensive shelf legislation in the manner of States where such questions had been resolved or did not exist.[4]

In policy terms, the unsystematic treatment of the shelf can be contrasted with the approach of Canadian governments and legislators to the fishing zones or to Arctic waters. A major objective of successive federal governments, certainly from the 1960s onward, was the promotion of a new legal regime for fisheries that would

---

[2] In the *Re Newfoundland Continental Shelf*, [1984] 1 S.C.R. 86, the Supreme Court of Canada held that when Newfoundland entered Confederation in 1949, it did not have the requisite external sovereignty to acquire what the court described as extraterritorial rights over the shelf, and that in any event the institution of the shelf had not by that time crystallized in international law. It followed that by the time the continental shelf emerged as a concept in international law, the federal government was the sole possessor of external sovereignty for Canada. Legislative jurisdiction fell to Parliament under the "peace, order and good government" residual clause in the Constitution.

[3] In *Reference re Offshore Mineral Rights of British Columbia*, [1967] S.C.R. 792, the Supreme Court of Canada held that the territorial sea did not form part of the colony of British Columbia at the time of union with Canada in 1871. It followed automatically that Canada, not the province, had the right to explore and exploit the continental shelf beyond the territorial sea.

[4] See, for example, the United States Submerged Lands Act, 43 U.S. Code § 1333, which extends federal and state laws to the outer continental shelf, or the British Continental Shelf Act 1964, (U.K.) c. 29, which applies civil and criminal law to acts and omissions on continental shelf installations.

recognize the predominant interest of coastal states in the living resources off their coasts. Canada was one of the first countries to extend its exclusive fishing zone beyond the traditional limit of the 3-mile territorial sea: first to 12 miles in 1964[5] and then to 200 miles on January 1, 1977.[6] These measures reflected part of a coherent and sometime vigorous strategy to promote and establish responsible fisheries management in the oceans adjacent to Canada.[7] Evidence of this policy is found in the fact that developments in international law and domestic legislation proceeded in tandem. Indeed, some have suggested that Canada was prepared to act unilaterally in advance of the emergence of a consensus on coastal State rights under international law, when its vital national interests were threatened such as in the Arctic.[8]

The incorporation of rights over the continental shelf into Canadian law, on the other hand, was ad hoc and frequently lagged behind developments in international law.[9] The Government of Canada reacted cautiously to the Truman Proclamation of 1945, in which the United States claimed "jurisdiction and control" over the natural resources of the seabed and subsoil adjacent to its coasts.[10] Canada did not adopt regulations authorizing oil and gas operations in offshore areas until 1960,[11] and did so under the auspices of a regime designed for land-based activities. Individuals could

[5] Territorial Sea and Fishing Zones Act, S.C. 1964-65, c. 22.

[6] Fishing Zones of Canada (Zones 4 and 5) Order, SOR/77-62. The legislative basis for the extension of jurisdiction over fisheries to 200 miles was set out as early as 1970 in An Act to Amend the Territorial Sea and Fishing Zones Act, R.S.C. 1970, Supp. I, c. 45.

[7] A. E. Gotlieb, "The Canadian Contribution to the Concept of a Fishing Zone in International Law" (1964) 2 Canadian Yearbook of International Law 55.

[8] Allan Gotlieb and Charles Dalfen, "National Jurisdiction and International Responsibility: New Canadian Approaches to International Law" (1973) 67 Am. J. Int'l L. 229, at 235.

[9] L. L. Herman, "The Need for a Canadian Submerged Lands Act: Some Further Thoughts on Canada's Problems" (1980) 58 Can. B. Rev. 518, at 521.

[10] Proclamation No. 2667, 10 *Federal Register* 12303; reprinted in (1946) 40 Am. J. Int'l L. Supp. 45. The United States transmitted to the Canadian embassy in Washington both a draft copy and the final version of the Proclamation. Canada adknowledged receipt of the proclamation without comment. For copies of the relevant diplomatic correspondence see *Gulf of Maine* case, U.S. Memorial, p. 81, para. 133 and annexes.

[11] Canada Oil and Gas Regulations, P.C. 1960-474, April 13, 1960, adopted pursuant to the Territorial Lands Act, S.C. 1950, c. 22, and the Public Lands Grants Act, S.C. 1950, c. 19.

apply for permits for exploratory work in areas defined in the regulations as "Canada lands" — federal Crown lands, in other words, which only hypothetically included submerged lands under the sea. The first offshore permits off the Atlantic coast were issued not long after the 1960 regulations came into force.[12]

The explanation for the difference in treatment between the shelf and superjacent waters is threefold. First, there was the federal/provincial dispute over jurisdiction referred to above. Second, there was no crisis in relation to the resources of the continental shelf to bring the subject to the top of the political agenda, such as occurred in the fisheries with overfishing by distant-water fleets, or in the Arctic with the threat posed to territorial integrity by the voyage of the tanker *Manhattan*. Third, there was little need to perfect the regime applicable to the shelf, because as the concept developed in international law, it was clear that no claim or proclamation was necessary for a coastal State to exercise jurisdiction in respect of the seabed. Under Article 2, paragraph 3 of the 1958 Geneva Convention on the Continental Shelf, the rights of the coastal State do not depend on occupation, effective or notional, or on any express proclamation. In the words of the International Court of Justice in the 1969 *North Sea* cases, such rights exist "*ipso facto* and *ab initio*."[13] This is not the case with an exclusive fishing zone, or the exclusive economic zone (EEZ), which must be expressly claimed and established in order to assert exclusive jurisdiction to the exclusion of all other states.[14]

II. THE CANADIAN LAWS OFFSHORE APPLICATION ACT

Following the *Hibernia Reference* and its elimination of any significant doubt over federal jurisdiction, preparation of comprehensive

[12] The original permit and licence regime for oil and gas activities was modified on a number of occasions over the years: in 1961 the Canada Oil and Gas Land Regulations, and the Canada Oil and Gas Drilling and Production regulations, P.C. 1961-797, June 6, 1961 revoked and repealed the Canada Oil and Gas Regulations to divide the regulations concerning technical standards for drilling, etc., from those concerning the disposition of interests in oil and gas; in 1977 Order in Council, P.C. 1977, 2155, July 28, 1977 authorized exploration agreements and provided certain exploration rights to Petro-Canada; in 1982 the Canada Oil and Gas Act, S.C. 1980-81-82, c. 81 implemented the National Energy Program; and more recently the Canada Petroleum Resources Act, R.S.C. 1985, c. C-8.5, overhauled the legislative framework for oil and gas activities on federal lands.

[13] *North Sea Continental Shelf, Judgment* [1969] I.C.J. Rep. 22, para. 19.

[14] Rudolf Bernhardt, "Custom and Treaty in the Law of the Sea," Rec. des Cours, 1987, V (tome 205) 247, at 294.

legislation incorporating rights over the shelf into Canadian law began in earnest. The resulting Canadian Laws Offshore Application Act, although primarily concerned with the shelf, sets out the regime for the application of both federal and provincial laws to the entire offshore, including the internal waters and territorial sea of Canada, the continental shelf and any exclusive economic zone that Canada might create in the future. This multiplicity of zones makes the Act complex. As a result, the technique for applying laws offshore must be adjusted to reflect the difference in legal status between the various zones in which laws are being applied. Thus, laws are applied without qualification to the internal waters and territorial sea, where Canada possesses full territorial sovereignty, subject only to certain navigational rights of other States in the territorial sea. With respect to the shelf or EEZ, over which Canada has only those sovereign rights accorded to coastal States under international law, the regime is adapted so that laws can be applied in a manner that respects the rights of other states under the law of the sea.

A. FEDERAL LAW

1. *Internal Waters and Territorial Sea*

The Act defines internal waters and the territorial sea by reference to the Territorial Sea and Fishing Zones Act.[15] By virtue of that statute the internal waters and territorial sea are incontestably part of Canada. Moreover, under section 8 of the Interpretation Act,[16] every federal enactment applies to the whole of Canada, unless a contrary intention is expressed therein. Consequently, at least since the 1964 enactment of the Territorial Sea and Fishing Zones Act, it should have been clear that federal laws apply to the internal waters and the territorial sea, making any reference in the Canadian Laws Offshore Application Act to these zones unnecessary. However, confusion has bedevilled the application of laws beyond the land territory for many years. Therefore, in a declaratory provision, the Act stipulates, "for greater certainty," that federal laws apply in the internal waters and the territorial sea.[17] This

---

[15] Canadian Laws Offshore Application Act, s. 2(1) incorporates the definition of "internal waters" and "territorial sea" from s. 3 of the Territorial Sea and Fishing Zones Act, R.S.C. 1985, c. T-8.

[16] R.S.C. 1985, c. I-21.

[17] Canadian Laws Offshore Application Act, s. 4.

provision should not be regarded as new law, but as a useful clarification.

The historic source of the confusion over the territorial operation of laws was at least in part due to the bewildering complexity of the old case, *R.* v. *Keyn*,[18] which is said to have held that there was no application of English law to the territorial sea without an explicit enactment to that effect.[19] As a result of the Canadian Laws Offshore Application Act, no further misunderstanding over the territorial principle of application should occur.

Questions could still arise in proceedings in which the exact extent of the internal waters and the location of the territorial sea is in issue. Amendments in the Act to the definition of baselines in the Territorial Sea and Fishing Zones Act should eliminate any future uncertainty in domestic court proceedings over the existence or validity of Canada's claims of internal waters by virtue of historic title. Until the amendment, baselines comprised only the low-water line along the coast, or straight baselines established pursuant to an order under the Territorial Sea and Fishing Zones Act. Baselines henceforth include the outer limits of waters with respect to which Canada has a historic title or other title under international law.[20]

This amendment to the definition of baselines operates in conjunction with section 10 of the Canadian Laws Offshore Application Act, which confers a statutory basis on certificates of the Secretary of State for External Affairs with respect to the legal status of geographical locations in the internal waters, territorial sea, continental shelf, or future EEZ. Such certificates will be particularly useful with respect to areas where the extent of Canada's internal waters claims have not been clarified by the creation of straight baselines, such as, in the Gulf of St. Lawrence or Dixon Entrance. Under subsection 10(1), certificates of the Secretary of State for External Affairs are conclusive proof of the legal status of offshore zones over which Canada exercises jurisdiction. A cross-reference to this evidentiary provision of the Act has been added to subsection 477(3) of the Criminal Code, which in addition provides that certificates of

[18] (1876) 2 Ex.D. 63.

[19] D. P. O'Connell, *The International Law of the Sea,* Vol. II, ed. I. A. Shearer (Oxford: Clarendon Press, 1984), 739.

[20] Section 19 of the Act amends subsection 5(3) of the Territorial Sea and Fishing Zones Act and adds subsection 5(3.1) on baselines where there is historic title and baselines in other areas.

the Secretary of State for External Affairs are conclusive proof that any geographical location is in a fishing zone of Canada or outside the territory of any state.[21]

The certificates, of course, relate to a question of law, that is, whether a given geographical location is in the internal waters, territorial sea, continental shelf, fishing zones, or future EEZ of Canada and therefore subject, with certain restrictions imposed by international law, to Canadian criminal jurisdiction. Their conclusiveness should not infringe on any presumption of innocence guaranteed under the Charter, as the court would only be taking judicial notice of the existence, extent, and geographical location of Canadian criminal jurisdiction.[22] It would not be determining factual elements of the offence, but the legal issue from which flows the application of Canadian law and the jurisdiction of the court.

The first certificate under section 10 of the Act was issued in August 1991, with respect to the status of the waters of the Gulf of St. Lawrence. It is a statement of remarkable simplicity, in which the delegate of the Secretary of State for External Affairs says: "J'atteste, conformément à l'article 10(1) de la Loi sur l'application extra côtière des lois canadiennes, que les eaux du Golfe du St-Laurent sont des eaux intérieures du Canada."

Taken together, these provisions amending the definition of baselines and establishing a statutory basis for the conclusiveness of certificates will make it difficult to challenge the government's view of the internal waters, territorial sea, continental shelf, or fishing zones. The situation which occurred in the *Sea Shepherd* case, where a Quebec provincial court judge acquitted on jurisdictional grounds a number of persons accused of interfering with the seal hunt could, in theory, no longer occur.[23]

---

[21] Criminal Code, s. 477.4 (3).

[22] In *R.* v. *Vaillancourt*, [1987] 2 S.C.R. 636, the Supreme Court of Canada held that the presumption of innocence in s. 11(d) of the Charter is offended when legislation omits an essential element of the definition of an offence or if it substitutes proof of an essential element.

[23] In *R.* c. *Paul Franck Watson*, the court disputed the federal claim that the Gulf of St. Lawrence is internal to Canada, notwithstanding the issuance of a certificate by the Secretary of State for External Affairs to this effect. The court held that the 1964 Territorial Sea and Fishing Zones Act repealed any prerogative power with respect to the extent of the maritime realm of the Crown. In the absence of straight baselines, the court concluded that the baselines of the territorial sea was the low-water line along the coast, with the result that the Gulf of St. Lawrence fell outside the territorial sea, depriving the court of jurisdiction over citizens of a foreign state on the high seas. Cour des sessions de la paix, Canada, Province

2. *The Continental Shelf*

Prior to the entry into force of the Canadian Laws Offshore Application Act, the Canadian rule of statutory interpretation was that federal laws applied only within Canadian territory unless they contained a specific provision respecting their extraterritorial reach.[24] The Act now sets out the conditions under which federal law is applied to the continental shelf.

"Federal laws" is a defined term in section 2 of the Act and includes any Act of Parliament, regulations, or other "rules of law." Territorial ordinances under the Northwest Territories Act or the Yukon Act are specifically excluded from the definition of federal laws. They will therefore be picked up under the term "provincial laws" by the operation of subsection 35(1) of the Interpretation Act, which provides that the term "province" includes "territory" unless otherwise indicated. The concept of "rules of law" is intended to cover federal common law, such as the rules of admiralty incorporated in the term "maritime law" in the Federal Court Act, or any common law remedies that accompany matters that fall under the exclusive jurisdiction of Parliament, such as intellectual property.

The extension of laws under the Act should not be regarded as a "territorialization" of the continental shelf or future EEZ of Canada.[25] Unlike the case of the internal waters and territorial sea, with respect to which the conditions for the application of federal law have not been specified, the application of laws to the shelf has been circumscribed in the legislation to reflect the limited nature of the rights Canada enjoys over such extraterritorial zones under

de Québec, District de Gaspé, nᵒ 110-01-000306, 20 décembre 1983. Upheld on appeal by Cour supérieure, chambre criminelle, nᵒ 110-38-000001-849, 17 mars 1987, Desjardins, jcs. For comment, see France Morrissette, "Le statut du golfe du Saint-Laurent en droit international et en droit interne" (1985) Revue générale de droit 273.

[24] E. A. Driedger, *The Construction of Statutes* (Toronto: Butterworths, 1974), 166.

[25] The Counter-Memorial submitted by Canada on February 1, 1991 in the case concerning the delimitation of the maritime boundary between Canada and France answers the allegation it says was made in the French Memorial that the Act goes beyond what is permitted by international law. *Canadian Counter-Memorial*, para. 203.

[26] Article 76 of the Convention defines the shelf in the following terms:
The continental shelf of a coastal State comprises the sea-bed and subsoil of the submarine areas that extend beyond its territorial sea throughout the natural prolongation of its land territory to the outer edge of the continental margin, or to a distance of 200 nautical miles from the baselines from which the breadth of the territorial sea is measured where the continental margin does not extend up to that distance.

international law. In the first instance, laws are applied only to marine installations and structures attached to the continental shelf, to artificial islands, and to safety zones. Although the Governor in Council is authorized to apply laws "in or above" any location on the shelf in regulations, which might appear to be a very wide discretionary power, section 6 provides that "federal laws shall be applied...in a manner that is consistent with the rights and freedoms of other states under international law and, in particular, with the rights and freedoms of other states in relation to navigation and overflight." Furthermore, the Governor in Council is empowered in subsection 5(3) to specify in the regulations the circumstances in which laws will be applied beyond marine installations and structures. This power could be used to ensure compliance with international law.

(a) Definition of the Shelf

The definition of the continental shelf in the Act is in terms borrowed largely from the 1982 United Nations Convention on the Law of the Sea, that is, the seabed and subsoil of those submarine areas that extend beyond the territorial sea to the greater of 200 miles or the outer edge of the continental margin. Thus, the shelf begins twelve miles from the baselines of the territorial sea, whether these are low-water lines along the coast, straight baselines established pursuant to the Territorial Sea and Fishing Zones Act, or the outer limits of Canada's historic waters. The legal, as opposed to the physical shelf, therefore, does not begin at the shoreline.

Over the last decade, with a few exceptions, federal legislative drafters have attempted to use this internationally accepted definition of the shelf from the 1982 Montego Bay Convention in defining the shelf or in setting out the scope of application of statutes that apply to it. The Income Tax Act, the Customs and Excise Offshore Application Act,[27] the Canada-Newfoundland Atlantic Accord Implementation Act,[28] the Hibernia Project Development Act,[29] and so on, all use similar language to describe the shelf. The reason why is obvious: since the continental shelf is primarily a juridical rather than physical concept, and is derived from international law, it makes sense to have the greatest degree of compatibility between

[27] R.S.C. 1985, c. C-53.

[28] S.C. 1987, c. 3.

[29] S.C. 1990, c. 41.

the language of domestic statutes and the various international instruments defining the shelf. This provides greater legal certainty and helps to assure other nations who continue to enjoy important navigational rights in the waters above the shelf that Canada is acting in accordance with international law in enacting legislation applicable to it.

The Canadian Laws Offshore Application Act is interesting in that it extends all laws offshore in specified circumstances, merely reserving the power to exclude the application of certain laws or parts of laws to the Governor in Council. An alternative would have been to empower the Governor in Council to apply prescribed laws through regulations. Instead, the comprehensive approach set out in section 5 of the Act reserves the power for the Governor in Council to exclude through regulations any Act or part of an Act that, for whatever reason, is determined to be inappropriate for offshore application.[30] The justification for this choice appears to be that it favours simplicity. If laws were prescribed, lists would have to be regularly updated. Applying all laws will result in fewer regulations under the Act.

(b) The "attachment" criterion

An additional safeguard to ensure that laws are applied extraterritorially only to the extent permitted under international law is the provision that stipulates that federal laws are only applied by the Act to "marine installations or structures" that are "attached" to the shelf, to artificial islands, and to their safety zones. Absent regulations to the contrary, federal laws are not being applied to the whole continental shelf. This "attachment criterion" is very important to understanding the scheme of the Act. It ensures that there is a nexus between the application of laws to the shelf and resource exploration or exploitation. In this way, it reflects the limited nature of the sovereign rights Canada enjoys over the continental shelf by eliminating the likelihood of any interference with the navigational rights of other States under international law.

The "attachment criterion" works as follows. If a foreign-flagged rig is being towed, for example, from the North Sea to the Grand Banks of Newfoundland, Canadian laws will not apply to the rig until it arrives at its destination and is attached to the continental shelf by anchors or any other method. This means that even if during

---

[30] Canadian Laws Offshore Application Act, s. 5(2).

its transit the rig crosses hundreds of miles of waters above the Canadian shelf, the laws of Canada will not apply to it under this Act. The Canadian Bar Association suggested to the legislative committee of the House of Commons that studied the bill that laws should begin to apply to the rig as soon as it enters waters above the Canadian shelf, in many cases well before it arrives at its final destination.[31] However, the bill was adopted as drafted.

The purpose of the "attachment criterion" is to provide an objective standard by which to judge whether a "marine installation or structure" is engaged in resource exploitation. Under international law, Canada would have no jurisdiction over a rig that was merely transitting the shelf. The Canadian Bar Association's proposal would have made it necessary to prove a subjective intention to exploit resources as a precondition to the application of Canadian laws. In addition, it would have required the identification of the outer limits of the Canadian shelf in order to know when our laws would begin to apply in the hypothetical voyage from the North Sea to the Grand Banks or the use of a compulsory proof certificate of the Secretary of State for External Affairs under section 10. The identification of the outer edge of the continental margin in accordance with Article 76 of the United Nations Convention on the Law of the Sea would involve an enormous amount of geophysical work. Although the Act does authorize the Governor in Council to determine the extent of the shelf in regulations,[32] this power appears to have been contemplated to be used in circumstances where it might be convenient (either for technical or diplomatic reasons) to eliminate any doubts about whether a given area forms part of the continental shelf of Canada without defining the outer limits per se. It was not intended to replace altogether the technical provisions of Article 76 of the 1982 convention respecting outer limits.

The "attachment criterion" only relates to the initial application of Canadian laws to a marine installation or structure. Once the structure is attached, Canadian laws will apply to it until it moves off the continental shelf of Canada. That means even if the rig becomes temporarily unattached for operational reasons, or is on its voyage of departure, Canadian laws apply. This should alleviate any fears that a "marine installation or structure" would

[31] Canada, House of Commons, Minutes of Proceedings and Evidence of the Legislative Committee on Bill C-39, May 29, 1990.
[32] Canadian Laws Offshore Application Act, s. 2(2)(a).

circumvent the application of Canadian laws by pulling up its anchors.

3. *Beyond the Continental Shelf*

Section 5(3)(c) of the Act also authorizes the Governor in Council to apply Canadian laws beyond the continental shelf of Canada through regulations. This power can only be exercised pursuant to an international agreement or arrangement entered into by Canada. Its purpose is to enable Canadian laws to apply to joint resource development zones straddling one of the maritime boundaries of Canada, where an agreement exists on joint exploitation. There is a precedent for this type of arrangement in the North Sea and one can imagine its utility in boundary areas in the Gulf of Maine or Beaufort Sea.

The provision, however, is drafted widely and confers the authority on the Governor in Council to apply Canadian laws anywhere beyond the Canadian shelf. Such a power may be useful to prohibit drift net fishing on the high sea pursuant to a future international convention, or to implement other international agreements where Canada is required to prohibit conduct on the high seas by the nationals of other parties, provided there is an applicable provision in Canadian law that can be extended.

B. PROVINCIAL LAWS

1. *Application*

Paragraph 7(1)(a) of the Act provides for provincial laws to be applied to the internal waters and territorial sea in the offshore area adjacent to but outside a province. Paragraph (b) of the subsection further applies provincial laws to the adjacent offshore area on the seaward side of the internal waters and territorial sea "to the same extent as federal laws." In other words, by virtue of these provisions, all provincial laws will be applied to the internal waters, the territorial sea, and to "marine installations or structures" attached to the continental shelf upon the entry into force of the section for each coastal province. The Governor in Council enjoys the same power to make regulations respecting the exclusion or application of provincial laws in or above the entire shelf or any portion thereof that it has with respect to federal laws.

Subsection 7(2) eliminates any confusion with respect to federal control over offshore resources by excluding from application any provision of a provincial law that imposes a tax or royalty or that relates to mineral or other non-living natural resources. A similar result is found in the section of the United States Submerged Lands Act extending state laws offshore.[33] Nevertheless, the Governor in Council can make regulations on the terms and conditions under which provincial tax or royalty laws can be extended, for example, pursuant to a future federal/provincial accord on resource revenue.

Section 7 has not yet entered into force. Therefore, although federal laws are currently being applied offshore through the operation of the Act, no provincial laws have been extended under it. Section 7 will come into force with respect to an offshore area adjacent to a province only on a day to be fixed by order of the Governor in Council. The Act requires sixty days' notice in the Canada Gazette for comments and representations to be made to the government prior to the application of provincial laws offshore.[34]

All this means that section 7 is essentially enabling legislation. It will come into force not automatically but separately for each province. If there is no practical need for the application of provincial laws in the area adjacent to any given province there may be no need to make the section applicable to that area.

The purpose of applying provincial laws offshore is to cover the complete range of private law matters that are of obvious importance to the development of the resources of the continental shelf. To mention only a few: personal property security laws, social legislation, as well as the common law, including such matters as provincial tort law with its distinct human dimension, all have significant implications for offshore development. Under the Constitution, provincial laws have no extraterritorial effect, although occasionally courts have managed to apply provincial law to activities occurring offshore.[35] The Act is intended to provide a secure statutory basis for the extension of provincial laws, creating conditions of legal certainty. In this connection, the jurisdiction of provincial and superior courts is extended to the offshore areas adjacent to each coastal province.[36]

The technique used for the application of provincial laws outside the boundaries of the provinces is incorporation by reference.

[33] Submerged Lands Act, 43 U.S. Code s. 1333(a)(3).
[34] Canadian Laws Offshore Application Act, s. 21.
[35] *Workmen's Compensation Board* v. *C.P.R.* [1920] A.C. 1984 (P.C.).
[36] Canadian Laws Offshore Application Act, s. 9.

Rather than re-enact the entire body of provincial law, the Act simply incorporates provincial law, including the common law, as it may from time to time exist for the purposes of application offshore. The constitutionality of the technique has been considered by the courts on numerous occasions, most notably in *Coughlin* v. *Ontario Highway Transport Board*.[37] In that case, the Court upheld the validity of a federal scheme which incorporated provincial law relating to intraprovincial trucking for extraprovincial carriers.

Some provincial legislation is already applied offshore through the technique of incorporation by reference into federal law. The Canada-Newfoundland Atlantic Accord Implementation Act,[38] and the Canada-Nova Scotia Offshore Petroleum Resources Accord Implementation Act,[39] apply Newfoundland and Nova Scotia "social legislation" to the offshore zones defined therein. The Hibernia Development Project Act[40] permits the Governor in Council to apply and modify Newfoundland personal property security legislation to the offshore area defined in the Atlantic Accord legislation. In the case of any inconsistency with the application of provincial laws under the Canadian Laws Offshore Application Act and the Hibernia legislation, the latter will prevail.

2. *"Offshore Area" with Respect to a Province*

The means to establish the extent of the offshore area adjacent to any particular province is set out in section 2 of the Act. Basically, the offshore area is a zone determined in accordance with the equidistance method, that is, in the terms of the legislation, "any area of the sea that *is not within any province* that is . . . nearer to the coast of that province than to the coast of any other province." However, under paragraph (b) of subsection (1), the power is reserved for the Governor in Council to prescribe under subsection 2(2)(c) of the Act, any other area of the sea adjacent to a province as the "offshore area." Presumably, this is to permit recourse to some other method of delimitation, such as an enclave, parallels and meridians, and so on, where the coastal geography is such that application of the equidistance method would produce an unusually

---

[37] [1968] S.C.R. 569. The *Coughlin* principle has been recently approved by the Supreme Court of Canada in *R.* v. *Furtney*, [1991] S.C.R.

[38] S.C. 1987, c. 3.

[39] S.C. 1988, c. 28.

[40] *Supra* note 29.

shaped or unworkable offshore area.

The Act provides no guidance to the Governor in Council on when to exercise this power to abandon equidistance. One plausible situation would be where the equidistance method would produce inequitable results in a delimitation between sovereign states effected in accordance with principles of international law. For example, when small islands belonging to one province lie close off the coast of another province, on the "wrong side" of the median line, a regulation could be used to prescribe something other than an equidistance zone for the purposes of the definition "offshore area."

It must be emphasized that the offshore area with respect to a province is only that part of the internal waters, territorial sea, and continental shelf that lies outside the province. Parliament has no power unilaterally to change provincial boundaries, and federal legislation could not deal with the application of provincial laws in maritime areas that are inside a province, such as the Strait of Georgia or Conception Bay. This falls within the ordinary constitutional jurisdiction of the province. It follows logically that section 8 of the Act makes clear that a province may not claim jurisdiction over an adjacent offshore area merely by virtue of the application of its laws there pursuant to the federal statute.

Of course, the normal rule in Canada is that the provinces end at the low-water line along the coast. Practically speaking, the Act will be required for the application of provincial laws to most sea areas adjacent to Canada, except where there are waters *intra fauces terrae* or in the few cases where historic waters, the territorial sea, or part thereof already lay within the province at the time of its entry into Confederation. Reflecting this predominant federal interest in the offshore, subsection 3(1) of the Act vests in Her Majesty in right of Canada the seabed and subsoil below the internal waters and territorial and any rights of Canada beyond. Subsection 3(2) is a saving clause to ensure that no legal right or interest held prior to the coming into force of the legislation is abrogated by this vesting provision. It will preserve any claim by a province, individual or other group that may exist.

III. CRIMINAL CODE AMENDMENTS

The Canadian Laws Offshore Application Act enacts several important changes to the Criminal Code respecting its application to the internal waters, territorial sea, and beyond.

To reflect the full sovereignty of Canada over its internal waters, the Code no longer requires the consent of the Attorney General of Canada for the prosecution of offences alleged to have been committed there. Consent is still required for prosecutions involving foreigners on board foreign-registered vessels in the territorial sea. This was maintained to provide the opportunity to consider any navigational rights of other states, such as the right of innocent passage, prior to proceeding with a prosecution.[41]

The Code also applies to marine installations and structures on the continental shelf, regardless of the flag they are flying.[42] This means Canadian courts now have jurisdiction over any offences committed on the rigs and platforms by Canadians or foreign workers. The consent of the Attorney General of Canada is required for the prosecution of foreigners in relation to offences alleged to have been committed on board foreign-flagged rigs.[43] As in the case of the territorial sea, there will be cases where it may be desirable for the Attorney General of Canada to waive jurisdiction in favour of another country's courts, such as where an offence involves two foreigners on board a foreign vessel.

The prosecution of fisheries offences will be assisted by the new application of the Criminal Code to acts or omissions committed on board foreign fishing vessels. International law does not permit the full application of criminal law to persons on board foreign fishing vessels in Canadian fisheries waters except in relation to offences connected with the fishery. Hence, two restrictions on the application of the Code to foreign vessels have been added in subsection 477.1(2) to safeguard the rights of foreign states. First, the vessel must be in the Canadian zone in connection with the exploration, exploitation, management, or conservation of the living resources thereof. Second, the act of omission must be committed by or in relation to a Canadian citizen or permanent resident. The measure is designed primarily to protect Canadian fisheries officers carrying out inspections or enforcing Canadian fisheries laws on board foreign vessels, and is therefore limited in scope this way.

There is now a statutory basis for hot pursuit beyond the fisher-

[41] Criminal Code, s. 477.2.

[42] *Ibid.*, s. 477.1.

[43] *Ibid.*, s. 477.2 (2).

ies waters of Canada right up to the territorial sea of other states.[44] New paragraph 477.1(1)(d) of the Criminal Code deems an offence to have occurred in Canada if it is committed "outside Canada, in the course of hot pursuit." It is not limited to pursuit from the territorial sea, but permits pursuit from any maritime zone of Canada in relation to an act or omission that is an offence by virtue of the extension of laws under the Canadian Laws Offshore Application Act[45] or of the independent operation of any other Act of Parliament.[46] Thus, if an offence under the Coastal Fisheries Protection Act, the statute which prohibits unauthorized foreign fishing in the fisheries waters of Canada, is committed in the 200-mile zone, that is, outside the territory of Canada, this provision authorizes pursuit onto the high seas. It is not intended to cover criminal offences involving only foreign nationals on board the vessel.

Paragraph 477.3(1) of the Criminal Code confers every power of arrest, search, or seizure that can be exercised in Canada to offences that occur outside of Canada by virtue of the extension of laws under subsection 477.1(1). The consent of the Attorney General of Canada is required for exercise of any power of arrest, entry, search, or seizure on board any ship registered outside Canada in respect of any act or omission that is an offence only by virtue of the hot pursuit provision of the Code or the new provisions extending the application of laws offshore.[47] Thus, in the case of a hot pursuit of a foreign fishing vessel from the fisheries waters of Canada on to the high seas, consent would not be required for the exercise of any power of arrest, as the act or omission is an offence by virtue of the independent operation of Canadian fisheries legislation and not the extension of laws under the Canadian Laws Offshore Application Act or the Criminal Code. However, consent will be required for any prosecution in relation to offences committed in the course the pursuit.

CONCLUSION

The Canadian Laws Offshore Application Act modernizes the legal regime applicable to the offshore by providing a comprehen-

[44] *Ibid.*, s. 477.1(1)(d).
[45] *Ibid.*, s. 477.1(1)(a).
[46] *Ibid.*, s. 477(2).
[47] *Ibid.*, s. 477.3(3).

sive framework for the application of federal and provincial laws
to the maritime zones off Canada's coasts. It places this country
in the same position as other nations that have taken legislative measures to incorporate into their internal legal system the rights granted
coastal states under international law. In doing so, it replaces an
antiquated legal approach to the offshore that has existed virtually
unchanged since colonial times. In sharp contrast to the old system,
the new legislation is forward-looking and potentially adaptable to
new forms of jurisdiction that may emerge in the future. The inclusion of a reference to a future EEZ in the legislation indicates
that the Act itself foresees the natural evolution of the law relating
to the offshore in accordance with the development of international law. Sound policy reasons support the continued modernization
of legislation, and the incorporation of new rights and jurisdictions
into the domestic law of Canada as they emerge and are accepted
internationally. It makes sense to continue the process of updating
laws to reflect the institutions set out in the law of the sea and to
bring our maritime zones into line with those of other States. The
Canadian Laws Offshore Application Act provides the vehicle for
doing so.

Ross Hornby

Sommaire

La Loi sur l'application extracotière des lois canadiennes

La Loi sur l'application extracotière des lois canadiennes *est entrée en vigueur
le 4 février 1991, à l'exception de l'article 7 visant l'application des lois provinciales aux
zones maritimes à l'extérieur de toute province. La loi rend le régime d'application des
lois fédérales et provinciales dans les zones extracôtières conforme au droit de la mer moderne.
Premièrement, la loi précise que les eaux intérieures et la mer territoriale font partie du
Canada et que les lois fédérales s'y appliquent. Deuxièment, elle précise les conditions
dans lesquelles les lois fédérales s'appliquent au plateau continental. Troisièment, la loi
établit la procédure pour faire appliquer les lois provinciales aux zones extracôtières ad-
jacentes à une province et la procédure de délimination de ces zones. En outre, la loi
énonce dans quelles conditions le Code criminel s'applique aux zones maritimes, y
compris aux eaux sur lesquelles le Canada a un titre de souveraineté historique.*

Canadian Investment Promotion
and Protection Treaties

OVER THE PAST TWO YEARS a major development has occurred in Canadian treaty practice with the signing of five bilateral investment promotion and protection treaties (BITs) with the USSR, Poland, Czechoslovakia, Uruguay, and Hungary.[1] In signing these accords, Canada joined the ranks of most OECD members with similar agreements in force.[2]

Canada has a long history of bilateral agreements impinging on investment. These start with various friendship, commerce, and navigation (FCN) treaties concluded by Great Britain before Canada assumed independent responsibility for its treaty relationships.[3] FCN treaties are now generally seen as insufficient to deal with the more specific contemporary demands of investors — particularly those concerning effective dispute settlement mechanisms. Like most countries, Canada no longer negotiates FCN treaties.

More recently, Canada has entered into numerous bilateral investment insurance agreements to guarantee subrogation rights under political risk insurance policies issued by the Export Develop-

---

[1] See Agreement between the Government of Canada and the Government of the Union of Soviet Socialist Republics for the Promotion and Reciprocal Protection of Investments, Moscow, November 20, 1989; Agreement between the Government of Canada and the Government of the Republic of Poland for the Promotion and Reciprocal Protection of Investments, Warsaw, April 6, 1990; Agreement between the Government of Canada and the Government of the Czech and Slovak Federal Republic for the Promotion and Protection of Investments, Prague, November 15, 1990; Agreement between the Government of Canada and the Government of the Oriental Republic of Uruguay for the Promotion and Protection of Investments, Ottawa, May 16, 1991; and Agreement between the Government of Canada and the Government of the Republic of Hungary for the Promotion and Reciprocal Protection of Investments, Ottawa, October 3, 1991.

[2] For a broad discussion of such agreements, see Bilateral Investment Treaties (United Nations Centre on Transnational Corporations) (1988).

[3] See (1974) 12 *Canadian Yearbook of International Law* 276-77.

ment Corporation to Canadian investors abroad.[4] While not normally dealing with such general matters as non-discrimination, these agreements establish a mode to arbitrate investment disputes between Canada and the host state. Despite this, investment insurance agreements are now also seen, like FCN treaties, as inadequate to deal with the wider issues affecting Canadian investors abroad.[5]

At the multilateral level, serious attempts to develop sophisticated investment conventions have emanated from the OECD. Though never ratified, the 1967 OECD Draft Convention on the Protection of Foreign Property represents the basis for many of the some 265 bilateral investment promotion and protection treaties in force by the late 1980s.[6] While typically BITs are seen as a way of addressing the problems of the property rights of developed source country investors in developing host countries, the pattern of these agreements is now more broadly based. Many BITs are in place between industrial countries and less developed states, but they also exist between market economies and centrally planned economies, between newly industrialized countries, and other countries, and between developing countries themselves. The first BIT was a 1959 agreement between the Federal Republic of Germany and Pakistan; Germany now has sixty-six of them.[7] Other countries have enthusiastically signed such agreements; they include France (28), Switzerland (34), the United Kingdom (37), and The Netherlands (30). The United States has signed only 11 bilateral investment treaties.

By dealing in a more detailed way with controversial issues such as expropriation and currency transfer, the BIT is more sophisticated

---

[4] For a sourcebook concerning these accords, see Meron, *Investment Insurance in International Law* (1976). Subrogation refers to the insurance law doctrine whereby, in consideration of meeting the insured's claim, the insurer can recover the value of any benefits available to the insured incidental to the loss. The bilateral investment insurance agreements oblige recognition by host states of EDC's subrogation rights as an insurer.

[5] See Paterson (ed.), *Canadian Regulation of International Trade and Investment 294* (1986).

[6] Draft Convention on the Protection of Foreign Property and Resolution of the OECD on the Draft Convention, OECD Paris, 1967.

[7] See Voss, "The Protection and Promotion of Foreign Direct Investment in Developing Countries; Interests, Interdependencies, Intricacies," (1982) 31 Int'l and Comp. L.Q. 686. For a compilation of all BITs extant, see *Investment Laws of the World: Investment Treaties*, Vols. 1-3 (ICSID) (1991).

than its predecessors. Most BITs provide for the free transfer of capital and profits and confer most-favoured nation and national treatment by the host country towards source country investors. While the original appeal of these treaties may have been their attempt to finesse some of the problems surrounding the international law of expropriation, their current attraction seems to have more to do with securing a favourable investment environment in the host state.

Given its membership in the OECD and the Group of Seven, it is puzzling that Canada has waited so long to sign its first BIT. There may be several reasons for this inactivity, though no one of them alone seems to offer a complete explanation. In its earlier history, the BIT was viewed largely as a device to enhance protection of source country investments in developing countries. By 1989, of almost $80 billion in total Canadian foreign investment, only $11.76 billion was in developing countries, mostly in Asia and the Americas.[8] On the other hand, Canada (unlike many European countries) lacks historical and political ties with most of these countries and the BIT might have been seen as compensating for some of these deficiencies. During the 1970s and early 1980s, Canada, like Australia and New Zealand, had a comprehensive foreign investment screening process, administered by the Foreign Investment Review Agency.[9] Australia and New Zealand signed their first BITs in 1988, both with China.[10] Canada may have regarded the BIT as incompatible with a high-profile domestic investment policy that many saw as hostile towards foreign ownership. On several occasions, Canada has justified its failure to enter into such agreements on the basis that they deal partly with matters within provincial jurisdiction. Whatever the reason for past intransigence, the five BITs Canada has signed seem to be part of a new Canadian willingness to support the dismantling of barriers to foreign investment, both here and abroad.

[8] Canada's International Investment Position (1989) (Statistics Canada). The largest host countries were Brazil ($1.5 billion), Indonesia ($0.9 billion), and Mexico ($0.17 billion).

[9] For an excellent historical analysis of FIRA, see Franck and Gudgeon, "Canada's Foreign Investment Control Experiment: The Law, the Context and the Practice," (1975) 50 N.Y.U.L. Rev. 74.

[10] See Mo, "Some Aspects of the Australia-China Investment Protection Treaty," (1991) 25 J. of World Trade 43.

CANADIAN INVESTMENT IN THE USSR

The Canada-USSR BIT, signed on November 20, 1989 in Moscow, reflects the USSR's new interest in attracting investment from market economy countries like Canada. Similar agreements have been signed by the USSR with France, The Netherlands, Germany, Finland, the United Kingdom, and Belgium. Canada has reinforced its commitment to enhanced commercial relations with the USSR by funding pre-investment studies and establishing a $500 million Export Development Corporation line of credit.[11] Despite recent events in that country, the increased openness of the USSR economy is evidenced through moves to advance earlier reforms allowing joint ventures between Soviets and foreigners, and by allowing foreign-owned subsidiaries and the repatriation of hard currency profits by investors. Furthermore, these legislative changes seem to be reflected in real expansion of foreign investment. In the first three months of 1991, total sales by USSR joint ventures stood at U.S. $11.4 billion (four times as much as a year earlier).[12] Meanwhile, the most serious obstacle to new investment in the USSR continues to be the inconvertibility of the ruble, rather than the existence of outdated structural legal problems.

The Canada-Poland BIT was signed at Warsaw on April 6, 1990 and other Canadian BITs have since been signed with Czechoslovakia and Hungary. Like the USSR, Poland has recently embarked on a modification of its domestic laws relating to foreign investment. Its joint venture regulations are among the most liberal in Eastern Europe and in 1989 a Foreign Investment Agency was established to promote and supervise foreign investment. Despite this liberalization of laws, Poland with an external debt of around U.S. $40 billion, high inflation, and an antiquated industrial infrastructure remains an unattractive host country for many investors. Much of the liberalization of Polish foreign investment controls are designed around linkage of new investment with privatization of government enterprise, rather than according investors

[11] See Notes for a Speech by the Minister for International Trade to the Canada-U.S.S.R. Business Council, Moscow, October 24, 1990. For up-to-date perspectives on investment in Eastern Europe and the USSR, see "Special Symposium Issue: Trade and Foreign Investment in Eastern Europe and the Soviet Union," (1991) 24 Vanderbilt J. of Transnational Law 205-448.

[12] "Joint Ventures Grow Amid Soviet Gloom," *Globe and Mail,* Toronto, September 10, 1991.

freedom as to the form their investment might take.[13] Canada has so far co-ordinated its economic assistance to Poland with the other members of the OECD and the Group of Seven.[14]

The Canada-Uruguay BIT was executed in Ottawa on May 16, 1991. A Canada-Argentina BIT is forthcoming and other Canadian BITs are planned with South American and South-East Asian nations. In expanding its BIT negotiations to include Latin American states, Canada will confront different interpretations of legitimate diplomatic protection such as those upon which the Calvo clause and the Drago doctrine are based.[15] The following discussion focuses on the text of the Canada-USSR BIT, but where significant differences exist reference will also be made to provisions of the other Canadian BITs.

The Canada-USSR Agreement for the Promotion and Protection of Investment

SCOPE OF APPLICATION

The scope of the Canadian BITs turns largely on the meaning of terms that they employ.[16] The USSR BIT defines "investment" in broad terms as any type of asset invested by an investor of one party in the territory of the other, including loans, shares in a business enterprise, private contractual rights, and public rights, such as those under licensing procedures.[17] It is striking that the USSR, Polish, Czech, and Hungarian BITs do not refer specifically to any of the specialized forms of economic association sometimes found in socialist states, but the width of the definition of "investment" may have been intended to avoid these differences arising out of domestic laws and policies. The USSR BIT provides that any change in the form of an investment does not affect its character as such.[18] Some BITs stipulate that such an altered investment must not vary

---

[13] See *Financial Post,* February 27, 1990, at 6.

[14] See *Financial Post,* August 28, 1989, at 10.

[15] See Shea, *The Calvo Clause* (1955).

[16] Article 1 of the USSR BIT defines the words "territory," "investment," "returns," and "investor."

[17] Article 1(b). This functional definition can be contrasted with that contained in Article 1611 of the Canada-United States Free Trade Agreement, which requires a permanent establishment in the host state.

[18] *Ibid.*

from the form of investment that was originally approved.[19] The USSR BIT has not been implemented by a Canadian enactment, so presumably its existence would not affect the application of the Investment Canada Act and other domestic review laws to an investment sufficiently altered to require separate approval.

BITs do not create rights of establishment exceeding those arising under domestic laws. Article 2(2) of the USSR BIT allows the host state to retain its laws and policies concerning the admission of investments from the other state. The treaty also allows the host state to introduce future restrictions on establishment of foreign investment, provided such rules are applied equally to all foreign investors.[20] The protections afforded by the BIT do not, therefore, apply to foreign investments that have not received the preliminary approvals required under domestic law. As in the case of the Canada-United States Free Trade Agreement, rulings under that law are not amenable to the dispute settlement procedures established under the BIT itself.[21]

The scope of the BIT is also affected by its duration. The USSR BIT provides that the agreement does not apply to investments made before January 1, 1950.[22] The other four BITs have differing commencement dates.[23]

The scope of the BIT is significantly affected by the legal persons to whom it applies. The term investor is defined in Article 1 of the USSR BIT as meaning, in the case of natural persons, those who are citizens or permanent residents of either party. Corporations and other legal entities are defined according to the law under which they are constituted or incorporated. The status of natural persons or corporations is thus dependent on the domestic laws of either Party. It appears that a corporate investor established under the laws of a state of the United States, controlled by a Canadian citizen and carrying on business in Canada, will not obtain protection under the USSR BIT. Problems could arise as to the application of the USSR BIT if a Soviet citizen with landed immigrant status in Canada were to invest in the USSR. If the individual is seen as a USSR citizen, he or she may not be eligible

---

[19] See *supra* note 2, at 22-23.

[20] Article 2(3).

[21] *Ibid.;* cf. Canada-United States Free Trade Agreement, Article 1608.1.

[22] Article 14 (2).

[23] Inquiries of the Department of External Affairs about these variations in the commencement of treaty coverage failed to reveal any explanation of them.

for protection under the treaty. The Uruguayan BIT expressly provides that it does not extend to natural persons who are citizens of both contracting parties.

TREATMENT OF INVESTMENTS

"Fair and Equitable Treatment"

Article 3(1) of the USSR BIT provides that investments or returns of investors receive fair and equitable treatment ''in accordance with principles of international law.'' This formula reflects the basic minimum standard of international law, though not all states currently accept it. As well as reiterating mutual adherence to a basic principle, the inclusion of Article 3(1) provides a principle for resolving the interpretation of ambiguities arising under other provisions of the accord.

Most-Favoured Nation Treatment

Article 3(2) and (3) provides parties must grant investments and investors of each other no less favourable treatment than they grant investors and investments of third states. This guarantees each party that more favourable investment terms granted by the other party to a third state will also be extended to its investors and their investments. In the case of investors, this treatment only extends to the ''management, use, enjoyment or disposal of their investments or returns.'' It is doubtful if Article 3 could be interpreted as requiring that special advantages granted an individual third state investor must be extended to investors of the other party. The use of the terms ''investors'' and ''investments'' in their plural, rather than their singular form, supports this interpretation, as does the limit of the exceptions enumerated in Article 4 to matters dealt with by treaty. The most-favoured nation standard only applies to more favourable treatment afforded by treaty, despite ad hoc preferences being inconsistent, in principle, with the standard of fair and equitable treatment set out in Article 3(1).

National Treatment

Article 3(4) of the USSR BIT requires each party to treat investments or returns of investors of the other ''no less favourably than it treats investors or returns of its own investors.'' Of course, this standard does not affect the host state rules applicable to the entry of foreign investment.[24] While a basic requisite for capital-exporting countries, national treatment clauses have historically been absent from investment treaties involving socialist states, which have been concerned that they might favour foreign enterprises over domestic firms. It is therefore evidence of the abandonment of this concern that all of the Canadian BITs contain national treatment provisions. On the other hand, the national treatment obligation in Article 3(4) is significantly qualified by the phrase "to the extent possible and in accordance with its laws and regulations." Canadian investors in the USSR should, therefore, be concerned that they will continue to be subject to a discriminatory investment regime applicable to foreign investors but not to local citizens.

The preferential treatment of United States investors pursuant to Chapter 16 of the Canada-United States Free Trade Agreement does not flow to the USSR as a result of Article 3. This is because Article 4 provides that none of the benefits of any existing or future free trade area or customs union need be extended by one party to investors of the other.[25]

The co-existence of the "fair and equitable" standard, alongside the most-favoured nation and national treatment principles, may mean that where the application of either of the latter gives rise to difficulty — such as when financing incentives are only extended to nationals — the "fair and equitable" standard can be used to prevent claims to the advantages of such incentives by capital-exporting investors on the basis that the local program does not substantially impair their activities in the host state and was not intended to benefit more advantaged investors like themselves. However, in the case of host countries with the serious domestic economic problems of Poland and the USSR, foreign investors are likely to demand that such incentives be made available as an inducement to invest.

COMPENSATION

Most BITs contain provisions on compensation for losses caused by armed conflict or domestic disorder. Article 5 of the USSR BIT provides a most-favoured nation standard regarding settlement (including restitution, indemnification, and compensation) of losses

[24] Article 2(2).

[25] The inapplicability of Article 24 of the GATT to preferences regarding investment necessitates a specific provision of this kind.

arising from these events. Thus, no absolute right to compensation is granted but the foreign investor must be treated no less favourably than investors of a third state. The USSR BIT provides, however, that such payments as are made must be "prompt, adequate, effective and freely transferable." Two of the Canadian BITs — with Czechoslovakia and Uruguay — also apply a national treatment standard in respect to compensation for armed conflict or domestic disturbance.

EXPROPRIATION

Article 6 of the USSR BIT sets out a detailed expropriation provision consisting of four elements. First, there is a broad definition of expropriation (to include nationalization, expropriation, or measures having similar effect). Second, there is a prohibition of expropriation except for a public purpose, under due process of law, and on a non-discriminatory basis. Third, expropriation is to be accompanied by "prompt, adequate and effective compensation" based on the "real value" of the investment at the time of expropriation. Finally, the affected investor is entitled to prompt review by a judicial or other independent authority of its case and of the question of valuation.

The first two elements reflect contemporary customary international law. The meaning of "public purpose" is determined by the law of the host state. While most developing countries acknowledge a duty to pay compensation, they would prefer that it be measured according to the law of the expropriating state. The USSR BIT reflects the view of most capital-exporting states, that compensation be "prompt, adequate and effective." Most BITs contain this definition of compensation which may be seen to represent an attempt by Western developed countries, like Canada, to prevent a re-examination of the international legal standards for compensation, unchallenged until the Russian and Mexican revolutions.[26]

There is also reference to judicial review of the taking under the laws of the host state. The language of Article 6 repeats that of the United Kingdom Model BIT on this issue. It would appear that while the law of the host state governs matters of procedure, that law must adjust, if necessary, to afford the minimum protection afforded by the substantive criteria set out in Article 6.

---

[26] See *supra* note 2, at 70.

Most BITs provide that investors have the right to freely transfer all income and other proceeds from their investments. Article 7 of the USSR BIT requires that each party guarantee prompt (within two years) transfer in convertible currencies of investment returns, proceeds of the liquidation of an investment, loan repayments, wages, and compensation for expropriation or war losses.[27] The list of monies set out in Article 7 does not include depreciation or contributions of capital to the investment. There is a most-favoured nation obligation in respect of funds transfer.[28] Article 7 also provides for an extension of the transfer period from two to five years in case of exceptional balance of payments difficulties. This appears to be based on the model treaty of the Federal Republic of Germany and is realistic in view of the limited abilities of many host states to perform currency convertibility obligations.[29]

SUBROGATION

Canada since 1969 has entered into specialized bilateral investment insurance agreements with several countries. A major effect of these accords has been to ensure the recognition of the insurer's rights as subrogee under political risk insurance policies issued by the Export Development Corporation. Subrogation clauses are also characteristic of most BITs. The subrogation provided for under Article 8 of the USSR BIT is not expressed in as much detail as in typical Canadian investment insurance agreements, but it does ensure that, despite being subrogated to the investor's rights, the source state can authorize the investor to pursue its claim to compensation. This is sometimes advantageous, such as when the source state wishes, for political reasons, to minimize its profile in an expropriation claim.

DISPUTE SETTLEMENT

International law is replete with instances of attempts by source states to resolve investment claims regarding impugned conduct on

[27] Article 1 defines "returns" as "all amounts yielded by an investment and, in particular, though not exclusively, profits, interest, capital gains, dividends, royalties, fees or other current income."

[28] Article 7(3).

[29] Article 5(2).

the part of host countries. The BIT represents a pragmatic attempt to ameliorate the perceived inadequacy of international law to satisfactorily resolve claims in such cases. Since there is no established institutional venue to which investor claimants can resort and the courts of the host state are often perceived as unreliable in such cases, BIT dispute resolution provisions appear as the most satisfactory solution for many investors and capital-exporting countries. Like most BITs, the Canada-USSR example deals separately with disputes between the source and host states on the one hand, and host states and foreign investors on the other.

Disputes between an Investor and the Host Contracting Party (Article IX)

In the case of disputes between investors and host governments, most BITs provide for submission to the International Centre for the Settlement of Investment Disputes between States and Nationals of Other States (ICSID).[30] ICSID was established in 1966 under a World Bank-sponsored convention, as part of that institution's interest in encouraging investment in developing countries. ICSID is a novel form of dispute resolution, supplementing litigation, private arbitration, and diplomatic protection. ICSID is not an arbitral tribunal in its own right but acts to facilitate the establishment of arbitral tribunals to resolve investment disputes between contracting states and nationals of other contracting states. The jurisdiction of the centre rests on the prior consent of the parties but none may withdraw its consent unilaterally. Advance consent to ICSID arbitration, typical of most BITs, has the effect of removing investment disputes from the territory of either disputant and increases the likelihood of enforcement of any subsequent award.[31] Canada has never ratified the ICSID Convention, though ninety-five other states have — including such federal states as Australia, Nigeria, and the United States. The USSR, Poland, and Uruguay have not signed the ICSID Convention. Czechoslovakia has signed, but not ratified the Convention, and Hungary has ratified it.

The ICSID framework is clearly designed with the political dynamics of a dispute between a private investor and a host state in mind and most non-Canadian BITs incorporate reference to ICSID for the resolution of such disputes. By contrast, the USSR BIT, in Article 9, provides for arbitration of such disputes pursuant

[30] For the text of the Convention, see (1965) 4 Int'l Leg. Mat. 524.

[31] *Ibid.,* Article 54(1).

to the 1976 Arbitration Rules of the United Nations Commission on International Trade Law (UNCITRAL).[32] Because these rules were primarily designed to govern private arbitrations, they would seem much less suitable than ICSID procedures to resolve investment disputes where one side is a sovereign state. It is regrettable that the treaty did not at least adopt the ICSID Arbitration Rules, rather than those of UNCITRAL, leaving the parties free to agree otherwise. This situation was adjusted by the time the Uruguayan and Hungarian BITs were signed; these agreements both provide for ICSID arbitration as an alternative but only where both states are ICSID parties. This is presumably indicative of Canadian intention to sign the World Bank treaty in the near future.

Differing attitudes towards sovereignty over investments are revealed by Article 10 of the Canada-Uruguay BIT, dealing with disputes between investors and the host state. Arbitration under either UNCITRAL rules or ICSID auspices is possible at the investor's option but only if a host country tribunal has not rendered a decision within eighteen months or its ruling is considered manifestly unjust or in violation of the accord.

Until recently, Canadians faced substantial legal difficulties in connection with resolving by arbitration any international commercial disputes in which they were involved.[33] For constitutional and other reasons, Canada had not acceded to the 1958 United Nations Convention on the Recognition and Enforcement of Foreign Arbitral Awards (the "New York Convention").[34] Primarily as a result of initiatives taken by the province of British Columbia in 1986 to modernize its arbitration statutes, Canada acceded to the New York Convention on May 12, 1986. The New York Convention provides a mechanism for enforcing awards given in the territory of members, irrespective of the citizenship of the parties.[35] It also applies to the enforcement of agreements to arbitrate.[36] Now that the Con-

---

[32] As adopted by the United Nations Commission on International Trade Law on April 28, 1976 (UN Sales No. E.77.V.6). For the text of the Rules, see Paterson and Thompson (eds.), *UNCITRAL Arbitration Model in Canada,* Appendix 6 (1987).

[33] See Brierley, "International Trade Arbitration: The Canadian Viewpoint," in Macdonald, Morris, and Johnson (eds.), *Canadian Perspectives on International Law and Organization* 826 (1974).

[34] Convention on the Recognition and Enforcement of Foreign Arbitral Awards, done at New York, July 10, 1958, U.N. Doc. No. E/Conf. 26/9, Rev. 1. As of June 1989, 83 states had ratified the convention.

[35] *Ibid.,* Article 3.

[36] *Ibid.,* Article 2.

vention is part of the federal and provincial laws of Canada, the security of Canadian investment in developing countries should be enhanced.[37] On the other hand, accession to the New York Convention undermines the long-standing explanation of the federal government for Canada's non-accession to ICSID on the basis that it relates to matters within provincial competence.

In the past two years, along with implementing the New York Convention, Canadian jurisdictions have enacted legislation based on the UNCITRAL Model Law on International Commercial Arbitration, adopted by UNCITRAL on June 21, 1985.[38] This legislation applies to arbitrations of international commercial disputes that occur in Canada and places considerable limits on the scope for judicial intervention in the conduct of these private proceedings. The legislation may increase the probability of arbitration in Canada of a dispute involving a Canadian investment in a host country.

Disputes between the Contracting Parties (Article 2)

Like most BITs, the USSR BIT provides for diplomatic solutions to disputes between the two states concerning the interpretation or application of the treaty. If such avenues fail, though no time limit is provided, the matter can be submitted, at the request of either side, to an ad hoc arbitration tribunal. Provision is made for the appointment of an independent chairman, in addition to a nominee from each party. The tribunal may determine its own procedure and must report its decision within six months from the appointment of its chairman.

There is no reference to the law applicable to such a dispute in Article 2. This is characteristic of most BITs and presumably implies that the matter is for the arbitral tribunal to determine. The United States prototype BIT refers to "the applicable rules of international law." It is unlikely that the tribunal would confine itself to the law of the host state, and the rules of international law and widespread commercial practice are likely to be addressed as well.

CANADIAN INVESTMENT POLICY, 1974-90

Events in Canada during the 1980s made it clear that there had

---

[37] For an inventory of Canadian laws, see Paterson and Thompson, *op. cit. supra* note 32, at 165.
[38] See (1985) 24 Int'l Leg. Mat. 1302.

been a substantial change in the government's attitude towards restrictions on foreign investment. The Trudeau governments of the seventies witnessed an expansion of economic nationalism in Canada. Many Canadians began to question whether economic benefits were being secured to Canada by transnational investment. Specifically, concerns were raised about such matters as the unlimited exports of unprocessed primary products and the tendency of American branch plants to use imports from United States manufacturers, rather than Canadian suppliers. While resembling the concerns of many developing countries, Canada's arguments were reinforced by the geographical proximity of the United States and related issues of cultural and social independence.

Canadian law and policy during the 1970s was in direct response to the above concerns. These measures included the Foreign Investment Review Act, the National Energy Policy, and provincial and federal legislation dealing with the extraterritorial application of foreign regulatory legislation and corporate management directives. In international venues, Canada's investment perspective was reflected in lack of participation in arrangements designed to facilitate the resolution of investment disputes. Canada did not accede to the United Nations Convention on the Reciprocal Recognition and Enforcement of Foreign Arbitral Awards and the World Bank Convention establishing ICSID. Nor did Canada, unlike the United States and several European countries, enter into any BITs. Even when adopting the 1976 OECD Declaration on International Investment and Multinational Enterprises, Canada simultaneously expressed its resolve to retain the right to impose future restrictions upon the entry of foreign investment.

By the mid-1980s, however, there had been a distinct change in Canadian foreign investment policy. This change was symbolized for many by the Prime Minister's sentiment that Canada was now "open for business." The Foreign Investment Review Act was repealed and replaced by the Investment Canada Act in 1985, thus limiting the categories of reviewable foreign investments. Along with a new foreign investment screening agency, Investment Canada, amendments were also made to the Bank Act, expanding the scope for foreign banking operations in Canada. Canada's international positions regarding investment also reflected this overall change in policy. In 1985 Canada became part of the OECD Code on Capital Movements. The Uruguay Round of Multilateral Trade Negotiations, commencing in 1986, also saw Canada more or less allied with the United States in supporting liberalized trade in services and other related GATT initiatives. In 1988, the execution of the Canada-United States Free Trade Agreement also signalled Canadian willingness to agree to freer rights of establishment —at least as far as the United States was concerned. The decade closed with Canada's first BIT being signed with the Soviet Union.

Why did Canadian investment policy undergo the major shift just described? At least three reasons suggest themselves. First, American investment in Canada had largely stabilized by 1980, and investments from other countries, especially those in the Asia-Pacific region, was increasing at a faster rate. Also, Canada itself was becoming a more significant investor abroad than earlier, especially in the United States. Second, there was a greater realization in Canada by the early 1980s that continued economic growth was dependent on international competitiveness. The Canadian government increasingly saw this as better secured if Canada participated in effective international agreements, rather than independently reacting to isolated domestic concerns. Finally, the movement to deregulate the Canadian economy in the 1980s increased the likelihood that Canada would enter into international accords to reduce artificial barriers to economic transactions.

LACK OF A COHERENT NATIONAL POLICY ON FOREIGN INVESTMENT CONTROLS

While a perceptible change in Canada's policy concerning restrictions on foreign investment has occurred since the 1970s, there has not been a clear statement of the nature of this change. Canada's restrictive investment regime of the 1970s received extensive publicity, but this was in some measure because Canada had, through most of its history, remained relatively open to foreign investment. This fact is best proven by the high levels of American and European investment that have long existed in Canada. What restrictions continue to exist are fairly transparent and affect areas of economic activity that are restricted from foreign access in most countries, such as banking, broadcasting, insurance, and transportation.

The most clearly articulated Canadian concerns about foreign investment have surrounded the investment coming from abroad into Canada. First, there is concern to restrict foreign investment in areas of the economy that are seen to have strategic significance; this was illustrated during the public debate about whether the Free

388 *Annuaire canadien de Droit international 1991*

Trade Agreement with the United States (FTA) obliged Canada to sell water to the United States. These sorts of concerns are evidenced by Chapter 9 of the FTA, which deals with trade in energy. Second, there is long-standing Canadian concern about the protection of cultural industries (such as book publishing) from foreign ownership and control; the FTA contains an explicit exemption for cultural industries from all provisions of the treaty and a similar exemption is apparently being sought by Canada in its negotiations with Mexico and the United States concerning a North American Free Trade Agreement.

While concerns about foreign investment in Canada have been well documented, there has been much less force behind Canada's support for international agreement about limits on foreign investment restrictions. In part, this is simply a result of the absence of major international initiatives affecting foreign direct investment, at least until the current round of Multilateral Trade Negotiations. However, it also apparently reflects a decision to separate national investment policy and Canada's position on investment issues in multilateral fora. It is hard to gauge this latter point in the absence of available recent statements, but it appears to amount to support for continuing liberalization of existing restrictive measures, as well as restrictions on the introduction of new measures. The reasons for Canadian passivity on these questions are elusive. They probably include the small scale of Canadian foreign direct investment in developing countries (which usually have restrictive investment regimes) and the large scale of Canadian investment in Europe and the United States (where investment restrictions are relatively modest or, at least, visible).

While there have been major international undertakings by Canada recently concerning foreign investment (the FTA, the OECD Codes, and BITs), these steps have not occurred in the context of a clearly articulated Canadian policy on the topic. Canada risks being perceived as having an investment policy that is the same as that of the United States, unless it explains its position on the changes that have occurred. In the absence of this explanation, observers may think that Canadian policy has not changed since the 1970s, except in relation to privileges granted American investors under the FTA. Other OECD countries have already started informally to pressure Canada to extend to them the benefits conferred upon the United States under the FTA regarding investment and trade in services.

If no coherent Canadian foreign investment policy is forthcoming, Canada risks losing its credibility in what is shaping up to be a heated debate between developed and developing countries over investment issues. If Canada is seen as aligned with the developed countries (particularly the United States) in this policy confrontation, it may not receive the benefit of concessions granted by the developing countries. Another risk of a passive investment policy is that the sort of strategic and cultural justifications for controls that have been developed in relation to Canada's domestic investment regime, may lose support in the process of developing a broad international investment consensus.

CONCLUSION

Canada has signed its first BITs at a time when these accords are increasingly seen as inherently biased in favour of capital exporting states.[39] The intent of Canada in executing these agreements appears to be to improve the climate for its investors, but they may actually do little to improve the economic rights of Canadians under the laws of the host state. The critical achievement of the BIT appears to be the framework it provides for dispute settlement between investors and host states. The Canadian BITs are seriously flawed in that access to ICSIDs binding arbitral procedures is impossible or will only be possible once Canada adheres to that multilateral accord.

ROBERT K. PATERSON
Faculty of Law, University of British Columbia

Sommaire

Progrès récents dans l'investissement canadien à l'étranger et l'entente conclue entre le Canada et l'URSS sur la promotion et la protection réciproque de l'investissement

Depuis 1990, le Canada a signé ses cinq premières ententes bilatérales sur la promotion et la protection réciproque de l'investissement. Ce type de traité, que l'Allemagne a été la première à conclure, est répandu et n'est plus conclu uniquement entre États développés exportateurs de capitaux et États en développement.
L'article analyse d'abord les dispositions du premier traité sur l'investissement conclu

[39] See *A Multilateral Investment Accord: Issues, Models and Options,* Working Paper Number 8, (1991) *Investment Canada* 32.

entre le Canada et l'URSS. Les obligations qu'il impose ressemblent à celles que l'on trouve habituellement dans d'autres ententes de ce genre et elles ont pour but de garantir le respect de normes minimales d'équité. On peut douter cependant qu'un grand nombre d'investisseurs canadiens à l'étranger trouveront dans ces traités les droits et les recours juridiques particuliers dont ils aimeraient être investis. De plus, les dispositions des ententes canadiennes sur le règlement des différends n'offrent pas nécessairement les moyen efficaces pour résoudre les différends en matière d'investissement impliquant des investisseurs privés et des gouvernements qui accueillent les investissements.

Cette entente sur l'investissement constitue un jalon dans l'élaboration de la politique canadienne contemporaine en matière d'investissement. Depuis 1974, la réglementation canadienne de l'investissement étranger a été marquée par deux périodes distinctes. Pendant la première période, le Parlement a adopté la Loi sur l'examen de l'investissement étranger *et la participation du Canada aux ententes internationales relatives à l'investissement est restée limitée. Cependant, à la suite de l'élection du gouvernement conservateur dans le milieu des années 1980, une approche très différente de la réglementation de l'investissement a été adoptée, entraînant avec elle l'abrogation de la* Loi sur l'examen de l'investissement étranger *et l'octroi de concessions aux investisseurs américains dans le cadre de l'*Accord de libre-échange entre le Canada et les États-Unis. *Les ententes sur l'investissement conclues récemment, comme celle à laquelle on est arrivé avec l'URSS, concordent avec cette libéralisation du droit interne. Elles mettent toutefois en évidence l'absence de politique canadienne claire en matière de réglementation de l'investissement à l'étranger ainsi que la nécessité de maintenir une telle réglementation au Canada.*

Self-Defence as a Justification for Disregarding Diplomatic Immunity

FROM THE NEED TO FACILITATE INTERNATIONAL RELATIONS, there has evolved in customary international law the venerable practice by host states of affording various privileges to the envoys of foreign states. A personal immunity from arrest or detention by the receiving state, a personal immunity from the criminal, civil, and administrative jurisdiction of the receiving state, and an inviolability for the mission's premises are among the most rudimentary of these prerogatives. However, from time to time, these privileges are abused to no greater end than the insulation of a foreign diplomat from the consequences of his own criminal behaviour. Faced with this situation, receiving states have traditionally reacted by expelling the diplomat, a power now codified in Article 9 of the 1964 Vienna Convention on Diplomatic Relations,[1] but, to ensure the safety of persons and property, it may be necessary sometimes to restrain the emissary until such time as he can be removed.

But by what authority may a receiving state take this action against a diplomat? There are no grounds within the Vienna Convention that would sanction it, no matter what threat the diplomat posed to the receiving state or its residents. However, the principle of self-defence is relevant in diplomatic law, and it may provide a legitimate pretext for acting in violation of diplomatic immunity. Self-defence is an important principle of customary international law, exemplified by Article 51 of the United Nations Charter; it comes into play when acts of force are committed by states, although it is not limited to such contingencies.[2] The ques-

---

[1] 500 UNTS 95.
[2] U.K. House of Commons Foreign Affairs Committee, Paper No. 127, First Report, The Abuse of Diplomatic Immunities and Privileges, Report with an Annex [hereinafter cited as First Report]; Together with the Proceedings of the Committee [hereinafter cited as Proceedings]; Minutes of Evidence Taken on 20 June and 2 and 18 July in the Last Session of Parliament [hereinafter cited as Minutes]; and Appendices at xxxviii-x (1984) [hereinafter cited as Appendices]. Appendices, Appendix 4, at 71.

tions to be considered here are whether or not self-defence in fact provides the receiving state with a legal justification for the restraint of a diplomat and, if so, what is the legitimate scope of such defensive actions; specifically, can a foreign diplomat be subject to the local criminal jurisdiction in the name of self-defence?

LEGITIMACY OF SELF-DEFENCE IN DIPLOMATIC LAW

The academic discourses on diplomatic law reveal a general consensus in favour of permitting a receiving state to violate a diplomat's immunity on the basis of self-defence where the diplomat has personally engaged in violence against the receiving state or its citizens. In *De Jure Belli ac Pacis Libris Tres*, Grotius stated that "all human laws have been so adjusted that in case of dire necessity they are not binding; and so the same rule will hold in regard to the law of the inviolability of ambassadors. Therefore, that an immediately threatening peril may be met, if there is no other proper recourse, ambassadors can be detained and questioned. But if an ambassador should attempt armed force he can indeed be killed, not by way of penalty, but in natural defence."[3] Bynkershoek, in *De Foro Legatorum*, concurred with Grotius, citing with approval his words quoted above and stating:

Still another problem has its origins here, whether an ambassador who initiates violence cannot be repelled with violence when he acts publicly, perhaps joining enemies or rebels in arms against us, or privately by assaulting or killing our citizens or something of the sort. Whosoever uses force, him it has always been permissible to repel by force, nor is there any exception in the case of ambassadors. When in Euripides' *Heraclidae*, Copreus, the ambassador said, "Do not by the Gods dare to strike an ambassador," Demophon replied, "Unless the ambassador shall learn to act with self-restraint," that is, unless he shall refrain from using the violence which Corpreus was threatening.

Grotius also rightly permits the return of a blow, not as a measure of punishment, but as a measure of natural defence to save one's self from imminent peril.[4]

Among the other seminal authors on diplomatic law, Johann Textor concurred with Grotius and Bynkershoek. In *Synopsis Juris Gentium*, he maintained that "The guarantee of public safety [afforded to diplomats] is put to an end if the legate himself resorts

---

[3] Hugo Grotius, *De Jure Belli ac Pacis Libris Tres* 444.

[4] Cornelius van Bynkershoek, *DeForo Legatorum* 89-90.

to violence. For, it being permissible to repel force by force, according to the principles of the Law of Nature, even to the killing of an assailant, a legate who makes a forcible attack on any other may undoubtedly be resisted and even killed by the attacked party."[5] Has this view as to the propriety of a receiving state's right of self-defence against the violent actions of foreign diplomats survived to the present?

On April 17, 1984, an orderly demonstration was held by opponents of Colonel Qaddafi's government on the pavement in St. James' Square, London, opposite the Libyan People's Bureau. Both the Foreign Office in London and the British ambassador in Tripoli had been warned the day before that if the demonstration would be allowed to go ahead, Libya "would not be responsible for its consequences." During the demonstration, shots were fired from the windows of the Bureau, killing Woman Police Constable Fletcher, who was on duty in the square.[6] This shooting incident impelled the British government to undertake an investigation into abuses of diplomatic privileges and immunities. The investigation was made the responsibility of the Foreign Affairs Committee of the U.K. Parliament. The Committee heard testimony from various prominent international lawyers, and questions concerning the right of a receiving state to act in self-defence against the violent acts of foreign diplomats were considered extensively.

In testimony given before the Committee, Sir John Freeland, legal adviser to the Permanent Undersecretary of State and Head of the Diplomatic Service, noted that the doctrine of self-defence in international law can only be utilized under specific conditions:

Question: If we had a right in self-defence in international law or domestic law to protect ourselves against attack, what was to stop the police going into the embassy building immediately that they heard firing to seize, the guns, the ammunition, or the firer in self-defence?

Sir John Freeland: Perhaps I might reply initially rather generally. It is, of course, the case that the doctrine of self-defence in international law is a very restrictive one. The classic formulation is that self-defence is justified where there is "a necessity of self-defence instant, overwhelming [and] leaving no choice of means and no moment for deliberation."[7]

---

[5] Johann Wolfgang Textor, *Synopsis Juris Gentium* 143; see also *United States* v. *Benner* (1830), 1 Baldwin's Reps. (Amer.) 240.
[6] Rosalyn Higgins, "The Abuse of Diplomatic Privileges and Immunities: Recent United Kingdom Experience," 79 Am. J. Int'l L. 641, at 643 (1985).
[7] This *locus classicus* of the right of self-defence in international law comes from the *Caroline* case. In asking Great Britain to show cause why a British subject should

In more modern parlance, we would take the view that the right to resort to self-defence arises where there is a serious threat or actual danger, where there is no other means of averting it or bringing it to an end, and that the action taken in self-defence must be limited to what is necessary and what is proportionate.[8]

Similar testimony was given by Sir Francis Vallat;[9] he agreed that the doctrine of self-defence in international law could legitimately be employed in violation of diplomatic privilege in appropriate circumstances. In fact, he went so far as to outline what such circumstances might be:

Question: [D]o you agree that if, on hearing the guns being fired, the police had rushed into the Embassy, on the basis that they had no idea when the guns would stop firing, and they were acting to [prevent] further shooting, that would come into the heading of "self-defence" justifiable in international law?

Sir Francis Vallat: I did not say that, or I certainly did not intend to say that. What might be possible, and one has got to remember when dealing with the Embassy premises that you are dealing with Article 22 of the [Vienna Convention on Diplomatic Relations], which is fairly absolute in granting inviolability of the premises of diplomatic missions. But there may be certain circumstances, and I would not like to put it higher than this, in which it might be justifiable. Suppose the embassy were being used as a kind of fortress for a running battle with people in the street, it might then become justifiable, but I find it difficult to imagine that before an international tribunal of repute, one would be held to be justified to run into an embassy because there had been one or two shots fired, even if that happened to cause an injury or a death.[10]

All the authorities canvassed by the Committee agreed that self-defence was a valid option against diplomats who abused their privilege in a manner which posed an immediate threat to the receiving state. Yet there was no consensus as to whether the shots fired

---

not be tried for arson and murder in connection with an 1837 foray undertaken into U.S. territory to destroy a steamship being used to supply reinforcements to a group planning an insurrection against British rule in Canada, the U.S. Secretary of State required that the British show "a necessity of self-defence, instant, overwhelming, leaving no choice of means, and no moment for deliberation." See D. W. Bowett, *Self-Defence in International Law* 58-60 (1958).

[8] Minutes, June 20, 1984 at 28, see 48-50 and 53.

[9] Sir Francis Vallat was Deputy Legal Adviser to the Foreign Office, 1954-60; Legal Adviser, 1960-68; member of the International Law Commission, 1973-81; and member of the drafting committee of the conference that drew up the Vienna Convention in 1961.

[10] Minutes, July 2, 1984, at 34, sec. 78.

from the Libyan embassy constituted a threat of sufficient magnitude as to justify reliance upon the doctrine. Though Sir John Freeland and Sir Francis Vallat seemed to think that an abuse of sufficient magnitude had not occurred, in a memorandum submitted by Colonel Professor G.I.A.D. Draper, it was suggested otherwise:

> Thus, in the incident of the shooting of Woman Police Constable Fletcher on 17 April, 1984, by an inmate within the Libyan embassy whose status and identity were unknown, it can be properly contended that, in immediate response, counter-fire might have been directed at the Libyan Embassy windows by the police. Further, in the period immediately after the firing from the embassy, entry might have been carried out by the police, with firearms, if available, and sufficient force used within the embassy to overpower the assailant or any person armed and remove all weapons found inside. Such acts would, in exercise of the right of self-defence, probably have been required immediately after the firing from within or during continued firing.
>
> It is probably a valid contention in law that an immediate and forcible entry into [the] diplomatic premises of Libya, after the firing incident, was a measure designed to prevent the offender repeating the offence, and the overpowering of him within the embassy precincts would have been a legitimate exercise of the inherent right of self-defence enjoyed by the UK.[11]

Research could discover no case law discussing the propriety of a state's reliance upon the doctrine of self-defence as against an extreme abuse of diplomatic privilege. Yet there are instances where states have professed to act in violation of a diplomat's immunity on the basis of self-defence.

On January 29, 1717, having learned of a conspiracy to invade England and dethrone the King, the government ordered the arrest of Gyllenburg, the Swedish ambassador, who was the author of the conspiracy. Gyllenburg complained that his arrest was a direct breach of the law of nations, and some of the foreign ministers at the Court of London agreed. The Secretaries of State consequently wrote letters to the diplomatic corps in London to assign reasons for the arrest, and justifying it on the basis of self-defence. The letters satisfied all of the ambassadors except Montleone, the Spanish Ambassador, who observed that he was sorry no other way could be fallen upon for preserving the peace of the kingdom other than the arrest of a public minister.[12]

---

[11] Appendices, Appendix 6, at 71-72.

[12] Robert Phillmore, *Commentaries upon International Law*, Vol. 2, sec. 181 (Philadelphia:

More recently in 1984, British authorities justified the searching of Libyan diplomats as they left the Embassy at the end of the siege on the basis of self-defence, saying that "The Foreign and Commonwealth Office have taken the view that the physical search of persons emerging from the Bureau (whether or not they were later found to be persons who had previously been recognised as having diplomatic status) was justified by reference to self defence in domestic and international law."[13] Having surveyed the authorities, it is reasonable to conclude that the doctrine of self-defence in international law is a valid basis upon which a receiving state may properly justify a violation of diplomatic immunity. While the scope of the abuse required to justify reliance upon the doctrine is uncertain, the fact that the doctrine may be employed is not. However, the argument may be made that the doctrine of self-defence has had no application in the context of diplomatic law since the adoption of the Vienna Convention on Diplomatic Relations. The Vienna Convention is a general codification of diplomatic law,[14] yet it allows for absolutely no exceptions to the principle of diplomatic inviolability. Therefore, no exceptions to diplomatic inviolability being recognized, it may be argued that the doctrine of self-defence should not provide an exception to diplomatic immunity.

Michael Hardy, in his book *Modern Diplomatic Law,* stated that the idea of allowing for any exceptions to diplomatic inviolability was expressly rejected by both the International Law Commission and by the Vienna Conference. He put it thus: "After long discussion, the International Law Commission decided that no exceptions should be made to this rule [of inviolability,] even in the event of emergency, a decision upheld at the Conference. If a unilateral power of determination were given to the receiving State in one context, for example, with respect to the outbreak of fire, by parity of reasoning, the power should extend, or might in practice be extended, to acts based on other paramount necessities, such as those of state security — and this no sending State wished to see."[15] This was confirmed by Sir Francis Vallat in his testimony before the U.K. Foreign Affairs Committee:

T. & J. W. Johnson, Law Booksellers, 1855).

[13] First Report, xxxii, sec. 102. For a discussion of self-defence used by individuals against diplomats, see *United States* v. *Ortega* [1825] (Case No. 15,971) 27 Fed. Cas. 3959; see also *United States* v. *Liddle,* [1808] (Case No. 15,598) 26 Fed. Cas. 936.

[14] First Report, viii, sec. 13.

[15] Michael Hardy. *Modern Diplomatic Law* 44 (1968).

Question: Can you remember why the idea of specified exceptions in the event of manifest abuse was rejected?

Sir Francis Vallat: It was rejected both by the International Law Commission and virtually unanimously, I say virtually unanimously, by an overwhelming majority of the Conference because it was considered that in the interests of international relations there should really be a protection of embassies, an inviolability of premises, without exception. One of the fears was that if specific exceptions were made in the Convention, this would give rise to doubts; it would also give a certain power of appreciation to the receiving state which it was thought might lead to trouble and be undesirable and really for those two main reasons, I would say, the idea was objected to by the vast majority of the Conference.[16]

Prima facie, therefore, the argument against the use of the doctrine of self-defence as an exception to diplomatic inviolability is well founded. Yet a closer examination of both the Convention itself and of commentary submitted by the International Law Commission prior to the Vienna Conference reveals that the doctrine of self-defence was not within the scope of the Convention's general ban on all exceptions to the principle of diplomatic inviolability.

Scrutiny of the Convention discloses that, although it was intended to be a general codification of diplomatic law, it does not purport to be an exhaustive codification. In its preamble, the Convention affirms that the rules of customary international law should continue to govern questions not expressly regulated by the provisions of the Convention.[17] Therefore, as there is no article in the Vienna Convention expressly regulating the employment of self-defence, and as the use of self-defence has long been a recognized principle relevant to diplomatic law, the doctrine may still be legitimately employed in that context.

Moreover, the International Law Commission expressly stated in 1957 that the doctrine of self-defence was not within the ambit of the Convention's denial of any exceptions to diplomatic immunity. In the commentary made with respect to the personal inviolability of the diplomat, the Commission stated that:

[Article 22 of the Vienna Convention] confirms the principle of the personal inviolability of the diplomatic agent. From the receiving States' point of view, this inviolability implies, as in the case of the mission's premises, the obligation to respect, and to ensure respect for, the person of the diplomatic agent. The receiving State must take all reasonable steps to that

---

[16] Minutes, July 2, 1984, at 35, sec. 85.

[17] Preamble to the Vienna Convention on Diplomatic Relations (1961), 500 UNTS 95.

end, possibly including a special guard where circumstances so require. Being inviolable, the diplomatic agent is exempted from certain measures that would amount to coercion. *This principle does not exclude either self-defence or, in exceptional circumstances, measures to prevent the diplomatic agent from committing crimes or offences.*[18]

It would seem, therefore, that the doctrine of self-defence remains, in the proper context, a legitimate exception to the general principle of diplomatic inviolability.

SCOPE OF SELF-DEFENCE IN DIPLOMATIC LAW

In view of the conclusion that the doctrine of self-defence permits a receiving state to breach the inviolability of diplomatic agents legitimately in certain circumstances, the permissible scope of such a breach must be considered. Having violated the diplomat's personal immunity and removed the immediate threat that the diplomat posed, may the receiving state, under the guise of self-defence, validly continue to subject the diplomat to local criminal jurisdiction?

It is evident that those writers who recognize the right of the receiving state to exercise self-defence against diplomats would not permit the receiving state to subject such offenders to the domestic criminal authority. Grotius stated that the right of self-defence is to be employed only to prevent harm from occurring and may not be employed to bring the diplomat within the local criminal jurisdiction. Bynkershoek agreed,[19] noting with approval these words of Grotius: "[T]his extreme necessity does not warrant the infliction of punishment, which in other cases is also removed by the law of nations, as will appear below, when we treat of the effects of regular warfare. Such extreme necessity will be concerned with guarding against serious hurt, especially to the state."[20]

This view is still the predominant view today, supported by Article 31 of the Vienna Convention which provides that "a diplomatic agent shall enjoy immunity from the criminal jurisdiction of the receiving state." And arguments were submitted to the U.K. Foreign Affairs Committee to the effect that, if, in the legitimate exercise of self-defence, British police had entered the Libyan embassy upon the outbreak of machine-gun fire from its windows, the assailant could not have been detained any longer than was necessary to stop

---

[18] [1957] Yearbook of the International Law Commission, Vol. II, pt. 2, at 138.

[19] *Op. cit. supra* note 4, at 90.

[20] *Op. cit. supra* note 3, at 444.

the firing. As was said, ''Had the assailant been established at the time of entry and overpowered by the police, as a member of the mission, it would not have been lawful to detain him in custody in order to bring him to trial before the criminal courts [of Great Britain.] That is precluded by Article 31 of the Convention which confers immunity, in the absence of waiver by the Government of the [sending] State. This immunity is complete.''[21] Other academic authorities concur. In Volume I of Oppenheim's *International Law,* it is stated that ''As diplomatic envoys are sacrosanct, the principle of their inviolability is generally recognised. But there is one exception. For if a diplomatic envoy commits an act of violence which disturbs the internal order of the receiving State in such a manner as makes it necessary to put him under restraint for the purpose of preventing similar acts, he may be arrested for the time being, although he must in due time be safely sent home.''[22] This view is also supported by *United States* v. *Benner.* In that case, the defendant constable executed a warrant of arrest against an attache of the Danish legation; a scuffle ensued and blows were exchanged between Constable Benner and the attache Mr. Brandis. Charges were brought against the constable and, with respect to the assault, the Court stated that ''if a minister assaults another, he may [even] be killed in self-defence, *though not by way of punishment.*''[23]

A receiving state which, in the name of self-defence, acts against a diplomat's personal inviolability, therefore, is confined to acting only to remove the immediate threat posed by the diplomat. Self-defence will not sanction the exposure of the diplomat to the domestic criminal proceedings.

RECIPROCITY: THE LIMITING FACTOR

As with all other sanctions available to receiving states against foreign diplomats within their jurisdiction, self-defence and all measures taken in reliance thereon are subject to the restraining influence of considerations of reciprocity. Reciprocity stands as the keystone in the construction of diplomatic privilege. Every state that maintains missions abroad and admits diplomats into its own territory is both a sending and a receiving state. All diplomatic privileges are extended on the understanding that such privileges will be

[21] Appendices, Appendix 6, p. 72.

[22] L. Oppenheim. *International Law* Vol. I (1912) sec. 388.

[23] *United States* v. *Benner,* (Case No. 14, 568) 24 Fed. Cas. 1084, 1085 (1830).

reciprocally accorded, and that their infringement by a state will
prejudicially affect that state's own representatives abroad.[24] The
sending state's own representatives abroad are in a sense hostages,
and, even in minor matters, their treatment will depend upon that
accorded to the receiving state's representatives in the sending
state.[25] In a real sense, therefore, reciprocity is the truest sanction
provided by diplomatic law, and can confound almost any attempt
to chastise or punish diplomats stationed in the sending state.[26]

Apprehension about reciprocal actions against their own diplomats stationed abroad frequently prevents states from fully utiliz-
ing their powers under the Vienna Convention and customary
international law to deal with abuses of diplomatic privilege. In
the 1984 shooting at the Libyan embassy in London, the occupants
of the embassy claimed that the gunman — whichever occupant
of the embassy he may have been — was immune from prosecution because he had diplomatic immunity. British authorities agreed
and escorted the embassy's residents out of the country. The British
government responded with prudence to this incident; it did not
hastily expel the entire Libyan mission because Britain feared that
Libya would retaliate excessively against British diplomats and
citizens still in Libya.[27] The Libyan press had already threatened
that any "humiliation" of Libyan or Arab citizens in Britain would
be met with "tenfold humiliation for Britons staying in Libya and
the rest of the Arab homeland."[28]

For large western states, the problems presented by reciprocity
are often magnified by the presence abroad of large expatriate communities.[29] When an intolerable abuse of diplomatic privilege has
been committed by a sending state, the receiving state must consider not just how the livelihood of its diplomats is endangered by
any actions taken against those of the sending state; it also must

[24] James T. Southwick, "Abuse of Diplomatic Privilege and Immunity: Compensatory and Restrictive Reforms," 15 Syracuse J. of Int'l & Com. L. 89 (1988).

[25] Eileen Denza, *Diplomatic Law* 2 (1976).

[26] *Supra* note 24 at 89.

[27] David H. Goodman, "Reciprocation as a Means of Curtailing Diplomatic
Immunity Abuses in the United States: The United States Needs to Play Hard-
ball," 11 Houston J. of Int'l L. 394, fn. 7 (1989).

[28] "An Undiplomatic Outrage," *The Times* (London), April 18, 1984, at 13.

[29] Rosalyn Higgins, "The Abuse of Diplomatic Privileges and Immunities: Recent
United Kingdom Experience," 79 Am. J. of Int'l L. 645 (1985).

be mindful of the safety of its expatriates and their families.[30] Though there is no legal basis in international law for retaliation against a state's expatriates, experience has shown that such a response is often undertaken.[31]

The threat of reciprocal action will not always deter a state from acting against foreign diplomats who have abused the position of their post. For example, on May 11, 1986, Britain expelled three Syrian diplomats for their alleged involvement in an attempt to smuggle a bomb aboard an Israeli jumbo jet at Heathrow airport. The expulsions came after more than a week of discussions between British officials and Syrian diplomats, who refused to waive the suspects' diplomatic immunity so that they might be questioned by police. The move was made despite the recognition that it courted the risk of diplomatic countermeasures by Syria.[32] The next day Syria expelled three British envoys. The three were declared *persona non grata* by Damascus and given one week to leave.[33] This series of expulsions, coupled with further evidence of the participation of Syrian diplomats in terrorist attacks, led the U.K. to terminate its diplomatic relations with Syria on October 25, 1986.[34]

Though the threat of reciprocal action is not always sufficient to deter a state from acting against foreign diplomats, its restraining influence is a consideration whenever such actions are proposed. In the evidence presented to the U.K. House of Commons Foreign Affairs Committee in 1984 in hearings on the Libyan embassy incident, there is the following statement:

In considering the question of reciprocity, which is of such central importance, it is vital to keep in mind the possibility of retaliatory action, however baseless and illegal it may be. We have to consider these questions on the basis of worst case assumptions. But that should not, of course,

---

[30] *Supra* note 24.

[31] "Syria Responds by Cutting Ties with Britain," *New York Timess,* October 25, 1986, at A4: "Two British teachers and an American librarian were murdered in Moslem West Beirut in April 1986 in what was called a retaliation to Britain's allowing American bombers to take off from British bases to attack Libya."

[32] "Britain Expels 3 Syrian Attaches: London Reports It Has 'Plenty' on Diplomats but Gives No Details," *The New York Times,* May 11, 1986, at A1 and A15.

[33] "Damascus Expels Three British Envoys," *The New York Times,* May 12, 1986, at A5.

[34] "Britain Breaks Syrian Ties; Cites Proof of Terror Role; El Al Suspect Is Convicted," *The New York Times,* October 25, 1986, at A1. For an example of diplomatic sanctions and counter-sanctions involving Canada, see "Spy Wars with Moscow," *Maclean's,* July 4, 1988, at 10-11.

prevent us taking action where action is justifiable, necessary, and likely to have the desired result. In certain cases, it is inevitable that there will be a deterioration or disruption in official relations with a foreign government. That will often be accompanied or followed by the loss of trade and other commercial opportunities. Where it is necessary to consider such action, it is vital to minimise the risk to the personal safety of Britons abroad as well as to our material intrests. When considering action in any particular case, it would be the height of folly not to make the most careful assessment of the implications for the full range of Britain's interests.[35]

Thus, whenever a receiving state takes punitive action against any foreign emissary within its jurisdiction upon the basis of self-defence or otherwise, so long as states both dispatch and receive envoys, the exercise of sanctions against foreign diplomats must always be undertaken with due consideration to the possibility of reprisals.

JOHN S. BEAUMONT
Sherwood Park, Alberta

Sommaire

La légitime défense: un motif permettant de ne pas respecter l'immunité diplomatique

Dans l'intervalle entre la déclaration d'un État accréditaire selon laquelle un diplomate est persona non grata et le départ effectif de ce diplomate du territoire de l'État accréditaire, l'État accréditaire peut légitimement se fonder sur la légitime défense pour faire cesser les actes de ce diplomate qui menacent la population ou les biens de l'État accréditaire.

Les discours universitaires influents en droit diplomatique reconnaissent la pertinence de la légitime défense dans ce domaine et soutiennent qu'elle constitue un motif valable pour ne pas respecter l'immunité d'un diplomate. Ce propositions ont été suivies et appliquées en droit contemporain.

Cependant, le principe de légitime défense ne donne pas à l'État accréditaire le pouvoir d'assujettir les diplomates au droit pénal interne. Il lui permet seulement d'éliminer toute menace immédiate que le diplomate peut présenter sans toutefois l'autoriser à punir l'émissaire fautif.

Peu importe le motif sur lequel l'État accréditaire s'appuie pour prendre des mesures contre un diplomate qui a un comportement répréhensible, ces mesures doivent toujours tenir compte du fait que les diplomates d'un État accréditant sont en réalité les hotages de l'État accréditaire. Le traitement de ces diplomates sera donc déterminé par la conduite du premier à l'égard des propres émissaires du second.

---

[35] Minutes, July 18, 1984, at 45, sec. 134.

International Arbitration and International Adjudication: The Different Contemporary Lots of the Two Hague Tribunals*

A CELEBRATION IN 1988 of the centenary of the birth of the great contemporary Dutch jurist, J. H. W. Verzijl (1888-1987), coincided with the seventy-fifth anniversary of the Peace Palace in The Hague, the official residence of the International Court of Justice. The irony, noted by a participant in the Verzijl centenary symposium, *International Arbitration: Past and Prospects,* Professor Kooijmans (at 23), is that the Peace Palace was originally built for that "other" Hague tribunal, the Permanent Court of Arbitration, one of the more notable concrete achievements of the First Hague Peace Conference of 1899. Today, the International Court of Justice, with a rapidly expanding number of client states (including Third World and former Soviet bloc states, after the lean years of the 1960s and 1970s when it was widely perceived as a European, Eurocentrist institution), has taken over virtually all the old building and has had to have a new annex built to house its judges. By comparison, the Permanent Court of Arbitration, for lack of business since the Second World War, has dwindled away to a single room on the second floor that seems to be opened once or twice a year only so that distinguished visitors can admire its exotic oriental art furnishings. Both the monograph published by the secretariat of the Permanent Court of Arbitration in co-operation with the T. M. C.

---

* This note draws upon, and constitutes a review of, three recent, challenging surveys of aspects of the international arbitral and adjudicatory processes: *International Arbitration: Past and Prospects.* Edited by A.H.A. Soons. Dordrecht/Boston/London: Martinus Nijhoff, 1990. Pp. xx, 221 (U.S. $85.00; £54.00); *The Permanent Court of Arbitration: New Directions.* Edited by P.J.H. Jonkman. The Hague: International Bureau of the Permanent Court of Arbitration, 1991. Pp. vii, 67; and *Aspects of the Administration of International Justice.* By Eli Lauterpacht. Cambridge: Grotius Publications Limited, 1991. Pp. xxxiv, 166 (U.S. $70.00; £35.00).

Asser Institute, *The Permanent Court of Arbitration: New Directions,* and also to a considerable extent the Verzijl symposium edited by Professor A. H. A. Soons, address the remarkable decline of the Permanent Court of Arbitration itself, after the original high hopes of its founding fathers at the turn of the century, and also to the reasons for the perhaps diminishing role of international arbitration in the contemporary era.

Professor Kooijmans in *International Arbitration* (at 23), refers to the public dissatisfaction of a Netherlands participant in the First Hague Peace Conference: "Instead of a Permanent Court, the Convention of 1899 only created the phantom of a Court, an impalpable ghost, or, to speak more plainly, it created a clerk's office with a list" (quoted in James Brown Scott, Introduction, *Hague Court Reports* (1916), at xviii). A background paper, prepared by a Working Group on Improving the Functioning of the Permanent Court of Arbitration, and published in *The Permanent Court of Arbitration: New Directions* (at 21), also recurs to James Brown Scott: "[The Permanent Court of Arbitration] is not permanent because it is not composed of permanent judges; it is not accessible because it has to be formed for each individual case; finally, it is not a court, because it is not composed of judges" *(The Proceedings of The Hague Peace Conference: Conference of 1907,* James Brown Scott ed., (1921), Vol. 2, at 319).

The Permanent Court of Arbitration is, in fact, a panel of potential arbitrators from whom contending states may select, if they so wish, once they have decided to submit their difference to arbitration. The panel is constituted by each state, party to the Hague Convention of 1907 on Pacific Settlement of International Disputes, nominating, for a renewable term of six years, four persons who, according to Article 44 of the Convention, are "of known competency in questions of international law, of the highest moral reputation, and disposed to accept the duties of Arbitrator." The political reality, however, is that less than half the 160-odd members of the United Nations were, in the 1980s, officially participating in the Arbitration Court (76 in 1987, according to the author's own studies: *Judicial Settlement of International Disputes* (1991), at 97), while an even smaller number (63 in 1987, *ibid.*) had actually gone on to name its national panel of four potential arbitrators on the Court. Even more noteworthy is the fact that, among the states that had managed to name national panels on the Court, four had, in the 1980s, members first appointed in the 1940s and still on the list four decades later (Dominican Republic, Ecuador, Paraguay, Switzerland); while appointments to national panels within the Court, dating back three decades and more were commonplace and also involved major powers (Austria, Brazil, El Salvador, Ecuador, France, Hungary, Italy, Japan, Poland, Spain). What all this suggests—beyond the more obvious explanation of administrative inertia in the national foreign ministries charged with preparing, and then maintaining, such national panels within the Court—is that the job that members of the panels may eventually be called on to perform is hardly considered to involve vital state interests or to risk major internal political controversy. This seems to be the conclusion of the richly talented and experienced Working Group assembled by the Permanent Court of Arbitration's Secretariat, which was presided over by Judge Lachs and which included several other members of the International Court of Justice (Judges Aguilar, Bedjaoui, Guillaume, Jennings [Court President], and Tarassov).

In the view of the Working Group:

Non-recourse to the PCA may also be attributed to certain constitutional, procedural and organizational deficiencies of the Court. While many States Parties to the Conventions do select as members of the PCA— 'persons. . .of known competence in question of international law. . .and disposed to accept the duties of arbitrator. . .'—it often appears that persons are selected more with a view to their function in a 'national group' for nominating candidates to the International Court of Justice, than to their serving as arbitrators, since they hold public offices of a quality likely, in practice, to preclude their appointment to tribunals which the parties to a dispute would want to convene and function expeditiously, and for which independence and the appearance thereof, are of critical importance.

To this may be added the further qualification that even when functioning (in terms of Articles 4, 5, and 6 of the Statute of the International Court of Justice), as, in effect the national selection committees for nomination of candidates for election to the International Court of Justice, the contrast between the law-as-written and actual state practice is substantial. Not merely, as already noted, have more than half the members of the United Nations failed to constitute national panels within the Permanent Court of Arbitration that could function as such national selection committees, but also the officially published voting statistics of the actual Security Council/General Assembly ballotings on the candidates for election to the International Court reveal that states whose national panels have nominated particular candidates do not regard themselves as necessarily bound to respect those nominations and in fact some have cast their actual votes for others (*Judicial Settlement of International Disputes* (1991), at 99-100).

If it is the national foreign ministries themselves that, for the most part, will determine the actual nominations for candidates for election to the International Court (see, in this regard, Article 4(2) of the Statute of the ICJ), and that, in all cases, control the national votes cast in the Security Council and General Assembly in the actual elections, one may ask how much of a role is left for the national panels within the Permanent Court of Arbitration. The Working Group on the Permanent Court of Arbitration itself poses the dilemma with the rhetorical question, "venerable anachronism or neglected asset?" (*The Permanent Court of Arbitration: New Directions* (1991), at 19). Professor Kooijmans, addressing the Verzijl centenary symposium, throws out the challenge to states that are members of the Permanent Court of Arbitration: "It might be interesting to ask the governments concerned why they keep in existence (keep alive would be a rather weird expression in this respect) an institution which they steadfastly refuse to use. Frankly spoken, I do not expect too many honest replies," (*International Arbitration: Past and Prospects* (1991), at 25). The more substantial question—going beyond the immediate issue of the atrophy or possible revival of a particular institution, the Permanent Court of Arbitration, is posed by Judge Lachs in his paper to the Verzijl symposium—namely the nature of the distinction between arbitration and adjudication, whether it be viewed in *a priori*, purely conceptual terms or else on a thoroughly empirical, experiential basis as evidenced in the record of concrete disputes between states. While taking note of "the increasing assimilation of arbitration to adjudication," he suggests that:

some arbitral tribunals, even in the modern context, do not have to be guided solely by law. I do not by this mean that they also apply equity, for it is sufficiently evident by now that equity is an omnipresent rule within international law itself. But, generally speaking, arbitration opens the way to reaching solutions which produce in both parties a sense of having been treated fairly where the application of strict law might have produced a solution less persuasive to the layman or politician. The arbitral solution may furthermore be more pragmatic and practical than could have been reached by adjudication without necessarily differing in the final balance of gains and losses for either side. (*International Arbitration: Past and Prospects* (1991), at 41)

Judge Lachs goes on to pose the question "whether arbitration and adjudication can be fused into one under the mantle of the International Court of Justice" (*ibid.*, 46). He refers to Article 26(2) of the ICJ Statute, empowering the Court at any time to form a chamber for dealing with a particular case, with "the number of judges to constitute such a chamber [to] be determined by the Court with the approval of the parties," as amplified in Article 17(2) and (3) of the 1978 Revised Rules of Court. He regards this provision, taken together with the preserving of the right of the parties in regard to naming judges ad hoc, as involving the addition of "an existing remnant of arbitral practice. . . to the new quasi-judicial element in respect of composition. This is about as close as we can get to structuring a bench of the Court in accordance with arbitral prac- tice. . . Provided that the judicial character of the proceedings is respected, I see little reason to spurn this injection into adjudica- tion of some aspects of arbitral practice which States find attrac- tive" (*ibid.*, 47-48). As Judge Lachs suggests, "to take a sterner view would simply invite a repetition of the *Beagle Channel* situation, where five members of the International Court sat ostensibly as arbitra- tors but in reality as judges on another bench" (*ibid.*, 48). On the further question that the comment implies, as to what was to be gained by coming to the International Court, Judge Lachs suggests that the two maritime boundary delimitation cases, *Beagle Channel* and *Gulf of Maine*— the first an ad hoc arbitral tribunal formed out- side of and separately from the Permanent Court of Arbitration, and the second a Chamber (the first such Chamber) created wi- thin the International Court—provide the answer: the vicissitudes of the arbitral award in *Beagle Channel,* as compared to the "greater security of the result" of the judgment of the five-judge Chamber of the International Court in *Gulf of Maine (ibid.).*

On the issue of the relative appropriateness of disputes for ar- bitration as opposed to adjudication—whether some disputes are *inherently* appropriate for the one mode of settlement rather than the other, Judge Lachs suggests that the criterion may be found in the *type of law* to be applied. He contends that in *Barcelona Traction,* the International Court would have been "eminently fitted to con- sider the allegations of denial of justice, had it permitted itself to venture this far into the merits, but the questions of company law and the rights of stockholders were not quite 'up its street.' Likewise in *Western Sahara,* an advisory case with strong contentious aspects, the Court was precisely the right forum for disposing of the concept of *res nullius* but in handling matters of religious allegiance and the territorial rights of nomads it was on unfamiliar grounds'' (*ibid.,* 50). What Judge Lachs essays experientially, on a basis of the Court's jurisprudence in concrete cases—namely the delimitation of the boundaries of the arbitrable and the justiciable— is picked up also by Professor Kooijmans, who looks to that earlier Gulf War between Iraq and Iran that began in 1979 and lasted throughout most of the 1980s: ''Although this dispute was partly a purely legal dispute, since it involved the unilateral denunciation by Iraq of the 1975 Algiers Agreement including the settlement procedure provided for in that agreement, it obviously did not lend itself for judicial settlement because of the heavy political overtones''(*ibid.,* 34).

One might argue, nevertheless, that Professor Kooijmans devotes more time than is really needed to abstract, *a priori* conceptual categories like ''non-legal disputes'' (raised in Professor Sohn's valuable historical survey, at 9 et seq.), even while he expresses his own misgivings as to conventional legal antinomies—rejected, by now, by major national courts and, increasingly, by the International Court itself—of ''legal disputes''/''political disputes,'' or ''justiciable disputes''/''non-justiciable disputes'' (*ibid.,* 26 et seq.). Charles De Visscher (as noted by another symposium participant, T. D. Gill, *ibid.,* 196) had insisted, much earlier, that ''Since there is no firm criterion derived from the object or nature of the dispute by which to classify disputes *a priori* as political or legal, the attitude of the parties is alone decisive on the procedural plane'' (*Theory and Reality in Public International Law* (1954) (English edition, by P. E. Corbett (1968), at 353).

The reasoned doubts as to the validity of any *a priori* distinction between arbitration and adjudication in the settlement of international disputes receive additional support from another intellectual-legal viewpoint in Elihu Lauterpacht's monograph, *Aspects of the Administration of International Justice,* offered as part of the Hersch Lauterpacht Memorial Lectures series. While Lauterpacht's main focus is upon the International Court of Justice, he does offer some comments (pp. 85-86) upon the classical distinction between arbitration and judicial settlement, which saw ''judicial settlement institutionalized in the form of a pre-established court while arbitration is conducted by arbitrators selected for each case and thus lacks judicial continuity.'' He suggests that the lines have become blurred since arbitration has in a number of instances become institutionalized, as in the Permanent Court of Arbitration and even the Iran-U.S. Claims Tribunal.

On a further point of claimed distinction, namely that arbitration is really an extension of the diplomatic process and that, in consequence, arbitrators are freer than are judges to depart from the strict application of the law, Lauterpacht cites the U.S. Judge Kellogg in his Observations (Separate Opinion) in *Free Zones of Upper Savoy and the District of Gex* (PCIJ, Ser. A No. 24, 4, at 29 et seq.) Judge Kellogg had adopted, in his Opinion, the instructions given by U.S. Secretary of State Elihu Root to U.S. delegates to the Second Hague Peace Conference of 1907: ''It has been a very general practice for arbitrators to act, not as judges deciding questions of fact and law upon the record before them under a sense of judicial responsibility, but as negotiators effecting settlement of the questions brought before them in accordance with the traditions and usages and subject to all the considerations and influences which affect diplomatic agents'' (*ibid.*, 36). This having been said, Lauterpacht goes on to criticize the dissenting opinion of Judge Shahabuddeen in *Application for Permission by Nicaragua to Intervene in the El Salvador/Honduras Case* (ICJ Reports 1990, at 92). The issue was whether the application by Nicaragua to intervene in a case which, at the request of the parties, El Salvador and Honduras, had been referred to a Chamber of the International Court, should be heard by the full fifteen-member Court as Nicaragua contended, rather than by the Chamber. The full Court, by twelve votes to three, rejected Nicaragua's contention, on the score that the Chamber should be competent to deal with incidental questions, including therein applications to intervene. Judge Shahabuddeen's dissent focused on the institution of Chambers of the Court which, in his view, with the according to the parties of a right to be consulted about the composition of the Chamber, amounted to a form of arbitration and therefore departed from the basic requirement of acting as a court of law (*ibid.*, 18 et seq.) Lauterpacht's conclusion, from the Court majority's rejection of Judge Shahabuddeen's argument, is that it did not attribute the same fundamental significance to the distinction between arbitration and judicial settlement (*Aspects of the Administration of International Justice* (1991), at

91). Lauterpacht also considers that Judge Shahabuddeen was pitting the strict words of the ICJ Statute (which, in Shahabuddeen's interpretation, would not allow the parties to control, or even influence, the composition of Chambers) "against a trend, albeit insufficiently articulated, that favours settlement by any means, provided it is a settlement" (*ibid.*, 93).

It is this emphasis on the International Court's choosing to apply a beneficial construction of its Statute and Rules in the interests of problem-solving and dispute settlement in the concrete case that provides something of a leitmotiv for Lauterpacht's interpretation of the Court's approach to the issue of consent of the parties as a basis for Court exercise of jurisdiction. Lauterpacht here cites *Nicaragua: Jurisdiction and Admissibility* (ICJ Reports 1984, at 392), where the Court, by a very large majority, held that an unratified declaration by Nicaragua under Article 36(2) of the Statute of the PCIJ was capable of founding the jurisdiction of the ICJ under Article 36(5) of the ICJ Statute. In referring to the classical concept of consent of the parties as basic to Court jurisdiction in a case, he considers that, now, "some cracks in the edifice are developing, though, it would seem, less from any critical approach to the concept of consent than from the seeming disinclination of the Court to forego jurisdiction in certain cases in which there is at any rate an arguable case that consent has been given" (*Aspects of the Administration of International Justice* (1991), at 23). He likewise cites the Court's later judgment in the case brought by Nicaragua against Honduras in *Border and Transborder Armed Actions: Jurisdiction and Admissibility* (ICJ Reports 1988, at 69), as evidence of "the same [judicial] predisposition to find a source of consent" (*Aspects of the Administration of International Justice* (1991), at 23).

Further to his theme that "evidence is accumulating that it is not correct to assume that jurisdiction is only exercised where there is a clear consent" of state parties (*ibid.*, 25), Lauterpacht looks to the International Court's recent rejection of the need for a jurisdictional link in intervention proceedings under Article 62 of the ICJ Statute: see *ibid.*, 26-30, citing *Land, Island and Maritime Frontier Dispute (El Salvador/Honduras), Application to Intervene, Judgment,* ICJ Reports 1990, at 92 (Application by Nicaragua); also *Tunisia/Libya Continental Shelf,* ICJ Reports 1981, at 3 (Application by Malta); and *Libya/Malta Continental Shelf,* ICJ Reports 1984, at 3 (Application by Italy), where the Court found other grounds for rejecting the applications to intervene.

Professor Brownlie, writing before the Court's 1990 decision in *Land, Island and Maritime Frontier Dispute (El Salvador/Honduras)*, was critical of the Court's refusal to permit Italy to intervene in *Libya/Malta Continental Shelf* (ICJ Reports 1984, at 3), viewing the Court majority as being influenced by "the problem of competition between the idea of arbitration, which is that essentially of a *private* litigation, and the system of the International Court" (*International Arbitration: Past and Prospects* (1990), at 60). As Brownlie further argues: "If intervention were allowed on a very generous basis, then it is thought that States would avoid the Court and go to arbitration more often, because there is no possibility of someone breaking into your private litigation; and it has been said that the pressure on the Court, so to speak, to be 'user-friendly' when chambers are being constituted, results from the feeling which the Court may have that if it does not play ball then the parties will go to arbitration" (*ibid.*). Brownlie's conclusion, in any case, is that arbitration and adjudication are "essentially the same process. . .and that in general the relation is one of complementarity" (*ibid.*).

CONCLUSIONS

1   Classical distinctions between international arbitration and international adjudication, that are cast in abstract, *a priori* terms and based on notions that the arbitral process is more flexible and permits access to larger and looser issues of equity and comparative justice and the search for compromise between the competing state interests, while the adjudicatory process is limited to technical-legal decisions and the search for "black-letter law," are denied by the empirical record of the two types of international tribunals.

2   The international judicial decision-making process in particular—as shown in the contemporary jurisprudence of the International Court—shows full awareness of the relation and interaction between law and society, and of the relevance and utility of an interests-balancing approach to international dispute settlement. Further, both in terms of the specific injunctions of recent international treaties and also of its own *jurisprudence constante*, the International Court sees itself as called upon to determine and to apply equitable principles in its decisions.

3   The opting by state parties for ad hoc arbitral tribunals of their

own creation, rather than the International Court, for purposes
of their conflicts resolution, seems related more substantially
to procedural, adjectival law advantages as conceived by "like-
minded" states, such as the ability to confine the tribunal
membership to "like-minded" judges, rather than to any
perceived intrinsic differences between arbitration and
adjudication as such.

4   The international Court's tolerance of a "gloss" on the strict
words of the Court Statute and Rules of Court, whereby the
state parties are now permitted a substantial, if not determinative
role in the choice of judges for ad hoc chambers, appears in
retrospect as a defensive reaction by the Court, at a time when
its docket of cases was sparse, to the potential loss of business
and client states to arbitral tribunals. That gloss on the Court
Statute seems by now to be well accepted and well established,
and to operate by pragmatic consensus between the Court and
the parties as to choice of the judges for a chamber as well as
their number.

5   The atrophy of the Permanent Court of Arbitration, at a time
when recourse to ad hoc arbitral tribunals outside that Court
is still frequent, seems attributable, in considerable measure,
to a blurring of its role, in which an intendedly purely ancillary
function of its designated members—screening of potential
candidates for nomination by individual states for purposes of
election to the International Court—has overpowered the original purpose and historical raison d'être of furnishing an
authoritative list of distinguished international jurists on whom
states would draw when they opted to go to arbitration. The
obvious and necessary remedy for the Permanent Court of
Arbitration is to amend its statute and to slough off the business
of prescreening of candidates for election to the International
Court and return it, instead, to national governments and their
foreign ministries.

6   The International Court of Justice, in its contemporary phase,
seems to be applying a good deal of the procedural flexibility
and informality traditionally associated with arbitral and other
non-judicial tribunals. In the area of jurisdiction and the basic
notion of consent of states as the basis thereof, the Court will
not allow itself to be frustrated by technical points or minor
defects in procedural forms so long as it is persuaded that the

will of the party concerned was there, at the relevant time, to accept jurisdiction. The moving principle here appears to be that procedure is, and should be, subordinate to substance; and that the Court should not try to avoid substantive (policy) issues on adjectival law grounds. It all seems part of the larger trends in the Court's philosophy, manifest since the *Namibia* ruling in 1971, that the Court's problem-solving potential should be facilitated, in the interest of non-prolongation of international disputes and of restoring harmony to the parties. (See, in this regard, the author's *Judicial Settlement of International Disputes* (1991), at 122 et seq.)

EDWARD McWHINNEY
Simon Fraser University, Burnaby, BC

Information Note:
Secretary-General's Trust Fund*

IN RESPONSE TO THE NEED of developing countries, the Secretary-General of the United Nations established in 1989 a Trust Fund. The purpose of the Fund is to provide financial assistance in order to encourage states to seek a solution to their legal disputes through the International Court of Justice.

Legal disputes exist in various parts of the world. The high costs incurred in proceedings often constitute a financial obstacle to the seeking of a judicial settlement through the Court. This is particularly true in many developing countries where multiple needs compete for very limited funds. There are known cases where the parties are prepared to resort to judicial settlement but are in need of funds or legal expertise or both. There have also been cases where the parties were willing but unable to implement an ICJ Judgement. The availability of external resources in such cases can therefore be extremely helpful in their search for peaceful means through the Court for the settlement of disputes. The Trust Fund offers limited financial assistance for the purpose of defraying expenditures incurred in Court proceedings. It thus encourages states to make better use of the International Court of Justice and also actively foster the peaceful settlement of disputes.

The Fund has received worldwide support and some thirty states from all regions of the world have made financial contributions. It received its first application in March 1991 and an award was subsequently made in May to a developing country which is seeking a solution to a dispute with its neighbour through the International Court of Justice. A second application, also from a developing country, is now pending. The present assets of the Fund are, however, very limited.

Relations in many regions of the world will indeed be greatly improved if more legal disputes can be settled through the

---

* Published at the request of the Secretary-General of the United Nations.

International Court of Justice, the legal arm of the United Nations. The Fund relies on voluntary contributions and is open to all entities. It welcomes contributions from states, individuals, institutions, corporations, and non-governmental organizations. Contributions may be made in monetary terms (to the Secretary-General's Trust Fund to Assist States in the Judicial Settlement of Disputes, Chemical Bank, UN Branch Account No. 015-004473). Further information may be obtained from the Office of Legal Affairs, Office of the Legal Counsel, United Nations Secretariat, New York, NY 10017.

October 1991

Chronique de droit international économique en 1990 / Digest of International Economic Law in 1990

I

Commerce

préparé par

MARTIN ST-AMANT*

E N 1990, L'ACTION JURIDIQUE DU CANADA en matière de commerce international se sera principalement manifestée au GATT, comme le démontre les conflits relativement nombreux dans lesquels le Canada fut impliqué ainsi que l'activité qu'il aura dépolyé cette année là. L'action juridique du Canada se sera en outre révélée en cette année, par l'entremise d'actes unilatéraux et d'accords commerciaux conclus avec d'autres États. La mise en oeuvre de l'Accord de libre-échange Canada-États-Unis constitue un dernier aspect qui aura préoccupé, par la force des choses, le Canada en cette année 1990.

I. CONFLITS ET ACTIVITÉS DANS LE CADRE DU GATT

Dans le cadre du GATT, les contentieux impliquant le Canada auront sensiblement diminué par rapport à l'année précédente.[1] Ainsi, aucun litige n'aura connu un dénouement par l'adoption de rapports des Groupes spéciaux par le Conseil du GATT. Dans un dossier, un Groupe spécial présenta néanmoins son rapport aux

---

* Avocat, Leduc Lebel (Montréal); candidat au Doctorat en droit commercial international (Université de Paris I — Panthéon-Sorbonne).

---

[1] Sur les litiges survenus en 1989, voir M. ST-AMANT, "Chronique de droit économique international," (1990) 28 *A.C.D.I.*, 433-37.

parties impliquées, mais ce dernier du fait de l'opposition des États-Unis, n'aura pu être adopté en 1990 par le Conseil.[2] Le 3 août, un Groupe spécial faisait ainsi droit à la revendication du Canada, selon laquelle les droits compensateurs institués par les États-Unis sur la viande de porc canadienne furent perçus de façon contraire à l'article VI:3 de l'Accord général.[3] Dans les conclusions de son rapport, le Groupe spécial rejetait l'allégation américaine à l'effet que les subventions accordées aux éleveurs de porcs se répercutaient entièrement, en raison du processus de production, sur les producteurs de viande de porc.[4] De façon plus précise, le Groupe spécial notait qu'il ne suffisait pas simplement à cet égard de démontrer que le commerce de la viande de porc pouvait être affecté par les subventions versées aux éleveurs de porc. Selon le Groupe spécial, puisque des branches de production distinctes existaient au Canada pour l'élevage des porcs et la production de viande de porc, pour considérer l'octroi de telles subventions comme des subventions aux producteurs de viande de porc il fallait que ces dernières profitent à ces producteurs par le truchement d'une baisse du prix du porc, ce qui n'était ici manifestement pas le cas. Le Groupe spécial recommandait donc, soit le remboursement des droits compensateurs correspondant au montant des subventions octroyées aux éleveurs de porcs, ou soit encore une nouvelle détermination sur la base de la présente décision.

D'autres contentieux reliés à l'adoption de rapports antérieurs par le Conseil du GATT auront marqué l'année 1990. Ainsi, le litige entre le Canada et les États-Unis concernant les restrictions canadiennes à l'importation de crème glacée et de yoghourt aura continué de retenir l'attention. Suite au rapport du Groupe spécial adopté par le Conseil du GATT en 1989 et concluant que ces restrictions à l'importation ne pouvaient se justifier eu égard à l'Accord général,[5] les États-Unis, à maintes occasions, auront insisté

---

[3] Voir le texte du rapport du Groupe spécial dans le document du GATT: L/6721 (1990).

[4] On se souviendra qu'en 1984, le Congrès américain ajouta une disposition à la Loi douanière américaine de 1930 indiquant les critères pour compenser les subventions accordées aux produits primaires agricoles (upstream subsidies). Voir *Tariff Act of 1930* 771B, 19 U.S.C. 1677-2 (Supp. IV 1986). C'est sur la base de cette disposition que le Département du commerce des États-Unis détermina que plusieurs programmes fédéraux et provinciaux canadiens octroyant des subventions aux éleveurs de porc, profitaient également aux producteurs de viande de porc. Voir *Fresh, Chilled and Frozen Pork from Canada,* 54 Fed. Reg. 30,774 (Dep't Comm. 1989) (final determination).

[5] Voir M. ST-AMANT, *loc. cit. supra* note 1, p.434 On se rappellera que le Groupe

auprès du Canada afin que ce dernier pays mettre en oeuvre les conclusions du rapport.[6] En réponse, le Canada a rétorqué qu'il donnerait effet au rapport, mais seulement en fonction des résultats de l'Uruguay Round.[7]

Les États-Unis ont d'autre part exigé au titre de l'article XXIII:I, que des consultations avec le Canada soient ouvertes sur la mise en oeuvre du rapport du Groupe d'experts concernant les pratiques canadiennes relatives aux boissons alcooliques importées.[8] Non seulement le Canada n'aurait pas selon ce pays, éliminé les pratiques discriminatoires à l'égard de la bière importée, mais en outre, plusieurs provinces canadiennes auraient depuis lors, instauré de nouvelles pratiques jugées elles aussi incompatibles avec le rapport du Groupe spécial.[9] La procédure de consultation n'ayant pas permis de résoudre le différend, les États-Unis demandaient le 12 décembre, l'établissement d'un nouveau Groupe spécial pour examiner si le Canada s'était conformé au rapport et si les droits que les États-Unis détenaient en vertu de l'Accord général avaient été annulés ou compromis.[10]

D'autres événements survenus dans le cadre du GATT et concernant le Canada auront su retenir notre attention en 1990. Soulignons en premier lieu la conclusion d'une série d'accords lesquels

---

spécial a conclu que les restrictions canadiennes à l'importation de crème glacée et de yoghourt étaient incompatibles avec l'article XI:I de l'Accord général et ne pouvaient se justifier au titre de l'article XI:2 c) i).

[6] Voir *Focus, Bulletin d'information du GATT,* no 72, 1990, p. 10; no 73, 1990, p. 5; no 75, 1990, p. 3; no 76, 1990, p. 6. Les États-Unis auront d'ailleurs signalé qu'ils avaient établi une liste de produits pouvant servir de base au retrait des concessions. Voir *Focus, Bulletin d'information du GATT,* no 77, 1990, p. 7.

[7] *Ibid.* Le Canada aura dans l'intervalle présenté une proposition de réforme de l'article XI de l'Accord général au Groupe de négociation sur l'agriculture de l'Uruguay Round afin de légaliser ce type de restriction à l'importation. Voir Ministre du Commerce extérieur, *Communiqué de presse,* no 068, 14 mars 1990.

[8] GATT Doc. DS17/1 (1990). Sur ce rapport voir par ailleurs, M. ST-AMANT "Chronique de droit économique international en 1988," (1989) 27 *A.C.D.I.,* 339-340.

[9] Les pratiques jugées discriminatoires par les États-Unis étaient le "listing," c'est-à-dire l'inscription au catalogue, la majoration des prix et les restrictions concernant les points de vente. Voir *Focus, Bulletin d'information du GATT,* no 75, 1990, p. 3.

[10] Voir *Focus, Bulletin d'information du GATT,* no 77, 1990, p. 7. Pour davantage de détails relativement à ce différend, voir B. SWICK-MARTIN, "Canadian Trade Update," (1991) 12 *Can. Competition Policy Record,* 24-25; *Focus, Bulletin d'information du GATT,* no 75, 1990, p. 3. Soulignons d'autre part qu'en parallèle le gouvernement américain a décidé le 29 juin d'ouvrir une enquête, en vertu de la Section 301 du "Trade Act" of 1974 sur les pratiques canadiennes en matière de commercialisation de la bière. Voir 27 *Int'l Trade Rep.* (BNA) 998 (1990).

seront toutefois conclus à titre provisoire en attendant le résultat final de l'Uruguay Round. Ainsi, des décisions sur l'inscription des «autres droits ou imposition» aux listes de concessions tarifaires,[11] et sur les entreprises commerciales d'État,[12] de même que des textes révisés sur l'Accord relatif aux obstacles techniques au commerce,[13] l'Accord sur les procédures en matière de licences d'importation[14] et sur l'Accord relatif à la mise en oeuvre de l'article VII de l'Accord général sur les tarifs douaniers et le commerce,[15] auront été adoptés. Par ailleurs, en vertu du Mécanisme d'examen des politiques commerciales institué à titre provisoire lors de l'examen à mi-parcours de l'Uruguay Round, le Conseil aura procédé le 30 juillet à l'examen de la politique commerciale et économique du Canada.[16] Les membres du Conseil notaient plus particulièrement le niveau général d'ouverture du marché canadien ainsi que l'effet bénéfique de ses récentes initiatives économiques. Des préoccupations auront cependant été exprimées sur différents sujets tels que la complexité du régime tarifaire, la mise en oeuvre des engagements interna-

---

[11] Voir *Nouvelles de l'Uruguay Round,* NUR 037, 1990. Cette décision, a pour objet de modifier l'article II:I b) de l'Accord général afin d'inscrire ces autres droits ou impositions (droit de timbre, taxes fiscales...) sur les listes de position tarifaire consolidées et ce, en vue d'accroître la transparence des impositions à l'importation.

[12] Voir *Nouvelles de l'Uruguay Round,* NUR 040, 1990. Cette décision vient compléter l'article XVII de l'Accord général en prévoyant que les entreprises commerciales d'Etat, telles que définies, devront faire l'objet de notification afin qu'un groupe de travail, établi par la décision, les examine. Une procédure de contre notification est également prévu si une partie juge inadéquate les notifications d'une autre partie. La décision vise ainsi à assurer la transparence des activités des entreprises commerciales d'État.

[13] Voir *Nouvelles de l'Uruguay Round,* NUR 042, 1990. Le texte révisé étend la portée de l'accord, pour y inclure les prescriptions fondées sur des procédés et méthodes de production, clarifie la notion d'"obstacle non nécessaire," accroit la transparence des organismes de normalisation nationales et régionales et contient enfin des dispositons détaillées relativement à la reconnaissance de l'évaluation de la conformité opérée par d'autres pays.

[14] *Ibid.* Le texte révisé prévoit notamment la limitation des licences non automatiques à ce qui est nécessaire à l'administration des mesures auxquelles elles s'appliquent et l'établissement de critères pour déterminer si les procédures de licences automatiques constituent des restrictions aux échanges.

[15] *Ibid.* Le texte révisé du Code de la valeur en douane concerne plus spécifiquement les règles à respecter lorsque l'administration des douanes a des raisons de douter de l'exactitude de la valeur déclarée.

[16] Voir à cet égard le rapport préparé par le Secrétariat du GATT, à titre d'information pour les Parties Contractantes, dans le document GATT/1484 (1990). Ce rapport fera l'objet prochainement d'une publication du secrétariat à l'intention de la population.

tionaux par les gouvernements provinciaux, les niveaux élevés des subventions octroyées aux producteurs agricoles ainsi que le peu d'échanges commerciaux avec les pays en voie de développement. Le Canada aura en outre présenté le 19 avril, une proposition ambitieuse pour le renforcement du système du GATT,[17] proposition qui fut dans l'ensemble bien accueillie mais jugée néanmoins prématurée par certains partenaires commerciaux du Canada.[18]

II. Actes unilatéraux du Canada

En ce qui concerne les actes unilatéraux en 1990, il faudra retenir particulièrement la réforme fiscale d'envergure engagée au Canada et qui a abouti à la suppression de la taxe de vente fédérale et son remplacement par une taxe générale multistade de 7% sur la plupart des biens et services transigés au pays.[19] En vertu de cette réforme, laquelle entrera en vigueur le 1er janvier 1991, non seulement les exportations de biens et de services seront détaxées, donc non taxables, mais les exportateurs se feront également rembourser la totalité des taxes payées sur les achats de produits ou de services liés à leurs activités commerciales.[20] Quant aux produits et services importés, ils seront généralement imposés comme s'ils avaient été produits au Canada.[21] Le Canada aura en outre, en 1990, modifié pour une seconde année consécutive la *Liste des marchandises d'exportation contrôlée* (LMEC),[22] pour l'aligner avec les listes internationales

---

[17] Voir Ministre du Commerce extérieur, *Communiqué de presse*, no 082, 19 avril 1990. Selon cette proposition intitulée *Renforcement du système commercial multilatéral ouvert*, il aurait lieu d'entreprendre une réforme institutionnelle significative, laquelle devrait comprendre les éléments suivants: amélioration de la transparence, confirmation du Mécanisme d'examen des politiques commerciales, règlement efficace des différends par la consolidation et la restructuration des mécanismes de règlement des litiges, création d'une organisation mondiale du commerce, renforcement des liens existant entre les questions commerciales et financières.

[18] Voir L. HOSSIE, "Little Headway Seen on Old Sore Points as Informal GATT Talks Start in Mexico," dans *Globe and Mail*, 20 avril 1990, p. B6; 17 *Int'l. Trade Rep.* (BNA) 588 (1990).

[19] Voir *Loi modifiant la Loi sur la taxe d'accise, le Code criminel, la Loi sur les douanes, le Tarif des douanes, la Loi sur l'accise, la Loi de l'impôt sur le revenu, la Loi sur les statistiques et la Loi sur la Cour canadienne de l'impôt*, S.C. 1990, c45.

[20] Annexe VI.

[21] Une personne important un service dans le cadre de son entreprise ne sera toutefois pas assujettie à la taxe. Sur toutes ces questions voir P. MARCEAU, "La TPS et les marchés internationaux," (1990) 3 *Bulletin de la Société de droit international économique*, 11-12.

[22] *Liste des marchandises d'exportation contrôlée*, (1989) 123 Gaz. Can. II 2101 adoptée en vertu de l'article 6 de la *Loi sur les licences d'exportation et d'importation*, S.R.C. 1985, c. E-19.

élaborées dans le cadre du COCOM (Comité de coordination pour le contrôle multilatéral des exportations).[23] Deux modifications auront également été apportées à la *Liste des marchandises d'importation contrôlée* (LMIC),[24] exigeant dorénavant pour les marchandises visées, l'obtention d'une licence d'importation. C'est le cas pour le matériel militaire en provenance de la République d'Afrique du Sud,[25] et pour certains produits en acier spécialisé.[26] Soulignons en dernier lieu, la décision canadienne de réduire dès le 1er novembre le droit à l'exportation sur le bois d'oeuvre québécois à destination du marché américain tel que le permet le mémorandum d'entente sur le bois d'oeuvre entre le gouvernement canadien et américain,[27] ainsi que l'arrêté visant l'interdiction de respecter l'application extra-territoriale d'un règlement américain prohibant tout échange commercial avec Cuba.[28]

---

[23] *Liste des marchandises d'exportation contrôlée — Modification*, (1990) 124 Gaz. Can. II 3300. La modification la plus significative concerne l'abrogation de certains groupes de marchandises pour lesquels l'obtention d'une licence d'exportation est requise et leur remplacement par un renvoi explicite aux Listes Industrielles et de Matériel de Guerre du COCOM. Selon le résumé d'impact du règlement, ce renvoi contribuera notamment à réviser plus rapidement la LMEC pour tenir compte des listes internationales tout en faisant en sorte que les exportateurs canadiens ne soient pas soumis à des restrictions commerciales plus lourdes que ses concurrents.

[24] *Liste des marchandises d'importation contrôlée*, (1989) 123 Gaz. Can. II 2569 adoptée en vertu de l'article 5 de la *Loi sur les licences d'exportation et d'importation*, S.R.C. 1985, c. E-19.

[25] *Liste des marchandises d'importation contrôlée — Modification*, (1990) 124 Gaz. Can. II 1435. L'ajout sur la Liste vise à mettre en oeuvre les engagements du Canada au terme des résolutions 418 et 591 du Conseil de sécurité des Nations Unies à l'égard de l'embargo sur les armes d'origine sud-africaine.

[26] *Liste des marchandises d'importation contrôlée — Modification*, (1990) 124 Gaz. Can. II 2314. L'ajout sur la Liste vise ici à s'assurer que la surveillance des importations de produits en acier spécialisé soit poursuivie puisque le décret du 1er janvier 1987 exigeant une telle surveillance expirait le 1er juin 1990. Cette mesure ne prévoit donc que la collecte de renseignements sur ces produits nonobstant l'introduction de contingent.

[27] Voir Ministre du Commerce extérieur, *Communiqué de presse*, no 250, 1er novembre 1990. Le droit passe de 8% à 6,2% le 1er novembre 1990 et sera ramené à 3,1% le 1er novembre 1991, et à 3% le 1er novembre 1992 et ce jusqu'au 31 octobre 1994. Il s'agit du *Memorandum of understanding of Dec. 30, 1986, for the Secretary of Commerce and the United States Trade Representative*, 52 Fed. Reg. 231 (1987).

[28] *Arrêté de 1990 sur les mesures extra-territoriales étrangères (États-Unis)*, (1990) 124 Gaz. Can. II 4918, adopté en vertu de la *Loi sur les mesures extraterritoriales étrangères*, S.R.C. 1985, c. F-29. Cet arrêté fait suite à l'adoption par le Congrès américain du ''mack amendment,'' lequel aurait pour effet de prohiber, en vertu du droit américain, tout commerce avec Cuba même pour les compagnies situées sur le territoire canadien et contrôlées par les États-Unis. Selon le résumé d'impact de l'arrêté, cette application extraterritoriale du droit américain, compromet les échanges commerciaux entre le Canada et Cuba et constitue ainsi un empiétement sur la souveraineté canadienne.

III. Accords commerciaux conclus par le Canada

Relativement à la conclusion de traités multilatéraux de nature commerciale, on peut noter que le Canada a adhéré, le 19 septembre 1990, à la Convention internationale d'assistance mutuelle administrative en vue de prévenir, de rechercher et de réprimer les infractions douanières.[29] Cette Convention, négociée sous l'égide du Conseil de coopération douanière en 1977[30] a comme objectif principal de développer la coopération entre les administrations en vue de lutter contre les infractions à la législation douanière.[31]

Au niveau bilatéral, mentionnons l'Accord avec le gouvernement Mexicain sur l'assistance et la collaboration entre les administrations douanières canadienne et mexicaine,[32] rendu nécessaire faute de ratification par le Mexique de la Convention internationale d'assistance mutuelle administrative, en vue de lutter contre les infractions douanières; l'Accord de coopération commerciale, économique et industrielle avec la Bulgarie,[33] venant se greffer à un réseau fort élaboré d'accords du même genre; et l'Échange de Lettres constituant un Accord avec les États-Unis sur les importations d'oeufs d'incubation de poulets de chair et de poussins.[34]

[29] *Convention internationale d'assistance mutuelle administrative en vue de prévenir, de rechercher et de réprimer les infractions douanières (avec Annexes),* (1990) R.T. Can. no 41. L'instrument d'adhésion du Canada a été déposé le 19 septembre 1990 et la Convention est entrée en vigueur pour le Canada le 19 décembre 1990. Sur cette convention, voir B. COLAS (éd.), *Accords économiques internationaux: répertoire des accords et des institutions,* (1990), pp. 65-66.

[30] *Convention portant création d'un Conseil de coopération douanière,* (1971) R.T. Can. no 38.

[31] À cette fin, une partie au traité peut au cours d'une enquête ou dans le cadre d'une procédure judiciaire ou administrative nationale, demander l'assistance d'une autre administration en vue de prévenir, de rechercher et réprimer les infractions douanières lorsque ces deux parties ont accepté la même obligation. Les obligations de la Convention font l'objet d'une série d'annexes susceptibles d'être adoptées indépendamment les unes des autres et qui portent sur des champs d'assistance aussi variés que l'assistance en matière de détermination des droits et taxes à l'importation ou à l'exportation, la participation à des enquêtes à l'étranger, l'assistance sur demande en matière de contrôle, la déposition des agents de douane devant les tribunaux à l'étranger et l'assistance spontanée.

[32] *Accord entre le gouvernement du Canada et le gouvernement des États-Unis Mexicains concernant l'assistance et la collaboration mutuelles entre leurs administrations douanières,* (1990) R.T. Can. no 31.

[33] *Accord à long terme entre le gouvernement du Canada et le gouvernement de la République populaire de Bulgarie sur le développement de la coopération commerciale, économique et industrielle,* (1990) R.T. Can. no 6.

[34] *Échange de Lettres constituant un Accord entre le gouvernement du Canada et le gouvernement des États-Unis d'Amérique sur les importations d'oeufs d'incubation de poulet de chair et de poussins,*

IV. MISE EN OEUVRE DE L'ACCORD DE LIBRE-ÉCHANGE CANADA-
ÉTATS-UNIS

La seconde année de mise en oeuvre de l'Accord de libre-échange Canada-États-Unis,[35] s'est poursuivie de façon "constructive et équilibrée" aux dires des gouvernements canadien et américain.[36] Alors que les deux pays s'entendent à ce que les échanges commerciaux s'accroissent encore davantage,[37] les statistiques économiques démontrent que le commerce entre le Canada et les États-Unis se chiffrait à 197 milliards de dollars, en 1989, soit une augmentation de 4% sur l'année 1988 et 12,2% de plus qu'en 1987.[38] Par ailleurs, le Groupe de travail du GATT chargé d'examiner la compatibilité de l'Accord avec l'article XXIV de l'Accord général, n'aura pas au cours de l'année 1990 présenté son rapport aux Parties Contractantes. Le Canada et les États-Unis auront cependant eu l'opportunité de répondre à certaines questions soulevées à ce sujet.[39] Alors que s'amorce les négociations sur un Accord de libre-échange tripartite,[40] il est approprié de décrire de quelle façon la mise en oeuvre législative et jurisprudentielle de l'Accord de libre-échange Canada-États-Unis s'est dans les faits réalisée en 1990.

A. MISE EN OEUVRE LÉGISLATIVE

Outre, la réduction graduelle des droits de douanes, laquelle s'es-teffectuée conformément aux dispositions de l'Accord de libre-

entré en vigueur le 13 septembre 1990. Cet Echange de Lettres, impose des contrôles annuels à l'importation et plus spécifiquement pour l'année 1990, des contrôles sur les oeufs d'incubation de poulets de chair et de poussins. Les parties prennent soin d'indiquer que cet accord d'autolimitation des exportations, ne préjudicie en rien aux droits et obligations découlant de l'Accord général sur les tarifs douaniers et le commerce et qu'il ne doit pas être interprété comme étant conforme ou non conforme au GATT.

[35] *Accord de libre-échange entre le Gouvernement du Canada et le Gouvernement des États-Unis d'Amérique,* signé le 2 janvier 1988, en vigueur le 1er janvier 1989. Reprinted in (1988) 27 I.L.M. 281 (ci-après dénommé l'Accord de libre-échange).

[36] Voir Ministre du Commerce extérieur, *Communiqué de presse,* no 104, 18 mai 1990.

[37] *Ibid.*

[38] Voir *Statistiques Canada,* 1987-1988-1989.

[39] Voir GATT Doc. L/6739 (1990).

[40] Le 24 septembre 1990, le ministre canadien du commerce extérieur annonçait en effet la participation du Canada aux négociations sur le libre-échange avec les Etats-Unis et le Mexique. Voir Ministre du Commerce extérieur, *Communiqué de presse,* no 114, 24 septembre 1990. Voir également les développements sous la chronique "investissement" du présent annuaire.

échange,[41] il y a lieu de souligner l'application à titre provisoire
le 1er avril, de l'entente de 1989 sur l'accélération de la réduction
des droits applicables à certains produits,[42] et sa mise en vigueur
formelle finalisée par un Échange de Notes entre les deux gouvernements le 18 mai avec effet le 1er avril.[43] Une seconde série de consultations pour devancer l'échéance prévue pour l'abolition
progressive des tarifs douaniers a été engagée en 1990 et les modifications qui seront apportées aux listes tarifaires des deux pays,
devraient entrer en vigueur le 1er juillet 1991.[44] Dans le secteur de
l'agriculture, les deux parties se sont entendues sur le calcul des
niveaux de soutien gouvernemental accordé dans chaque pays pour
le blé et l'orge et au vu et su des résultats de ces calculs, des licences d'importation continueront d'être exigées par le Canada pour
ces céréales.[45] Par ailleurs, conformément à la clause de sauvegarde

[41] Tel que le prévoit l'Accord, une seconde réduction tarifaire de 20% et de 10% s'est
opérée le 1er janvier 1990 respectivement sur les produits de la catégorie d'échelonne-
ment B et C. *Accord de libre-échange, supra,* note 35, art. 401 (2)(b) et 401 (2)(c). Mentionnons également la réduction de l'écart de majoration des prix du vin supérieur,
lequel le 1er janvier 1990 ne devrait plus dépasser 50% de l'écart de base entre
l'écart de majoration appliqué en 1987 et l'écart des frais de services réels. *Id.,* art.
803 (b), ainsi que l'élimination progressive des restrictions à l'importation des au-
tomobiles d'occasion et la première étape d'élimination des redevances pour opérations douanières. *Id.,* art. 1003 (b) et 403.

[42] Voir Ministre du Commerce extérieur, *Communiqué de presse,* no 064, 2 avril 1990.
Cette entente négociée en vertu de l'article 401 (5) de l'Accord de libre-échange,
couvre 400 numéros tarifaires pour des échanges bilatéraux d'une valeur de 6 milliards de dollars. Sur cette entente, voir par ailleurs M. St. Amant, *loc. cit. supra,*
note 1 p. 442.

[43] *Échange de Notes constituant un Accord entre le gouvernement du Canada et le gouvernement des
Etats-Unis d'Amérique modifiant les listes tarifaires contenues à l'Annexe 401.2-A et à l'Annexe
401.2-B de l'Accord de libre-échange fait à Ottawa, Washington et Palm Springs les 22 décembre
1987 et 2 Janvier 1988,* (1990) R.T. Can. no 49. Pour la mise en oeuvre en droit cana-
dien voir par ailleurs, *Décret no 1 de réduction accélérée des droits de douane,* (1990) 124 Gaz.
Can. II 2213; *Décret no 2 de réduction accélérée des droits de douane,* (1990) 124 Gaz. Can.
II 2721; *Décret no 3 de réduction accélérée des droits de douane,* (1990) 124 Gaz. Can. II 2922;
Décret no 4 de réduction acélérée des droits de douane, (1990) 124 Gaz. Can. II, 2987.

[44] Voir Gouvernement du Canada, *Communiqué de presse,* (1990) no 024, 6 février 1990;
no 228, 4 octobre 1990. A noter que ces réductions s'exécutent en tenant dûment
compte des demandes soumises par les industries des deux pays. Pour un aperçu
de ces consultations voir M. DROHAN et J. LEWINGTON, "U.S., Canada Get
490 Petitions for Speedier Tariff Relief," dans le *Globe and Mail,* 20 avril 1990, p.B3.

[45] Voir Ministre du Commerce extérieur, *Communiqué de presse,* no 089, 2 mai 1990.
Rappelons que le Canada s'est engagé en vertu de l'article 705 de l'Accord de libre-
échange à éliminer les licences d'importation qu'il exige pour l'avoine, le blé et
l'orge lorsque les niveaux de soutien américain seront égaux ou inférieurs aux niveaux de soutien des mêmes céréales au Canada. D'autre part, un Accord est intervenu pour modifier la méthode utilisée pour calculer ces niveaux de soutien décrite

prévue à l'article 702 pour les fruits et légumes frais, le Canada a imposé un droit temporaire additionnel pour une certaine période sur les importations d'asperges à l'état frais ou réfrigérés originaires des États-Unis.[46] Un accord informel d'une année sur une base expérimentale est également intervenu entre les deux pays, lequel facilitera le commerce de la volaille et de la viande.[47]

Au niveau des Groupes de travail créés en vertu de l'Accord, les progrès auront été à peine perceptibles. Le Comité sélect de l'automobile chargé selon l'article 1004 de l'Accord de conseiller les deux gouvernements sur la façon d'améliorer la compétitivité de cette industrie en Amérique du Nord, aura continué ses travaux tout en recommandant au cours de l'année que les règles d'origine autorisant le commerce en franchise des produits de l'automobile passent, de 50%, tel que le prévoit présentement l'Accord de libre-échange, à 60%.[48] Le Groupe de travail sur les services créé pour mettre en oeuvre le chapitre 14 de l'Accord aura quant à lui présenté son premier rapport à la Commission mixte du commerce canado-américain, rapport qui ne fait toutefois qu'esquiver les questions à examiner et le plan de travail proposé.[49] L'important Groupe de travail chargé en vertu du chapitre 19 de développer un cadre juridique pour une règlementation commune en matière de subventions et mesures compensatoires aura lui aussi remis son premier rapport à la Commission, mai ce futur cadre n'aura pas encore

à l'annexe 705.4 de l'Accord. Voir *Echange de Notes constituant un Accord entre le gouvernement du Canada et le Gouvernement des États-Unis d'Amérique modifiant les Appendices 1 et 2 de l'Annexe 705.4 de l'Accord de libre-échange fait à Ottawa, Washington et Palm Springs les 22 décembre 1987 et 2 janvier 1988,* entré en vigueur le 2 mai 1990.

[46] *Arrêté visant le droit temporaire imposé sur les asperges à l'état frais ou réfrigérés, 1990,* (1990) 124 Gaz. Can. II 2008. Le droit additionnel est égal à la différence entre le Tarif des Etats-Unis et le Tarif de la nation la plus favorisée. Il fut abrogé le 6 juin 1990. Voir *Arrêté visant le droit temporaire imposé sur les asperges à l'état frais ou réfrigéré, 1990 — abrogation,* (1990) 124 Gaz. Can. II 2168.

[47] Selon cet Accord, dès que ces deux produits feront l'objet d'inspection alimentaire selon la procédure de l'un ou de l'autre pays, ils pourront circuler librement entre les deux frontières. Pour plus de détails sur cet Accord qui pourrait, s'il est mutuellement acceptable aux deux parties, être entériné législativement et devenir ainsi permanent, voir 9 *Int'l Trade Rep.,* (BNA) 310 (1990).

[48] Voir 33 *Int'l Trade Rep.* (BNA) 1262 (1990). Le Canada par la voie de son ministre du Commerce extérieur aura cependant fortement critiqué cette recommandation. Voir Ministre du Commerce extérieur, *Communiqué de presse,* no 163, 3 août 1990.

[49] Voir le sommaire des décisions de la Commission mixte du commerce canado-américain, Ministre du Commerce extérieur, *Communiqué de presse,* no 104, 18 mai 1990.

fait l'objet de négociations.⁵⁰ En dernier lieu, les membres du Groupe de travail sur les règles d'origine et les autres questions douanières se seront entendus sur plusieurs modifications de forme aux règles d'origine⁵¹ et la Commission mixte du commerce canado-américain approuva de nouvelles recommandations concernant des modifications à apporter au chapitre 15 de l'Accord de libre-échange.⁵²

B. MISE EN OEUVRE JURISPRUDENTIELLE

Les mécanismes de règlement des différends auront pendant la seconde année de mise en oeuvre continué de démontrer leur efficacité. En vertu de la procédure générale de règlement des différends prévue au chapitre 18 de l'Accord de libre-échange, le Groupe spécial institué pour examiner les prescriptions américaines sur la taille du homard aura présenté son rapport final à la Commission mixte du commerce canado-américain.⁵³ Le Groupe spécial dans une décision partagée (trois juges contre deux) rejeta l'argument du Canada à l'effet que la prescription américaine visant l'interdiction de vente ou de transport vers les États-Unis de homards d'une taille inférieure à la taille minimum fixée par la loi fédérale, contrevenait à l'article 407 de l'Accord, lequel incorpore l'article XI:I du GATT. Selon le Groupe, les mesures adoptées constituent des mesures intérieures et ne relèvent pas de l'article XI:I mais de l'article III du GATT car cesdites mesures ne s'appliquent pas exclusivement aux homards importés mais également aux homards américains.⁵⁴ Par ailleurs, si aucune solution mutuellement avantageuse n'a pu émerger en 1990 sur la question du commerce du homard, une entente est intervenue sur la mise en oeuvre du rapport du Groupe spécial sur le saumon et le hareng,

⁵⁰ *Ibid.*

⁵¹ Voir le sommaire des décisions de la Commission mixte du commerce canado-américain, Ministre du Commerce extérieur, *communiqué de presse*, no 235, 11 octobre 1990.

⁵² *Ibid.* Ces nouvelles recommandations portent sur l'établissement d'exigences ou d'équivalence en termes d'études pour un certain nombre de professions ainsi que sur l'ajout d'un certain nombre d'autres professions à l'annexe 1502.1 de l'Accord.

⁵³ Voir *Dans l'affaire des homards du Canada,* dossier USA-89-1807-01, 25 mai 1990.

⁵⁴ Le Groupe ne s'est toutefois pas prononcé sur la question de savoir si la prescription américaine était compatible ou non avec l'article III de l'Accord général. Pour un commentaire plus approfondi de cette décision, voir N. J. SCHULTZ, ''Lobster Dispute Settlement Panel Reads 'Do unto Others' Principle into GATT,'' (1990) 11 *Can. Competition Policy Record,* 22-24.

rapport présenté aux parties en 1989.[55]

Quant au mécanisme particulier de règlement de différends en matière de droits antidumping et compensateurs, les décisions des groupes spéciaux formés au terme du chapitre 19 de l'Accord de libre-échange, auront été nombreuses. Dans le cadre de la présente chronique limitons nous à indiquer sommairement les décisions nationales contestées ainsi que les principales questions en litige,[56] tout en soulignant que toutes les décisions des Groupes spéciaux concernent des décisions administratives du Département du Commerce des États-Unis ou des décisions judiciaires rendues par la Commission américaine du commerce international. Aucune ordonnance ou conclusion du Tribunal canadien du commerce extérieur ou décision ou réexamen du Sous-ministre du Revenu national pour les douanes et l'accise n'a donc fait l'objet en 1990 d'un examen par les Groupes spéciaux. Les décisions du Département du commerce examinées portent ainsi sur les pièces de rechange pour les épandeuses automotrices de revêtements bitumineux du Canada,[57] sur les nouveaux rails d'acier du Canada[58]

---

[55] Voir Gouvernement du Canada, *Communiqué de presse*, no 038, 22 février 1990. Pour la mise en oeuvre en droit interne canadien de cette entente, voir *Règlement de pêche du hareng du Pacifique — Modification*, (1990) 124 Gaz. Can. II 1048; *Règlement de pêche commerciale du saumon dans le Pacifique — Modification*, (1990) 124 Gaz. Can. II 1042; *Liste des marchandises d'exportation contrôlée — Modification*, (1190) 124 Gaz. Can. II 1051.

[56] Le lecteur pourra cependant avantageusement consulter le Bulletin du libre-échange pour un commentaire judicieux sur chacune de ses décisions. Voir I. BERNIER et B. LAPOINTE, *Accord de libre-échange entre le Canada et les États-Unis — Annoté*, (1989).

[57] *Pièces de rechange pour Les épandeuses automotrices de revêtements bitumineux du Canada*, Dossier USA-89-1904-02. Il s'agissait dans ce dossier de déterminer si la décision du Département sur le champ d'application de son ordonnance était appuyée par des preuves solides au dossier et conforme à la législation, critères d'examen énoncés par le Tariff Act of 1930 et dont le Groupe en vertu de l'article 1904 paragraphe 3 de l'Accord de libre-échange se devait d'appliquer. Le Groupe confirmait la décision sur le champ d'application. Deux autres affaires sur le même produit aura en outre été réunies et font l'objet d'une seule décision par le Groupe Spécial. *Pièces de rechange pour les épandeuses automotrices de revêtements bitumineux du Canada*, Dossier USA-89-1904-03 et 05. Parmi les questions portées à l'étude du Groupe, figuraient les dispositions du Tariff Act de 1930 concernant les rectifications du prix d'achat et du prix de vente à l'exportation et les rectifications en matière de circonstances de vente, de même que l'épuisement des recours administratifs et subsidiairement la valeur des précédents sur la procédure de révision du Groupe spécial. Le Groupe confirmait sur tous ces aspects, les décisions du Département du Commerce.

[58] *Dans l'affaire des nouveaux rails d'acier du Canada, à l'exception des rails légers*, Dossier USA-89-1904-07. En tenant dûment compte des critères d'examen figurant dans le Tariff Act de 1930, le Groupe devait examiner les aspects de la décision du Département portant sur l'allocation des subventions versées pour le paiement des débentures, la garantie donnée pour un prêt par le Gouvernement canadien à une filiale

et sur le porc frais, frigorifié et congelé du Canada.[59] Les décisions de la Commission américaine du commerce international qui auront fait l'objet d'un examen par des Groupes spéciaux visent les nouveaux rails d'acier[60] et le porc frais frigorifié et congelé du Canada.[61]

En terminant, mentionnons qu'un Groupe spécial aura pour la première fois rendu une décision sur un renvoi et ayant constaté que le Département du commerce américain n'avait pas rempli de nouveau son obligation, retourna une seconde fois le dossier à ce dernier pour une décision définitive.[62]

---

laquelle fut jugée comme une subvention susceptible de faire l'objet de droits compensateurs et le calcul de la subvention. Sur les deux premiers points le Groupe renvoyait au Département ces aspects de la décision et sur le troisième confirmait le calcul effectué par le Département. Une autre décision sur le même produit fut rendue le 30 août 1990; *dans l'affaire des nouveaux rails d'acier du Canada à l'exception des rails légers,* Dossier USA-89-1904-08. La question examinée ici eu égard aux critères d'examen prévus dans le Tariff Act de 1930 concernait l'utilisation de la meilleure information disponible pour établir les coûts de production. Le Groupe confirmait la décision du Département du commerce.

[59] *Dans l'affaire du porc frais, frigorifié et congelé du Canada,* Dossier USA-89-1904-06. Les questions à décider eu égard au critères d'examen du Tariff Act de 1930 portaient en autres sur l'application et l'interprétation de l'article 771B (upstream subsidy), sur les facteurs de conversion employés pour ventiler la subvention, sur le caractère de spécificité, le calcul de la subvention, sur les meilleurs renseignements possibles, et l'épuisement des recours administratifs. Le Groupe confirmait en partie et renvoyait en partie la décision du Département.

[60] *Dans l'affaire des nouveaux rails d'acier du Canada,* Dossier USA-89-1904-09 et 10, il s'agissait d'appels regroupés de décisions concluant à une menace de préjudice à l'industrie américaine en raison du dumping et de l'octroi de subventions. Les questions examinées portaient notamment sur le champ d'application d'une décision concluant à une menace de préjudice, sur la possible cumulation des importations faisant l'objet d'un dumping avec les importations subventionnées, et sur l'application des critères d'examen au Tariff Act de 1930 à l'égard de la décision concluant à une menace de préjudice et à celle concluant à l'absence de lien de causalité entre les importations et le préjudice important. Le Groupe confirmait la décision de la Commission.

[61] *Dans l'affaire du porc frais, frigorifié et congelé du Canada,* Dossier USA-89-1904-11. Il s'agissait en l'espèce d'un examen d'une décision concluant à une menace de préjudice à l'industrie américaine en raison de l'octroi de subventions. Eu égard aux critères d'examen figurant dans le Tariff Act de 1930, la question en litige était de savoir si la menace de préjudice reposait sur une preuve d'une menace de préjudice réelle et imminente. Puisque l'utilisation par la Commission de certaines statistiques étaient de l'avis du Groupe erronée, ce dernier renvoyait le dossier à la dite Commission afin qu'elle réexamine de nouveau la preuve.

[62] *Dans l'affaire des framboises rouges du Canada,* Dossier USA-89-1904-01. Pour un commentaire de la première décision du Groupe spécial, voir M. ST-AMANT, *loc. cit. supra* note 1, 447.

II

Le Canada et le système monétaire international en 1990

préparé par

BERNARD COLAS*

L A TRANSITION DES PAYS D'EUROPE centrale et orientale d'une économie à planification centralisée vers une économie de marché, l'invasion du Koweît et la persistance de la crise de l'endettement ont particulièrement marqué le système monétaire international au cours de l'année 1990.

Peu d'initiatives majeures ont été prises cette année afin d'alléger la dette extérieure des pays en développement. La conclusion d'accords de restructuration entre les banques créancières et le Mexique, les Philippines, le Costa Rica, le Venezuela, l'Uruguay dans le cadre du Plan Brady, ainsi qu'avec le Chili et le Maroc sont toutefois à souligner.[1] De plus, les Chefs d'État et de gouvernement des sept pays les plus industrialisés, réunis à Houston du 9 au 11 juillet 1990, ont décidé d'encourager le Club de Paris à allonger les périodes de remboursement de la dette des pays à revenu moyen inférieur. Cette démarche concerne les pays dont la dette officielle est importante et pour lesquels le recours au plan Brady aurait peu d'effets; la Pologne a été l'un des premiers pays à avoir bénéficié

---

[1] Pour tenir compte des incidences que de telles opérations ont sur les banques, le Bureau du Surintendant des banques du Canada a émis, le 25 octobre 1990, une Ligne directrice [PPP 1990/10] qui ajoute aux instructions comptables relatives à la création de comptes de réserves pour créances irrécouvrables, des conventions en matière d'évaluation et d'inscription des titres acquis: (1) à l'occasion d'échanges de dettes contre des participations avec des pays désignés, (2) d'acquisition de dettes d'un pays désigné par suite d'une transaction sans lien de dépendance et (3) d'acquisition de titres pour fins de restructuration des prêts accordés aux pays désignés. Celle-ci remplace la Ligne directrice du 30 septembre 1989 [G-20]. Une seconde Ligne directrice [PPD 1990/10] remplace la G-8 sur la constitution de provisions à l'égard des risque-pays et met à jour la liste des 43 pays désignés.

de cette initiative.[2] Les Sept ont également souligné la décision prise par le Canada d'annuler les prêts d'aide publique au développement remboursables par II pays des Caraï bes membres du Commonwealth à concurrence de II millions CAD.[3]

L'attention des acteurs internationaux a surtout porté sur les aspects institutionnels; notre analyse visera cette année à souligner la contribution canadienne au succès des négociations destinées à augmenter la capacité d'assistance des institutions financières internationales (partie I) et à assurer une meilleure coopération entre banques centrales et autorités de surveillance des institutions financières (partie II). Nous apprécierons l'effort poursuivi par le Canada — en tant que puissance moyenne parmi les grands — afin de promouvoir la coopération multilatérale et les principes de l'économie de marché dans le respect des valeurs de démocratie, des droits de la personne et de développement durable.

I. RENFORCEMENT DE LA CAPACITÉ D'ASSISTANCE DES INSTITUTIONS FINANCIÈRES INTERNATIONALES

De façon générale, les institutions financières internationales puisent leurs ressources de contributions des pays membres (quotes-parts) ainsi que d'emprunts. Celles-ci leur permettent d'apporter une assistance technique ou financière aux États membres, selon des conditions qui varient d'une institution à l'autre. Le Fonds Monétaire International (FMI) en plus de s'acquitter d'une fonction de surveillance du système monétaire et financier international, apporte traditionnellement son aide aux pays qui connaissent des difficultés de balance de paiements. Les banques de développement ont plutôt pour objet de financer des projets de développement dont certains, à la suite de mesures prises en 1990, doivent tenir compte des incidences environnementales.

A. FONDS MONÉTAIRE INTERNATIONAL (FMI)

Le FMI a joué un rôle de premier plan en faveur du maintien de la stabilité du système monétaire international, dont l'extrême

[2] *Rapport annuel de la Banque des règlements internationaux* (1991), p. 168. J. POWELL, "Nouvelles stratégies en matière de dette internationale," *Revue de la Banque du Canada* (1990) décembre, p. 21.

[3] Soulignons également la proposition Britannique d'alléger la dette des pays les plus pauvres fortement endettés présentée le 20 septembre 1990 à la Conférence du Commonwealth à Trinidad.

fragilité a été mise en évidence par la crise du Golfe.[4] Le Canada a souligné l'appui qu'il apporte à cette institution multilatérale à l'occasion de la ratification[5] de deux accords relatifs l'augmentation des quotes-parts[6] des pays membres et au troisième amendement des statuts du FMI. Ces textes avaient été adoptées le 28 juin 1990 par le Conseil des gouverneurs du FMI sous forme de résolutions[7] sur la base des considérations et ententes convenues au sein du Comité intérimaire, organe consultatif du FMI, lors de sa réunion de mai 1990.

Cette entente représente un compromis pour lequel M. Michael Wilson,[8] Président du Comité intérimaire et Ministre des Finances du Canada, est en grande partie responsable. Rappelons que les États Unis et la Grande-Bretagne étaient réticents à toute augmentation des quotes-parts alors que les autres pays industrialisés étaient favorables à une majoration des quotes-parts située entre 66 et 100%. Les pays en développement souhaitaient quant à eux leur doublement.

Lorsqu'il entrera en vigueur, le relèvement des quotes-parts convenu augmentera de 50% les ressources de FMI. Le niveau actuel de 90,1 milliards de DTS sera porté à environ 135,2 milliards de DTS.[9]

---

[4] Afin de répondre aux besoins des pays affectés par la crise du Golfe, il a été convenu, conformément aux recommandations du Comité intérimaire à sa réunion des 23 et 24 septembre 1990, que le Fonds adapte ses mécanismes actuels de prêts et fasse en sorte qu'ils soient plus souples. De plus, un élément lié à l'importation de pétrole a été intégré de façon temporaire (jusqu'à la fin de 1991) au mécanisme de financement compensatoire et de prévoyance afin de couvrir l'excédent des coûts des importations de pétrole brut.

[5] *Loi modifiant la Loi sur les accords de Bretton Woods et des accords connexes,* Projet de loi C-93 (adoptée par la Chambre des communes le 25 février 1991), 2ème session, 34ème Législature, (Can.).

[6] Les quotes-parts ont deux objets: (1) elles fixent l'accès aux ressources du FMI, les limites des emprunts inconditonnels ou conditionnels que chaque État peut contracter auprès du FMI, et (2) elles déterminent le poids relatif des pays dans les prises de décision puisque le droit de vote des pays à l'Assemblée des gouverneurs, et leur représentation au sein du Conseil d'administration et du Comité intérimaire, sont proportionnés au montant de leur quote-part.

[7] Résolutions 45-2 et 45-3. Notons que le Conseil des gouverneurs, organe suprême du FMI, est tenu en vertu de l'article III-2-a de ses Statuts de procéder, tous les cinq ans, à un examen général des quotes-parts des États membres et, s'il le juge approprié, d'en proposer la révision.

[8] M. Wilson est devenu président du Comité intérimaire le 3 janvier 1990 et le demeurera tant qu'il conservera son poste de Ministre des Finances.

[9] L'augmentation des quotes-parts ne pourra entrer en vigueur avant la date à laquelle le FMI déterminera que, pendant la période prenant fin le 30 décembre 1991, des pays membres dont la somme des quotes-parts représente au moins 85%

Parallèlement à l'augmentation, il est proposé une modification de la quote-part relative des États: 60% de l'augmentation sont distribués à tous les membres du Fonds en proportion de leur quote-part actuelle et 40% sont répartis selon une clé spécifique destinée à tenir compte de l'évolution de leurs poids respectifs dans l'économie mondiale.[10] Cette modalité de calcul sur 40% fait passer le Japon du 5e au 2e rang des détenteurs de quotes-parts ex-aequo avec l'Allemagne (6, 1% de parts chacun). Inversement, le Royaume-Uni régresse de la 2e place à la 4e place, ex-aequo avec la France[11] (5,48% de parts chacun). Le Canada passe du 7e au 8e rang au profit de l'Italie avec respectivement 3,19 et 3,39% des parts.[12] Les États-Unis demeurent le principal actionnaire avec 19,61% des parts et l'Arabie Saoudite le 6e actionnaire avec 3,79% des parts sur un total d'environ 151 actionnaires.

La prise d'effet de cette augmentation est toutefois conditionnée par l'entrée en vigueur du projet de troisième amendement aux statuts du FMI.[13] Cet amendement, dont l'adoption avait été demandée par les États-Unis en échange de l'obtention de leur accord pour augmenter les quotes-parts, vise principalement à régler le problème des impayés au titre d'obligations financières envers le Fonds qui, au 30 avril 1990, se chiffraient à 3,27 milliards de DTS à l'encontre de 11 pays.[14] Il prévoit que le Conseil d'administration peut décider à une majorité de 70% du total des voix attribuées, de suspendre les droits de vote d'un pays membre et certains droits

des quotes-parts actuelles — et 70% au-delà de cette date — ont consenti à l'augmentation qui leur a été proposée.

[10] Cinq critères ont été utilisés pour déterminer la part de chaque pays membre dans cette seconde distribution: le PIB, le niveau des recettes courantes, celui des dépenses courantes, le niveau de variabilité des recettes courantes et les réserves de change sur la période des douze derniers mois.

[11] Un compromis s'est apparemment dessiné entre le Royaume-Uni et la France pour l'obtention de cet ex-aequo. Le Royaume-Uni aurait accepté de partager sa quatrième place avec la France en échange de l'obtention du siège de la BERD à Londres. Voir S. FIDLER, ''Paris Faces Pressure in Dispute over IMF'' dans *Financial Times (London)*, 2 mai 1990.

[12] La quote-part du Canada passerait de 2,9 à 4,3 milliards DTS, obligeant ainsi le Canada à verser 5,8 millions CAD, au titre de dépenses non-budgétaires, et 25% de ce qui reste à payer en DTS à partir de ses réserves internationales.

[13] Cet amendement entrera en vigueur lorsque le FMI certifiera qu'il a été accepté par les 3/5 des pays membres, détenant 85% du total des voix.

[14] *Rapport annuel du Fonds monétaire international* (1990), p. 69. Les pays membres visés sont le Cambodge, le Libéria, le Panama, le Pérou, le Sierra Leone, la Somalie, le Soudan, le Viet Nam et la Zambie ainsi que le Guyana et le Honduras.

connexes si ce pays persiste à ne pas s'acquitter de ses obligations aux termes des Statuts. Il s'agit d'une étape intermédiaire entre la suspension des droits d'emprunts et l'explusion, pouvoirs que le FMI possède déjà.

D'autres mesures correctives ont été proposées pour faire face à ce probléme des impayés qui entrave les opérations du FMI et affaiblit sa crédibilité.[15] Le Comité intérimaire a approuvé en mai 1990 la méthode "d'accumulation des droits." Cette méthode s'applique aux pays membres en situation d'arriérés persistants envers le FMI à la fin de 1989 qui adopteront un vaste programme d'ajustement économique avant la réunion du Comité intérimaire du printemps de 1991. Il s'agit pour les pays d'acquérir des droits, fondés sur une amélioration soutenue de leurs résultats économiques dans le cadre d'un programme suivi par le FMI, en vue d'obtenir ultérieurement, après liquidation des arriérés, un financement de la part du FMI. De plus, des groupes de soutien multilatéraux au Guyana et au Honduras ont aidé ces pays à rembourser les arriérés accumulés envers le FMI respectivement les 20 et 28 juin 1990 et être de nouveau admis à utiliser les ressources générales du Fonds.[16] Le Canada a présidé le groupe de soutien en faveur du Guyana.[17]

B. BANQUES DE DÉVELOPPEMENT

L'augmentation de la capacité financière d'institutions multilatérales de développement s'est également accompagnée en 1990 de l'adoption de mesures visant à favoriser la conservation de l'environnement.

La Banque européenne pour la reconstruction et le développement (BERD), dont l'acte constitutif a été signé par le Canada à Paris le 29 mai 1990,[18] constitue la première institution internationale

---

[15] Notons que des communications ont été envoyées aux dirigeants de certaines institutions financières internationales signalant le manquement aux obligations financières envers le FMI de quatre pays et une déclaration de non-coopération a été prononcée à l'égard du Libéria.

[16] C'était la première fois qu'une décision d'irrévocabilité est révoquée dans le cadre de l'approche fondée sur une collaboration intensifiée, approuvée par le Comité intérimaire du Fonds en 1988; voir *Bulletin du FMI*, 9 juillet 1990, p. 206.

[17] *Rapport annuel du FMI, op. cit. supra*, note 14, p. 68. Dans le cadre de l'opération en faveur du Guyana, la part souscrite par la Banque du Canada au crédit-relais, avec le consentement du Ministre des finances, s'est élevée à 31,75 millions USD. Voir *Rapport de la Banque du Canada* (1990), p. 40.

[18] *Loi concernant la participation du Canada à la Banque européenne pour la reconstruction et le développement*, Projet de loi C-88 (adoptée par la Chambre des communes le 21

associant l'ensemble des pays d'Europe centrale et orientale — Albanie exceptée — aux pays occidentaux à économie de marché. De plus, elle s'avère être la première banque multilatérale de développement qui statutairement doit tenir compte des aspects environnementaux dans l'exécution de ses actions.

Cette banque,[19] née d'une initiative française, a un triple objectif: favoriser la transition des économies des pays d'Europe centrale et orientale vers des économies de marché, promouvoir l'initiative privée et l'esprit d'entreprise et encourager le progrès et la reconstruction économique de ces pays. Elle est tenue de coopérer avec d'autres organisations internationales concernées par le développement économique et l'investissement des pays bénéficiaires, soient les pays membres d'Europe centrale et orientale qui procèdent à une "transition résolue vers l'économie de marché, participent à la promotion de l'initiative privée et de l'esprit d'entreprise et appliquent les principes de la démocratie pluraliste et du pluralisme."[20]

Les moyens d'action de cette nouvelle banque sont multiples. Ils peuvent prendre la forme d'assistance technique, de participation financière ou de prêts principalement en faveur des entreprises du secteur privé; les Statuts de la BERD prévoient qu'au moins 60% de ses crédits sont destinés à ces entreprises. Les entreprises d'État pourront bénéficier de son assistance, sans toutefois dépasser 40% des crédits, dans la mesure où cela favorise leur transition du système de contrôle étatique centralisé vers la "démonopolisation, la décentralisation ou la privatisation."

Pour ce faire, la BERD dispose d'un capital initial de 10 milliards d'écus contrôlé à 51% par les États membres de la Communauté économique européenne (CEE), la Commission des Communautés européennes et la Banque européenne d'investissement. Les États Unis sont le principal actionnaire avec une participation de 10% proche de la minorité de blocage fixée à 15% pour les principales décisions. Le Japon dispose de 8,58% et les pays

---

janvier 1991), 2ème session, 34ème législature, permet au Canada de ratifier l'acte constitutif, entré en vigueur le 15 avril 1991.

[19] J. MAJEU, "La BERD: beaucoup plus qu'un plaidoyer," *Bulletin de la SDIE* (1990), Vol.3, No. 3, pp. 3-5.

[20] Une proposition canadienne retenue dans l'acte constitutif prévoit qu'à l'occasion de l'examen annuel de la stratégie de prêt pour un pays bénéficiare, la BERD peut mettre fin au financement si les 2/3 des pays qui représentent les 3/4 des votes considèrent que ce pays n'applique pas de façon cohérente les principes de la démocratie, du pluralisme et de l'économie de marché.

d'Europe centrale et orientale détiennent 13,5% du capital dont 6% pour l'URSS. Le Canada est le huitième actionnaire avec une participation de 3,4% du capital, soit un capital versé d'environ 120 millions USD et 400 millions USD sujet à appel.[21]

Le Canada a également participé en juin 1990 à la création du Fonds de Montréal sur la protection de la couche d'ozone[22] et en novembre 1990 à la création du Fonds pour l'environnement mondial (FEM).[23] Sur le continent américain, la Banque interaméricaine de développement (BID) a créé en 1990, dans le cadre de la réorganisation de la Banque, la Division de la protection de l'environnement dont l'objectif est d'atténuer l'impact sur l'environnement des projets d'investissements et d'aider à mettre au point des projets ayant un impact environnemental favorable. L'Assemblée a approuvé l'entrée en vigueur de la septième augmentation générale des ressources de la Banque[24] et en octobre 1990, la création d'un mécanisme de réduction de la dette et du service de la dette pour aider les pays emprunteurs à réduire leur dette publique extérieure et le service de la dette avec les banques commerciales.[25]

II. COOPÉRATION ENTRE AUTORITÉS DE CONTRÔLE BANCAIRE

L'intégration des marchés financiers au plan international a mis en relief l'interdépendance des économies et a motivé l'adoption d'initiatives en 1990 par les banques centrales et autorités de contrôle bancaire pour assurer la cohérence du système financier privé dans son ensemble. Celles-ci ont adopté des principes de base, qu'elles se sont engagés à appliquer selon les moyens dont elles

---

[21] Cette initiative s'inscrit dans un cadre plus large des mesures du Canada sur le plan bilatéral et multilatéral, qui comprennent l'aide de 72 millions à laquelle s'est ajoutée 60 millions CAD sur trois ans accordée à la Hongrie et à la Pologne. Voir MINISTÈRE DES FINANCE, *Information* n° 90-135, Ottawa, 22 octobre 1990.

[22] Voir B. COLAS, R. OSTERWALDT, ''Le Canada et la protection internationale de l'environnement en 1989,'' *ACDI* (1990).

[23] Ce Fonds sera géré conjointement par la Banque mondiale, le Programme des Nations Unies pour le développement (PNUD) et le Programme des Nations Unies pour l'environnement (PNUE). Avec une dotation initiale de 1,5 milliards USD sous forme d'engagements, le FEM devrait être opérationnel au milieu de 1991. Voir: *Rapport annuel de la Banque mondiale* (1991), p. 63.

[24] Résolution AG-2/90. Cet accord accroît le capital autorisé de 26,5 milliards USD et le porte à un montant total de 61 milliards USD. La portion libérée de la souscription de chaque pays membre est de 2,5% souscrite en monnaies convertibles; les 97,5% restants consistant en capital exigible.

[25] *Rapport annuel de la Banque interaméricaine de développement* (1990), p. 24.

disposent, et à coopérer entre elles principalement par voie d'échange d'informations et de consultation.

A. CONTRÔLE DES ÉTABLISSEMENTS DES BANQUES À L'ÉTRANGER

Sept ans après l'adoption du Concordat de Bâle[26] de 1983, le Comité de Bâle sur le contrôle bancaire[27] a adopté un "Supplément au Concordat" qui l'élargit et le complète. Le Concordat traite exclusivement des responsabilités des autorités de contrôle bancaire dans la surveillance de la gestion prudentielle et de la solidité de l'activité des établissements des banques à l'étranger.[28] Le Supplément vise à encourager une collaboration plus régulière et mieux structurée la qualité et l'étendue de la surveillance de l'activité bancaire transfrontière.

Par exemple, l'une des premières recommandations du Supplément vise la procédure d'autorisation d'établissement; elle indique qu'au moment où une banque dépose une demande d'ouverture d'un nouvel établissement à l'étranger, l'autorité d'accueil, avant l'octroi d'une licence bancaire, devrait s'assurer que les autorités d'origine n'y voient pas d'objection. Les recommandations contiennent également des dispositions qui visent à satisfaire les besoins d'information des autorités d'origine et des autorités d'accueil, à supprimer les entraves à l'échange d'informations prudentielles dues aux règles du secret bancaire et à assurer la vérification comptable externe des établissements à l'étranger. Les instances chargées de l'activité d'assurance y ont également souscrit.[29]

B. SYSTÈMES DE COMPENSATION INTERBANCAIRE

La Banque des règlements internationaux (BRI) a publié en novembre 1990 le "Rapport du Comité sur les systèmes de compensation interbancaires des banques centrales des pays du groupe des Dix."[30] Ce Comité a examiné l'apport aux systèmes de com-

---

[26] Concordat de Bâle sur le contrôle des établissements des banques à l'étranger, voir B. COLAS (éd.), *Accords économiques internationaux: répertoire des accords et des institutions* (1990), p. 238.

[27] Le Comité se compose des représentants des banques centrales et des autorités de surveillance des pays membres du groupe des Dix et du Luxembourg.

[28] Le Concordat tient compte du principe selon lequel les autorités d'origine doivent examiner l'ensemble des activités, à l'échelle mondiale de chaque banque, au moyen de la technique de la consolidation, afin d'être pleinement satisfaites de leur solidité.

[29] *Rapport annuel de la BRI, op.cit. supra,* note 2, p. 133.

[30] Le Canada, membre du groupe des Dix, était représenté par M. G. G. Thiessen,

pensation des ordres de paiement interbancaires et des opérations de change. Il recommande des normes minimales en ce qui concerne la conception et le fonctionnement de tels systèmes afin que soit garantie la gestion prudente du risque de crédit et du risque de liquidité et propose un cadre de suivi effectif concerté des banques centrales.

Les paiements interbancaires dans une devise donnée s'effectuent toujours en définitive par l'intermédiaire de comptes auprès de banques centrales émettrices. Toutefois, le secteur privé développe des systèmes de règlements interbancaires véritablement transnationaux qui dissocient la compensation interbancaire réalisée dans un centre financier du règlement définitif des positions dans un autre centre.

Un nombre restreint de systèmes transfrontières de compensation de paiements sont actuellement en service. Leurs développements préoccupent les banques centrales en raison des conséquences qu'ils peuvent avoir pour la structure globale du crédit des marchés financiers et, en particulier, des marchés de change et des fonds interbancaires. L'objectif plus vaste poursuivi par les banques centrales du fait de l'adoption de ce texte est de restreindre le risque systémique[31] dans les systèmes de paiement et sur les marchés financiers.

C. BLANCHIMENT DES CAPITAUX

Afin de prévenir l'utilisation du système bancaire et des institutions financières aux fins de blanchir l'argent de la drogue, un Groupe d'action financière sur le blanchiment de capitaux[32] a été mis sur pied à l'issue de la réunion du G-7 en Juillet 1989. Il a produit un Rapport que le ministre d'État (Finances), l'honorable Gilles Loiselle, a publié en avril 1990. Ce rapport propose une quarantaine de recommandations en faveur desquelles le Canada, membre du groupe, s'est prononcé. Le Ministre a créé un Comité consultatif sur le blanchiment de fonds le 18 janvier 1990 et a notamment proposé l'adoption de mesures législatives portant sur les exigences

---

Premier sous-gouverneur de la Banque du Canada.

[31] Le risque systémique est le risque que l'illiquidité ou la défaillance d'un établissement et, partant, son incapacité à faire face à ses obligations venant à échéance n'entraînent l'illiquidité ou la défaillance d'autres établissements.

[32] Les pays membres du G-7 ainsi que l'Australie, l'Autriche, la Belgique, l'Espagne, le Luxembourg, les Pays-Bas, la Suède et la Suisse ont participé aux travaux du Groupe.

de maintien de documents pour assister les enquêtes policières en matière de blanchiment de fonds.[33] De plus, le Bureau du Surintendant des banques examine, depuis le 1er janvier 1990, les méthodes de détection des opérations de blanchiment de fonds dans le cadre de l'inspection annuelle de toutes les institutions financières.[34]

---

[33] Le Canada a de plus modifié le Code criminel, la Loi sur les aliments et drogues et la loi sur les stupéfiants [Projet de loi C-61, entré en vigueur le 1.1.1989] et a signé un document intitulé "Prévention de l'utilisation du système bancaire pour le blanchiment de fonds d'origine criminelle" en janvier 1989 avec d'autres membres du Comité Cooke de la BRI. GOUVERNEMENT DU CANADA, *Communiqué* n° 90-055, 19 avril 1990.

[34] Il a également publié un document intitulé "Mécanismes efficaces de repérage et d'élimination des opérations de blanchiment de fonds." Voir *Rapport annuel du Bureau du Surintendant des institutions financières* (1990), p. 23.

III

Investissement

préparé par

PIERRE RATELLE*

I. Contexte général

E N 1990, la conjoncture politique et économique canadienne a été défavorable à l'investissement international. D'abord, au niveau politique, plusieurs événements ont ébranlé sérieusement le Canada.[1] Ensuite, au niveau économique, d'autres événements ont sérieusement affecté le Canada.[2] Par rapport à 1989, il en a

---

* Avocat au Barreau du Québec et Docteur en droit (Université de Paris 1 — Panthéon-Sorbonne); D.E.A. de droit international économique (Université de Paris 1 — Panthéon-Sorbonne); D.E.A. de droit international public (Université de Paris 2 — Panthéon - Assas); LL.B. (Université Laval).

---

[1] D'une part, le Canada a essuyé l'échec de l'"Accord du Lac Meech," lequel devait ramener dans le "giron constitutionnel canadien" la province de Québec, mais qui n'a jamais pu être ratifié. Voir C. HEBERT, "Meech est bel et bien mort," dans *Le Devoir,* 23 juin 1990, p. 1. ceci a amené cette province à laisser planer la menace de sa séparation du reste du Canada et de son accession unilatérale à la souveraineté. Cf. D. LESSARD et A. PEPIN, "Le Québec est libre et capable d'assurer son destin, réplique Bourassa," dans *La Presse,* 23 juin 1990, p. A1. D'autre part, la province de l'Ontario, qui représente 40 pour cent du produit intérieur brut (PIB) canadien, a élu pour la première fois de son histoire un gouvernement néo-démocrate, beaucoup plus "à gauche" que le gouvernement libéral précédent; ce qui a inquiété les milieux financiers et des affaires canadiens et étrangers. Cf. notamment "Ontario Will Pay Dearly for NDP, [Conrad] Black: Press Baron Predicts Economic Slowdown if Rae Has His Way," in *the Gazette,* 12 septembre 1990, p. B1.

[2] D'une part, le Canada a connu sa pire récession depuis celle de 1982; ce qui a entraîné une augmentation importante du nombre des faillites, des mises-à-pied, mais aussi du pessimisme des consommateurs canadiens envers l'économie du pays. Cf. OCDE, *Perspectives économiques de l'OCDE* (décembre 1990), pp. 91-92; "Recession Far from Bottom: It's Not Over Yet," in *Winnipeg Free Press,* 6 novembre 1990, p. C1. D'autre part, son déficit budgétaire annuel a atteint près de 29 milliards

résulté une chute spectaculaire des investissements directs étrangers au Canada et des investissements directs canadiens à l'étranger.[3]

II. Actions unilatérales

A. Mise en oeuvre de l'accord de libre—échange avec les états-unis

Le 1er janvier 1990 était le premier anniversaire de l'Accord de libre-échange entre le Canada et les États-Unis (ALÉ), mais aussi le début de sa deuxième période de transition devant conduire à sa pleine réalisation en matière d'investissement.[4] À cet égard, il convient de noter que, dans le cadre de la *Loi sur Investissement Canada* (LIC),[5] le seuil donnant ouverture à l'examen de l'acquisition directe du contrôle d'une entreprise canadienne par une entreprise américaine a été haussé à 50 millions de dollars canadiens.[6] Quant au seuil donnant ouverture à l'examen de l'acquisition indirecte du contrôle d'une entreprise canadienne par une entreprise américaine, il a été accrû à 250 millions de dollars canadiens.[7] Les investissements étrangers autres qu'américains ne bénéficient pas de ces augmentations et demeurent assujettis aux seuils actuels de la LIC, lesquels sont fixés à cinq millions de dollars canadiens pour les acquisitions directes et à 25 millions de dollars canadiens pour les acquisitions indirectes.[8]

---

de dollars canadiens, gonflant ainsi son déficit budgétaire total à 358 milliards de dollars canadiens. Près de 26 pour cent des recettes budgétaires annuelles du gouvernement canadien vont maintenant aux frais de la dette publique. Cf. MINIST E RE DES FINANCES DU CANADA, ''Faits saillants des résultats financiers d'avril 1990,'' dans *La Revue financière*, novembre 1990, Tableau de référence financier récapitulatif.

[3] En 1990, les nouveaux investissements canadiens à l'étranger ont totalisé 5.2 milliards de dollars canadiens, soit 20 pour cent de moins que l'année précédente. Quant au nouveaux investissements étrangers au Canada, ils ont atteint, en 1990, la somme de neuf milliards dollars canadiens, soit 25 pour cent de moins qu'en 1989. Cf. STATISTIQUE CANADA, *Bilan des investissements internationaux du Canada 1988-1990* (avril 1991), pp. 11 et ss.

[4] Les versions françaises et anglaises font partie de la *Loi de mise en oeuvre de l'Accord de libre-échange entre le Gouvernement du Canada et le Gouvernement des États-Unis d'Amérique*, S.C. 1988, c. 65; une version en langue anglaise est reproduite dans *United States-Canada Free Trade Agreement Implementation Act of 1988*, Pub. L. 100-4449, 102 Stat. 1851 (1988) ainsi que dans (1988) 27 *I.L.M.* 281.

[5] Voir S.C. 1985, c. 20.

[6] Voir ALÉ, Annexe 1607.3, art. 2 § (a) (i) (A).

[7] *Id.*, art. 2 § (a) (ii) (A).

[8] Voir LIC, art. 14 et 15.

B. MODIFICATIONS AU PROGRAMME D'IMMIGRATION DES INVESTISSEURS

La ministre fédérale de l'Emploi et de l'Immigration a annoncé, au mois d'août 1990, des modifications importantes à la composante immigrants investisseurs du Programme d'immigration des gens d'affaires.[9]

D'abord, afin que les investissements puissent bénéficier d'une période suffisante pour rapporter des dividendes, la période minimale d'immobilisation passe de trois à cinq ans.[10] Ensuite, les règles d'admissibilité de la catégorie I sont révisées de manière à permettre aux provinces qui ont accueilli moins de dix pour cent des gens d'affaires immigrants (au lieu de trois pour cent), au cours d'une année civile, de satisfaire aux exigences de cette catégorie.[11] Grâce à cette modification, les provinces des Prairies et de l'Atlantique seront maintenant admissibles à cette catégorie. Enfin, les investissements minimaux pour les catégories I et II sont accrûs de 100 000 dollars canadiens pour être portés respectivement à 250 000 dollars canadiens et à 350 000 dollars canadiens; le montant minimal requis pour la catégorie III est maintenu à 500 000 dollars canadiens.[12] Les investisseurs dans les provinces de l'Ontario, du Québec et de la Colombie Britannique devront donc, dorénavant, effectuer des investissements minimaux de 350 000 dollars canadiens, alors que ceux des provinces des Prairies et de l'Atlantique devront investir au moins 250 000 dollars canadiens.[13]

---

[9] Voir MINISTRE DE L'EMPLOI ET DE L'IMMIGRATION, *Déclaration*, N° 90-23, 20 août 1990. La composante immigrants investisseurs du Programme d'immigration des gens d'affaires à été mise en place, en 1986, afin de permettre d'admettre au Canada des personnes ayant des compétences et de l'expérience dans le domaine des affaires dont pourrait tirer profit le Canada, et qui seraient prêtes à investir dans des entreprises canadiennes. Ces entreprises doivent être jugées par les Provinces comme étant importantes pour leur développement économique, tout en permettant de créer ou de conserver des emplois. En pratique, les investisseurs doivent faire une proposition d'investir dans une petite et moyenne entreprise qui doit obtenir au préalable l'approbation du gouvernement fédéral. Trois catégories d'investissements minimaux sont prévues: catégorie I: 150 000 dollars canadiens; catégorie II: 250 000 dollars canadiens; catégorie III: 500 000 dollars canadiens.

[10] Voir *Règlement sur l'immigration de 1978 — Modification*, (1990) 124 Gaz. Can. II 4888, art. 1 (1).

[11] *Ibid.*

[12] *Ibid.*

[13] *Ibid.*

C. GEL DES AVOIRS IRAQIENS ET KOWEITIENS

Suite à l'invasion du Koweït par les troupes iraqiennes, le 2 août 1990, le Canada a vigoureusement condamné cette agression armée.[14] Sous l'égide du Conseil de sécurité des Nations Unies, le Canada s'est mis immédiatement à la tâche en vue de rédiger une réponse commune claire et sans équivoque à l'attaque militaire iraqienne.[15] Cette réponse s'est traduite par la Résolution 661 adoptée, le 6 août 1990, par le Conseil de sécurité, laquelle prévoit l'imposition de sanctions par les pays membres de l'Organisation des Nations Unies (ONU).[16]

Par la suite, le gouvernement canadien a approuvé un règlement en vertu de l'article 2 de sa *Loi sur les Nations Unies*,[17] afin que le Canada puisse participer à l'engagement international prévu dans cette résolution.[18] Ce règlement prévoit, notamment, le gel des avoirs iraqiens et koweïtiens au Canada,[19] lesquels incluent les investissements directs qui s'élevaient à un peu plus de 100 millions de dollars canadiens en 1989.[20]

D. AUTORISATION À AMERICAN EXPRESS POUR OUVRIR SA PROPRE BANQUE

Le ministre d'État aux Finances a annoncé, au mois de février 1990, que le gouvernement canadien avait l'intention d'autoriser la compagnie American Express Canada Inc., filiale en propriété entière du conglomérat American Express Company (Amex), de New York, à établir une banque en sol canadien.[21]

[14] La journée même, le secrétaire d'État aux Affaires extérieures du Canada a fait une déclaration à ce sujet. Voir SECRETAIRE D'ÉTAT AUX AFFAIRES EXTÉRIEURES, Communiqué, N° 162, 2 août 1990.

[15] Cf. SECRETARY OF STATE FOR EXTERNAL AFFAIRS, *News Release*, N° 166, 4 août 1990.

[16] Voir C.S. Rés. 661 (1990), Doc. N.U. S/RES/661 (1990).

[17] Voir L.R.C. 1985, c. U-3.

[18] Voir *Règlement des Nations Unies sur l'Iraq*, (1990) 124 Gaz. Can. II 3629.

[19] *Id.*, art. 6.

[20] Cf. STATISTIQUE CANADA, *op. cit. supra*, note 3, p. 60.

[21] Cf. CANADA, CHAMBRE DES COMMUNES, *Compte rendu officiel (Hansard)*, 34e législature, 2e session, vol. 131, N° 128, 6 février 1990, p. 7898. Amex est un chef de file international en matière de services de paiement et l'un des principaux émetteurs de cartes de crédit dans le monde (36.5 millions de cartes en circulation) tout en dominant le marché international des chèques de voyage (sa part de marché est supérieure d'au-delà de 50 pour cent à celle de ses plus proches concurrents). Amex exerce la plupart de ses activités bancaires par le biais de quatre filiales bancaires. Quelques données financières qui donnent une idée de la puissance économique de ce conglomérat: en 1989, ses revenus excédaient les 23

Plusieurs intervenants du milieu financier au Canada, en particulier l'Association des banquiers canadiens (Association), se sont
opposés à ce qu'Amex fasse son entrée sur le marché bancaire canadien. Selon l'Association, il était totalement injustifié q'Amex puisse
offrir au consommateur canadien, par l'entreprise de sa filiale bancaire canadienne, une gamme de produits financiers plus étendue
que celle qui est permise aux institutions financières canadiennes.[22]
Ensuite, au dire de l'Association, il n'était pas dans l'intérêt public que le gouvernement canadien permette à des multinationales
étrangères, comme Amex, de percer davantage les marchés financiers de détail du pays avant que la nouvelle législation financiè-
rene soit entrée en vigueur.[23] Enfin, pour l'Association, la décision
du gouvernement canadien de donner le "feu vert" à Amex risquait
de créer un dangereux précédent au Canada.[24]

Les doléances de l'Association ne semblent pas avoir ébranlé la
volonté du gouvernement canadien puisqu'au mois d'avril 1990,
il octroyait des lettres patentes à American Express Canada Inc.
pour ouvrir Amex Banque du Canada.[25] Selon les informations

---

milliards de dollars américains (par comparaison, le budget de la province de
Québec, pour la même année, était d'environ 27.5 milliards de dollars américains),
ses actifs totalisaient plus de 143 milliards de dollars américains, incluant les actifs
de ses quatre filiales bancaires qui atteignaient, à eux seuls, les 30 milliards de
dollars américains, soit plus que les actifs de la sixième banque au Canada. Cf.
AMERICAN EXPRESS COMPANY, *Our 1990 Annual Report and History of Growth*
(1991), pp. 41-46; GOUVERNEMENT DU QUEBEC, CONSEIL DU TRÉSOR,
Budget 1989-1990 (1989), p. vii.

[22] Voir ASSOCIATION DES BANQUIERS CANADIENS, *Le droit à la concurrence?*
(1990), p. 1. Par exemple, Amex pourrait offrir aux détenteurs de ses cartes de crédit
des produits et des services d'assurance, de voyage, d'activités de marketing direct
par le biais de catalogue et de magazines, de crédit-bail, de gestion de portefeuille
et de conseil en placement, etc., ce qu'interdit la législation bancaire canadienne.
Voir *Loi sur les banques*, L.R.C. 1985, c. B-1, art. 302.

[23] *Ibid.* Comme nous allons le voir, un nouveau cadre législatif et réglementaire allait être présenté à l'automne 1990.

[24] Selon l'Association, quatre autres conglomérats ayant un profil semblable à Amex
— tel que General Electric Company, qui oeuvre dans les secteurs traditionnels
de l'éclairage, des électroménagers et des moteurs, mais qui possède également
un large éventail d'activités dont des services financiers hautement diversifiés offerts
à l'échelle planétaire — pourraient théoriquement déposer une requête officielle
d'établissement de banque au Canada. *Id.*, pp. 1-2.

[25] Voir *Avis du Bureau du Surintendant des institutions financières*, (1990) 124 Gaz. Can. I 1951.
L'octroi de lettres patentes constitue le premier pas pour obtenir une licence bancaire canadienne, laquelle est accordée dès que le requérant a tenu une réunion
du premier conseil d'administration et une première assemblée des actionnaires
et que la banque a reçu au moins cinq millions de dollars canadiens en contrepar-
tie de l'émission de ses actions. Voir *Loi sur les banques, supra*, note 22, art. 26, 27

disponibles, Amex ne désirerait pas ouvrir de succursales au Canada ni accepter de dépôts.[26] Cependant, elle serait intéressée à s'infiltrer dans le système de paiements canadiens afin que les titulaires canadiens de ses cartes de crédit puissent avoir accès aux réseaux de guichets automatiques bancaires canadiens.[27]

E. MODIFICATION AUX RÈGLES DE PROPRIÉTÉ ÉTRANGÈRE DES SOCIÉTÉS DE FIDUCIE ET DE PRÊTS

En septembre 1990, le ministre fédéral d'État aux Finances a déposé à la Chambre des Communes, en première lecture, un projet de loi visant notamment à modifier les règles concernant la propriété étrangère des sociétés fédérales de fiducie et de prêts (Projet de loi C-83).[28]

Le Projet de loi C-83 est le premier élément du nouveau cadre législatif et de la nouvelle réglementation que le gouvernement canadien se propose d'appliquer aux institutions financières fédérales.[29] En ce qui a trait à la propriété étrangère, il établit des règles de propriété permettant d'avoir des sociétés fédérales de fiducie et de prêts à capital fermé aussi bien qu'à capital élargi.[30] En pratique,

---

et 29 § 2; *adde* BUREAU DU SURINTENDANT DES INSTITUTIONS FINAN-CIÈRES, *Guide à l'intention des banques étrangères. Renseignements relatifs à la constitution de filiales de banques étrangères et à l'immatriculation des bureaux de représentation en vertu de la Loi canadienne sur les banques* (décembre 1989), pp. 9-10.

[26] Voir ASSOCIATION DES BANQUIERS CANADIENS, *op. cit. supra*, note 22, p. 30.

[27] Voir P. R. HAYDEN, J. H. BURNS et al., "Amex Gets Green Light to Open Bank in Canada," in CCH, *Foreign-Investment in Canada; A Guide to the Law* (1990), vol. 1, Report Bulletin IC56-2.

[28] Voir *Loi remaniant et modifiant la législation régissant les sociétés de fiducie et de prêts fédérales et comportant des mesures connexes et corrélatives*, Projet de loi C-83 (1ère lecture, 27 septembre 1990), 2e session, 34e législature (Can.).

[29] D'autres projets de loi à venir viseront à modifier la *Loi sur les banques, supra*, note 22, la *Loi sur les compagnies d'assurance*, L.R.C. 1985, c. I-14, la *Loi sur les associations coopératives de crédit*, L.R.C. 1985, c. C-41, et les lois connexes. Cf. MINISTÈRE DES FINANCES DU CANADA, *Réforme des lois sur les institutions financières fédérales. Aperçu des propositions législatives* (automne 1990), p. 3.

[30] Voir Projet de loi C-83, art. 395-400. Par opposition à la propriété à capital fermé, la propriété à capital élargi pose des limites au nombre d'actions que peuvent détenir une ou plusieurs personnes étrangères dans les sociétés fédérales de fiducie ou de prêts. Le but est évidemment d'éviter que des étrangers ne prennent le contrôle de ces institutions de dépôt. Au Canada, la traduction juridique est l'existence d'une règle interdisant à toute personne ou groupe de personnes associées étrangères de détenir respectivement plus de dix et 25 pour cent d'une catégorie d'actions d'une société fédérale de fiducie ou de prêts. Cette règle est appelée com-

ce sont les Américains qui bénéficieront de ces nouvelles règles puisqu'en vertu de l'ALÉ,[31] ils ne sont pas assujettis à la règle de propriété étrangère, dite "10/25," qui est contenue dans le Projet de loi C-83.[32] En d'autres termes, les Américains seront les seuls investisseurs étrangers à tirer profit des règles relatives à la propriété étrangère à capital fermé des sociétés fédérales de fiducie et de prêts que le Projet de loi C-83 met de l'avant.

Ces nouvelles règles de propriété étrangère, que comporte le Projet de loi C-83, n'ont pas été sans ressusciter de vieux démons au sein du milieu financier canadien. Celui-ci s'est montré particulièrement inquiet face aux répercussions défavorables que ces nouvelles règles pourraient causer au système financier canadien, en particulier aux systèmes de paiement et d'assurance-dépôt.[33] De plus, à la lumière de la libéralisation des échanges de services en général,[34] il n'est pas interdit de croire que d'énormes pressions pourraient être exercées par les principaux partenaires commerciaux du Canada afin, qu'en matière de propriété de sociétés fédérales de fiducie et de prêt, celui-ci leur accorde un traitement similaire à celui dont bénéficient les États-Unis dans le cadre de l'ALÉ.[35]

munément dans le jargon juridique: la "règle 10/25." Voir *Loi sur les sociétés de fiducie, supra,* art. 40; *Loi sur les sociétés de prêts,* L.R.C. 1985, c.L-12, art. 44 § 3 et 45 § 1.

[31] Voir ALÉ, art. 1703 § (d) et (e).

[32] Voir Projet de loi C-83, art. 395 § 2.

[33] Voir en particulier la lettre, du 20 septembre 1990, adressée au premier ministre du Canada, Brian Mulroney, par l'Association des banquiers canadiens, 17 p. De nombreuses études sur le système financier en général et sur la faillite d'institutions financières en particulier reconnaissent la pertinence de la propriété à capital élargi par opposition à la propriété à capital fermé en tant que moyen de réduire les risques de transactions intéressées, c'est-à-dire l'usage abusif des fonds des déposants par les propriétaires de ces institutions financières. Voir notamment CONSEIL ÉCONOMIQUE DU CANADA, *Le nouvel espace financier — Les marchés canadiens et la mondialisation* (1989), pp. 55 et 56; et du même organisme, *L'encadrement du système financier* (1987), p. 98; E.G. CORRIGAN, *Financial Market Structure: A Longer View* (1987), pp. 25-26; voir aussi J.-L. SANTINI, "La crise des caisses d'épargne américaines tourne au cauchemar." Dans *Le Devoir,* 2 août 1990, p. 5.

[34] À ce sujet, voir notamment D. J. GERVAIS, "Les services et l'Uruguay Round: un bref état des lieux," (1991) 2 *Bulletin de la Société de droit international économique — Canada* 12-13; K. L. KELLER-HOBSON, "La Communauté européenne à l'aube de 1992," déjeuner-causerie tenu à Montréal, le 1er février 1991, par le bureau d'avocats montréalais DESJARDINS DUCHARME, pp. 7-8.

[35] Cf. CHAMBRE DES COMMUNES DU CANADA, *Rapport du Comité permanent des Affaires étrangères et du Commerce extérieur,* fascicule No 76, 12 décembre 1990, p. 11.

III. Actions bilatérales

A. conventions bilatérales d'investissement

Dû aux changements historiques d'ordre politique et économique dont est le théatre depuis un an l'Est européen, il est maintenant possible pour le Canada de conclure des conventions de promotion et de protection des investissements avec des pays qui originent de cette région du monde. Le Canada a d'ailleurs conclu, en 1990, deux accords de ce type avec, dans l'ordre chronologique, la Pologne[36] et la Tchécoslovaquie.[37] Comme le Canada a conclu pour la première fois, en 1989, un semblable accord avec l'Union des Républiques Socialistes Soviétiques,[38] le réseau canadien des conventions de promotion et de protection des investissements avec les pays socialistes se met donc progressivement en place.

Par ailleurs, le Canada a conclu, en 1990, un accord d'assurance-investissement avec le Bangladesh (Accord avec le Bangladesh),[39] lequel s'intègre à un réseau déjà constitué de 41 accords.[40] L'Accord avec le Bangladesh constitue, en définitive, une "copie carbone" des accords précédents puisqu'il prévoit: 1⁰ la reconnaissance par le Bangladesh de la subrogation des droits de l'investisseur canadien en faveur de la Société pour l'expansion des exportations (SEE), lorsque celle-ci a versé une indemnité à cet investisseur en vertu d'un contrat d'assurance;[41] 2⁰ qu'un tribunal arbitral ad hoc tranchera tout différend entre le Canada et le Bangladesh qui portera sur l'interprétation et l'application de l'Accord;[42] 3⁰ que l'autorisation préalable du Bangladesh est une condition *sine qua non* pour qu'un investisseur puisse se voir octroyer l'assurance de la SEE;[43] 4⁰ que les fonds en monnaie locale, qu'acquiert la SEE par la subro-

---

[36] Voir *Accord entre le Gouvernement du Canada et le Gouvernement de la République de Pologne sur l'encouragement et la protection réciproque des investissements,* [1990] R.T. Can., N⁰ 43.

[37] Voir *Accord entre le Gouvernement du Canada et la Gouvernement de la République fédérale tchèque et slovaque sur l'encouragement et la protection des investissements,* [1990] R.T. Can., N⁰ 19.

[38] À ce sujet, voir P. RATELLE, "Chronique de droit économique international en 1989. Investissement," (1990) 28 *A.C.D.I.* 449, 453-4.

[39] Voir *Accord entre le Gouvernement du Canada et le Gouvernement de la République du Bangladesh relatif à l'assurance-investissement,* [1990] R.T. Can., N⁰ 4.

[40] Voir MINIST E RE DES AFFAIRES EXTÉRIEURES DU CANADA, *Liste des traités bilatéraux et multilatéraux du Canada en vigueur au 1ᵉʳ janvier 1988* (1989), pp. 1-1 et ss.; et du même ministère, *Bilateral Treaty Actions Taken by Canada in 1989* (1990), pp. 1 et ss.; *Bilateral Treaty Actions Taken by Canada in 1990* (1991), pp. 1 et ss.

[41] Voir Accord avec le Bangladesh, art. I (d) *in fine.*

[42] *Id.,* art. VI.

[43] *Id.,* art. V.

gation, bénéficient d'un traitement similaire à celui dont jouirait l'investisseur s'il les conservait, et qu'ils peuvent être librement utilisés par le Canada pour ses dépenses sur le territoire du Bangladesh;[44] 5⁰ que dans la mesure où la législation du Bangladesh interdit à la SEE d'acquérir les droits sur un bien de son assuré, le gouvernement du Bangladesh permettra à cet investisseur et à la SEE de transférer ces droits à une entité autorisée à le faire conformément à la législation du Bangladesh.[45]

B. CONVENTIONS FISCALES

Le maillage conventionnel canadien en matière fiscale se fait toujours plus imposant à chaque année.[46] Quatre autres conventions ont été conclues par le Canada, en 1990, avec, dans l'ordre chronologique, le Mexique,[47] la Finlande,[48] le Venezuela[49] et la Tchécoslovaquie.[50] À l'instar des conventions antérieures, ces conventions s'inspirent de modèles communs qui ne sont autres que les modèles de convention de l'Organisation de Coopération et de Développement économiques (OCDE).[51] Leur principal objectif est de faciliter les échanges et les investissements internationaux notamment en apportant une certaine clarté et stabilité concernant l'application des dispositions fiscales aux revenus internationaux.[52] Ces

[44] *Id.,* art. IV.
[45] *Id.,* art. II.
[46] Selon des données fournies par le ministère des Affaires extérieures du Canada, plus de 50 conventions ont été jusqu'à maintenant conclues par le Canada. Voir *supra,* note 40.
[47] Voir *Convention entre le Gouvernement du Canada et le Gouvernement des États mexicains sur l'échange de renseignements en matière fiscale,* Mexico, signée le 16 mars 1990.
[48] Voir *Convention entre le Gouvernement du Canada et le Gouvernement de la Finlande en vue d'éviter les doubles impositions et de prévenir l'évasion fiscale en matière d'impôts sur le revenu et sur la fortune,* Helsinski, signée le 28 mai 1990.
[49] Voir *Accord entre le Gouvernement du Canada et le Gouvernement de la République du Vénézuela en vue d'éviter les doubles impositions concernant le transport maritime et aérien,* Caracas, signé le 26 juin 1990.
[50] Voir *Convention entre le Gouvernement du Canada et le Gouvernement de la République fédérale Tchèque et Slovaque en vue d'éviter les doubles impositions et de prévenir l'évasion fiscale en matière d'impôts sur le revenu et sur la fortune,* Prague, signée le 30 août 1990.
[51] Le texte de ces modèles de conventions est reproduit dans OCDE, *Modèle de convention de double imposition concernant le revenu et la fortune* (septembre 1977), 226 p.; *Modèle de convention de double imposition concernant les successions et les donations* (mai 1983), 152 p.; voir aussi D. J. ALBRECHT, "Canadian Foreign Policy and the International Politico-Legal Process," (1983) 21 *A.C.D.I.* 149, 157-161.
[52] Cf. SÉNAT DU CANADA, *Délibérations du Comité sénatorial permanent des Affaires étrangères,* fascicule N⁰ 1, 20 juin 1990, pp. 1:10-1:11.

conventions prévoient ainsi des dispositions permettant d'éviter, d'une part, la double imposition des revenus circulant entre le Canada et les pays signataires et, d'autre part, de prévenir la fraude et l'évasion fiscales.[53] Enfin, elles incluent un mécanisme de règlement des différends ayant trait à leur application et à leur interprétation.[54]

IV. ACTIONS MULTILATÉRALES

A. CYCLE D'URUGUAY DU GATT

L'année 1990 coïncidait avec la phase finale du huitième cycle de négociations commerciales multilatérales de l'Accord général sur les Tarifs douaniers et le Commerce (GATT) amorcé quatre ans plus tôt à Punta del Este, en Uruguay. Un des domaines de négociations de ce Cycle d'"Uruguay" sont les "mesures concernant les investissements et liées au commerce", que l'on appelle plus communément dans le jargon du GATT: les "TRIM."[55]

Afin que soient résolues rapidement les questions en suspens en ce domaine, de manière à ce que les négociations puissent se poursuivre sur la base d'un texte unique, le grand défi que se devaient de surmonter, en 1990, les participants à la table de négociations G-12, table qui concerne les TRIM, était fondamentalement d'aplanir l'opposition entre les pays moins avancés et les pays développés, laquelle perdurait depuis le début du Cycle d'Uruguay.[56] Pratiquement, l'une des décisions politiques essentielles que se

[53] Cf. Convention avec le Mexique, art. 4; Convention avec la Finlande, art. 22 et 25; Convention avec la Tchècoslovaquie, art. 23 et 26; Accord avec le Venezuela, art. 1.

[54] Cf. Convention avec le Mexique, art. 5; Convention avec la Finlande, art. 24; Convention avec la Tchècoslovaquie, art. 25; Accord avec le Vénézuela, art. 5.

[55] Il s'agit de l'abréviation anglaise pour les *Trade-Related Investment Measures*. Les TRIM sont, en gros, des conditions imposées aux investisseurs étrangers par les États d'accueil qui modifient artificiellement les flux des échanges. Ce peut être, par exemple, des prescriptions relatives à la teneur en produits nationaux. À ce sujet, voir A. KLEITZ, "Les entraves à l'investissement et distortions commerciales," (1990) 162 *l'Observateur de l'OCDE* 23-27.

[56] La dynamique interne fondamentale de cette opposition s'explique de la manière suivante. D'une part, les pays moins avancés craignent que l'interdiction ou l'encadrement des TRIM compromette gravement leur souveraineté nationale en matière de politiques d'investissement et nuise aux objectifs de celles-ci. D'autre part, les pays développés, qui sont les plus importants pays d'origine des investissements internationaux, sont, au contraire, favorables à l'idée que les mouvements transfrontières de capitaux soient les plus fluides possible.

devaient de prendre les participants était de savoir si certaines TRIM devaient être expressément interdites parce qu'elles ont intrinsèquement un effet de restriction ou de distortion des échanges, ou si les effets de toutes les TRIM sur le commerce devaient être traités strictement cas par cas.[57] Plus important encore, les participants se devaient de tomber d'accord sur l'éventail des TRIM à considérer.[58]

Malgré les propositions mises de l'avant et la bonne volonté démontrée par les participants à la table G-12, l'opposition entre pays moins avancés et pays développés est demeurée présente à chacune des réunions tenues au cours de 1990.[59] En fait, à mesure que les négociations approchaient de leur conclusion, plus les choses apparaissaient sous un jour sombre. À l'issue de la réunion ministérielle finale du Comité des négociations commerciales, tenue à Bruxelles, en décembre 1990, les participants n'ont d'ailleurs pu que constater que le Cycle d'Uruguay ne pouvait être conclu dans les délais prévus, en particulier concernant les TRIM.[60] Ils ont donc décidé de suspendre les négociations qui se poursuivront à Genève, au début de 1991, sous la responsabilité du Directeur général du GATT, Arthur Dunkel, afin de parvenir notamment à un accord dans le domaine des TRIM.[61]

À l'instar des années précédentes, le Canada n'a présenté, en 1990, aucune communication aux réunions tenues à la table G-12. Toutefois, au mois d'avril, il a mis de l'avant l'idée d'établir une nouvelle organisation mondiale du commerce qui se fonderait sur les droits et obligations découlant fondamentalement du Cycle d'Uruguay et qui aurait notamment pour mandat d'administrer le nouvel accord sur les TRIM.[62]

[57] Cf. *Focus, Bulletin d'information du GATT,* N° 76, 1990, p. 2.

[58] *Ibid.*

[59] Voir *Nouvelles de l'Uruguay Round,* N° 35, 1990, pp. 18-19; *id.,* N° 41, 1990, p. 6.

[60] Voir *Nouvelles de l'Uruguay Round,* N° 44, 1990, p. 1.

[61] Voir *Focus, Bulletin d'information du GATT,* N° 77, 1990, pp. 1 et 2. Ces négociations seront fondées sur le Projet d'Acte final reprenant les résultats des négociations commerciales du Cycle d'Uruguay qu'Arthur Dunkel a présenté au Comité des négociations commerciales lors de la réunion de Bruxelles. Voir document MTN.TNC/W/35/Rev.1 du 3 décembre 1990.

[62] Voir MINISTRE DU COMMERCE EXTÉRIEUR, *Communiqué,* N° 82, 19 avril 1990; *adde* MINISTÈRES DES AFFAIRES EXTÉRIEURES ET DU COMMERCE EXTÉRIEUR DU CANADA, BUREAU DES NÉGOCIATIONS COMMERCIALES MULTILATÉRALES, *Les négociations commerciales multilatérales du Cycle d'Uruguay* (mai 1990), p. 2.

B. RÈGLEMENTATION DE L'OCDE

En 1990, des efforts ont été déployés sur deux fronts afin de rendre plus efficace l'Instrument relatif au Traitement national (ITN).[63] D'une part, les négociations menées par le Comité sur l'investissement et les entreprises multinationales (CIME), lequel est chargé de la mise en oeuvre de l'ITN, pour définir la portée et la teneur d'un nouvel ITN renforcé, ont progressé.[64] À sa réunion annuelle de 1990, le Conseil de l'OCDE a d'ailleurs confirmé la nécessité d'un ITN renforcé.[65] Bien que deux problèmes principaux préoccupant le Canada demeurent toujours en suspens, soit l'application de l'ITN dans les subdivisions territoriales des pays membres et l'octroi du traitement national aux entreprises étrangères pour les mesures touchant la culture, le CIME devrait néanmoins être en mesure de soumettre au Conseil de l'OCDE, avant la réunion annuelle de 1991 de celui-ci, le texte de ce nouvel ITN renforcé.[66] D'autre part, le CIME a réalisé des progrès sensibles afin de renforcer les engagements pris par les pays membres au titre de l'ITN, notamment en compilant et en revisant les listes complètes des dérogations et des exceptions au traitement national qui ont été

---

[63] L'ITN est une décision du Conseil de l'OCDE qui résulte de la Déclaration de 1976 sur l'investissement international et les entreprises multinationales. En gros, l'ITN requiert de tous les pays membres qu'ils fassent bénéficier les entreprises étrangères ou sous contrôle étranger, qui sont déjà établies sur leur territoire, d'un régime non moins favorable que celui qui est appliqué aux entreprises nationales dans les mêmes circonstances, c'est-à-dire bénéficier du traitement national. Le texte de l'ITN est reproduit dans OCDE, *Traitement national des entreprises sous contrôles étrangers* (avril 1985), 82 p.; pour le texte de la Déclaration de 1976, voir de la même organisation, *Le réexamen de 1984 de la déclaration et des décisions de 1976* (juillet 1984), 70 p.

[64] Le nouvel ITN, qui serait proposé par le CIME au Conseil de l'OCDE, aura force obligatoire pour tous les pays membres, y compris leurs subdivisions territoriales, telles que les provinces canadiennes, et comprendrait un "mécanisme de cliquet" destiné à interdire que soient réinstaurées des exceptions, et aux termes duquel les pays s'engageraient à n'opérer aucune discrimination. Voir OCDE, *Activités de l'OCDE 1990* (1991), p. 33.

[65] *Id.*, p. 130.

[66] *Id.*, p. 33. Bien que la position du Canada concernant ce nouvel ITN n'ait pas été encore rendue publique, des informations obtenues du ministère des Affaires extérieures et de la Délégation permanente du Canada auprès de l'OCDE sont à l'effet que le Canada devrait formuler une réserve de type "fédérale" et recourir à une réserve lui permettant de promouvoir et de préserver son identité culturelle. Dans ce dernier cas, ceci signifierait pratiquement que le Canada pourrait prendre de nouvelles mesures dans le domaine culturel qui pourraient favoriser les entreprises canadiennes au détriment des entreprises étrangères, ce à quoi se seraient opposé les États-Unis.

préparées par eux.[67]

Par ailleurs, selon des informations obtenues du ministère des Affaires extérieures et de la Délégation permanente du Canada auprès de l'OCDE, le Conseil de l'OCDE aurait considéré dans un rapport confidentiel, que les obligations auxquelles est assujetti le Canada dans le cadre de l'ALÉ, notamment en ce qui concerne les seuils d'examen des investissements américains et les règles de propriété de certaines institutions financières, contrevenaient au Code de libération des mouvements de capitaux auquel est partie le Canada.[68] Une des caractéristiques essentielles de ce Code est le principe de non discrimination.[69] En pratique, ce principe signifie que les mesures de libération des mouvements de capitaux, qui sont contenues dans l'ALÉ, et dont le Canada a fait bénéficier les États-Unis, doivent être étendues également à tous les autres pays membres qui sont parties à ce Code.

C. ANNONCE DE DISCUSSIONS POUR UN ACCORD DE LIBRE-ÉCHANGE NORD-
AMÉRICAIN

Le ministre canadien du Commerce extérieur a annoncé, en septembre 1990, la décision du Canada de participer avec le Mexique et les États-Unis à des discussions visant à établir les bases d'éventuelles négociations officielles qui mèneront à la conclusion d'un accord de libre-échange entre eux.[70] Bien que les éléments, la portée et les modalités de ces négociations ne soient pas encore établis, on sait d'ores et déjà que cet accord de libre-échange nord-américain (ALÉNA) comprendra non seulement des règles

---

[67] *Ibid.*

[68] Ce Code vient compléter et renforcer un certain nombre d'instruments visant la libéralisation de la vie économique internationale, tels que le Code de l'OCDE portant sur la libération des opérations invisibles courantes, le GATT et les Statuts du Fonds monétaire international (FMI). En simplifiant, on peut dire que ce Code a pour objectif final d'obtenir que les résidents des différents pays membres puissent opérer entre eux des transactions aussi librement que les résidents d'un seul et même pays membre. Le texte de ce Code est reproduit dans OCDE, *Code sur la libération des mouvements de capitaux* (décembre 1990), 144 p.

[69] Cf. OCDE, *Introduction aux code de l'OCDE* (juin 1987), pp. 13-14.

[70] Voir MINISTRE DU COMMERCE EXTÉRIEUR, *Communiqué,* N° 114, 24 septembre 1990. Le marché qu'il régira sera le plus grand du monde avec un PIB de 6,300 milliards de dollars américains et une population de 360 millions d'habitants, surpassant celui de la Communauté économique européenne (CEE) qui a un PIB de 4,800 milliards de dollars américains et un population de 320 millions d'habitants. Cf. M. BYFIELD, "Crafting the World's Biggest Trade Bloc: Mexico, the U.S. and Canada," (1991) 18 *Alberta Western Report* 32-33.

en matière de biens et services, mais aussi des règles en matière d'investissement et un mécanisme de règlement des différends.[71]

Bien que le milieu canadien des affaires ait bien accueilli, dans son ensemble, la création d'une zone de libre-échange nord-américaine,[72] l'unanimité n'est pas acquise pour autant au Canada. Le Mexique n'est pas un important pays d'accueil des investissements canadiens.[73] Néanmoins, certains intervenants, notamment des partis politiques et des centrales syndicales, ont craint que la mise en place d'un ALÉNA jointe à d'autres facteurs, tels que l'existence de la zone franche mexicaine dite des "Maquiladoras,"[74] la nouvelle réglementation mexicaine des investissements étrangers qui est plus favorable que jamais à ceux-ci[75] et, finalement, les coûts de la main-d'oeuvre mexicaine qui sont nettement inférieurs à ceux qui prévalent au Canada,[76] n'amènent de nombreuses sociétés commerciales canadiennes et étrangères, en particulier américaines, non seulement à investir au Mexique plutôt qu'au Canada, mais aussi à déménager leurs usines installées sur le territoire canadien, entraînant ainsi la fermeture de celles-ci et des pertes d'emplois importantes au Canada.[77] En outre, au dire même du ministre canadien du Commerce extérieur, rien n'exclut que les négotia-

---

[71] Voir la déclaration du représentant du Canada aux discussions entourant cet ALÉNA dans CHAMBRE DES COMMUNES DU CANADA, *op. cit. supra*, note 35, p. 8.

[72] Cf. notamment "Le Canada doit être présent aux négociations États-Unis — Mexique," dans CONSEIL DU PATRONAT DU QUÉBEC, *Communiqué*, 27 août 1990.

[73] En 1989, le Mexique se classait au 19ᵉ rang des pays d'accueil des investissements canadiens n'accueillant environ que deux pour cent de ceux-ci. Cf. STATISTIQUE CANADA, *op. cit., supra*, note 3, pp. 50 et 60.

[74] À ce sujet, voir S. WARD et al., "Maquiladoras 'as the Investor Sees It'," (1990) 2 *Gestion 2000* 83-103.

[75] À ce sujet, voir D. J. KAYE, "Recent Developments. Mexico: Liberalizing Foreign Investment," (1990) 4 *Temple Int'l & Comp. L.J.* 79-90.

[76] À ce sujet, voir G. SCHOEPPLE et J. F. PEREZ-LOPEZ, "Export Assembly Operations in Mexico and the Caribbean," (1989) 31 *Interamerican Studies and World Affairs* 131-161.

[77] Pour connaître la position des Parti libéral et Nouveau parti démocratique fédéraux ainsi que du Congrès du travail du Canada et de la *United Radio and Machine Workers of Canada*, voir CHAMBRE DES COMMUNES DU CANADA, *op. cit. supra*, note 35, pp. 11, 29-37. Pour connaître la position du gouvernement néo-démocrate de l'Ontario, voir J. McNISH, "Rae Warns US of Free-Trade Deal: Ontario's NDP Government May Have a Little Room to Move," in *The Globe and Mail*, 31 octobre 1990, p. B5.

tions qui entoureront cet ALÉNA n'entraînent la réouverture de l'ALÉ,[78] avec les dangers que cela comporte pour certains.[79]

Bien que les négociations officielles n'aient pas encore commencé, des discussions ont été amorcées, le 18 octobre 1990, à Houston, au Texas, entre le représentant du Canada à ces discussions et ses homologues américain et mexicain.[80] Le calendrier des négociations officielles devrait être fonction de la procédure législative aux États-Unis et de l'urgence avec laquelle ceux-ci et le Mexique chercheront à conclure cet ALÉNA.[81]

---

[78] Voir CHAMBRE DES COMMUNES DU CANADA, *op. cit. supra,* note 35, pp. 12-13.

[79] Selon Gordon Ritchie, notamment, ancien négociateur en chef adjoint du Canada pour l'ALÉ, des pourparlers tripartites donneraient la possibilité aux États-Unis de revenir à la charge sur de nombreuses questions qui n'ont pas été réglées à leur satisfaction lors des négociations entourant l'ALÉ, telles que les industries culturelles qui, en vertu de l'article 2005 de l'ALÉ, ne sont pas assujetties aux règles d'investissement qui sont contenues dans cet accord. Cf. STRATEGICO INC., ''Le libre-échange tripartite et l'intérêt canadien,'' (1991) 4 *Information de la Société international économique — Canada* 3, 7.

[80] Cf. SÉNAT DU CANADA, *Délibérations du Comité sénatorial permanent des Affaires étrangères,* fasicule N° 33, 23 octobre 1990, p. 33:5.

[81] Cf. SÉNAT DU CANADA, *Rapport du Comité sénatorial permanent des Affaires étrangères,* fasicule N° 34, 20 novembre 1990, pp. 69 et ss.

Canadian Practice in International Law/ La pratique canadienne en matière de droit international public At the Department of External Affairs in 1990-91 / Au ministère des Affaires extérieures en 1990-91

compiled by/préparé par

BARRY MAWHINNEY*

INTERNATIONAL ECONOMIC .LAW

Canada's Legal Obligations in International Commodity Bodies

In a memorandum dated August 16, 1991, the Legal Bureau wrote:

Canada is under treaty obligations, binding at public international law, to pay its assessed contribution towards the administrative expenses of the International Wheat Council, the International Tropical Timber Organization, the International Customs Bureau, and the OECD Steel Committee. Although the legal situation is not clear, we believe that Canada is under a constructive (but not treaty) legal obligation at public international law to the other members to pay its assessed contribution towards the administrative expenses of the International Lead and Zinc Study Group, the International Rubber Study Group and the Inter-

---

* Barry Mawhinney, Legal Adviser, Department of External Affairs, Ottawa. The extracts from official correspondence contained in this survey have been made available by courtesy of the Department of External Affairs. Material appearing in the House of Commons Debates is not included. Some of the correspondence from which extracts are given was provided for the general guidance of the enquirer in relation to specific facts which are often not described in full in the extracts contained in this compilation. The statements of law and practice should not necessarily be regarded as a definitive general statement by the Department of External Affairs of that law or practice.

national Nickel Study Group. In addition, under the laws of the host country for each of these three Study Groups, Canada may be under a contractual or quasi-contractual legal obligation to the organization itself to pay its assessed contribution towards administrative expenses. . . .

Of course, Canada is under no legal obligation to join or to remain a member of any international organization. To address Canada's legal obligations at that level of generality would be meaningless, and consequently we will not examine the provisions for withdrawal from the organizations or the provisions for amending or renewing their constitutive instruments. We would note, however, that the instruments establishing many commodity organizations have definite terms and must, therefore, be renewed or renegotiated periodically.

Although a legal obligation to contribute to administrative expenses of an international commodity organization usually would exist under public international law, it could exist under a system of domestic law, such as the law of the country where the commodity organization has its headquarters. The character of an obligation under domestic law would be different qualitatively from an obligation under public international law. However, if one assumes that it is the policy of the Government of Canada to respect its legal obligations, the effect would be the same. Canada would be committed in law to paying its share of administrative expenses.

The Foreign Extraterritorial Measures Act and the Mack Amendment

In an opinion dated September 18, 1991, the Legal Bureau wrote:

On October 31, 1991, the Attorney General for Canada, with the concurrence of the SSEA, issued the first ever blocking order under the Foreign Extraterritorial Measures Act (FEMA) to counteract the provisions of the Mack Amendment that formed part of the U.S. Export Administration Re-authorization Bill of 1990. In the end, President Bush vetoed the measure containing the Mack Amendment. Nevertheless, the Mack Amendment provides a useful example of the different approaches to jurisdictional issues adopted by the U.S. compared with Canada. Since the Mack Amendment has been subsequently attached to two further Senate bills, it also promises to remain a significant issue of the Canada/U.S. bilateral agenda for the foreseeable future. . . .

From 1975 to passage of the Mack Amendment by the U.S. Congress in 1990, U.S. law focused directly on the subsidiary itself, although regulatory language provided a clear signal that licences would be granted if transactions fell within particular categories. In fact, serious incidents arising from the extraterritorial application of the CACRs [U.S. Cuban Assets Control Regulations] declined during this period.

The Mack Amendment represented an aggravation of the impact of the post-1975 U.S. rule, although not literally an extension of its jurisdictional reach. By prohibiting the issuance of licenses while at the same time requiring them, the Mack Amendment prevented the case by case negotiation of incidents which enabled licenses to be issued even though the Canadian and U.S. governments continued to disagree over the principles that underlay each country's exercise of jurisdiction over subsidiaries.

The U.S. bases its legal position on the relatively uncontroversial international law principles for exerting jurisdiction in which it is recognized that states may exercise control over persons on the basis of territory and nationality. However, the provisions of the post-1975 U.S. CACRs and the Mack Amendment are to many countries, including Canada, an unacceptable extension of these basic principles in that both the CACRs and Mack extend the nationality principle to enable U.S. law to proscribe conduct by not only U.S. citizens, but as well any corporations, wherever organized, that are owned and controlled by such persons.

The Canadian position, shared by almost all other western countries, rejects the contention that the nationality principle can be so extended to enable a state to regulate the conduct of corporations organized in foreign states on the basis of the ownership or control of their citizens. From the Canadian perspective, these corporations, by the act of incorporation in Canada, are "nationals" of Canada. The fact that investment enabling such companies to be created came from outside the jurisdiction cannot act as a basis for the laws of that country to follow them over the border.

As such, the Canadian position avoids the balancing tests utilized by the U.S. in cases where they take the position that they exercise a concurrent jurisdiction over subsidiaries with the territorial state.

To strengthen the ability of the Canadian government to combat this and other unacceptable U.S. assertions of extraterritorial jurisdiction, the Canadian Parliament passed the FEMA in 1984. It provides to the government a legislative basis to counteract the extraterritorial assertion of jurisdiction by foreign law in a number of instances, in particular, for discovery of documents, anti-trust litigation and the application of foreign laws that purport to regulate conduct in Canada. At the time of passage, it was made clear by the government that the FEMA represented a weapon of last resort since the effect of blocking orders is to place persons in the position of conflicting requirements between any Canadian order and the extraterritorial order of the foreign state. Given that the U.S. already exercised an unacceptable jurisdiction to Canada that offended international law and given that the Mack Amendment prevented any political solution where the U.S. CACRs collided with Canadian law and trade policy, the adoption of the Mack Amendment was a classic case justifying the usage of the FEMA.

Access to U.S. Market for Canadian Meat

In a memorandum dated December 21, 1990, the Legal Bureau wrote:

it remains possible for the U.S. to put restrictions on Canadian beef exports to the U.S. in certain circumstances including when:
  (i) the conditions of Article 704(2) of the FTA (Free Trade Agreement) are met,
  (ii) the conditions of global emergency action (safeguards) under Article 1102 are met.
. . . Article 704(1) prohibits the introduction or maintenance of any quantitative restriction or any measure having equivalent effect except as otherwise provided in this Agreement. Thus, the prohibition on quantitative or equivalent restrictions is expressly made subject to other provisions of the FTA. Any other provision of the FTA that permits a quantitative or equivalent restriction that does not, in turn, exempt meat goods thereby prevails over Article 704.
  The most immediate example of the FTA "providing otherwise" is contained in Article 704(2) which permits the imposition of import restrictions against Canada in circumstances where the U.S. had imposed a quantitative restriction against third countries and Canada had not taken equivalent action — only to the extent and for such period of time as is "sufficient to prevent frustration of the action taken on imports of the meat good from third countries."
  As for safeguard actions pursuant to Chapter 11 of the FTA, there is no exemption in Chapter 11 for meat products. We have examined the U.S. domestic law implementing the emergency global actions in Chapter 1102 carefully and have not found any exception for meat products. Thus, we would conclude that provided all the conditions for FTA Chapter 1102 action are met, a safeguard action which could include a quantitative restriction can still theoretically be taken by the U.S. against meat imports from Canada. For the U.S. to impose import restrictions on Canadian meat pursuant to Article 1102, it would have to find that imports from Canada are greater than 5-10 per cent and are "contributing importantly" to the serious injury or threat thereof caused by meat imports. Furthermore, the process for imposing a safeguard action would appear, from our reading of the U.S. legislation, to be much more onerous than the imposition of a quota pursuant to the Meat Import Act.
  In the elements text that preceded the legal text of the FTA, the intention of the parties in drafting Article 704 is stated as follows:

Both Parties have agreed to exempt each other from their respective Meat Import Laws. Rules of origin and meat inspection requirements will prevent trans-shipment through either Party from third countries. The agreement language will also prevent either Party from displacing domestic meat with third countries' meat imports in order to increase exports to the other Party.''

The only amendments to U.S. law made to implement Article 704, were made to the Meat Inspection Act of 1979 to delete Canada from the calculation of the quantity of meat articles that may be imported without triggering an import quota under the Act as required under Article 704(1). It also provides authority for the President to impose import restrictions on Canadian meat articles under the limited circumstances envisaged in Article 704(2). No other exemptions in U.S. domestic law were made to exempt Canadian meat from other U.S. trade laws.

In the 1989 Edition of ''Overview and Compilation of U.S. Trade Statutes'' prepared for the Committee on Ways and Means of the U.S. House of Representatives, the U.S. government provides its interpretation of Article 704 as follows:

> In the free trade agreement that the United States and Canada signed in January 1988, the two governments agreed to exempt each other from import quotas applied *under their respective meat import laws.* (emphasis added)

A footnote to this entry goes on to explain:

> U.S. meat producers may still petition the U.S. International Trade Commission to impose countervailing duties on meat imports from Canada if they think that subsidized imports are injuring the U.S. industry.

This extract emphasizes the U.S. view, supported by the record of the negotiating history, that the prohibition on import restrictions contained in Article 704 is limited to those previously imposed under the Meat Import Act. Restrictions pursuant to other provisions of the FTA, remain permissible as do restrictions to prevent the frustration of VRAs or quotas against third countries.

GATT Panel on Beer

In a memorandum dated May 16, 1991, the Legal Bureau wrote:

Technically, the consistency of provincial measures with the GATT is a different issue from Canada's obligations once a provincial inconsistency is found. The 1988 Panel made this distinction in finding certain provincial measures inconsistent with the GATT and then giving Canada time to fulfil its obligation to take reasonable measures. For Canada to argue that provincial measures were not inconsistent with the GATT because they qualify under the PPA [Protocol of Provisional Application], does not necessarily recognize that GATT obligations are directly applicable to the provinces, but recognizes that their practices can and have been considered for consistency with the GATT and therefore should benefit from PPA cover if it is applicable. In any case, it is clear that GATT thinking (Gold Coins, Liquor Boards panels; MTN discussions) has moved beyond the point where one could argue that the *only* obligation of a federal state is to take reasonable measures rather than to account for inconsistent measures of sub-national units through compensation. If Canada is in fact accountable for the GATT consistency of provincial measures it may be idle to engage in debate on whether the GATT is directly applicable to provincial measures.

No GATT panel has examined the question of the applicability of the PPA to provincial law, so there is no definitive answer. An answer can only be deduced from the scholarly writings on this issue and a discussion of the intent and scope of the PPA.

There is very little comment on the applicability of the PPA to provincial laws by Canadian authors. Jon Johnson states: "One commentator suggests that "local legislation 'existing' at the time the GATT was completed was not within the exception." (The Free Trade Agreement: A Comprehensive Guide, page 51). The commentator he is referring to is John Jackson whose 1969 book remains the main source of discussion on this issue. Other authors (American) have either not commented on the issue or cite Jackson's views without substantive comment. . . .

Jackson's conclusion, to which Johnson refers, would suggest that the PPA does not apply to any sub-national unit. However, he reaches this conclusion after a discussion that relates the problem to the U.S. system in which he says the federal executive authority to implement treaties can override local legislation. Therefore if the purpose of the PPA was to require a country to apply the GATT to the fullest extent of its executive power and its executive power extends to override state law, then the PPA cannot be invoked to justify inconsistent state law. By negative implication, this suggests that in a different federal state where the "federal executive authority" cannot override provincial legislation, the PPA could apply to justify inconsistent sub-national law.

Applying this reasoning to Canada, a panel would probably inquire about what the equivalent in Canada is to the U.S. federal executive authority. Technically, the Canadian executive branch consists of the Governor-General, the cabinet (including the prime minister) and the Privy Council. If we were to take a literal view of Jackson's comment, then the federal executive could not override provincial jurisdiction unless there were an appropriate (and constitutionally valid) regulation making power authorized by statute. No such power existed in 1947.

However, given GATT panels' predilection to construe the PPA very narrowly, we question whether this technical assertion will be sufficient to satisfy the panel. More probable in our view will be further exploratory questions from the panel trying to translate Jackson's views more completely into the Canadian context. . . .

Legal Status of GATT Decisions

In a memorandum dated July 6, 1990, the Legal Bureau wrote:

By way of comparison, the legal status of amendments or additions to the GATT that are made pursuant to the amending procedure in Article XXX of the GATT is clear. Once the relevant number (which depends on the Article amended) of Contracting Parties (CPs) accept the amendment it is in effect in respect of those Contracting Parties that have accepted it. Until that time, the amendment is not legally in effect. While this situation is clear, it is also time consuming and rather rigid.

International legal obligations do not find their source in treaties alone. The traditional sources of international law as listed in Article 38 of the Statute of the International Court of Justice, are as follows:

(a) international conventions, whether general or particular, establishing rules expressly recognized by the contesting States;
(b) international custom, as evidence of a general practice accepted as law;
(c) the general principles of law recognized by civilized nations;
(d) subject to the provisions of Article 59, judicial decisions and the teachings of the most highly qualified publicists of the various nations, as subsidiary means for the determination of the rules of law.

If decisions, declarations, understandings adopted by the GATT CPs can be fitted into any of the above categories, they could be said to be sources of international law and likely constitute legally binding obligations. The reason for our comment that such decisions are legally ambiguous relates to the lack of a "bright line test" by which one can easily fit them into one of the above categories. In the event that one CP sought to rely on a decision, declaration or understanding and another CP claimed that it did not create legally binding obligations, a complex series of considerations would have to be weighed to resolve the question. Considering each of the 4 categories listed above in relation to GATT decisions of the CPs (whatever title they may be given — understanding, declaration, decision) the following factors would be relevant.

I. Re (a) — Conventions (including the GATT itself)

The GATT does not expressly provide for, nor comment on, the legal status of decisions adopted by the CPs. Article XXV of the GATT does envisage meetings of the CPs to facilitate the operation and further the objectives of the GATT. To the extent that there is much discussion of the legal basis for decisions of the CPs, it is this provision of the GATT that is generally referred to. See, for example, the Note by the Secretariat (MTN.GNG/NG7/W/61) on the legal procedures for changing the applicable date in Article II:1 (b) of the GATT. Article XXV does not on its face permit the CPs to amend the GATT by a decision of the CPs. Given that the GATT contains an express provision in Article XXX for amending the GATT, a reasonable interpretation of Article XXV would not support it being used to amend the GATT. In practice, however, we understand that it has been used to justify decisions such as the "Enabling Clause" and this subsequent practice raises questions as to the scope and interpretation to be given to Article XXV. In this regard, Article 31 of the Vienna Convention on the Law of Treaties provides some guidance.

Article 31(3)(a) and (b) of the Vienna Convention on the Law of Treaties provide as follows:

> There shall be taken into account together with the context:
> (a) any agreement between the parties regarding the interpretation of the treaty or the application of its provisions;
> (b) any subsequent practice in the application of the treaty which establishes the agreement of the parties regarding its interpretation.

One could characterize a decision of the CPs (particularly a decision that takes the form of an interpretive note), provided it was reached by consensus, as an agreement between the parties within the context of Article 31 (3) (a) of the Vienna Convention. One could argue that a decision of the CPs, or for that matter any application of GATT procedures or disciplines, if it is consistently applied by all GATT CPs, constitutes a subsequent practice that should be used to interpret the meaning of provisions of the GATT. . . .

Reliance on Article 31 of the Vienna Convention is justifiable, in our opinion, for a GATT Decision that is an elaboration of the meaning of an Article or that relates to a minor technical matter. If the decision was broader in scope, the question would arise as to whether it is merely an interpretation or goes further and actually modifies the terms of the treaty. It may be difficult at times to determine with certainty whether a particular decision merely interprets the GATT or goes further and amends it.

An international arbitral award made in 1963 concerning the interpretation of the United States/France Air Service Agreement of 1946, did consider that a consistent course of conduct could be taken into account as a source of subsequent modification (ie, not just an interpretation) of the terms of a treaty. An approach such as this should be tempered with caution, since too liberal an acceptance of subsequent conduct modifying a treaty would diminish the purpose of the certainties of legal obligation that treaty law and practice attempt to achieve, including the safeguards that are built into a formal amending procedure.

The success of an argument that a GATT Council decision of the CPs interprets or modifies the GATT in a manner that is legally binding will depend on factors such as the manner in which the decision was adopted and the scope of the decision. If a decision is reached by a vote rather than by consensus, it is more difficult to argue credibly that a subsequent agreement has been reached or that subsequent practice is common and consistent. Interpretive notes are more likely to find quick acceptance as binding than a decision that alters substantive obligations in a major fashion.

II. Re (b) — Customary International Law

Customary international law in classical terms was determined by evidence of the "customs and usages of civilized nations." It is sometimes referred to as state practice. . . In GATT terms, one might argue that the practice of CPs has been to abide by Decisions of the CPs (at least as far as interpretive notes, understandings and declarations are concerned) , thus evincing an acceptance of the binding character of at least some types of Decisions of the CPs. We would highlight, however, that customary international law usually refers to substantive rules of law and generally does not intervene in procedural issues related to the practice of states under a particular Convention.

III. Re (c) — General Principles of Law Recognized by Civilized Nations

This is generally considered to relate to broad principles that cut across a number of substantive areas, such as reciprocity and proportionality. Depending on the actual content of a decision of the GATT CPs we could envisage circumstances when one could argue that it is legally binding as a reflection of a general principle of international law. For example, a decision that stated that retaliation must be proportionate to the injury suffered might fall into this category.

IV. Re (d) — Judicial Decisions and Legal Scholars

To the extent that GATT Panels rely on interpretive notes or other matters that have been concluded by Decision of the GATT CPs, the legalcharacter of the Decision is enhanced. Similarly, the views of eminent scholars on the legal character of a particular GATT Council decision or indeed GATT Council decisions in general, can contribute to its binding character. Incidentally, in this regard, Jackson's views, including his concerns about too broad an interpretation of Article XXV of the GATT, may be cited as a source of international law.

V. Conclusions

Some might argue that it is inappropriate to measure GATT obligations solely against the traditional standards of the sources of international law. Rather than attempt as we have done above, to fit decisions of GATT CPs within or to analogize them into one of the traditional sources, perhaps there is room to argue that GATT practice and theology supports the position that at least certain of the agreements that are reached after detailed tariff round negotiations can become binding obligations through adoption by Decisions of the CPs. Indeed, such a view would have some credibility in international legal circles since some legal scholars argue that modern realities dictate that decisions or recommendations of specialized agencies that relate to their specific field of competence, should be considered to create legal obligations. . . . Whether the scope of a specific agreement reached in the Uruguay Round would qualify under this approach remains to be determined. We do not consider that this approach holds any merit for an agreement that would impose major new substantive obligations on states — such as a services agreement. It might be considered for a more detailed elaboration of an already existing obligation.

Of course, if states were to accept the notion that decisions of the GATT are legally binding per se, more attention might be paid to expressing objections to Council decisions rather than passively allowing them to be adopted. Ideally, if CPs want the flexibility of adopting certain of the results of tariff rounds by decisions of the CP's, then they should seriously consider enshrining this in the GATT in a manner similar to the Convention on the Organization of the OECD, Article 5(a) of which permits the OECD to take decisions "which, unless otherwise provided, shall be binding on all Members." This puts the onus on states to decide at the time a decision is made whether it is prepared to accept the decision as legally binding.

Discussion of the legal status of decisions of the CPs reached after lengthy discussions in the Uruguay or future rounds should ensure that the special character of the GATT, the lengthy negotiating process and the positive impact on commercial transactions of some of the understandings that might be reached is taken into account. At the same time, these considerations must be carefully balanced against the need for legal certainty that is greatly enhanced by agreements being translated into treaty form.

It is for these reasons that we would hesitate to dismiss any and all decisions of the CPs as non-legally binding. Nor would we want to categorically state that all of them are legally binding. The nature and scope of the decision, the degree of consensus, the policy reasons for or against considering a decision as legally binding would all have a bearing, hence the comment in our memorandum under reference that the legal status of decisions, understandings and declarations in the GATT is ambiguous.

Relationship between FTA and Any Agreement on Services in Uruguay Round

In a memorandum dated June 29, 1990, the Legal Bureau wrote:

The Free Trade Agreement (FTA) makes provision in Article 104 for the relationship between it and pre-existing bilateral and multilateral agreements between Canada and the United States. Basically it affirms the rights under agreements in force before January 1, 1989 and provides that in the event of any inconsistency between the FTA and a pre-existing agreement, the FTA is to take precedence.

The FTA does not provide for its relation to subsequent bilateral or multilateral agreements. The relevant principle of international law is contained in the Vienna Convention on the Law of Treaties, Article 30 (3), which provides:

When all the parties to the earlier treaty are parties also to the later treaty but the earlier treaty is not terminated or suspended in operation under article 59, the earlier treaty applies only to the extent that its provisions are compatible with those of the later treaty.

Therefore, in the absence of an express treaty provision regarding priority, as between parties to a treaty who become parties to a later, inconsistent, treaty, the earlier treaty will apply only where its provisions are not incompatible with the later treaty.

Whether the subsequent treaty relates to the same subject matter and whether there is an inconsistency between the provisions

will normally be construed strictly. If it is possible to interpret both the earlier and later treaties in a consistent fashion, there will be a tendency to do so. A later multilateral treaty that does not go as far as a bilateral treaty is not incompatible and therefore does not implicitly substitute the lesser standards of a later multilateral agreement between the bilateral treaty partners. If it goes further in some respect, then the FTA could be displaced by the later treaty in that regard. If a multilateral agreement on services contains an MFN obligation, and no implied or express exception for free trade areas, then Canada's services sector obligations to the United States under the FTA would extend to all states party to the later treaty. However, Canada's rights vis-à-vis parties other than the United States might not be similarly extended because MFN is not by its nature a reciprocal obligation.

In addition, the general legal principle that the specific takes precedence over the general could result, in certain circumstances, in some provisions of a more specific prior treaty being upheld over a general subsequent treaty. It is a question of interpretation in each case whether this principle is relevant.

Retaliation and Cross-Retaliation

In a memorandum dated September 26, 1990, the Legal Bureau wrote:

There is a customary legal right to retaliate, proportionately, for the failure of one party to a treaty to meet its international obligations. This can involve suspension of an obligation owed under a different treaty than that originally breached. Although there could be arguments to the contrary, our view is that the right to retaliate unilaterally by suspending GATT obligations for a breach of the GATT has been displaced (in all but the most exceptional circumstances) by the dispute settlement mechanism: council must authorize retaliation. It does not have the right to do so in respect of violations of treaties other than the General Agreement. It could be argued, again by reference to customary principles, that a party to another agreement (e.g., TRIPS, services) could suspend its obligations under such agreement in retaliation for breach of the GATT, or another trade treaty, unless those agreements expressly provide otherwise.

What this means is that MTN negotiators should not assume that cross-retaliation is impermissible or even that a reference to a dispute settlement procedure necessarily disciplines the right of unilateral retaliation in appropriate circumstances. Rather, there are good legal reasons supporting what is clearly a negotiating objective — to obtain a specific commitment eschewing unilateral retaliation and to specify clearly when and in what circumstances cross-retaliation is to be permitted...

Retaliation under the GATS: Possible Problems

In a memorandum dated May 23, 1991, the Legal Bureau wrote:

Unlike the GATT, retaliation in the GATS [General Agreement on Trade in Services] could potentially involve retaliation against the nationals of other GATS Parties, be they natural or juridical persons, resident in the territory of the Party taking the retaliatory action.

The questions that arise are to what extent, if any, will retaliation under the GATS be affected by the rules of customary international law regarding the protection of aliens, other relevant international agreements, in particular bilateral "friendship, commerce and navigation" and "investment protection" agreements, and the operation of the domestic laws of the Parties to the GATS...

The GATS will prevail over conflicting rules of customary international law and the provisions of pre-existing agreements that protect the rights of aliens. However, unless it is clearly stipulated in the GATS that its provisions will prevail in the case of conflict with the provisions of subsequent agreements, then the provisions of these subsequent agreements will prevail.

In the case where a Party has given investment guarantees to the national of another Party for the latter's investment in the former's territory, particularly if the investment guarantee agreement is subject to arbitration under the International Convention for the Settlement of Investment Disputes, then it will not be practical for the host Party to retaliate against the guaranteed investment.

If retaliation against resident foreign service providers is to be pursued as a possible option under the GATS, Canada and other GATS Parties will have to determine to what extent their constitutional laws protect the resident nationals of other Parties and to what extent such laws are capable of being overridden by legislation implementing their GATS obligations.

In general it will be more feasible for a GATS Party to retaliate against the service providers of another GATS Party that sell or wish to sell services to its consumers but who are not yet resident in its territory than against those service providers who are resident in its territory....

USE OF FORCE

Droit des Réclamations Internationales

Dans une opinion du 3 juin 1991, le Bureau juridique a écrit:

La doctrine classique de droit international coutumier de "l'état de guerre" (state of war), quoique toujours valide, n'a plus l'importance qu'elle a déjà eu parce qu'elle n'est plus utilisée. Pour éviter d'être soumis aux implications juridiques et politiques de la guerre, les États parlent aujourd'hui d'agressions, d'hostilités ou d'attaques armées. La signification du mot "guerre" est des plus incertaine de nos jours. Un pays sera responsable des dommages causés par la guerre à la condition évidente qu'il y ait effectivement un état de guerre. Autrement, l'État n'encourra pour ses fautes que sa responsabilité de droit international coutumier, sans que ni le droit de la guerre coutumier ni le droit des réclamations de guerre ne soient invoqués.

Peut-on considérer l'application par les pays membres des Nations-Unies des résolutions du Conseil de sécurité comme un "état de guerre"? D'abord, la définition de la guerre que donne le droit international exige la présence d'au moins deux États, et les Nations Unies n'en sont pas un. Mais surtout, on ne peut, selon la majorité des auteurs, identifier la notion technique de la guerre aux actions entreprises au nom de la communauté internationale dans l'intérêt commun. De pareilles actions ont des objectifs limités. De plus, la Charte des Nations Unies affecte grandement l'application du droit de la neutralité qui s'applique normalement en temps de guerre. Par contre, sur le plan strictement juridique, la situation de l'action contre l'Irak n'est pas aussi claire. Le contrôle effectif de la force des Nations Unies ne relevait pas de l'ONU, et ce critère est important pour déterminer les responsabilitées de chacun des belligérants lorsque les forces des Nations Unies sont en cause. La résolution 678 (1990) du Conseil de sécurité de l'ONU *autorise* les États membres à prendre les mesures nécéssaires pour appliquer les résolutions précédentes qui demandaient le retrait de l'Irak du Koweïit. . . .

Le principe selon lequel l'action concertée des États en application des résolutions des Nation-Unies ne constitue pas un état de guerre prédomine, mais il n'est pas absolu. En effet, les circonstances de chaque conflit peuvent rapprocher celui-ci de la "guerre." C'est par exemple le cas quand un seul pays encourage et obtient l'adoption de résolutions auxquelles il est à peu près seul à répondre, comme lors de l'intervention américaine en Corée en 1950. C'est aussi le cas lorsque les Nations-Unies s'en prennent à un État souverain et membre de l'ONU, à l'encontre de groupes désorganisés comme au Congo en 1960. Le fait que les belligérants de la guerre de Corée (UN, Corée du Nord et Chine) aient reconnu officiellement l'application de la convention de Genève de 1949 sur les prisonniers de guerre et qu'aucun d'eux n'ait nié l'applicabilité du droit coutumier de la guerre démontre que la distinction entre état de guerre et application des résolutions des Nations-Unies est très théorique.

Il existe donc une certaine incertitude sur la relation juridique entre les belligérants, ou du moins sur la relation entre l'État visé par l'action des Nations Unies et les États concrétisant cette action pour les Nations

Unies. Cela a des conséquences directes sur les sources du droit des réclamations suite à ces conflits. En effet, les États "vainqueurs" à travers l'action des Nations Unies font face à peu de restrictions sur la façon d'établir le système de réclamations d'après conflit et en même temps toutes les possibilités juridiques sont justifiables. C'est surtout la règle éternelle du Gaulois Brennus, *vae victis,* qui risque alors de s'appliquer. . . .

Le droit susceptible de s'appliquer à des réclamations internationales en temps de guerre peut varier selon la formule adoptée pour l'adjudication de ces réclamations. Il est donc important de prévoir immédiatement les différentes possibilités. . . .

Les Nations Unies avaient le choix entre trois possibilités quant à l'administration des réclamations qui seront faites contre l'Irak.

(a) Une commission des réclamations de guerre

La première possibilité suit la méthode utilisée lors de la deuxième guerre mondiale. À cette époque, l'Acte final de la Conférence de Paris sur les réparation allemandes (AFCPRA) avait créé l'Agence interalliée des réparations (AIR). Dix-hui⁺ États en faisaient partie. Cette agence devait répartir les réparations allemandes parmi les États membres en fonction d'un pourcentage indiqué dans l'AFCPRA. Chaque pays membre était ensuite chargé de redistribuer à ses citoyens les sommes ainsi recouvrées, à l'aide d'organismes nationaux. C'est la Commission des réclamations de guerre (CRG) qui, au Canada, eut cette responsabilité. La CRG appliqua un code d'adjudication établi par règlement selon le rapport d'un commissaire consultatif sur les réclamations de guerre. Le droit contenu dans ce code était autant de nature international qu'interne. C'était une sorte de droit "sui generis." Selon le rapport final, il semble que les résultats obtenus par cette Commission ont été très satisfaisants.

(b) Un tribunal international des réclamations de guerre

La seconde possibilité est la création d'un tribunal international où chaque pays présenterait ses réclamations au nom de ses citoyens. Cette possibilité présente de grandes difficultés pratiques. L'exemple le plus proche en est le tribunal des réclamations Iran-É.U., qui n'implique que deux pays et qui après plus de dix années d'opérations n'a réellement traité qu'un faible pourcentage de toutes les réclamations qu'il a reçues. Les principes juridiques mis en oeuvre par ce tribunal se trouvent à l'article 5 de la Déclaration d'Alger de 1981:

> The tribunal shall decide all cases on the basis of respect for law, applying such choice of law rules and principles of commercial and international law as the Tribunal determines to be applicable, taking into account relevant usages of the trade, contract provisions and changed circumstances.

Ces principes furent très influencés par les négociations entre les deux protagonistes. Par exemple, ce tribunal ne traite que les réclamations de citoyens à État et non entre États, et il ne reçoit que les réclamations pour pertes matérielles.

(c) Un tribunal bilatéral pour chaque État réclamant

La troisième possibilité d'instance de règlement des réclamations contre l'Irak serait que chaque État réclamant crée un tribunal bilatéral avec l'Irak. Les difficultés juridiques de cette solution sont énormes: source du droit, répartition équitable des réparations, application uniforme du droit, etc. Dans l'histoire, de tels tribunaux ont en général appliqué les règles de: "international law, justice and equity" selon l'expression souvent employée.

(d) L'existence de règles générales

De ce qui précède, il faut conclure qu'il n'est possible de connaître le droit qui s'appliquera à une réclamation que lorsqu'on connaît le forum qui aura à juger de cette réclamation, s'il y en a un. Même encore, il ne sera pas possible de prévoir les règles spécifiques qui s'appliqueront. . . .

UN Sanctions against IRAQ: Food Supplies

In a memorandum dated August 16, 1990, the Legal Bureau advised:

[Concerning UN Security Council resolution 661] . . . the key part of the resolution is paragraph 3(c) which reads in part, "The sale or supply. . .of any commodities or products. . .but not including supplies intended strictly for medical purposes and, in humanitarian circumstances, foodstuffs. . . ."

It is clear from the phrasing of this exception to the economic sanctions put in place through resolution 661 that not all shipments of food are covered. Only those shipments made in "humanitarian circumstances" are excluded from the sanctions. This phrase is, admittedly, open to interpretation and there is little authority available to shed definitive light on the scope of the exception. . .

In the absence of a clearer interpretation of the relevant phrase from UN sources, some insight can be obtained by resort to humanitarian rules. Under the latter, there are restrictions on the concept of "total war," a concept which excludes the possibility of starvation of the civilian population. The Hague Rules of 1907 qualify the concept of total war by the requirement that military actions be taken only for the "imperative demands of the necessities of war." A further restriction was placed on states by the 1949 Geneva Conventions, which apply to the situation in the Gulf since all countries so far involved are parties to those instruments. Article 23 of the Fourth Geneva Convention requires states to allow free passage of essential foodstuffs intended for children under fifteen, expectant mothers and maternity cases. The free passage could, however, be interrupted if the food was being diverted to military purposes.

Further rules in this area were adopted in the 1977 Protocols to the Geneva Conventions. Under Protocol I, starvation of the civilian population is expressly prohibited. Nonetheless, the Red Cross commentary to the Protocols makes it clear that this rule does not require that all foodstuffs be allowed into the territory of the adverse party. . .

INTERNATIONAL ENVIRONMENTAL LAW

Energy and the Environment

In a note dated March 26, 1990, the Legal Bureau wrote:

In November 1988, as a response to growing public and political interest in global warming induced by greenhouse gases and related atmospheric problems, an Intergovernmental Panel on Climate Change (IPCC) was established, under the auspices of the World Meteorological Organization and the United Nations Environment Programme (UNEP), to study the impacts of climate change and to develop policies and strategies for dealing with their environmental consequences. Canada is an active participant in the IPCC and, as member of the IPCC Bureau and vicechairperson of the response strategies Working Group, contributes effectively to the deliberations of that body.

There is a general view that while existing legal instruments and institutions with a bearing on climate should be fully utilized and further strengthened, they are insufficient alone to meet the challenge. A very broad international consensus has therefore emerged in the IPCC, confirmed notably at the 44th United Nations General Assembly, on the need for a framework Convention on Climate Change. Such a convention should be framed in such a way as to gain the adherence of the largest possible number and most suitably balanced spread of countries; contain provision for separate annexes/protocols to deal with specific obligations. As part of the commitment of the parties to deal with greenhouse gas emissions and the adverse effects of global warming, the convention would also address the particular financial needs of the developing countries and the question of the access to and transfer of technology.

There are a number of issues to be decided in the negotiation of such a Convention. These might include:

—the political imperative of striking the correct balance between the arguments for a far-reaching action-orientated framework Convention and the need for urgent adoption of such a Convention so as to begin tackling the problem of climate change;

—the extent to which specific obligations, particularly on the control of emissions of carbon dioxide and other greenhouse gases, should be included in the Convention itself or be the subject of separate protocols;

—the timing of negotiation of such protocols in relation to the negotiations on the framework Convention.

Basel Convention: Protocol on Liability

In a memorandum dated March 12, 1991, the Legal Bureau wrote:

The second and last meeting of the "Ad hoc working group of legal and technical experts to develop elements which might be included in a Protocol on liability and compensation for damage resulting from the transboundary movements and disposal of hazardous wastes and other wastes" took place at UNEP headquarters in Nairobi, March 6-9...

The discussion on international liability and compensation led the delegates to agree on the need for a general introductory paragraph to the Protocol outlining its purpose. The concepts of "adequate and prompt compensation for damage" (India), "to deter violations of the Convention" (USA), "promote the protection of human health and the environment" (Netherlands), and "to enable the restoration of the environment" (Netherlands, Canada) were included and accepted by all delegates as valid aims for the Protocol...there was general consensus on draft elements outlining a three-tier approach to this question:

—first, civil liability as described in Part One of the elements;
—second, to the extent that compensation for damage under Part One is inadequate or not available, recourse to an international fund for immediate response action and supplementary compensation;
—third, to the extent that compensation for damage under Part One or the International Fund is inadequate or not available, State liability.

State liability was not defined further, except that, at the initiative of the Netherlands, a footnote was added to the effect that some delegations noted that State responsibility, and thus State liability for wrongful acts, was not covered... .

There was consensus on the primacy of recourse through domestic courts, although the Netherlands introduced as a footnote the notion of an international tribunal. The need for an international advisory body for the assessment of clean-up and remedial action, as well as the evaluation of environmental damage, was agreed on...

Although an almost exact copy of the Basel Convention, the Bamako Convention contains significant differences to the Basel regime, notably a ban on the import of hazardous wastes into Africa, and a ban on the dumping of hazardous wastes at sea. It imposes "strict liability as well as joint and several liability on generators." The Convention also has a section on the adoption of the precautionary approach, mentioning the need to "prevent the release in the environment of substances. . .without waiting for scientific proof regarding such harm'' and ''the application of clean-production methods, rather than the pursuit of a permissible emissions approach based on assimilative capacity assumptions''. Sub-paragraph 4(9)(b) of Basel, concerning export of hazardous wastes in cases where wastes are required as a raw material for the recycling industry of the country of import, was dropped. . .

FISHERIES

Straddling Stocks

In a briefing note dated October 26, 1990, the Legal Bureau wrote:

Canadian government efforts to end overfishing in the northwest Atlantic include an initiative directed at ensuring the application of the provisions of the United Nations Convention on the Law of the Sea on conservation of the living resources of the high seas and strengthening Canada's position concerning the management of fish stocks straddling the Canadian 200-mile zone.

In that connection, a conference of legal and scientific experts from 15 countries, from the provinces of Newfoundland, Nova Scotia and British Columbia, and high level officials from the FAO and the United Nations was held in St. John's Newfoundland, in September 1990. Participants exchanged views on certain activities and practices on the high seas, such as unregulated fishing, vessel reflagging and overfishing, which are inconsistent with sound conservation and management policies, and have an adverse impact on the fisheries resources under the jurisdiction of coastal states.

Participants were of the view that while the provisions of the Law of the Sea Convention provide a sound framework for conservation of high seas resources, they must be given full effect in order to achieve the basic objectives of conservation. They supported the principle, consistent with the Convention, that states whose nationals fish on the high seas must ensure that such activities do not have an adverse impact on living resources under the jurisdiction of coastal states. With respect to straddling stocks, participants agreed that conservation measures applied to the high seas portion of the stocks should be consistent with the management regime of the coastal state in its exclusive economic zone. Other harmful practices such as reflagging of vessels and unregulated fishing were denounced.

While the conclusions of the St. John's conference do not provide instant international law, they are reflective of increasingly shared views as to how the Law of the Sea Convention should be interpreted and applied. The document provides a good basis to build on and ultimately achieve recognition of the principles embodied therein.

Participants in the conference did not support unilateral extension of jurisdiction beyond the 200 mile zones permitted by the Law of the Sea Convention to address problems relating to high seas fishing.

TREATY INTERPRETATION

Les Règles de rédaction et d'interprétation dans le contexte de l'Article 304 de l'ALE

Dans un mémorandum du 15 juillet 1991, le Bureau juridique a écrit:

Le présent ouvrage concernera principalement. . . la nécessité d'éviter une interprétation donnant un résultat absurde ou déraisonnable ainsi que celle conduisant à une absence de conséquence pour un ou plusieurs mots (doctrine de l'effet utile ou encore de l'interprétation effective, ce qui correspond à une traduction littérale de *rule of effectiveness*). Nous soumettons que ce dernier point est le plus important à cause de la force probante de l'argument (défaut de raison d'être de passages importants de l'article 304). . . puisqu'une interprétation conduisant à une absence d'effet utile sera inévitablement absurde et déraisonnable. Incidemment, comme le démontrera la définition qu'en fait Fitzmaurice, la règle de l'effet utile se fonde en partie sur la prise en compte de l'intention générale à la base du traité. . . .

L'argument le plus fort quant à l'existence d'une telle règle en droit international reste sans contredit le paragraphe 32 (b) de la Convention de Vienne sur le droit des traités qui permet de faire appel à des moyens complémentaires d'interprétation lorsque l'interprétation en vertu de la règle générale (article 31) "conduit à un résultat qui est manifestement absurde ou déraisonnable." La doctrine consultée estime d'ailleurs que "toute interprétation qui mène à l'absurde doit être rejetée." Au niveau jurisprudentiel, la Cour de Justice des Communautés Européennes a fait appel à plusieurs reprises à la nécessité d'écarter toute interprétation susceptible de conduite à un résultat absurde. . .

Dans l'arrêt *Iranian Oil* la Cour Internationale de Justice statua:

The Government of the United Kingdom has further argued that the Declaration would contain some superfluous words if it is interpreted as contended by Iran. It asserts that a legal text should be interpreted in such a way that a reason and meaning can be attributed to every word in the text. It may be said that this principle should in general be applied when interpreting the text of a treaty. . . resulting from negotiations between two or more States.

Dans la décision *Cayuga Indians Claims*, il fut soumis qu'un article précis du Traité de Ghent. . .

was only a "nominal" provision, not intended to have any definite application. We cannot agree to such interpretation. Nothing is better settled, as a canon of interpretation in all systems of law, than that a clause must be so interpreted as to give it a meaning rather than so as to deprive it of meaning. We are not asked to choose between possible meanings, we are asked to reject the apparent meaning and to hold that the provision has no meaning. This we cannot do. . . .

La doctrine de l'effet utile va plus loin que de requérir qu'une norme produise un effet, car encore faut-il que celui-ci soit "utile." L'appréciation de cette utilité renvoie nécessairement à des données extérieures à la disposition en cause: la recherche de l'effet utile suppose une référence implicite soit au contexte, soit au but de l'accord ou de la convention.

Le changement fondamental de circonstances

Dans une note du 7 juin 1991, le Bureau juridique a écrit:

La théorie du changement fondamental de circonstances, aussi exprimée par la maxime "rebus sic stantibus" est bien établie en droit international. Explicitement reconnue par la Cour internationale de Justice comme faisant partie du droit coutumier, la règle a été codifiée à l'article 62 de la Convention de Vienne sur le droit des traités (1969) (la "Convention de Vienne"). Il est utile de reproduire le premier paragraphe de cet article:

1. Un changement fondamental de circonstances qui s'est produit par rapport à celles qui existaient au moment de la conclusion d'un traité et qui n'avait pas été prévu par les Parties ne peut pas être invoqué comme motif pour mettre fin au traité ou pour s'en retirer, à moins que:
    (a) l'existence de ces circonstances n'ait constitué une base essentielle du consentement des parties à être liées par le traité; et que
    (b) ce changement n'ait pour effet de transformer radicalement la portée des obligations qui restent à exécuter en vertu du traité. . . .

À la lecture du paragraphe 62(1), on remarquera qu'on y édicte avant tout une *interdiction* d'invoquer la théorie, à une seule exception près. . . Il s'agit en effet d'un recours qui doit être utilisé avec prudence, afin de conserver un certain équilibre entre l'important principe de la stabilité des traités internationaux et la nécessité de répondre aux exigences du changement.

Le texte du paragraphe 62(1) requiert donc le respect des conditions suivantes, telles que proposées par la Commission du droit international, pour que s'applique l'exception à l'interdiction générale contenue à l'article:
— il faut que le changement porte sur les circonstances qui existaient au moment de la conclusion du traité;
— il faut que le changement soit fondamental;
— il faut qu'il n'ait pas été prévu par les Parties;

— il faut que l'existence des circonstances dont il est question ait constitué une base essentielle du consentement des parties à être liées par le traité;
— il faut que le changement ait pour effet de transformer radicalement la portée des obligations qui restent à être exécutées en vertu du traité.
On notera par ailleurs qu'invoquer ce motif d'extinction ne suffit pas pour que le traité cesse de produire tout effet. La Convention de Vienne prévoit effectivement, à ses articles 65 à 67, une procédure devant être respectée pour faire valoir de telles prétentions.

Brièvement, cette procédure prévoit la nécessité d'aviser les autres États concernés de notre intention d'invoquer cette théorie. Ceux-ci pourront alors faire connaître leur opposition à l'extinction du traité, auquel cas les parties devront tenter de s'entendre à l'aide de moyens tels que la négociation, l'enquête, l'arbitrage, etc. À défaut d'entente, toute partie pourra exiger la mise en place d'une commission de conciliation qui entendra les parties et émettra des recommandations quant à l'issue du différend. Ces recommandations ne lieront cependant pas les États concernés. . . . nous en retiendrons que les conséquences qui découlent du changement invoqué doivent avoir un impact majeur sur la situation du pays qui l'invoque. . .

En vertu de l'article 62 de la Convention de Vienne, un traité sera éteint si on peut invoquer avec succès un changement fondamental de circonstances qui répond aux critères établis à l'article. L'article 44 de cette même convention prévoit pour sa part que l'extinction peut n'être prononcé qu'à l'égard de certaines clauses du traité lorsque:

(1) les clauses sont séparables du reste du traité en ce qui concerne leur exécution;
(2) l'acceptation des clauses en question n'a pas constitué une *base essentielle* du consentement à être lié par l'ensemble du traité; et
(3) il n'est pas *injuste* de continuer à exécuter ce qui subsiste du traité (nos soulignements). . .

Interpretation of GATT Article XXV

In a memorandum dated July 9, 1991, the Legal Bureau wrote:

Considering the express terms of Article XXV and the object and purpose of the Article and the GATT as a whole, we consider that the withdrawal of a waiver should only require a simple majority of votes cast on the issue. The withdrawal of a waiver is not expressly mentioned in Article XXV:5, which refers only to the initial waiver of an obligation as requiring a ⅔ majority of votes cast by a majority of CONTRACTING PARTIES. Since a withdrawal restores the rights between contracting parties to their previous position, the rationale for requiring a higher level of majority for the grant of a waiver does not apply to its subsequent withdrawal.

Canadian Practice in International Law / La pratique canadienne en matière de droit international public

Parliamentary Declarations in 1990-91 / Déclarations parlementaires en 1990-91

compiled by / préparé par

MAUREEN IRISH*

A. RESOLUTIONS / RÉSOLUTIONS

(a) *L'Irak/Iraq*

La Chambre passe à l'étude de la motion no 16 de M. Clark (Yellowhead):

> Que cette Chambre condamne l'invasion du Koweit par l'Iraq et, stimulée par le consensus international sans précédent exigeant le retrait immédiat et sans condition des forces iraqiennes du Koweit et le rétablissement complet du gouvernement légitime du Koweit, proclame ouvertement son appui aux résolutions pertinentes du Conseil de sécurité des Nations Unies qui ont été adoptées depuis le 2 août, et à l'envoi de membres, de navires et d'appareils des Forces armées canadiennes pour prendre part à l'effort militaire multinational dans la région de la péninsule arabique, et accepte, étant donné le sérieux de la situation, l'engagement du gouvernement de déposer une nouvelle résolution devant la Chambre dans l'éventualité du déclenchement d'hostilités mettant en cause les Forces armées canadiennes dans la région de la péninsule arabique; et
>
> Que, sur adoption de la présente motion, celle-ci sera réputée avoir

* Associate Professor, Faculty of Law, University of Windsor.

été renvoyée au Comité permanent des affaires étrangères et du commerce extérieur. . . .

La motion de M. Clark (Yellowhead), mise aux voix, est adoptée.

(House of Commons Debates, October 23, 1990, pp. 14612-13)
(Débats de la Chambre des Communes, le 23 octobre 1990, pp. 14612-13)

The House resumed from Wednesday, November 28, the adjourned debate on the motion of Mr. Clark (Yellowhead):

That this House, noting that the Government of Iraq has not complied with the United Nations Security Council resolutions concerning the invasion of Kuwait and the detention of third country nationals, supports the United Nations in its efforts to ensure compliance with Security Council resolution 660 and subsequent resolutions. . . .

The House divided on the motion, which was agreed to on . . . division. . . .

(House of Commons Debates, November 29, 1990, pp. 15957, 15972-73)
(Débats de la Chambre des Communes, le 29 novembre 1990, pp. 15957, 15972-73)

La Chambre reprend l'étude, interrompue le 17 janvier, de la motion de M. Clark (Yellowhead):

Que la Chambre réaffirme son appui aux Nations Unies pour mettre fin à l'agression du Koweit par l'Irak. . . .

The House divided on the motion, which was agreed to on . . . division.

(House of Commons Debates, January 22, 1991, pp. 17557, 17567-68)
(Débats de la Chambre des Communes, le 22 janvier 1991, pp. 17557, 17567-68)

(b) *Lithuania / La Lituanie*

Right Hon. Joe Clark (Secretary of State for External Affairs):

Mr. Speaker, there have been extensive consultations, carried out principally by the member for Scarborough Centre and I think you would find there is unanimous agreement in the House to adopt, without debate, the following resolution which I would propose to move, seconded by my colleagues from Parkdale — High Park and Winnipeg Transcona:

Be it resolved
    That this House condemns the brutal and unacceptable Soviet crackdown in Lithuania, and calls upon President Gorbachev and U.S.S.R. authorities to refrain from using further violence against the people and democratically elected governments of Lithuania, Latvia and Estonia.
    Cette Chambre demande à l'URSS de respecter ses obligations en vertu des accords d'Helsinki et de la Charte de Paris, et de trouver des solutions respectant les droits et les libertés fondamentaux.
    Reconnaissant la politique du gouvernement canadien de ne pas reconnaître juridiquement l'annexion des États baltes, cette Chambre réitère sa résolution de mars 1990 et continue d'appuyer le droit des peuples Baltes de définir leur avenir.

Mr. Speaker: The House has heard the motion. Is there agreement? Some hon. members: Agreed. Motion agreed to.

(House of Commons Debates, January 15, 1991, pp. 16983-84)
(Débats de la Chambre des Communes, le 15 janvier 1991, pp. 16983-84)

B. GOVERNMENT STATEMENTS / DÉCLARATIONS GOUVERNEMENTALES

1 . *International disputes and Peacekeeping / Les différends internationaux et le maintien de la paix*

(a) *Iraq / L'Irak*

Hon. Bill McKnight (Minister of National Defence): Mr. Speaker, it gives me pleasure to table PC1990-1995 dated September 15, 1990, an Order in Council, deploying Canadian troops, in response to Iraqi aggression.

(House of Commons Debates, September 24, 1990, p. 13218)
(Débats de la Chambre des Communes, le 24 septembre 1990, p. 13218)

Right Hon. Brian Mulroney (Prime Minister): Mr. Speaker, last August 2 without provocation or warning, Iraq invaded Kuwait. Having overrun his smaller neighbour, Saddam Hussein claimed that Kuwaiti territory henceforth belonged to Iraq. Although he said that he had no further territorial ambitions, such assurances have been heard before. Fifty-two years ago this month, in Munich, the world learned a hard lesson about aggression and appeasement.

The world may have been surprised by the Iraqi invasion of Kuwait but no one was taken in by the justifications given for it. The invasion of Kuwait was seen for exactly what it was: a brutal aggression, a flagrant violation of international law and a challenge to the principles of the international order on which world peace depends. Iraq's aggression demonstrated how important that order is. . . .

The United Nations has emerged from this crisis in the gulf with new life born at the end of the Cold War under the renewed determination on the part of many countries including, most importantly, former adversaries to make the idea of collective security work. In the seven weeks that have followed the Iraqi invasion of Kuwait, we have seen the United Nations operate I think precisely as its founders would have envisaged and would have hoped. The Security Council has condemned the invasion. It has passed seven resolutions, the most recent following the armed entry by Iraqi soldiers into Canadian and other diplomatic residences in Kuwait and the detention by force of our representatives. . . .

Saddam Hussein is facing the military forces of more than 25 nations. The determination of Egypt and Syria to play a significant role in the collective defence of Saudi Arabia was not only unusual and remarkable, but I think a most encouraging development not only for the present situation which we confront but future developments in the Middle East.

Throughout this crisis Canada has been active in a number of ways and the Secretary of State for External Affairs has played a vigorous and a most effective role in representing Canada throughout. We have focused our activities on three fronts, which the Secretary of State for External Affairs will elaborate on in much greater detail. First of all, diplomatic, in helping to orchestrate the United Nations embargo and in helping Canadians in the region. Second, economic, through respect of the embargo ourselves, not without cost. This has been a very costly. In fact I believe that the first effect of the biting of the embargo took place in Vancouver where

60,000 tonnes of Canadian wheat destined for Iraq were stopped in Vancouver harbour. This was a great hardship for Canadian farmers but all Canadians have respected that embargo, and that too is most important.

Par la façon dont il a traité des étrangers qui menaient une vie pacifique et productive au Koweït et en Iraq, Saddam Hussein a exhibé à la face du monde la banque-route morale de son régime. Sans le moindre égard pour leur sécurité ou leur survie, le gouvernement irakien a forcé des milliers de travailleurs étrangers à travers les déserts, sous la chaleur mortelle du mois d'août, pour se réfugier en Jordanie. Le Canada a été l'un des premiers pays à mettre des fonds à la disposition d'organisations internationales afin de les aider à faire face aux problèmes complexes que pose cet exode massif de réfugiés, particulièrement en Jordanie.

Nous avons plus tard annoncé une augmentation très considérable de cette aide et approuvé une série de mesures supplémentaires, ce qui représente en tout des déboursés de l'ordre de quelque 75 millions de dollars qui visent essentiellement le bien-être des réfugiés. Nous allons, par exemple, assurer le transport aérien de personnes déplacées qui retournent dans leur pays d'origine et fournir une aide spéciale à certains des pays les moins en mesure d'absorber d'un seul coup des milliers de leurs propres ressortissants. Nous allons aussi venir en aide aux pays de la région qui subissent durement les contrecoups de la crise et des sanctions prises contre l'Iraq, notamment la Jordanie, la Turquie et, par exemple, l'Égypte. . . .

Canada's response to the Gulf crisis was quick, clear, and unequivocal. When we dispatched three ships carrying almost 1,000 personnel, we decided at that time not to give their crews their specific mission tasking because we wanted to take into account the important evolution of developments internationally before doing so, given the normal time it would take for the Canadian ships to reach the Gulf. Subsequent UN resolutions, particularly resolution 665, confirmed, I believe, the appropriateness of this initial position and helped Canada define the ships' current mission, I believe, to the satisfaction of the military advisers of the Government of Canada.

On September 15, when our troops entered the operations zone, the Governor General signed the Order in Council placing them on active service for this mission. The Order in Council was tabled earlier this afternoon by the Minister of National Defence, consistent with parliamentary traditions. Members of this House have the opportunity to debate this matter fully before the ships arrive at station on October 2.

When it became clear 10 days ago that an additional contribution in the form of air support would be extremely helpful, not only for our own ships and the protection of our own personnel but for those of friendly nations as well, the Government of Canada decided to despatch a squadron of CF-18 fighter aircraft from Lahr, West Germany to the Gulf to protect Canadian lives and the Canadian operation. They will arrive in the area shortly and will be sustained by another 450 military personnel. We are also making Canadian civilian aircraft available to assist other countries in moving their forces to Saudi Arabia. . . .

Throughout this crisis the protection of Canadians put in jeopardy by Saddam Hussein has been a major concern for the Government of Canada. We have evacuated as many Canadian citizens as possible and we have stayed in touch with those still there to offer whatever material, logistic, and moral support we can. I know that many Canadians are worried about members of their families still caught there and I know that all members of the House join me today in praying that those Canadians detained in Iraq and Kuwait against their will will not be harmed. Our hearts go out to these families and I give them the assurance of all members of the House that we will continue to do all that we humanly can to make sure that we get their loved ones out and back to Canada.

We, and all other civilized nations in the world, are going to hold Saddam Hussein responsible for the well-being of our own citizens.

(House of Commons Debates, September 24, 1990, pp. 13232-35) (Débats de la Chambre des Communes, le 24 septembre 1990, pp. 13232-35)

Mr. Patrick Boyer (Parliamentary Secretary to Secretary of State for External Affairs): . . . On August 2, 1990 Security Council resolution No. 660 condemned the invasion of Kuwait. On August 6, resolution 661 instituted sanctions against Iraq and occupied Kuwait. August 9, resolution 662 condemned the annexation of Kuwait by Iraq. On August 18, resolution 664 called on Iraq to allow other nationals to leave Iraq and occupied Kuwait. On August 25, resolution 665 authorized the use of reasonable force to inspect shipping and ensure that the sanctions outlined in resolution 664 were in fact being respected.

On September 13, resolution 666 set out the conditions under which humanitarian shipments of food and medicine could be made to Iraq and occupied Kuwait. On September 16, resolution 667 condemned Iraq's incursion into diplomatic premises in occupied Kuwait — I would note that that included premises of the Canadian mission there — and the detention of diplomatic personnel. On September 25, resolution 670 was adopted limiting air transport into Iraq in furtherance of the sanctions.

Never in peacetime has any country, which has violated international law the way Iraq has, faced such a solid wall of sanctions. Many of us have looked at previous examples of the use of sanctions and felt that it was a flawed instrument, an effort that was often circumvented and of very little effect. Certainly in this case the United Nations support — and I mean the 158 or so countries of the United Nations that are behind these eight Security Council resolutions — indicates that this very serious situation is being well handled and the aggression that was anticipated has to date been contained to the invasion of Kuwait.

Any suggestion that Canada's actions in the gulf crisis have been contrary to our tradition as peacekeepers reflects an opinion that has been overtaken by the facts. This is both peacekeeping and peace making. That is the theme I want again to emphasize as we now look at the new possibilities in the post-cold war era of finding co-operation to make the United Nations all that it was dreamt it could be in 1945.

Peacekeepers have traditionally been deployed under the United Nations flag between the parties to a conflict following a truce. Certainly in the case of the current conflict, Canada would support the placing of peacekeepers between Iraq and Kuwait once Baghdad withdraws from the country it has invaded.

(House of Commons Debates, September 27, 1990, p. 13492)
(Débats de la Chambre des Communes, le 27 septembre 1990, p. 13492)

Hon. Lloyd Axworthy (Winnipeg South Centre): . . . I ask the minister if the government has now decided whether to take some special actions, such as sending a delegation, or would it be asking the Secretary General of the UN whether he would undertake to go to Iraq and make the case to free the foreign nationals presently detained by the Iraqi government?

Right Hon. Joe Clark (Secretary of State for External Affairs): . . . I have indicated privately to the hon. member, and I think publicly on other occasions, that there will not be an official mission on the part of Canada to seek the release of these persons because we think that would be used for propaganda purposes by the Saddam Hussein regime.

(House of Commons Debates, November 5, 1990, p. 15125)
(Débats de la Chambre des Communes, le 5 novembre 1990, p. 15125)

Hon. Lloyd Axworthy (Winnipeg South Centre): . . . As the minister is aware, there are efforts under way to organize an unofficial all-party delegation to go to Baghdad to make a case for the release of hostages.

I would like to ask the minister if he could confirm comments he made outside the House yesterday where he indicated that the government would be prepared to provide information on the Canadians presently being detained in Kuwait and Iraq, and also provide assistance and services to the embassy and other agencies of the government.

Could the minister tell us exactly what kind of support and co-operation the government would provide to this effort?

Right Hon. Joe Clark (Secretary of State for External Affairs): Mr. Speaker, the member has been quite precise in his question. This government will not authorize a delegation by representatives of Canada to Baghdad. Individual members of Parliament are free to act as they choose.

When individual members of Parliament travel abroad, they are naturally eligible to have the help of Canadian embassy officials. That would be the case with any Canadian members of Parliament who are in Baghdad.

If members of Parliament require a briefing in their private, unofficial capacities, that briefing will be available, whether they undertake a trip there or anywhere.

(House of Commons Debates, November 7, 1990, p. 15248)
(Débats de la Chambre des Communes, le 7 novembre 1990, p. 15248)

Hon. Lloyd Axworthy (Winnipeg South Centre): . . . Has there yet been at the United Nations or within the Department of External Affairs a clear assessment of the effectiveness of the present economic embargo? Will the Government of Canada as a member of the Security Council be putting forward measures at that council which would broaden and strengthen the application of economic sanctions as a way of giving a clear message to Iraq without continuing to talk about an escalation of military hostilities?

Right Hon. Joe Clark (Secretary of State for External Affairs): Mr. Speaker, there is a continuing assessment of the effectiveness of sanctions. I think that question has to be answered in two ways. Are they effective in their breadth and in the degree of support by the outside world? Are they effective in changing behaviour in Iraq?

The answer to the first question, are they effective in their breadth and in the degree to which they are respected, is very much yes. That has to do in part with the existence of a very effective naval blockade in which Canada is playing, I may say, a commendable role. It also indicates the degree to which there is firm international support. We are monitoring that. We are the vice-chair of the Security Council subcommittee on sanctions.

As to the other question, the impact on Iraq itself, there is some impact. It is not an impact, I have to tell the House, that looks like it will change Iraqi behaviour in the short term. Nonetheless I agree with the hon. member in his observation that we want to continue to press on sanctions and other peaceful means to make Saddam Hussein understand that the world is resolute in requiring him to leave Kuwait.

(House of Commons Debates, November 8, 1990, pp. 15322-23)
(Débats de la Chambre des Communes, le 8 novembre 1990, pp. 15322-23)

Mr. John Brewin (Victoria): . . . On September 26 the Minister of National Defence made a solemn commitment to this House:

— before any changes are made to the mission that Canadian forces are involved in at this time in support of the United Nations sanctions, resolution 665, that of deterring aggression, they will have to be consulted and we will have to make that change in Canada.

This weekend there were reports, apparently clear and documented, that Canadian forces in the gulf were going far beyond the enforcement of the UN sanctions and were in fact involved, albeit in a defensive way, in the support of so-called Operation Imminent

Thunder, an offensive exercise near the Kuwaiti border. . . .

Hon. Mary Collins (Associate Minister of National Defence and Minister responsible for Status of Women): . . . I would like to assure my colleague that our role in the Persian Gulf has not changed. Our role is to enforce the UN sanctions against Iraq and to deter aggression. That will continue to be our role. Any change in that mandate would have to be considered by the government and, we would hope, by Parliament.

Yes, we did participate in the exercise over the weekend, albeit, as the member indicated, in a minor role. We assisted in the patrols; we assisted in escorting the U.S. hospital ships; and we participated, as the member has indicated, in a defensive capacity in an air operation to test out command and control capabilities of the multinational forces which are operating in the area.

(House of Commons Debates, November 19, 1990, p. 15385)
(Débats de la Chambre des Communes, le 19 novembre 1990, p. 15385)

Right Hon. Joe Clark (Secretary of State for External Affairs): . . . Mr. Speaker, today we are on the eve of another important Security Council vote. I think it is right for Parliament to consider the implications of the crisis that prompts this vote. . . . I want to take this opportunity to set out the thinking of the government on the decision that is before us in the Security Council tomorrow and my view of the context in which that decision will be taken. . . . Iraq is still occupying Kuwait, in spite of universal condemnation and the near universal application of sanctions.

We, of course, hope that sanctions will help to persuade Saddam Hussein to withdraw. We continue to believe that they help make clear our resolve, but we also now recognize that sanctions in and of themselves are not sufficient to force a withdrawal, if the Iraqi government places a higher priority on holding onto its territorial gains than on the resumption of normal life for its citizenry. We simply have to face that fact.

The government in Baghdad, as the House knows, has been using innocent civilians of third countries, including Canada, in its efforts to wrest concessions from the international community and to try to win propaganda points with its own supporters. It has proceeded at the same time with a ruthless program to annihilate all traces of Kuwait's separate existence. In short, Iraq has repeatedly ignored the demands of the international community in successive Security Council resolutions passed since August 2. It has failed to comply with the obligations incumbent upon it on the basis of international law, on the basis of the principles of civilized behaviour, and on the basis of its own membership in the United Nations. . . .

Tomorrow's resolution will demand full compliance with previous council resolutions. If Iraq does not fully implement those resolutions, the text will authorize member states co-operating with the government of Kuwait to use all necessary means to see they are implemented and to restore international peace and security in the area. Does this mean that force will be used? That is up to Iraq.

That resolution will probably be approved tomorrow, November 29. In normal cases, that would mean the capacity to act, with whatever means, would exist tomorrow, November 29. Now there is a serious and constructive proposal that the resolution build in a pause between the day in November when the authority is vested, and some specific later date on which it might be used. That proposal reflects the call for a pause which Canada and other countries proposed after discussion during the United Nations General Assembly. A deadline which implied an ultimatum could be counterproductive and artificial, and that is not what is proposed. As the Prime Minister said yesterday, what is contemplated is, instead, a pause of goodwill to allow Saddam Hussein one more opportunity to reflect on his options. Naturally, that time must be used by all nations to seek a basis for the peaceful acceptance of Security Council resolutions. But, in particular, it gives Iraq an opportunity to seek a peaceful end to the war it began when it invaded Kuwait.

(House of Commons Debates, November 28, 1990, pp. 15859, 15861-63)
(Débats de la Chambre des Communes, le 28 novembre 1990, pp. 15859, 15861-63)

Right Hon. Joe Clark (Secretary of State for External Affairs): The Security Council resolution that was voted yesterday, supported and indeed sponsored by Canada along with the Union of Soviet Socialist Republics and others, talks about a pause of goodwill.

As I indicated yesterday in some comments, that pause of goodwill proposal was in fact proposed by Mr. Gorbachev on behalf of the Soviet Union in negotiations of which Canada was a very active and full partner. We were seeking to have a resolution which could send a very clear, unmistakable signal to Saddam Hussein that force would be used but that it would not be triggered with the adoption of the resolution yesterday.

What would begin with the adoption of the resolution yesterday was a period of time, some 47 days, in which it would be possible for all of us to try to seek some basis on which the Security Council resolutions could be respected, Kuwait could be restored to her sovereignty and the world could get on with the rest of its business. . . .

Mrs. Coline Campbell (South West Nova): . . . The Order in Council passed September 15 sending our forces to the Persian Gulf cited only those Security Council resolutions related to the enforcement of economic sanctions against Iraq.

Can the minister say whether this government will bring forward a new Order in Council to cover the resolutions passed yesterday at the UN, calling for the use of "all necessary means" to get Iraq out of Kuwait?

Hon. Bill McKnight (Minister of National Defence): Madam Speaker, the hon. member forgot to mention that in the Order in Council which dispatched Canadian men and women to serve in the multinational effort was the deterrence of aggression.

I informed the House during the debate that took place the day before yesterday that if there was a change in the commitment of the Canadian forces, if there was a need to bring about that change, it would be brought forward to the House at that time.

This time what is covered in the Order in Council, the presence of the Canadian forces there and their capability and the tasks they have assumed, are perfectly concurrent and will remain that way. If there is any change, we will inform the House in due time.

Mrs. Coline Campbell (South West Nova): My supplementary is to the Minister of National Defence. Again, it is a question of interpretation, I am sure. Yes, the Order in Council used military forces, but it was to enforce economic sanctions of resolution 665.

We have had many resolutions since that, particularly yesterday's. The National Defence Act says that there must be an Order in Council specifying why our forces are going over there, particularly in light of yesterday, whereby after January 15 we will be sending them into a forum of war. . . .

Hon. Bill McKnight (Minister of National Defence): Madam Speaker, I would ask my hon. colleague to review the National Defence Act. What the government did was comply with convention.

We felt it was important to have a debate that would allow us to bring forward the Order in Council. It was not a legal requirement. It was something the government did because we believed it was important that the House put its signature on what we were doing at the time.

As I said earlier to the hon. member, if there is a change in the role of the Canadian forces, we have said, the Secretary of State for External Affairs has said, the Prime Minister has said, that we would bring it forward to the House for debate in due course.

I can assure the hon. member that there has been no change in the role of the Canadian forces in their function, in reality and in practice. They are there to enforce the world's condemnation of Iraq.

(House of Commons Debates, November 30, 1990, pp. 16040-41)
(Débats de la Chambre des Communes, le 30 novembre 1990, pp. 16040-41)

Hon. Lloyd Axworthy (Winnipeg South Centre):. . . When the United Nations Security Council imposed economic sanctions, it established a special committee of the council to assess and report on the effectiveness of those sanctions. That committee has yet to report. Yet various experts, including the director of the CIA, have said that sanctions are having a very deep impact, including the war-fighting capacity of Iraq.

How can Canada commit this country to go to war when the United Nations Security Council has yet to decide on the effectiveness of sanctions, as it must do under the charter, before it initiates any further military action?. . .

Right Hon. Joe Clark (Secretary of State for External Affairs): Mr. Speaker, the question as to how long one would wait for sanctions to take effect on Iraq, if they would ever take effect on Iraq, is an important question.

The hon. member knows, because he has been a member of the parliamentary committee before which these matters have been discussed, that it is possible to have reports. We have already had reports. Some have been circulated from the committee to which he refers.

There is no obligation, unless he has just invented one in his own mind, for that committee to make a report as a condition precedent to other decisions being taken by the Security Council. He knows that. . . .

Hon. Lloyd Axworthy (Winnipeg South Centre): The government has talked about defending the charter. Under Article 42 of the Charter of the United Nations no military action can be initiated until the Security Council has decided on the adequacy or inadequacy of sanctions. The Security Council has not made that decision.

How can the minister and the Prime Minister send Canada to war when a fundamental principle and fundamental requirement of the charter has not yet been met? You are denying the Charter of the United Nations.

Right Hon. Joe Clark (Secretary of State for External Affairs): Mr. Speaker, if Canada is denying the Charter of the United Nations, so, too, is Javier Perez de Cuellar; so, too, is the Government of France; so, too, is the Government of the United Kingdom; so, too, are all the members — permanent and those with two-year terms — of the Security Council; and so, too, are other countries which recognize, as the Prime Minister said so eloquently this morning, that the initial purpose of the United Nations when it was established by Mr. Pearson, among others, was to provide the capacity to talk as long as talk would work. But then, under the charter, when it became clear that talk would not persuade —

Mr. Axworthy (Winnipeg South Centre): Article 42 under the charter is being evaded — which is to obey the charter, not evade it.

Mr. Clark (Yellowhead): it was in the interests of world order for force to be deployed. That is the charter. It has been decades since we have been able to realize the effectiveness to accomplish what Lester Pearson dreamed of.

We are now in a situation where it is possible for us to have the full authority of the United Nations Charter, the authority to talk and the authority to act.

(House of Commons Debates, January 15, 1991, pp. 17006-7)
(Débats de la Chambre des Communes, le 15 janvier 1991, pp. 17006-7)

Hon. Audrey McLaughlin (Yukon): . . . We are now at January 15, a date which has been set for the consideration of war, but many countries continue peace proposals. Britain has made some, as has France and some of the Arab countries. There are initiatives being pursued even at this late date.

My question to the Prime Minister is this. What initiatives are

being taken by his government today, January 15, to either participate or to initiate peace proposals and options to war?

Right Hon. Joe Clark (Secretary of State for External Affairs):
Mr. Speaker, one of the proposals that has come forward in the
last 36 hours is a proposal by the Government of France that is being
considered in the Security Council. It contains six elements. The
most important is the first because it requires a very clear signal
on the part of Iraq that it will take actions immediately to respect
the Security Council resolutions.

The other five points in that proposal reflect to a remarkable
degree the proposals that were contained in a letter written by the
Prime Minister of Canada to the Secretary General of the United
Nations, Mr. Perez de Cuellar, which I delivered to him the night
before he left for Baghdad. Those proposals had been drawn from
conversations that the Prime Minister and I, the Minister of National Defence, the Associate Minister and others, have had with
various leaders of other countries, including several in the Arab
world. One of the realities of which we are acutely conscious is that
very often countries will say things to Canada that they will not
say to superpowers or will not say to countries which are directly
involved in negotiations.

As a result of that good standing of Canada, we were able to
take these various proposals, synthesize them and draw from them
what we considered to be elements of a potential proposal. Those
elements were in the possession of the Secretary General when he
went to Baghdad. He was deeply apppreciative of the Canadian
initiative. As I understand it, he did not have the opportunity to
discuss those with Saddam Hussein because Saddam Hussein was
not prepared to discuss at that time even the least adherence to
Security Council resolutions.

(House of Commons Debates, January 15, 1991, pp. 17007-8)
(Débats de la Chambre des Communes, le 15 janvier 1991, pp. 17007-8)

Hon. Kim Campbell (Minister of Justice and Attorney General
of Canada):. . . I would like to speak of the legal aspects of this
crisis, both in Canadian and international law, and talk of the respective roles of the government, Parliament and the United Nations.

En droit canadien, le recours à la force armée par le Canada,
soit de sa propre initiative, soit dans le cadre du système de sécurité
collective des Nations Unies, a toujours relevé de la prérogative de

la Couronne au même titre que le pouvoir de conclure des traités et de reconnaître les États étrangers. C'est l'essence même de la conduite des relations extérieures. Pas plus tard qu'en 1981, la Cour suprême du Canada a affirmé que le pouvoir de déclarer la guerre faisait partie de la prérogative royale. Nos experts en matière constitutionnelle sont du même avis. Une mesure d'exécution autorisée par l'ONU est certainement un recours à la force armée qui ne dépasse pas les limites de la prérogative traditionnelle.

Monsieur le Président, l'article 31 de la Loi sur la Défense nationale traite de la situation du personnel des Forces armées. Il prévoit que le gouverneur en conseil peut mettre en service actif les Forces canadiennes en conséquence d'une action entreprise par le Canada aux termes de la Charte des Nations Unies.

The House will recall that an Order in Council was passed on September 15, 1990 under this provision, placing the Canadian component of the multinational military coalition on active service. This measure was stated to apply not only to the implementation of United Nations measures that had then been passed. It also referred to participation in "such other actions as may be appropriate under the charter of the United Nations".

Le gouvernement a veillé à ce que la Chambre soit informée de tous les événements qui se sont produits depuis le début de la crise. C'est notre respect profond pour le régime parlementaire, la démocratie et le principe selon lequel un gouvernement responsable doit rendre compte à la Chambre de toutes les mesures importantes qu'il prend qui nous a incités à agir de cette façon.

Aujourd'hui, nous soumettons cette question à la Chambre pour une troisième fois parce que la situation est à ce point grave qu'il convient que la Chambre l'examine à un moment aussi critique.

Hon. members will no doubt recall the resolution passed on October 23 which condemned the Iraqi invasion, affirmed support for Canadian actions, and contained an undertaking on the part of the government to present a further resolution in the event of an outbreak of hostilities.

This was followed by a resolution of November 29 which supported the efforts of the UN under the original resolution and subsequent UN resolutions including resolution 678. Notwithstanding that there has not been an outbreak of hostilities, the government has ensured that the House has been recalled to consider this motion as the expiry of the UN deadline draws near.

The measures the government has taken in bringing develop-

before Parliament go beyond what happened in the case of the Korean conflict. There Parliament was indeed informed and given an opportunity to debate the issue, but it was after the fact. Here the government has consistently brought matters to the House in a timely way. . . .

Jusqu'à maintenant, je n'ai parlé que des diverses mesures prises par le Canada et du cadre constitutionnel dans lequel elles s'insèrent. Permettez-moi de vous donner un aperçu des mesures des Nations Unies, dans l'ordre où elles ont été prises, ainsi que des principes de la Charte des Nations Unies qui les sous-tendent.

In the exercise of its responsibilities under the United Nations charter to maintain or restore international peace and security, the Security Council adopted resolutions under chapter VII of the charter. The first resolution, resolution 660 of August 2, 1990, determined that there was a breach of international peace and security as regards the Iraqi invasion of Kuwait on August 2, 1990. It condemned the invasion, demanded immediate withdrawal by Iraq, and called upon Iraq and Kuwait to begin immediately intensive negotiations for the resolution of their differences.

Four days later, on August 6, in resolution 661, the Security Council, deeply concerned that resolution 660 had not been implemented and noting that the legitimate Government of Kuwait had expressed its readiness to comply with resolution 660, decided to impose economic sanctions under chapter VII of the charter.

Aux termes d'autres résolutions, le Conseil de sécurité déclare légalement invalide l'annexion du Koweït par l'Irak. Il demande à l'Irak de faciliter le départ immédiat des ressortissants d'États tiers présents en Irak ou au Koweït, condamne l'agression iraquienne à l'égard des diplomates et des locaux diplomatiques et fait appel aux États membres qui ont actuellement des forces navales dans la région afin qu'ils prennent toutes les mesures nécessaires et justifiées selon les circonstances pour intercepter les navires en vue d'assurer l'application des sanctions économiques.

Finally, by resolution 678 of November 29, 1990, the Security Council, recalling and reaffirming its 11 resolutions relating to the Iraqi invasion of Kuwait and mindful of its duties and responsibilities under the charter of the United Nations for the maintenance and preservation of international peace and security, gave Iraq until the end of January 15, 1991 to comply fully with resolution 660 and all subsequent relevant resolutions requiring Iraq to withdraw from Kuwait. Failing this, member states are authorized to use all necessary means to implement those resolutions and to restore international peace and security in the area. Furthermore, resolution 678 requested all states to provide support for these actions.

The overriding principle of the United Nations is the maintenance of international peace and security through collective action. The most fundamental principle of the charter is article 2, paragraph 4, which prohibits the use of force in international relations, especially aggression against the territorial integrity of any state.

Article 2, paragraph 5, requires all the members of the United Nations to render assistance to the organization in actions which it undertakes under its authority.

Article 25 stipulates that the members of the United Nations agree to accept and carry out the decisions of the Security Council. The House approved the charter and Canada's membership in the United Nations with all the obligations that entails by a motion passed on October 19, 1945, shortly after the birth of the new organization.

What this House is discussing today is no more and no less than the fulfilment of its obligations under international law and specifically under the charter of the United Nations to which Canada has committed its full support.

Mr. Joseph Volpe (Eglinton — Lawrence): . . . Inasmuch as I have heard this type of speech on several occasions this evening, would she tell this House whether it is her understanding that a positive response to the resolution means in fact that the government will engage in armed intervention without further consultation with Parliament? . . .

Ms. Campbell (Vancouver Centre): The troops that are in the gulf to fulfil their obligations under sanctions have always been in a position where they might have to engage in combat. They are vulnerable and, if they had been attacked, they would have had to respond.

What I have tried to point out is that the constitutional, legal authority to change that mandate, which has not been changed, is the royal prerogative. That decision has not yet been made and it is why this debate is taking place. I want to say that as a member of the government I have been very grateful for the insightful and thoughtful comments that have been made in this House today. . . .

It is a misconception on the part of some Canadians that their being in the gulf now to enforce sanctions means that they would not possibly become involved in combat. That could have happened

494 The Canadian Yearbook of International Law 1991

at any given time and they would of course have behaved appropriately.

(House of Commons Debates, January 15, 1991, pp. 17072-75)
(Débats de la Chambre des Communes, le 15 janvier 1991, pp. 17072-75)

Right Hon. Brian Mulroney (Prime Minister): Mr. Speaker, hon. members will know that military action began in the Persian Gulf today, as announced at 7 p.m. eastern standard time.

President Bush called me beforehand to apprise me that he had authorized such action. We understand at the moment that the participants of this first wave included forces from the United States, the United Kingdom, Saudi Arabia and Kuwait.

The fighting is a direct consequence of Saddam Hussein's determination to maintain his brutal occupation and his illegal annexation of Kuwait in defiance of world opinion. He has chosen to ignore the numerous opportunities that were open to him to withdraw. He has had 167 days since his illegal and brutal invasion of Kuwait on August 2, and 48 full days since the United Nations Security Council passed Resolution 678 on November 29.

In all of that time, with all of the requests, with all of the appeals from leaders around the world, his answer has been no. Resolution 678 provided a pause for peace and gave Saddam Hussein one final opportunity to comply with the will of the world community, as duly expressed through the United Nations. He refused again and again to take that opportunity. Diplomacy has been given every chance to end this conflict peacefully, but regrettably has failed in the face of Saddam Hussein's intransigence. That same intransigence and his indifference to the suffering of his own people, especially the children, made it clear that sanctions alone were not going to force him to leave Kuwait.

There has not been a single iota of interest on his part in complying with the United Nations directives. The time has regrettably come therefore to act in the interests of preserving world order and in safeguarding the effectiveness of the United Nations. A failure by the world community to act would have undermined the United Nations, turned a blind eye to naked aggression, condoned violations of international law and encouraged other potential aggressors to defy world opinion in the pursuit of their own criminal ambitions. If Canada had stood aside, we would have betrayed our own national interests, repudiated our own responsibilities and dishonoured our own traditions. . . .

We have joined with other UN members in expelling Saddam Hussein from Kuwait by force. At this moment our CF-18s are flying combat air patrol in the northern Persian Gulf, protecting Canadian and allied ships and personnel in the gulf and the Arabian Peninsula. Canadian ships are now engaged in the company of others playing a vital role in assuring the support of the seaborne arm of the coalition in the Persian Gulf.

Earlier this evening, the cabinet met and gave the Chief of the Defence Staff, General de Chastelain, authority for the Canadian forces to carry out sweep and escort missions over Kuwait and Iraq, if necessary and appropriate. All Canadian forces in the gulf will nevertheless remain under Canadian command.

I profoundly regret, as I am sure, Mr. Speaker, all members of this House do, that it has come to this. It is with no satisfaction that we take up arms, because war is always a tragedy, but the greater tragedy would have been for criminal aggression to go unchecked.

(House of Commons Debates, January 16, 1991, p. 17164)
(Débats de la Chambre des Communes, le 16 janvier 1991, p. 17164)

Hon. William Rompkey (Labrador): . . . Canadians will want to know exactly what role Canadian forces are playing in the gulf now, specifically what missions they will be carrying out — both the planes and the ships.

Can the minister tell us what that role is, will be, and exactly what danger it is likely to put our forces in now and in the future.

Hon. Bill McKnight (Minister of National Defence): Mr. Speaker, as the hon. member is aware, since hostilities commenced, as the January 15 deadline established by the United Nations had passed, the role of Canada's fighter squadron has been that of combat air patrol, the same role that was provided before January 15, before the change in circumstances. That was the responsibility of the Canadian forces last evening. For the near term, I anticipate that to be the role which they will take.

The authorization of sweep and escort for the Canadian fighter squadron does not mean that they will participate in that role, but it means that they are available to the tactical commanders to participate if they can assist in removing Saddam Hussein from Kuwait.

As to our naval task force, it is assembled to provide defensive support and resupply among a group of other nations. The two destroyers are providing, along with vessels of other nations, air defensive support to the combat logistic group. They, as the hon. member and others are aware, would not operate in the very northern tip of the gulf. They would operate in providing resupply at sea in a less hostile area. They, along with the Canadian destroyers and air defence vessels of other nations, are providing the defensive task force or the grouping for those Canadian ships and ships of other nations. . . .

Mr. Fred J. Mifflin (Bonavista – Trinity – Conception): . . . Given the reaction of the Secretary General of the United Nations after hostilities commenced last night, and given the announcement by White House spokesman Marvin Fitzwater that the coalition forces have joined the United States in the liberation of Kuwait, I would like to ask the Minister of National Defence whether the government considers what is going on now in the Persian Gulf a United Nations controlled operation, or does it not?

Hon. Bill McKnight (Minister of National Defence): Mr. Speaker, part of the answer to the hon. member's question is that the authority for the activity that is taking place now, that of hostility and the use of force to remove Saddam Hussein from Kuwait, falls under the auspices of the United Nations and the authority of the United Nations to the collaborating nations.

As the hon. member would know, Canada has tactical command of assets, materiel and personnel of other nations. That being said, the over-all command of the assets of all the collaborating nations involved in the hostilities in enforcing the UN resolution 678 to remove Saddam Hussein fall under the over-all command of General Norm Schwarzkoff. That being said, we must recognize that when Canada accepts tactical control and command of assets and personnel of other nations, naturally Canada has assigned the tactical control of its assets to the over-all command.

Mr. Fred J. Mifflin (Bonavista – Trinity – Conception): . . . I would like to ask the minister perhaps in another way, does the Government of Canada intend to ask the Secretary General of the United Nations to invoke the necessary measures in the United Nations charter to make this a UN-controlled operation?

Hon. Bill McKnight (Minister of National Defence): Mr. Speaker, as the answer to the hon. member's first question dealt with the authority, he knows the only appropriate instrument to my knowledge within the United Nations charter at this time for this event happens to be the military committee. I think he realizes and understands the military committee of the United Nations has been inactive for several years. Because of the cold war, that may change in the future, but it has not changed at this date.

I am sure the hon. member would agree with me that having national command, Canadian command of Canadian men and women and assets in the Persian Gulf, is much better than abdicating the command to a committee.

(House of Commons Debates, January 17, 1991, pp. 17197-98)
(Débats de la Chambre des Communes, le 17 janvier 1991, pp. 17197-98)

Hon. Jean Chrétien (Leader of the Opposition):... Last night Canadians were horrified to learn of the unprovoked attack by Iraq on Tel Aviv and Haifa, the two largest cities of Israel.

I am sure that all members of the House and all Canadians will share with me in expressing our deep sympathy and solidarity with our friends in Israel. It is clear that Israel has shown remarkable restraint in the face of a very real threat to its own people.

Will the Prime Minister tell the House what decisions his government has made in response to the attack of last night?...

Right Hon. Brian Mulroney (Prime Minister):... Last night, in the face of this unprovoked attack, I communicated with the Government of Israel and then sent a letter to the Prime Minister in which I said:

You may be aware that I have strongly condemned Saddam Hussein's missile attack on your country tonight. However, I am writing to you to express my profound sympathy to you and to the people of Israel.

Canada deplores this criminal and unprovoked act. It demonstrates, if anyone was still in doubt, the threat that Saddam Hussein poses to international peace and security.

The attack on Israel was a clear attempt to provoke retaliation in order to bring your country into the war. I know this will not escape your government.

Our thoughts are with you tonight. I wish to express the sympathy of the Canadian Government to the victims and their families. I convey the best wishes of all Canadians to them for a speedy recovery.

(House of Commons Debates, January 17, 1991, p. 17283)

(Débats de la Chambre des Communes, le 17 janvier 1991, p. 17283)

Hon. Audrey McLaughlin (Yukon):... Iraqi troops are now withdrawing from Kuwait, and yet President Bush has decided to pursue the war and to reject every proposal to bring this war to an end....

Today the Prime Minister made a statement that he would like to see the Security Council hold a meeting to discuss compliance of Iraq with the resolutions.

I would ask the Prime Minister, in addition to that, will the government also support a cease-fire which can be monitored by the United Nations and support that cease-fire immediately? By any standards the war is won. When is enough enough?

Right Hon. Brian Mulroney (Prime Minister): Mr. Speaker, enough is enough when an aggressor nation indicates once and for all that it is going to honour all of the resolutions of the UN Security Council. Iraq's Ambassador to the United Nations was asked at 12:30 today whether or not Iraq intends to honour all 12 resolutions of the Security Council, and his answer was no. He said: "Some of these resolutions may be invalid. We have our own reservations. Some of them sort of lend themselves to different interpretations. So we really have to take it step by step."

All members of the coalition, from Denmark to Great Britain to France, the socialist Government of France, today said the position put forward by the Leader of the NDP is unacceptable....

Hon. Audrey McLaughlin (Yukon):... We know that much of Iraq's military force has been destroyed, that in fact the UN resolutions that authorized force to ensure that Iraq withdrew from Kuwait, which is what the last resolution says, is being done, we understand, by the retreat of Iraqi troops. U.S. pilots have told reporters that while Iraqi troops are fleeing from Kuwait, they are bombing them with cluster bombs on the highways north of Kuwait City. In the words of one pilot, "we hit the jackpot."

My question to the Prime Minister is: Are Canadian pilots involved in this bombing of the retreat of Iraqi forces?

Right Hon. Brian Mulroney (Prime Minister): Mr. Speaker, Canadian pilots and CF-18 aircraft are fully engaged in the prosecution of the effort to ensure that the President of Iraq conveys, unmistakably, his complete acceptance of the 12 United Nations resolutions to the Security Council. At that time and at that time alone would a cease-fire be appropriate, and would the Government of Canada instruct its CF-18s to cease and desist from the kind of action in which they are engaged in prosecution of the defence of the United Nations.

Hon. William Rompkey (Labrador): . . . Our planes in the gulf have had a number of roles throughout the war: air patrol, sweep and escort and, more recently, a bombing mission. I want to ask the Minister of National Defence: What is the role of the CF-18s in the gulf at this moment? Is it business as usual? Have any new orders been issued or are they contemplated to the CF-18s in the gulf by the minister or by the Canadian commander in the gulf?

Hon. Bill McKnight (Minister of National Defence): No, Mr. Speaker. I have said on several occasions that the role of the CF-18 squadron, under the air tasking orders as agreed to by the Canadian commander in the Middle East, is that of combat air patrol, sweep and escort, and air to ground interdiction.

There has been no change, and I do not anticipate any until the results of the coalition effort have brought about a compliance with the United Nations resolutions under which the CF-18 squadron and all Canadian personnel are involved in enforcing.

(House of Commons Debates, February 26, 1991, pp. 17660-62)
(Débats de la Chambre des Communes, le 26 février 1991, pp. 17660-62)

Right Hon. Joe Clark (Secretary of State for External Affairs): . . . Today Kuwait is again a free country, though deeply scarred by its ordeal.

I visited free Kuwait five days ago. I raised over the Canadian Embassy there, the flag our diplomats so reluctantly took down when they were forced by lack of food and water to leave on October 19.

I wish now to report to the House on that trip which began, quite deliberately, with a call on the Secretary-General of the United Nations in New York and which took me to Jordan, Israel, Saudi Arabia, Syria and Iran as well as Kuwait and the United States. I met with leaders of those countries and with the foreign ministers of Egypt and of Italy, and with leading Palestinians from the Occupied Territories. . . .

Madam Speaker, I believed that my trip to the area should begin with the government of Kuwait. The Emir of Kuwait was still in Taif, in Saudi Arabia, where he had spent the occupation. His appreciation for Canada's contribution to the liberation of Kuwait was heartfelt. The Emir was deeply concerned at the damage to his people and to his state. Plans are already beginning for the massive reconstruction of Kuwait and I welcomed the clear assurances that the expertise of Canadian companies will enjoy opportunities commensurate with the important role Canada played in liberating Kuwait.

The senseless damage to Kuwait must be seen to be believed. Across the limitless desert landscape burn innumerable fires, each set deliberately with powerful charges of high explosives. Downtown, on the waterfront, are burned-out building after building, looted store after store, museums, homes, things of value or merit, trashed. This was not war damage; this city was put to the torch in the last 48 hours of occupation.

For the Kuwaitis, the ending of sanctions against Iraq is therefore a major problem. Should oil exports again earn revenues for Iraq when Kuwait remains crippled? On the other hand, Iraq itself is badly damaged and needs to finance its own recovery. One idea being explored by countries of the region is the dedication of a proportion of Iraq's oil revenues to repair the damage Saddam Hussein has done.

Much will depend on what kind of regime survives in Iraq. Saddam Hussein is now being challenged by his own people. But through the force of arms and oppression he can cling to power. As long as he does, the countries of the region will be wary of his designs and will want continued sanctions on anything enabling him to rebuild his armies.

In Kuwait, there is a mood calling for change in the way the country governs itself. The government says it is anxious to open up the regime, to institute more democracy. I encouraged that development and urged that particular care be taken to allow the reintegration of Palestinian residents of Kuwait, many of whom, most of whom, were intensely loyal to Kuwait.

Almost everyone with whom I met indicated that the Palestinian problem is the key issue to be resolved in the region. The answer will have to be found in greater security for all states of the area. The issue has three essential elements which all must be respected. They are the security of the state of Israel, the rights of the Palestinians and territory. . . .

Much time in this discussion is devoted to technique, to whether it should be an international conference, at the United Nations or not at the United Nations, or whether it should be separate bilateral negotiations, and whether discussion between the Palestinians and the Israelis should be part of that or separate, and, in any case, who should represent the Palestinians, and so on.

On that last point, Canada can only agree with the Secretary-General of the United Nations; the Palestinians should be represented by the organizations or representatives they choose. Our distaste for the support for Saddam Hussein by the leader of the Palestine Liberation Organization should not disqualify Palestinians from coming to their conclusions on what we have always said was fundamental; their right to choose their own leadership in the search for realization of their legitimate rights.

(House of Commons Debates, March 15, 1991, pp. 18534-36)
(Débats de la Chambre des Communes, le 15 mars 1991, pp. 18534-36)

L'hon. Audrey McLaughlin (Yukon): . . . Les Kurdes du Canada sont très inquiets concernant leurs familles en Irak. Je voudrais demander au ministre ce que va faire le gouvernement pour aider les familles kurdes, les Kurdes ici au Canada, afin qu'ils puissent obtenir l'information concernant leurs familles en Irak?

Le très hon. Joe Clark (secrétaire d'État aux Affaires extérieures): Monsieur le Président, nous avons déjà eu des conversations entre certains représentants de mon ministère et les porte-paroles et les représentants de la communauté canadienne d'origine kurde. Nous avons l'intention de continuer ces consultations.

Bien sûr, il est difficile pour nous ou pour quiconque de chercher et d'avoir l'information exacte en ce qui concerne la situation des Kurdes en Irak. Une grande partie de cette région de l'Irak est en train de bouger; il y a un grand mouvement de personnes: plus d'un million de personnes sont maintenant dans le processus de voyager vers les frontières d'Iran et de la Turquie.

Je crois que la meilleure garantie que nous puissions donner aux Canadiens et aux autres, c'est de trouver les moyens d'arrêter les activités de Saddam Hussein, d'arrêter les attaques contre les Kurdes. Et nous sommes en train, aux Nations Unies, et par voie de nos gestes humanitaires, de chercher les moyens de faire cesser cette tragédie.

Hon. Audrey McLaughlin (Yukon): Mr. Speaker, certainly we all agree that it is necessary that the Kurds be protected and be given the protection of the United Nations. I am sure that the minister would agree that part of that in the long term is to ensure that we have arms control in the world. The United Nations should take a strong stand on arms control and let Canada be a participant in that. . . .

Right Hon. Joe Clark (Secretary of State for External Affairs): The hon. member has raised questions with regard to the role of the United Nations in this crisis with respect to the Kurds and I think the House may be interested to know the current situation as Canada sees it.

The House will know that the European Community has proposed a sort of enclave under UN protection. We share some of the concerns of the Secretary General of the United Nations with respect to jurisdiction. But in the circumstances, we would nonetheless support that European Community proposal.

However, if the enclave idea is not acceptable, we have set out an alternative Canadian proposal. There was a discussion on Saturday between my office and Ambassador Yves Fortier. Yesterday afternoon, Ambassador Fortier, on behalf of Canada, made a formal proposal to Jean Claude Aimé, the Assistant Secretary General of the United Nations, regarding an alternative Canadian proposal, which we believe avoids the problem of sovereignty. That proposal would involve. . .two elements. It involves the sending into Iraq of a civilian United Nations presence which would have in the first instance a responsibility for ensuring the co-ordination of delivery of humanitarian and other assistance. It would also assign to that civilian United Nations presence a sort of ombudsman role which would be able to guarantee, as best the world can, that undertakings with respect to amnesty are being honoured and would be able to offer some indication to citizens of Kurdish origin in Canada and to concerned citizens around the world.

(House of Commons Debates, April 9, 1991, pp. 19225-26)
(Débats de la Chambre des Communes, le 9 avril 1991, pp. 19225-26)

(b) Europe / *L'Europe*

Hon. Warren Allmand (Notre-Dame-de-Grâce): Today, the countries of NATO and the Warsaw Pact have concluded an historic agreement to significantly cut military forces in Europe and have virtually ended the cold war.

As a result of this treaty, I would like to ask the minister what will be the impact on Canada's military and foreign policy. In particular, what are the government's plans to redeploy Canadian forces in Europe, either to bring them home or to give them a new role as a result of these significant changes?

Hon. Mary Collins (Associate Minister of National Defence and Minister responsible for Status of Women): . . . It is recognized that the signing of the CFE treaty is indeed an historic event. I was there when they started this discussion a year and a half ago. We were all delighted at the outcome.

I think the hon. member also realizes that the reductions provided for in the first CFE are primarily on the eastern European side. On the NATO side, they are not as considerable at this point in time. Although all the details are not known, we do not expect that it will actually affect our Canadian troops in Europe.

Nevertheless, we have already decided that we are going to be reducing our forces by about 1,400. We will be looking, as we proceed, with CFE-IA as to what the potential impacts on Canadian military participation in Europe might be. I would also like to advise my hon. colleague that one role that Canada will be playing as a result of the CFE agreement is in the area of verification. We have taken an active part and we look forward to participating in what we think can be very important long-term benefits for the security of Europe through that participation.

(House of Commons Debates, November 19, 1990, p. 15391)
(Débats de la Chambre des Communes, le 19 novembre, 1990, p. 15391)

Hon. Bill McKnight (for the Minister of Finance) moved that Bill C-88, an act to provide for the membership of Canada in the European Bank for Reconstruction and Development, be read the second time and referred to a legislative committee.

Mr. William Scott (Parliamentary Secretary to Minister of Veterans Affairs): . . . The concept of the EBRD originated from a French proposal that was quickly endorsed at a meeting of the European community in Paris in November 1989. Canada quickly endorsed this principle of a broad based bank to provide a focus for world-wide financial assistance to central and eastern Europe, in support of the process of political and economic change then beginning in that region. . . .

This process culminated in the representatives of potential member countries signing the bank's Articles of Agreement, entitled

Agreement Establishing the European Bank for Reconstruction and Development (Schedule — Section 2 of the bill), in Paris on May 29, 1990. . . .

Mr. Speaker, it is the government's view that enhanced economic co-operation and integration among the countries of central and eastern Europe, and more broadly, will be vital to the process of structural adjustment that they require and would reduce the likelihood of regional conflict. . . .

The EBRD is loosely modelled on the existing regional development banks in Latin America, Asia, Africa and the Caribbean. However, unlike these banks, the EBRD has a distinctive political mandate to support the transition to the market-based economies through the particular encouragement of private enterprise in those countries of central and eastern Europe adopting both political and economic reforms. The contracting parties of the EBRD have used the articles of agreement to state their commitment to democracy, the rule of law, respect for human rights and market economics. . . .

The bank is to be European in character, but broadly international in membership. Its membership will include the 12 member states of the European community; the European Economic Commission, the European Investment Bank, the countries of central and eastern Europe including the U.S.S.R., and other European and non-European countries that are also members of the International Monetary Fund. . . .

The main objective of the bank is to promote the development of the private sector by focusing on those countries undergoing economic liberalization and democratization. To do so, it will need to co-ordinate its work closely with existing institutions such as the International Monetary Fund and World Bank. In order to establish a mechanism for selecting those countries eligible to borrow and to ward against possible backsliding on reforms, the Articles of Agreement provide for an annual review of the bank's lending strategy in each borrowing country. This review, which was proposed by Canada during the negotiations, should ensure that only those countries consistently applying the principles of democracy, pluralism and market economics continue to be eligible for borrowing.

The bank's central task is to build a vibrant private sector in countries that have been dominated for the past 45 years by inefficient state planning and almost total state ownership. The articles specify that at least 60 per cent of bank funding will be targeted toward lending and equity participation in private sector enterprises. Lending to the public sector will be aimed at assisting in the transition toward greater competitiveness and eventual possible privatization of public sector firms. There may also be limited lending for infrastructure projects required to support the free market economy.

I would also note that, for the first time in the articles of agreement of any such international institution, direct reference has been made to the bank's role in promoting environmentally sound and sustainable development. The Government of Canada attaches special importance to this element of the European Bank's objectives.

(House of Commons Debates, November 30, 1990, pp. 16023-24)
(Débats de la Chambre des Communes, le 30 novembre 1990, pp. 16023-24)

2. *Les droits de la personne / Human Rights*

(a) *Oka-Kanesatake*

Hon. Herb Gray (Leader of the Opposition): . . . Canadians have watched with shock and dismay while the neglect and ineptitude of the Prime Minister and his government has meant that the crisis at Oka-Kanesatake has gone on for more than 75 days without a fair and reasonable solution being arrived at. . . .

Right Hon. Brian Mulroney (Prime Minister): With regard to the problem at Oka that my hon. friend raises, we have taken actions which will be the subject of debate in the House tomorrow. We purchased the land and are ready to transfer that land to the natives and the leadership at Oka, as soon as the guns are put down and the acceptance of law and order, which must prevail across Canada, is accepted by those who have hijacked an otherwise entirely peaceful community. . . .

Hon. Herb Gray (Leader of the Opposition): Mr. Speaker, our Canadian Constitution also guarantees rights of association, movement, and communication, including rights of freedom of the press. Yet, in recent days we have seen all too many breaches of those rights at Oka-Kanesatake. . . .

Hon. Kim Campbell (Minister of Justice and Attorney General of Canada): Mr. Speaker, I think the hon. member should bear in mind what the situation is in Oka, where we have the *dénouement* of the situation. It has resulted in a situation where in the treatment centre, in addition to journalists, there are people who are suspected of being in violation of the criminal law of Canada. The law enforcement authorities are attempting to bring those people before the appropriate authorities to determine whether charges should be laid and to allow the judicial process to go forward.

A review of the law of freedom of speech in Canada and the right of freedom of the press would reveal that that law, as it has been discussed by the court, contemplates, depending on the circumstances, that some limitations might be imposed on the access by the press of information.

(House of Commons Debates, September 24, 1990, pp. 13204-5)
(Débats de la Chambre des Communes, le 24 septembre 1990, pp. 13204-5)

Mr. Robert E. Skelly (Comox — Alberni): Mr. Speaker, yesterday in the House of Commons, the Prime Minister said:

The Government of Canada responded to a — request from the Government of Quebec pursuant to the National Defence Act to provide the Canadian army for peacekeeping purposes —

However, at a news conference on August 8 to announce the decision, the Prime Minister contradicted his friend, the Liberal premier of Quebec, and said that it would be inappropriate and misleading to describe the army's role at Oka as one of peacekeeping. Can the Prime Minister explain to the House on which occasion he was telling the truth?

Hon. Bill McKnight (Minister of National Defence): Mr. Speaker, rather than play on words, I think it is more important that the NDP recognize that the Canadian forces have been requisitioned under the National Defence Act in the aid to the civil power. It is a provision in the act that is available to every province in Canada when they need assistance because they cannot enforce civil law, have peace and security for their people, by either the municipal policing authorities, their provincial policing authorities or, in this case, the Royal Canadian Mounted Police.

The Canadian forces were called in, have responded and, to the greatest extent possible, carried out their responsibilities with diligence, patience and understanding that I think even the hon. member would recognize.

Mr. Robert E. Skelly (Comox — Alberni): Mr. Speaker, given that the army has been accused of provoking hostility, withholding food, denying human rights and trampling freedom of the press, why does the Prime Minister, with his Minister of Indian Affairs, continue to hide behind the army and why will he not take the responsibility now and commit himself to finding a political solution to this three-month-old conflict?

Hon. Thomas Siddon (Minister of Indian Affairs and Northern Development): Mr. Speaker, this government has been committed to finding a political solution to these matters for at least three years. . . .

Mme Sheila Finestone (Mount Royal): Monsieur le Président, dans une lettre adressée à John Ralston Saul, le président du groupe d'écrivains PEN International, le ministère de la Défense affirmait, et je cite: ''que l'équipement et les films appartenant aux journalistes pourraient passer les barricades militaires et qu'on permettrait aussi aux journalistes de s'approvisionner en nourriture.'' Le ministre refuse d'honorer ses engagements.

Voici donc ma question qui s'adresse au ministre des Affaires indiennes. Pourquoi refuse-t-il de reconnaître que ces droits sont absolument fondamentaux dans une société démocratique?

Hon. Bill McKnight (Minister of National Defence): Mr. Speaker, I think the hon. member has to understand that there are basic rights in a democratic society. The first right is that of respect of law. There are suspected law-breakers in the treatment centre at this time. The Canadian forces are acting as peacemakers and peace officers in this instance. With regard to food, I can tell the hon. member that we estimate there are some 53 people in the treatment centre. We are providing rations for 60 people. The other day we provided four eggs per person, some 240 eggs. They were so desperate for food that the warriors threw them at the army. . . .

Mrs. Sheila Finestone (Mount Royal): Mr. Speaker, first, I would like the minister to tell us what laws the journalists have broken.

Second, I would like the minister to tell us whether or not he believes that the public's right to know the real story at Oka, Kanesatake and the treatment centre is not a fundamental right.

Does the minister think that stopping access to films and tapes and the filing of stories is an absolute abridgement of fundamental rights in this democracy, that it is censorship?

Hon. Bill McKnight (Minister of National Defence): Mr. Speaker, the hon. member should recognize that there are suspected law-breakers in the treatment centre. . . . If that is recognized by the hon. member then she, I believe, will concur with the actions that have been taken by the Canadian forces to limit inflow. There has been no limit to reporters wanting to leave. If reporters wish to leave, the door is open. If anyone wishes to leave, the door is open.

I ask the hon. member to understand that this is not a public event. These are actions that have taken place by people suspected of breaking the law. The Canadian forces are acting as peace officers under the jurisdiction of Canada. Perhaps the member will understand that these are not equals: one is enforcing law and the other is attempting to break law. We are making every effort possible to make sure there is a peaceful resolution.

(House of Commons Debates, September 25, 1990, pp. 13297-98) (Débats de la Chambre des Communes, le 25 septembre 1990, pp. 13297-98)

Le très hon. Brian Mulroney (premier ministre): Madame la Présidente, depuis le mois de juillet, la télévision inonde les foyers canadiens d'images troublantes de barricades et d'hommes masqués brandissant des fusils d'assaut. Un groupe d'individus fortement armés et aux visées idéologiques a récupéré un différend territorial qui avait éclaté à Oka et s'en est servi pour tenter de protéger, entre autres choses, des activités commerciales illégales. Leurs tactiques ont été celles de terroristes. Les *warriors* ont prétendu agir en représentants légitimes des Indiens, mais se sont complètement discrédités en brandissant des armes de grande puissance, en proférant des menaces contre les autorités, en se livrant à la contrebande, en intimidant des Mohawks respectueux de la loi, en bloquant des voies de transport et en saccageant des propriétés privées.

Ce qui se passe à Oka n'est pas de la désobéissance civile: il s'y passe des activités violentes qu'aucune collectivité ne peut accepter de quelque façon que ce soit de tolérer. Le différend territorial qui a servi de prétexte au conflit d'Oka, et je ne veux pas du tout, madame la Présidente, minimiser les revendications territoriales importantes et historiques des peuples autochtones...mais le différend territorial en question qui a servi de prétexte au conflit d'Oka est réglé effectivement depuis longtemps, soit depuis que le gouvernement fédéral a fait l'acquisition du terrain en litige en juillet, avant que n'éclatent les incidents, en vue de le remettre aux

Mohawks en cause. . . .

What has been at issue these past weeks is not the land, rather the warriors acting against all of the peaceful and noble traditions of Canada's Mohawks. The warriors, advised by foreign legal counsel, have been seeking recognition that their communities are independent and that the laws of Canada do not apply to their lands and to their activities which in the past have included smuggling and gambling on a very large scale. They have sought by various means to circumvent the Canadian justice system.

The warriors' demands are not simply ideas on which reasonable people can agree or simply agree to disagree. They strike at the very heart of what Canada is all about.

The warriors have been acting as if the concept of native self-government means national independence. I want to be very clear on this point. Native self-government is something that can bring great honour, great accomplishment, and great justice to native peoples and, indeed, it shall. But it does not and cannot ever mean sovereign independence within Canadian territory. Mohawk lands are part of Canadian territory and Canadian law must and does apply to us all. Everyone in Canada — members of this House, members of every house, warriors included — is subject to the Criminal Code of Canada. If exceptions to the Criminal Code were made on the basis of colour, race, or creed, where could the line be drawn in a country as diverse and as complex as Canada? What could be more repugnant in a democracy than a legal system based on birth rather than equality?

(House of Commons Debates, September 25, 1990, pp. 13316-17) (Débats de la Chambre des Communes, le 25 septembre 1990, pp. 13316-17)

(b) *South Africa / L'Afrique du Sud*

Right Hon. Joe Clark (Secretary of State for External Affairs): Mr. Speaker, the Commonwealth Committee of Foreign Ministers on Southern Africa met in special session on February 16 in London to discuss Commonwealth policy in light of recent developments in South Africa, including the statement made by President de Klerk on February 1, 1991 which committed the South African government to repeal the remaining legislative pillars of apartheid. . . .

The world is involved in South Africa precisely because the system of apartheid is so powerful and so deliberate a denial of basic human equality, so singular an instrument of racial prejudice. Just as many South Africans show remarkable responsibility in facing their new challenges, so must the world community weigh and apply our influence with great care. The moral imperative remains: to end apartheid. Now, the change in the air, the question of how we contribute to that goal becomes more complex.

Commonwealth foreign ministers, after extensive debate, reflecting the representative nature of that group, agreed unanimously on a position that recognizes a commitment to real reform, but will only reward actual changes which dismantle the system of apartheid. We believe our strongest sanctions should remain until the system is, effectively, abolished; but that lesser sanctions should be lifted in response to tangible proof of a determination to end apartheid irreversibly.

The committee, therefore, decided to adopt a "programmed management approach" that would reward concrete action in South Africa. The first stage in the program would be reached when the remaining political prisoners are released, when the way is cleared for exiles to return home, when repressive provisions of security legislation are repealed and when the group areas act, the Population Registration and Land Act are repealed.

Ces changements peuvent tous être apportés d'ici la prochaine réunion des ministres du Commonwealth, qui aura lieu à la fin du printemps ou en été. Pendant cette rencontre, les ministres examineront les progrès accomplis et décideront s'ils justifient la levée de certaines sanctions comme les restrictions touchant les visas, l'embargo sur le tourisme et les liaisons aériennes, ainsi que les restrictions relatives aux contacts officiels.

Mes collègues et moi craignions entre autres que l'actuelle législation sur la sécurité ne pose un obstacle important à la liberté politique. Nous avons appelé le gouvernement sud-africain à mettre fin aux détentions sans procès, ainsi qu'aux restrictions touchant les assemblées publiques et à accorder aux Sud-Africains les droits universels à la liberté de réunion, à la liberté d'expression et à l'application régulière de la loi. Des progrès substantiels doivent être enregistrés en ce qui concerne le retour des exilés et la libération des prisonniers politiques, d'ici le 30 avril prochain, comme il a été convenu dans le compte rendu de Pretoria d'août dernier.

The committee also addressed the question of sporting contacts. In future, the embargo on sporting contacts will be treated independently from other sanctions. The committee agreed to be guided by representative sports bodies at South African, African and, in the fullness of time, international Olympic levels. These organizations will provide the signal for the re-admission of South African sports to international competition. Indications are that this will probably take place on a sport-by-sport basis. . . . Sanctions have been crucial in bringing about the changes that have occurred to date, and will go on being crucial if the destruction of apartheid is to be ultimately assured.

(House of Commons Debates, February 28, 1991, pp. 17790-92)
(Débats de la Chambre des Communes, le 28 février 1991, pp. 17790-92)

(c) *Convention on the Rights of the Child / La Convention relative aux droits de l'enfant*

Mr. Russell MacLellan (Cape Breton — The Sydneys): . . . As the minister knows, the government co-sponsored and signed the UN Convention on the Rights of the Child; yet in that convention it says that "any child that is deprived of liberty shall be held separate and apart from adults unless it is not in the interests of that child to do so."

Yet this government proceeds to house and jail children and young offenders with adult criminals. . . . It has been over a year since this convention was signed and co-sponsored by this government and yet it has not been ratified. I realize that the provinces have to agree, but the provinces also had to agree to housing young offenders separate and apart, which this government has just insisted on letting slide.

Why does the government not admit that it has no intention of fulfilling the mandate of the UN charter on the rights of the child? When, if it does have an intention of signing it, is this very important convention going to be ratified in this country?

Hon. Benoît Bouchard (Minister of National Health and Welfare): . . . As my friend said before, the convention has been accepted and has been given to the provinces. We are still working with the provinces toward the ratification of the convention. It should be done normally this fall. It is going well.

(House of Commons Debates, June 14, 1991, pp. 1741-42)

(Débats de la Chambre des Communes, le 14 juin 1991, pp. 1741-42)

3. *Diplomatic Relations / Les relations diplomatiques*

(a) *Les États Baltes / Baltic States*

Hon. Jean Chrétien (Leader of the Opposition):. . . As the Prime Minister knows, this past weekend, Soviet troops attacked the Latvian Department of the Interior, and at least five people were killed, some of whom were civilians and some of whom were press people. This crackdown came just one week after Soviet troops moved into Lithuania, killing 14 people. Will the government call in the ambassador of the U.S.S.R. and express to him the outrage of the people of Canada at this use of force?

Right Hon. Joe Clark (Secretary of State for External Affairs): Mr. Speaker, we have already called in the Soviet ambassador, again today, to make precisely that point, that Canada strongly condemns the brutal and unwarranted military force used against the people in the democratically-elected government of Latvia.

(House of Commons Debates, January 21, 1991, p. 17495)
(Débats de la Chambre des Communes, le 21 janvier 1991, p. 17495)

M. Alfonso Gagliano (Saint-Léonard): Monsieur le Président, ma question s'adresse à la ministre de l'Emploi et de l'Immigration. À cause des événements tragiques dans les pays baltes et la mobilisation de l'armée russe, est-ce que la ministre va arrêter la déportation des réfugiés de ce pays, particulièrement ceux qui ne veulent pas faire partie de l'armée de l'Union soviétique?

L'hon. Barbara McDougall (ministre de l'Emploi et de l'Immigration): Monsieur le Président, nous avons une politique de déportation qui est très sensible à la situation dans les pays qui font partie de l'Union soviétique. Également, les personnes de l'Union soviétique qui sont ici peuvent demander une prolongation de leur visa au Canada.

Mr. Alfonso Gagliano (Saint-Léonard): Mr. Speaker, my colleagues and I have been informed this weekend that some refugees from the Baltic states presently in Canada are being deported. They believe that once they are in the Soviet Union they will be drafted by the army.

Will the minister make sure there is no deportation into the Baltic states?

Hon. Barbara McDougall (Minister of Employment and Immigration): Mr. Speaker, we have been very sensitive to the situation in the Baltic states. Of course the people from these states carry Soviet passports, so it is up to them to identify themselves as being from a Baltic state.

(House of Commons Debates, January 21, 1991, p. 17498)
(Débats de la Chambre des Communes, le 21 janvier 1991, p. 17498)

Right Hon. Joe Clark (Secretary of State for External Affairs): Mr. Speaker, there is not very often uanimity in this House, even on questions of international policy, but I think that this is one of those occasions in which the House of Commons of Canada speaks, if not with on voice, then certainly with one purpose and one conviction, and that is to send the clearest possible signal to the leadership of the Soviet Union and to the Baltic peoples that Canada, each and every one of us, each and every Canadian, opposes absolutely the crackdown that has begun to develop in the Soviet Union against aspirations and governments which have a legitimacy in the Baltic states. . . .

Canada's support for the Baltic states has been unwavering. We recognize their *de jure* independence. We have never accepted their forcible annexation. We support the right of their peoples to determine their own future. The question for us is what practical help can we offer now. . . .

Le printemps dernier, les trois républiques ont tenu des élections justes et libres. . . .

À l'initiative de la Lituanie, le 11 mars, ces gouvernements démocratiquement élus ont déclaré leur indépendance de l'URSS. Ils ont tenté de négocier avec Moscou, comme le prévoit la Constitution actuelle. Ils ont, au lieu de cela, fait l'objet de pressions politiques et économiques.

Cinq ans de dimunution du mode de vie ont amené la perestroïka au point critique. L'économie soviétique est en miettes. Les pressions indépendantistes et l'opinion publique défavorable sont à la hausse. M. Gorbatchev doit choisir d'avancer ou de reculer.

Les défendeurs de Gorbatchev réclament que la loi et l'ordre sont les seules armes contre l'anarchie. Ses opposants disent qu'en le réprimant il deviendra l'otage des forces réactionnaires. Avec la polarisation, l'instabilité s'installe rapidement.

Cet hiver, l'URSS a réclamé l'assistance du Canada et des autres pays occidentaux. Nous avons choisi d'appuyer les réformes en diminuant le coût de la transition. Suite à mes entretiens avec l'ancien ministre des Affaires étrangères, M. Chevardnadze, le premier ministre du Canada a offert des mesures d'assistance concrètes à l'occasion du dernier sommet de la CSCE à Paris. Tout ceci est en danger. . . . Canada's reaction to the tragic events in Vilnius was among the strongest to come from any democracy in the western world.

The Prime Minister wrote immediately to President Gorbachev. He issued a strong condemnation, calling on the Soviet President to show restraint and to negotiate settlements based on the Helsinki Final Act and the Charter of Paris. He reminded him that at this time of heightened international tension, Canadians were watching events in the U.S.S.R. just as we were watching events in the gulf.

At the same time, the Prime Minister announced that Canada was reviewing its offer of technical assistance and the new $150 million line of credit. That is not food aid, but a commercial sale. We have drawn a direct linkage between Canadian assistance and the continuation of Soviet reform. . . . I want to advise the House that we have now suspended any action under those programs that had not taken place before the actions in Lithuana. On January 15, this House passed a unanimous resolution condemning the brutal violence used against the people and democratically elected Government of Lithuania.

Saturday I received a communication from the Soviet Ambassador giving the official explanation for the tragic events in Lithuania. The note rejected Moscow's responsibility for what happened, blaming instead the Lithuanian leaders who were claimed to have held extremist positions. That, however, was before the equally tragic events in Riga yesterday.

No one knows if Mr. Gorbachev is still in charge or, more worrying, whether he remains committed to the reforms that began in his name. . . .

Mr. Flis: On a point of order, Mr. Speaker, we definitely would like to hear a little longer from the Secretary of State for External Affairs, but in his three minutes I wonder if he could clarify this point. He keeps saying that he met with the Vice-President in his parliamentary capacity. I was under the impression he was meeting these people as Secretary of State for External Affairs.

Mr. Clark (Yellowhead): Mr. Speaker, I think the hon. member understands, as others in the House do, the constraints that are upon us as a country. I have made it very clear that the circumstances under which I could meet elected leaders, other parliamentarians who hold government office from the Baltic States, was in my capacity as a parliamentarian. That has been understood by all of them and I think clearly understood by members of the Baltic community in Canada. It was certainly in that capacity that I met the parliamentarian who is vice-president of Latvia today.

(House of Commons Debates, January 21, 1991, pp. 17529-33)
(Débats de la Chambre des Communes, le 21 janvier 1991, pp. 17529-33)

(b) *L'auto-détermination — Québec — Self-determination*

L'hon. Jean Lapierre (Shefford):... Monsieur le Président, ma question s'adresse au très honorable premier ministre. A plusieurs reprises, le premier ministre a reconnu publiquement la légitimité et la légalité de la Commission Bélanger-Campeau. Je demande donc au premier ministre: Est-ce qu'il est aussi d'accord avec le préambule de la loi établissant cette commission, qui stipule, et je cite: "Considérant que les Québécoises et les Québécois sont libres d'assumer leur propre destin, de déterminer leur statut politique et d'assurer leur développement économique, social et culturel"?

Est-ce le premier ministre peut nous dire une fois pour toutes s'il est oui ou non d'accord avec le droit à l'autodétermination du peuple du Québec?

Le très hon. Brian Mulroney (premier ministre): Monsieur le Président, je n'ai jamais examiné le préambule dont parle mon ami. J'en ai lu de larges extraits, mais je ne l'ai pas examiné en détail. Je serai donc obligé de le relire attentivement avant de donner suite à sa question.

Je pense que mon ami sait fort bien que la participation du premier ministre du Canada et des chefs de l'opposition, de la quasi totalité des premiers ministres des autres provinces et de lui-même, d'ailleurs, qui était député fédéral, au référendum de 1980, implique bien sûr l'acceptation par tous les Canadiens d'un vote démocratique et libre selon les circonstances et les critères normaux et acceptables.

Alors, sans entrer dans un domaine que je ne peux pas toucher à cause de la raison que je viens de mentionner, je pense que l'expérience de M. Trudeau, du secrétaire d'État aux Affaires extérieures, en 1980, de la quasi totalité des membres de la Chambre et des premiers ministres indique la volonté démocratique de tous les Canadiens.

(House of Commons Debates, November 7, 1990, p. 15254)
(Débats de la Chambre des Communes, le 7 novembre 1990, p. 15254)

4. *Le territoire / Territory*

(a) *Arctic Sovereignty / La souveraineté dans l'Arctique*

Hon. Audrey McLaughlin (Yukon): For a number of years now we have been discussing in the Arctic the infringement on Canadian territory by the United States in terms of issuing oil and gas drilling leases on Canadian territory.

Once again, this year, May 20, 1991, the Department of the Interior says that under sale 124, it is going to issue oil and gas drilling licences in the Beaufort Sea in Canadian territory.

Just four years ago, in 1987, this same issue arose. What has this government done in four years to establish Canadian sovereignty in the Arctic north?

Hon. Jake Epp (Minister of Energy, Mines and Resources): Mr. Speaker, I want to indicate to the Leader of the NDP that... as recently as two days ago I was able to speak to Secretary Watkins at the International Energy Agency and raise these issues with him directly.

Hon. Audrey McLaughlin (Yukon):.... This report from the Department of the Interior of the United States says that it will issue leases in Canadian waters, if it is in the U.S. interest. What about the Canadian interest and what is this government doing specifically to stand up to the U.S. government and say that this is unacceptable and Canadian sovereignty is just that, it is Canadian sovereignty.

Hon. Jake Epp (Ministrer of Energy, Mines and Resources): Mr. Speaker, the Leader of the NDP asks what will we do directly.

I have already indicated to her how direct we had been. Additionally, I can point out to her that through the Canadian Embassy and directly through Ambassador Burney these issues have been raised, and also directly with various officials in the United States. . . .

I say to the hon. member that our position from 1987 has not changed. Canada's position on sovereignty has not changed. The United States government can have whatever position it wants. Our position has not changed on that sovereignty question.

(House of Commons Debates, June 5, 1991 pp. 1199-1200)
(Débats de la Chambre des Communes, le 5 juin 1991, pp. 1199-1200)

5. *Environmental Law / Le droit de l'environnement*

(a) *Le réchauffement de la planète / World Climate Conference*

Ms. Lynn Hunter (Saanich — Gulf Islands): Mr. Speaker, at the Second World Climate Conference in Geneva over 700 scientists from 120 countries concluded in their final statement that immediate action is required to reduce carbon dioxide emissions if we are to avoid destructive impacts of global warming. They said also that it was technically feasible to achieve the required goal of at least a 20 per cent reduction in CO_2 emissions. The United States, the Soviet Union, and Saudi Arabia have all made it quite clear that they are unwilling to take any action.

I ask the Prime Minister: Why has Canada sided with the United States on this issue, instead of working with progressive countries for a declaration that heeds the calls of the scientists?

Mr. Lee Clark (Parliamentary Secretary to Minister of the Environment): Mr. Speaker, I want to make it very clear to the House and to all interested parties that Canada has not sided with the United States, or the Soviet Union, or Saudi Arabia or any other nation which is seeking to retard progress at this particular convention.

In fact, if I may, I would like to read from the final communique, which states: "Taking into account that the developed world is responsible for about three-quarters of all emissions of greenhouse gases, we welcome the decisions and commitments undertaken by the European Community with its member states, Australia, Austria, Canada, Finland, Japan, New Zealand, Norway, Sweden,

Switzerland, and other developed countries to take actions aimed at stabilizing emissions of CO_2 or CO_2 and other greenhouse gases not controlled by the Montreal protocol by the year 2000 in general at 1990 levels.''

(House of Commons Debates, November 7, 1990, pp. 15253-54)
(Débats de la Chambre des Communes, le 7 novembre 1990, pp. 15253-54)

(b) *Les pluies acides — Air Quality Accord*

M. Guy Saint-Julien (Abitibi):... Le Congrès des États-Unis a adopté une nouvelle Loi sur la salubrité de l'air. C'est une excellente nouvelle pour les générations actuelles et futures de Canadiens, de Québécois et d'Américains.... Le premier ministre peut-il nous assurer que l'entrée en vigueur des mesures de cette nouvelle Loi américaine va permettre de réduire considérablement les émissions de produits chimiques toxiques et les pluies acides qui ont ravagé les lacs, rivières et forêts du Québec, des Maritimes et du Canada?

Le très hon. Brian Mulroney (premier ministre):... La législation de la semaine dernière a été une très bonne nouvelle pour le Canada. La Loi prévoit une réduction de dix millions de tonnes des émissions, ce qui réduira les dommages causés aux lacs et aux forêts de l'est du Canada. Je note, monsieur le Président, que la troisième séance des négociations bilatérales entre le Canada et les États-Unis en vue de la conclusion d'un accord sur les pluies acides se tiendra à Ottawa, cette semaine....

(House of Commons Debates, October 29, 1990, p. 14809)
(Débats de la Chambre des Communes, le 29 octobre 1990, p. 14809)

M. Paul Martin (LaSalle — Émard):...Une entente environnementale, pour être valable, doit contenir les critères suivants: sanctions, coercition, mécanismes d'examen public, mécanismes de surveillance indépendants du gouvernement. Voici donc ma question: Le vice-premier ministre peut-il nous assurer que l'entente sur la pollution atmosphérique à être signée aujourd'hui rencontre tous ces critères? Peut-il nous assurer que ce ne sera pas une entente vide de sens, de la poudre aux yeux, comme le Plan vert?

L'hon. Gerry Weiner (secrétaire d'État du Canada et ministre d'État (Multiculturalisme et Citoyenneté)): Madame la Présidente, aujourd'hui est une journée historique pour le Canada. Notre premier ministre et le président Bush vont signer un accord bientôt. Je sais, pour certains députés de cette Chambre qui étaient ici et pour les autres qui n'ont pas participé, que depuis 1978 nous avons discuté des possibilités...Today is a day to reflect on achievement and accomplishment, to celebrate what we have been able to do together. A vigorous new partnership has been brought together. Why not congratulate today instead of belittling. Today is a day to reflect on this success.

(House of Commons Debates, March 13, 1991, p. 18394)
(Débats de la Chambre des Communes, le 13 mars 1991, p. 18394)

(c) *Chlorofluorocarbons*

Hon. Chas. L. Caccia (Davenport):... We learned today from the National Aeronautics Space Agency that the ozone layer in southern Canada has thinned by 5 per cent. The medical profession is of the view that every percentage decrease in the ozone layer leads to an increase of 3 to 4 per cent in the incidence of skin cancer. Therefore, this becomes a matter of urgent public concern.

Will the minister indicate in the House whether he is willing to commit himself today to the deadline of 1995 for the date when chlorofluorocarbons and similar chemical substances will be fully phased out in Canada?

Mr. Lee Clark (Parliamentary Secretary to Minister of the Environment): Mr. Speaker, I am happy to have this opportunity to say, first of all, that this government is, and has been for many years, very concerned with the issue of CFC emissions and their impact on the ozone layer, as the hon. member has just expressed.

I am very proud of the fact that this government has displayed a greater amount of leadership on this issues than many other countries in the world. In fact, as you know, the Montreal protocol talks in terms of the total elimination of the manufacture and import of CFCs by the year 2000. I am delighted that this government has already made a commitment to do that by the year 1997.

We have shown leadership in the past and we will continue to do so now and in the future. I am also pleased to say that almost 85 per cent, I believe, of the use of CFCs will be prohibited in this country by the year 1995.

(House of Commons Debates, June 3, 1991, p. 971)
(Débats de la Chambre des Communes, le 3 juin 1991, p. 971)

6. *International Trade / Le commerce extérieur*

(a) *Mexico / Le Mexique*

Mr. John C. Crosbie (Minister for International Trade):... I point
out to the House that if the hon. members opposite would do some
research, they would see that of 140 international instruments on
the environment, Mexico has ratified 27. It has adhered to the 1985
Vienna Convention for the Protection of the Ozone Layer and the
1987 Montreal protocol on substances that deplete the ozone layer.
They passed extensive domestic legislation and environmental
standards. They still have difficulties in implementation and
enforcement because of their financial limitations. They are a
developing country with a large foreign debt.

I point out that during his official visit to Mexico last year the
Prime Minister signed an environmental co-operation agreement
between Canada and Mexico and we are implementing several small
scale but useful bilateral economic co-operation projects in
Mexico. . . . Mexico has ratified 61 of more than 170 International
Labour Organization conventions, including eight of what are
known as the II core conventions, for example, freedom of association, abolition of forced labour, equal remuneration, and non-
discrimination.

This compares to the United States which has ratified only seven
of these ILO conventions, none of them core, and Canada which
has adhered to 26, four of which are core. Mexico actually has a
better record than either the United States or Canada in adhering
to international conventions dealing with labour matters. One has
to wonder about all these attacks on Mexico and unjustified asper-
sions with reference to the labour situation in Mexico.

In addition, the 1969 Inter-American Convention on Human
Rights contains a basic freedom of association provision. That instrument was ratified by Mexico. It has not been ratified by the
United States, nor has it been ratified by Canada, so when we start
to examine the actual situation in Mexico with respect to legislation and the adherence to international conventions, both with
respect to the environment and to labour matters, Mexico actually
has quite a fair record. They doubtless have difficulties in implemen-

tation because of its economic situation, because of the fact it is undeveloped, and its rapidly increasing population, now 85 millin people. Mexico is trying to pull itself up by its bootstraps.

The same thing applies to the criticism of the so-called Maquiladora areas which, in the eyes of the hon. personages opposite, are supposed to be very retrograde.

In the opinion of Mexicans it is far better to obtain entry level jobs which give them some income, experience, and hope for the future than to have no jobs at all.

(House of Commons Debates, March 15, 1991, pp. 18545-46)
(Débats de la Chambre des Communes, le 15 mars 1991, pp. 18545-46)

L'hon. Jean Chrétien (chef de l'opposition):... On s'attend aujourd'hui à ce que le Congrès américain donne son approbation afin de faciliter les négociations du libre-échange entre les États-Unis, le Canada et le Mexique. Le Président Bush avait déjà communiqué ses objectifs aux membres du Congrès il y a plusieurs semaines et avait clairement expliqué ce qui ferait ou ne ferait pas partie de ces négociations. Je demande donc au ministre: Quand va-t-il faire comme le Président Bush? Quand va-t-il communiquer aux députés de cette Chambre et à la population canadienne les objectifs clairs et précis de son gouvernement pour ces négociations très importantes?

Hon. Michael Wilson (Minister of Industry, Science and Technology and Minister for International Trade): Mr. Speaker, the negotiations we hope will be commencing shortly on the North American free trade agreement will involve, we expect and we hope, an opening up of the Mexican market to Canadian exporters.

We expect also that there will be an element of the free trade agreement which will involve an opening up of investment possibilities between Canada and Mexico.

I have made it very clear that the question of cultural industries is not one that we are prepared to negotiate. We believe the position we took in the free trade agreement with the United States is one that we should continue in these negotiations.

Hon. Jean Chrétien (Leader of the Opposition): Mr. Speaker, before President Bush can even begin fast track negotiations with Mexico, he has to get the approval not only of committees of the Congress, but of Congress itself.

That process gave the American people a chance to express their concerns. When will the government give the Canadian people the same opportunity and agree to public hearings on these very important negotiations?

Hon. Michael Wilson (Minister of Industry, Science and Technology and Minister for International Trade):... I have had some preliminary discussions with the chairman of the Standing Committee on External Affairs and International Trade. We are also going to be following the same process of very open and ongoing consultations with people in the private sector, both business and labour.

We are also going to be having extensive consultations with the provinces so that they will be totally aware of the positions that we take in the free trade agreement negotiations, as well as be able to give us their advice, their guidance and their judgement as to positions we should be taking in relation to their own interests as provinces.

Hon. Jean Chrétien (Leader of the Opposition): Mr. Speaker, in order to win support in Congress for these negotiations with Mexico, President Bush promised to bring in adjustment programs for American workers who will lose their jobs because of the trilateral trade agreement.

I ask the minister: What about Canadian workers? When will we see a commitment by this government, the government of the Canadian people, for a program of adjustment for the Canadian workers who will lose their jobs because of these negotiations?

Hon. Michael Wilson (Minister of Industry, Science and Technology and Minister for International Trade): Mr. Speaker, my friend opposite jumps to the conclusion that free trade results in lost jobs. I question that because in the last 45 years, as tariff barriers and non-tariff barriers have been falling, we have seen a continuation of growth in jobs from trade. Trade has grown from about 15 per cent of our economy to 30 per cent of our economy and has provided jobs for over three million Canadians....

He asks what our position has been on adjustment for workers who lose their jobs. We have far better adjustment programs than the United States has.

(House of Commons Debates, May 22, 1991, pp. 375-76)
(Débats de la Chambre des Communes, le 22 mai 1991, pp. 375-76)

M. Paul Martin (LaSalle — Émard):... Le président Bush a

annoncé des mesures pour protéger certains des intérêts environnementaux des États-Unis dans l'Accord de libre échange avec le
Mexique. . . . On a nos propres exigences environnementales, même
si le ministre ne veut pas les reconnaî tre.

Je lui adresse cette question: Quand le ministre a-t-il l'intention
de déposer, ici en Chambre, une politique indépendante qui
protégera les intérêts environnementaux du Canada dans ces
négociations?

L'hon. Jean J. Charest (ministre de l'Environnement): Monsieur
le Président, dans le cadre des négociations, l'environnement sera
traité à trois niveaux en ce qui concerne le Canada. Dans le cadre
de l'entente comme telle, les sujets qui sont négociés dans le cadre
de l'entente auront une dimension environnementale dont le
Canada se préoccupera. Dans le cadre des sujets qui sont à
l'extérieur de l'entente, le Canada souhaite qu'il y ait une négociation parallèle sur ces sujets-là.

Finalement, monsieur le Président, nous avons déjà eu l'occasion de dire en cette Chambre qu'une fois l'entente conclue, comme
toutes les autres politiques du gouvernement, elle devra faire l'objet d'une évaluation environnementale lorsqu'elle sera soumise au
Cabinet. À ce moment-là, le gouvernement aura à tirer un certains
nombre de conclusions et à les rendre publiques, monsieur le
Président.

(House of Commons Debates, May 22, 1991, pp. 378-79)
(Débats de la Chambre des Communes, le 22 mai 1991, pp. 378-79)

(b) *Dispute Settlement / Le libre-échange*

Hon. Ralph Ferguson (Lambton – Middlesex): Madam Speaker,
in March 1987, Canadian pork producers were assured by the Prime
Minister in this House of Commons that a free trade agreement
with the United States would help Canadian farmers by increasing
predictability and security of access of exports by the farm sector
to United States markets.

Now, four years later, the United States is refusing to accept the
January decision of the free trade dispute settling mechanism on
Canadian pork exports. . . .

Hon. John C. Crosbie (Minister for International Trade):
Madam Speaker, the series of actions that we have taken together
with Canadian pork producers in connection with pork has been

an unparalleled example of success. We have been successful in the
GATT panel with reference to this question. We have been suc-
cessful with respect to a panel under the U.S. – Canada Free Trade
Agreement.

Now, in desperation, the U.S. National Pork Producers Council
has filed a petition asking United States trade representatives to
establish an extraordinary challenge committee to review the panel's
action. That is an act of desperation on its part. It is an extraordinary procedure the council is asking to be used which has not been
used so far. It can only properly be used with respect to some
misbehaviour of panel members. It is extremely unlikely, if the
USTR gives permission for it to go forward, that it would be
successful.

To date our record is unparalleled in the success we have had
under the U.S. – Canada Free Trade Agreement in this important
area.

(House of Commons Debates, March 13, 1991, p. 18400)
(Débats de la Chambre des Communes, le 13 mars 1991, p. 18400)

Hon. Michael Wilson (Minister of Industry, Science and Technology
and Minister for International Trade):. . . I might say that we on
the government side are very pleased, as I am sure colleagues on
the other side of the House are also very pleased, with the results
of the extraordinary challenge result that we heard today. We expect
that this will be the end of the matter. The extraordinary challenge
committee ruling today was binding. The countervailing duty will
be revoked. It was a 3-0 decision on the matter.

(House of Commons Debates, June 14, 1991, p. 1742)
(Débats de la Chambre des Communes, le 14 juin 1991, p. 1742)

(c) *Softwood lumber / Le bois d'oeuvre*

Mrs. Dorothy Dobbie (Parliamentary Secretary to the Minister of
Indian Affairs and Northern Development):. . . On the larger question of addressing the memorandum of understanding itself, the
hon. member will know that the Minister for International Trade
is consulting closely with the provinces and the industry on this
issue. . . . The memorandum of understanding never was envisioned
as a permanent arrangement. It was understood during negotiations

of the Canada – U.S. Free Trade Agreement that the MOU would not exist forever and that the government would want to revisit this issue.

Circumstances have changed significantly since the memorandum of understanding was negotiated in 1986. Stumpage rates have increased in British Columbia and Quebec. These provinces together account for 90 per cent of Canada's exports of softwood lumber to the U.S.

The value of the Canadian dollar has appreciated significantly, vis-à-vis the U.S. dollar since 1986. Canada's market share in the U.S. has dropped by six points from 33 per cent to 27 per cent. Based on a reasonable and objective review, the memorandum of understanding has served its purpose. There are no subsidies now to the Canadian lumber industry. The memorandum of understanding is being re-examined in consultation with the provinces and with industry, and a decision to take up the issue with the U.S. will depend solely on the outcome of these consultations.

(House of Commons Debates, March 18, 1991, p. 18644)
(Débats de la Chambre des Communes, le 18 mars 1991, p. 18644)

(d) *Agriculture — GATT — L'agriculture*

Hon. John C. Crosbie (Minister for International Trade): . . . Madam Speaker, I believe that the Uruguay round of the multilateral trade negotiations is the most important single economic decision-making event that will take place in the 1990s — or at least as far as one can see ahead in the 1990s. . . .

It is widely agreed by those participating in the negotiations that, unless there is a satisfactory resolution of the agricultural issues, there will be no satisfactory ending to the Uruguay round in December in Brussels. . . .

There have been efforts in the past to deal with agricultural trade, but they have been largely unsuccessful in dealing with non-tariff import barriers and the question of subsidies, and in particular export subsidies. Many areas of agriculture are not subject to effective GATT rules at all.

As we all know, the United States has had a waiver in many of these areas since 1954 or 1955. The offer we have made in the GATT negotiations, of course, is subject to all of this being removed. We will not sustain our offer, for example, if there was any suggestion

526   *The Canadian Yearbook of International Law 1991*

that the waiver the United States now has is to continue in the future. Our offer is made subject to certain conditions being met.

What is our offer? It is an initial and conditional offer, conditional on other countries agreeing to negotiate a substantial agricultural trade reform package with concrete benefits for our own agriculture. It is designed to achieve, over a 10-year period, an end to the international subsidy war through total elimination and prohibition of export subsidies. That is the first objective. . . .

One of the difficulties with the European Community is that the European Community appears determined not to agree to any restrictions with respect to export subsidies. If the European Community is not going to agree to any restriction on its right to give the tremendous export subsidies it is now giving its grain and other farmers, then Canada is going to continue to be savaged in the competition between the EC, the U.S., and others through the use of export subsidies. That is one objective.

The second objective is greater market orientation through a reduction of up to 50 per cent in trade distorting, internal subsidies, combined with clearer rules on what is to constitute non-countervailable or non-trade distorting support for agriculture. This is most important.

It is not all internal subsidies, Madam Speaker. It is trade distorting internal subsidies and clear rules. What kind of support can you give which will not be subject to countervail and will be non-trade distorting? That is to be decided in this round, some clear rules on those subjects.

Our third objective is improved market access through a one-third reduction of normal tariffs, resulting on bound rates no higher than 20 per cent.

The final, major objective is greater security for supply management through a strengthened and clarified Article XI of the GATT, in accordance with the proposal we made in March of this year, and which would include minimum market access levels pursuant to our international obligations.

A strengthened and clarified Article XI is needed if our dairy farmers are to be properly protected with the supply management system we now have. They know and understand that. The *status quo* will not adequately protect Canadian dairy farmers today. That is why it is so important that we reach success in these negotiations. That is an additional reason. Without a strengthened and clarified Article XI, a GATT panel has already indicated that dairy farmers are going to be in difficulty as a result of an interpretation of the present rules of the GATT.

With respect to minimum market access levels, all that has been suggested is that, over a 10-year period, the minimum market access levels with respect to supply management programs would increase to 5 per cent of the domestic market.

(House of Commons Debates, November 2, 1990, pp. 15084-86)
(Débats de la Chambre des Communes, le 2 novembre, 1990, pp. 15084-86)

Mr. Maurice Foster (Algoma): . . . Last year the government agreed to give the United States access to the Canadian market for ice-cream and yogurt after the GATT negotiations this fall. Now that the negotiations have been suspended, or at least put in limbo for the next several weeks. I want to know if the government plans to allow access for processed dairy products from the United States, like ice-cream and yogurt. . . .

Hon. Don Mazankowski (Deputy Prime Minister, President of the Privy Council and Minister of Agriculture): Mr. Speaker, the hon. member is wrong in his assumption. We did not agree to give the United States access to the ice-cream and yogurt market. We did say that we would be prepared to sit down and negotiate, but it would have to be within the terms of the over-all objectives achieved through the MTN.

After all, we did lose a GATT panel on the issues. The hon. member is a great fan of the GATT in this particular case and I can assure him that we will not negotiate any access with the Americans until such time as the MTN is concluded. The hon. member knows as well that the position we advanced with regard to the Canadian agriculture position at the MTN was fully consistent with his goals and objectives and the goals and objectives of Canadian agriculture. It would be commensurate, and reciprocal with us getting access to the American market under their removal of the section 22 waiver.

(House of Commons Debates, December 10, 1990 p. 16486)
(Débats de la Chambre des Communes, le 10 décembre 1990, p. 16486)

(e) *Sale of Goods* — *Les contrats de vente de marchandises*

Mr. Rob Nicholson (Parliamentary Secretary to Minister of Justice and Attorney General of Canada): . . . The purpose of this bill is to implement the United Nations Convention on Contracts for the International Sale of Goods thus allowing departments, departmental corporations, and agent Crown corporations to benefit from its provisions. It does so by resorting to the usual practice of giving force of law to the convention which is reproduced in a schedule to the act.

A convention on contracts for the international sale of goods applies to transactions involving the sale of goods for business use between parties whose place of businesses are located in different contracting states.

It establishes a uniform system of rules for the international sale of goods and gives access to legal rules that are compatible with Canadian law. . . .

There are now 28 contracting states to the convention, some of which like the United States, France, the Federal Republic of Germany, Italy, China, are among our largest trading partners. Thus, the adoption of federal implementing legislation will enable federal entities to avail themselves of the benefits of the regime established under the convention in a large number of transactions.

The convention facilitates trade by providing parties to a contract for the international sale of goods with a uniform system of rights, but it also preserves their freedom to contract by allowing them to derogate from the convention by means of an express clause. . . .

The convention on contracts for the international sale of goods was submitted to the provinces and their reaction has been very positive. Eight provinces, Prince Edward Island, Nova Scotia, New Brunswick, Newfoundland, Ontario, Manitoba, Alberta and British Columbia, as well as the Northwest Territories have already passed implementing legislation. . . .

(House of Commons Debates, November 5, 1990, pp. 15136-37)
(Débats de la Chambre des Communes, le 5 novembre 1990, pp. 15136-37)

Treaty Action Taken by Canada in 1990-91 / Mesures prises par le Canada en matière de traités en 1990-91

compiled by / préparé par

FRANÇOISE PLANTE* AND / ET CÉLINE BLAIS**

I. BILATERAL

Argentina

Agreement on Film Relations, Montreal, September 22, 1988; *in force* October 11, 1990; *signed and applied provisionally* September 22, 1988.

Australia

Film Co-production Agreement (with Annex), Canberra, July 23, 1990; *in force* September 26, 1990.

Treaty on Mutual Assistance in Criminal Matters (with Annex), Ottawa, June 19, 1989; *in force* March 14, 1990.

Protocol amending the Reciprocal Agreement on Social Security, Ottawa, October 11, 1990.

Bahamas

Treaty on Mutual Legal Assistance in Criminal Matters (with Annex), Nassau, March 13, 1990; *in force* July 10, 1990.

Bangladesh

Agreement concerning Investment Insurance, Dhaka, July 12, 1990; *in force* July 12, 1990.

Belize

General Agreement on Development Co-Operation (with Annexes), Belmopan, May 15, 1990.

Brazil

Agreement on Air Transport, Brasilia, May 15, 1986; *in force* July 26, 1990.

Exchange of Notes constituting an Agreement to amend the May 15, 1986 Air Transport Agreement, Ottawa, December 20, 1990; *in force* December 20, 1990.

Bulgaria

Long Term Agreement on Development of Trade, Economic and Industrial Cooperation, Sofia, May 22, 1990; *in force* May 22, 1990.

Burundi

General Agreement on Development Cooperation (with Annexes), Ottawa, September 24, 1990; *in force* September 24, 1990.

Chile

Agreement on Air Transport (with Annex), Santiago, July 6, 1990; *applied provisionally* from July 6, 1990.

* Françoise Plante, Treaty Registrar, Legal Advisory Division, Department of External Affairs. Françoise Plante, Greffie des Traités; Direction des consultations juridiques, Ministère des Affaires extérieurs.

** Céline Blais, Legal Advisory Division, Department of External Affairs. Céline Blais, Direction des consultations juridiques, Ministère des Affaires extérieures.

Côte d'Ivoire

Agreement on Air Transport (with Memorandum of Agreement and Annex), Quebec, September 3, 1987; *in force* April 23, 1990; *applied provisionally* September 3, 1987.

Cyprus

Agreement on Social Security, Ottawa, January 24, 1990.

Czechoslovakia

Agreement for the Promotion and Protection of Investments, Prague, November 15, 1990.

Convention for the Avoidance of Double Taxation and the Prevention of Fiscal Evasion with Respect to Taxes on Income and on Capital, Prague, August 30, 1990.

Finland

Agreement for Air Services between and beyond their Respective Territories (with Annexes), Helsinki, May 28, 1990; *applied provisionally* from date of signature.

Convention for the Avoidance of Double Taxation and the Prevention of Fiscal Evasion with Respect to Taxes on Income, Helsinki, May 28, 1990.

France

Agreement regarding the Development of French Language Audiovisual Co-Production Projects for Television, Ottawa, March 14, 1990; *in force* March 14, 1990.

Agreement regarding Co-operation and Exchanges in the Museums Field, Paris, November 26, 1990; *in force* April 1, 1991.

Protocol to the Agreement on Mutual Assistance for the Prevention, Investigation and Suppression by the Customs Administrations of Both Countries of Customs Offences, Ottawa, November 6, 1990.

Exchange of Notes amending the Agreement of March 30, 1989 Establishing a Court of Arbitration for the Purpose of Carrying Out the Delimitation of Maritime Areas between Canada and France, Paris, July 10, 1990; *in force* July 10, 1990.

Hong Kong

Agreement concerning the Investigation of Drug Trafficking and Confiscation of the Proceeds of Drug Trafficking, Hong Kong, November 14, 1990; *in force* February 17, 1991.

ICAO

Headquarters Agreement, Calgary and Montreal, October 4 and 9, 1990.

Ireland

Agreement on Social Security, Ottawa, November 29, 1990.

Italy

Treaty on Mutual Assistance in Criminal Matters, Rome, December 6, 1990.

Jordan

Agreement on Air Transport (with Annexes), Amman, May 10, 1990; *in force* May 10, 1990.

Luxembourg

Convention on Social Security (with Protocol), Ottawa, May 22, 1986; *in force* April 1, 1990.

Mexico

Agreement on Tourism Cooperation, Ottawa, May 8, 1984; *in force* January 17, 1985; *terminated* September 21, 1990.

Agreement on Tourism Co-operation, Mexico, March 16, 1990; *in force* September 21, 1990.

Agreement regarding Mutual Assistance and Co-operation between their Customs Administrations, Mexico, March 16, 1990; *in force* September 21, 1990.

Agreement on Environmental Co-operation, Mexico, March 16, 1990; *in force* September 21, 1990.

Treaty between the United Kingdom of Great Britain and Mexico for the Mutual Surrender of Fugitive Criminals, Mexico, September 7, 1886; *in force* April 19, 1889; *terminated* October 21, 1990.

Treaty of Extradition, Mexico, March 16, 1990; *in force* October 21, 1990.

Treaty on Mutual Legal Assistance in Criminal Matters, Mexico, March 16, 1990; *in force* September 21, 1990.

Convention for the Exchange of Information with Respect to Taxes, Mexico, March 16, 1990.

Multinational Force and Observers
Exchange of Notes between the Government of Canada and the Multinational Force and Observers constituting an Agreement further amending the Agreement on the Participation of Canada in the Sinai Multinational Force and Observers, signed June 28, 1985, as amended March 18, 1986 (with Annex), Rome, March 14, 1990; *in force* March 28, 1990.

Netherlands, The
Air Transport Agreement, Ottawa, June 17, 1974; *in force* June 15, 1975; *terminated* February 1, 1990, in respect of the Kingdom of the Netherlands in Europe.
Exchange of Notes constituting an Agreement relating to the Operation of Nonscheduled (charter) Flights, Ottawa, June 2, 1989; *in force* February 1, 1990.
Agreement relating to Air Transport (with Annex), Ottawa, June 2, 1989; *in force* February 1, 1990.
Agreement on Film and Video Relations (with Rules of Procedure), Ottawa, October 18, 1989; *in force* November 26, 1990; Applied from the date of signature.
Agreement on Social Security, The Hague, February 26, 1987; *in force* October 1, 1990.
Supplementary Agreement amending the Agreement on Social Security, Ottawa, July 26, 1989; *in force* October 1, 1990.

Nicaragua
General Agreement on Development Cooperation (with Annexes), Managua, December 18, 1990; *in force* December 18, 1990.

Philippines
Treaty on Extradition, Ottawa, November 7, 1989; *in force* November 12, 1990.

Poland
Agreement for the Promotion and Reciprocal Protection of Investments, Warsaw, April 6, 1990; *in force* November 22, 1990

Saudi Arabia
Air Transport Agreement (with Annex), Riyadh, November 14, 1990; *in force* June 9, 1991;

Spain
Agreement Relating to the Free Exercise of Remunerative Activities by Dependents of Employees of Diplomatic Missions, Consular Posts or Permanent Missions to International Organizations, Madrid, February 8, 1990; *in effect provisionally* from February 8, 1990.
Treaty between the United Kingdom and Spain for the Mutual Surrender of Fugitive Criminals, London, June 4, 1878; *in force* December 9, 1878; *terminated* August 15, 1990.
Treaty of Extradition, Madrid, May 31, 1989; *in force* August 15, 1990.

Thailand
Agreement for the Training in Canada of Personnel of the Armed Forces of the Kingdom of Thailand, Bangkok, July 30, 1990; *in force* July 30, 1990.

United Kingdom
A Treaty on Mutual Assistance in Criminal Matters (Drug Trafficking) (with Annex), Ottawa, June 22, 1988; *in force* August 4, 1990.

United Nations
Agreement concerning the Establishment and Support of an Information Office for North America and the Caribbean of the United Nations Centre for Human Settlements (Habitat), Nairobi. Signed and entered into force on March 27, 1990 with effect from October 1, 1989.
Exchange of Letters constituting an Interim Agreement on the Status of the Interim Multilateral Fund for the Implementation of the Montreal Protocol on Substances that Deplete the Ozone Layer, Montreal, December 17, 1990; *in force* December 17, 1990.

United States of America
Exchange of Notes constituting an Agreement amending Schedules 1 and 2 of Annex 705.4 of the Free Trade Agreement, Washington, May 2, 1990; *in force* May 2, 1990.
Exchange of Notes constituting an Agreement amending the Tariff Schedules contained in Annex 401.2-A and Annex 401.2-B of the Free Trade Agreement (Washington and Palm Springs, Dec. 22, 1987 and Jan. 2, 1988), Toronto, May 18, 1990; *in force* May 18, 1990.

Exchange of Notes constituting an Agreement Concerning Imports of Broiler Hatching Eggs and Chicks, Washington, September 13, 1990; *in force* September 13, 1990.

Agreement on Fisheries Enforcement, Ottawa, September 26, 1990.

Treaty on Mutual Legal Assistance in Criminal Matters, Québec, March 18, 1985; *in force* January 24, 1990; Canadian Ratification subject to a declaration.

Exchange of Notes constituting an Agreement to extend the October 28, 1980 Agreement providing for Coordination of the Icebreaking Activities on the Great Lakes, Ottawa, December 4, 1990; *in force* December 5, 1990.

Agreement for the Establishment of a Binational Educational Exchange Foundation, Ottawa, February 13, 1990; *in force* February 13, 1990.

Venezuela

Convention on Air Transport (with Annexes), Caracas, June 26, 1990.

Agreement for the Avoidance of Double Taxation regarding Shipping and Air Transport, Caracas, June 26, 1990.

II. MULTILATERAL

Agreement Establishing the International Network for the Improvement of Banana and Plantain, Paris, October 27, 1988; *signed* by Canada, October 27, 1988; Canada's Instrument of Ratification deposited September 8, 1989; *in force* October 18, 1990; *in force* for Canada October 18, 1990.

Protocol relating to an Amendment to the Convention on International Civil Aviation (Article 50(a)), Montreal, October 26, 1990; Canada's Instrument of Ratification deposited April 19, 1991.

Convention for the Conservation of Antarctic Seals, London, June 1, 1972; Canada's Instrument of Accession deposited October 4, 1990; *in force* March 11, 1978; *in force* for Canada November 3, 1990.

International Convention on Mutual Administrative Assistance for the Prevention, Investigation and Repression of Customs Offences, Nairobi, June 9, 1977; Canada's Instrument of Accession deposited September-

ber 19, 1990; *in force* May 21, 1980; *in force* for Canada December 19, 1990.

Exchange of Notes constituting an Agreement amending the Agreement between the Parties to NATO regarding the Status of their Forces, and the Supplementary Agreement with respect to Foreign Forces stationed in the FRG, Bonn, September 25, 1990; *signed* by Canada, September 25, 1990.

Exchange of Notes constituting an Agreement concerning the Convention on the Presence of Foreign Forces in the Federal Republic of Germany of 23 October 1954, Bonn, September 25, 1990; *signed* by Canada, September 25, 1990; *in force* September 25, 1990; *in force* for Canada September 25, 1990.

Treaty on Conventional Forces in Europe (with Protocols), Paris, November 19, 1990; *signed* by Canada, November 19, 1990.

Convention for the Recognition of Studies, Diplomas and Degrees concerning Higher Education in the States belonging to the Europe Region, Paris, December 21, 1979; Canada's Instrument of Ratification deposited March 6, 1990; *in force* February 19, 1982; *in force* for Canada April 6, 1990.

Foundation Charter of the Regional Center for Central and Eastern Europe, Budapest, June 20, 1990; *signed* by Canada, September 5, 1990; *in force* September 5, 1990; *in force* for Canada September 5, 1990; Canada was a founding member.

Amendment to the Montreal Protocol on Substances that Deplete the Ozone layer, London, June 29, 1990; Canada's Instrument of Acceptance deposited on June 29, 1990.

Agreement establishing the European Bank for Reconstruction and Development, Paris, May 29, 1990; *signed* by Canada, May 29, 1990; Canada's Instrument of Ratification deposited February 25, 1991; *in force* March 28, 1991; *in force* for Canada March 28, 1991.

Convention on the Rights of the Child, New York, November 20, 1989; *signed* by Canada, May 28, 1990. *inforce* September 2, 1990, not yet in force for Canada.

Constitution of the International Organization for Migration, Venice, October 19, 1953; Canada's Instrument of Accession deposited November 9, 1990; *in force* November 30, 1954; *in force* for Canada May 23, 1990.

Convention against the Illicit Traffic in

Narcotic Drugs and Psychotropic Substances, Vienna, December 20, 1988; *signed* by Canada, December 20, 1988; Canada's Instrument of Ratification deposited July 5, 1990; *in force* November 11, 1990; *in force* for Canada November 11, 1990.

International Convention on Salvage, London, April 28, 1989; *signed* by Canada, June 11, 1990.

Convention on Early Notification of a Nuclear Accident, Vienna, September 26, 1986; *signed* by Canada, September 26, 1986; Canada's Instrument of Ratification deposited January 19, 1990; *in force* October 27, 1986; *in force* for Canada February 18, 1990.

Charter of the Organization of American States as amended, Bogota, April 30, 1948; *signed* by Canada, November 13, 1989; Canada's Instrument of Ratification deposited January 8, 1990; *in force* for Canada January 8, 1990. Amended by Protocol of Buenos Aires, Feb 27, 1967 and by Protocol of Cartegena de Indias, Dec 5, 1985. Canadian declaration annexed to Instrument of Ratification.

Patent Cooperation Treaty, Washington, June 19, 1970; *signed* by Canada, June 19, 1970; Canada's Instrument of Ratification deposited October 2, 1989; *in force* January 24, 1978; *in force* for Canada January 2, 1990. Chapter II of Treaty entered into force on 29 March 1978.

Final Acts of the Regional Administrative Radio Conference to Establish a Plan for the Broadcasting Service in the Band 1605-1705 kHz in Region 2, Rio de Janeiro, 1988, Rio de Janeiro, June 8, 1988; Canada's Instrument of Ratification deposited February 20, 1991; *in force* July 1, 1990; *in force* for Canada February 20, 1991; Applied with effect from July 1, 1990. Available for reference purposes from the Library at Communications Canada.

Resolutions on the crisis in the Persian Gulf by the UN Security Council acting under Chapter VII of the Charter of the United Nations, New York, beginning August 6, 1990; *in force* for Canada when passed by the Security Council.

Protocol Additional to the Geneva Conventions of 12 August 1949, and relating to the protection of Victims of International Armed Conflicts (Protocol I) (with Annexes), Geneva, June 8, 1977; *signed* by Canada, June 8, 1977; Canada's Instrument of Ratification deposited November 20, 1990; *in force* December 7, 1978; *in force* for Canada May 20, 1991.

Protocol Additional to the Geneva Conventions of 12, August 1949, relating to the Protection of Victims of Non-International Armed Conflicts (Protocol II), Geneva, June 8, 1977; *signed* by Canada, December 12, 1977; Canada's Instrument of Ratification deposited November 20, 1990; *in force* December 7, 1978; *in force* for Canada May 20, 1991.

Agreement between the Governments of Canada, the United Kingdom, Australia, New Zealand and India, and the Government of the Tunisian Republic concerning Commonwealth War Cemeteries, Graves, and Memorials in Tunisia, Tunis, May 2, 1990; *signed* by Canada, May 2, 1990.

I. BILATÉRAUX

Arabie Saoudite

Accord sur le transport aérien (avec annexe), Riyadh, le 14 novembre 1990; *en vigueur* le 9 juin 1991.

Argentine

Accord sur les relations cinématographiques, Montréal, le 22 septembre 1988; *en vigueur* le 11 octobre 1990; signé et appliqué provisoirement le 22 septembre 1988.

Australie

Accord de coproduction cinématographique (avec annexe), Canberra, le 23 juillet 1990; *en vigueur* le 26 septembre 1990.

Convention d'entraide juridique en matière pénale (avec annexe), Ottawa, le 19 juin 1989; *en vigueur* le 14 mars 1990.

Protocole modifiant l'Accord réciproque de sécurité sociale, Ottawa, le 11 octobre 1990.

Bahamas

Traité d'entraide juridique en matière pénale, Nassau, le 13 mars 1990; *en vigueur* le 10 juillet 1990.

Bangladesh

Accord relatif à l'assurance-investissement, Dhaka, le 12 juillet 1990; *en vigueur* le 12 juillet 1990.

Bélize

Accord général de coopération et développement (avec annexes), Belmopan, le 15 mai 1990.

Brésil

Accord sur le transport aérien, Brasilia, le 15 mai 1986; *en vigueur* le 26 juillet 1990.
Échange de Notes constituant un Accord modifiant l'Accord sur le transport aérien signé le 15 mai 1986, Ottawa, le 20 décembre 1990; *en vigueur* le 20 décembre 1990.

Bulgarie

Accord à long terme sur le développement de la coopération commerciale, économique et industrielle, Sofia, le 22 mai 1990; *en vigueur* le 22 mai 1990.

Burundi

Accord général de coopération au développement (avec annexes), Ottawa, le 24 septembre 1990; *en vigueur* le 24 septembre 1990.

Chili

Accord sur le transport aérien (avec annexe), Santiago, le 6 juillet 1990; *appliqué provisoirement* à partir du 6 juillet 1990.

Chypre

Accord sur la sécurité sociale, Ottawa, le 24 janvier 1990.

Côte d'Ivoire

Accord sur le transport aérien (avec Mémoire d'entente et annexe), Québec, le 3 septembre 1987; *en vigueur* le 23 avril 1990; *appliqué provisoirement* le 3 septembre 1987.

Espagne

Accord relativement au libre exercice d'activités rémunératrices par des personnes à la charge d'employés de missions diplomatiques, de postes consulaires et missions permanentes auprès d'organisations internationales, Madrid, le 8 Février 1990. A pris effet à titre conditionnel à compter du 8 février 1990
Traité d'extradition, Madrid, le 31 mai 1989; *en vigueur* le 15 août 1990.
Traité d' extradition entre le Royaume-Uni et l'Espagne, Londres, le 4 juin 1878; *en vigueur* le 9 décembre 1878; *terminé* le 15 août 1990.

États-Unis d'Amérique

Échange de Notes constituant un accord sur les importations d'oeufs d'incubation de poulet de chair et de poussins, Washington, le 13 septembre 1990; *en vigueur* le 13 septembre 1990.
Échange de notes constituant un Accord modifiant les Appendices 1 et 2 de l'Annexe 705.4 de l'Accord de libre-échange, Washington, le 2 mai 1990; *en vigueur* le 2 mai 1990.
Échange de Notes constituant un Accord modifiant les listes tarifaires contenues à l'Annexe 401.2-A et à l'Annexe 401.2-B de l'Accord de libre-échange (Washington et Palm Springs, 22 déc. 1987 et 2 janv. 1988), Toronto, le 18 mai 1990; *en vigueur* le 18 mai 1990.
Accord portant création d'une fondation binationale pour les échanges dans le domaine de l'éducation, Ottawa, le 13 février 1990; *en vigueur* le 13 février 1990.
Traité d'entraide juridique en matière pénale, Québec, le 18 mars 1985; *en vigueur* le 24 janvier 1990. Instrument de ratification canadien accompagné d'une déclaration
Échange de Notes constituant un Accord prolongeant l'Accord prévoyant la coordination des activités de brisage des glaces dans les Grands lacs, Ottawa, le 4 décembre 1990; *en vigueur* le 5 décembre 1990.
Accord concernant l'application de la législation sur les pêches, Ottawa, le 26 septembre 1990.

Finlande

Accord concernant le transport aérien entre leurs territoires respectifs et au-delà (avec annexes), Helsinki, le 28 mai 1990; *appliqué provisoirement* à partir de la date de signature.
Convention en vue d'éviter les doubles impositions et de prévenir l'évasion fiscale en matière d'impôts sur le revenu, Helsinki, le 28 mai 1990.

Force Multinationale et Observateurs (FMO)

Échange de Notes entre le gouvernement du Canada et la Force multinationale et d'Observateurs constituant un Accord modifiant davantage l'Accord relatif à la participation du Canada à la Force multinationale et d'Observateurs du Sinaï, signé le 28 juin 1985, tel que modifié le 18 mars 1986 (avec annexe), Rome, le 14 mars 1990; *en vigueur* le 28 mars 1990.

France

Accord relatif au développement de projets de coproduction audiovisuelle télévisée de langue française, Ottawa, le 14 mars 1990; *en vigueur* le 14 mars 1990.

Accord concernant la coopération et les échanges dans le domaine des musées, Paris, le 26 novembre 1990; *en vigueur* le 1er avril 1991.

Échange de Notes constituant un Accord modifiant l'Accord du 30 mars 1989 instituant un tribunal d'arbitrage chargé d'établir la délimitation des espaces maritimes, Paris, le 10 juillet 1990; *en vigueur* le 10 juillet 1990.

Avenant à l'Accord d'assistance mutuelle visant à la prévention, la recherche et la répression des fraudes douanières par les administrations douanières des deux pays, Ottawa, le 6 novembre 1990.

Hong Kong

Accord concernant les enquêtes sur le trafic des drogues et la confiscation du produit du trafic des drogues, Hong Kong, le 14 novembre 1990; *en vigueur* le 17 février 1991.

Irlande

Accord sur la sécurité sociale, Ottawa, le 29 novembre 1990.

Italie

Traité d'entraide en matière juridique, Rome, le 6 décembre 1990.

Jordanie

Accord sur le transport aérien (avec annexes), Amman, le 10 mai 1990; *en vigueur* le 10 mai 1990.

Luxembourg

Convention sur la sécurité sociale (avec Protocole), Ottawa, le 22 mai 1986; *en vigueur* le 1er avril 1990.

Mexique

Accord concernant la coopération touristique, Ottawa, le 8 mai 1984; *en vigueur* le 17 janvier 1985; *terminé* le 21 septembre 1990.

Accord de coopération touristique, Mexico, le 16 mars 1990; *en vigueur* le 21 septembre 1990.

Accord concernant l'assistance et la collaboration mutuelles entre leurs administrations douanières, Mexico, le 16 mars 1990; *en vigueur* le 21 septembre 1990.

Traité d'entraide juridique en matière pénale, Mexico, le 16 mars 1990; *en vigueur* le 21 septembre 1990.

Accord de coopération dans le domaine de l'environnement, Mexico, le 16 mars 1990; *en vigueur* le 21 septembre 1990.

Traité d'extradition, Mexico, le 16 mars 1990; *en vigueur* le 21 octobre 1990.

Traité entre le Royaume Uni et les États-Unis du Mexique pour l'extradition mutuelle de criminels fugitifs, Mexico, le 7 septembre, 1886; *en vigueur* le 19 avril, 1889; *terminé* le 21 octobre 1990.

Convention sur l'échange de renseignements en matière fiscale, Mexico, le 16 mars 1990.

Nations Unies

Échange de lettres constituant un Accord provisoire sur le statut du Secrétariat du fonds multilatéral provisoire qui est chargé de la mise en oeuvre du Protocole de Montréal relatif à des substances qui appauvrissent la couche d'ozone, Montréal, le 17 décembre 1990; *en vigueur* le 17 décembre 1990.

Accord concernant l'établissement et le financement d'un bureau d'information pour l'Amérique du Nord et les Antilles du Centre des Nations Unies pour les établissements humains (Habitat), Nairobi. *Signé et entré en vigueur* le 27 mars 1990 avec effet à partir du 1er octobre 1989.

Nicaragua

Accord général sur la coopération au développement (avec annexes), Managua, le 18 décembre 1990; *en vigueur* le 18 décembre 1990.

Oaci

Accord de siège, Calgary et Montréal, les 4 et 9 octobre 1990.

Pays-Bas

Accord relatif au transport aérien, Ottawa, le 17 juin 1974; *en vigueur* le 15 juin 1975; *terminé* le 1er février 1990. Terminé pour le Royaume des Pays-Bas en Europe.

Accord sur le transport aérien (avec annexe), Ottawa, le 2 juin 1989; *en vigueur* le 1er février 1990.

Échange de Notes constituant un Accord relatif à l'exploitation de vols non réguliers (affrétés), Ottawa, le 2 juin 1989; *en vigueur* le 1er février 1990.

Accord sur les relations cinématographiques et audiovisuelles (avec règles de procédure), Ottawa, le 18 octobre 1989; *en vigueur* le 26 novembre 1990; *appliqué* à partir du jour de sa signature.

Accord sur la sécurité sociale, La Haye, le 26 février 1987; *en vigueur* le 1er octobre 1990.

Accord supplémentaire modifiant l'Accord sur la sécurité sociale, Ottawa, le 26 juillet 1989; *en vigueur* le 1er octobre 1990.

Philippines

Traité d'extradition, Ottawa, le 7 novembre 1989; *en vigueur* le 12 novembre 1990.

Pologne

Accord sur l'encouragement et la protection des investissements, Varsovie, le 6 avril 1990; *en vigueur* le 22 novembre 1990.

Royaume-Uni

Traité d'entraide en matière pénale (trafic de drogue) (avec annexe), Ottawa, le 22 juin 1988; *en vigueur* le 4 août 1990.

Tchécoslovaquie

Accord sur l'encouragement et la protection des investissements, Prague, le 15 novembre 1990.

Convention en vue d'éviter les doubles impositions et de prévenir l'évasion fiscale en matière d'impôts sur le revenu et sur la fortune, Prague, le 30 août 1990.

Thaïlande

Accord concernant le stage de formation au Canada de personnel des Forces Armées du Royaume de Thaïlande, Bangkok, le 30 juillet 1990; *en vigueur* le 30 juillet 1990.

Venezuela

Accord relatif au transport aérien (avec annexes), Caracas, le 26 juin 1990.

Accord tendant à éviter la double imposition dans le domaine du transport maritime et aérien, Caracas, le 26 juin 1990.

II. MULTILATÉRAUX

Convention portant création d'un réseau international pour l'amélioration de la production de la banane et de la banane plantain, Paris, le 27 octobre 1988; *signée* par le Canada, le 27 octobre 1988; l'instrument de ratifi-

cation du Canada a été déposé le 8 septembre 1989; *en vigueur* le 18 octobre 1990; *en vigueur* pour le Canada le 18 octobre 1990.

Protocole portant amendement de la Convention relative à l'aviation civile internationale (article 50(a)), Montréal, le 26 octobre 1990; l'instrument de ratification du Canada a été déposé le 19 avril 1991.

Convention pour la protection des phoques de l'Antarctique, *fait à* Londres, le 1er juin 1972; l'instrument d'adhésion du Canada a été déposé le 4 octobre 1990; *en vigueur* le 11 mars 1978; *en vigueur* pour le Canada le 3 novembre 1990.

Convention internationale d'assistance mutuelle administrative en vue de prévenir, de rechercher et de réprimer les infractions douanières, Nairobi, le 9 juin 1977; l'instrument d'adhésion du Canada a été déposé le 19 septembre 1990; *en vigueur* le 21 mai 1980; *en vigueur* pour le Canada le 19 décembre 1990.

Échange de Notes constituant un Accord au sujet de la Convention entre les États Parties à l'OTAN sur le statut de leurs forces, de l'Accord complétant cette Convention en ce qui concerne les forces étrangères stationnées en RFA et des accords qui s'y rapportent, Bonn, le 25 septembre 1990; *signé* par le Canada, le 25 septembre 1990.

Échange de Notes constituant un Accord au sujet de la Convention du 23 octobre 1954 sur la présence de forces étrangères en République fédérale d'Allemagne, Bonn, le 25 septembre 1990; *signé* par le Canada, le 25 septembre 1990; *en vigueur* le 25 septembre 1990; *en vigueur* pour le Canada le 25 septembre 1990.

Traité sur les forces armées conventionnelles en Europe (avec Protocoles), Paris, le 19 novembre 1990; *signé* par le Canada, le 19 novembre 1990.

Convention sur la reconnaissance des études et des diplômes relatifs à l'enseignement supérieur dans les États de la région Europe, Paris, le 21 décembre 1979; l'instrument de ratification du Canada a été déposé le 6 mars 1990; *en vigueur* le 19 février 1982; *en vigueur* pour le Canada le 6 avril 1990.

Charte de Fondation du Centre régional de l'environnement pour l'Europe centrale et l'Europe de l'Est, Budapest, le 20 juin 1990; *signé* par le Canada, le 5 septembre 1990; *en vigueur* le 5 septembre 1990; *en vigueur* pour le Canada le 5 septembre 1990. Le Canada est un membre fondateur.

Amendement au Protocole de Montréal relatif à des subsances qui appauvrissent la couche d'ozone, Londres, le 29 juin 1990; l'instrument d'acceptation du Canada a été déposé le 29 juin 1990.

Accord portant création de la Banque Européenne pour la reconstruction et le développement, Paris, le 29 mai 1990; *signée* par le Canada, le 29 mai 1990; l'instrument de ratification du Canada a été déposé le 25 février 1991; *en vigueur* le 28 mars 1991; *en vigueur* pour le Canada le 28 mars 1991.

Convention relative aux droits de l'enfant, New York, le 20 novembre 1989; *signé* par le Canada, le 28 mai 1990; *en vigueur* le 2 septembre 1990; pas encore en vigueur pour le Canada.

Constitution de l'Organisation internationale pour les migrations, *fait à* Venise, le 19 octobre 1953; l'instrument d'adhésion du Canada a été déposé le 9 novembre 1990; *en vigueur* le 30 novembre 1954; *en vigueur* pour le Canada le 23 mai 1990.

Convention contre le trafic illicite des stupéfiants et des substances psychotropes, Vienne, le 20 décembre 1988; *signée* par le Canada, le 20 décembre 1988; l'instrument de ratification du Canada a été déposé le 5 juillet 1990; *en vigueur* le 11 novembre 1990; *en vigueur* pour le Canada le 11 novembre 1990.

Convention sur l'assurance [et le sauvetage maritime], Londres, le 28 avril 1989; *signée* par le Canada, le 11 juin 1990.

Convention sur la notification rapide d'un accident nucléaire, Vienne, le 26 septembre 1986; *signée* par le Canada, le 26 septembre 1986; l'instrument de ratification du Canada a été déposé le 19 janvier 1990; *en vigueur* le 27 octobre 1986; *en vigueur* pour le Canada le 18 février 1990.

Charte de l'Organisation des États Américains telle que modifiée, Bogota, le 30 avril 1948; *signée* par le Canada, le 13 novembre 1989; l'instrument de ratification du Canada a été déposé le 8 janvier 1990; *en vigueur* pour le Canada le 8 janvier 1990; Amendée le 27 février 1967 et le 5 décembre 1985. Déclaration du Canada annexée à l'Instrument de ratification.

Traité de coopération en matière de brevets, Washington, le 19 juin 1970; *signé* par le Canada, le 19 juin 1970; l'instrument de ratifica-

tion du Canada a été déposé le 2 octobre 1989; *en vigueur* le 24 janvier 1978; *en vigueur* pour le Canada le 2 janvier 1990. Le chapitre II est entré en vigueur le 29 mars 1978.

Actes finals de la Conférence administrative régionale des radiocommunications chargée d'établir un Plan pour le service de radiodiffusion dans la bande 1605-1705 kHz dans la Région 2, Rio de Janeiro 1988, Rio de Janeiro, le 8 juin 1988; l'instrument de ratification du Canada a été déposé le 20 février 1991; *en vigueur* le 1er juillet 1990; *en vigueur* pour le Canada le 20 février 1991; *appliqués* avec effet à partir du 1er juillet 1990. Matériaux de renseignements disponibles à la Bibliothèque, Communications Canada.

Actes finals de la Conférence administrative mondiale des radiocommunications sur l'utilisation de l'orbite des satellites géostationnaires et la planification des services spatiaux utilisant cette orbite (ORB- 88), Genève 1988, Genève, le 6 octobre 1988; l'instrument de ratification du Canada a été déposé le 20 février 1991; *en vigueur* le 16 mars 1990; *en vigueur* pour le Canada le 20 février 1991; *appliqués* avec effet à partir du 16 mars 1990, compte tenu d'une déclaration. Matériaux de renseignements disponibles à la Bibliothèque, Communications Canada.

Actes finals de la Conférence administrative mondiale télégraphique et téléphonique (CAMTT-88), Melbourne 1988, Melbourne, le 9 décembre 1988; l'instrument de ratification du Canada a été déposé le 20 février 1991; *en vigueur* le 4 juillet 1990; *en vigueur* pour le Canada le 20 février 1991; *appliqués* avec effet à partir du 4 juillet 1990. Matériaux de renseignements disponibles à la Bibliothèque, Communications Canada.

Amendements de la Convention portant création de l'Organisation internationale de télécommunications maritimes par satellites (INMARSAT), Londres, le 19 janvier 1989; l'instrument d'adhésion du Canada a été déposé le 13 juin 1990.

Résolutions concernant la situation dans le Golfe persique adoptées par le Conseil de sécurité des Nations Unies, agissant en vertu du Chapitre VII de la Charte des Nations Unies, New York, à compter du 6 août 1990; *en vigueur* pour le Canada dès leur adoption par le Conseil de sécurité.

Protocole additionel aux Conventions de

Genève du 12 août 1949 relatif à la protection des victimes des conflits armés internationaux (Protocole I) (avec annexes), Genève, le 8 juin 1977; *signé* par le Canada, le 8 juin 1977; l'instrument de ratification du Canada a été déposé le 20 novembre 1990; *en vigueur* le 7 décembre 1978; *en vigueur* pour le Canada le 20 mai 1991.

Protocole additionnel aux Conventions de Genève du 12 août 1949 relatif à la protection des victimes des conflits armés non internationaux (Protocole II), Genève, le 8 juin 1977; *signé* par le Canada, le 12 décembre 1977; l'instrument de ratification du Canada a été déposé le 20 novembre 1990; *en vigueur* le 7 décembre 1978; *en vigueur* pour le Canada le 20 mai 1991.

Accord entre les gouvernements du Canada, du Royaume-Uni de Grande-Bretagne et d'Irlande du Nord, de l'Australie, de la Nouvelle-Zélande et de l'Inde et le gouvernement de la République Tunisienne concernant les cimetières, sépultures et monuments militaires du Commonwealth en Tunisie, Tunis, le 2 mai 1990; *signé* par le Canada, le 2 mai 1990.

Canadian Cases in International Law in 1990-91 / La jurisprudence canadienne en matière de droit international en 1990-91,

compiled by / préparé par

JOOST BLOM*

I. PUBLIC INTERNATIONAL LAW /DROIT INTERNATIONAL PUBLIC

Seas — fishing zone

Note. See *R.* v. *Alvarez (No. 2)* (1990), 81 Nfld. & P.E.I. R. 23 (Nfld. T.D.), which held that Canada's fishing zones, in which two ship's masters were accused of fishing illegally, were validly proclaimed by regulations under section 4 of the Territorial Sea and Fishing Zones Act, R.S.C. 1970, c. T-7. This conclusion involved construction of the authorizing statute in the light of customary international law. A similar conclusion was reached, after similar arguments, in *R.* v. *Alegria* (1987), 67 Nfld. & P.E.I. R. 256 (Nfld. T.D.), noted in the 1988 volume of this *Yearbook* at p. 402.

Seas — inland waters — application of federal maritime law

Note. *Whitbread* v. *Walley*, [1990] 3 S.C.R. 1273, 77 D.L.R. (4th) 23, decided that the federal jurisdiction over maritime law extended to navigable waters in a province, whether or not they were within the ebb and flow of the tide.

Sovereign immunity

Jaffe v. *Miller* (1990), 73 D.L.R. (4th) 420. Ontario Court, General Division.

In 1980 the plaintiff was charged in Florida with various criminal

* Professor of Law, University of British Columbia.

offences. In 1982 he was kidnapped in Toronto, forcibly removed to Florida, imprisoned there, and charged with further offences in 1983. He brought the present action against lawyers and an investigator working for the State of Florida, claiming damages for conspiracy to lay charges without reasonable and probable cause and with malice, and conspiracy to kidnap him. The defendants included a Florida District Attorney, an Assistant District Attorney, an investigator employed by them, and a lawyer who was counsel to the Florida Department of Business Regulation. The Attorney General of Florida and the Florida Board of Risk Management were sued as being vicariously liable for the torts of the other defendants.

Sutherland, J. dismissed the action against all the defendants on the ground that the State of Florida and these persons were entitled to immunity under the State Immunity Act, R.S.C. 1985, c. S-18. The acts complained of were public, governmental acts of the state, not within any of the exceptions in the act. The immunity applied to all the individual defendants. They were functionaries of the state whose positions were created by the state Constitution and they were acting within the scope of their duties. They had not waived their immunity by also applying to have the action stayed on the ground of *forum non conveniens;* the relevant rule (Ont. Civ. Proc. R. 17.06(4)) said expressly that such an application was not an attornment to the jurisdiction.

Treaties — implementing legislation — construction

National Corn Growers Association v. *Canada (Canadian Import Tribunal),* [1990] 2 S.C.R. 1324, 74 D.L.R. (4th) 449. Supreme Court of Canada.

This was an application to set aside a decision of the Canadian Import Tribunal. The tribunal had made a determination under the Special Import Measures Act, S.C. 1984, c. 25 [now R.S.C. 1985, c. S-15], that the subsidizing by the United States of growers of grain corn had caused and was causing material injury to Canadian corn producers. This determination was a prerequisite to the imposition of a countervailing duty on grain corn imported from the United States.

The principal argument of the applicant, an association of American corn producers, was that the tribunal had misapplied section 42(1) of the Special Import Measures Act. This directed the tribunal to inquire "whether the...subsidizing of the goods...has caused, is causing or is likely to cause material injury [to the production in Canada of like goods].'' The applicant had argued before the tribunal that "the goods" meant imported goods. The main support for this argument was the 1979 GATT Subsidies Code (Agreement on Interpretation and Application of Articles 6, 16, and 23 of the General Agreement on Tariffs and Trade), Article 6(1) of which provides that a determination of injury "shall involve an objective examination of both (a) the volume of subsidized imports and their effect on prices in the domestic market for like products and (b) the consequent impact of these imports on domestic producers of such products." It was argued that the tribunal should have interpreted section 42(1) of the act consistently with Canada's international obligations as set out in the GATT Subsidies Code, and that the Code specified subsidized imports as the subject of the inquiry. In fact there had been only a modest level of imports of American grain corn into Canada. The argument by Canadian corn producers was that potential imports could be taken into account, and that the injury in this case, which involved a virtually open international market, resulted from Canadian producers having to lower their prices or lose market share to imported American corn.

The tribunal had considered the GATT Subsidies Code as well as the act, and concluded that it could take cognizance of potential or likely imports in the determination of material injury. The Federal Court, Trial Division, and the Federal Court of Appeal (in a decision noted in the 1989 volume of this *Yearbook* at p. 43) held that the tribunal's decision should not be set aside.

In unanimously dismissing the appeal the Supreme Court held that the issue upon a review of a decision of an administrative tribunal, whose decisions were declared in the empowering statute to be final and binding, was whether the tribunal's interpretation of the applicable statutory provisions was patently unreasonable. This review included (three out of seven judges dissenting on this point) a consideration of whether it was patently unreasonable to give consideration to the terms of the GATT in interpreting section 42 of the act. The majority, speaking through Gonthier, J., held that it was reasonable for the tribunal to do so. One should strive, he said, to expound an interpretation of domestic law that was consonant with the relevant international obligations. Further, it was reasonable to make the reference to an international agreement at the very outset of the inquiry, to determine if there was any ambiguity, even latent, in the domestic legislation. He rejected the

Court of Appeal's suggestion that recourse to the international obligations should only be had if the domestic legislation was found to be ambiguous on its face. As a latent ambiguity must arise out of matters external to the text to be interpreted, the international agreement was relevant in determining whether an ambiguity existed.

Gonthier, J. held further that the tribunal had not taken an unreasonable view of either section 42 of the act or of the GATT Code provisions, in finding that both were consistent with taking potential as well as actual imports into account.

II. CONFLICT OF LAWS / DROIT INTERNATIONAL PRIVÉ

A. *Jurisdiction / Compétence des tribunaux*

1. *Common law and federal*

(a) *Service* ex juris

Service ex juris — *claim in contract*

Note. Fleming v. *Samuelsohn Ltd.,* [1991] W.W.R. 176, 49 B.C.L.R. (2d) 391 (S.C.), found that a wrongful dismissal was a breach of contract that took place in British Columbia because the notice of termination was received there. Service *ex juris* was thus possible without leave. *National Bank of Can.* v. *Cedar Dale Industries Inc.* (1989), 97 N.B.R. (2d) 352 (C.A.), held that a contract by telephone had been made in Vermont, where the acceptance was received, not in New Brunswick, so service *ex juris* was improper. *Northern Sales Co. Ltd.* v. *Government Trading Corp of Iran* (1991), 81 D.L.R. (4th) 316, [1991] 5 W.W.R. 758 (B.C.C.A.), held that the transitory presence in the province of cargoes belonging to the defendant, around the time the writ was issued but not on the exact day, did not satisfy Rule 13(1)(j) of the B.C. Rules of Court, which authorizes service *ex juris* without leave where it appears "that the plaintiff has a good cause of action . . . upon a contract . . . and that the defendant has assets within the jurisdiction of the value of $200 at least."

Service ex juris - *claim in tort*

G.W.L. Properties Ltd. v. *W.R. Grace & Co. — Conn.* (1990), 50 B.C.L.R. (2d) 260. British Columbia Court of Appeal.

The Court of Appeal held that an American manufacturer had

been properly served *ex juris* in an action for negligence in manufacturing and supplying an asbestos product that was incorporated into the plaintiff's buildings in British Columbia, and in failing to warn the plaintiff of the dangers of such a product when the defendant knew or ought to have known of the dangers. Although the defendant did not distribute or market its products in Canada it was arguable that it could reasonably have foreseen that the product would reach British Columbia consumers through normal channels of trade. If so, there would be a tort in British Columbia, within Rule 13(1)(h) of the B.C. Rules of Court, if the product caused damage when used in the province. The failure to warn would also be a tort in British Columbia, because the duty alleged was one to warn the consumer in British Columbia.

Service ex juris — *action against an estate*

Canadian Commercial Bank v. *Belkin* (1990), 73 D.L.R. (4th) 678, 107 A.R. 232. Alberta Court of Appeal.

A resident of British Columbia, a director of the plaintiff bank, was served *ex juris* in an Alberta action. He died before the hearing. The plaintiffs obtained orders for service *ex juris* on the British Columbia executors of the estate, the assets of which were almost all situated in that province. The only assets in Alberta were certain real property, amounting in value to less than one percent of the estate. The Alberta Court of Appeal held that the service was improper. The question whether the action survived against the estate was a matter of Alberta law, but the relevant statute (the Survival of Actions Act, R.S.A. 1980, c. S-30) could not have an extraterritorial effect so as to authorize impleading a non-resident upon whom the estate had devolved. An Alberta court could not assume jurisdiction over a personal representative appointed under a foreign law, because that would be to interfere in the administration of a foreign estate. An exception should not be made for estates being administered elsewhere in Canada; it would leave a Canadian citizen's estate hostage to litigation in every other part of the federation that assumed a jurisdiction to establish a liability of the estate.

An action in Alberta was possible against a personal representative appointed in Alberta as an administrator of Alberta assets, an administrator *ad litem* or an administrator under some other special grant. That would not be a patent interference with an administration outside of Alberta. But the plaintiffs here might not be content with a proceeding against such a representative, since they sought a right to share in the assets under administration in British Columbia. (The claim was for an amount greater than the whole of the estate.) An argument that the executors had made themselves executors *de son tort* in Alberta was rejected on the ground that there was no evidence of the executors' intermeddling with the land that was the only asset of the estate in Alberta. In any event recovery against the executors on this ground would be limited to the assets with which they had intermeddled.

The plaintiffs might be right in saying that Alberta was not only the convenient forum to try these proceedings, but it was also unfortunate or unwise to have parallel proceedings in British Columbia. That was a matter that the executors and the courts responsible for the administration of the estate had to consider and decide.

Service ex juris — *procedure generally*

Note. Three Canadian jurisdictions (federal, Alberta, Newfoundland) still require leave for any service *ex juris.* Several cases have discussed the type and amount of evidence needed to support an application for leave: *Iona Appliances Inc.* v. *Amway of Canada Ltd.* (1990), 31 C.P.R. (3d) 571 (F.C.T.D.); *Esso Resources Canada Ltd.* v. *Stearns Catalytic Ltd.* (1990), 41 C.P.C. (2d) 228 (Alta. Q.B.); *Sopol-Pacific Ltd.* v. *Schreier Malting Co.* (1991), 45 C.P.C. (2d) 235 (Alta. Q.B. (M.C.)).

In the jurisdictions where no leave is required for service *ex juris* in defined types of action, leave may be given for such service in a case that does not fall under any of the defined types. See *Exta-Sea Charters Ltd.* v. *Formalog Ltd.* (1991), 55 B.C.L.R. (2d) 197 (S.C. (M.C.)), applying a test based on real and substantial connection with the province to decide whether leave should be given.

In *Technaflow Inc.* v. *Minti Sales Ltd.,* [1991] 5 W.W.R. 692 (Alta. Q.B. (M.C.)), it was held that a garnishing order could not be issued against an American company with no presence in Alberta; as with any order of execution, the person sought to be bound had to be within the jurisdiction.

(b)   *Declining jurisdiction — agreed choice of forum*

Note. In *Corostel Trading Ltd.* v. *Secunda Marine Services Ltd.* (1990), 38 F.T.R. 232 (F.C.T.D.), the court took jurisdiction despite an exclusive choice of forum clause in favour of London, England, because the case was predominantly connected with Canada and the plaintiff would not have access to important witnesses if the clause were enforced. See also *Fleming* v. *Samuelsohn Ltd.,* [1991] 1 W.W.R. 176, 49 B.C.L.R. (2d) 391 (S.C.) (clause not enforced), and *Fairfield* v. *Low* (1990), 44 C.P.C. (2d) 65 (Ont. H.C.) (clause enforced).

(c) *Declining jurisdiction:* forum non conveniens

Defendant served in the jurisdiction

Kornberg v. *Kornberg* (1990), 76 D.L.R. (4th) 379, [1991] 2 W.W.R. 594; leave to appeal refused, [1991] 1 S.C.R. x. Manitoba Court of Appeal.

A husband and wife, who were married in 1958, had lived all their lives in Manitoba until they separated in 1987. The husband later moved permanently to Minnesota. On 6 September 1989 the wife, still resident in Manitoba, petitioned before a court in Minnesota for divorce and a disposition of the matrimonial assets. The husband sought unsuccessfully to have the Minnesota court stay these proceedings. On October 19, 1989 he also began proceedings in Manitoba for divorce and property relief. The husband applied to the Manitoba Queen's Bench for an injunction against the wife's continuing the proceedings in Minnesota. The wife applied to the same court for a stay of the husband's action in that court. The property at issue included substantial holdings of real estate in Manitoba, Saskatchewan, and the United States.

The Manitoba Court of Appeal reversed the trial judge's decision that the Minnesota proceedings should be enjoined because Manitoba was the *forum conveniens.* This was not the test. The husband had failed to establish that the Minnesota proceedings were vexatious or oppressive, or that they would result in injustice to him. The wife had chosen the forum in which he usually lived and her proceedings had very real connections with that jurisdiction. The Court of Appeal further held that the Manitoba proceedings should be allowed to continue as well. The wife had not established that Minnesota was a clearly or distinctly more appropriate forum for the trial of the action. It was not *prima facie* unjust or vexatious to commence two actions about the same subject-matter, one in Manitoba and the other in a foreign court. The courts would lean against this inference even more strongly where the plaintiff in one jurisdiction was the defendant in the other. It might well be that

as the proceedings continued in Manitoba and in Minnesota, one
forum would emerge as the natural forum for the resolution of the
parties' matrimonial and property disputes. That, however, was a
matter beyond the record in this appeal. So was the question of
interjurisdictional cooperation that could make discovery and other
pre-trial procedures in one forum available for use in the other
forum.

Note. Other cases where defendants who were served in the
province sought a stay of proceedings on the ground of *forum non
conveniens* were *Saint John Shipbuilding Ltd.. v. The Eldir,* [1991] 1 F.C.
D-34 (T.D.) (stay refused); *Halifax Grain Elevator Ltd.* v. *Cargill Ltd.*
(1990), 96 N.S.R. (2d) 234 (T.D.) (stay granted); and *Thorpe Bros.
Ltd.* v. *Saan Stores Ltd.* (1990), 89 Sask. R. 106 (Q.B.) (stay refused).

Defendant served ex juris

Westminer Canada Holdings Ltd. v. *Coughlan* (1990), 73 D.L.R. (4th) 584,
75 O.R. (2d) 405. Ontario Divisional Court.

The plaintiffs, federally incorporated companies with head offices
in Ontario, purchased the majority of the shares in a mining company incorporated in Nova Scotia, whose shares traded on both
the Toronto and Montreal Stock Exchanges. The plaintiffs subsequently brought an action in Ontario against the former directors
of the mining company for fraud, conspiracy, wilful misrepresentation and illegal insider trading in the company's ore reserves. The
action included claims based on failure by these directors to file
material information under the Ontario Securities Act, R.S.O. 1980,
c. 466, whose rules applied to the mining company as a "reporting issuer." The company was not a reporting issuer under the
equivalent Nova Scotia legislation and was not required to file the
information in Nova Scotia that it had allegedly failed to file in
Ontario. All but one of these directors were served *ex juris,* in Nova
Scotia. The service was admittedly within the Rules of Civil
Procedure, but the defendants sought a stay of the action under
Rule 17.06 on the ground that Ontario was *forum non conveniens.* The
Master ordered a stay, principally because most of the witnesses
were in Nova Scotia and most of the material facts were connected
with Nova Scotia.

The Divisional Court reversed the Master's decision on the
ground that in two respects the stay would deprive the plaintiffs
of a legitimate juridical advantage they might have in an Ontario

court. First, a Nova Scotia court might not apply the Ontario statute or the rules of the Toronto Stock Exchange, since it might apply the common law rule that a claim on a foreign tort could succeed only if the wrong was actionable under the *lex fori*. Second, the claim would now be statute-barred in Nova Scotia. The defendants' undertaking not to raise the limitation defence in Nova Scotia did not end the matter. The juridical disadvantage remained because a bare promise not to rely on the limitation (the plaintiffs had not agreed to the undertaking) was short of a binding contract to that effect, and because various other circumstances might make the waiver ineffective.

A further reason for denying a stay was that the action arose out of a shareholders' lock-out agreement that was expressly governed by Ontario law, and a take-over bid that also included a choice of law in favour of Ontario. The defendants listed the shares on the Toronto Stock Exchange and thus were subject to that exchange's rules as well as the Ontario Securities Act with regard to disclosures and filings as directors and insiders.

Note. Another case of *forum non conveniens* in litigation relating to the sale of corporate shares was *Paterson* v. *Hamilton* (1991), 79 Alta. L.R. (2d) 111, 111 A.R. 1 (C.A.).

In *Buchar* v. *Weber* (1990), 71 D.L.R. (4th) 544 (Ont. H.C.), a plaintiff who had been injured as a passenger in a motor vehicle accident in Alberta argued that his action against the Alberta-resident driver and owner should be allowed to continue in Ontario, because he had the advantage there that the Alberta "guest statute," requiring him to show gross negligence, would not be applied by an Ontario court. The court held, first, that this was incorrect because an Ontario court would apply the civil law of the *lex loci delicti* in a case of this kind; and, secondly, that the *forum conveniens* was Alberta.

(d) *Actions concerning property*

Matrimonial property

Note. In making orders under the matrimonial property statutes of the common law provinces, the courts have held that they have no jurisdiction to order the conveyance of immovables outside the province from one spouse to another. They can, however, make *in personam* orders that effect an apportionment of the value of such immovables. See, this year, *Gomez-Morales* v. *Gomez-Morales* (1990), 30 R.F.L. (3d) 426 (N.S.C.A.), and *Laurence* v. *Laurence* (1991), 56 B.C.L.R.

(2d) 254 (C.A.).

On jurisdiction to deal with immovables in the province, see *Fareed* v. *Latif* (1991), 31 R.F.L. (3d) 354 (Man. Q.B.).

(e)   *Infants and children*

Custody — no extraprovincial order

Note. In the common law provinces jurisdiction in custody is subject to three different sets of rules. First, if custody is sought as corollary relief in divorce proceedings, or a corollary order for custody is sought to be varied, the provisions of the Divorce Act, R.S.C. 1985, c. 3 (2nd Supp.), apply. These include the ability of the court with jurisdiction in divorce to order a transfer of custody proceedings to another province if it would be a more appropriate forum (s. 6). For cases applying the relevant provisions, see *Cormier* v. *Cormier* (1990), 107 N.B.R. (2d) 442 (Q.B.); *Ketler* v. *Peacey* (1990), 28 R.F.L. (3d) 266 (N.W.T. S.C.); and *Staranowicz* v. *Staranowicz* (1990), 30 R.F.L. (3d) 185 (Ont. Gen. Div.). Second, where custody is litigated independently, many common law provinces have statutory rules for jurisdiction that are based on a real and substantial connection with the province. Third, in the remaining provinces jurisdiction in custody depends on common law rules based on the child's ordinary residence. The child's presence in the jurisdiction can also suffice, but a court will usually decline jurisdiction on the ground that the ordinary residence is usually *forum conveniens;* see *Sutton* v. *Sodhi* (1989), 94 N.S.R. (2d) 126 (Fam. Ct.). At common law jurisdiction to vary a custody order cannot be based on the fact that the court had jurisdiction to make the original order; if the child has moved out of the province, jurisdiction is lost. See *C.(T.S.)* v. *N.(D.L.)* (1990), 28 R.F.L. (2d) 353 (N.B.C.A.).

Extraprovincial custody orders — enforcement and variation

Note. See *Miller* v. *Miller* (1990), 30 R.F.L. (3d) 204 (Alta. C.A.), where the Alberta court ordered a child, who had been brought by her father to Alberta, returned to Saskatchewan. The latter province's court had awarded custody to the mother and further disputes as to custody would best be heard there as well, since it was still the child's ordinary residence.

(f) Injunctions against carrying on legal proceedings in another jurisdiction

Amchem Products Inc. v. *British Columbia (Workers' Compensation Board)* (1990), 75 D.L.R. (4th) 1, [1991] 1 W.W.R. 243; leave to appeal granted, [1991] 1 S.C.R. xv. British Columbia Court of Appeal.

A large number of individuals brought an action in a District Court in Texas against various manufacturers of asbestos products, claiming damages for having been exposed to those asbestos products in the workplace. In most cases the claimants were resident in British Columbia and alleged their injuries had been suffered there. The action was being prosecuted on their behalf by the Workers' Compensation Board of that province, under a statutory right of subrogation to their claims as a result of paying benefits for the claimants' injuries. All except two of the companies were incorporated in the United States, but not in Texas; the two others were incorporated in Quebec and the United Kingdom. The jurisdiction of the Texas court was based on each company's doing business and selling its products in that state.

The companies began proceedings in British Columbia, claiming a declaration that they were not liable to the claimants, and a permanent injunction against the claimants' continuing their proceedings in Texas. They also sought an interim injunction against the claimants' seeking an order from the Texas court to enjoin the companies from carrying on these proceedings in British Columbia. The chambers judge, Esson C.J.S.C., granted the interim injunction against any Texan proceedings to enjoin the continuation of those in British Columbia, and his order was upheld by the Court of Appeal.

The critical question on an application for an injunction to restrain a party from continuing foreign legal proceedings was whether the continuation would be oppressive or vexatious as against the party seeking the injunction. On this point *Société Nationale Industrielle Aérospatiale* v. *Lee Kui Jak,* [1987] A.C. 897I (P.C.), should be followed. In the present case any attempt by the claimants to preempt by Texan court orders the hearing of the companies' case in British Columbia would be vexatious and oppressive. British Columbia was the only natural forum for the claimants' action. The acts and omissions that were the subject of the claims all occurred in Canada, the claimants were currently or at the material times British Columbia residents, and it was in British Columbia that they suffered the injury and were admitted to compensation. The companies had no natural connection with Texas. In addition it appeared that the court in Texas would not hear any argument based on *forum non conveniens*. The denial to the companies of even a hearing on the merits of such a plea, albeit as a result of a rule of Texas law, was enough to tip the scales to a finding of oppression. This was so even taking into account the advantages on both liability and damages that the claimants might enjoy in Texas, assuming that Texas law would be applied to the claims. Neither the natural forum being in this province, nor the absence of a doctrine of *forum non conveniens* in Texas, was by itself decisive. The oppression was shown by a combination of all the circumstances.

It was of no significance that the injunction the companies sought was not ancillary to any other claim by the companies, and did not relate to any legal proceedings in British Columbia by the claimants. Injunctions of this sort were an exception to the basic principle restricting the grant of injunctions to certain exclusive categories.

Note. An injunction against proceeding against a manufacturer in Texas was refused in *Bell Helicopter Textron Inc.* v. *Brown*, [1991] 5 W.W.R. 374, 55 B.C.L.R. (2d) 310 (S.C.), because Texas was the defendant's home state and thus a natural forum. See also *Kornberg* v. *Kornberg*, noted above under (c) declining jurisdiction: *forum non conveniens*, and *Aikmac Hldg. Ltd.* v. *Loewen* (1989), 66 Man. R. (2d) 295, 42 C.P.C. (2d) 139 (Man C.A.), where injunctions were also refused.

2. *Québec*

Compétence territoriale — défendeur domicilié hors du Québec -article 68 C.P.

Dargaud Éditeur c. *Presse-Import Léo Brunelle Inc.*, [1990] R.D.J. 341. Cour d'appel du Québec.

Par des contrats conclus à diverses époques à compter du 23 février 1978, Dargaud Éditeur, une société française, accordait à Presse-Import, une société canadienne, l'exclusivité de la distribution des produits de Dargaud Éditeur au Canada. L'une de ces conventions, passée le 27 novembre 1984, et renouvelée par un avenant du 26 juin 1986, liait les parties et réglait leurs relations contractuelles pour une période expirant le 31 décembre 1989. Le 11 juillet 1988, on a signé une nouvelle entente pour prolonger la convention du 1ᵉʳ janvier 1990 au 31 décembre 1992.

Le 24 mars 1989, à Paris, Dargaud Éditeur a donné au représentant de Presse-Import un avis de dénonciation du contrat, à prendre effet immédiatement. A la même époque, Dargaud Éditeur a transféré au Groupe Quebecor le privilége de l'exclusivité de ses produits. Presse-Import l'a poursuivi en dommages. Elle a demandé qu'une injonction interlocutoire soit émise pour forcer Dargaud Éditeur et Dargaud Canada à respecter leurs engagements et pour qu'il soit interdit à Quebecor de distribuer les produits dont elle réclamait le droit à l'exclusivité. La Cour supérieure s'est déclaré compétente pour entendre l'affaire et a ordonné l'émission de l'injonction sollicitée. L'appel ne contestait pas le bien-fondé du jugement quant au mérite de la demande d'injonction. L'appel portait exclusivement sur un moyen déclinatoire.

Les appelantes ont soutenu que la Cour supérieure était incompétente *ratione loci* pour entendre l'affaire. Ils ont dit que toute la cause d'action n'avait pas pris naissance au Québec (Art. 68(2)) parce que le contrat dont il s'agissait a été conclu en France. En outre, ils ont dit que le respect de l'ordonnance impliquée ne pouvait être assuré vu l'impossibilité de prononcer contre Dargaud Éditeur, en cas de non-observance, une sanction ayant un caractére exécutoire.

La Cour d'appel a conclu que la Cour supérieure n'était pas compétente selon Art. 68(2). Il est vrai que toute la cause d'action n'avait pas pris naissance dans la province. Le contrat de 1984 avait été conclu en France. Il n'importait plus de rechercher où ont eu lieu les accords de volontés ou même les signatures relatives aux écrits subséquents à celui de 1984, vu qu'ils n'étaient que des avenants ou renouvellements de celui-ci. Or, un des éléments constitutifs et essentiels de cette cause s'était produit à l'extérieur de la province.

L'art. 68(1) C.P. s'appliquait cependant en l'espèce. Au moment de l'institution des procédures, Dargaud Éditeur était créancière de Presse-Import pour une somme de 500 000 FF. Il ne s'agissait pas en l'occurrence d'un actif existant à l'occasion d'une circonstance qui tenait purement du hasard ou d'une conjonction unique. Une créance due au défendeur constitue un bien au sens de l'article 68 C.P. L'endroit où il est situé est celui où le débiteur a son domicile ou sa résidence. Or, l'existence de cette créance suffisait à attribuer juridiction à la Cour supérieure.

L'argument selon lequel la Cour supérieure ne devait pas exercer sa juridiction parce que l'injonction serait inefficace, a été rejeté. L'injonction visait à empêcher toute entreprise autre que Presse-Import de faire la distribution des ouvrages de Dargaud Éditeur. Quebecor avait été mise en cause dans la requête. Son siège social était au Québec et toute velléité de sa part de transgresser l'ordonnance le rendrait passible d'une déclaration d'outrage et des peines qui peuvent en être la sanction. La même remarque s'appliquait à toute autre entreprise faisant des affaires au Québec qui voudrait se substituer à Presse-Import dans ses relations contractuelles avec l'éditeur. Tout en admettant qu'on ne pouvait exclure d'une façon absolue la possibilité que Dargaud Éditeur prenne la décision de cesser ces envois, il n'apparaissait pas qu'une attitude aussi radicale de sa part soit envisageable, puisqu'elle la priverait d'un marché important.

Morel c. *Parrot,* [1990] R.D.J. 246. Cour d'appel du Québec.

L'appelant a assigné en dommages pour atteinte à sa réputation le Syndicat des postiers du Canada (le syndicat), sa section locale de Montréal et les huit membres de son exécutif, ceux-ci, tant personnellement qu'ès qualités. Il a allégué qu'une lettre écrite à Ottawa, signée par chacun des membres de l'exécutif et ensuite diffusée à tous les membres du syndicat résidents au Québec et à tous les présidents et secrétaires de chaque association locale du pays était diffamatoire. Il a introduit son recours dans le district de Montréal. Les huit intimés, membres de l'exécutif, ont présenté une exception déclinatoire au motif qu'aucune des dispositions de l'article 68 C.P. n'était satisfaite. Le juge de la Cour supérieure a accueilli la requête.

La Cour d'appel a rejeté l'appel. Toute la cause d'action n'avait pas pris naissance à Montréal (article 68(2)). En matière quasi-délictuelle, chacun des trois éléments (faute, dommage et lien de causalité) de la responsabilité devait prendre naissance au district de la Cour supérieure. La faute alléguée en l'espèce était la publication d'une lettre diffamatoire; cette faute s'est produite aux lieus de réception, parmi lesquels Montréal n'était qu'un endroit parmi plusieurs autres.

Le syndicat était une association *bona fide,* non une corporation, et n'avait aucun bien au Québec (article 68(1) C.P.). L'appelant l'avait assigné sous son nom collectif comme permet l'article 115 C.P., et il ne pouvait pas en même temps agir et plaider comme s'il avait poursuivi chaque membre de l'association. L'article 68(3) C.P. ("lieu où a été conclu le contrat qui donne lieu à la demande") ne s'appliquait pas non plus; l'action était de nature délictuelle et ne dépendait d'aucune maniére de la nature des liens qui l'unissaient à son syndicat.

Note. Veuillez comparer *Trans-Dominion Energy Corp.* c. *Total Return Fund Inc.,* [1990] A.J.Q. 719, No 2126 (C.A.). L'intimée, une société dont la siège social était à Montréal, était actionnaire de l'appelante, une société constituée en vertu des lois de la Colombie-Britannique. L'intimée a intenté une action contre l'appelante en réclamation de la perte subie en raison de la diminution de valeur de ses actions depuis la tenue d'une assemblée générale spéciale. Elle a allégué que l'appelante avait erronément envoyé l'avis de cette assemblée à Calgary au lieu de Montréal, et qu'en raison de cette erreur de procédure, elle n'avait pas pu s'opposer au projet de modification du statut de la compagnie. La Cour d'appel a décidé que toute la cause d'action avait pris naissance au Québec, puisque le lieu d'omission d'avertir est l'endroit où l'avertissement aurait dû être reçu.

Association canadienne d'athlétisme c. *St-Hilaire,* [1990] R.D.J. 132. Cour d'appel du Québec.

L'intimé a présenté une requête en injonction interlocutoire afin qu'il soit, entre autres, ordonné aux deux appelantes, l'Association canadienne des Jeux du Commonwealth Inc. (l'A.C.J.C.) et l'Association canadienne d'athlétisme (l'A.C.A.), et à la Fédération d'athlétisme du Québec (F.A.Q.) de l'intégrer à titre d'entraîneur à la délégation canadienne d'athlétisme devant se rendre en Nouvelle-Zélande. Il a allégué en effet que si l'A.C.A., dont il était devenu membre en règle à Montréal, avait respecté ses propres règlements et critères, il aurait été sélectionné pour se rendre en Nouvelle-Zélande. La requête a été signifiée aux appelantes en Ontario, lieu de leur siège social. Une exception déclinatoire a été rejetée par le juge de la Cour supérieure. La pourvoi des appelantes a également été rejetée. L'article 68(2) C.P. ne s'appliquait pas, parce que l'intimé n'avait pas établi que la décision de ne pas l'intégrer fut prise à Hull ou ailleurs au Québec. Mais il alléguait, sans employer le mot, la violation d'un contrat avec l'A.C.A. Ce contrat, qui "donne lieu à la demande," fut conclu à Montréal. St-Hilaire était membre de l'A.C.A. en tant que membre de la F.A.Q., et il est devenu membre de la F.A.Q. à Montréal. Mais pour ce qui était de l'A.C.J.Q. on ne pouvait parler de contract avec l'intimé.

L'A.C.J.Q. n'était pas obligée de suivre les recommandations de l'A.C.A., et même si l'A.C.J.Q. n'avait pas respecté ses propres règlements et critères, l'intimé ne pouvait s'en plaindre sur une base contractuelle quelconque.

Note. Deux autres décisions au sujet de l'article 68 C.P., dans lesquelles la Cour s'est déclarée incompétente, sont *Systèmes de rebuts médicaux Decom* c. *Simonds Manufacturing Co.,* [1990] A.J.Q. 719, No 2128 (C.S.), et *Carver Boat Corp.* c. *Arcand,* [1990] A.J.Q. 723, No 2137 (C.A.).

Demande en matière familiale — article 70 C.P.

Note. Veuillez voir *Droit de la famille — 831,* [1990] A.J.Q. 720, No 2132 (action intentée par des enfants, domiciliés dans le district de Montréal, contre leur père, domicilié au Nouveau-Brunswick; compétence de la Cour en raison du domicile de l'une des parties au Québec).

B. *Procedure / Procédure*

Common law and federal

(a) *Pretrial procedure*

Discovery of documents — blocking legislation

Hunt v. T & N plc. (1991), 81 D.L.R. (4th) 764, [1991] 5 W.W.R. 475. British Columbia Court of Appeal.

In one of many actions pending in British Columbia for asbestos-related injury, for aggregate damages of more than $200 million, certain of the defendants objected as a test case to producing or even identifying documents kept at their offices in Quebec. They relied upon that province's Business Concerns Records Act, R.S.Q. 1977, c. D-12, section 2 of which prohibits any person from removing from Quebec any document (as defined) "or résumé or digest of any document" relating to any business concern in Quebec.

The Court of Appeal, upholding the decision of Esson C.J.S.C., held the defence to be valid. In this case the public policies of British Columbia, as reflected in its Rules of Court and principles of practice and procedure, conflicted with the policies of Quebec as reflected in the Business Concerns Records Act. Comity as between Canadian provinces required recognition of and deference to the validly enacted legislation of a province by the courts of another province. A court might examine the constitutional validity of legislation of another province designed to intrude into the exclusive legislative field of the court's own province, but this was not such a case. The Quebec statute dated from 1958; there was an identical statute in Ontario. It appeared to be true that some of the defendants had deliberately solicited orders from the Quebec courts prohibiting disclosure of documents in this case. But the deliberate courting of a legal impediment to production was of no significance if, without the order, there was an effective right to refuse production. On the basis of expert evidence as to the law of Quebec, a "résumé or digest" in section 2 should be construed as extending even to indirect disclosure in a list of documents.

(b)   *Trial procedure*

Remedy — damages for foreign currency loss

Note. See *McCutcheon* v. *McCutcheon* (1989), 102 N.B.R. (2d) 271 (Q.B.), and *Ripulone* v. *Pontecorvo* (1989), 98 N.B.R. (2d) 267 (Q.B.), affd. on other grounds (1989), 104 N.B.R. (2d) 56 (C.A.), in both of which a claim calculated in foreign currency was converted into Canadian dollars using the exchange rate at the date of the hearing.

(c)   *Evidence obtained locally for foreign proceedings*

Letters rogatory

Note. See *Gourmet Resources Int'l Inc. Estate* v. *Paramount Capital Corp.* (1991), 3 O.R. (3d) 286 (Gen. Div.), in which a debtor was ordered to answer questions in Ontario in aid of execution on a United States judgment, pursuant to an order given on letters rogatory from the United States Bankruptcy Court.

See also *Coats Co.* v. *Bruno Wessel Ltd.* (1990), 46 C.P.C. (2d) 316 (Ont. Gen. Div.), where the Ontario court refused to enforce letters rogatory issued by a United States District Court, on the ground that the request for documents was overbroad.

C.   *Foreign judgements / jugements étrangers*

1.   *Common law and federal*

(a)   *Conditions for enforcement by action or registration*

Finality of judgment — default judgment set aside in original jurisdiction

Note. In *Toronto-Dominion Bank* v. *Prairie Gold Oilfield Servicing Ltd.*

(1990), 71 D.L.R. (4th) 738, [1990] 6 W.W.R. 16 (Sask. Q.B.), an Alberta default judgment that had already been registered in Saskatchewan was set aside in Alberta so the debtor could defend. It was held that the appropriate course was to leave the Saskatchewan judgments and executions in place while staying any enforcement of them pending the outcome of the Alberta proceedings.

Jurisdiction of original court — submission by the defendant

Note. Carrick Estates Ltd. v. *MacKinnon* (1990), 86 Sask. R. 232 (C.A.), affirmed the decision noted in the 1990 volume of this *Yearbook* at p. 618. See also *Hoopman Estate* v. *Imrie* (1991), 57 B.C.L.R. (2d) 310 (S.C. (M.C.)).

Jurisdiction of original court — real and substantial connection

Morguard Investments Ltd. v. *De Savoye,* [1990] 3 S.C.R. 1077, 76 D.L.R. (4th) 256. Supreme Court of Canada.

Two lenders brought foreclosure proceedings on a mortgage over real estate in Alberta. The defendant, who had assumed the obligations of mortgagee, was served with process in British Columbia but did not appear and took no part in the action. The lenders obtained judgments in default for sale of the property and for personal judgment against the defendant for the balance owing after sale. They were unable to register the money judgment under the reciprocal enforcement of judgments legislation in British Columbia (Court Order Enforcement Act, R.S.B.C. 1979, c. 75, Part 2), because section 31(6)(b) precluded registration, the defendant having neither voluntarily appeared nor otherwise submitted during the proceedings to the Alberta court's jurisdiction. The lenders therefore brought an action on their judgments, arguing they were enforceable at common law.

The chambers judge and the Court of Appeal held for the plaintiff lenders. The Court of Appeal (whose decision is noted in the 1988 volume of this *Yearbook* at p. 417) relied expressly on the ground that the traditional common law insistence on the defendant having been served with process in the foreign country or having submitted to its courts' jurisdiction was obsolete. Judgments, at least those from within Canada, should also be recognized on the ground of "reciprocity," that is, if the British Columbia courts would have taken jurisdiction under circumstances parallel to those in which the foreign court took jurisdiction.

The Supreme Court of Canada affirmed the decision, but on different grounds. Speaking through La Forest, J., the court stressed that the basis of the rules of private international law was comity, which today meant the need to facilitate the flow of wealth, skills and people across state boundaries in a fair and orderly manner. The traditional common law limitations on the recognition and enforcement of foreign judgments had been formulated in a world of slow movement and inadequate communications, and needed to be reassessed. In any event these limitations should never have been applied as between the Canadian provinces and territories. Comity applied with much greater force between the units of a federal state. The English rules flew in the face of the intent, apparent in the Canadian constitution, to create a single country. Citizens had the right of mobility across provincial boundaries; there was a common market and federal regulation of interprovincial trade; and the Canadian judicial structure imposed a uniform standard of procedural fairness on the courts of the provinces and territories, through the federal appointment of all superior court judges and the supervising role of the Supreme Court of Canada in appeals.

The rules of private international law as between the provinces must be shaped to conform to the federal structure of the constitution. The decision of any Canadian court was entitled to recognition in any other Canadian court, provided there was a real and substantial connection between the original province and the subject-matter of the action. In the present case such a connection was obviously present; it was difficult to imagine a more reasonable place for the action for the deficiencies to take place than Alberta. The judgments were therefore enforceable. The fact that the statutory rules for jurisdiction in the Court Order Enforcement Act reflected the narrower, traditional common law grounds was irrelevant; that could not inhibit the development of the common law.

Note. The *Morguard* decision is of the greatest importance for Canadian private international law, in two ways: first, because of what it says generally about a modern form of comity being the basic organizing principle of this branch of the common law; and, secondly, because of what it says specifically about the enforcement of judgments. It leaves four major questions to be answered by future decisions or, possibly, by legislation.

One is whether its expanded grounds for recognizing and enforcing judgments apply to judgments from outside Canada. One

case has already held that it does: *Clarke* v. *Lo Bianco* (1991), 59
B.C.L.R. (2d) 334 (S.C.) (compare *Hoopman Estate* v. *Imrie* (1991), 57
B.C.L.R. (2d) 310 (S.C. (M.C.)), decided before *Morguard* but after
a precursor to it). This may be doubted. The stress La Forest, J.
laid on the importance of the federal setting, and the potential
difficulties of recognizing default judgments from distant countries,
probably militate against such an extension of *Morguard.*

The second is whether a default judgment entitled to recognition by the *Morguard* rule can be reopened in any way on the merits
in the recognizing court. There is no sign in *Morguard* itself that
the conclusiveness principle which obtains under the traditional
common law rules will not apply equally to judgments recognized
under the new rule. One case decided after the Court of Appeal's
decision in *Morguard* did permit a reopening of the merits, but this
was probably a misapplication of the (already doubtful) British
Columbia doctrine that "manifest error" will vitiate a foreign
default judgment: *Alberta Mort. & Housing Corp.* v. *Pelkey* (1990), 46
C.P.C. (2d) 55 (B.C.S.C.).

A third issue is the exact nature of the "real and substantial
connection" test. La Forest, J. referred at various places to the original province's connection not only with the "subject matter of the
action," but also with the "damages suffered," the "legal obligation"
in question, the "transaction or the parties," and "the defendant."
All seem potentially relevant expressions, but they may have
divergent implications. The American due process doctrine focuses
almost exclusively on the connections with the defendant and the
defendant's activities, but it is unclear how far La Forest, J. drew
inspiration from that source.

Finally, it remains to be seen whether the real and substantial
connection idea becomes a principle of Canadian constitutional law
as well as the conflict of laws. La Forest, J. disclaimed any intention to decide the case on constitutional grounds, since the case
had not been argued as a constitutional one. Nevertheless there is
much in the judgment to support the argument that the jurisdiction of the courts of the provinces and territories is now subject
to a constitutionally binding limitation embodied in the phrase "real
and substantial connection". Similarly, it is arguable that the obligation to recognize judgments from elsewhere in Canada, subject
to the jurisdictional tests, has become a constitutionally mandated
one from which provincial laws may not derogate. That would be
a major inroad into what has been seen until now as an area of

provincial legislative competence. It is submitted that the definitive adoption of such constitutional restrictions should await a case in which the constitutional issues are fully argued.

(b)   *Defences to enforcement by action or registration*

Public policy

Honolulu Federal Savings & Loan Corp. v. *Robinson* (1990), 76 D.L.R. (4th) 103, [1991] 1 W.W.R. 174. Manitoba Court of Appeal.

Judgment was entered against the defendant mortgagor by a court in Hawaii for deficiencies owing after a mortgage sale of a condominium in that state. The defendant argued that the rule in section 16 of the Mortgage Act, R.S.M. 1987, c. M200, which restricts a mortgagee's remedy to the land itself, was one of public policy and precluded enforcement of the foreign judgment. The Court of Appeal affirmed the trial judge's rejection of this argument. The statute regulated mortgages of land in Manitoba, but not elsewhere.

Note. See also *Becker* v. *Peers* (1990), 106 A.R. 127 (Alta. Q.B. (M.C.)).

(c)   *Enforcement by registration under reciprocal enforcement of judgments legislation*

Note. James C. Bennett Hldgs. Ltd. v. *EMD Mgmt. Ltd.* (1991), 47 C.P.C. (2d) 13 (Man. Q.B.), held that the time limit on moving to set aside registration was not binding if the registration had been procured by false or fraudulent statements as to service in the original action. In *Bennett* v. *Cultural Tours* (1991), 58 B.C.L.R. (2d) 225 (S.C.), the defendant was held not to have been "duly served" in the Ontario court's jurisdiction, for the purposes of the uniform reciprocal enforcement legislation, when the plaintiff had handed the defendant the statement of claim with the words that he (the plaintiff) was not officially serving him and would not do so unless the parties could not negotiate a settlement. *Ruf* v. *Walter,* [1990] 6 W.W.R. 661, 43 C.P.C. (2d) 307 (Sask. Q.B.), held that a judgment for costs was within the scope of the reciprocal enforcement legislation and thus registrable.

(d)   *Enforcement by registration under reciprocal enforcement of maintenance orders legislation*

Note. In *Mosseau* v. *Mosseau* (1990), 84 Sask. R. 271 (U.F.C.), the judge made a provisional variation order terminating a 1978 Manitoba maintenance order and cancelling the arrears.

2. *Québec*

Sentence arbitrale étrangère — homologation

Argos Films c. *Ciné 360 Inc.*, [1991] R.J.Q. 1602. Cour d'appel du Québec.

Argos (requérante appelante) et Ciné 360 (intimée) ont signé un contrat pour la distribution d'un film au Québec, qui prévoyait l'arbitrage en France et assujettissait les parties au droit français. La clause d'arbitrage stipulait que les litiges nés au contrat "se règleront au choix du demandeur, soit par la voie d'arbitrage [en France], soit par la voie judiciaire devant les tribunaux [français]" mais, "lorsque [Argos] sera demandeur, il pourra également saisir le tribunal du domicile de [Ciné 360]," au Québec.

Un litige est survenu et Argos, conformément aux termes du contrat, a demandé l'arbitrage. La sentence arbitrale fut prononcée, et Argos présenta une requête en homologation devant la Cour supérieure du district de Montréal. Le premier juge, par une décision notée dans le tome 1988 de cet *Annuaire* à la page 422, a rejeté la requête en homologation. Après avoir passé en revue la doctrine, qui était nettement divisée sur ce sujet, il a conclu que la Cour supérieure n'était pas un "tribunal compétent" au sens de l'ancien article 950 C.P., pour homologuer une sentence arbitrale prononcée dans un autre pays mais pas encore homologuée selon la loi qui s'y applique. Le nouvel article 948 C.P., qui fut adopté en novembre 1986, déclare que "Le présent titre s'applique à une sentence arbitrale rendue hors du Québec qu'elle ait été ou non confirmée par une autorité compétente."

La Cour d'appel a accueilli le pourvoi. Le nouvel article 948 ne venait que déclarer l'état du droit existant en novembre 1986 et non attribuer à la Cour supérieure une compétence qu'elle n'avait pas auparavant. Le tribunal compétent, au sens des anciennes dispositions relatives à l'arbitrage, était le tribunal qui aurait eu autrement compétence sur l'objet du litige, n'eût été de la clause de l'arbitrage. En l'instance, l'objet du contrat concernait exclusivement la distribution d'un film au Québec, et l'objet du litige portait essentiellement sur la manière dont Ciné 360 avait rempli ses obligations contractuelles au Québec. La clause sus-citée n'excluait la compétence du tribunal québécois, qui avait déjà compétence *ratione personae*. Parce que la Cour supérieure ne s'était pas prononcée sur les motifs que Ciné 360 pourrait normalement faire valoir à l'encontre d'une requête en homologation, c'est-à-dire de l'examen des nullités dont la sentence pourrait être entachée ou des autres questions de forme qui pourraient en empêcher l'homologation, il était nécessaire de retourner le dossier à la Cour supérieure pour qu'il y soit procédé sur le fond de la requête en homologation.

D.   *Choice of law (including status of persons) / Conflits de lois (y compris statut personnel)*

1.   *Common law and federal*

(a)   *Characterization*

Procedure or substance — right of subrogation

Note. Régie de l'assurance automobile du Québec v. *Brown* (1990), 71 D.L.R. (4th) 457 (N.B.C.A.); leave to appeal refused, [1991] 1 S.C.R. vi, held that the Régie's statutory right of subrogation under Quebec law was recognized in New Brunswick, but, according to New Brunswick law, the action had to be brought in the name of the insured whose claim was being pursued.

Procedure or substance — limitations statutes

Note. Clark v. *Naqvi* (1989), 99 N.B.R. (2d) 271 (C.A.), affirmed the decision noted in the 1990 volume of this *Yearbook* at p. 619, which sensibly, but contrary to most authority, applied the Nova Scotia limitation rules to an action governed by Nova Scotia law, on the ground that the rules were substantive rather than procedural. Like the trial judge, the Court of Appeal barely discussed the characterization issue.

Procedure or substance — amount of damages

Note. See *Metaxas* v. *The Galaxias,* [1990] 2 F.C. 400 (T.D.), which applied Greek law to determine how much certain seamen were entitled to in respect of the termination of their employment. Greek law was applied both as the proper law of the contracts of employment and, pursuant to s. 275 of the Canada Shipping Act, R.S.C.

1985, c. S-9, as the law of the ship's port of registry. See also another judgment in the same set of proceedings, noted in the 1989 volume of this *Yearbook* at p. 473.

(b)   *Exclusion of foreign law*

Public policy

Note. See *243930 Alberta Ltd.* v. *Wickham,* noted below under (e) contract, and *Honolulu Federal Savings & Loan Corp.* v. *Robinson,* noted above under C. foreign judgments, (b) defences to enforcement by action or registration.

(c)   *Domicile*

Note. See *Re Urquhart Estate* (1990), 74 O.R. (2d) 42, 38 E.T.R. 222 (Ont. H.C.), in which the deceased was held not to have lost a domicile of choice in Ontario, despite spending much of his time elsewhere in his last years. In *Fareed* v. *Latif* (1991), 31 R.F.L. (3d) 354 (Man. Q.B.), a matrimonial case, the court determined the husband's domicile by applying the "principal home" test in the Domicile and Habitual Residence Act, R.S.M. 1987, c. D96, s. 8.

(d)   *Legal personality and capacity to sue*

Note. *Lainière de Roubaix S.A.* v. *Craftsmen Distrs. Inc.,* [1991] 5 W.W.R. 217, 55 B.C.L.R. (2d) 103 (C.A.), held that carrying on business in the province did not include merely selling goods to a B.C. customer and accepting payment by a cheque drawn on a Canadian bank. A French seller could therefore sue in B.C. without registering as an extraprovincial company.

(e)   *Contract*

Proper law — no agreed choice

243930 Alberta Ltd. v. *Wickham* (1990), 73 D.L.R. (4th) 474, 75 O.R. (2d) 289. Ontario Court of Appeal.

The plaintiff was in the business of building, selling and administering multiple unit residential buildings, which were marketed as tax shelters. The plaintiff's shareholders and its sole director were all Ontario residents and its business was primarily conducted in Ontario, but the present action arose out of its sale of twelve units in a project situated in Alberta. The sale was to an Ontario land developer, who resold the units to individual investors, the defendants. All negotiations between the plaintiff and the Ontario developer, and between the developer and the investors, took place in Ontario. (Thus the findings of the trial judge; the Court of Appeal referred to evidence that at least one investor's negotiations took place in Alberta.) The contract of resale was made in Ontario. The investors signed agreements in Ontario by which they assumed the obligations under vendor's mortgage agreements securing payment of the balance of the purchase price. These had been entered into by the Ontario developer as trustee for the investors, and included an express waiver of section 41(1) of the Law of Property Act, R.S.A. 1980, c. L-8, which provides that a mortgagee's remedy against the mortgagor is restricted to the land and that "no action lies" on the personal covenant. Any waiver of the benefits of section 41(1) was, however, declared by section 41(5) to be against public policy and void. When the plaintiff brought action in Ontario for the balance owing on the mortgages, it argued that their proper law was that of Ontario and that the Alberta statute therefore did not apply. The trial judge held for the plaintiff on the ground that although the proper law of the mortgages was Alberta law, section 41 was a procedural provision and did not preclude this action.

The Court of Appeal agreed that the proper law was that of Alberta. The rule was that the proper law of a contract of mortgage of real property was the law of the situs of the property. As the plaintiff argued, the agreement could be seen as a tax-related one, made in Ontario between Ontario residents, rather than as a contract relating to real estate. Nevertheless, regardless of where the documents were executed, the carrying out of the contract in its major aspects — transfer of title, registration of title, and management of the units — all took place in Alberta. That was the province with which the contract as a whole had its closest and most substantial connection.

Section 41(1) was substantive, not procedural, because in effect it did away with any personal liability of the mortgagor. It therefore applied in an Ontario forum, as did the nullification of the waiver clause by section 41(5). It was argued that as section 41(5) expressly declared Alberta public policy it could not apply in Ontario, but there was no public policy rule in Ontario that Ontario residents should not be protected against this kind of litigation when the law of the situs afforded such protection. Moreover, it would be inappropriate to afford such protection to owners of Alberta real estate only if they were resident in Alberta.

Note. See also *Ridders* v. *Mercury Tanklines Ltd.* (1990), 106 A.R. 291 (Q.B.) (proper law of contract of employment as truck driver); *Rôtisserie May's Ltée* v. *Stoel-Tek Inc.* (1990), 104 N.B.R. (2d) 255 (Q.B.) (contract by company in one province to sell equipment for delivery and after-sales service in another province); *Campbell* v. *Pringle & Booth Ltd.* (1988), 30 C.C.E.L. 156 (Ont. H.C.) (contract of employment as manager of branch outside province where employer based). In each the proper law was found by the "closest and most substantial connection" test.

Third party rights

Note. A Saskatchewan court, in *Gregory* v. *Kryg* (1990), 87 Sask. R. 283 (C.A.), applied Alberta law to hold that the plaintiff's claim arising out of an automobile accident in Saskatchewan was reduced pro tanto by no-fault benefits he had received from his own insurer. Both parties were Alberta residents insured under Alberta insurance policies to which this rule applied under s. 327(1) of the Insurance Act, R.S.A. 1980, c. I-5. This deemed release should be given effect as the result of the proper law of both parties' insurance policies. The position might have been different if only one had been insured under an Alberta policy.

(f) Torts

Tort outside the province

Note. As a result of *Grimes* v. *Cloutier* (1989), 61 D.L.R. (4th) 505 (Ont. C.A.), noted in the 1990 volume of this *Yearbook* at p. 624, Canadian courts have begun to insist that a plaintiff suing on a tort outside the province must show a civil cause of action by the *lex loci delicti*, not merely that the defendant's act is criminally wrongful under that law. *McLean* v. *Pettigrew*, [1945] S.C.R. 62, which applied the latter criterion, was said to apply only to cases where the facts made it appropriate to dispense with the tort law of the *locus delicti*. There, both plaintiff and defendant had travelled in the same car from their homes in Quebec to Ontario, where the accident occurred. In *Gagnon* v. *Gagnon* (1991) 3 O.R. (3d) 38 (Gen. Div.), the parties had travelled together from Ontario to Quebec and had an accident there. The bar to a civil action imposed by Quebec's no-fault insurance scheme was held inapplicable and criminal "wrongfulness" by Quebec law to be sufficient. Liability was thus based exclusively on Ontario law. In *Buchar* v. *Weber* (1990), 71 D.L.R. (4th) 544 (Ont. H.C.), the tort law of the *locus delicti*, Alberta, was applied since the parties were both resident there at the time of the accident.

The tort of inducing breach of contract was at issue in *Banco do Brasil S.A.* v. *Ship 'Alexandros G. Tsavliris,"* [1990] 3 F.C. 260, 35 F.T.R. 122 (T.D.). By asserting its claims under a mortgage over a Liberian ship in various ways, and threatening to have it arrested in Panama, the Brazilian bank had delayed the ship in performing a voyage charterparty from Europe to Canada. This was held to be an unreasonable exercise of the mortgagee's rights, and consequently to amount to inducement of breach of contract, which was actionable as a tort under Canadian maritime law and not justifiable under English law as the *lex loci delicti*. The *locus delicti* was England because the threats to the shipowners had been made there and solicitors had been instructed from there to arrest the ship.

Tort in the province

United States of America v. *Bulley* (1991), 79 D.L.R. (4th) 108, 55 B.C.L.R. (2d) 212. British Columbia Court of Appeal.

The United States claimed, by virtue of rights it had by United States law, to recover for medical expenses it had had to pay for a U.S. serviceman's wife who was injured in an accident in British Columbia. The court held that B.C. law applied to claims arising out of the accident, and that under the B.C. common law the United States had no independent cause of action for those expenses. The asserted right was purely a creation of the U.S. statute. Nor could the U.S. claim by way of subrogation, since under B.C. law it was not an insurer. The trial decision, noted in the 1988 volume of this *Yearbook* at p. 427, was affirmed.

(g) *Property*

Movables — title — personal property security

Note. See *Royal Bank* v. *Pattison Bros. Agro Ltd.* (1990), 1 P.P.S.A.C. (2d) 136 (Sask. Q.B.), in which a security interest perfected in Ontario was lost through sale of the goods in Saskatchewan. The holder had perfected its interest by registration in Saskatchewan, but that was ineffective as against a prior bona fide purchaser since it took place more than sixty days after the goods came into the province. According to the statute, only if the interest had been registered within the sixty days would it have "continued perfected" throughout.

Succession — will — interpretation

Note. In *Re Barna Estate* (1990), 40 E.T.R. 89 (B.C.S.C.), a will of movables made in British Columbia by a testatrix domiciled in France at her death was interpreted according to B.C. law. The presumption was that interpretation should be according to the *lex domicilii*, but the facts showed a contrary intention.

Bankruptcy and insolvency

Note. See *Canadian Imperial Bank of Commerce* v. *Idanell Korner Ranch Ltd.* (1990), 87 Sask. R. 123 (Q.B.), in which a receiver appointed in British Columbia was held entitled to rely on its rights in Saskatchewan.

(h)   *Husband and wife*

Marriage — capacity — prohibited degrees

Canada (Minister of Employment & Immigration) v. *Narwal*, [1990] 2 F.C. 385. Federal Court of Appeal.

The validity of a marriage celebrated in England between a woman domiciled and resident in Canada and her divorced husband's brother, who was domiciled and resident in India, was challenged in the context of the woman's sponsorship of the man's application for landed immigrant status in Canada. It was argued that they were not married because they were within the prohibited degrees under Indian law, which applied as the law of the alleged husband's antenuptial domicile. The Federal Court of Appeal held the marriage valid by applying the theory that since the intended matrimonial home was Canada, the Indian restriction on capacity to marry did not apply. The fact that the parties had not yet succeeded in establishing their matrimonial home in Canada was due to their inability to convince the Canadian authorities of the merit of the immigration application. The spirit of the intended matrimonial home theory was met.

Note. The correctness of the intended matrimonial home theory, as distinct from the antenuptial domicile theory, for determining capacity to marry is disputed. In the few English and Canadian cases that support this theory the assumption has always been made that the parties must actually establish their home in the new country soon after the marriage. The *Narwal* case extends the theory to a situation where the intention had not yet been carried out — and, as it happened, could not be carried out unless the marriage was first recognized as valid.

(i) *Infants and children*

Adoption — effect on status

Note. See *Oliphant* v. *Oliphant Estate* (1990), 38 E.T.R. 133 (Sask. Q.B.), which applied the law of a child's domicile at the time of its adoption to determine that all legal ties between the natural father and the child came to an end and the child was therefore not "issue" of the father for the purpose of succession to his estate.

2. *Québec*

(a) *Ordre public*

Note. Veuillez voir *Bélisle National Leasing* c. *Bertrand,* [1991] R.J.Q. 194 (C.S.). La Cour a rejeté la prétention d'un débiteur que l'avis préalable requis par la Loi sur la protection du consommateur, L.R.Q., c. P-40, art. 34-35, s'appliquait comme règle d'ordre public à une créancière qui s'est prévalue de son droit de revendication en vertu d'un contrat de louage d'une automobile, qui était conclu en Ontario.

(b) *Biens*

Successions — testament — validité — domicile de la testatrice

Feltrinelli c. *Barzini* (1990), 40 E.T.R. 136. Cour supérieure du Québec.

La testatrice est née en Italie en 1903. Patricienne de naissance et fortunée de par son mariage, elle a vécu de 1950 à New-York. En 1951 elle a constitué une corporation, Merida, dont le siège social était à Stanbrige East, au Québec. Merida a acquis une grande ferme dans cette endroit et a entrepris la rénovation d'une maison en pierre située sur la propriété. La testatrice n'a fait que des visites sporadiques au Canada, et n'a jamais demeuré à Stanbridge. L'acquisition de la ferme avait pour but principal de faciliter l'obtention de la citoyenneté canadienne. Dans sa requête pour obtenir cette citoyenneté, présentée en décembre 1955, lorsqu'elle était déjà rentrée en Europe, elle a fait des déclarations fausses concernant sa résidence au Canada. Elle a obtenu la citoyenneté canadienne en avril 1956. De 1956 à 1976 elle a voyagé presque continuellement entre ses diverses domiciles en Europe, surtout ceux de Rome, Milan et Genève. En 1976 elle est tombée sérieusement malade et à compter de cette date elle a vécu de façon permanente dans sa maison à Milan. Elle y est décédée en août 1981.

Elle a laissé un testament signé à Milan en Mars 1981 en vertu duquel elle léguait tous ses biens à une de ses deux filles de son second mariage. L'autre fille de ce mariage, et un fils et une fille du premier mariage, ne recevaient rien. Ceux-ci ont présenté devant la Cour supérieure une pétition d'héridité accompagnée d'une demande de déclaration de nullité du testament. Le testament, quant à sa forme, était conforme aux exigences de l'article 851 C.C. [testament suivant la forme dérivée de la Loi d'Angleterre], mais elle ne satisfait pas les exigences de la loi italienne, de sorte que selon le droit italien ce testament était nul de plein droit.

M. le juge Toth a conclu que la testatrice était domiciliée en Italie à son décès. Sa naturalisation ne créait aucune présomption quant à un éventuel domicile au Québec. L'article 80 C.C. dit que: "le changement de domicile s'opère par le fait d'une habitation réelle dans un autre lieu, jointe à l'intention d'y faire son principal établissement." Par le "principal établissement" des articles 79 et 80 C.C. on entend "le centre de gravité" des intérêts d'une personne, ce qui présuppose, normalement, une assez grande permanence d'habitation. L'appréciation de l'intention relative à la fixation du domicile est essentiellement une question de faits. En l'espèce, il n'y a jamais eu d'habitation réelle au Québec au sens de l'article 80 C.C. Les défendeurs se sont efforcés de prouver que la testatrice avait l'intention d'acquérir le statut juridique d'une personne domiciliée au Québec au lieu de prouver qu'elle avait l'intention de faire de Stanbridge son principal établissement. La volonté est examinée en fonction de l'intention de faire d'un lieu son établissement principal et non en fonction des effets juridiques que cela peut comporter.

Les défendeurs ont soutenu qu'en droit italien, le facteur de rattachement en matière de succession était la nationalité, en ce cas la nationalité canadienne, mais la Cour a décidé que, selon la loi italienne, la testatrice avait réacquis la nationalité italienne et perdu la nationalité canadienne plus de deux ans avant son décès.

L'article 7 C.C. consacre, en matière de forme, le principe de *locus regit actum.* Cette règle est facultative et le testateur a le choix entre la loi du lieu où le testament est fait et la loi québécoise de son domicile. En outre, en ce qui concerne les immeubles situés au Québec, la *lex rei sitae* s'applique. Le testament était donc valide en ce qui concernait des immeubles au Québec que la testatrice avait acquis en 1955. En ce qui concernait les biens meubles ni les articles du Code civil, ni la jurisprudence, ne permettent d'appliquer d'autres lois que soit la *lex loci actus,* soit la *lex domicilii.* Dans les deux cas c'était la loi italienne. Or, quant aux biens meubles (par exemple les actions de Merida) le testament était nul. Que le même testament soit valide quant aux immeubles situés au Québec et nul quant aux biens meubles résultait du fait que le Québec soumet les successions au régime de la scission. La réserve de la loi italienne en faveur des descendants ne s'appliquait pas aux immeubles situés au Québec. La restriction à la liberté de tester a été qualifiée comme étant une de droit testamentaire, c'est-à-dire tombant sous l'application de la loi successorale.

Book Reviews / Recensions de livres

The Non-Use of Force in International Law. Edited by W. E. Butler. Dordrecht: Martinus Nijhoff, 1989. Pp. 247. ISBN 0-7923-0293-1 (U.S. $67.50); World Security for the 21st Century: Challenges and Solutions. Edited by B. B. Ferencz. Dobbs Ferry: Oceana Publications, 1991. Pp. vi, 228. ISBN 0-379-20466-5.

Since the advent of President Gorbachev and the initiation of *glasnost* and *perestroika,* there has been an increasing understanding between the Soviet Union and the West. Even before this, however, a certain number of academic exchanges had been taking place among legal thinkers from both sides of what was formerly known as the Iron Curtain. From the English point of view many of these exchanges have been organized by Professor Butler at University College London, often in association with the Institute of State and Law of the Soviet Academy of Sciences. *The Non-Use of Force in International Law* consists of essays based on discussion at the Second Anglo-Soviet Symposium held in Moscow in May 1988. *World Security for the 21st Century* is almost a verbatim reproduction of discussions that took place at the Pace Peace Center in 1990 among a group of lawyers from the United States, the Soviet Union, and the United Nations. The Anglo-Soviet volume is much easier to deal with since it consists of a series of academic papers, while the Pace volume is the record of verbal interchanges.

One of the most notable things about the essays in *The Non-Use of Force in International Law* is the extent to which the World Court's judgment in the *Nicaragua* case figures in the Soviet contributions. In addition, a number of the contributions frequently reflect ideological positions as much as they do legal regulations. Thus, Professor Brownlie states (p. 21) that "the Second World War was fought to vindicate [the] principle. . .[that] the resort to force except in case of self-defence or collective self-defence was generally denied to states." Again, "The Israeli claim that anticipatory action was taken against Egypt in 1967 cannot be assessed without investigation of the assurances given by the United States to Israel and Egypt respectively. If, *as may have been the case* [italics added], Egypt was warned that any attack on Israel would lead to immediate United States intervention, the need for Israeli action would be difficult to justify'' (p. 24). The anti-Israel bias of a number of the contributions is also to be seen, for example, by the Soviet scholar, Dr. Müllerson (p. 30). This author also contends that ''the use of force to combat international terrorism is contrary to international law. Recent experience indicates [although he provides no evidence of this other than a statement by Gorbachev] that self-defence against international terrorism turns into State terrorism'' (p. 33). Is it true, as Dr. Shinkaretskaia would have us believe, that

the principle of peaceful settlement is one of the principles of customary international law set out in Article 33 of the United Nations Charter. . .[so that] the principle of peaceful settlement, being a generally recognized imperative principle of international law, cannot cease to be operative under any circumstances, irrespective of the state of relations between subjects of international law. [And does] international practice serve as confirmation of this? (p. 48)

Dr. Carty of the University of Glasgow presents an interesting analysis of the *Nicaragua* decision based on the contention that ''Western international lawyers tend to go directly to the dangers of a security nature involved in putting faith in the effective legal power of declarations on the use of force. . . . This is because they operate upon implicit Hobbesian assumptions about the nature of international society and the role of such declarations in that society'' (p. 54). By way of contrast, the Court's approach was ''that favoured predominantly by third world states and socialist states, which prefer to treat United Nations declarations as statements of the legal conscience of mankind'' (p. 57). This raises the question whether a single declaration or one that has not received the general support of Third World and socialist states is also entitled to be regarded in this fashion. What is one to say of the balanced character of a paper which states that ''Western States have long decided that they owe their security to an unconditional willingness to use nuclear weapons *specifically* against enemy civilian populations. It is the unconditional quality of this readiness which renders the no first use rule particularly objectionable'' (Carty, p. 64, italics added)?

Many of the papers, and not only those presented by Soviet scholars, refer to the 1987 General Assembly Declaration on the

Enhancement of the Effectiveness of the Principle of Non-Use of Force on International Relations. Dr. Fedorov emphasizes that this was "elaborated at the initiative of the Soviet Union [and] constitutes an important milestone in the process of the progressive development and codification of fundamental principles and provisions of the United Nations Charter and contemporary international law within the United Nations framework" (p. 77). While he concedes (p. 83) that "from the legal point of view the Declaration is of a recommendatory character," he nevertheless maintains that it "is a fundamental political and *legal* document which orients all States of the world towards real and effective actions aimed at preventing and excluding the use of force in all its forms and manifestations, especially nuclear, and directed at the realization of the long-standing dream of mankind: a world without weapons, a world without wars" (p. 84).

In view of the somewhat uncritical praise accorded to the Court's *Nicaragua* decision by so many of the participants, it is almost with a sense of relief that one reads Professor Mendelson's analysis of the decision in the light of customary international law. He criticizes the "surprising readiness of the Court to regard voting for General Assembly resolutions as a form of practice... [and] allowed [such] resolutions to be used as evidence of *opinio juris* [which] would seem to elevate General Assembly resolutions to a particularly potent form of 'instant customary law'" (pp. 91-92). He also questions the Court's use of the prohibition of force in the Helsinki Accord, pointing out that "some explanation of how a non-binding agreement can be said to constitute or evidence rules of customary law would have been appropriate" (p. 94). Finally, he suggests that the majority's desire to declare the United States

guilty of grave violations of international law. . . may perhaps explain the somewhat cursory treatment, or even in some cases neglect, of the problem of sources. It is, nevertheless, unfortunate that the majority did not treat this problem more thoroughly. A more rigorous analysis might not necessarily have led to a different conclusion; but it could have rendered the Judgment more credible in the eyes of the legal community, and it would have avoided muddying further the already murky pool of customary law and the methods of its formation. (p. 97)

Dr. Danilenko also subjects the decision to careful analysis and some of his remarks are of interest in relation to the recent war in the Gulf:

As regards the lawfulness of the exercise of collective self-defence, the Court held that the State for whose benefit the right is used must itself form and declare the view that it is the victim of an armed attack. The Court observed that international law does not allow another State to exercise the right of collective self-defence on the basis of its own assessment of the situation. An additional requirement is the existence of a request by the State which regards itself as the victim of an armed attack to the supportive State'' (p. 106).

This suggests that action by way of preventive self-defence can never be collective, and this view is supported by his citation of the Court's view that "under existing international law the State which considers itself the victim of any use of force may take only 'proportionate' counter-measures...The Court emphasized that 'while an armed attack would give rise to an entitlement to collective self-defence, a use of force of a lesser degree of gravity cannot produce any entitlement to take collective counter-measures involving the use of force'' (p. 106). At what point does one hold that the collective counter-measures involve the use of force? Was the decision of some states to strengthen Saudi Arabia's military potential after Iraq's attack on Kuwait such use?

In this connection, one might refer to the comments of Dr. Krylov: "The United Nations is an organization of sovereign states. It cannot be regarded as the principal guarantor against a nuclear war, nor can it prevent or eliminate all contradictions between countries'' (p. 111). However, can one accept so readily his contention that "the functioning of the United Nations for more than forty years has convincingly demonstrated that whenever members of the Organization have sincerely manifested interest in seeking mutually advantageous solutions, the United Nations was able to act resolutely and energetically. This has enabled the United Nations to perform the function of real machinery for the settlement of international conflicts, to further the development of cooperation between States, and to work out useful resolutions regarding arms limitation and disarmament'' (pp. 111-12)? In view of the Security Council Resolutions condemning Iraq's invasion of Kuwait and authorizing action of a military character against the invader — all of which received support from the Soviet Union — it would be interesting to know whether Dr. Krylov would still write: "The United Nations may adopt specific sanctions against member States in order to ensure compliance with resolutions. Of course, these are not sanctions in the strict sense of the term, but measures approximating certain legal sanctions. Applied by international organizations on the basis of legal norms in their charters, they bear a certain legal element, although they are not law'' (p. 117).

One of the stranger statements appearing in this collection of essays is that by Dr. Slinn of the School of Oriental Studies in his comments on the role of the Commonwealth. He points out that the Commonwealth does not seek to rival the United Nations and praises its role in the creation of Zimbabwe, although he tends to minimize or ignore such issues as Grenada, Indo-Pakistan differences, and other inter-Commonwealth disputes. He states that ''it remains a curious anomaly that the only 'formal' qualifications for membership of the Commonwealth today are full independence...and acceptance of the Queen as 'the symbol of the free association of its independent member nations and *as such* the Head of the Commonwealth','' and he goes on to state that ''as the Queen in her personal capacity, not the Crown as an institution, is Head of the Commonwealth.... The Headship is quite distinct from the Queen's role as Head of State of [some] Commonwealth member States. However...if a monarchy which acknowledges the Queen as its Head of State adopts a republican constitution, the consent of the other members must be obtained in order for the State to remain a member of the organization.... Students of international organizations may consider it remarkable that purely internal constitutional changes in an independent state may affect that State's membership of an international body'' (p. 121). But was this not the case with Egypt, Syria and the United Arab Republic, with the Federal and People's Republics of Germany, or even Singapore when it ceased to be part of Malaysia?

By way of contrast it is interesting to note some of the comments of a Soviet scholar on the Commonwealth. Dr. Krylov describes the Commonwealth as a ''political and legal reality'' (p. 137), with Canada, Australia, and New Zealand claiming ''the role of regional leaders'' (p. 139). In her view, ''the Commonwealth is moving in the direction of working out a new list of principles which all members of the association must adhere to and which correspond to generally recognized principles of international law'' (p. 140). She, too, tends to ignore the Grenada crisis and inter-member disputes while, perhaps, exaggerating the institutional aspects of the Commonwealth Secretariat. Her analysis of the Headship of the Commonwealth differs somewhat from that of Dr. Slinn (pp. 145-47). It is hardly true to say today that ''sometimes the Judicial

Committee of the Privy Council is classified as a tribunal of the Commonwealth'' (p. 148), although this may possibly have still been true when de Smith published the 1971 edition of his *Constitutional and Administrative Law*.

Among papers concerned with the actual resort to force, Dr. Kolesnik of the Soviet Foreign Office, regards an armed attack as a priority before there may be any resort to self-defence, contending that a mere threat would never suffice, for self-defence must always be retaliatory (p. 154). While he argues that ''armed attack embraces primarily the cases of the direct use of armed force that violate the territorial integrity and political independence of another State. . .it would be erroneous to assert that acts of indirect aggression are completely beyond the concept of armed attack'' (p. 155). This leads him to point out that the Security Council possesses the discretion to find an act of aggression even in the absence of an armed attack, although it must be recognized that ''at least the right of the preliminary identification of the fact of armed attack belongs to the victim State of the aggression'' subject, of course, ''to final assessment of the Security Council at a later stage'' (p. 156). Nevertheless, ''Having the right of initial identification of the fact of armed attack and without being bound by a peaceful settlement obligation with respect to the attacking side, the victim state itself determines the moment for starting defensive action, its nature, and means of implementation. Action in self-defence may be offensive militarily and may extend to the territory of the attacking side to the degree necessary to eliminate and prevent a renewal of armed attacks [as happened with Iraq in 1991]. Any types of weapons at the disposal of the defending State and not prohibited by international law may be used as a means of self-defence. The USSR and the People's Republic of China, having undertaken not to be the first to use nuclear weapons, proceed from the assumption that such weapons cannot be used in self-defence in response to non-nuclear armed attack, whereas the United States, Great Britain, and France retain the right to be the first to use nuclear weapons in an outbreak of armed conflict which runs counter to the principle of proportionality, traditionally recognized, among others, by the supporters of the concept of 'self-defence under general international law'. . . . [But this] concept amounts to the complete isolation of the United Nations from the process of ensuring international peace as it broadens the range of military activity beyond the Security Council's control'' (p. 157).

While one may feel at times, particularly in view of the abandonment of the cult of personality, that there is too much reference in some of the Soviet contributions to the views of Gorbachev as if he were an authority on the law, it cannot be denied that many of the papers in this collection — and it has not been considered necessary to refer to them all — are enlightening on a variety of views, particularly by Soviet scholars, on different aspects of the use or non-use of force. Whatever criticisms one might have of some of the comments, one must be thankful for the opportunity to have these contributions in whatever form they appear.

World Security in the 21st Century frequently reflects the same ideological influences and differences (see, e.g., p. 175 re the ''debate'' between Dr. Furkalo and Professor Ferencz on U.S. attitudes to the ABM Treaty). As regards the future and generating political will, a comment by Dr. Evintov is interesting. In the Soviet Union, he said, ''lawyers were ready to draw up documents expressing the stated norms, but these laws were without any force. They were artificial because they conveyed only the political will of the moment. I think it is better to weigh and balance the interests rather than to impose laws based on the omnipotent power of the state. Only such rules will be effective. I think the ILC and the Sixth Committee of the United Nations can work out and codify minimum norms of international behavior. We must make an inventory of such norms that already exist, including the accepted *jus cogens,* 'general principles' of law. We must enumerate the existing rules of international behavior in every field of international relations and publish the results in many volumes. It's a big job but within the framework of the declared United Nations Decade of International Law, it's absolutely necessary'' (p. 176). He makes this sound almost easy even if it is ''a big job.'' It is, however, a time-consuming undertaking and probably would not be considered pressing by either the Commission or the Sixth Committee, particularly as the American Society of International Law is already working with an international committee in seeking this objective.

While some of the discussions and comments in this volume are interesting, one is left with the feeling that the whole thing was somewhat too ''folksy.'' It would have been much more useful had there been initial discussion papers published in full with summaries of what followed.

L. C. GREEN
University of Alberta

Dominique Carreau, Thiébaut Flory et Patrick Juillard. *Droit international économique.* Paris: LGDJ, 1990. Pp. 725 (220F).

La troisième édition de ce manuel est une version refondue et augmentée d'un ouvrage publié en 1978 et revisé une première fois en 1980. L'objectif des trois auteurs (qui signent depuis plus de vingt ans les chroniques sur la monnaie, le commerce et l'investissement publiées dans l'*Annuaire français de droit international*) demeure le même: présenter une synthèse de l'aspect juridique des relations économiques internationales.

Mais les transformations rapides des relations économiques internationales au cours de la décennie écoulée ont été si importantes qu'elles n'ont pas pu ne pas affecter le droit qui les régit. Elles justifient amplement l'adaptation et la mise à jour de la matière.

Les changements dans l'environnement économique international, conjugué au succès du manuel, avaient déjà incité les auteurs en 1980 à remodeler l'ouvrage deux ans seulement après la parution de l'édition originale. Ils s'agissait essentiellement à l'époque de repenser les écrits sur les mécanismes monétaires (système monétaire européen) et le système commercial international (Tokyo Round), qui semblaient le plus affectés par la chaîne des événements. Les auteurs y ajoutèrent également des analyses sur l'établissement des personnes et la prestation des services.

Dix ans plus tard c'est l'ensemble des relations économiques internationales qui a subi des modifications majeures. Le retournement du marché pétrolier international porta un coup dur — certains diront fatal — au Nouvel ordre économique international. Les bouleversements à l'Est amplifièrent le mouvement et les entreprises de privatisation amorcés au Nord et au Sud. La déréglementation et l'innovation dans le domaine de la finance contribua à l'expansion de l'euro-marché et au développement des marchés internationaux des capitaux. L'endettement du Tiers Monde entraîna un regain d'intérêt pour l'investissement direct au Sud. L'accroissement presque continu du commerce international depuis la fin de la second guerre mondiale s'accompagna de poussées protectionnistes.

Mais, en fait, les fluctuations des relations économiques internationales ne semblent pas avoir affecté véritablement la conception que les auteurs se font du droit international économique (DIE) en tant que branche ou discipline juridique: ceux-ci vont essentiellement affiner leurs définitions et analyses. Par contre, si changement il y-a eu, c'est surtout au plan des finalités qu'il se situe, ainsi que de l'ordre juridique sur lequel s'appuie le droit en question: celui-ci semble traversé par un mouvement de libéralisation progressive, même si le protectionnisme subsiste dans certains domaines et qu'il se développe dans d'autres.

Dans une introduction d'une quarantaine de pages, les auteurs commencent par définir la matière et à en dégager les caractères originaux, après quoi ils examinent la société internationale et l'ordre international économiques.

Le DIE est défini comme étant "cette branche du droit qui réglemente, d'une part, l'établissement et l'investissement internationaux et, d'autre part, la circulation internationale des marchandises, services et paiements" (p. 46). Les professeurs de Paris (MM. Carreau et Juillard) et de Lille (M. Flory) confirment leur attachement à la conception restrictive du DIE en précisant qu'il s'agit d'un "droit cadre," un "droit des grands ensembles économiques," qui réglemente "les relations macro-économiques par opposition à des relations micro-économiques" (p. 45). Aussi vont-ils chercher à dégager l'originalité du DIE en le comparant à "ce genre proche que serait le droit international général" (p. 47).

Cette originalité se manifeste notamment au plan des sources. Les sources du DIE — qui font l'objet d'une classification plus sûre et plus détaillée que dans la deuxième édition — sont essentiellement des sources internationales, mais les sources nationales et du tiers ordre, les sources publiques, privées et mixtes (les contrats d'État) jouent un rôle important. De plus, les sources internationales "s'infléchissent" au contact du DIE: préférence pour les principes généraux et les actes unilatéraux (des organisations internationales mais aussi des États) par rapport aux traités et à la coutume. De même, le bilatéralisme semble prédominer en matière conventionnelle (de sorte que les règles contenues dans les conventions bilatérales ne s'appliquent qu'aux États qui y sont parties) et les accords infra-étatiques jouent un rôle très important (accords conclus entre les administrations des États).

Cette originalité se manifeste également au plan des sanctions: flexibilité des mécanismes, importance de l'informalisme, allergie au juge international, sanctions relevant d'une multitude d'ordres juridiques, importance de l'arbitrage mixte en matière d'investissement international.

Le droit international économique contient donc des règles et mécanismes suffisamment souples pour régir une réalité fluctuante et mouvante, à la différence du droit international général plus rigide et précis. On peut noter, par ailleurs, que les auteurs ne cherchent pas à distinguer explicitement le DIE de disciplines apparemment connexes comme le droit commercial international ou, encore, le droit international du développement. En excluant de son domaine l'examen du financement international des investissements publics (qui faisait l'objet d'une sous-partie dans la deuxième édition), le DIE se distingue de cette "autre discipline [le droit international du développment] fort bien exposée par ailleurs dans des études spécifiques" (p. 5). Mais, en même temps, il s'en rapproche en traitant notamment des régimes particuliers de faveur dont bénéficient les pays en voie de développement en matière commerciale (aussi, les auteurs se réfèrent à plusieurs reprises à la Charte des droits et devoirs économiques des États dans la partie traitant de l'investissement international). Peut-on en déduire que le DIE et le droit international du développement, qui se rejoignent dans certains secteurs, tendent de plus en plus à se détacher l'un de l'autre? Le declin du Nouvel ordre économique international — en modérant les revendications des pays en voie de développement —n'aurait-il pas pu provoquer le phénomène inverse, à savoir une plus grande intégration du droit international du développement au DIE?

En fait, les auteurs semblent avoir privilégié une démarche pragmatique qui consiste à éviter les controverses doctrinales que suscitent ces notions nouvelles de droit international du développement ou de DIE. Cette dernière est-elle une discipline juridique autonome? Les auteurs ne se réfèrent même pas au concept d'"autonomie" qui a fait oculer beaucoup d'encre (dans la deuxième édition ils avaient soulevé la question sans y répondre). Ils se contentent de renvoyer le lecteur aux articles et ouvrages de doctrine qui analysent la question: que ce soit le rapport du professeur P. Weil au Colloque d'Orléans de 1971, ou les articles de Philippe Kahn et Michel Virally dans les Mélanges Goldman de 1982 ou, encore, le cours du professeur I. Seidl-Hohenveldern à l'Académie de droit international de La Haye de 1986.

Après avoir défini et délimité le DIE, les auteurs étudient la société internationale économique et l'ordre international économique. On peut regretter ici que certains questions méthodologiques abordées dans la version de 1980, et qui assuraient une transition entre les deux parties de l'introduction, n'aient pas été soulevées dans la troisième édition: notamment le lien entre l'ordre international économique et DIE.

Celui-ci régit une société internationale hétérogène composée de sujets divers: à côté des États et des organisations internationales on y trouve "les sujets nouveaux, encore mal intégrés par ce même droit international général, que sont les organisations gouvernementales et les entreprises multinationales" (p. 58). On voit donc ici que le DIE se distingue du droit international général par ses sujets et non seulement par ses sources et ses mécanismes de sanction. De plus, si les deux "disciplines" reconnaissent à l'État un rôle essentiel, le DIE attribue à chaque catégorie d'États un statut différent: États capitalistes et États socialistes; pays développés et pays en développement. Mais il apparait que ces distinctions sont de plus en plus dépassées. Les États de l'Est adoptent les mécanismes du marché et les pays en développement ne sont plus toujours unis par des intérêts communs.

Ceci ne pourra profiter qu'aux pays développés à économie de marché, qui jouent un rôle prédominant dans cette société internationale économique bien qu'ils aient été vivement critiqués et même parfois défiés par les autres États: "L'ordre international économique mis en place en 1945 est l'oeuvre des pays capitalistes, non des pays socialistes" (p. 61).

L'ordre international économique est défini comme "l'ensemble cohérent de règles juridiques orientées en fonction des finalités du système" (p. 81). L'édition de 1980 avait consacré des pages très intéressantes sur son évolution historique depuis le dix-neuvième siècle. Or la version récente n'en a tenu que très partiellement compte, ce qu'on ne peut que regretter.

Aussi, c'est sur un ordre international économique contemporain d'inspiration nettement "neo-libérale" que s'appuie le droit international économique aujourd'hui. Les "récents ralliements des pays socialistes d'Europe" (p. 82) et les "succès fragmentaires" du Nouvel ordre économique international sont très probablement à la fois la cause et la conséquence de cette évolution.

Cette libéralisation progressive se manifeste essentiellement au plan commercial et monétaire (même si des "zones d'ombres" subsistent à côté des "zones de lumière") plutôt qu'en matière d'investissement international privé (même "s'il existe des réalisations ponctuelles ou régionales"; p. 84).

Les deux parties de l'ouvrage traitent d'ailleurs de la circulation internationale des marchandises, services et paiements d'une part, et de l'établissement des personnes et de l'investissement international d'autre part.

La première partie examine successivement le système commercial international, la circulation des services et le système monétaire transnational. L'étude du système commercial international contient une analyse très claire du régime général du GATT ainsi que des régimes particuliers applicables à certains secteurs (produits de base, produits manufacturés et semi-manufacturés) et à certains pays (commerce Nord-Sud et commerce Sud-Sud). Elle est suivie de l'examen des mesures protectionnistes (échanges compensés, accords bilatéraux d'autolimitation et mesures unilatérales) ainsi que de certaines tentatives de libéralisation et de résistance à ce même protectionisme (à travers l'étude des zones franches et des négociations de l'Uruguay Round).

Le commerce international des services est également marqué par le protectionisme et par les efforts d'y mettre fin au sein de l'Uruguay Round. Ces deux points sont traités tour à tour dans la partie qui lui est consacrée.

Dans le chapitre relatif au système monétaire international sont abordés le système monétaire public (le système de Bretton Woods et les sous-systèmes régionaux — Banque des règlements internationaux, CEE) et le système monétaire privé (Euro-dépôt, euro-crédit, euro-obligation et nouveaux instruments financiers internationaux).

Il ressort que l'évolution des échanges internationaux s'est accompagnée d'une libéralisation du commerce (les droits de douane ne constituent plus un obstacle au commerce; les subventions sont contrôlées et les restrictions quantitatives négligeables), et d'une liberalisation au niveau monétaire et financier (convertibilité des monnaies des pays développés à économie de marché; développement des euro-marchés grâce à la liberté dont ont bénéficié notamment les banques internationales).

Mais, cette libéralisation n'a pas empêché, entre autres, le maintien du protectionisme ni les problèmes suscités par l'endettement international. En matière commerciale, les États auront recours soit au bilatéralisme soit à des mesures unilatérales afin de contrôler les échanges commerciaux. En matière monétaire et financière, ils vont implicitement intervenir pour inciter les banques à renégocier leurs dettes vis-à-vis du tiers-monde en ayant recours à des mécanismes informels et non aux dispositions très sophistiquées des contrats d'euro-crédit (contrats riches en clauses destinées à protéger les banques contre les risques d'insolvabilité de l'emprunteur).

La deuxième partie aborde l'établissement des personnes et

l'investissement international (définition; constitution et liquidation; traitement, protection et garantie; transferts de propriété; nationalisation, privatisation).

Certes, le droit des investissements est essentiellement fait de réglementations nationales qui reflètent les objectifs et stratégies économiques des États. Toutefois, une certaine évolution peut être constatée, marquée par un climat plus favorable aux investissements étrangers. Ceci est attester, entre autres, par les conventions bilatérales en matière d'investissements, les codes d'investissement, et par la convention de Séoul de 1985 portant création de l'Agence multilatérale de garantie des investissements (AMGI).

Malgré la multitude et la diversité des questions étudiées, les auteurs réussissent à nous donner une vue d'ensemble claire et cohérente de l'aspect juridique des relations économiques internationales. En outre, au-delà de leurs efforts de synthèse, ils n'hésitent pas à approfondir l'analyse de questions ou de techniques juridiques données, soulevant d'intéressants problèmes et suscitant la réflexion: nature juridique de l'euro-dollar, de l'accord de confirmation (standby arrangement), de la convention d'euro-crédit ayant pour objet le reéchelonnement des dettes commerciales; le régime juridique applicable au contrat de depôt en devises étrangères (illustré par le blocage des avoirs iraniens en 1979); le "droit jurisprudentiel" spécifique du GATT "issu des rapports des panels"; l'efficacité du système généralisé des préférences; le rapport entre la réglementation des changes et celle des investissements; la portée de l'affaire TOPCO; le rapport entre le traitement et la protection des investissements d'une part et la garantie internationale d'autre part.

Par ailleurs, la sélection bibliographique en tête de chaque chapitre complète parfaitement le texte qui l'accompagne. Indiquons également que M. Carreau a publié, en 1985 à la documentation française, un recueil de documents de droit international économique. Une version augmentée et mise à jour pourrait constituer un supplément précieux au manuel en question d'autant plus que les documents en langue française sont difficiles d'accès.

Ceci dit, c'est un ouvrage d'un très grand intérêt que nous présentent MM. Carreau, Flory et Juillard et dont la lecture est indispensable et est à recommander à la fois aux spécialistes et aux initiés.

YASSER SABRA
Chargé de cours, Université McGill

The Concept and Present Status of the International Protection of Human Rights.
By B. G. Ramcharan. Dordrecht: Martinus Nijhoff, 1989. Pp.
xi and 611. ISBN 9024737591. (U.S. $159.50).

Dr. Ramcharan in this work surveys the issue of protection of
human rights in the forty years since the adoption of the Universal
Declaration. His *dies ad quem* means that he has been unable to assess
the significance of the role of the United Nations or of the Coalition
forces acting under the umbrella of Security Council Resolutions,
in particular Resolution 687, in seeking to protect the human rights
of the Kurdish minority in Iraq after the conclusion of the Gulf
war — the first time that the United Nations has taken an activist
role to this end. This development, especially if followed in other
instances of the denial of human rights by a national government
— and of this there is as yet unfortunately no sign — would constitute a marked change from the situation as it existed in 1948 when
the Declaration was adopted. As Dr. Ramcharan points out, and
as the situation in Iraq demonstrates, "any international security
system has to come to grips with [gross] violations [of human
rights]...committed within the boundaries of States" (p. 1).
Moreover, it is being increasingly recognized that "in highly charged
situations, such as in international or internal conflicts, or in emergency situations, an international presence may be indispensable
if excesses or inhumane actions are to be avoided or minimised"
(p. 11).

A main criticism of the Universal Declaration was its lack of any
binding character and its complete silence on the protection of the
rights it proclaimed as being the inherent possession of all mankind.
To some extent the two International Covenants with their reporting and commenting systems — described by John Humphrey in
his preface as "the Organization of shame" (p. xi) — have made
some progress towards protection. But it has been on the regional
level, especially in Europe, and now also in Latin America, that
protection of human rights has become a reality through the
medium of international instruments. In addition, there have been
specific agreements, such as those on terrorism, torture, or the rights
of the child, which have enabled particular rights to be protected
at least on a limited scale, even if this only means relying on national law to impose punishment on those denying such rights.
However, by and large, the author is not interested in these regional
arrangements (pp. 33-36), tending to confine his comments to the

position as it is under the auspices of the United Nations taking the [so-called] International Bill of Human Rights as the legal basis of protection (Ch. 2).

As if quoting Vattel or Pufendorf, or the nineteenth-century writers on humanitarian intervention, Dr. Ramcharan asserts that the:

growing wave of international protection for the common good derives from general recognition in the international community that mankind cannot *and will not* allow a delinquent nation to endanger its survival, health or welfare by irresponsible behaviour. Hence, the international community's insistence on international scrutiny and control of individual state's actions in these domains. There is also growing recognition that human beings *will not* stand by idly and watch their fellow human beings murdered, tortured, enslaved or recklessly incarcerated by errant governments. There is therefore great insistence that international *protection* of human rights must become prompt, adequate and effective protection; that all must act for one and one for all (p. 2).

While this may well be the end that all humanists seek and one that governments should strive to instil in their populations, it must be recognized that with human nature as it is this ideal is far from realization. And the situation is not improved by citing such instruments as Article 19 of the International Law Commission's draft articles on state responsibility (p. 5).

The author maintains that if international protection is to have any real meaning, it must be "applicable to all individuals and groups in whatever part of the world they may be located," including their own countries or those of allied powers, and may be "anticipatory or preventive; curative or mitigatory; remedial or compensatory" (p. 18), and may be direct or indirect. "In seeking to protect human rights by halting gross violations of human rights, United Nations organs have employed a variety of methods including *urgent action,* such as the sending of telegrams, *mediatory and conciliatory measures* such as the use of the good offices of the United Nations Secretary-General, and the undertaking of direct contacts, *fact-finding, exposure and condemnation, sanctions,* and the provision of *assistance to victims*" (p. 29). Without being cynical, one might ask how often such actions have resulted in positive results and major improvements of a long-term character. Has it really mattered that the "United Nations has published a list of names of persons said to have committed the Crime of *Apartheid* and the *Ad Hoc* Working Group on the Situation of Human Rights in Chile published the

names of alleged torturers and called for their trial'' (p. 30)? Nor
has the fact that the Commission on Human Rights called on the
General Assembly to ask the world Court for an Opinion on the
''question of whether a State which pursues a policy of *apartheid* and
denies human rights, such as South Africa, may lawfully continue
to hold a place in the international community, in view of the provisions of the Charter of the United Nations, more particularly
Chapter II, Article 6'' *(ibid.)* come to any fruition — a fact which
suggests tht the majority of the members of the United Nations,
despite talk of respect for human rights, are not really concerned
in ensuring their protection. This statement is not affected in any
way by Dr. Ramcharan's question that ''in the face of the impressive
range of Charter-based activities and methods for the protection
of human rights, can any doubt still exist that the United Nations
is competent to act for the protection of human rights, especially
taking into account the authoritative [?] pronouncements by the
General Assembly?'' (p. 31). It should be borne in mind, of course,
that *competence* is not the same as *action*. It is not statements by the
Assembly or any other body that really matter: it is rather the willingness of the few ''democratic'' states that fall under criticism to
remedy the situation when brought to their attention, that is really
responsible for such improvement as there is.

While the author concedes that declarations, including the
Universal Declaration, do not constitute binding statements of law
(pp. 39-40), he argues that in the light of the practice of the world
Court, the General Assembly, and the UN Commission of Human
Rights, the standards laid down in the Declaration, together with
the two international covenants, constitute ''unequivocal world standards'' of human rights (p. 40), and that they now ''represent
minimal standards of conduct for all peoples and all nations... [while
s]ome parts of the Universal Declaration and the International
Covenants represent international customary law and, to that extent, are binding upon all States. Some provisions might even constitute norms of *Jus Cogens*'' (p. 59). It would have been helpful if
he had indicated which provisions he has in mind.

Chapter 3, constituting some 170 pages, is taken up with an in-
teresting and detailed account of the various ''strategies of protec-
tion'' that exist under the United Nations system, e.g., the
Commission, good offices, the role of the Secretary General under
Article 99 of the Charter, fact-finding, public debate, and the like.
Chapter 4 is concerned with discussion of problems relating to the

issue of protection at the international level. The author points out that, ''In the years that have elapsed since the establishment of the United Nations and the functioning of its human rights programme, the expectations of the peoples of the world that the organization will act effectively to protect human rights have remained largely in the realm of hope than in the realm of fact, notwithstanding impressive achievements in the field of standard-setting, research, studies and advisory services'' (p. 267). Among the reasons for this failure to achieve a realistic system, he cites problems of governmental commitment, of international structure and diplomatic framework, ideological competition, perspective and priorities, fact-finding, primitiveness of remedial responses, methods and procedures, responsibilities in the information process, and resources (pp. 269-73). To this may be added such matters as the failure to enforce treaty obligations, problems of state responsibility, and perhaps most significantly the unwillingness of states to give any reality to any system of international criminal law (pp. 277-300).

As to the trends in the United Nations activity in the field of human rights, Dr. Ramcharan cites six:

the expansion of the existing international code of human rights. . .practical implementation of the existing human rights norms and standards. . .encouraging all Governments to establish national human rights systems on the basis of the international code which has been set up by the United Nations [reference to British unwillingness to adopt a Bill of Rights embodying the European Convention merely emphasizes the difficulty in achieving this]. . .the further development of advisory services and technical assistance to Member States in need. . .endeavour[ing] to respond promptly and effectively in dealing with emerging problems and issues likely to affect individual liberty. . .[and maintaining the] trend towards international human rights protection,

with pressure from non-governmental organizations, among others, to move lackadaisical governments on whom it all depends (pp. 346-47).

It matters little whether one agrees with the philosophical basis of the present study or Dr. Ramcharan's belief that the Declaration and Covenants constitute a Bill of Rights which has become, whether in whole or part, an inherent segment of international law. His book is interesting and enlightening and a welcome addition to the growing library of human rights doctrine.

L.C. GREEN
University of Alberta

Judging the World: Law and Politics in the World's Leading Courts. Edited
  by Garry Sturgess and Phillip Chubb. Sydney; Toronto: Butterworths 1988. Pp. xiv:, 573. ISBN 0-409-30116-7. (C $49.95).

It has gradually become increasingly evident that courts around
the world, and particularly those in common law countries, are frequently called upon to decide the legality of political issues, both
national and international. *Judging the World* comprises the texts of
interviews with judges from the United Kingdom (House of Lords,
Judicial Committee, and the Court of Appeal); the United States
(Supreme Court and the Supreme Court of Wisconsin); Australia
(High Court and Court of Appeal, N.S.W.); New Zealand (Court
of Appeal); Canada (Supreme Court and Supreme Court, B.C.);
Ireland (Supreme Court); India (Supreme Court); Germany (Con-
stitutional Court); together with members of the International Court
of Justice, the Court of Justice of the European Communities, the
European Court and Commission of Human Rights, and the Inter-
American Court of Human Rights.

The aim of the collection is to discuss the ''extent to which judges
make the law; how they make it — by what rules and to what ends;
the extent to which their law making involves them in activity that
is inherently political; how they differ from politicians; how independent from the political process they really are; how they are appointed; how suitable they are as a group to be making decisions
that have such impact on the lives of ordinary citizens; and how
accountable they are. The book also looks at what happens when
the authority of governments and parliaments is challenged by
courts, when collisions occur'' (p. ix).

The first half of the book provides the editors' assessment of their
interviews with individual judges from the point of view of such
headings as ''The King and the Law''; ''The A-Bomb and the
Law'' — this is looked at from the standpoint of the United States,
Ireland, and India, but surprisingly there is no reference to any
decision relating to the bomb, even though one might have expected some reference to the Canadian Cruise Missile decision or that
of the World Court on the French nuclear tests; proliferation which
is concerned with bills of rights; the role of the various international courts; the issue of politics and judicial accountability; and
conflicts between courts and governments and between judges and
politics. For much of the discussion the emphasis is on judicial law-
making. In this connection it is interesting to read Denning's

comments on his own role and to note his comment concerning his retirement: "my hearing was beginning to go. So I realised I couldn't go on very much longer. I wouldn't want to ask for a hearing aid in a court or anything like that...and, of course, my arthritis was getting very bad. I was crawling across the street looking a very old man. It's a bad thing for a judge in a leading position to look a very old, doddery man" (p. 264). Equally interesting are the assessments of Denning's role by Lords Wilberforce and Ackner (pp. 271-73, 265-68).

It is interesting to note how outsiders view the impact upon Canada of the Charter of Rights and Freedoms:

The bomb is proliferating. Its explosive force in Canada has been dramatic, to say the least. Onlookers in Britain and Australia gaze in wonder at the mushroom cloud, at how the Charter has changed utterly the function of the country's Supreme Court and at how it is beginning to change the country itself. The Court has far greater power now than before and, surprisingly perhaps, this development has been as much regretted by some Canadians on the left of politics as it has been by the more traditional opponents of Bills of Rights. . . . Whether it is politics with a large or small 'p' it became clear from the earliest Charter decisions that the court was going to be the crucial determinant of what could and could not be done in Canada. . . . Whenever Parliament enacts legislation, the politicians ae looking over their shoulder not only at what the Charter says, but at what the court is doing and what it might do in the future. It is argued that this has chilled some legislative activity and that, rather than simply being accountable to the electorate, politicians now feel that their major responsibility is to tow [*sic*] the Judicial line. In Canada now, it is being argued, only the judiciary has the privilege of making mistakes. And, of course, when the judiciary makes a mistake it takes a very long time and a lot of money to correct. (pp. 59-63)

Is it true to say that under the "reasonable limits" provision, "if the federal parliament or one of the provinces enacts legislation which, it is found, will infringe one of the rights and freedoms guaranteed by the Charter, the legislation can still be saved if *parliament* can show that it is a reasonable limit which is obviously prescribed by law, and can show it to be demonstrably justified in a free and democratic society" (p. 63, italics added). For a more "Canadian" approach, reference should be made to the comments of Lamer, J. and Dickson, C.J. (pp. 387-99). Equally interesting is Tom Berger's account of his conflict with the Judicial Council and the reasons for his resignation from the B.C. bench (pp. 406-9).

Insofar as the international courts are concerned, the editorial notes are largely descriptive, although the comments on Judge Lachs — "the politician judge" — are interesting: "He has tried hard to change the court's public image. He has done this by pointing out that while it is an impartial legal tribunal, this does not mean it is entirely detached from international processes. When he was President of the court he was often at the United Nations General Assembly talking to people, letting them know that the court was available for the resolution of disputes and indicating those disputes for which he thought it would be a suitable venue. . . . Judge Lachs took the opportunity [in the *Tehran Embassy* case], as he has done so often, to push the law beyond the specifics of the case. He used his judgment to point to the broader implications of the illegal seizure of the embassy and also to the uses to which the law can be put in its march into the future. . . . In its relations with the countries under its jurisdiction the court, like national courts, obviously has to be careful. But when you are dealing with countries, an entirely new dimension is added to questions about the relationship between judging and politics. In the 1960's the International Court of Justice faced a fundamental challenge based upon hard questions about the nature of this relationship; with Judge Lachs as the severely pained catalyst" (pp. 89-94). (For Lachs' own view of his role, see pp. 464-66). Perhaps one of the most perspicacious remarks made by any of the judges interviewed in this collection and one that could have been made by Denning or Dickson, Berger or Mme Bertha Wilson had she been included, was made by Lachs: "There is a panorama of legal rules. You do not read the words only as words, you try to discover certain ideas behind them. And when the problem arises, do you seek the idea of those who wrote these words or the idea the words have today in the context of today's life? Because those who wrote them did so in different circumstances. I think a good judge should also have a vision of the possibilities the law can play and should play in the world of today and tomorrow. This is how I see the job of a judge. He should not close his eyes only to the text alone, limit himself to the text, but have some vision to make the words live. They must live, because you decide the cases between living beings, and from the moment the case comes to the court and you render your judgment, a lot of things may change. And they do change" (p. 467).

There are many gems to be found in the statements of some of the judges interviewed and these interviews are perhaps more important than the editorial introduction, though this too provides a useful overview of the topics with which it deals. One of the most useful functions of this volume is as a guide to students seeking to know what the law is, how judges approach it, and how similar are their approaches and respect for the law regardless of their backgrounds.

L.C. GREEN
University of Alberta

Judicial Settlement of International Disputes: Jurisdiction, Justiciability and Judicial Law-Making in the Contemporary International Court. By Edward McWhinney. Dordrecht: Martinus Nijhoff, 1991. Pp. xix, 189 (U.S. $89.00).

In many ways this collection of essays, based on lectures delivered at the Hague Academy in 1990, reads like a paean in praise of the activism of the World Court in recent years, especially since the "unfortunate" decision in the Second Phase of the *South West Africa* case, 1966. McWhinney distinguishes between the "old" Eurocentric and the "contemporary" Court (p. xvii) and pays tribute to Judge Lachs for having done so much to effect this transition (p. xix). He considers the present trends in the Court to reflect the influence of "major U.S. legal centres" upon law graduates from developing countries. This leads him to remark that "one of the curious historical ironies in the U.S. Administration's angry, reactive measures directed against the International Court after the Court's *Nicaragua* rulings of 1984-86, is that the Court majorities that decided against the U.S. on the issues under contest in the *Nicaragua* cases applied what amounted to a 'U.S. constitutional law' approach that the great liberal-activist judges on the U.S. Supreme Court in the Roosevelt era would certainly themselves have understood and approved" (p. xiv). Having taken the *South West Africa* cases as his watershed, it is unfortunate that McWhinney did not notice in checking his manuscript that he has described this mandated area as a "United Nations Trust Territory" (p. 17).

McWhinney has a lengthy critique of the use of chambers and is particularly critical of how the United States and Canada dictated membership of the bench in the *Gulf of Maine* case so as to exclude the two judges most competent in maritime matters (pp. 75-79) and points out how, in the *Continental Shelf (Libya)* case, one of these, Oda, wrote what was virtually a dissent on the *Maine* issue, leading the author to question how far chamber decisions really are decisions of the Court (p. 80).

As to the *Nicaragua* case, McWhinney makes clear the harm done to both the Court and the United States and reminds us of the rather disgraceful attack made upon the Court and some of its most eminent judges by Sofaer, legal adviser to the State Department, in relation to that judgment (p. 62 *et seq.*), and he does not fail to point out the satisfaction of the United States with the *Tehran Embassy* judgment, despite the presence of judges from the "Soviet bloc" and the Third World, although he is unhappy that the Court did not examine the history of U.S.-Iranian relations (pp. 138-39, 150).

One of the most interesting sections of the book is the chapter which examines how judges are selected and which makes a fairly strong case for choosing them on a regional basis (Ch. 4). It is also worth mentioning some causes that may be responsible for particular elections or defeats, particularly the election of Nagendra Singh's successor (pp. 99, 110) and the defeat of Bailey after Spender had cast the deciding vote on the South West Africa issue (pp. 104, 116). McWhinney's analysis of recent elections leads him to suggest that the present tendency is to look more than anything at a candidate's commitment to "progressive development" of the law (p. 114). At the same time he questions whether the Court should be sympathetic and even helpful in the course of a hearing to a poorer country that lacks a properly qualified bar so as to reduce the practice of Western counsel appearing against each other when the parties are from the Third World (p. 132).

McWhinney is convinced that, "in a very real sense, today, the International Court has become a representative tribunal, fully reflecting the legal-systemic, ethno-cultural, political-ideological, and geographical diversity of contemporary United Nations membership" (p. 116). This leads him to assert that "in the international 'Global Village' of today there is a sufficient interchange and interaction, between different legal systems, of jurists and of basic legal ideas, for the international legal culture to become increasingly homogenised, producing its own form of *Jus Gentium*-based common consensus on institutions like judicial review and its special modalities of operation. On this view, the judicial settlement of disputes is no longer a strictly 'Western' concept, but has become truly international; and Non-Western states that have participated in that creative evolution are not constrained by 'classical' Western legal definitions prescribing or restricting the permissible limits of its concrete operation and application" (p. 128).

McWhinney's account of contemporary *Judicial Settlement of International Disputes* is most interesting, even if one is not as enthusiastic as he is about the present somewhat anti-traditional activism of the Court. One might question his excessive use of capital letters and even the statement that "International Judicial Settlement, as a prime mode of international conflicts-resolution, was launched as a legal concept by Continental European (including Imperial Russian) jurists towards the close of the nineteenth century" (p. 156), which tends to ignore the efforts of such American peace activists as William Penn and the American and English Quaker movements, as well as the significance of the Jay arbitrations.

L.C. GREEN
University of Alberta

The Influence of Religion on the Development of International Law. By M. W. Janis (ed.). The Hague: Martinus Nijhoff, 1991. Pp. xii, 268 (£54).

For a discipline with a rich religious heritage, international law has often shown an almost adolescent ingratitude to its parentage. Whether or not one takes the view that international law was conceived in antiquity or in Reformation Europe, it is clear that the religious impulse, in particular Christianity, was present at its conception and throughout its birth and childhood. Even as late as the early twentieth century, it was possible for a leading international lawyer (Lawrence) to be a man of ordained orders. What possibility is there for such a man today to be an international lawyer and fully command undiluted professional respect?

Today, with legal positivism firmly gripping the horizons of the law schools, the fashionable international lawyer, like a teenager bowing to his peers, has found recourse to this parentage largely uninteresting and certainly unnecessary. One can look hard through the recent literature of international law and find very little on the relationship between international law and religion.[1] For a discipline that allegedly pays respect to precedent, this attitude is surprising.

Thus, it was with a considerable sense of homecoming (and of equal astonishment) that this reviewer alighted on *The Influence of Religion on the Development of International Law.* The work is a collection

[1] There are some exceptions, such as, certain contributors to the 1983 Colloque of the Hague Academy of International Law on "The Future of International Law in a Multicultural World" and also Falk, *Revitalizing International Law* (1989).

of eleven essays in two parts by various authors and embraces a wide range of matters connected by a religious motif and is the result of a panel meeting at the 1988 Annual Meeting of the American Society of International Law. The conclusions of the authors are perhaps tentative. However, there probably needs to be a period of mutual adjustment between international law and religion before there can be deeper communion, for so long have they wandered apart. Nevertheless, the reunion is welcomed.

The first part of the work is entitled ''History and Doctrine'' and consists of six essays intended, the preface states, ''to give the reader an idea of the influence of religion on the development of international law over time from the points of view of diverse cultures.'' However, the first essay, by Bederman, is of a general nature, being a treatment of the sources of international law and of international legal obligations in ancient times. This author's concern is to defend ancient international law from the charge of ''primitiveness,'' which is founded on its allegedly religious character. In defence of the charge, the author argues with conviction that religion was not the sole source of the ancient international legal systems of the world, but that ''instead, religion and ritual and rhetoric mixed to produce an idea of obligation.''

There then follow two short essays, one on the Confucian view of world order and the other a fairly traditional rehearsal of the thoughts of Kautilyan on international affairs and the application of Dharma in India. The author of the latter, Nanda, however, departs from some of his countrymen who have purported to find a direct link between ancient Hindu practices and modern international law.[2] He concludes that ''principles of interstate conduct in ancient Hindu India did not survive beyond the eighteenth century to have any tangible influence on modern international law.'' The thoughts of Confucius also seem to have had little influence on the development of modern international law.

The fourth and fifth essays relate to the impact of Christianity on international law. Janis provides an interesting survey of attitudes to and usages of religion in five standard law texts. The texts chosen are those of Grotius, Vattel, Wheaton, Oppenheim, and Brownlie. Janis helpfully affirms that the relationship of international law and religion is not completely one-way, the expansion

[2] For example, Singh, ''The Distinguishing Characteristics of the Concept of the Law of Nations as It Developed in Ancient India,'' in *Liber Amicorum for Lord Wilberforce* (1987) Brownlie & Bos 92 (eds.).

of the influence of secular thought on international law at the expense of religion. In the early nineteenth century, Wheaton and his contemporaries re-emphasized the importance of Christianity to international law when the Enlightenment had all but extinguished it. Noyes carries out a similar survey but limits it to the works of Lorimer and Phillimore, who wrote at the end of the nineteenth century. The final essay of Part I is entitled ''Islamic Fundamentalism and its Impact on International Laws and Politics.'' There is much more concerning the impact of Islamic fundamentalism on politics than international law in this essay.

The second part of the work is entitled ''Perspectives and Values'' and consists of five essays which, according to the preface, ''make more pointed arguments than the essays in Part I.'' The first by Kennedy is a rather breathless and compressed sketch of two different strategies of enquiry into the interaction of law and religion: first, what the author calls ''a strategy of narrative homology tracing structural similarities among the stories told by law and religion''; second, ''a strategy of recovery, recovery of the mutual participations of religious and legal in the construction of the state, the sovereign and his law.'' These strategies seem worthy of future exploration but as presented they are difficult to follow.

The second essay by Nafziger looks at five possible functions of religion in the international legal system. These functions he describes as ''creative,'' ''aspirational,'' ''didactic,'' ''custodial,'' and ''meditative.'' There then follows what is perhaps the most intriguing contribution to the work. Its author, Park, examines how religion as a matter of policy should (and should not) inform legal choices. It raises the insoluble issue of how a person with a belief that he believes comes from God, and that contradicts society's law, should act. Or to recall the view of the apostle Peter long ago, when the Jerusalem authorities prohibited the proclamation of the Gospel, ''we must obey God rather than men.''[3] The central core of the essay is taken up with an analysis of the famous trial of Servetus for heresy at the hands of Calvin and the consequent work of Castellion which did so much to bring about international religious toleration. The essay concludes with a brief consideration of the consequences of applying biblical principles to international economic life.

The final two essays consider the impact of two religious movements on particular aspects of international law. The first tells of

[3]   Acts 5:29.

the ultimately successful contribution of nineteenth-century American Protestants to the acceptance of the need for a world court; the second of the less successful attempts by Quakers in the United Kingdom to establish and enforce before the courts of that state the illegality of nuclear weapons under international law. These contributions are interesting to note at a time when the General Assembly's program for the Decade of International Law sees greater interest in and knowledge of international law by individuals as an essential means of strengthening the international legal system.

The Influence of Religion on the Development of International Law is a pioneering work charting much unfamiliar territory. It is not faultless, however, and if one has a criticism, it is that the book is too concerned with the externals of topography rather than the underlying structures and movements. This fault may be the inevitable result of an exploratory journey.

If there is to be a real purpose to the exploration of the relationship between international law and religion, rather than it simply be for amusement, that purpose must be to tell us how we have come to be where we are. To this reviewer the authors are perhaps too easily satisfied by the identification that the writer or the law in question was influenced by religion. This identification is, of course, fundamental to this work, but if it is to have real interest, there is a need to explain, or at least conjecture (however difficult), why a particular international lawyer or rule of international law was influenced by religion and what other forces were involved. Similarly, it is important to know why others, primarily later writers and rules of international law, were not so affected.

Further, if one is to be involved in the study of the relationship between law and religion, one inevitably must grasp the nettle of truth. In a sceptical age, particularly in its scholarly bastions, that is not a task which even the benefits of extirpation of truth makes attractive. However, it is the subject that lies at the heart of religion, if it is has any meaning.

Lack of concern for the truth also makes the subject all rather cold and uninteresting. Take Nafziger's article for instance (others might have been chosen). It looks at the five functions of religion within the international legal system which he identifies, as we have seen, as "creative," "aspirational," "didactic," "custodial," and "meditative." Now these functions may all be played by religion, but are they reflective of any greater purpose in the international legal system? Is the ultimate question for the international lawyer interested in religion to weigh the burden and benefit of religion to international law, as Nafziger thinks (a Benthamite view), or, are there equally important questions, such as, if there is a God, what does He say about the international legal system? Or, is He even concerned with the explicit content of rules rather than the response of humanity to such rules?

In biblical terms, "let your "Yes" be "Yes" and your "No" be "No.""[4] Or, could the international legal system ever have operated without the moral impulses and beliefs that come from God and impregnate even those who do not believe? Or, how will the international legal system and the people who operate it be judged on the basis of truth? Such questions are manifestly not ones within the normal ambit of the international lawyer and they are capable of a vast variety of answers from a human perspective, but they are ones that must be considered if the relationship between international law and religion is to be conducted properly. It is not enough to be like Pilate, to wash one's hands and ask "what is truth?"[5]

Further, there must be a deeper understanding of the world's religions if exploration of the relationship between international law and religion is to be helpful. They are not all the same. Christianity, for instance, does not consider itself to be a religion at all. You can search through the patriarchs, the prophets, and the apostles and on only two occasions will you find reference to religion.[6] That was not their concern. For them, the concern was truth, not religion; as the words of Jesus proclaim, "I am the way and the truth, and the life."[7] Equally, even within Christianity there are many views on minor matters. One could argue with Park that even on biblical grounds the Old Testament laws on international economic life ceased to apply with the new dispensation.

Notwithstanding these concluding carpings, this reviewer wholeheartedly welcomes this book. The authors are to be congratulated on their bravery in searching for the historical roots of international law and for finding a rich cavern of treasure for the better understanding of the world legal system. Let us all hope they return to

[4] Matthew 5:37.
[5] John 18:38.
[6] Acts 26:5 and James 1:26-27.
[7] John 14:6.

enter deeper into that cavern to bring to light more of those hidden riches.

JEREMY THOMAS, LL.B.(LON.), LL.M.(DAL.)
Assistant, Ashurst Morris Crisp, London, England, and Research Associate, Dalhousie Law School, Canada

Commonwealth International Law Cases, Vols. 12, 13. Edited by J. A. Hopkins. Dobbs Ferry: Oceana, 1990. ISBN 0-379-00962-5. (U.S. $60.00 per volume).

It is six years since the last volume of *Commonwealth International Law Cases* appeared with the collection only part way through the material on territorial jurisdiction. The newly published volume twelve continues with decisions relating to exceptions from and restrictions on territorial jurisdiction. As usual, the judgements are drawn from a variety of Commonwealth sources — Australia, Canada, Ceylon, Cyprus, East Africa, Fiji, Gibraltar, Hong Kong, India, Malaya, New Zealand, Singapore, and South Africa, and many of these countries are represented by different jurisdictions. Some of the cases are unreported, while others are drawn from series of reports with which many readers will probably be completely unacquainted. For this reason, it is unfortunate that the table of abbreviations is incomplete and it is only by looking at the actual report that one is able to ascertain the country from which it comes: D.C.A. — Queen's Bench, Quebec; M.P.R. — Supreme Court, Nova Scotia; N.S. — Supreme Court, Nova Scotia; W.W. & O.'B. — Supreme Court, Victoria, Australia.

The Canadian decisions in volume twelve are *Mehr v. Republic of China,* [1956] O.W.N. 218, on state immunity; *Peter Brown Jr. v. The S.S. Indochine* (1922), 1921 Ex.C.R. 406, recognizing the immunity of a state-owned vessel engaged in commerce, which must of course now be read in the light of the *Flota Maritima* decision [1962] S.C.R. 598. Closely related to these two decisions is that of the Hong Kong Supreme Court in *The Philippine Admiral,* [1974] H.K.L.R.111 — unfortunately the Privy Council decision in this case, [1977] A.C.373, has not been reproduced. Other Canadian cases in this volume are *Michigan State Bridge Commission v. Point Edward,* [1939] 3 D.L.R. 533, denying immunity to the plaintiff; *Municipality and Country of St. John v. Fraser-Brace Overseas Corporation,* [1958] S.C.R. 263, in which it held

an interest; this case should be read in conjunction with the decision in *Ogdensberg Bridge and Port Authority* v. *Township of Edwardsberg,* [1967] 1 O.R. 87. Finally, there is a group of cases concerning the position of visiting forces — *In re de Brujin,* [1942] 1 W.W.R. 105; *In re Romeijnsen,* [1942] 1 W.W.R. 119; *Reference re Exemption of U.S. Military and Naval Forces from Criminal Proceedings in Canadian Criminal Courts,* [1943] S.C.R. 483; *Gallant* v. *West,* [1955] 4 D.L.R. 209; and *Daroway* v. *The Queen,* [1956] Ex. C.R. 340 — the mink ranch case.

As to Canadian personal jurisdiction cases in volume thirteen, there are *The Queen* v. *Thomas Grey* (1951), 3 Newf. 205; *The Queen* v. *Hohn Kinsman* (1853), 2 N.S. 62, which provides an interesting analysis of the principles governing personal jurisdiction as well as the national character of a ship, and *The Queen* v. *Richard Moore* (1881), 2 D.C.A. 52; *Reg* v. *Pierce* (1887), 13 O.R. 226, on jurisdiction over bigamy committed outside of Canada, which should be read in conjunction with *Reg* v. *Brierly* (1887), 14 O.R. 525, *Reg.* v. *Plowman* (1893), 25 O.R. 656, and the *Reference re the Criminal Code* 1892, *ss.* 275-276, *relating to Bigamy* (1897), 27 S.C.R. 461. Other Canadian decisions concerning criminal jurisdiction are *The King* v. *Heckman* (1902), 5 C.C.C. 242; *R.* v. *Walkem* (1908), 14 B.C.R. 1; and *R.* v. *Neilson* (1918), 52 N.S. 42, in which Chisholm, J. of the Nova Scotia Supreme Court presented a careful analysis of *R.* v. *Keyn* (1876), (1876) 2 Exch. D. 63 and the Imperial Territorial Waters Jurisdiction Act.

These volumes are valuable because they not only make available a number of little-known decisions, but they also enable a reader to assess the contribution made by Commonwealth Judges to the interpretation of international law in relation to municipal law. At the same time they assist in assessing how far decisions from a variety of municipal jurisdictions reflect general principles of law recognized by civilized nations, providing evidence of different rules of what others would describe as customary international law by way of *opinio juris.* Both editor and publishers are to be congratulated.

L. C. Green
University of Alberta

American International Law Cases, 1986-1988. Second Series, Vols. 9-14. Edited by Bernard D. Reams, Jr. 1990. ISBN 0-579-20075-9. (U.S. $60.00 per volume).

Volumes 9-14 of the Second Series of *American International Law Cases* cover the years 1986-88, providing evidence of the fruitful jurisprudence of American federal and state courts in the field of international law. Taken together with the earlier series, edited first by Francis Deak and later by Frank S. Ruddy, and the other series published by Oceana on British and Commonwealth decisions respectively, they provide a veritable compendium of the decisions giving the views of the courts of English-speaking jurisdictions on what constitutes international law. They are a most useful tool for comparative study. Furthermore, with the reports of the International Court of Justice, the United Nations Reports of International Arbitral Awards, and the International Law Reports, they provide a comprehensive survey of the jurisprudence of the world in regard to this branch of law. One of the special values of the Oceana series is that they reproduce virtually all the decisions relating to a particular case, as well as a number tht would never find their way into the International Law Reports.

As is to be expected, these volumes continue to make use of the chapter headings and subheadings of earlier series, while Volume 13 introduces and 14 is devoted to a new section devoted to international trade, a topic that will become even more important than it already is with the development of free trade areas in which the United States is a party, and with the increasing significance of its relations with the European Economic Community, which will become even more significant after 1992, as will economic intercourse with the Soviet Union, in whatever form that empire might eventually evolve.

The classification used in these volumes for the section devoted to "War, Belligerency and Neutrality" (Vol. 12), the subheadings of which are "War and Espionage" and "Terrorism," is questionable. While a case might be made for including espionage, although even this is difficult (see *U.S.* v. *Morison* 844 F.2d 1057 (1988)), there seems to be no reason for including terrorism, especially as the United States has not ratified Protocol I, 1977, additional to the Geneva Conventions of 1949, whereby members of so-called national liberation movements may claim the rights of lawful combatants under the law of armed conflict. How does one justify the inclusion of *Chasser* v. *Achille Lauro Lines,* 844 F.2d 50 (1988), whereby the heirs of Leon Klinghoffer sought damages against the owners of the hijacked vessel?

Most international lawyers, including those in the United States, tend to regard terrorism as falling within the rubric of intrnational criminal law, as they do extradition — here treated as part of the law concerning aliens (Vol. II), where it appears together with deportation, and with *I.N.S.* v. *Cardoza-Fonseca*, No. 85-782, 1987, providing an interesting discussion on asylum for refugees. By separating terrorism and extradition as is done here, it becomes necessary to make a guess as to how a case will be reported. One might have expected the decision in the *Matter of Extradition of Atta*, 706 F.Supp. 1032 (1989), to be cross-referenced to terrorism, especially as this case also appears in Volume 12, and arose out of an Israeli request for the extradition of one accused of attacking an Egged bus on behalf of the Abu Nidal Organization. Under the heading of international organization, there are two or three cases referring to the Palestine Information Office and its closure, but surprisingly it also includes *Farrakhan* v. *Reagan*, 669 F. Supp. 506 (1987), concerning the claimant's rights to free speech and the right of the Muhammad Mosque Inc. to repay a loan it had received from the Islamic Call Society, an agency of the Libyan government.

Volume 10 deals, for the main part, with exceptions from and limitations upon the exercise of territorial jurisdiction, using the headings "sovereign immunity" and "act of state doctrine." The issues of diplomatic and consular immunity appear under the separate rubric of "diplomacy."

Since the adoption of the Canadian Charter of Rights and Freedoms, a number of attempts have been made to challenge government defence and foreign policy matters on constitutional grounds. Those who support these actions will find the first case in Volume 9 of major interest. *Committee of U.S. Citizens in Nicaragua* v. *Reagan*, 859 F.2d 929 (1888), which challenged the whole of official policy on behalf of the Contras. In his judgment, Circuit Judge Mikva made some interesting comments on the relation of international and national law: "When our government's two political branches, acting together, contravene an international legal norm, does this court have any authority to remedy the violation? The answer is "no" if the type of international obligation that Congress and the President violate is either a treaty or a rule of customary international law." His judgment also raises interesting questions as to whether submission to the jurisdiction of the World Court and agreeing to abide by its judgments constitute a rule of *jus cogens*. He held not. The whole judgment repays reading, as do some of the others concerning U.S. activities in Nicaragua. It should not be forgotten that the Canadian Charter contains the "reasonable limitation" provision, and one of the ways in which this may be assessed is by looking at the judgments in other jurisdictions.

Whatever criticisms one may have of the classification used in this series, there can be no denying the great value that is served by bringing all these United States cases together and making them available to the international law world at large. As with all similar series, both the editor and Oceana have put us deeply in their debt.

L. C. GREEN
University of Alberta

The Kuwait Crisis: Basic Documents. Edited by E. Lauterpacht et al. Cambridge: Grotius Publications, 1991. Pp. 330, including index. ISBN 0-949-009-86-5 (U.S. $70.00).

Perhaps one of the most serious problems confronting anyone trying to ascertain the history, politics, or law relating to the Iraq-Kuwait conflict is the difficulty of securing all the relevant documents. The Research Centre for International Law at the University of Cambridge and the editors of its Documents Series are therefore to be congratulated for having compiled the volume under review.

With the publication in Parts 5 and 6 of Volume 29 of International Legal Materials of Security Council Resolutions 660-78, starting with the condemnation of Iraq's invasion and culminating in the authorization of the use of all necessary means to secure its expulsion from Kuwait, that section of *The Kuwait Crisis* is perhaps not quite as essential as it might otherwise have been. But the volume contains the texts of such significant documents as the Secret Agreement of the British government with the Sheikh of Kuwait of 1899 and the Status Quo Agreements between the Ottoman and British governments of 1901, together with relevant extracts from the Treaties of Sevres and Lausanne. In addition there is all the material necessary to understand the basis on which Iraq became independent and the documents concerning the dispute between Iraq and Kuwait of 1961 as well as the 1963 agreement regarding the restoration of friendly relations, recognition, and the like.

Much has been made in the press of Iraqi demands upon Kuwait, and at pp. 73-83 will be found the September 1990 press release of the Iraqi Embassy in London together with the reply by the Association for Free Kuwait.

It is well known that the "Gulf debates" showed a unanimity of the Big Five in the Security Council that had not been seen for some years. Almost 100 pages of extracts from the debates are reproduced here, together with thirty other documents affecting the United Nations debates and actions. In addition to all this, there are also documents concerning the implementation of sanctions and their humanitarian exceptions, the naval and aerial interdictions, and a selection of materials concerning the treatment and protection of individuals and property in Kuwait and Iraq. The various peace proposals that were put forward in 1990 are reproduced, together with the reactions of a variety of regional organizations and other international institutions such as ICAO and the World Bank.

This volume clearly provides all that one needs in seeking to understand the background and progress of the Kuwait crisis prior to the outbreak of hostilities. The Cambridge Centre for International Law promises to bring out shortly a further volume dealing with sanctions and their economic consequences. It is to be hoped that a third volume carrying the story from Resolution 678, through the armed conflict, the truce, and subsequent activities will not be long delayed.

L. C. GREEN
University of Alberta

Consolidated Treaties & International Agreements Current Document Service: United States, Sept.-Dec. 1990. Edited by Erwin C. Surrency. Dobbs Ferry: Oceana, 1991. ISBN 1053-9905. Pp. xiii and 865. ($125.00 U.S.).

This volume of international agreements to which the United States is a party opens with a statement that applies to every major country and not merely the United States: "Finding the text of an American treaty or any other international agreement is often frustrating and time consuming because of [the] erratic form of public action. . . . Because of many factors other than the lack of determination on the part of the staff of the Department of State, the publication of the text of international agreements to which the United States is a party has fallen behind. Since the text of these agreements has not been published is any systematic way, it is hard to know exactly how far behind the official publication is lagging'' (p. xi).

The aim of the current series, of which this volume is part, is to ''include within 90 days of release or ratification, newly concluded international agreements,'' regardless of type — treaties and executive agreements, which have been ratified, even if they have not been officially published, and publication, as may be seen from the United Nations Treaty Series, may be almost light years behind. Moreover, frequently even a ratified document seems to get lost in the bureaucracy and never appears in an official publication.

The volume is published without a table of contents, but it contains appendices which are more useful than such a table. There is an index by country as well as a topical index, together with an index of multilateral treaties, and equally useful is a list of already published treaties to which reference is made in texts included in the volume. Finally, there is a list of officially unpublished agreements cited in documents included in the volume.

Those interested in the current state of United States international undertakings will be grateful to have documents made available to them regardless of the tardiness of the Government Printing House. Perhaps a Canadian publisher may be persuaded to undertake a similar task for Canadian treaties.

L. C. GREEN
University of Alberta

ANALYTICAL INDEX / INDEX ANALYTIQUE

THE CANADIAN YEARBOOK OF INTERNATIONAL LAW

1991

ANNUAIRE CANADIEN DE DROIT INTERNATIONAL

(A) Article; (NC) Notes and Comments;
(PR) Practice; (R) Review
(A) Article; (NC) Chronique; (PR) Pratique;
(R) Recension de livre